Yanmar

YANMAR MARINE DIESEL ENGINE 4JH2E, 4JH2-TE, 4JH2-HTE, 4JH2-DTE

Service Manual

Yanmar

YANMAR MARINE DIESEL ENGINE 4JH2E, 4JH2-TE, 4JH2-HTE, 4JH2-DTE

Service Manual

ISBN/EAN: 9783954272969
Erscheinungsjahr: 2013
Erscheinungsort: Bremen, Deutschland

© *marıtımepress in Europäischer Hochschulverlag GmbH & Co. KG, Fahrenheitstr. 1, 28359 Bremen. Alle Rechte beim Verlag und bei den jeweiligen Lizenzgebern.*

www.maritimepress.de | office@maritimepress.de

Bei diesem Titel handelt es sich um den Nachdruck eines historischen, lange vergriffenen Buches. Da elektronische Druckvorlagen für diese Titel nicht existieren, musste auf alte Vorlagen zurückgegriffen werden. Hieraus zwangsläufig resultierende Qualitätsverluste bitten wir zu entschuldigen.

YANMAR
SERVICE MANUAL
MARINE DIESEL ENGINE

MODELS
4JH2E
4JH2-TE
4JH2-HTE
4JH2-DTE

FOREWORD

This service manual has been compiled for engineers engaged in sales, service, inspection and maintenance. Accordingly, descriptions of the construction and functions of the engine are emphasized in this manual while items which should already be common knowledge are omitted.

One characteristic of a marine diesel engine is that its performance in a vessel is governed by its applicability to the vessel's hull construction and its steering system.

Engine installation, fitting out and propeller selection have a substantial effect on the performance of the engine and the vessel. Moreover, when the engine runs unevenly or when trouble occurs, it is essential to check a wide range of operating conditions — such as installation on the hull and suitability of the ship's piping and propeller — and not just the engine itself. To get maximum performance from this engine, you should completely understand its functions, construction and capabilities, as well as proper use and servicing.

Use this manual as a handy reference in daily inspection and maintenance, and as a text for engineering guidance.

Printed in Japan
A0A1029-9002

MODELS

4JH2E
4JH2-TE

4JH2-HTE
4JH2-DTE

Printed in Japan
A0A1029-9002

GENERAL

Printed in Japan
A0A1029-9002

1. Exterior Views

1-1 4JH2E

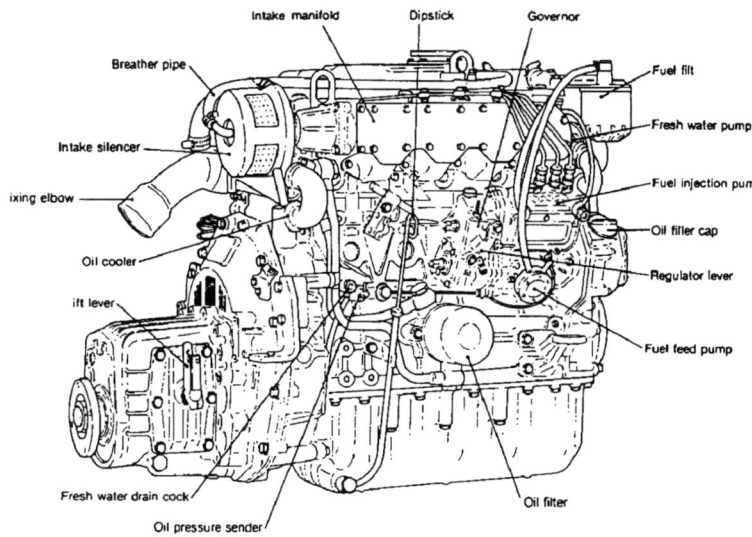

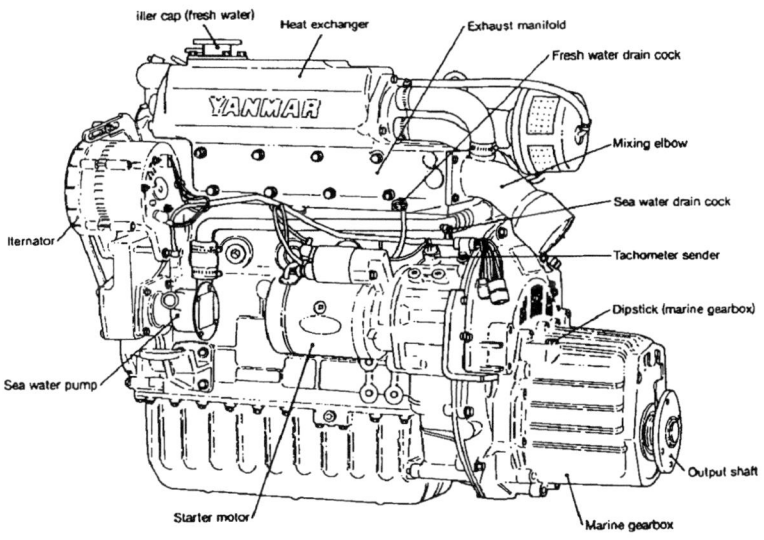

1·2 4JH2-TE

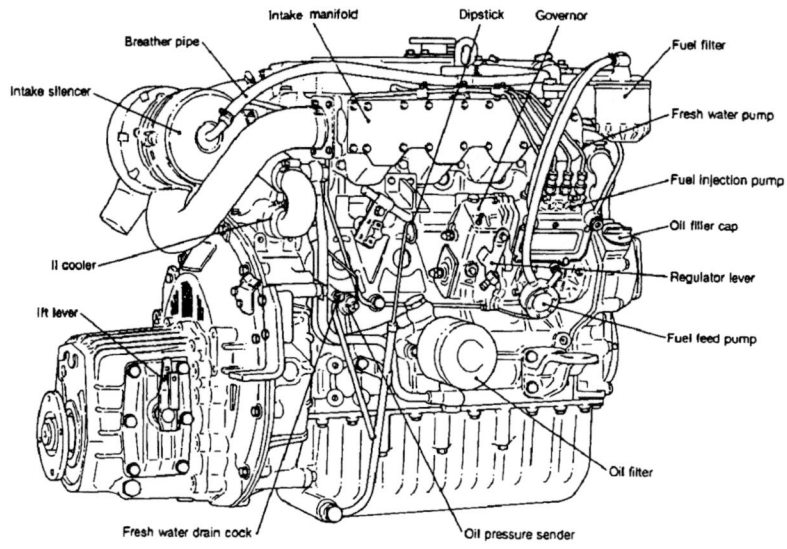

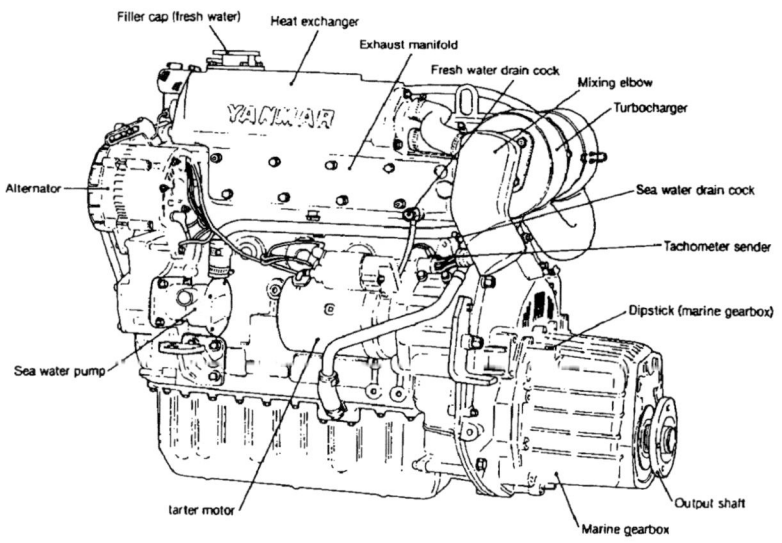

1-3 4JH2-HTE
 4JH2-DTE
 4JH2-UTE

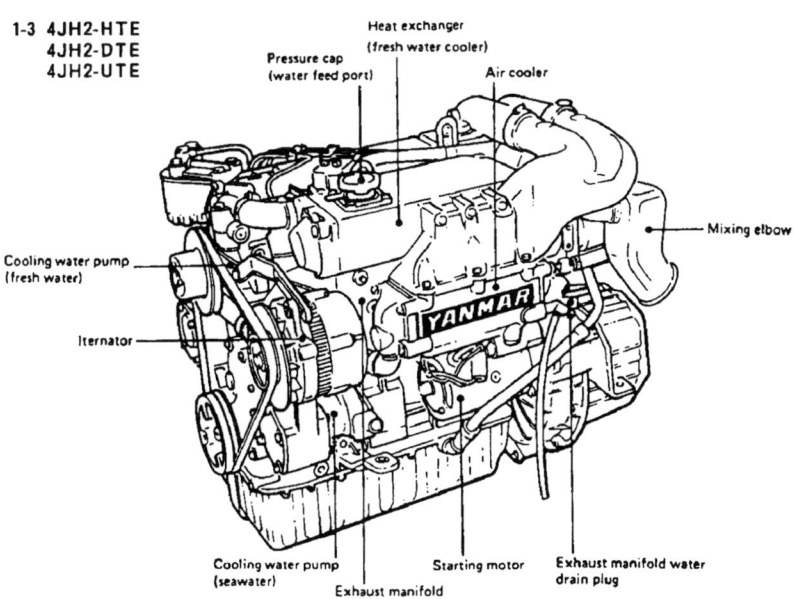

Heat exchanger
(fresh water cooler)

Pressure cap
(water feed port)

Air cooler

Mixing elbow

Cooling water pump
(fresh water)

Iternator

Cooling water pump
(seawater)

Exhaust manifold

Starting motor

Exhaust manifold water
drain plug

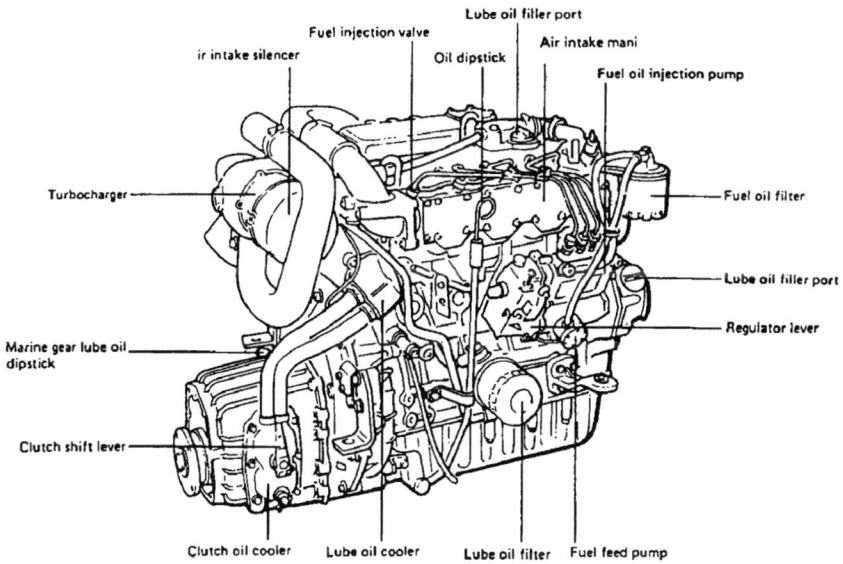

Lube oil filler port

Fuel injection valve

Air intake mani

ir intake silencer

Oil dipstick

Fuel oil injection pump

Turbocharger

Fuel oil filter

Lube oil filler port

Regulator lever

Marine gear lube oil
dipstick

Clutch shift lever

Clutch oil cooler

Lube oil cooler

Lube oil filter

Fuel feed pump

2-2 Marine Gear

	Model	KBW10E		KM3A		
Marine gear system	Type	Multiple friction disc cluth (Parallel drive)		Cone clutch (Angle drive)		
	Reduction ration (Forward/Reverse)	2.14/2.50	2.45/2.50	2.33/3.04	2.64/3.04	3.21/3.04
	Direction of rotation (Forward) Viewed from stam	Clock wise		Clock wise		
	Lubricating oil capacity Effect/max. ℓ (cu.in.)	0.2/0.7 (12.204/42.714)		0.05/0.35 (3.051/21.357)		
	Lubricating oil					
	Waight kg (ib.)	17.5 (38.588)		13 (28.665)		

2-3 Applicability of Marine gear & Reduction ratio

● : Standerd combination
○ : Optional combination
× : Inapplicable

Marine gear		Engine model	3JH2E	3JH2-TE
Model	Reduction ratio	I.D Merk		
KBW10E	2.14	S	●	●
	2.45	G	●	●
	2.83	GG	●	×
KM3A	2.33	S	●	●
	2.64	G	●	●
	3.21	GG	●	×

Printed in Japan
A0A1015-0104

2-2. Marine Gear

	Model		KBW20	KBW21	KM3P2	KM4A
Marine gear system	Type		Multiple friction disc clutch (Parallel drive)		One clutch (Parallel drive)	One clutch (Angle drive)
	Reduction ratio (Forward/Reverse)		2.17/ 2.62/ 3.28/ 3.06, 3.06, 3.06	2.17/ 2.62/ 3.06, 3.06	2.36/ 2.61	1.47/ 2.14/ 2.63/ 3.30/ 1.47/,2.14, 2.63, 3.30
	Reduction of rotation (Forward)		Clockwise			Bi-rotation
	Lubrication oil capacity Effect/max.	ℓ(cu.in.)	0.15/1.2	0.15/1.2	0.05/0.35	0.2/1.3
	Lubricating oil		Dexron, ATF		SAE 20/30. Same as Engine oil	
	Weight	kg(lb.)	26	30	15.5	28

2-3. Applicability of Marine gear & Redection rati

●:standard combinati
○:optional combinati
×:inapplicable

Marine Gear		Engine Model	4JH2E	4JH2-TE	4JH2-HTE	4JH2-DTE	4JH2-UTE
Model	Reduction ratio	I.D Mark					
KM3P2	2.36	S	●	×	×	×	×
	2.61	G	●	×	×	×	×
KBW20	2.17	S	●	●	×	×	×
	2.62	G	●	●	×	×	×
	3.28	GG	●	●	×	×	×
KBW21	2.17	S	○	○	●	●	●
	2.62	G	○	○	●	●	●
	3.28	GG	○	○	×	×	×
KM4A	1.47	SS	●	●	●	●	●
	2.14	S	●	●	●	●	●
	2.63	G	●	●	●	●	●
	3.30	GG	●	●	●	●	●

3. Construction

ENGINE MODEL		4JH2E	4JH2-TE	4JH2-HTE	4JH2-DTE	4JH2-UTE
Group	Part	Construction				
Engine Proper	Cylinder block	Integrally-cast water jacket and crankcase				
	Cylinder liner	Dry sleeve				
	Timing gear case	Cast aluminum				
	Oil sump	Cast aluminum, oil pan				
	Main bearings	Hanger-type bearing supports				
	Engine feet	Cylinder block and Flywheel mounting side				
Intake/Exhaust, Valve Drive	Cylinder head	Integrally-case type, jet cooling between valves, Intake/exhaust valve seat inserts				
	Intake/exhaust valves	Mushroom shaped, seat angle: Intake: 120° Exhaust: 90°				
	Intake manifold	Aluminum diecast integral				
	Exhaust manifold	Water cooled integral with water tank				
	Air cooler			Plate fin type	Corrugated fin type	
	Turbocharger			IHI RHB52 exhaust gas turbo	IHI RHB52HW exhaust gas turbo, Water cooled type	
	Valve drive	Overhead valve push rod rocker arm system				
	Timing gear	Helical gear				
Main Moving Parts	Crankshaft	Stamped forging				
	Flywheel	Cast iron static balance with ring gear				
	Pistons	Cast aluminum, oval type				
	Piston rings	2 compression rings, 1 oil ring				
	Piston pin	Floating type				
	Connecting rod	Forged steel				
	Crank pin bushings	Aluminum bushings				
Lube Oil System	Lube oil pump	Trochoid type				
	Oil filter	Full flow paper element cartridge type				
	Oil cooler	Sea water cooled pipe type		Sea water cooled multi-pipe type		
	Control valve	Cylindrical type with external adjusting shims				
Cooling Water System	Fresh water pump	V-pulley driven, centrifugal type				
	Sea water pump	Gear driven, rubber impeller type				
	Thermostat	Wax pellet type				
	Fresh water cooler	Multi-tube type integral with exhaust manifold				
Bilge	Bilge pump	Electric				
Fuel Injection Equipment	Fuel injection pump	YANMAR YPES-4CL				NP-VE4
	Fuel injection nozzles	Hole type				
	Fuel feed pump	Diaphragm type				Vane type
	Fuel filter	Paper element cartridge type				
Governor	Governor	Centrifugal all-speed mechanical type				
Remote Control Equipment	Engine speed & marine gearbox	Single control lever type with push-pull cable				
Starting Equipment	Electric starter	DC 12V, 1.4kW starter motor				
	Generator	12V, 55A with built-in IC regulator				
Marine Gearbox	Clutch	Multiple friction disc clutch/cone clutch				
	Reduction gear	Helical gear constant mesh type				

4-1. 4JH2E

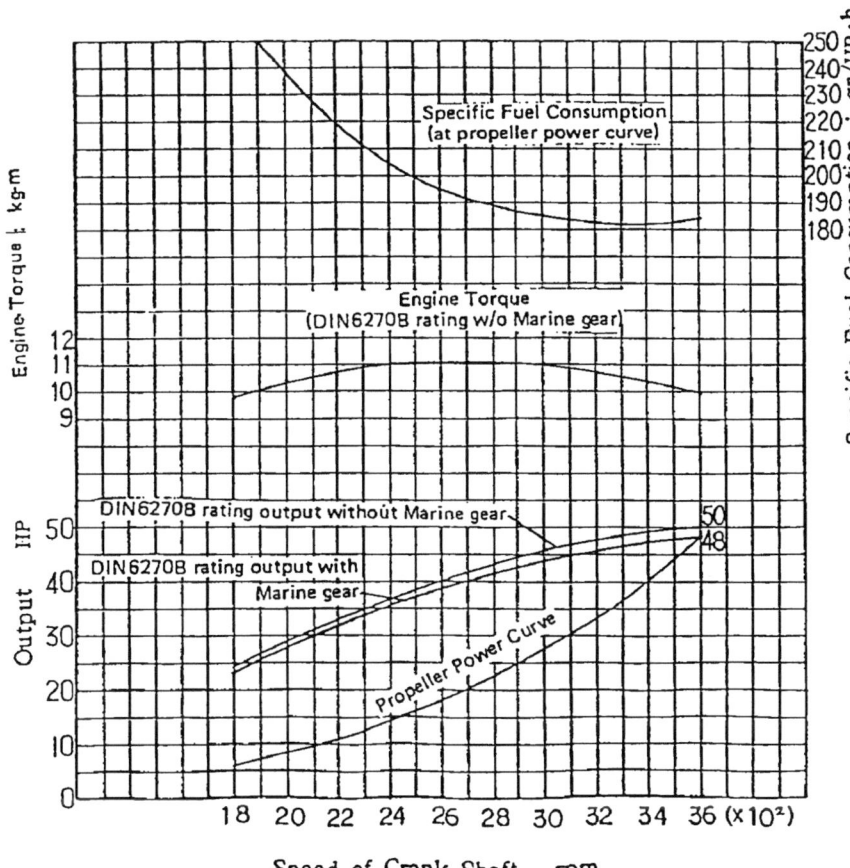

Speed of Crank Shaft   rpm

4-2. 4JH2-TE

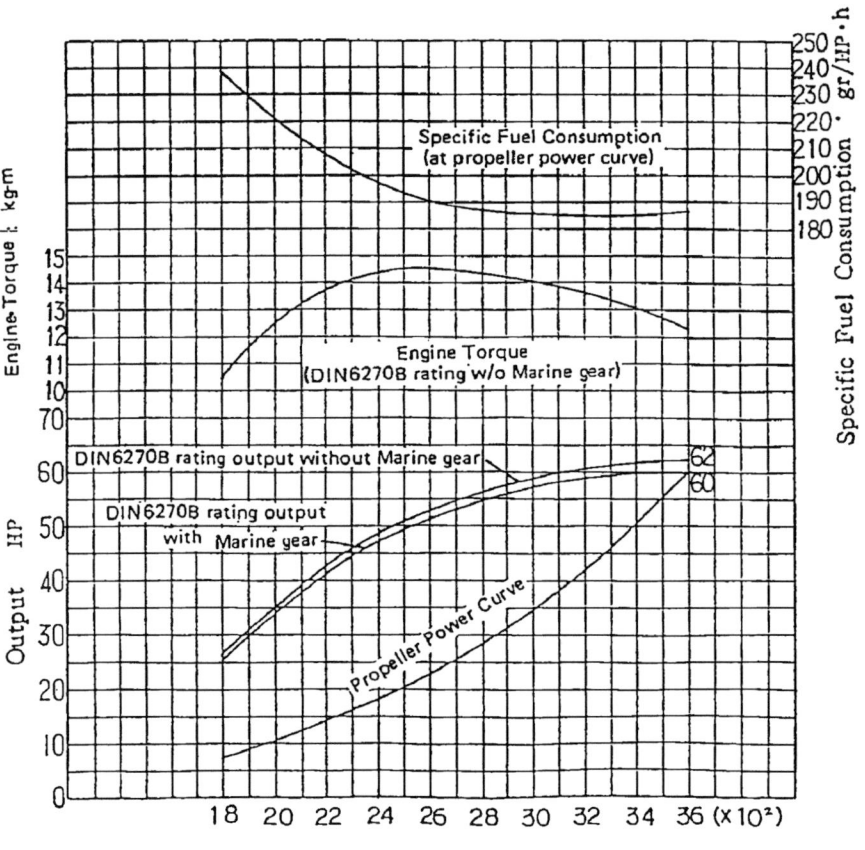

Speed of Crank Shaft   rpm

4-3. 4JH2-HTE

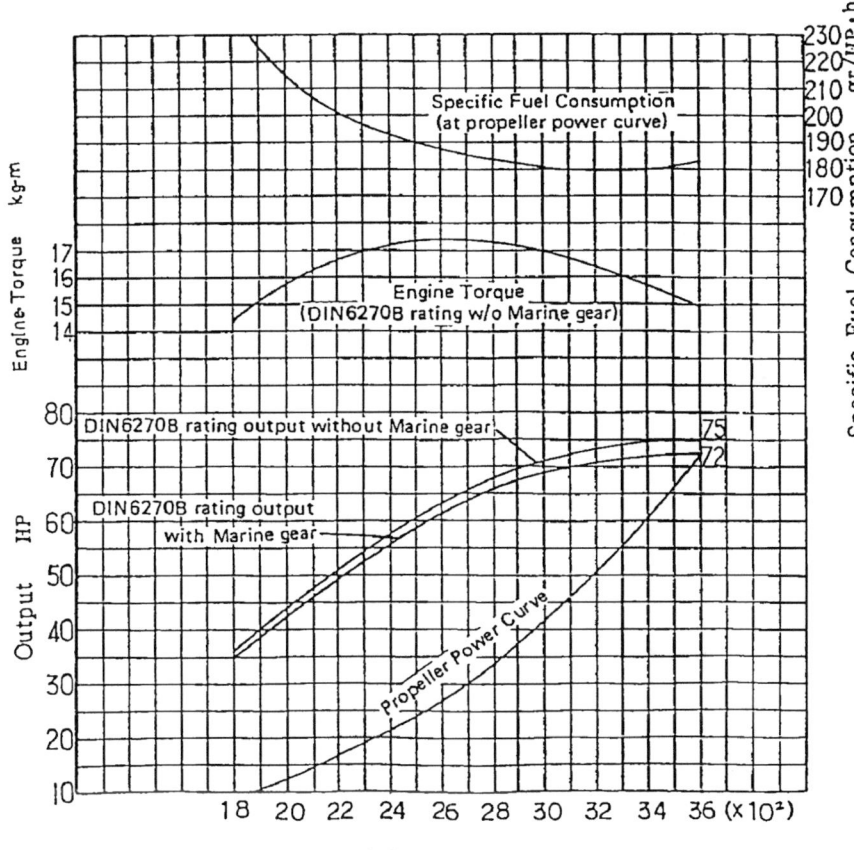

Speed of Crank Shaft   rpm

4-4. 4JH2-DT (B) E

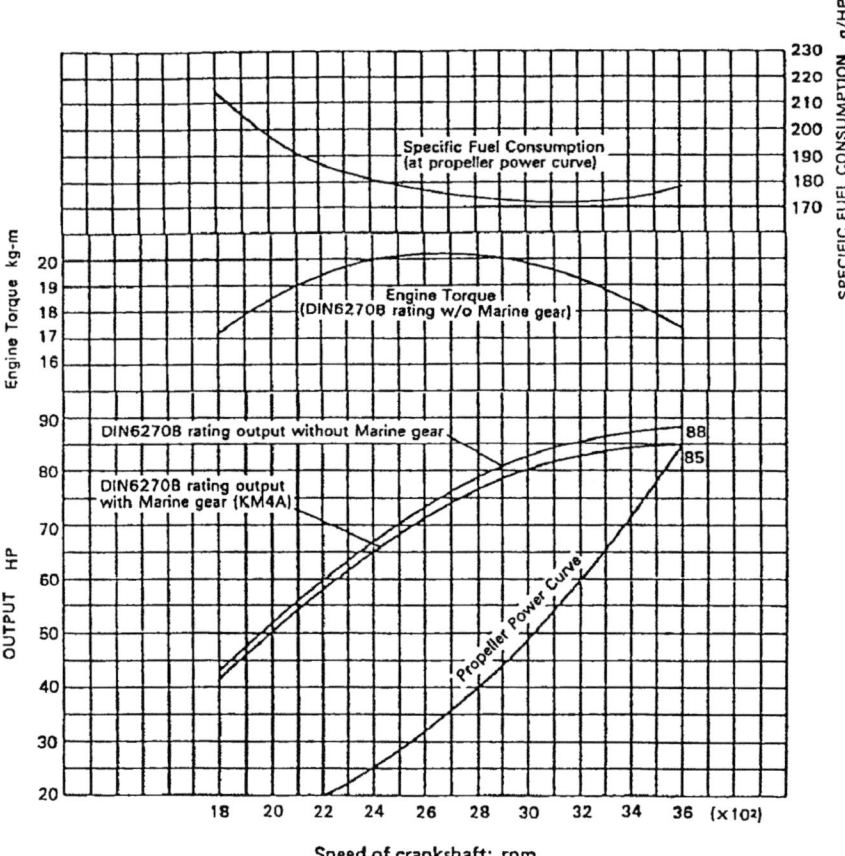

Speed of crankshaft: rpm

3-13.4JH2-UTE

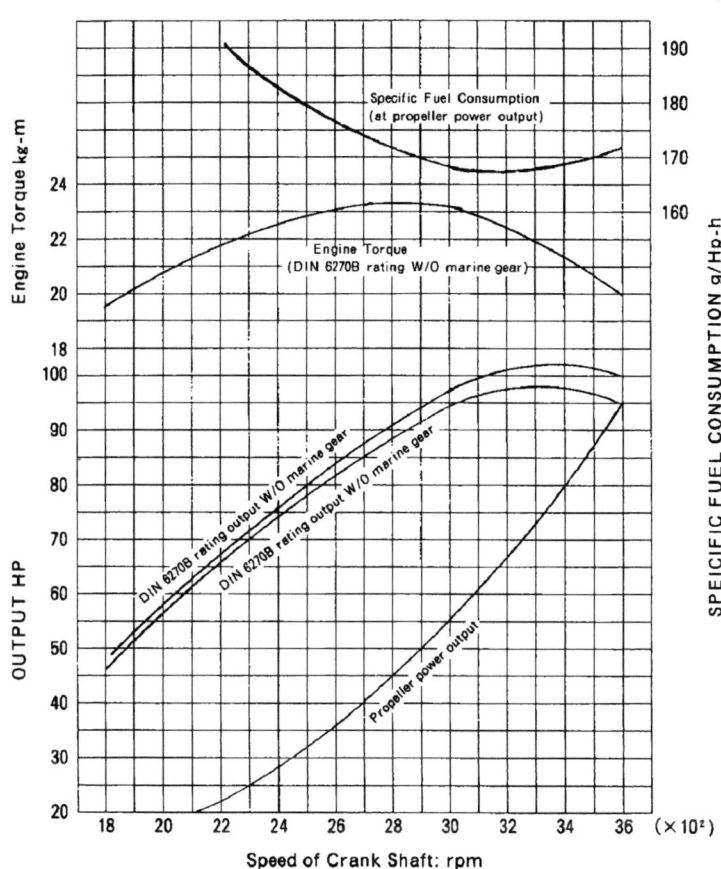

NOTE
Output, torque and specific fuel consumption are measured at the propeller shaft (The engine flywheel output is approx. 3% higher)

5. Engine Cross Section

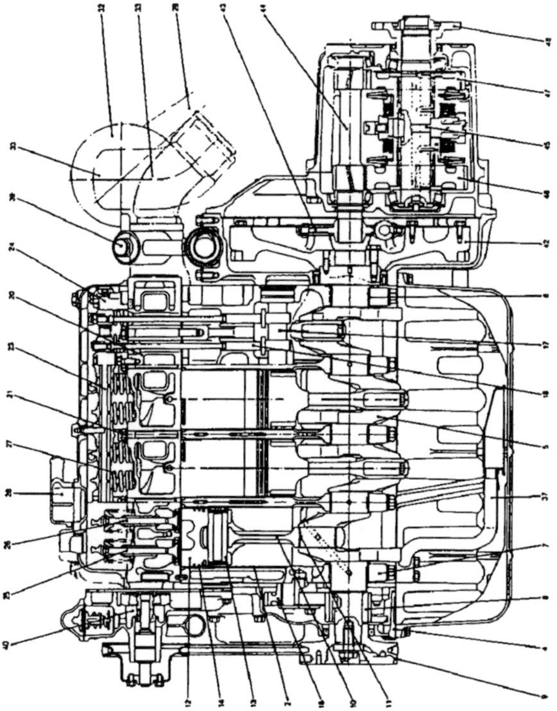

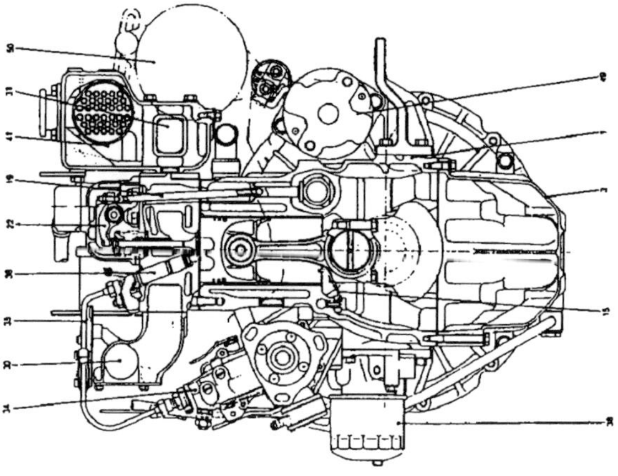

1. Cylinder block
2. Cylinder liner
3. Oil pan
4. Timing gear case
5. Crankshaft
6. Main bearing bushing
7. Main bearing cap
8. Crank gear
9. Crankshaft V-pulley
10. Connecting rod

11. Crank pin bushing
12. Piston
13. Piston pin
14. Piston ring
15. Piston cooling nozzle
16. Idle gear
17. Camshaft
18. Tappet
19. Push rod
20. Cylinder head

21. Cylinder head bolt
22. Valve rocker arm
23. Valve rocker arm shaft
24. Valve rocker arm shaft support
25. Intake valve
26. Exhaust valve
27. Valve spring
28. Breather
29. Intake silencer
30. Intake manifold

31. Exhaust manifold
32. Turbocharger
33. Mixing elbow
34. Fuel injection pump
35. Fuel pressure pump
36. Fuel injection nozzle
37. Lubricating oil inlet pipe
    Lubricating oil filter
    Lubricating oil cooler
    Cooling water pump

41. Heat exchanger
42. Flywheel
43. Damper disc
44. Input shaft
45. Output shaft
46. Forward gear
47. Reverse gear
48. Output shaft coupling
49. Starting motor
50. Alternator

4JH2E x KM3P2 Unit: mm (in.)

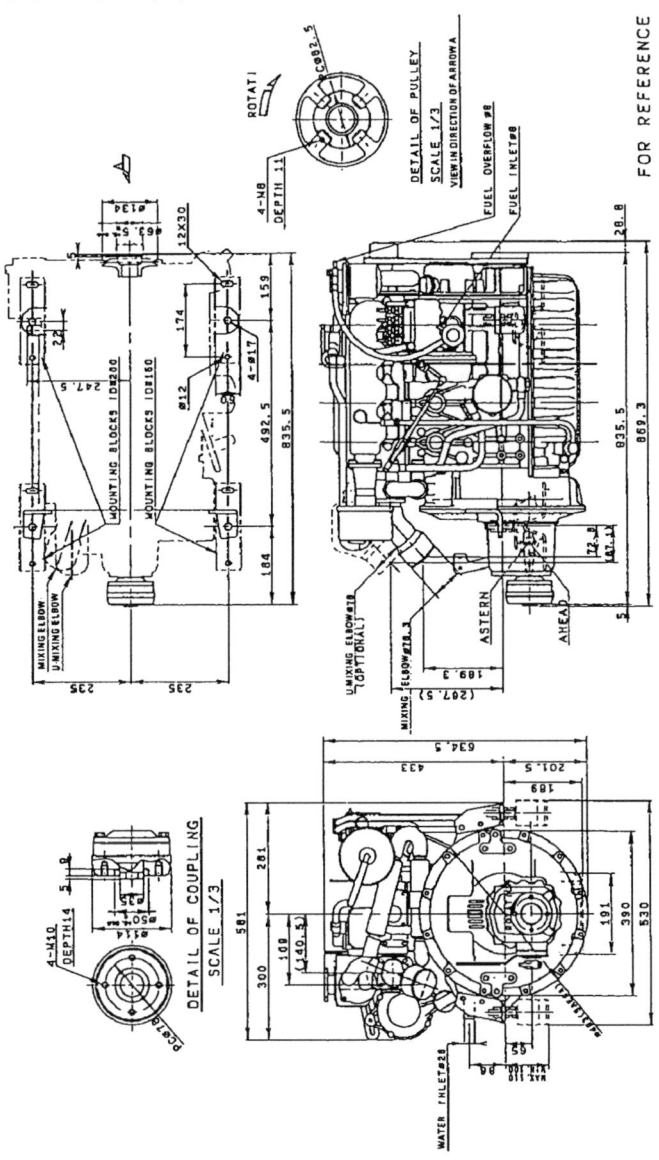

4JH2E x KBW20 Unit: mm (in.)

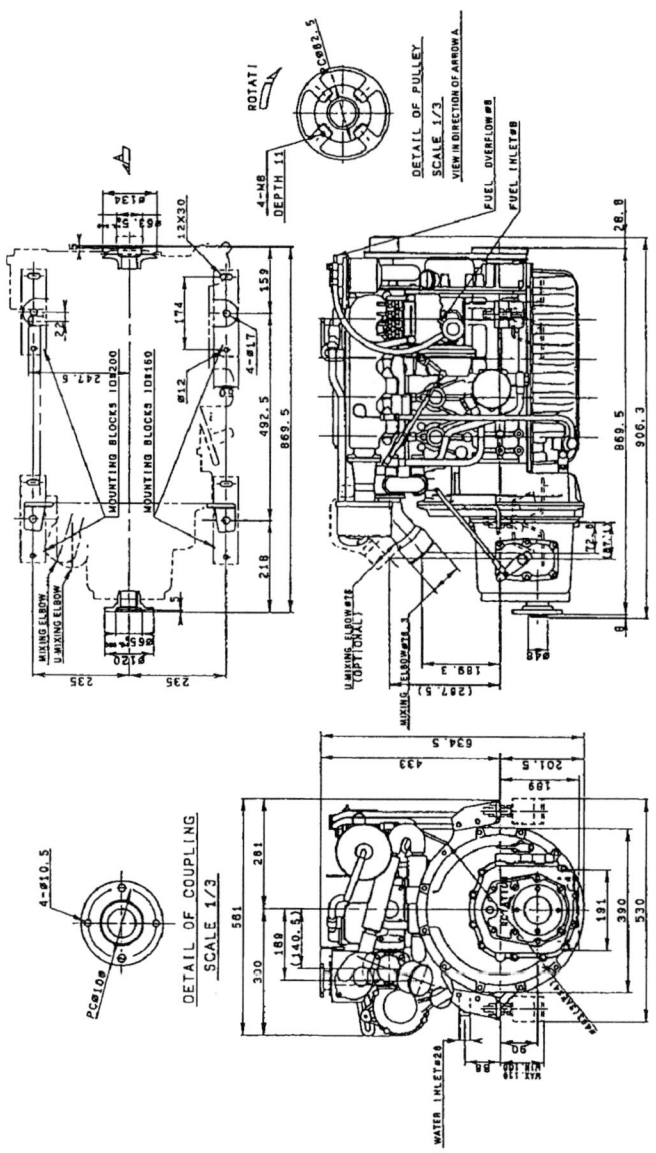

4JH2-HTE x KBW21   Unit: mm (in.)

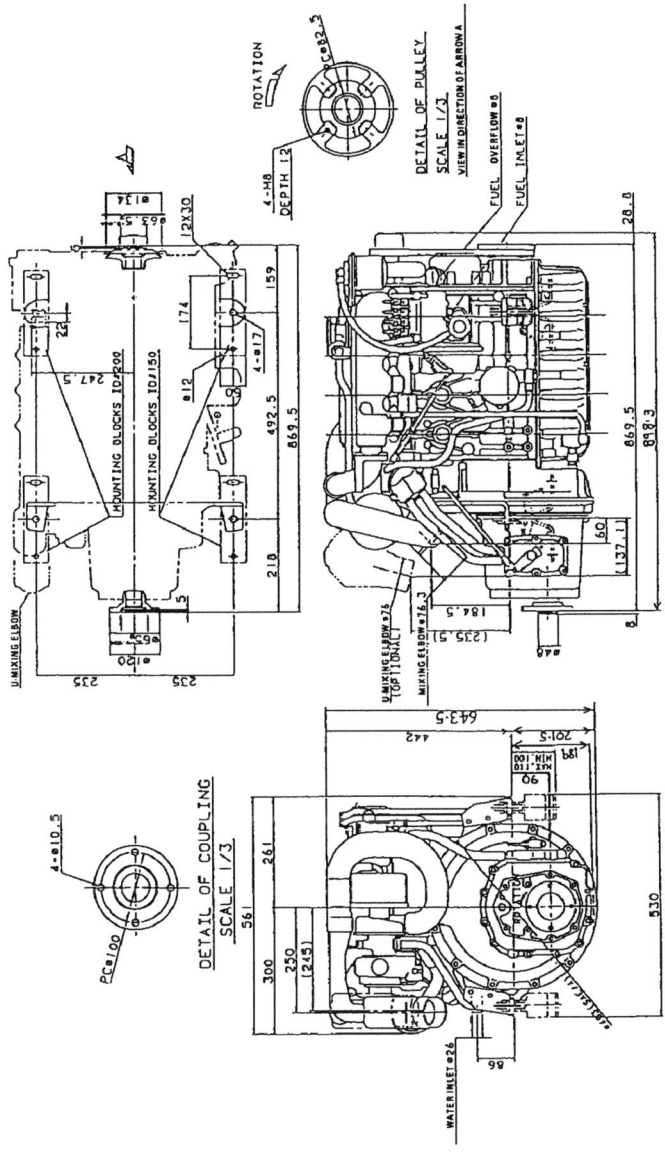

4JH2-TE x KM4A   Unit: mm (in.)

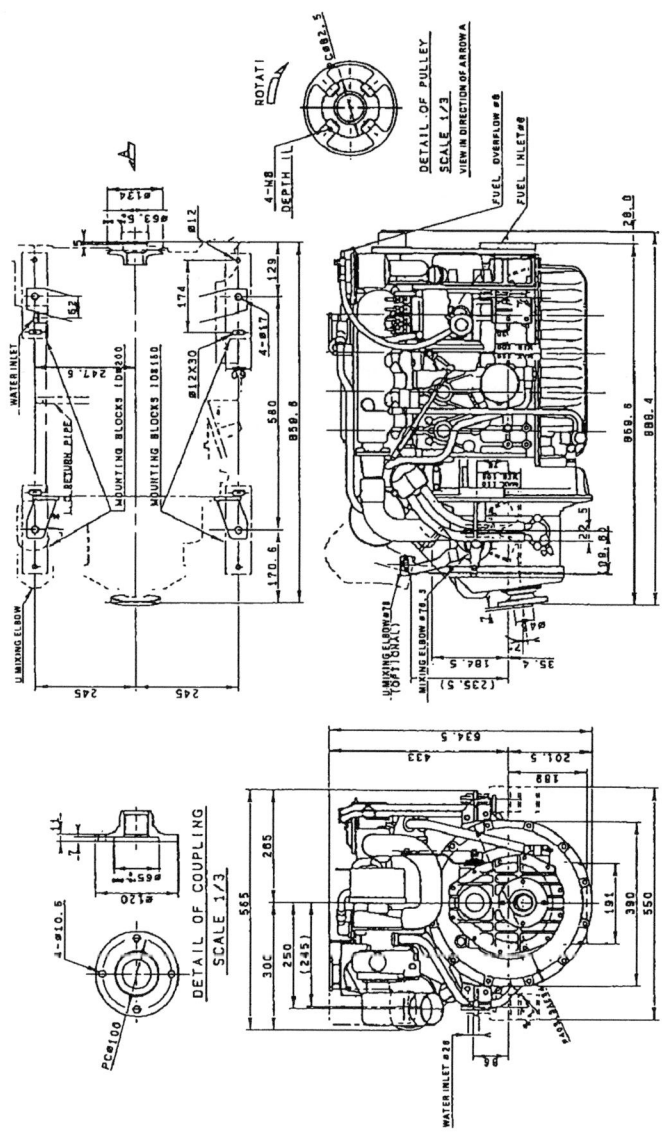

4JH2-TE x KBW20 Unit: mm (in.)

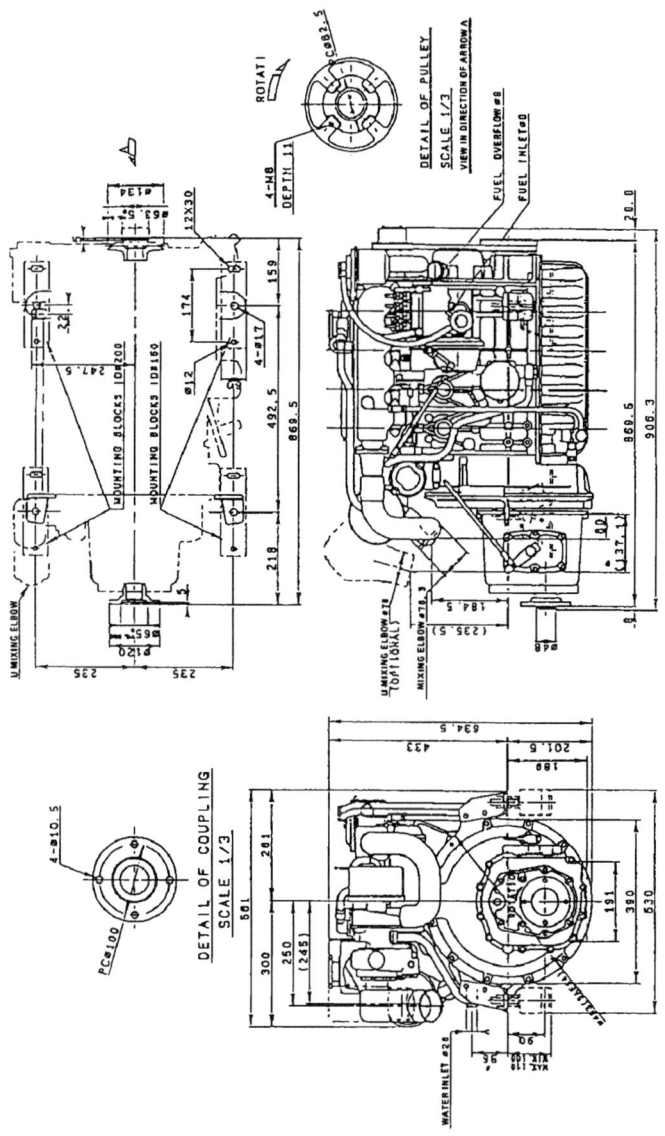

4JH2-HTE x KM4A   Unit: mm (in.)

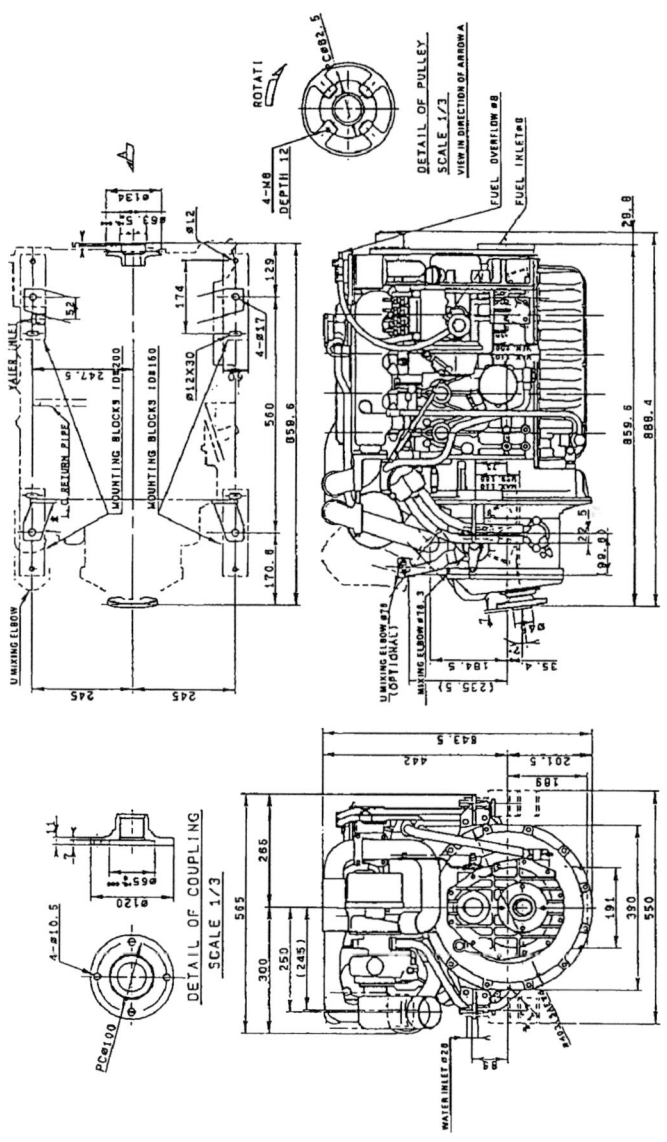

4JH2E x KM4A   Unit: mm (in.)

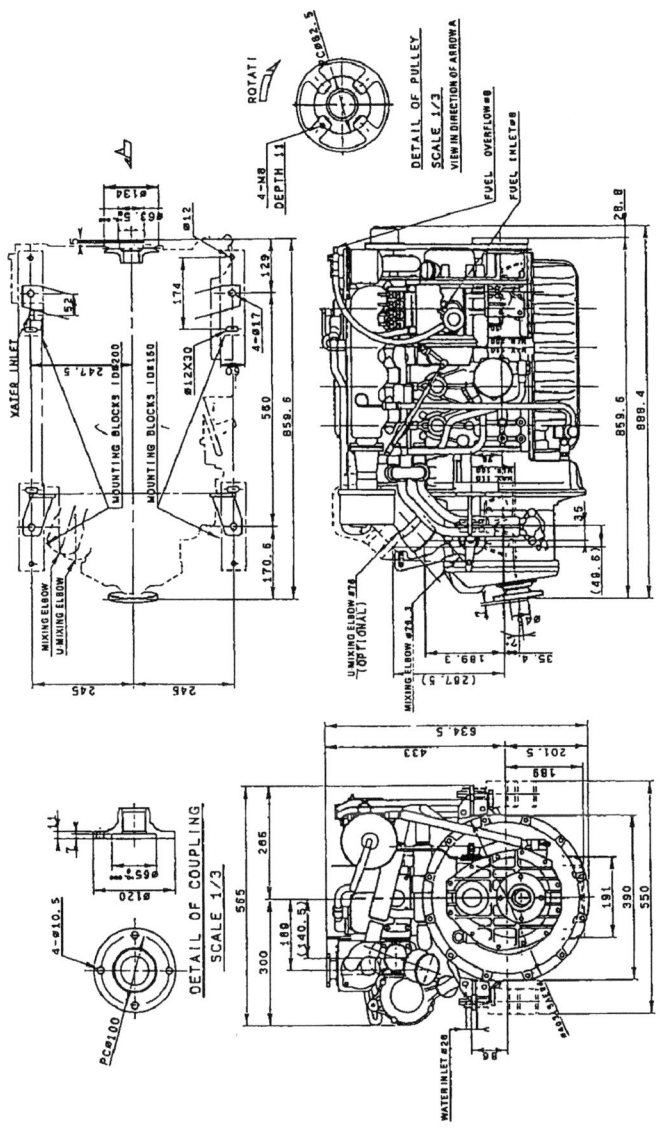

4JH2-DTE x KM4A Unit: mm (in.)

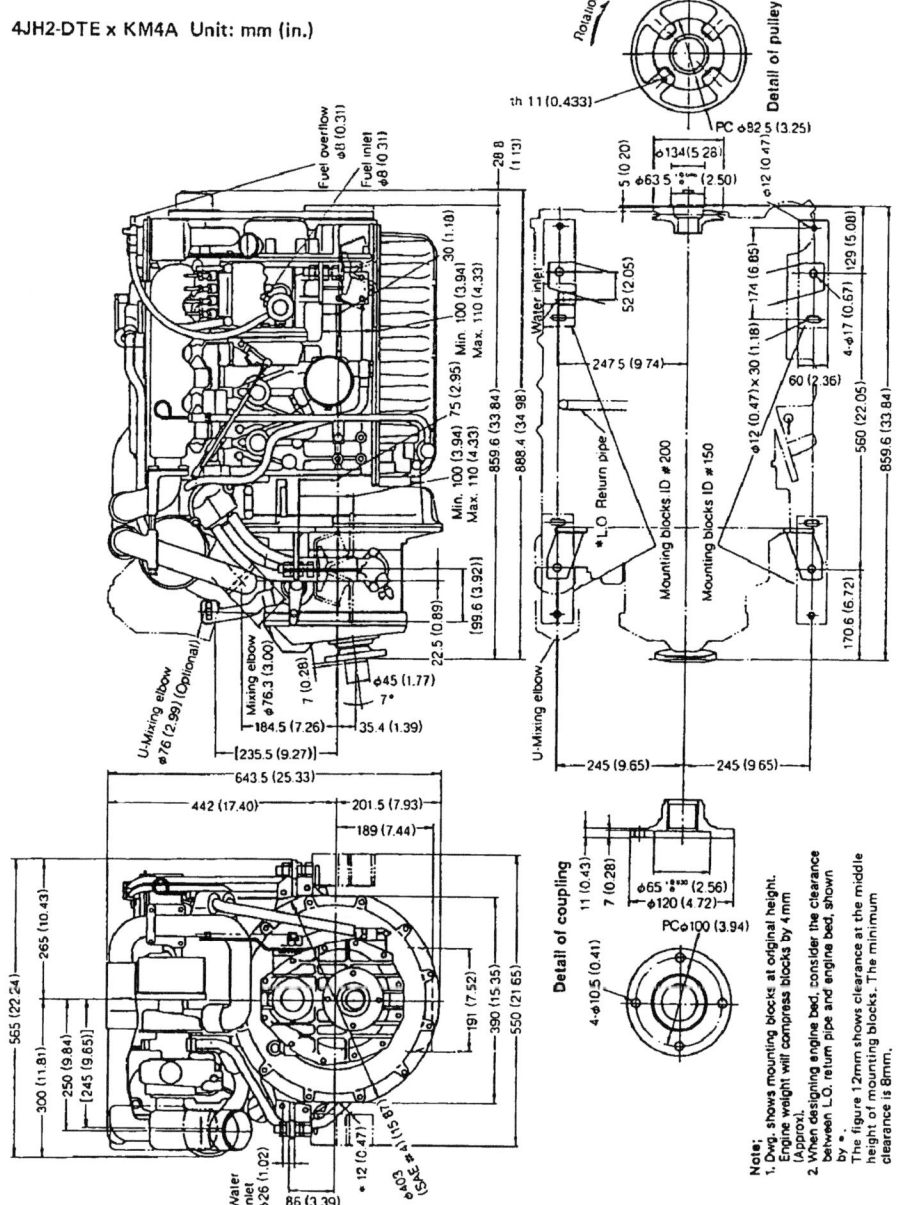

Detail of pulley

Detail of coupling

Note:
1. Dwg. shows mounting blocks at original height.
   Engine weight will compress blocks by 4mm
   (Approx.)
2. When designing engine bed, consider the clearance
   between L.O. return pipe and engine bed, shown
   by *.
   The figure 12mm shows clearance at the middle
   height of mounting blocks. The minimum
   clearance is 8mm.

4JH2-DTE x KBW21 Unit: mm (in.)

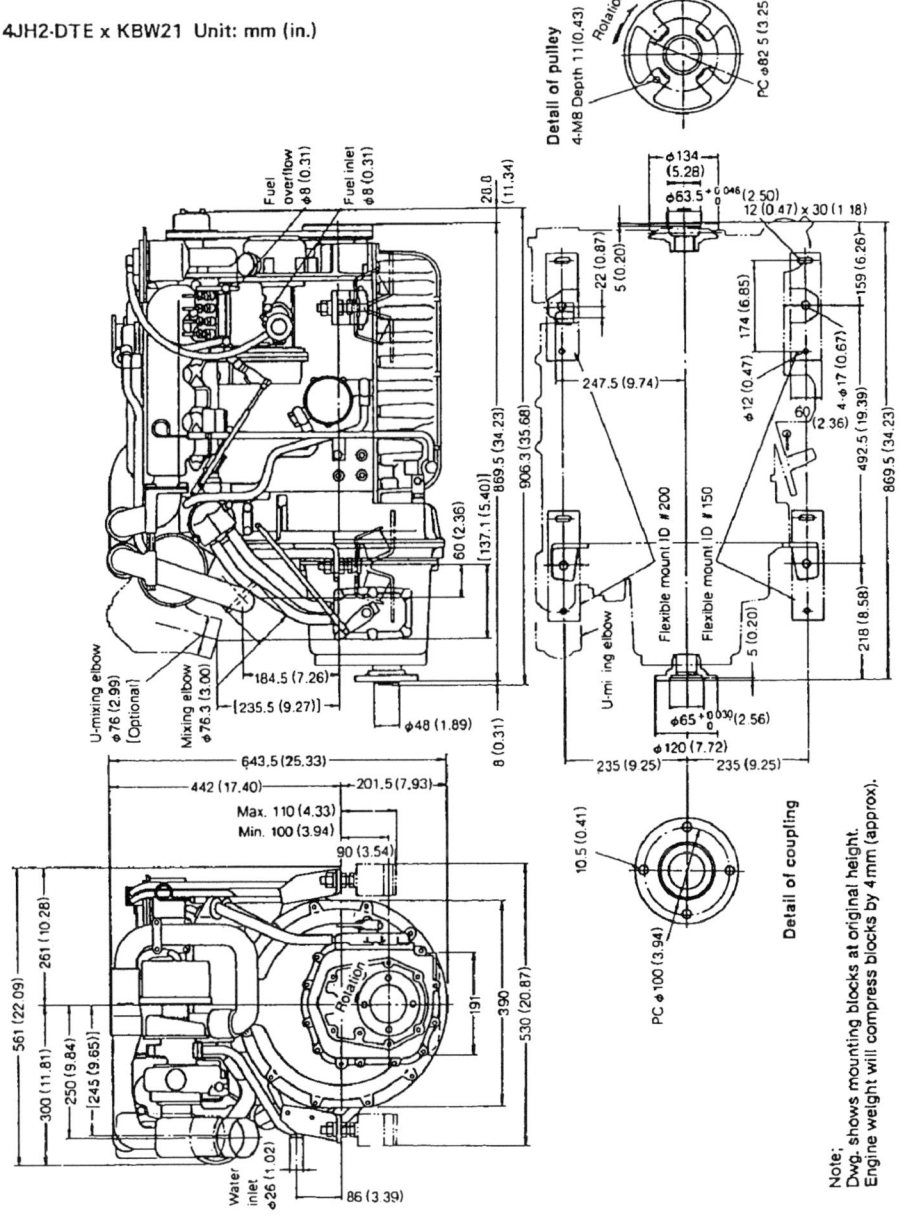

Detail of pulley
4-M8 Depth 11(0.43)
Rotation
PC ϕ82 5 (3 25)

Fuel overflow ϕ8 (0.31)
Fuel inlet ϕ8 (0.31)
20.0 (11.34)

ϕ134 (5.28)
ϕ63.5 $^{+0.046}_{0}$ (2 50)
12 (0 47) x 30 (1 18)

22 (0.87)
5 (0.20)

247.5 (9.74)

ϕ12 (0.47)
174 (6.85)
159 (6.26)
60 (2.36)
4 ϕ17 (0.67)
492.5 (19.39)
869.5 (34.23)

Flexible mount ID #200
Flexible mount ID #150

U-mixing elbow

5 (0.20)

218 (8.58)

U-mixing elbow ϕ76 (2.99) [Optional]
Mixing elbow ϕ76.3 (3.00)

184.5 (7.26)
[235.5 (9.27)]

ϕ48 (1.89)

8 (0.31)

ϕ65 $^{+0.030}_{0}$ (2 56)
ϕ120 (7.72)
235 (9 25) 235 (9.25)

U-mixing elbow

869.5 (34.23)
906.3 (35.68)
137.1 (5.40)
60 (2.36)

643.5 (25.33)
442 (17.40)
201.5 (7.93)
Max. 110 (4.33)
Min. 100 (3.94)
90 (3.54)

10 5 (0.41)

561 (22 09)
261 (10 28)
300 (11.81)
250 (9.84)
[245 (9.65)]

Rotation

191
390
530 (20.87)

PC ϕ100 (3.94)

Detail of coupling

Water inlet ϕ26 (1.02)
86 (3 39)

Note;
Dwg. shows mounting blocks at original height.
Engine weight will compress blocks by 4mm (approx).

Printed in Japan
A0A1029-9002

4JH2-UTE × KW4A
Unit:mm

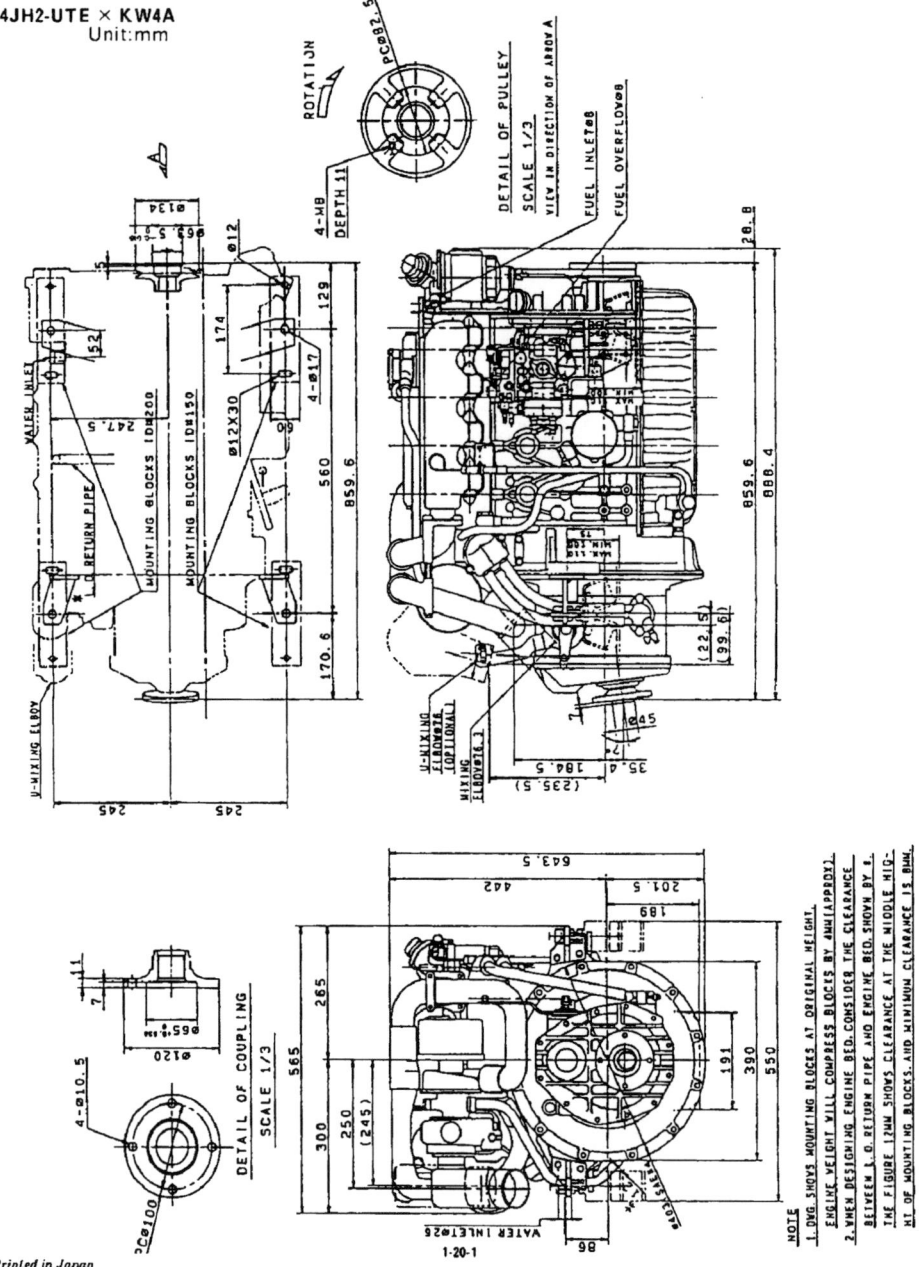

4JH2-UTE × KBW21
Unit:mm

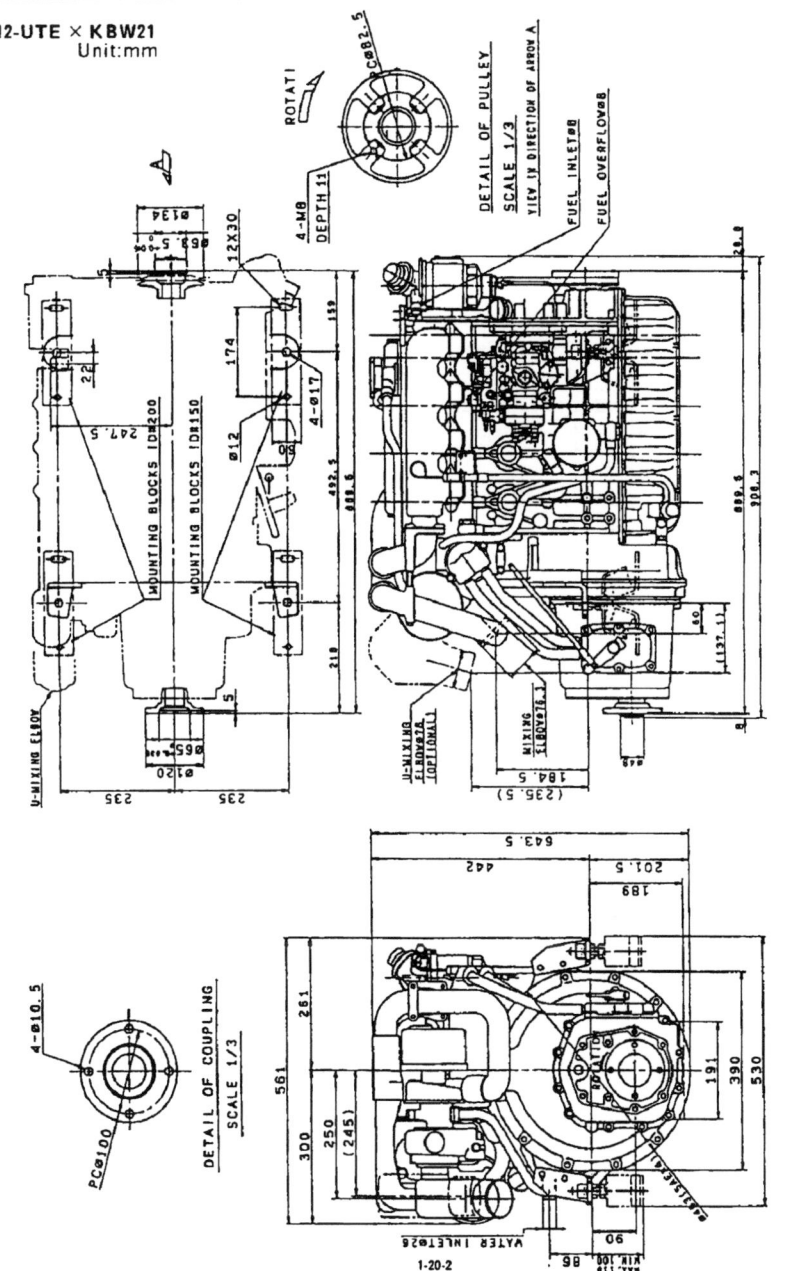

DETAIL OF PULLEY
SCALE 1/3
VIEW IN DIRECTION OF ARROW A

DETAIL OF COUPLING
SCALE 1/3

NOTE
1.DWG. SHOWS MOUNTING BLOCKS AT ORIGINAL HEIGHT.
ENGINE WEIGHT WILL COMPRESS BLOCKS BY 4MM(APPROX).

1-20-2

7. Piping Diagrams

7-1 4JH2E

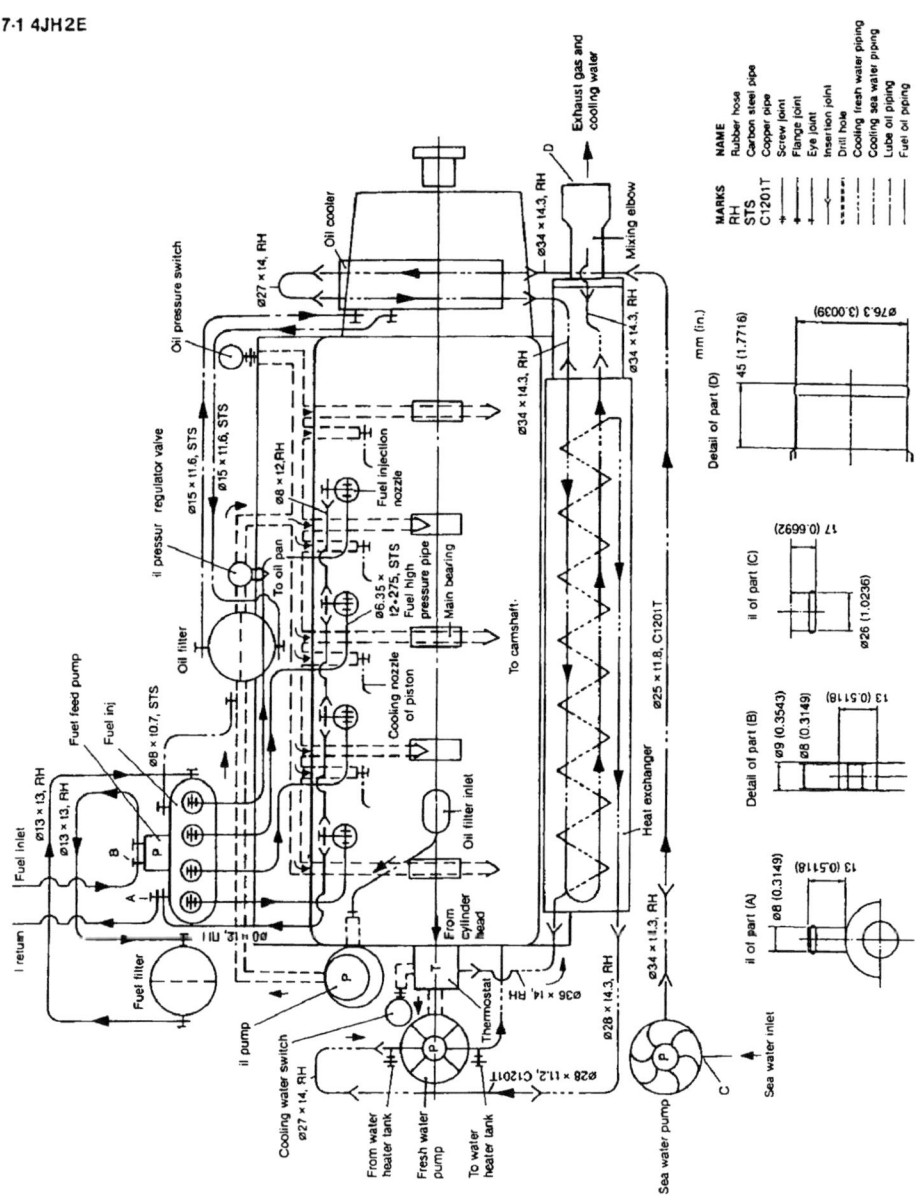

7·2 4JH2-TE

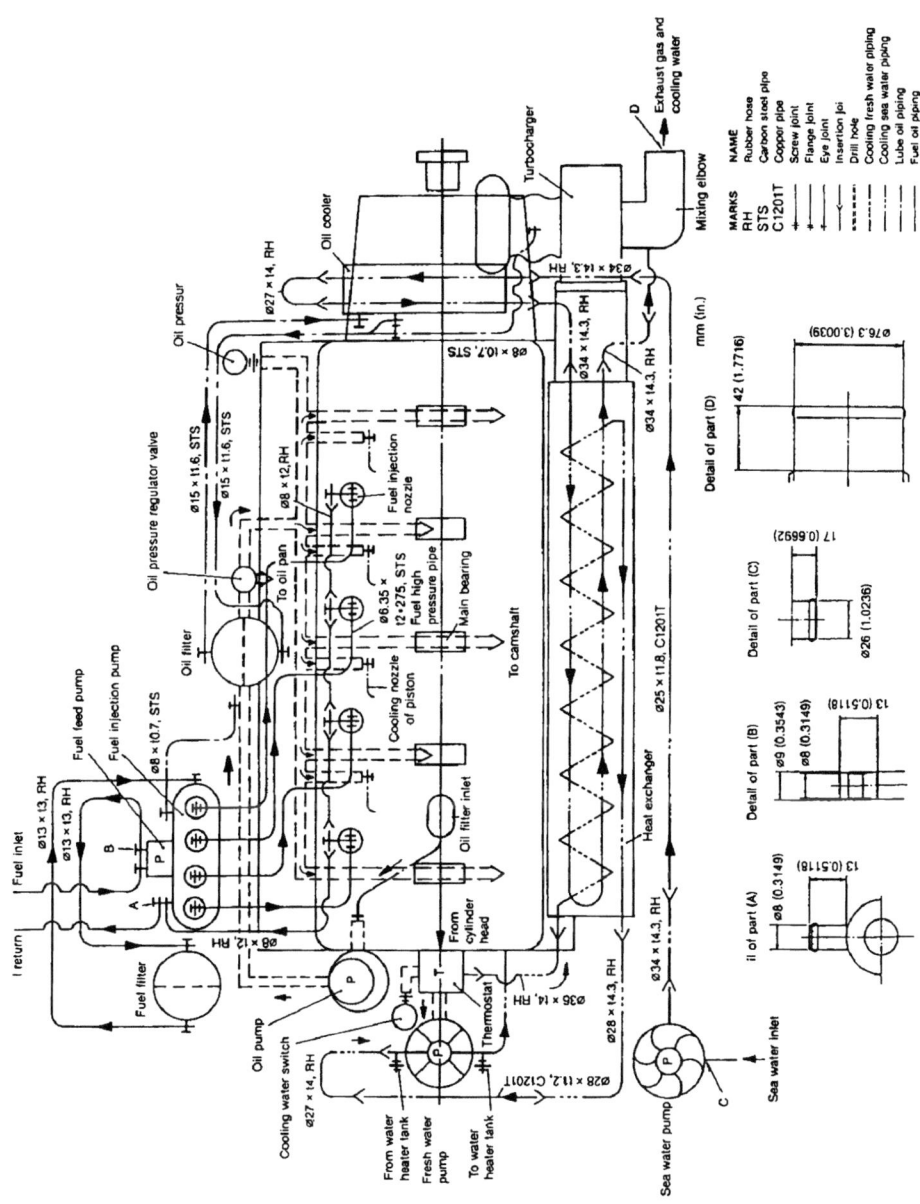

7-3. 4JH2-HT(B)E
4JH2-DT(B)E
4JH2-UT(B)E

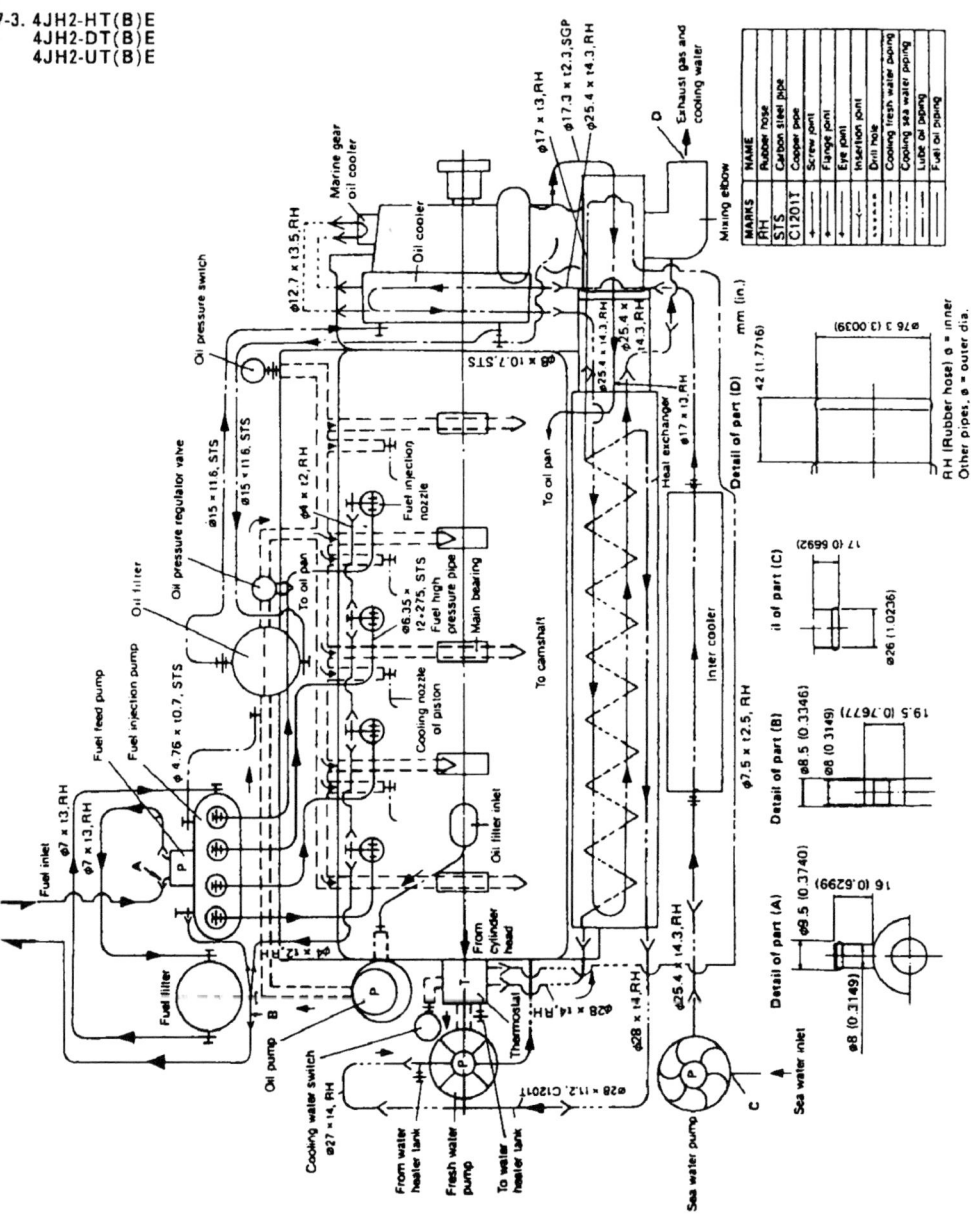

CHAPTER 2

INSPECTION AND SERVICING OF BASIC ENGINE PARTS

Printed in Japan
A0A1029-9002

1. Cylinder Block

The cylinder block is a thin-skinned, (low-weight), short skirt type with rationally placed ribs. The side walls are wave shaped to maximize ridigity for strength and low noise.

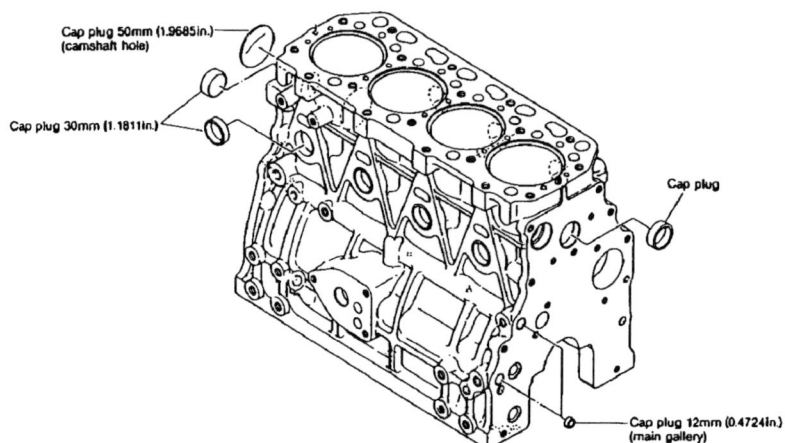

Cap plug 50mm (1.9685in.) (camshaft hole)

Cap plug 30mm (1.1811in.)

Cap plug

Cap plug 12mm (0.4724in.) (main gallery)

1-1 Inspection of parts

Make a visual inspection to check for cracks on engines that have frozen up, overturned or otherwise been subjected to undue stress. Perform a color check on any portions that appear to be cracked, and replace the cylinder block if the crack is not repairable.

1-2 Cleaning of oil holes

Clean all oil holes, making sure that none are clogged up and the blind plugs do not come off.

Color check kit
Part code No. 97550-004560

	Quantity
Penetrant	1
Developer	2
Cleaner	3

1-3 Color check procedure

(1) Clean the area to be inspected.
(2) Color check kit
The color check test kit consists of an aerosol cleaner, penetrant and developer.
(3) Clean the area to be inspected with the cleaner.
Either spray the cleaner on directly and wipe, or wipe the area with a cloth moistened with cleaner.
(4) Spray on red penetrant
After cleaning, spray on the red penetrant and allow 5 ~ 10 minutes for penetration. Spray on more red penetrant if it dries before it has been able to penetrate.
(5) Spray on developer
Remove any residual penetrant on the surface after the penetrant has penetrated, and spray on the developer. If there are any cracks in the surface, red dots or a red line will appear several minutes after the developer dries.
Hold the developer 300 ~ 400mm (11.8110 ~ 15.7480in.) away from the area being inspected when spraying, making sure to coat the surface uniformly.
(6) Clean the surface with the cleaner.

NOTE: *Without fail, read the instructions for the color check kit before use.*

2-1

1-4 Replacement of cup plugs

Step No.	Description	Procedure	Tool or material used
1.	Clean and remove grease from the hole into which the cup plug is to be driven. (Remove scale and sealing material previously applied.)	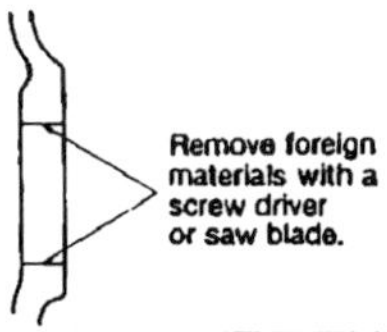 Remove foreign materials with a screw driver or saw blade.	•Screw driver or saw blade •Thinner
2.	Remove grease from the cup plug.	Visually check the nick around the plug.	•Thinner
3.	Apply Threebond No. 4 to the seat surface where the plug is to be driven in.	Apply over the whole outside of the plug.	•Threebond No. 4
4.	Insert the plug into the hole.	Insert the plug so that it sits correctly.	
5.	Place a driving tool on the cup plug and drive it in using a hammer.	Drive in the plug parallel to the seating surface.	•Driving tool

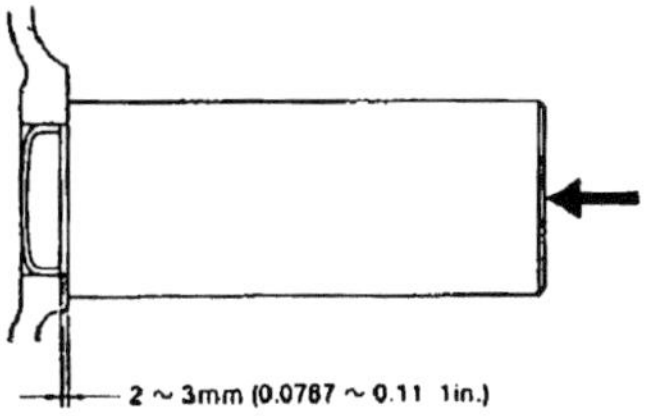

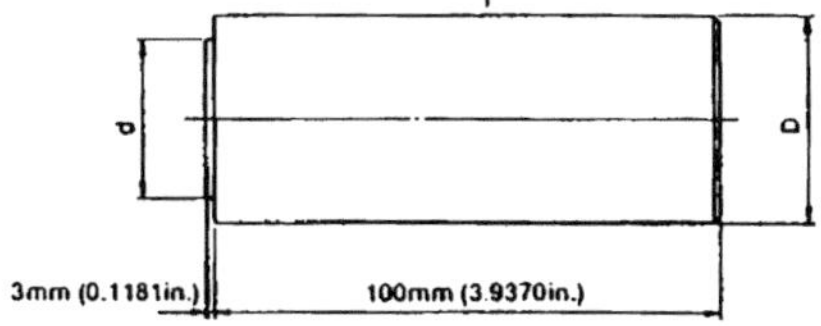

•Hammer |

2 ~ 3mm (0.0787 ~ 0.11 1in.)

3mm (0.1181in.)   100mm (3.9370in.)

*Using the special tool, drive the cup plug so that the edge of the plug is 2mm (0.0787in.) below the cylinder surface.

mm (in.)

Plug dia.	d	D
ø12	ø11.9 ~ 12.0 (ø0.4685 ~ 0.4724)	ø20 (ø0.7874)
ø30	ø29.9 ~ 30.0 (ø1.1770 ~ 1.8110)	ø40 (ø1.5748)

2-2

1-5 Cylinder bore measurement

Measure the bore diameter with a cylinder gauge at the positions shown in the figure.
Replace the cylinder bore when the measured value exceeds the wear limit. Measurement must be done at least at 3 positions as shown in the figure, namely, top, middle and bottom positions in both directions along the crankshaft rotation and crankshaft center lines.

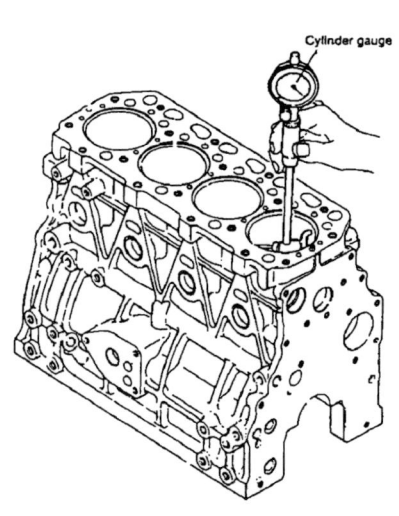

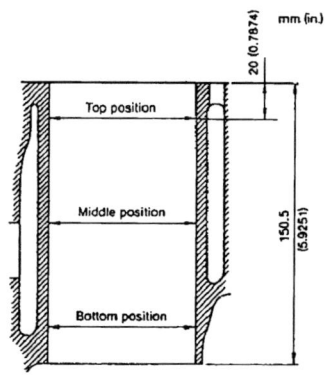

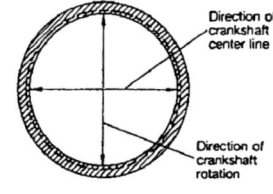

	Standard	Wear limit
Cylinder bore dia.	ø82.00 ~ 82.03 (3.2283 ~ 3.2295)	ø82.06 (3.2307)
Cylinder roundness	0 ~ 0.01 (0 ~ 0.0004)	0.02 (0.0008)

mm (in.)

Printed in Japan
A0A1029-9002

3. Cylinder Head

The cylinder head is of 4-cylinder integral constructi ,
mounted with 18 bolts. Special alloy stellite with superior
resistance to heat and wear is fitted on the seats, and the
area between the valves is cooled by a water jet.

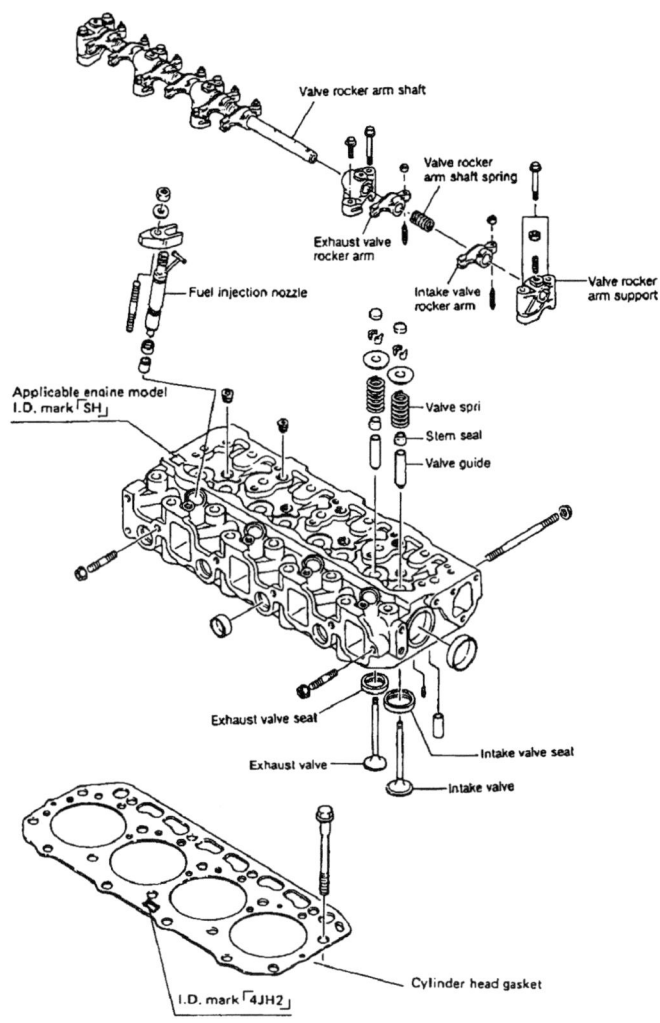

Valve rocker arm shaft

Valve rocker
arm shaft spring

Exhaust valve
rocker arm

Fuel injection nozzle

Intake valve
rocker arm

Valve rocker
arm support

Applicable engine model
I.D. mark 「SH」

Valve spri

Stem seal

Valve guide

Exhaust valve seat

Intake valve seat

Exhaust valve

Intake valve

Cylinder head gasket

I.D. mark 「4JH2」

2-6

3-1 Inspecting the cylinder head

The cylinder head is subjected to very severe operating conditions with repeated high pressure, high temperature and cooling. Thoroughly remove all the carbon and dirt after disassembly and carefully inspect all parts.

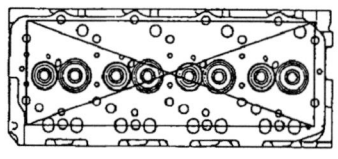

3-1.1 Distortion of the combustion surface

Carefully check for cylinder head distortion as this leads to gasket damage and compression leaks.
(1) Clean the cylinder head surface.
(2) Place a straight-edge along each of the four sides and each diagonal. Measure the clearance between the straight-edge and combustion surface with a feeler gauge.

Measurement procedure

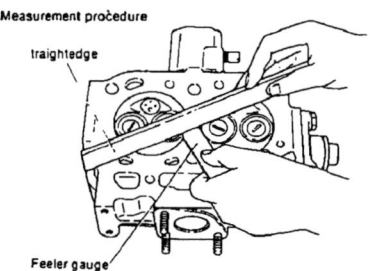

straightedge

Feeler gauge

mm (in.)

	Standard	Wear limit
Cylinder head distortion	0.05 (0.0019) or less	0.15 (0.0059)

3-1.2 Checking for cracks in the combustion surface

Remove the fuel injection nozzle, intake and exhaust valve and clean the combustion surface. Check for discoloration or distortion and conduct a color check test to check for any cracks.

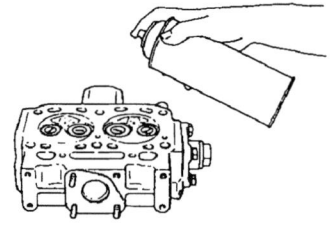

3-1.3 Checking the intake and exhaust valve seats

Check the surface and width of the valve seats.
If they are too wide, or if the surfaces are rough, correct to the following standards:

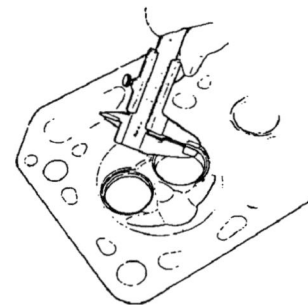

Seat angle	Intake	120°
	Exhaust	90°

mm (in.)

Seat width	Standard	Wear limit
Intake	1.28 (0.0504)	1.78 (0.0700)
Exhaust	1.77 (0.0697)	2.27 (0.0894)

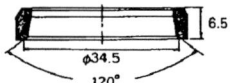

6.5
φ34.5
120°

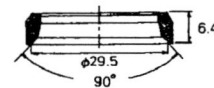

6.4
φ29.5
90°

Standard dimension

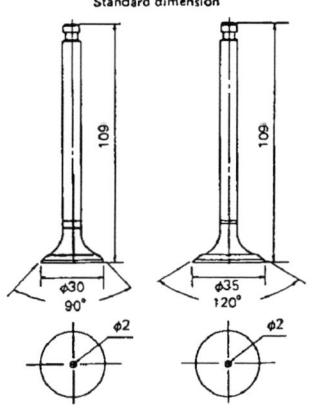

109

109

φ30
90°

φ35
120°

φ2

φ2

3-2 Valve seat correction procedure

The most common method for correcting unevenness of the seat surface with a seat grinder is as follows:

(1) Use a seat grinder to make the surface even.

As the valve seat width will be enlarged, first use a 70° grinder, then grind the seat to the standard dimension with a 15° grinder.

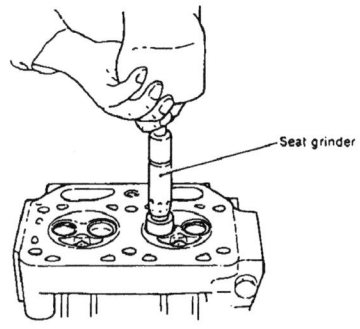

Seat grinder

Seat grinder	Intake valve	30°
	Exhaust valve	45°

NOTE: When seat adjustment is necessary, be sure to check the valve and valve guide. If the clearance exceeds the tolerance, replace the valve or the valve guide, and then grind the seat.

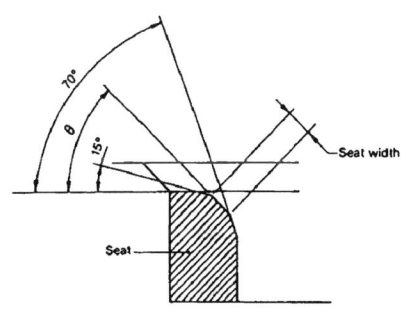

Seat width

Seat

(2) Knead valve compound with oil and finish the valve seat with a lapping tool.

(3) Final finishing should be done with oil only.

Lapping tool

Use a rubber cap type lapping tool for cylinders without a lapping tool groove slit.

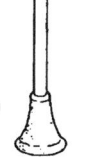

NOTE: Clean the valve and cylinder head with light oil or the equivalent after valve seat finishing is completed, and make sure that there are no grindings remaining.

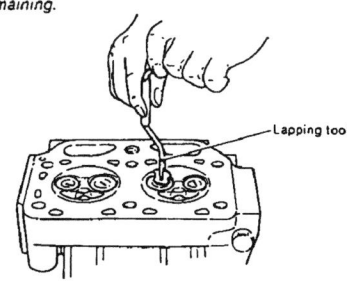

Lapping tool

NOTE: 1. Insert adjusting shims between the valve spring and cylinder head when seats have been refinished with a seat grinder.

2. Measure valve distortion after valve seat refinishing has been completed, and replace the valve and valve seat if it exceeds the tolerance.

3-3 Intake/exhaust valves, valve guides

3-3.1 Wearing and corrosion of valve stem

Replace the valve if the valve stem is excessively worn or corroded.

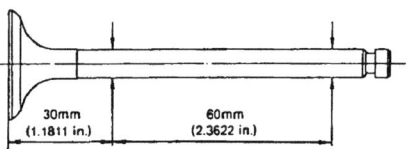

| | 30mm (1.1811 in.) | | 60mm (2.3622 in.) |

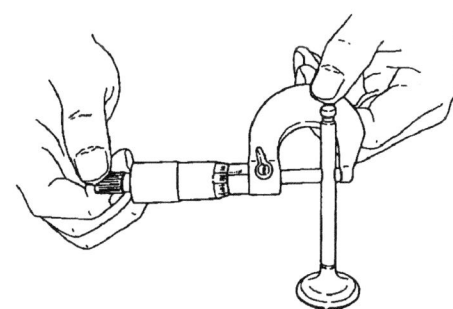

mm (in.)

Valve stem outside dia.	Standard	Wear limit
Intake	ø7.960 ~ 7.975 (ø0.3134 ~ 0.3140)	−0.13 (−0.0051)
Exhaust	ø7.955 ~ 7.970 (ø0.3132 ~ 0.3138)	−0.13 (−0.0051)

2-8

3-3.2 Inspection of valve seat wear and contact surface

Inspect for valve seat scratches and excessive wear. Check to make sure the contact surface is normal. The seat angle must be checked and adjusted if the valve seat contact surface is much smaller than the width of the valve seat.

NOTE: Keep in mind the fact that the intake and discharge valve have different diameters.

3-3.3 Valve sinking

Over long periods of use and repeated lappings, combustion efficiency may drop. Measure the sinking distance and replace the valve and valve seat if the valve sink exceeds the tolerance.

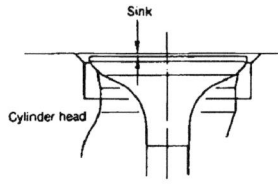

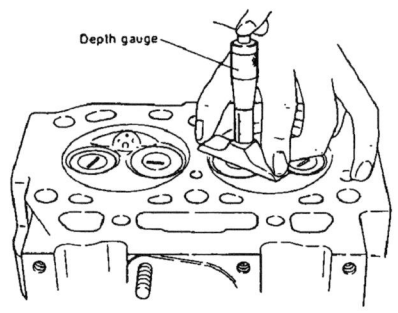

mm (in.)

	Standard	Wear limit
Valve sink	0.4 ~ 0.6 (0.0157 ~ 0.0236)	1.5 (0.0590)

3-3.4 Valve guide

(1) Measuring inner diameter of valve guide.
Measure the inner diameter of the valve guide and replace it if it exceeds the wear limit.

mm (in.)

		Standard	Wear limit
Valve guide inside dia.	Intake	φ8.010 ~ 8.025 (φ0.3154 ~ 0.3159)	+0.2 (0.0079)
	Exhaust	φ8.015 ~ 8.030 (φ0.3156 ~ 0.3161)	+0.2 (0.0079)

NOTE: The inner diameter standard dimensions assume a pressure fit.

(2) Replacing the valve guide
Use the insertion tool and tap in the guide with a mallet.

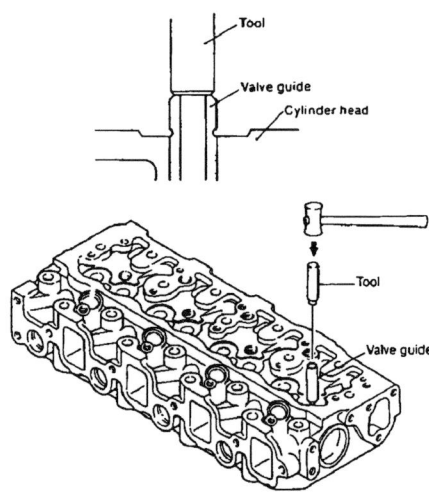

The intake valve guide and exhaust valve guide are of different shapes/dimensions. The one with a groove around it is the exhaust valve guide and the one without is the intake valve guide.

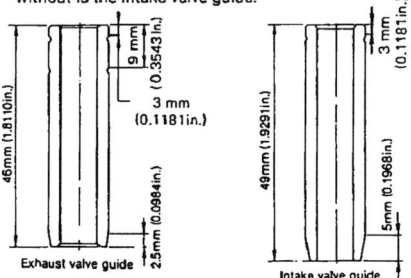

(3) Valve guide projection
The valve guide should project 15mm from the top of the cylinder head.

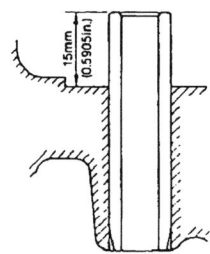

(4) Valve stem seals
The valve stem seals in the intake/exhaust valve guides cannot be re-used once they are removed—be sure to replace them.
When assembling the intake/exhaust valves, apply an adequate quantity of engine oil on the valve stem before inserting them.

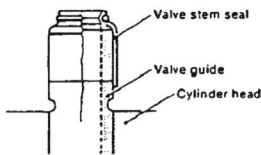

Valve stem seal
Valve guide
Cylinder head

3-4 Valve springs

3-4.1 Checking valve springs

(1) Check the spring for scratches or corrosion.
(2) Measure the free length of the spring.

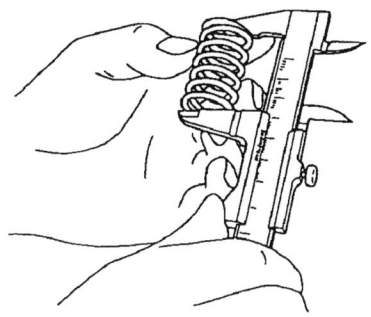

(3) Measure inclination.

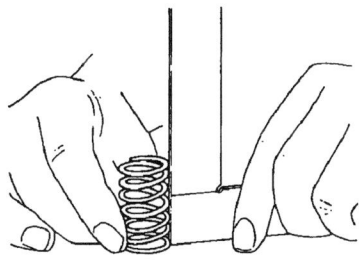

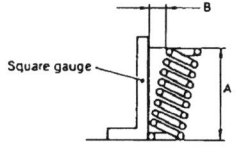

Square gauge

(4) Measure spring tensi

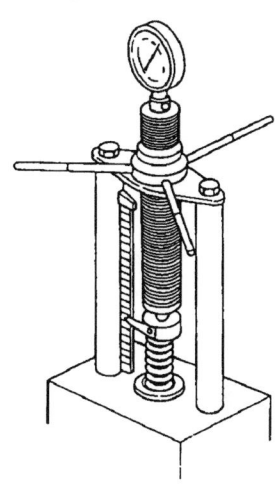

		mm (in.)
Valve spring	Standard	Wear limit
Free length	44.4 (1.7480)	43 (1.6929)
Length when attached	40 (1.5748)	—
Load when attached	12kg (26.46 lb.)	10kg (22.05 lb.)

Assembling valve springs .
The side with the smaller pitch (painted yellow) should face down (cylinder head).

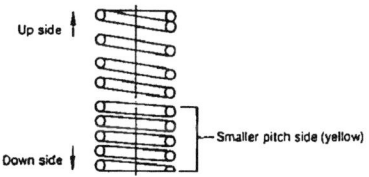

Up side
Down side
Smaller pitch side (yellow)

NOTE: The pitch of the valve spring is not even. The side with the smaller pitch (yellow) should face down (cylinder head) when assembled.

(5) Spring retainer and spring cotter
Inspect the inside face of the spring retainer, the outside surface of the spring cotter, the contact area of the spring cotter inside surface and the notch in the head of the valve stem. Replace the spring retainer and spring cotter when the contact area is less than 70%, or when the spring cotter has been recessed because of wear.

2-10

3-5 Assembling the cylinder head

Partially tighten the bolts in the specified order and then tighten to the specified torque, being careful that the head does not get distorted.

(1) Clean out the cylinder head bolt holes.
(2) Check for foreign matter on the cylinder head surface where it comes in contact with the block.
(3) Coat the head bolt threads and nut seats with lube oil.
(4) Use the positioning pins to line up the head gasket with the cylinder block.
(5) Match up the cylinder head with the head gasket and mount.

Exhaust manifold side

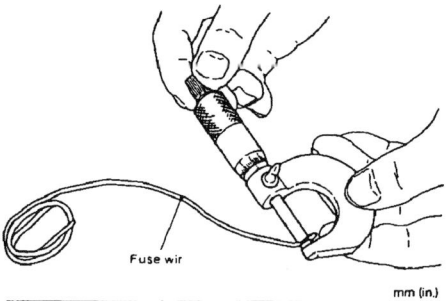

		First	Second
			kg-m (ft-lb)
Tightening torque		3.5 ~ 4.5 (25.32 ~ 32.55)	7.5 ~ 8.5 (54.25 ~ 61.48)

3-6 Measuring top clearance

(1) Place a high quality fuse (Ø1.5mm (0.0591in.), 10mm (0.3937in.) long) in three positions on the flat part of the piston head.
(2) Assemble the cylinder head gasket and the cylinder block and tighten the bolts in the specified order to the specified torque.
(3) Turn the crank, (in the direction of engine revolution), and press the fuse against the piston until it breaks.
(4) Remove the head and take out the broken fuse.
(5) Measure the three positions where each fuse is broken and calculate the average.
(0.71 ~ 0.75mm (0.0280 ~ 0.0295in.) is ideal)

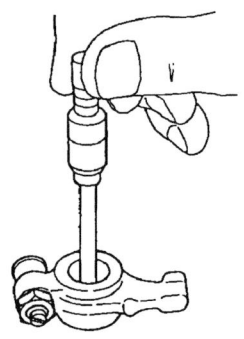

Fuse wir

	mm (in.)
Top clearance	0.71 ~ 0.89 (0.0280 ~ 0.0350)

3-7 Intake and exhaust valve arms

Valve arm and valve arm bushing wear may change opening/closing timing of the valve, and may in turn affect engine performance according to the extent of the change.

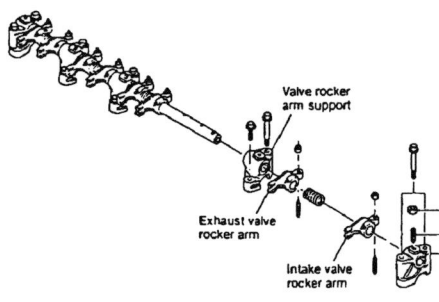

(1) Valve arm shaft and valve arm bushing
Measure the outer diameter of the shaft and the inner diameter of the bearing, and replace if wear exceeds the limit.

		Standard	Wear limit
			mm (in.)
Intake and exhaust valve rocker arm shaft outside dia.	A	15.966 ~ 15.988 (0.6285 ~ 0.6294)	15.955 (0.6281)
Intake and exhaust valve rocker arm inside dia.	B	16.000 ~ 16.027 (0.6299 ~ 0.6310)	16.090 (0.6334)
Valve rocker arm shaft and bushing clearance at assembly		0.012 ~ 0.061 (0.0005 ~ 0.0024)	0.135 (0.0053)

Replace the valve arm shaft bushing if it moves and replace the entire valve arm if there is no tightening clearance.

(2) Valve arm spring
Check the valve arm spring and replace it if it is corroded or worn.
(3) Valve arm and valve top retainer wear
Inspect the contact surface of the valve arm and replace it if there is abnormal wear or flaking.
(4) Inspect the contact surface of the valve clearance adjustment screw and push rod and replace if there is abnormal wear or flaking.

3-8 Adjustment of valve head clearance

(1) Make adjustments when the engine is cool.

	mm (in.)
Intake and exhaust head clearance	0.2 (0.0079)

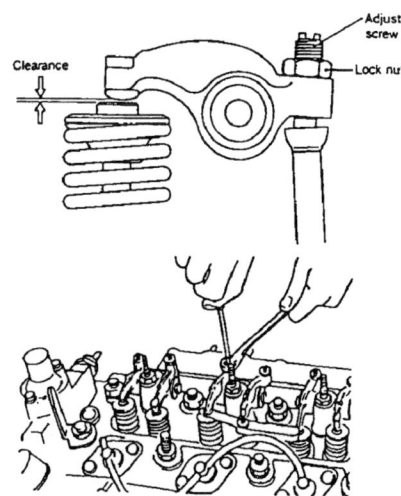

(2) Be sure that the opening and closing angles for both the intake and the exhaust valves are checked when the timing gear is disassembled (The gauge on the flywheel is read when the push rod turns the flywheel).

Model 4JH2-TE
4JH2-HTE
4JH2-DTE

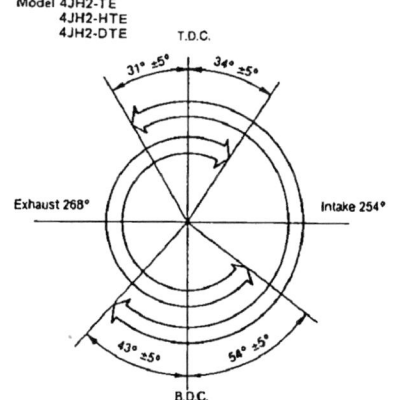

		4JH2E	4JH2-TE 4JH2-HTE 4JH2-DTE
Intake valve open	b. TDC	10° ~ 20°	26° ~ 36°
Intake valve closed	a. BDC	48° ~ 58°	38° ~ 48°
Exhaust valve open	b. BDC	51° ~ 61°	49° ~ 59°
Exhaust valve closed	a. TDC	13° ~ 23°	29° ~ 39°

2-12

4. Pistons and Piston Pins

Pistons are made of a special light alloy with superior thermal expansion characteristics, and the top of the piston forms a swirl type toroidal conbustion chamber. The opposite face of the piston combustion surface is ːil-jet cooled.
Pistion for engines with superchargers have a valve ress for the intake and exhaust valves.
The clearance between the piston and cylinder liner is kept at the pronper value by the piston cylinder liner property fit effected during assembly at the Yanmmar factory.

IMPORTANT:
Piston shape differs among engine models. If an incorrect pistion is installed, combustion performance will drop. Be sre to check the applicable engine model identification mark (I D Mark) on the piston to insure use of the correct part.

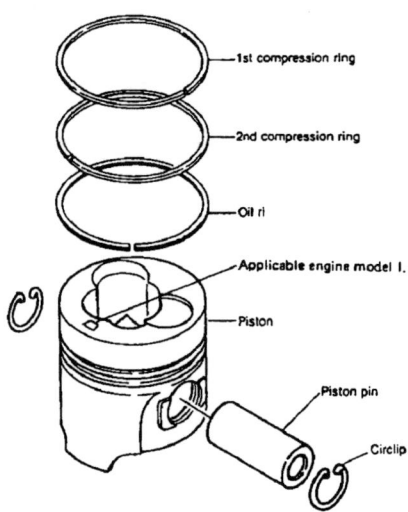

— 1st compression ring

— 2nd compression ring

— Oil rl

— Applicable engine model I.

— Piston

— Piston pin

— Circlip

I. D. Mark for Piston

Engine Model	I.D.mark
4JH2E	A
4JH2-TE	C
4JH2-HTE	C
4JH2-DTE	D
4JH2-UTE	D

Over Size Piston & Ring COMP.

I.D. Mark: OS25

Engine Model	Part No.
4JH2E	129570-22500
4JH2-TE 4JH2-HTE	129572-22500
4JH2-DTE 4JH2-UTE	129573-22500

4-1 Piston

4-1.1 Piston head and combustion surface

Remove the carbon that has accumulated on the piston head and combustion surface, taking care not to scratch the piston. Check the combustion surface for any damage.

4-1.2 Measurement of piston outside diameter/inspection

(1) Replace the piston if the outsides of the piston or ring grooves are worn.
(2) Measure the piston 22mm (0.8661in.) from the bottom at right angles to the piston pin.

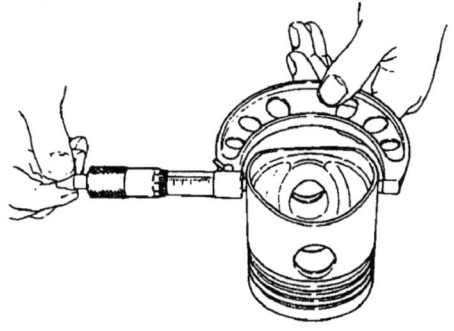

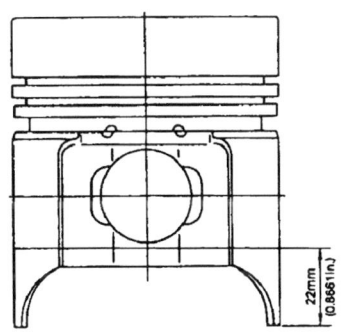

	mm (in.)
Standard	Wear limit
81.919 ~ 81.949 (3.22515 ~ 3.22634)	77.81 (3.0633)

4-1.3 Replacing the piston

A floating type piston pin is used in this engine. The piston pin can be pressed into the piston pin hole at room temperature (coat with oil to make it slide in easily).

4-2 Piston pin

Measure the outer diameter and replace the pin if it is excessively worn.

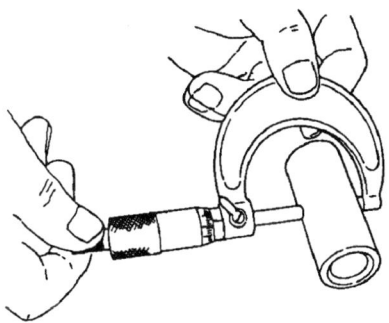

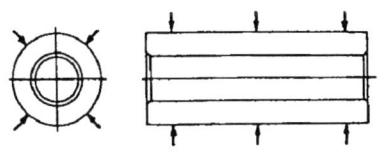

		mm (in.)
	Standard	Wear limit
Piston pin insert hole dia.	φ28.000 ~ 28.009 (φ1.10236 ~ 1.10272)	+0.020 (0.0008)
Piston pin outside dia.	φ27.987 ~ 28.000 (φ1.10185 ~ 1.10236)	−0.025 (0.0009)
Standard clearance	0 ~ 0.022 (0 ~ 0.0009)	0.045 (0.0018)

Printed in Japan
A0A1029-9109SP

4-3 Piston rings

There are 2 compression rings and 1 oil ring.
The absence of an oil ring on the piston skirt prevents oil from being kept on the thrust surface and in turn provides good lubrication.

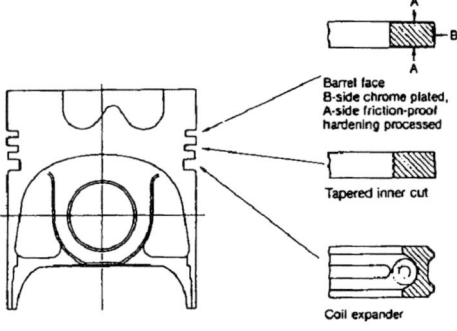

Barrel face
B-side chrome plated,
A-side friction-proof
hardening processed

Tapered inner cut

Coil expander

4-3.1 Measuring the rings

Measure the thickness and width of the rings, and the ring-to-groove clearance after installation. Replace if wear exceeds the limit.

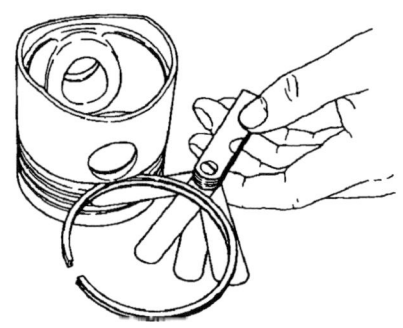

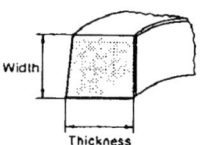

Width

Thickness

mm (in.)

		Standard	Wear limit
First piston ring	Groove width	2.060 ~ 2.075 (0.0811 ~ 0.0816)	—
	Ring width	1.975 ~ 1.990 (0.0777 ~ 0.0783)	—
	Groove and ring clearance	0.070 ~ 0.100 (0.0027 ~ 0.0039)	0.2 (0.0078)
Second piston ring	Groove width	2.025 ~ 2.040 (0.0797 ~ 0.0803)	—
	Ring width	1.970 ~ 1.990 (0.0776 ~0.0783)	—
	Groove and ring clearance	0.035 ~ 0.070 (0.0013 ~0.0027)	0.2 (0.0078)
il ring	Groove width	4.020 ~ 4.035 (0.1582 ~ 0.1588)	—
	Ring width	3.975 ~ 3.990 (0.1564 ~ 0.1570)	—
	Groove and ring clearance	0.030 ~ 0.060 (0.0011 ~ 0.0023)	0.2 (0.0078)

4-3.2 Measuring piston ring gap

Press the piston ring onto a piston liner and measure the piston ring gap with a gauge. Press on the ring about 30mm (1.811in.) from the bottom of the liner.

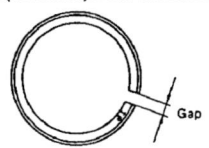

Gap

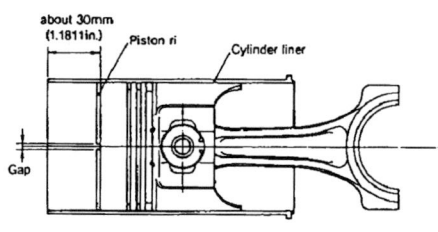

about 30mm (1.1811in.) Piston ri   Cylinder liner

Gap

mm (in.)

	Standard	Wear limit
First piston ring gap	0.25 ~ 0.40 (0.0098 ~ 0.0157)	1.5 (0.0590)
Second piston ring gap	0.20 ~ 0.40 (0.0078 ~ 0.0157)	1.5 (0.0590)
Oil ring gap	0.20 ~ 0.40 (0.0078 ~ 0.0157)	1.5 (0.0590)

4-3.3 Replacing the piston rings

(1) Thoroughly clean the ring grooves when replacing piston rings.

(2) The side with the manufacturer's mark (near piston ring gap) should face up.

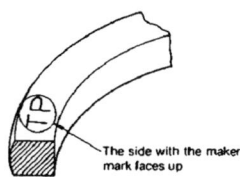

The side with the maker mark faces up

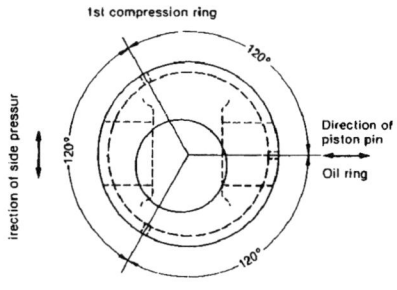

1st compression ring

Direction of piston pin

Oil ring

2nd compression ring

(3) After fitting the piston ring, make sure it moves easily and smoothly.

(4) Stagger the piston rings at 120° intervals, making sure none of them line up with the piston.

(5) The oil ring is provided with a coil expander. The coil expander joint should be opposite (staggered 180°) the oil ring gap.

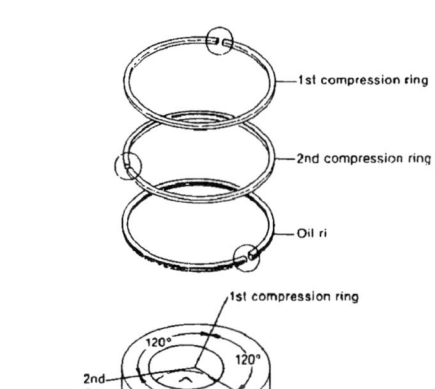

1st compression ring

2nd compression ring

Oil ri

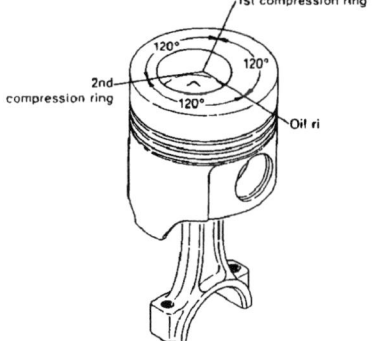

1st compression ring

2nd compression ring

120° 120° 120°

Oil ri

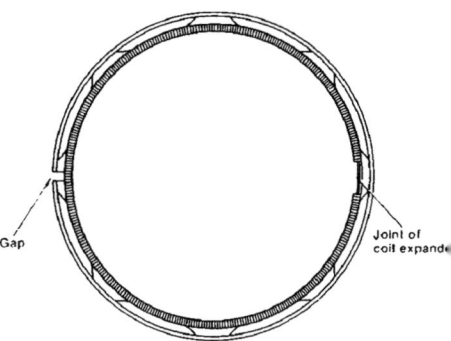

Gap

Joint of coil expande

2-16

5. Connecting Rod

The connecting rod is made of high-strength forged carbon steel.
The large end with the aluminium metal can be separated into two and the small end has a 2-layer copper alloy coil bushing.

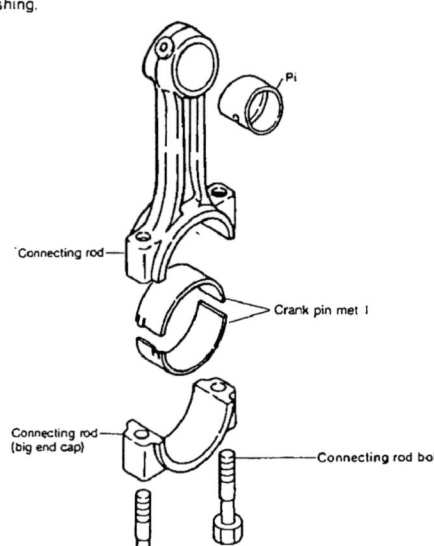

Connecting rod

Pi

Crank pin met I

Connecting rod (big end cap)

Connecting rod bolt

5-1 Inspecting the connection rod

5-1.1 Twist and parallelism of the large and small ends

Insert the measuring tool into the large and small ends of the connecting rod. Measure the extent of twist and parallelism and replace if they exceed the tolerance.

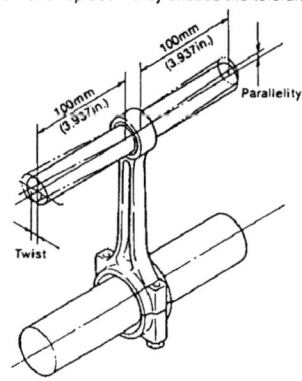

100mm (3.937in.)

100mm (3.937in.)

Parallelity

Twist

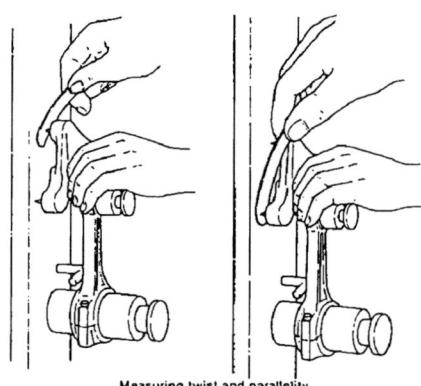

Measuring twist and parallelity

mm (in.)

	Standard	Wear limit
Connecting rod twist and parallelity	0.05 (0.0019)	0.07 (0.0027)

5-1.2 Checking thrust clearance

Fit the respective crank pins to the connecting rod and check to make sure that the clearance in the crankshaft direction is correct.

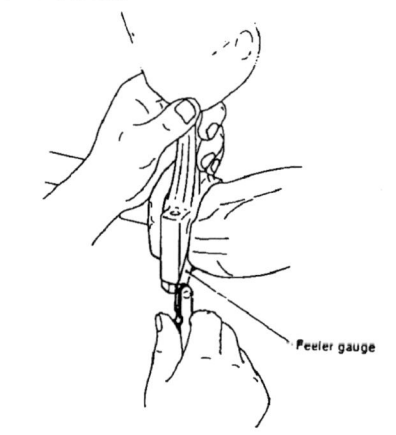

Feeler gauge

mm (in.)

	Standard	Wear limit
Connecting rod side clearance	0.20 ~ 0.40 (0.0078 ~ 0.0157)	0.55 (0.0216)

Printed in Japan
A0A1029-9002

5-2 Crank pin bushing

5-2.1 Checking crank pin bushing

Check for flaking, melting or seizure on the contact surface.

5-2.2 Measuring crank pin oil clearance

Use a plastic gauge.

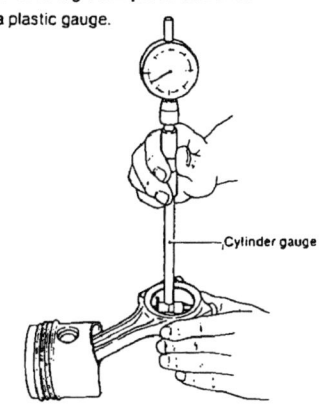

Cylinder gauge

Procedure

(1) Use the press gauge (Plastigage) for measuring oil clearance in the crank pin.

(2) Mount the connecting rod on the crank pin (tighten to specified torque).

Connecting rod tightening torque	5.0 ~ 5.5 kg-m (36.15 ~ 39.77 ft-lb)

(3) Remove the connecting rod and measure the broken plastic gauge with measuring paper.

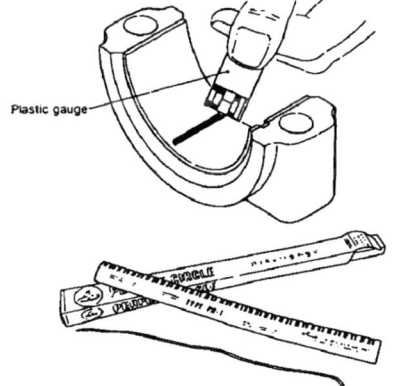

Plastic gauge

5-2.3 Precautions on replacement of crank pin bushing

(1) Wash the crank pin bushing.

(2) Wash the large end cap, mount the crank pin bushing and make sure that it fits tightly on the large end cap.

(3) When assembling the connecting rod, match up the large end and large end cap number. Coat the bolts with engine oil and gradually tighten them alternately to the specified torque.

If a torque wrench is not available, make match marks on the bolt heads and large end cap (to indicate the proper torque position) and retighten the bolts to those positions.

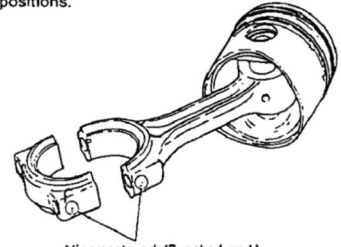

Alignment mark (Punched mark)

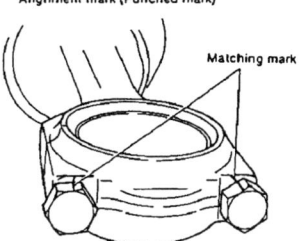

Matching mark

(4) Make sure there is no sand, metal cuttings or other foreign matter in the lube oil, and that the crankshaft is not scratched. Take special care in cleaning the oil holes.

5-3 Piston pin bushing

(1) Measuring piston pin clearance

Excessive piston pin bushing wear may result in damage to the piston pin or the piston itself.

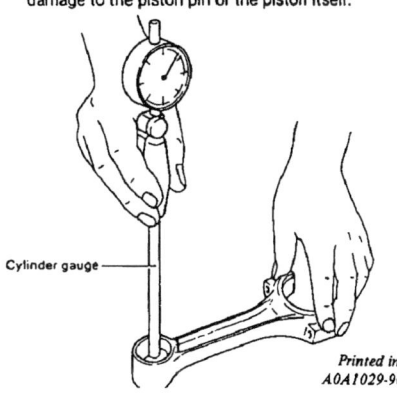

Cylinder gauge

Printed in Japan
A0A1029-9002

	Standard	Wear limit
		mm (in.)
Piston pin bushing inside dia.	28.025 ~ 28.038 (1.1033 ~ 1.1039)	28.1 (11.063)
Piston pin and bushing oil clearance	0.025 ~ 0.051 (0.0009 ~ 0.002)	0.11 (0.0043)

Since the small end in 4JH2 Series is tapered, bush insertion is extremely difficult. Any minor mistake will cause abnormalities such as twist and bite. Do not insert the bush on-site.
'(No piston pin bush spare part is available. It is included in the con-rod assembly supplied as a spare part.)

5-4 Assembling piston and connecting rod

The piston and connecting rod should be assembled so that the match mark on the connecting rod large end faces the fuel injection pump side and the combustion chamber above the piston is close to the fuel injection pump.

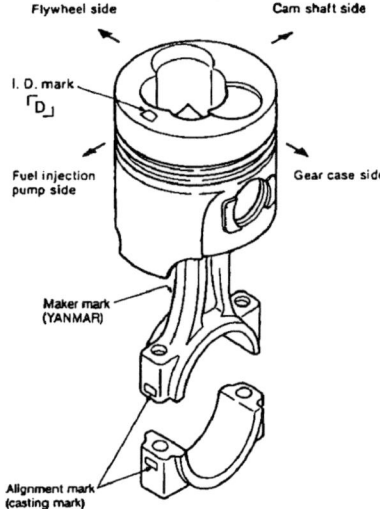

Flywheel side   Cam shaft side

I. D. mark
⌐D⌐

Fuel injection   Gear case side
pump side

Maker mark
(YANMAR)

Alignment mark
(casting mark)

6. Crankshaft and Main Bearing

The crank pin and crank journal have been induction hardened for superior durability, and the crankshaft is provided with four balance weights for optional balance. The crankshaft main bearing is of the hanger type. The upper metal (cylinder block side) is provided with an oil groove. There is no oil groove on the lower metal (bearing cap side). The bearing cap (location cap) of the flywheel side has a thrust metal which supports the thrust load.

IMPORTANT:
Although the size is identical, the crankshaft material of models 4JHE and 4JH-TE differ from that used in models 4JH-HTE and 4JH-DTE.
Please note that the crankshaft for models 4JHE and 4JH-TE cannot be used for models 4JH-HTE and 4JH-DTE since the crankshaft is not durable enough.

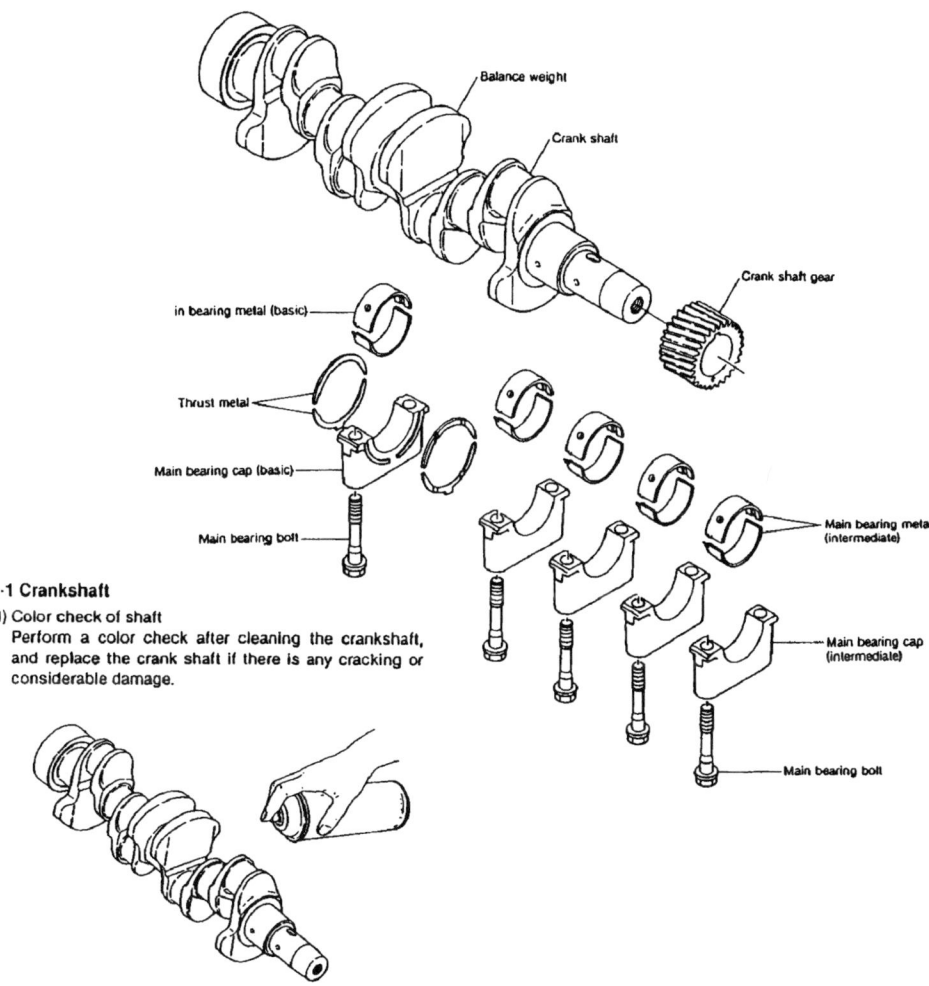

Balance weight

Crank shaft

Crank shaft gear

In bearing metal (basic)

Thrust metal

Main bearing cap (basic)

Main bearing bolt

Main bearing metal (intermediate)

Main bearing cap (intermediate)

Main bearing bolt

6-1 Crankshaft

(1) Color check of shaft
Perform a color check after cleaning the crankshaft, and replace the crank shaft if there is any cracking or considerable damage.

2-20

Printed in Japan
A0A1029-9002

(2) Bending of the crankshaft
Support the crankshaft with V-blocks at both ends
of the journals. Measure the deflection of the center
journal with a dial gauge while rotating the crankshaft
to check the extent of crankshaft bending.

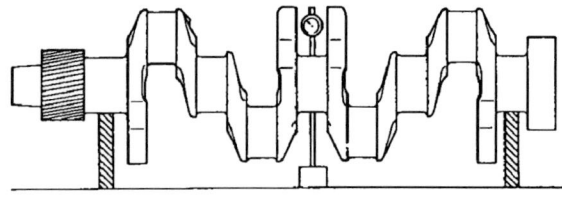 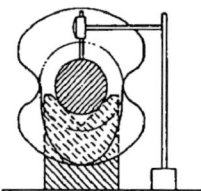

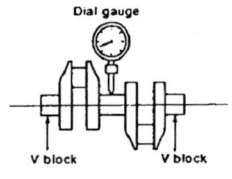 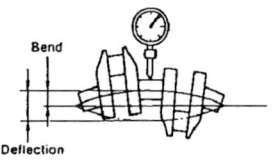

Crankshaft bend	Less than 0.03mm (0.0012 in.)

(3) Measuring the crank pin and journal
Measure the extent of journal wear (roundness, taper).
Regrind it to the proper shape if it is within the outer
diameter limit, and replace if not.

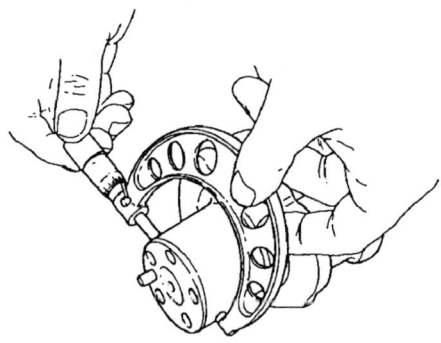 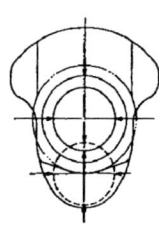 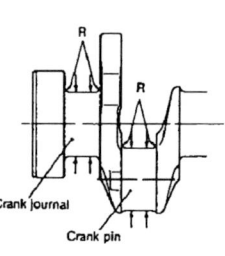

Crank journal

Crank pin

mm (in.)

		Standard	Wear limit
Crank pin	Outside dia.	47.952 ~ 47.962 (1.8878 ~ 1.8882)	47.75 (1.8799)
	Bushing inside dia.	48.000 ~ 48.045 (1.8897 ~ 1.8915)	48.10 (1.8937)
	Crank pin and bushing oil clearance	0.038 ~ 0.093 (0.0014 ~ 0.0036)	0.25 (0.0098)
Crank journal	Outside dia.	49.952 ~ 49.962 (1.9666 ~ 1.9670)	49.75 (1.9586)
	Bushing inside dia.	50.000 ~ 50.045 (1.9685 ~ 1.9702)	50.10 (1.9724)
	Crank journal and bushing oil clearance	0.038 ~ 0.093 (0.0014 ~ 0.0036)	0.25 (0.0098)
Fillet rounding of crank pin and journal		3.500 ~ 3.800 (0.1377 ~ 0.1496)	

(4) Checking side clearance of the crankshaft
After assembling the crankshaft, tighten the main bearing cap to the specified torque, and move the crankshaft to one side, placing a dial gauge on one end of the shaft to measure thrust clearance.
This measurement can also be effected by inserting the gauge directly into the clearance between the thrust bearing and crankshaft thrust surface.
Replace the thrust bearing if it is worn beyond the limit.

mm (in.)

	Standard	Wear limit
Crankshaft side gap	0.090 ~ 0.271 (0.0035 ~ 0.0106)	0.30 (0.0118)

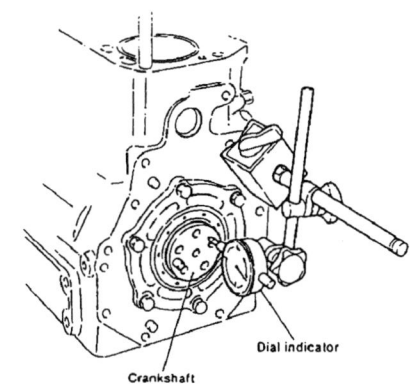

Dial indicator

Crankshaft

6-2 Main bearing

(1) Inspecting the main bearing
Check for flaking, seizure or burning of the contact surface and replace if necessary.
(2) Measuring the inner diameter of metal
Tighten the cap to the specified torque and measure the inner diameter of the metal.

Bearing cap bolt tightening torque	10.5 ~ 11.5 kg-m (75.92 ~ 83.15 ft-lb)

NOTE: When assembling the bearing cap, keep the following in mind.
1) The lower metal (cap side) has no oil groove.
2) The upper metal (cylinder block side) has an oil groove.
3) Check the cylinder block alignment No.
4) The "FW" on the cap lies on the flywheel side.

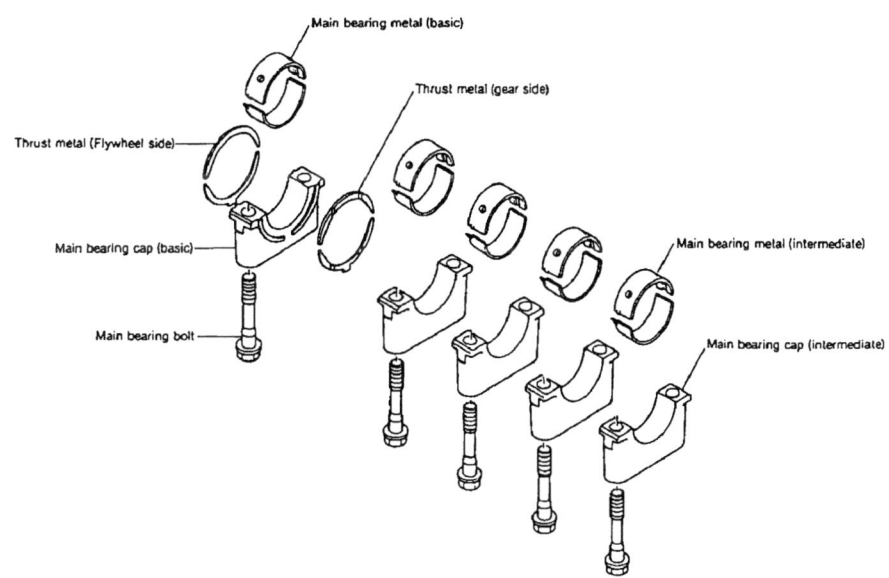

Main bearing metal (basic)

Thrust metal (gear side)

Thrust metal (Flywheel side)

Main bearing cap (basic)

Main bearing metal (intermediate)

Main bearing bolt

Main bearing cap (intermediate)

2-22

7. Camshaft and Tappets

7-1 Camshaft

The camshaft is normalized and the cam and bearing surfaces are surface hardened and ground. The cams have a curve that minimizes the repeated shocks on the valve seats and maximizes valve seat life.

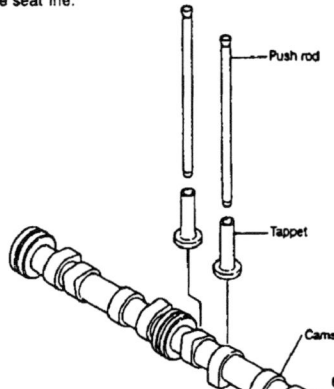

Push rod

Tappet

Camshaft

Camshaft bushing

Camshaft gear

Thrust metal

(1) Checking the camshaft side gap

The load is received by the standard bearing near the end of the camshaft by the cam gear, resulting in rapid wear of the end of the bearing and enlargement of the side gap. Therefore, measure the thrust gap before disassembly. As the cam gear is shrink-fitted to the cam, be careful when replacing the thrust bearing.

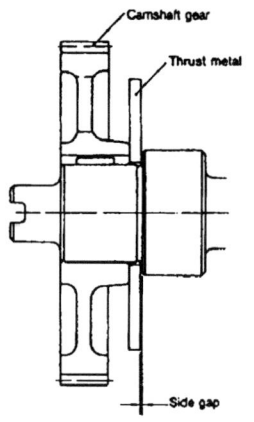

Camshaft gear

Thrust metal

Side gap

(2) Measure the camshaft height, and replace the cam if it is worn beyond the limit.

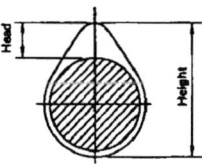

Head

Height

mm (in.)

	Standard	Wear limit
Camshaft side gap	0.05 ~ 0.20 (0.0019 ~ 0.0079)	0.4 (0.0157)

Camshaft height mm(in.)

Engine model		Standard	Wear limit
4JH2E	Intake cam	38.66 ~ 38.74 (1.5220 ~ 1.5251)	38.4 (1.5118)
	Exhaust cam		
4JH2-TE 4JH2-HTE 4JH2-DTE 4JH2-UTE	Intake cam	38.66 ~ 38.74 (1.5220 ~ 1.5251)	38.4 (1.5118)
	Exhaust cam	38.86 ~ 38.94 (1.5299 ~ 1.5330)	38.6 (1.5196)

(3) Measure the camshaft outer diameter and the camshaft bearing inner diameter. Replace if they exceed the wear limit or are damaged.

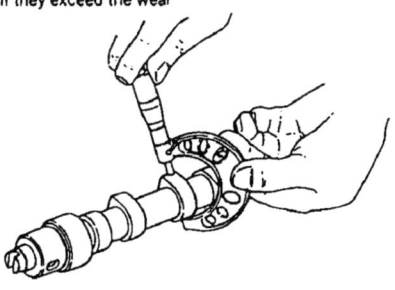

mm (in.)

	Standard			Wear limit
	Gear case side	Intermediate	Flywheel side	
Camshaft journal outside dia.	44.925 ~ 44.950 (1.7687 ~ 1.7696)	44.910 ~ 44.935 (1.7681 ~ 1.7690)	44.925 ~ 44.950 (1.7687 ~ 1.7696)	44.8 (1.7637)
Camshaft journal bushing inside dia.	44.990 ~ 45.050 (1.7712 ~ 1.7736)	—	—	—
Cylinder block bearing inside dia.	—	45.000 ~ 45.025 (1.7716 ~ 1.7726)	45.000 ~ 45.025 (1.7716 ~ 1.7726)	—
Oil clearance	0.040 ~ 0.125 (0.0015 ~ 0.0049)	0.065 ~ 0.115 (0.0025 ~ 0.0045)	0.050 ~ 0.100 (0.0019 ~ 0.0039)	0.2 (0.0078)

(4) Bending of the crankshaft

Support both ends of the crankshaft with V-blocks, place a dial gauge against the central bearing areas and measure bending. Replace if excessive.

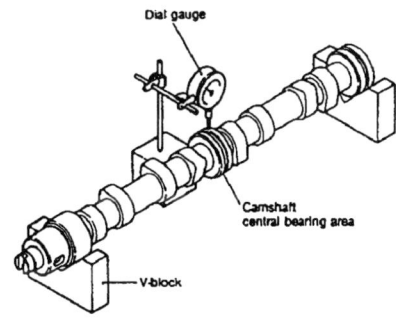

Dial gauge

Camshaft central bearing area

V-block

NOTE: The reading on the dial gauge is divided by two to obtain the extent of bending.

mm (in.)

	Wear limit
Camshaft deflection	0.02 (0.0007)

7-2 Tappets

(1) The tappets are offset to rotate during operation and thereby prevent uneven wearing. Check the contact of each tappet and replace if excessively or unevenly worn.

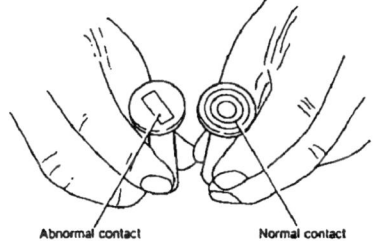

Abnormal contact   Normal contact

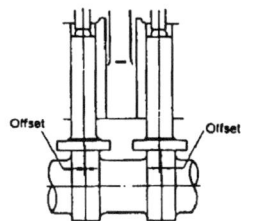

Offset   Offset

NOTE: When removing tappets, be sure to keep them separate for each cylinder and intake/exhaust valve.

2-24

Printed in Japan
A0A1029-9109SP

(2) Measure the outer diameter of the tappet, and replace if
worn beyond the limit.

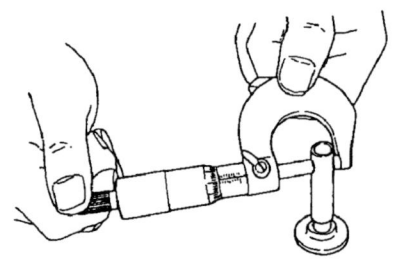

mm (in.)

	Standard	Wear limit
Tappet stem outside dia.	11.975 ~ 11.990 (0.4714 ~ 0.4720)	11.93 (0.4696)
Tappet guide hole inside dia. (cylinder block)	12.000 ~ 12.018 (0.4724 ~ 0.4731)	12.05 (0.4744)
Tappet stem and guide hole oil clearance	0.010 ~ 0.043 (0.0003 ~ 0.0016)	0.10 (0.0039)

(3) Measuring push rods.
Measure the length and bending of the push rods.

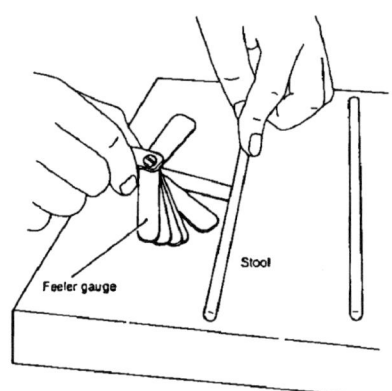

Stool

Feeler gauge

mm (in.)

	Standard	Wear limit
Push rod length	178.25 ~ 178.75 (7.0177 ~ 7.0374)	—
Push rod bend	Less than 0.03 (0.0011)	0.3 (0.0118)
Push rod dia.	8.5 (0.3346)	—

8. Timing Gear

The timing gear is helical type for minimum noise and specially treated for high durability.

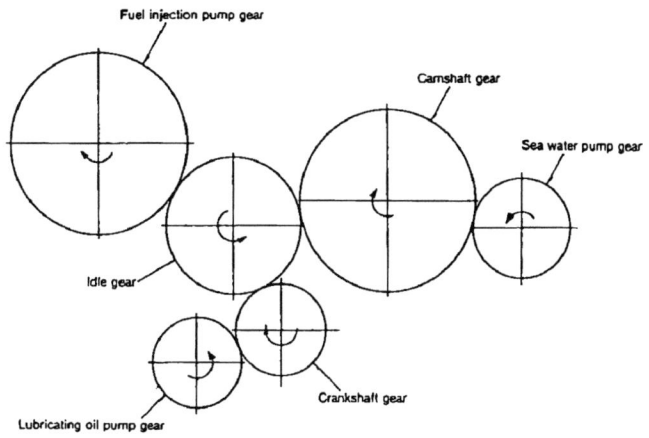

Fuel injection pump gear

Camshaft gear

Sea water pump gear

Idle gear

Crankshaft gear

Lubricating oil pump gear

mm (in.)

	No. of teeth	Face width	Spiral angle	Center distance	Back lash	Back lash Wear limit
Sea water pump gear	31	12.0	right	92.544 ~ 92.592 (3.6434 ~ 3.6453)	0.04 ~ 0.12 (0.0015 ~ 0.0047)	0.2 (0.0078)
Camshaft gear	56	18.0	left	105.318 ~ 105.380 (4.1463 ~ 4.1488)	0.04 ~ 0.12 (0.0015 ~ 0.0047)	0.2 (0.0078)
Idle gear	43	18.0	right	75.525 ~ 75.573 (2.9734 ~ 2.9753)	0.04 ~ 0.12 (0.0015 ~ 0.0047)	0.2 (0.0078)
Crankshaft gear	28	40.0	left	60.629 ~ 60.677 (2.3869 ~ 2.3888)	0.04 ~ 0.12 (0.0015 ~ 0.0047)	0.2 (0.0078)
Lubricating oil pump gear	29	8.0	right			
Idle gear	43	18.0	right	105.254 ~ 105.316 (4.1438 ~ 4.1462)	0.04 ~ 0.12 (0.0015 ~ 0.0047)	0.2 (0.0078)
Fuel injection pump gear	56	10.0	left			

8·1 Inspecting the gears

(1) Inspect the gears and replace if the teeth are damaged or worn.

(2) Measure the backlash of all gears that mesh, and replace the meshing gears as a set if wear exceeds the limit.

NOTE: *If backlash is excessive, it will not only result in ex-cessive noise and gear damage, but also lead to bad valve and fuel injection timing and a decrease in engine performance.*

(3) Idling gear

The bushing is pressure fitted into the idling gear. Measure the bushing inner diameter and the outer diameter of the shaft, and replace the bushing or idling gear shaft if the oil clearance exceeds the wear limit.

A, B and C are inscribed on the end of the idling gear. When assembling, these marks should align with those on the cylinder block.

2-26

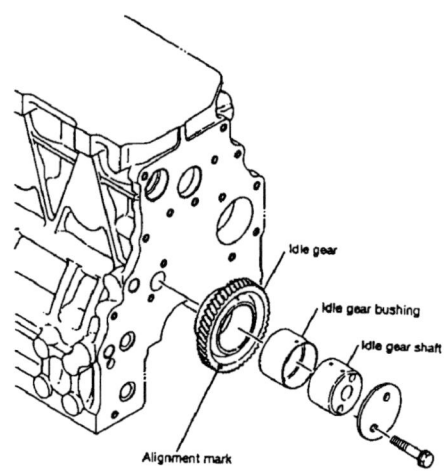

	Standard	Wear limit
		mm (in.)
Idle shaft dia.	45.950 ~ 45.975 (1.8090 ~ 1.8100)	45.88 (1.8062)
Idle shaft bushing inside dia.	46.000 ~ 46.025 (1.8110 ~ 1.8120)	—
Idle shaft and bushing oil clearance	0.025 ~ 0.075 (0.0009 ~ 0.0029)	0.15 (0.0059)

8-2 Gear timing marks

Match up the timing marks on each gear when assembling
(A, B and C).

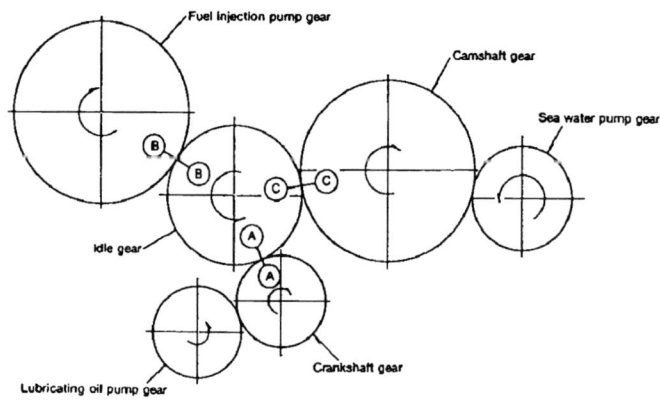

Printed in Japan
A0A1029-9002

9. Flywheel and Housing

The function of the flywheel is, through inertia, to rotate the crankshaft in a uniform and smooth manner by absorbing the turning force created during the combustion stroke of the engine, and by compensating for the decrease in turning force during the other strokes.

The flywheel is mounted and secured by 6 bolts on the crankshaft end at the opposite end to the gear case; it is covered by the mounting flange (flywheel housing) which is bolted to the cylinder block.

The fitting surface for the damper disc is on the crankshaft side of the flywheel. The rotation of the crankshaft is transmitted through this disc to the input shaft of the reduction and reversing gear. The reduction and reversing gear is fitted to the mounting flange.

The flywheel's unbalanced force on the shaft center must be kept below the specified value for the crankshaft as the flywheel rotates with the crankshaft at high speed. To achieve this, the balance is adjusted by drilling holes in the side of the flywheel, and the unbalanced momentum is adjusted by drilling holes in the circumference.

The ring gear is shrink fitted onto the circumference of the flywheel, and this ring gear serves to start the engine by meshing with the starter motor pinion.

The stamped letter and line which show top dead center of each cylinder are positioned on the flywheel circumference, and by matching these marks with the arrow mark at the hole of the flywheel housing, the rotary position of the crankshaft can be ascertained in order to adjust tappet clearance or fuel injection timing.

9-1 Specifications of flywheel

Outside dia. of flywheel		mm	φ339
Width of flywheel		mm	54
Weight of flywheel (including ring gear)		kg	15.6
GD' value		kg·m'	1.11
Circumferential speed		m/s	63.9 (3600rpm)
Speed fluctuation rate		δ	1/324 (3600rpm)
Allowable amount of unbalance		g-cm	26
Fixing part of damper disc	Pitch circle dia. of bolts	mm	170
	No. of bolts × bolt dia.		6-M8 thread equally spaced
Fixing part of crankshaft	Pitch circle dia. of bolts	mm	66
	No. of thread holes	mm	6-M10
	Fit joint dia.		ø85.000 ~ 85.035
Model of reduction and reversing gear			KM4A & KBW21
Mounting flange No.			SAE No.4 (in metric unit)
Ring gear	Center dia.	mm	322.58
	No of teeth		127

2-28

9-2 Dimensions of flywheel and mounting flange

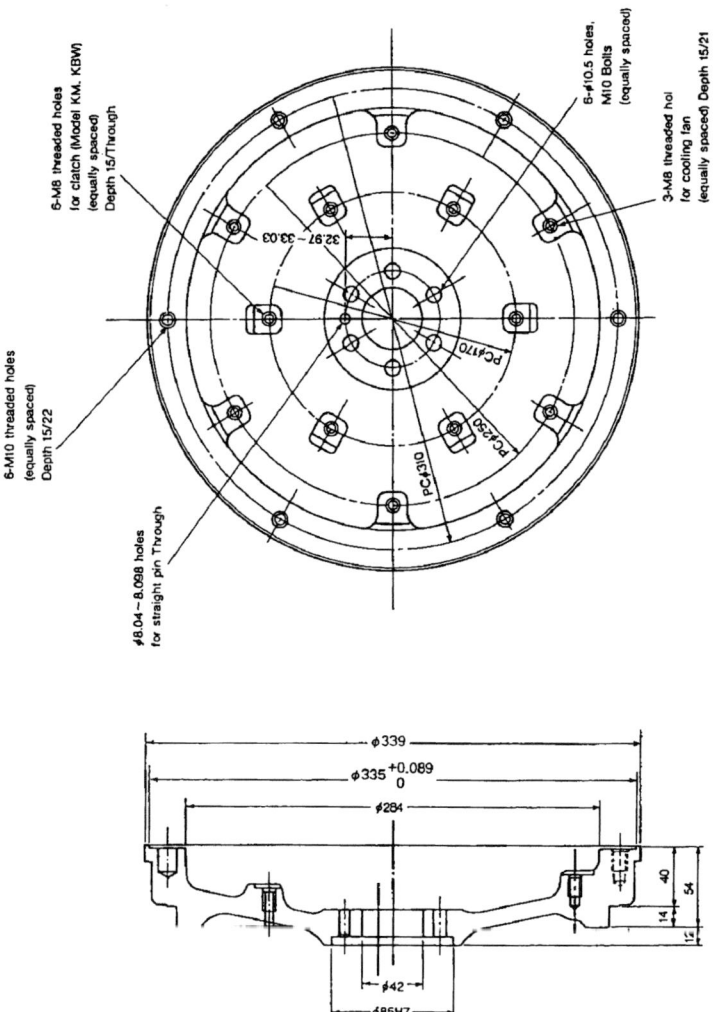

Printed in Japan
A0A1029-9002

9-3 Ring gear

When replacing the ring gear due to excessive wear or damaged teeth, heat the ring gear evenly at its circumference, and after it has expanded drive it gradually off the flywheel by tapping it with a hammer, a copper bar or something similar around the whole circumference.

	mm (in.)
Interference of ring gear	0.21 ~ 0.45 (0.0083 ~ 0.0177)

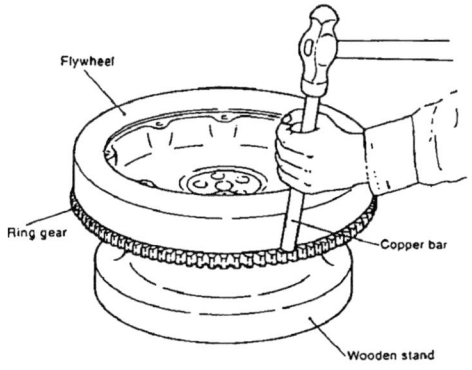

9-4 Position of top dead center and fuel injection timing

(1) Marking

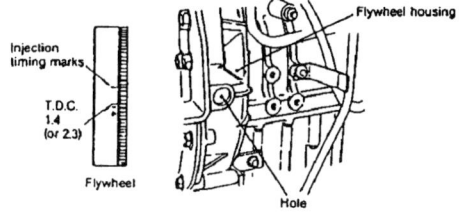

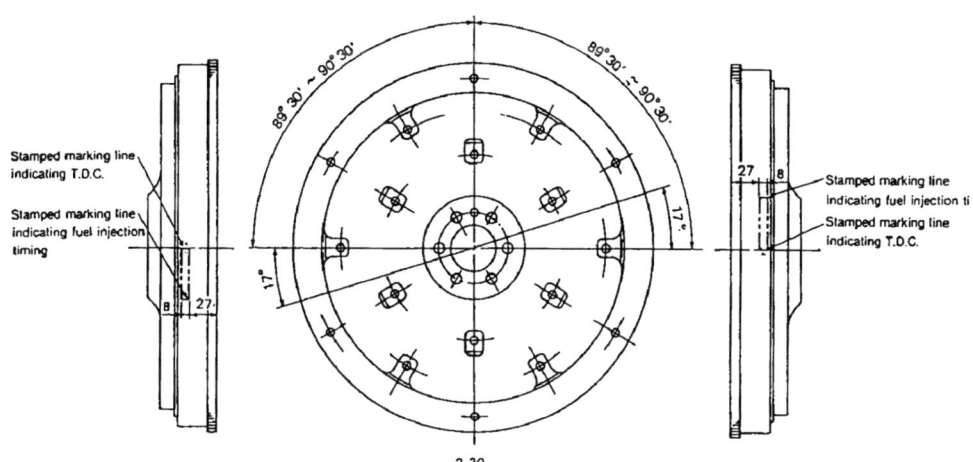

Printed in Japan
A0A1029-9002

(2) Matching mark

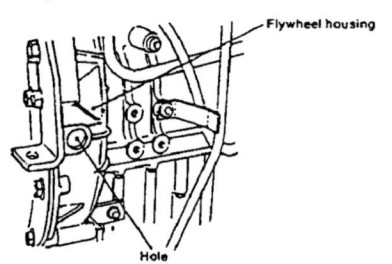

Flywheel housing

Hole

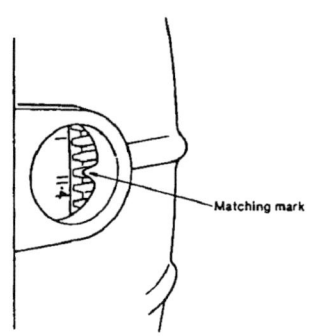

Matching mark

The matching mark is made at the hole of the flywheel housing.

9·5 Damper disc and cooling fan

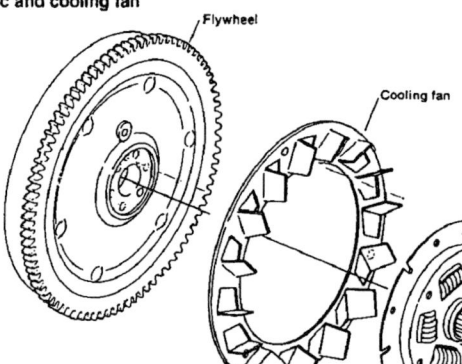

Flywheel

Cooling fan

Damper disc

Applicability of Cooling Fan

	4JH2E	4JH2-TE	4JH2-HTE	4JH2-DTE
KM3P3	O	—	—	—
KBW20	O	O	—	—
KBW21	—	—	—	—
KM4A	—	—	—	O

※ O Mark Cambination
Cooling Fan Equipipment

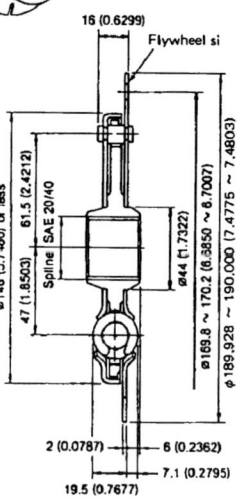

6-ø8.70 ~ 8.92
(0.3425 ~ 0.3511)

16 (0.6299)

Flywheel si

mm (in.)

ø146 (5.7480) or less

61.5 (2.4212)

Spline SAE 20/40

47 (1.8503)

ø44 (1.7322)

ø169.8 ~ 170.2 (6.6850 ~ 6.7007)

ø189.928 ~ 190.000 (7.4775 ~ 7.4803)

2 (0.0787)

6 (0.2362)

7.1 (0.2795)

19.5 (0.7677)

Torsional rigidity	421kg /rad (928.3 lb/rad)
Max. angle of torsion	7.3 × 10⁻³ rad
Stopper torque	37.7 kg·m (272.68 ft·lb)

Printed in Japan
A0A1029-9002

FUEL INJECTION EQUIPMENT

Printed in Japan
A0A1029-9002

1. Fuel Injection Pump Service Data (YANMAR TYPE : YPES-4CL)

Adjust-ment	Engine model / Item		4JH2-DTE						
	Assemble cord	Part No.	729570-51300		729571-51300		729572-51300		729573-51300
		I. D. mark	B471		B445		B438		B434
	Adjustment specs.		Engine specs.	Calibration specs.	Engine specs.	Calibration specs.	Engine specs.	Calibration specs.	Engine specs.	Calibration specs.
4-1-(1)	Nozzle type I. D. mark		155P235J20	DN-12SD12	140P255Z0	DN-12SD12	140P255Z0	DN-12SD12	140P265J20	DN-12SD12
	Injection starting kg/cm²		195~205	165~175	195~205	165~175	195~205	165~175	195~205	165~175
	pressure (lb/in²)		(2,773~2,915)	(2,346~2,489)	(2,773~2,915)	(2,346~2,489)	(2,773~2,915)	(2,346~2,489)	(2,773~2,915)	(2,346~2,489)
4-1-(2)	Fuel injection pipe mm		φ6/φ1.8×400	φ6/φ2×600	φ6/φ1.8×400	φ6/φ2×600	φ6/φ2×400	φ6/φ2×600	φ6/φ2×400	φ6/φ2×600
	OD φ/ ID φ×L (in)		(0.2362/0.078 ×15.748)	(0.2362/0.078 7×23.622)	(0.2362/0.070 8×15.748)	(0.2362/0.078 7×23.622)	(0.2362/0.078 7×15.748)	(0.2362/0.078 7×23.622)	(0.2362/0.078 7×15.748)	(0.2362/0.078 7×23.622)
4-2	Top clearance mm		0.45~0.55/3.0		0.45~0.55/3.0		0.45~0.55/3.0		0.45~0.55/3.0	
	/Prestroke (in)		(0.018~0.022/0.118)		(0.018~0.022/0.118)		(0.018~0.022/0.118)		(0.018~0.022/0.118)	
4-7-1	Rated load	Pump rpm: N1 rpm	1,800		1,800		1,800		1,800	
		Rack position: R1 mm(in.)	7(0.276)		7(0.276)		7(0.276)		8(0.315)	
		Measuring stroke St	1,000		1,000		1,000		1,000	
		Injection volume cc	27	29.5	33	36.5	39	46	45	52
		Nonuniformity %	±3		±3		±3		±3	
4-7-2	No load	Pump rpm: N2 rpm	1,950		1,950		1,950		1,950	
		Rack position: R2 mm(in.)	(4)		(3.5)		(3)		(3.5)	
4-7-3	Idling	Pump rpm: N3 rpm	400		400		400		400	
		Measuring stroke St	1,000		1,000		1,000		1,000	
		Injection volume cc	7~8	8~9	9~10	10~11	9~10	10~11	9~10	10~11
		Nonuniformity %	±10		±10		±10		±10	
4-7-4	Starting	Pump rpm: N4 rpm	200		200		200		200	
		Rack position mm(in.)	11.5~12.5(0.453~0.492)		11.5~12.5(0.453~0.492)		11.5~12.5(0.453~0.492)		11.5~12.5(0.453~0.492)	
		Measuring stroke St	1,000		1,000		1,000		1,000	
		Injection volume cc	60~70		60~70		60~70		60~70	
	Boost compensator	Standard	Non		Added		Added		Added	
		Pump rpm			900		900		900	
		Measuring stroke St			1,000		1,000		1,000	
		Injection volume cc			34~38		34~38		34~38	
Ref.	F. I Timing (F. I. D)deg.		b. T. D. C 12		b. T. D. C 17		b. T. D. C 17		b. T. D. C 17	

2. Governor

2-1. Boost compensator

(1) Objective of compensator

The boost compensator is a device mounted to the fuel injection pump for engines equipped with a turbocharger. The amount of air sent from the intake manifold by the linking function of the turbocharger increases in proportion to the amount of fuel injected from the injection pump (4JH2-TE, -HTE, -DTE). The boost compensator controls the injection quantity by responding to changes in pressure.

(2) Outline of structure and principle of operation

1 When the regulator handle is operated during abrupt acceleration, the control rack moves to the increase side as far as A.

2 Increase of engine speed drive the turbochanger to increase boosting pressure. This boosting pressure pushes the diaphragm in the boost compensator, moving the control rack to the fuel increase side by means of the boost compensator lever.

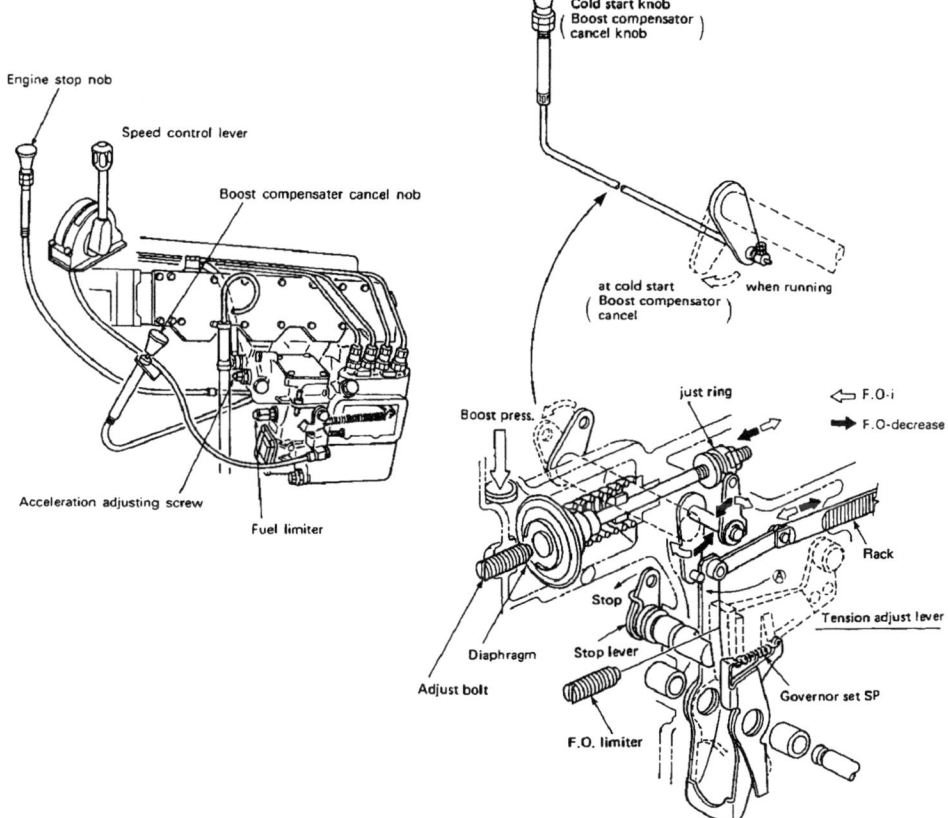

(3) Operation of cancel knob
   1 Since the boost compensator is the device that limits the fuel injection amount for starting the engine in cold temperatures (below -5°C), it is necessary to cancel the function of the boost compensator and increase the fuel injection amount.
   2 If the engine is hard to start in cold temperatures, start the engine by pulling the cancel knob (cold start knob).
   3 Once the engine is started, push the knob back into resume the function of the boost compensator.

(4) Adjustment of boost compensator
   The initial rack of the boost compensator has been adjusted properly at the time of shipment. However, the acceleration can be increased at the request of the customer. Watch the color of the exhaust while making the adjustment.

Adjust bolt

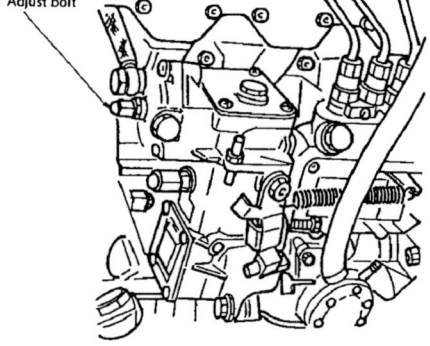

<Procedure>
Remove the cap nut of adjust bolt, loosen the lock nut and adjust the bolt with the blade-type screw driver.

Right turn	Large effect on boost comp.	• Higher acceleration • More black exhaust
Left turn	Small effect on boost comp.	• Lower acceleration • Less black exhaust

2-2. Disassembly, Reassembly and Inspection of Governor

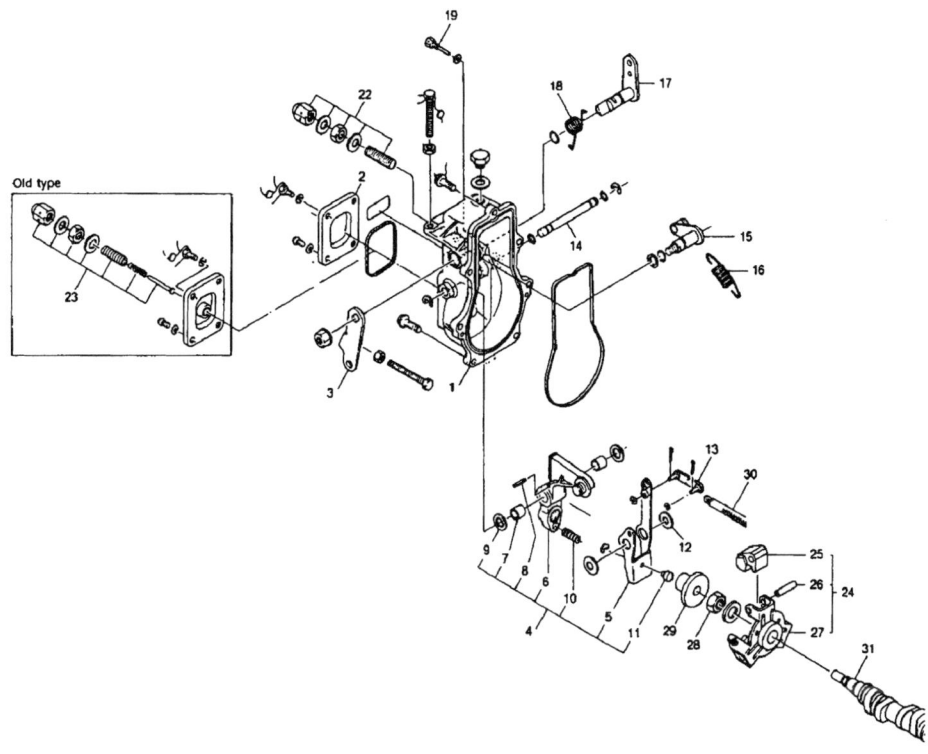

Old type

1. Governor case	12. Washer	24. Governor weight
2. Governor case cover	13. Governor link	25. Governor weight
3. Control lever	14. Governor shaft	26. Pin
4. Governor lever assembly 5. Governor lever	15. Control lever shaft	27. Governor weight support
6. Tension lever	16. Governor spring	28. Governor weight nut
7. Bushing	17. Stop lever	29. Governor sleeve
8. Spring pin	18. Stop lever return spring	30. Control rack
9. Shim	19. Stop lever stop pin	31. Fuel pump cam shaft
10. Throttle spri	22. Fuel stopper (limit bolt) assembly	
11. Shifter	23. Adjusting spring assembly	

2-2-1 Governor disassembly

(1) Remove the governor case.

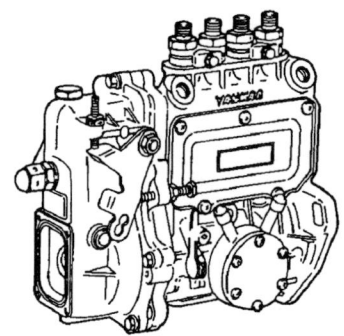

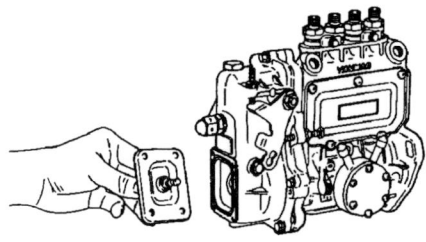

NOTE: *Loosen the hex bolt on models with an angleich spring.*

(2) Remove the control lever hex nut, and pull out the control lever from the control lever shaft.

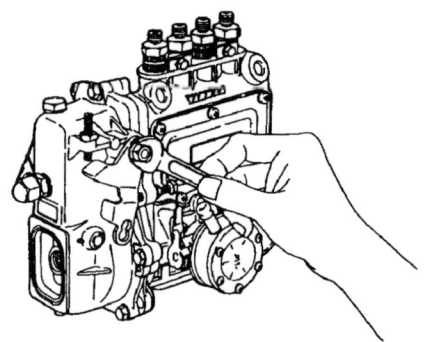

(3) Remove the governor case bolt. Remove the governor case (parallel pin) from the fuel pump until while lightly tapping the governor case with a wooden hammer. Create a gap between the governor case and fuel pump by moving parts of the governor lever.

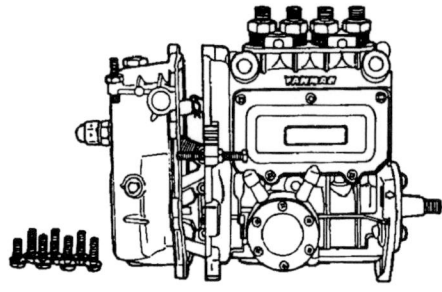

(4) Pull out the governor link snap pin by inserting needle nosed pliers between the fuel pump and governor case. case.

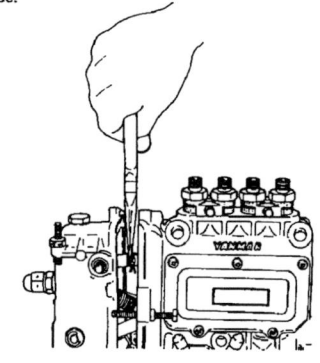

(5) The governor and fuel pump come apart by sliding the governor case and fuel pump apart and pulling out the link pin of the fuel control rack.

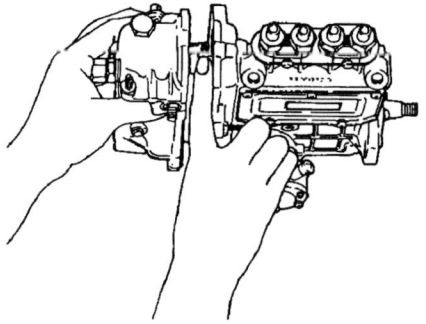

(8) Remove the snap-rings on both ends of the governor lever shaft.

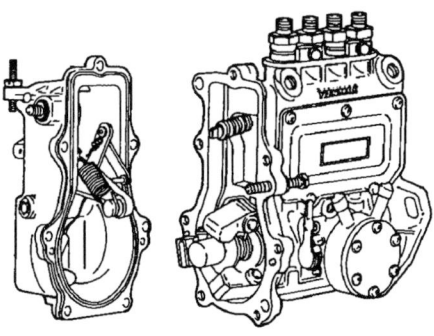

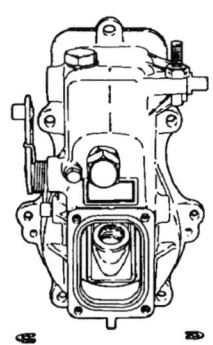

(6) Remove the stop lever return spring from the governor lever shaft.

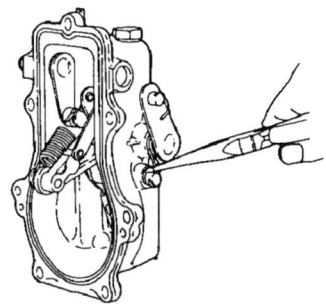

(9) Put a rod 8mm (0.3150in.) in dia. or less in one end of the governor lever shaft, and tap the governor shaft until the O-ring comes out the other side of the governor case.

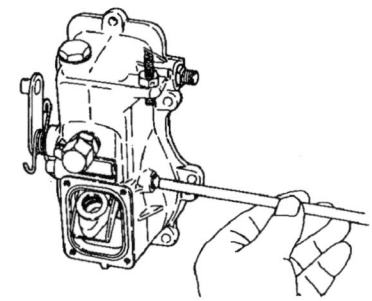

(7) Use needle nose pliers to unhook the governor spring from the tension lever and control lever shaft.

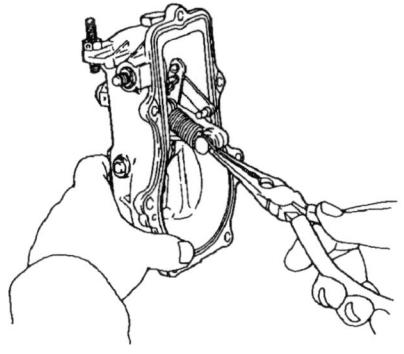

(10) After removing the O-ring, lightly tap the end of the shaft that you removed the O-ring from, and remove the governor lever shaft. Then remove the governor shaft assembly and washer.

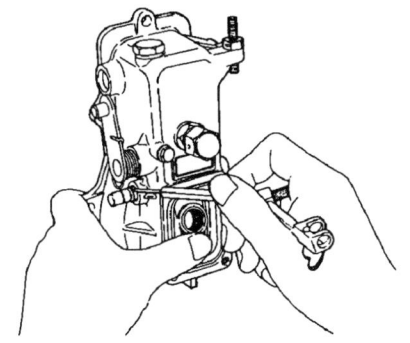

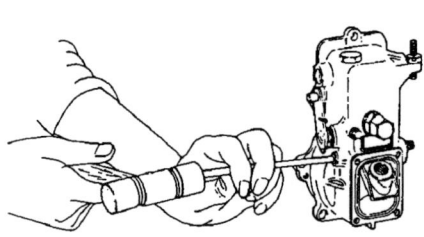

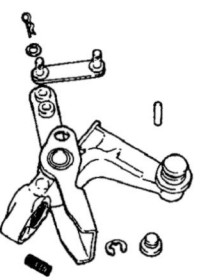

NOTE: *The governor assembly consists of the governor lever, tension bar, bushing, throttle spring and shifter, and is normally not disassembled.*
The spring pin is removed when you replace the shifter or throttle spring.

(12) When you need to pull out the stop lever, remove the stop lever shaft stop pin, and lightly tap the inside of the governor case.

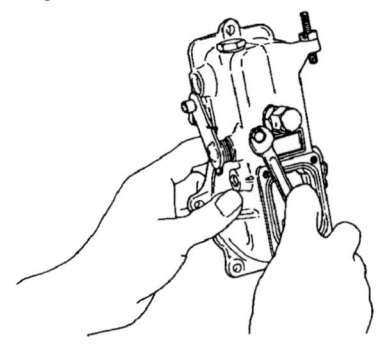

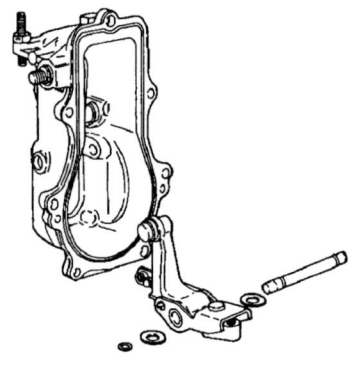

(11) Remove the governor link from the governor lever.

(13) When you need to pull out the control lever shaft, tap the end of the shaft with a wood hammer.

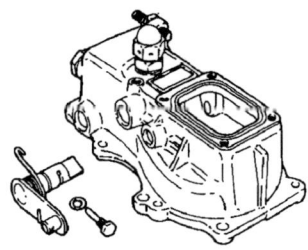

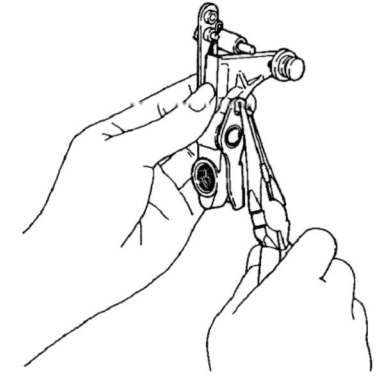

NOTE: 1. *Do not remove the fuel limit nut from the governor case unless necessary.*

(14) Pull out the governor sleeve on the end of the fuel camshaft by hand.

(16) Remove the governor weight assembly from the fuel pump cam using the governor weight pulling tools.

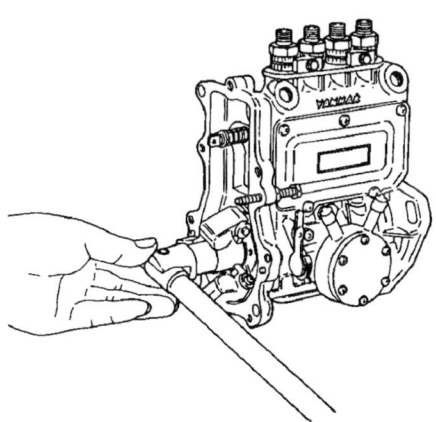

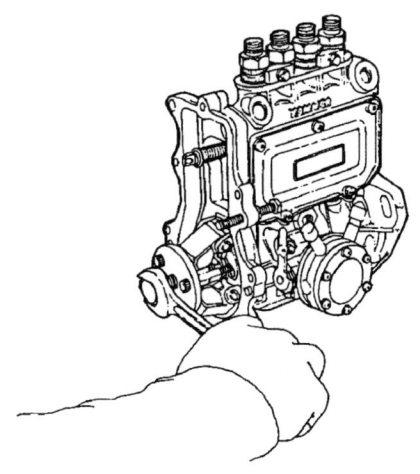

(15) Turn the governor weight with a box spanner two or three times to loosen it, stopping it with the hole in the fuel coupling ring or holding the coupling with a vise.

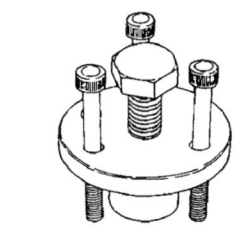

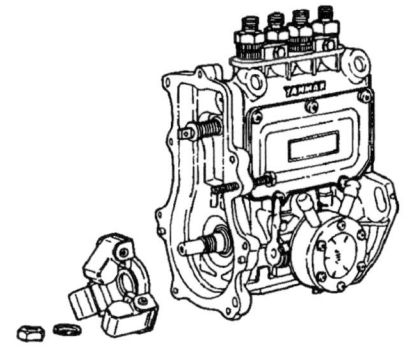

NOTE: When the taper fit comes apart after you have removed the nut, the governor weight may fly out —Be Careful.

NOTE: The governor weight assembly is made up of the governor weight, support and pin. Do not disassemble.

Printed in Japan
A0A1029-9002

2-2-2 Inspection of governor

Inspection of governor weight assembly
(1) Replace the governor weight if it does not open and close smoothly.

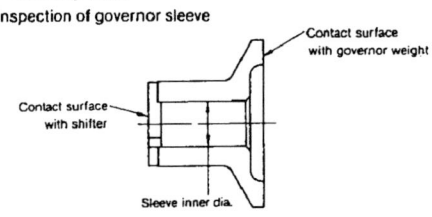

(2) Replace the governor weight if the contact surface with governor sleeve is extremely worn.
(3) Replace if there is governor weight support/pin wear or the caulking is loose.
(4) Replace if the governor weight support stopper is excessively worn.

Inspection of governor sleeve

Contact surface with governor weight

Contact surface with shifter

Sleeve inner dia.

(1) Replace the governor sleeve if the contact surface with governor weight is worn or there is pitching.
(2) Replace the governor sleeve if the contact surface with shifter is considerably worn or there is pitching.
(3) If the governor sleeve does not move smoothly above the cam shaft due to governor sleeve inner dia. wear or other reasons, replace.

Inspection of governor shaft assembly
(1) Measure the clearance between the governor shaft and bushing, and replace if it exceeds the limit.

mm (in.)

	Standard Dimension	Standard Clearance	Limit
Governor shaft outer dia.	7.986 ~ 7.995 (0.3144 ~ 0.3147)	0.065 ~ 0.124 (0.0025 ~ 0.0048)	0.5 (0.0196)
Bushing inner dia.	8.060 ~ 8.110 (0.3173 ~ 0.3192)		

(2) Inspect the shifter contact surface, and replace the shifter (always by removing the pin to disassemble) if it is worn or scorched.
(3) Disassemble and replace throttle springs that are settled, broken or corroded by pulling the spring pin.
(4) Check link parts for bends or kinks that will cause malfunctioning, and replace any parts as necessary.

NOTE: 1. Side gap on top of governor lever shaft.
mm (in.)

Standard side gap	0.4 (0.0157)

2. Replace the governor lever, tension bar, bushing, shifter and throttle spring as an assembly.

(5) Inspection of springs
1) Check the governor spring and other springs and replace if they are broken, settled or corroded.
2) Measure the free length of the governor spring, and replace if it exceeds the limit.
See service data sheet for free length of governor spring.

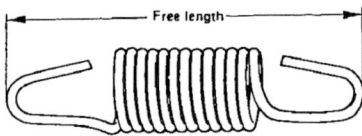

Free length

Governor spring spec. table

Engine model	4JH2E	4JH2-TE 4JH2-HTE, 4JH2-DTE
Part No.	129470-61650	129100-61730
Spring constant kg/mm	0.32	4.22
Free length mm	12	42

2-3 Assembling governor

Inspect all parts after disassembly and replace any parts as necessary. Before starting reassembly, clean new parts and parts to be reused, and put them in order.
Make sure to readjust the unit after reassembly to obtai the specified performance.

(1) Insert the governor weight assembly in the taper portion at the end of the fuel pump camshaft, stopping it with the hole in the fuel coupling ring or holding the coupling with a vise, mount the rest, and tighten the governor weight nut.

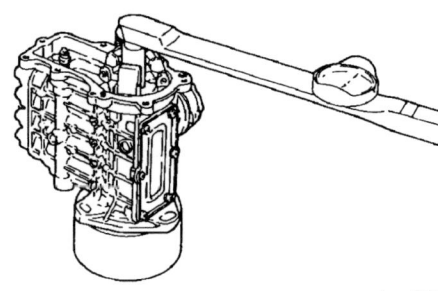

kg-m (ft-lb)

Governor weight nut tightening torque	4.5 ~ 5.0 (32.54 ~ 36.16)

(2) Open the governor weight to the outside, and insert the sleeve in the end of the fuel pump camshaft.

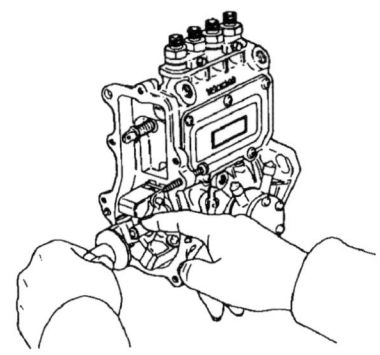

NOTE: Make sure that the sleeve moves smoothly after i serting it.

(3) When the stop lever has been disassembled, mount the stop lever return spring on the stop lever, tap the stop lever lightly with a wooden hammer to insert it, and tighten the stop lever stop pin.

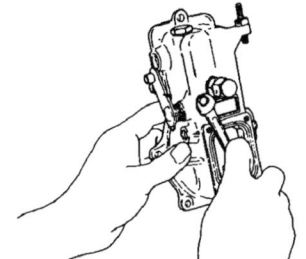

(4) When the control lever shaft has been removed, lightly tap the control lever shaft and washer from inside the governor case, using an appropriate plate.

(5) If the governor has been disassembled, tap in the spring pin.

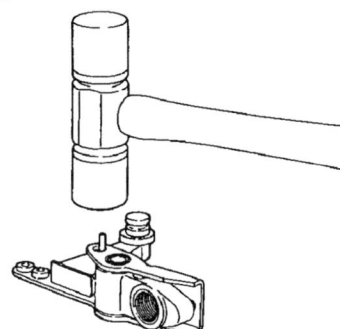

(6) Mount the governor lever assembly to the governor link.

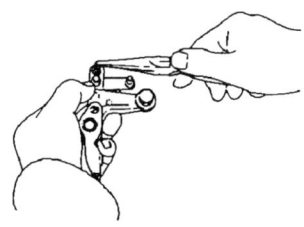

NOTE: 1. Make sure that the correct governor link mounting holes are used, and that it is mounted in the correct direction.
2. Make sure that the governor link moves smoothly.

(7) Put the governor lever shaft assembly in the governor case, insert the governor lever shaft, and tap it in until the O-ring groove comes out the opposite side of the governor case.

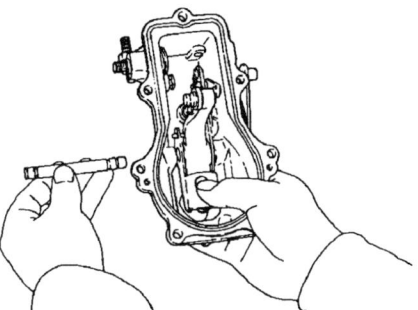

NOTE: 1. Fit the O-ring to the side you have tapped in.

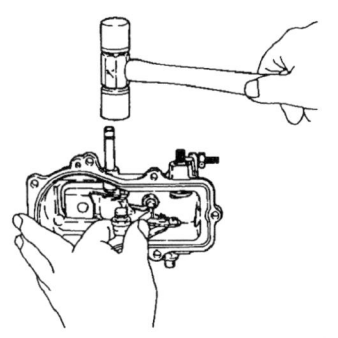

2. Be sure to insert the governor lever shaft i the correct direction.

Printed in Japan
A0A1029-9002

3. Don't forget to mount the washers to both sides of the governor lever.

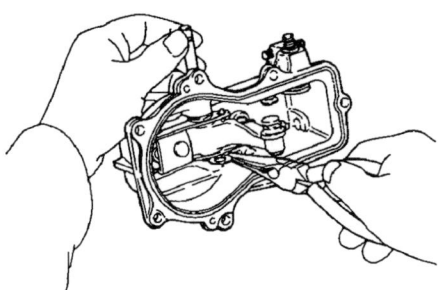

(8) After you have mounted the O-ring, tape the governor lever in the opposite direction, and mount the E-shaped stop rings on the grooves at both ends.

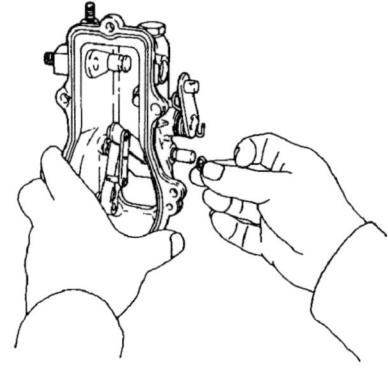

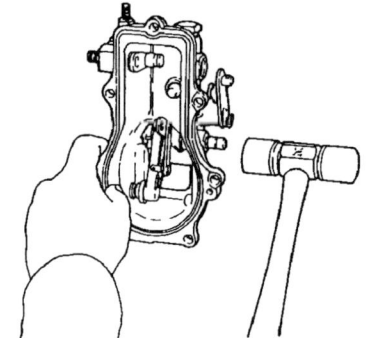

NOTE: After mounting the governor lever assembly, make sure the governor lever assembly moves smoothly.

(9) Fit the stop lever return spring to the end of the governor lever shaft.

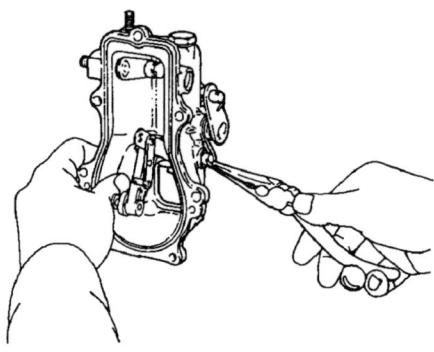

(10) Hook the governor spring on the control lever shaft and tension lever hook with radio pliers.

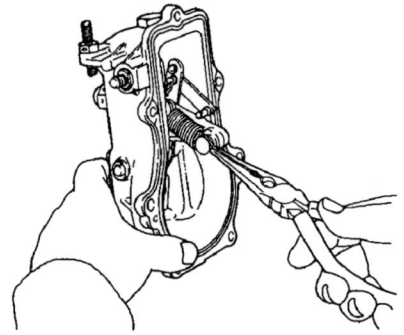

(11) Pull the governor link as far as possible towards the governor case mounting surface, insert the governor link pin in the fuel control rack pin hole and fit the snap pin on it.

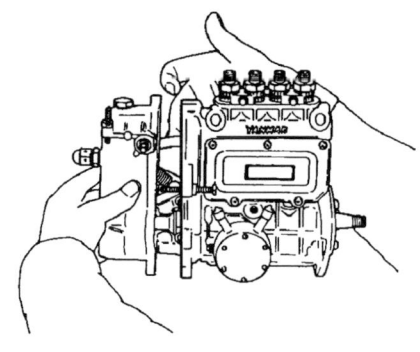

(12) Mount the governor case to the fuel pump unit while lightly tapping it with a wooden hammer, and tighten the bolts.

(13) Place the adjusting spring and adjusting rod on the governor case cover adjusting bolt, and mount the governor case cover.

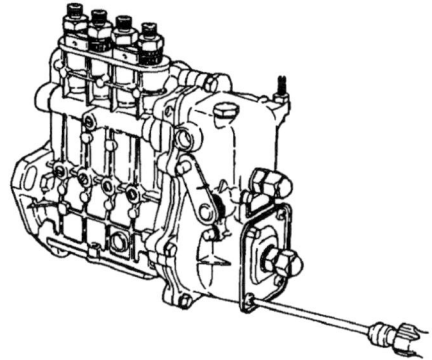

(14) Insert the control lever in the control lever shaft, and tighten the nut.

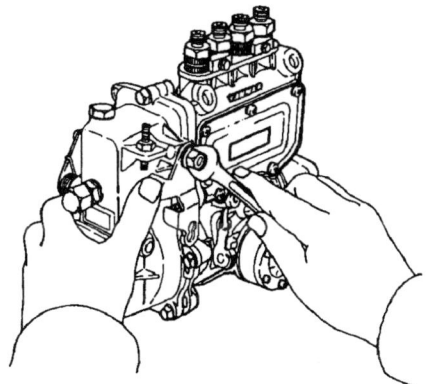

NOTE: Move the control lever back and forth to make sure that the entire link moves smoothly.

3. Disassembly, Reassembly and Inspection of Fuel Injection Pump

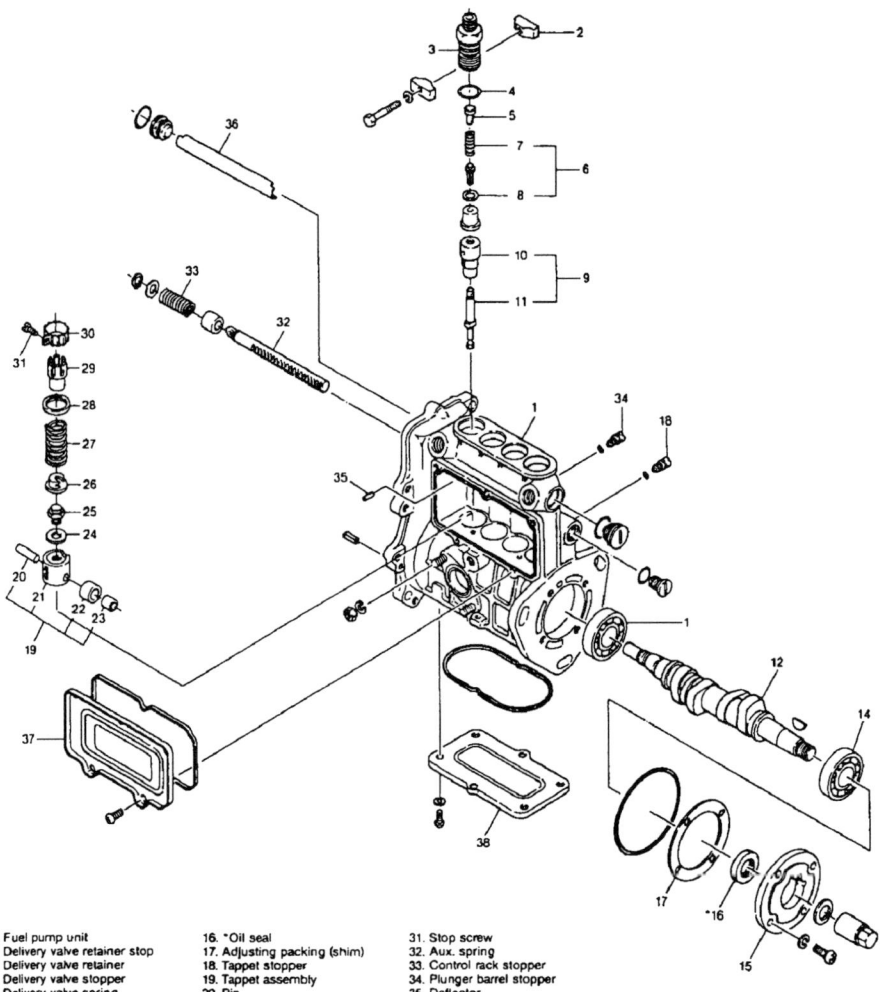

1. Fuel pump unit	16. *Oil seal	31. Stop screw
2. Delivery valve retainer stop	17. Adjusting packing (shim)	32. Aux. spring
3. Delivery valve retainer	18. Tappet stopper	33. Control rack stopper
4. Delivery valve stopper	19. Tappet assembly	34. Plunger barrel stopper
5. Delivery valve spring	20. Pin	35. Deflector
6. Delivery valve assembly	21. Roller guide	36. Pump side cover
7. Delivery valve	22. Roller (outer)	37. Pump bottom cover
8. Delivery valve seat	23. Roller (inner)	
9. Plunger assembly	24. Adjusting shim	
10. Plunger barrel	25. Adjusting bolt	
11. Plunger	26. Plunger spring rest B	
12. Fuel pump camshaft	27. Plunger spring	
13. Bearing	28. Plunger spring rest A	
14. Bearing	29. Control sleeve (reduction ring)	
15. Bearing holder	30. Control pinion B	

NOTE: 1. Some models are equipped with ball bearings and some with taper roller bearings.

2. *Oil seal: Some models are equipped with oil seals and some are not. The shape of the bearing holder differs for models with and without oil seals.

3-1 Disassembly of fuel injection pump

When disassembling the fuel pump, separate the parts for each cylinder and be careful not to get them mixed up. Be especially careful to keep the plunger/plunger barrel, delivery valve/delivery valve seat and other assemblies separate for each cylinder (the parts of each assembly must be kept with that assembly and put back in the same cylinder).

Preparation

1. Wash off the dirt and grease on the outside of the pump with cleaning oil (kerosene or diesel oil) before disassembly.
2. Perform work in a clean area.
3. Take off the fuel pump bottom cover and remove lubricant oil.
4. Turn the fuel pump upside down to drain fuel oil.

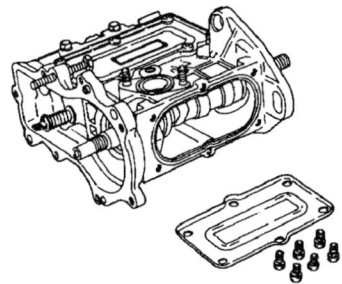

(1) Loosen the nut with a box spanner and take it off, holding it with the hole in the fuel coupling ring or holding the coupling with a vise and take out the governor weight assembly.

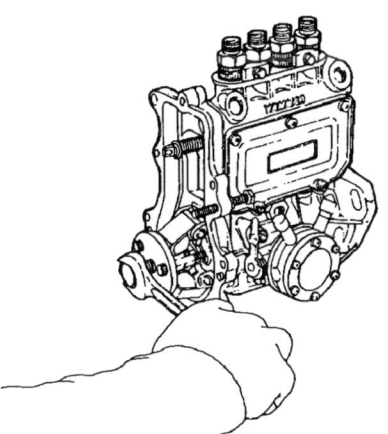

(2) Remove the fuel feed pump.

NOTE: Do not disassemble the fuel feed pump. See instructions for fuel feed pump for details.

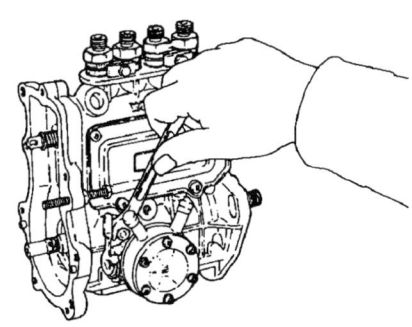

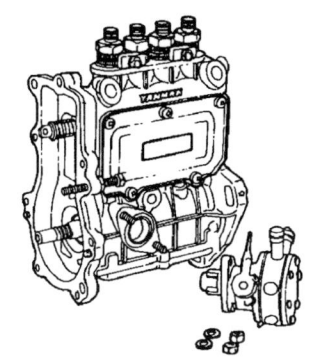

(3) Remove the fuel pump side cover.

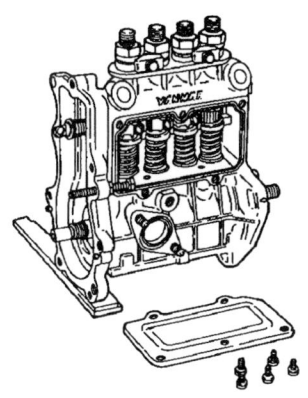

(4) Turn the camshaft until the roller guide is at the maximum head, and insert the plunger spring support plate in between the plunger spring washer B (lower side) and fuel pump unit.

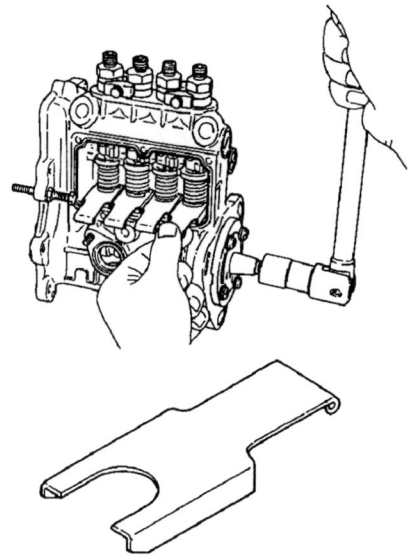

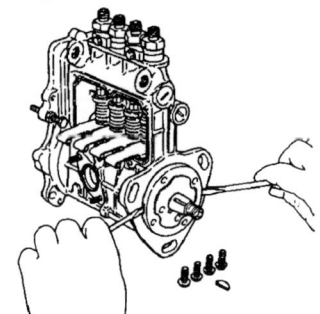

Plunger spring support plate

NOTE: If the camshaft does not turn, put double nuts on the end of the cam shaft or remove the coupling.

(5) Remove the camshaft wood ruff key.
(6) Put a screwdriver in the two grooves on the camshaft bearing holder mounting surface, and pull out the camshaft bearing holder.

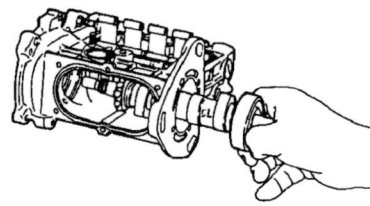

NOTE: 1. Be sure not to damage the oil seal with the threaded part of the camshaft.
2. Be careful not to loosen the shims in between the pump and bearing holder.

(7) Turn the fuel pump upside down, move all the roller guides to the plunger side, and then put the pump on its side. Turn the camshaft to a position so that none of the cylinder cams hit the tappets.
(8) Put a plate against the governor end side of the camshaft and lightly tap it, and pull out the camshaft and drive side bearing.

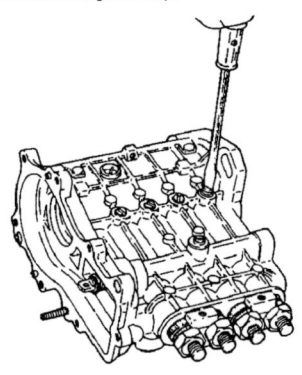

(9) Remove the roller guide stop.

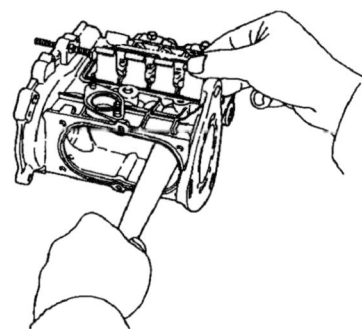

(10) Use a hammer handle or the like to push up the roller guide from the bottom of the pump, and remove the plunger spring support plate.

NOTE: The plunger spring may make the roller guide and plunger, etc. fly out when the plunger support plate is removed.

(11) Remove the roller guide.

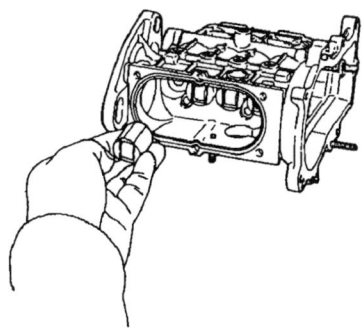

(13) Loosen the small screw on control pini

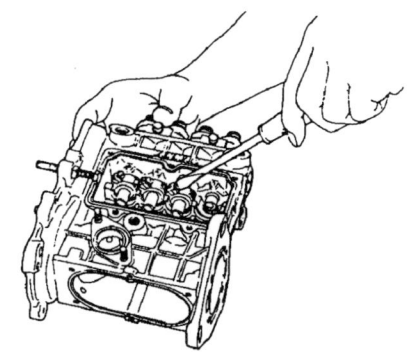

NOTE: When you stand the fuel pump up, all of the roller guides drop out at one time. Therefore, first remove the stop bolt for one cylinder at a time, and then the roller guide for each cylinder—continue this process.

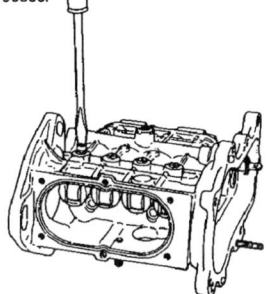

(12) Remove the plunger, plunger spring and lower washer from the lower part of the pump.

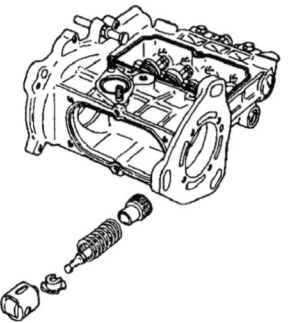

NOTE: Keep the parts separate for each cylinder.

NOTE: 1. Check to make sure the match marks on the pinion/sleeve are correct before loosening the small screw on the control pinion, as the pinion and sleeve come apart when the screw is loosened. If the mark is hard to read or off center, lightly inscribe a new mark. This will serve as a guide when adjusting injection volume later.

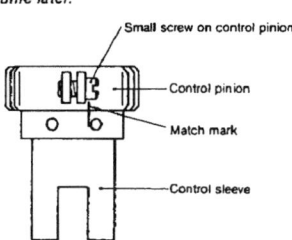

2. Keep parts separate for each cylinder.

(14) Remove the control pinion, sleeve and upper rest.

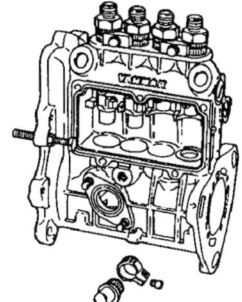

NOTE: Keep parts separate for each cylinder.

3-16

(15) Remove the control rack stop bolt and remove the rack.

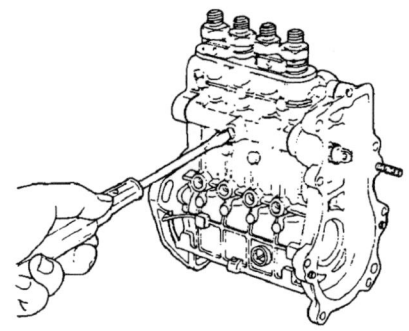

NOTE: Be careful not to lose the spring or rest on the control rack.

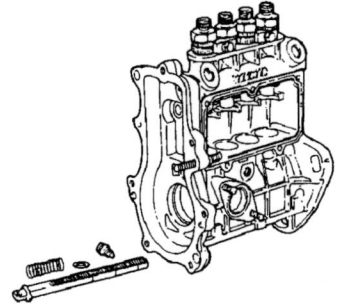

(16) Loosen the delivery valve retainer stop bolt, and remove the delivery valve holder stop.

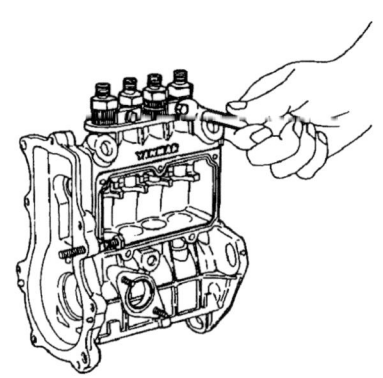

(17) Remove the delivery valve holder.

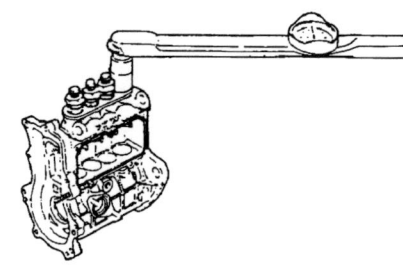

(18) Remove the delivery valve assembly.

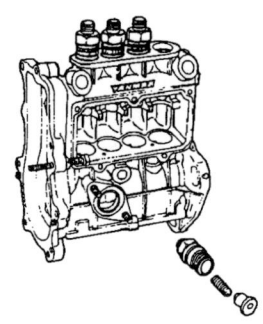

NOTE: 1. Be careful not to lose the delivery valve packing, delivery valve spring, delivery valve stopper or other small parts.
2. Keep the delivery valve assemblies for each cylinder clearly separated.

(19) Take the plunger barrel out from the top of pump.

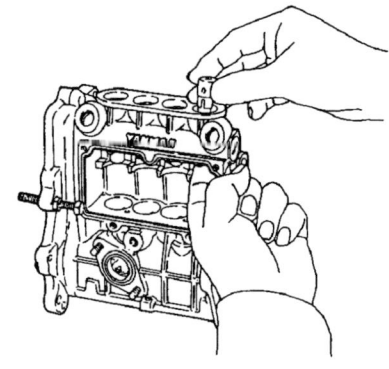

NOTE: Keep it as a set with the plunger that was removed earlier.

3-2 Inspection of fuel injection pump

(1) Inspection of plunger
1) Thoroughly wash the plungers, and replace plungers that have scratches on the plunger lead or are discolored.
2) The plunger is in good condition if it slides down smoothly when it is tilted about 60°. Repeat this several times while turning the plunger. Repair or replace if it slides down too quickly or if it stops part way.

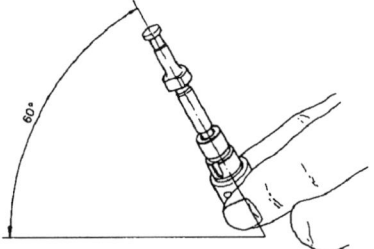

(2) Inspection of delivery valve

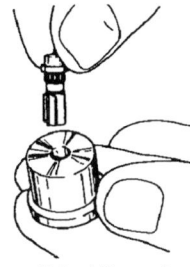

1) Replace as a set if the delivery valve suck-back collar or seat are scratched, scored, scuffed, worn, etc.
2) The valve is in good condition if it returns when released after being pushed it down with your finger (while the holes in the bottom of the delivery guide seat are covered). Replace if necessary.
3) Likewise, the valve should completely close by its own weight when you take your finger off the holes in the bottom of the delivery guide sheet.

NOTE: When fitting new parts, wash with diesel oil and perform the above inspection.

(3) Inspection of pump
1) Inspect for extreme wear of roller guide sliding surface. Scratches on the roller pin sliding surface are not a problem.
2) Inspect the plunger barrel seat.
If there are burrs or discoloration, repair or replace as this will lead to dilution of the lubricant.
(4) Inspection of fuel camshaft and bearings
1) Fuel camshaft
Inspect for scratches or wear of camshaft, deformation

of key grooves and deformation of screws on both ends, and replace if necessary.
2) Bearings
Replace if the taper rollers or outer race surface is flaked or worn.

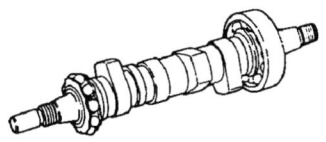

NOTE: Replace fuel camshafts and bearings together.

(5) Inspection of roller guide assembly
1) Roller

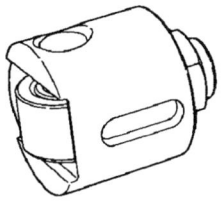

Replace if the surface is worn or flaked.
2) Roller Guide
Replace if the outer roller pin hole is extensively worn or there are many scratches.
3) Replace if the play of the roller guide assembly pin/roller is 0.2mm (0.0078in.) or more.
4) Injection timing adjustment bolt
Replace if the surface in contact with the plunger side is unevenly or excessively worn.
(6) Inspection of rack and pinion
1) Rack

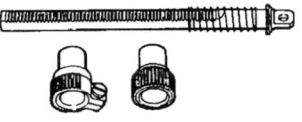

Inspect for bending of rack and wear or deformation of fit with pinion.
2) Pinion
Inspect for wear or deformation of fit with rack.

NOTE: If the tooth surface or sliding surface is not in good working order, rack resistance increases, affecting the condition of the engine (rough rpm, over running, etc.).

(7) Inspection of plunger spring and delivery spring
Inspect springs for scratches, cracks, breakage, uneven wear and rust.

(8) Inspection of oil seals
  Inspect oil seals to see if they are burred or scratched.
(9) Inspection of roller guide stop
  Inspect the side of the tip, replace if excessively worn.
(10) Inspection of O-rings
  Inspect and replace if they are burred or cracked.

3-3 Reassembly of fuel injection pump

Preparation

After inspection, put all parts in order and clean.
See Inspection of Fuel Pump for inspection procedure.

(1) Put in the plunger barrel from the top of pump.

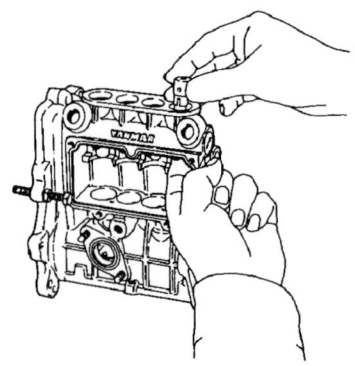

NOTE: Make sure the barrel key groove is fitted properly to the barrel stop pin.

(2) Place the delivery valve assembly, packing, spring and stopper from the top of the pump, in that order.

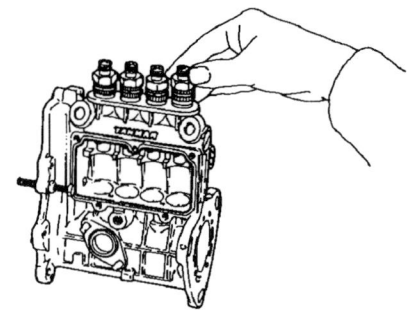

NOTE: Replace the delivery valve packing and O-ring.

(3) Place the control rack, and tighten the control rack stop bolt.

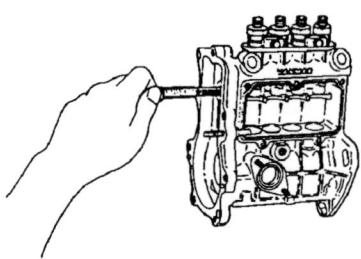

NOTE: 1. Do not forget the rack aux. spring.
2. Make sure the rack moves smoothly through a full cycle.

(4) Place the rack set screw (using the special tool) in the rack stop bolt screw hole to fix the rack.

(5) Looking from the bottom of pump, align the match marks on the rack and pinion.

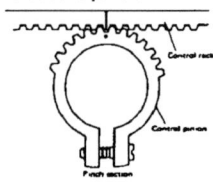

(6) While holding the pinion with one hand and keeping it aligned with the match mark, fit in the sleeve, and lightly tighten the small pinion screw.

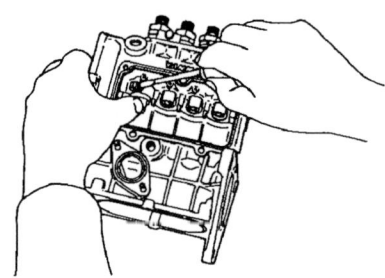

NOTE: Fitting of sleeve; Face towards small pini screws and align with match mark.

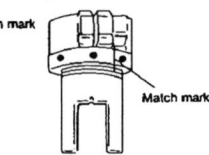

(7) Mount the plunger spring upper rest.

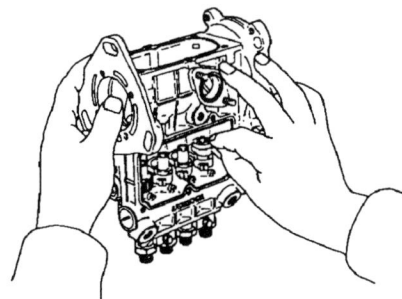

NOTE: 1. *Be sure to mount the upper rest with the hollow side facing down.*
2. *Recheck to make sure that the rack moves easily.*

(8) Mount the plunger spring.
(9) Mount the lower rest on the head of the plunger, and fit the plunger in the lower part of pump while aligning the match marks on the plunger flange and the sleeve.

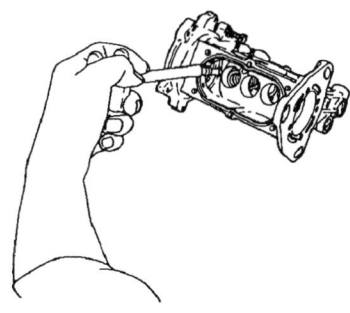

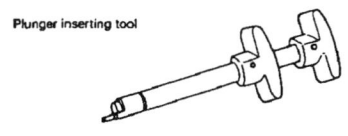

Plunger inserting tool

NOTE: *If the plunger is mounted in the opposite direction, the injection volume will increase abnormally and cannot be adjusted.*

(10) Insert the plunger spring support plate between the plunger spring seat B (lower) and fuel pump, by putting the handle of a hammer in the lower part of pump and pushing the roller guide up.

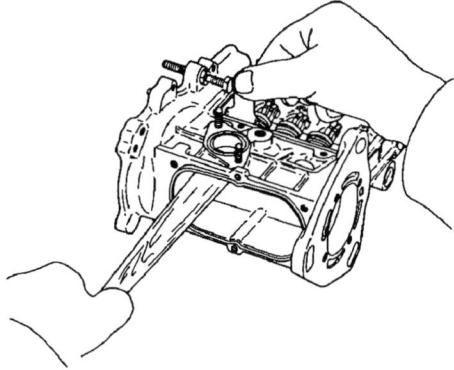

NOTE: 1. *Face the roller guide stop groove upwards, and align it with the stop screw hole on the pump.*

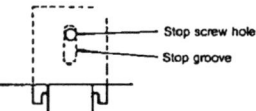

Stop screw hole
Stop groove

2. *Check the movement of the rack. The plunger spring may be out of place if the movement is heavy — insert a screwdriver and bring it to the correct position.*
3. *When replacing the roller guide assembly, fit shims and lightly tighten:*

Standard shim thickness	1.2 mm (0.0472 in.)
Part code number	129155-51600

(11) Make sure that the roller guide stop groove is in the correct position, and tighten the roller guide stop bolt.

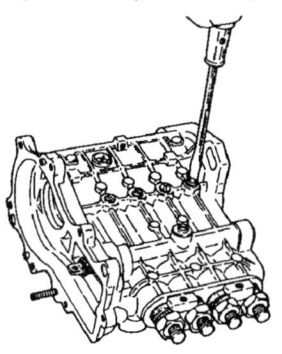

(12) Fit the bearings to both ends of the camshaft, and i
sert from the drive side by tapping lightly.

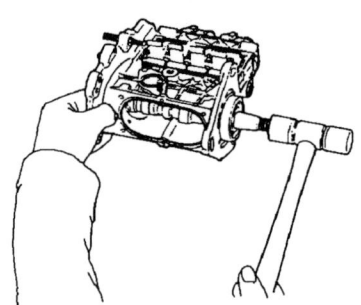

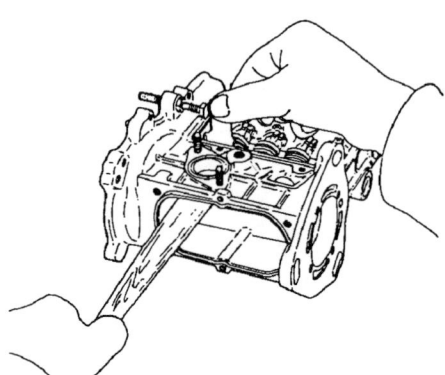

NOTE: Turn the pump upside down, and tap in the camshaft while moving the roller guide to the plunger
spring side.

(13) Fit the oil seal on the inside of the bearing retainer
and mount the bearing retainer.

(15) Mount the fuel pump side cover.
(16) Tap in the camshaft wood ruff key.
(17) Turn the camshaft, and pull out the plunger spring
support plate.

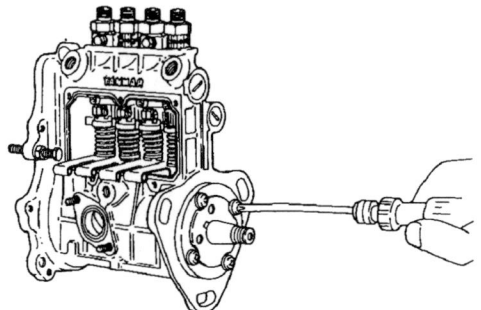

NOTE: Coat the camshaft and oil seal with oil to prevent
the oil seal from being scratched.

(14) Fix the pump, lightly tap both ends of the cam shaft with
a wooden hammer, and adjust the cam shaft side
clearance with the adjustment shims while checking
with a side clearance gauge.

	mm (in.)
Camshaft side clearance	0.02 ~ 0.05 (0.0007 ~ 0.0019)

Adjusting
Pull out the adjusting shims if the clearance is too small, and
add adjusting shims if it is too large.

	mm (in.)
Adjusting shim thickness	0.50 (0.0196)
	0.40 (0.0157)
	0.30 (0.0118)
	0.15 (0.0059)

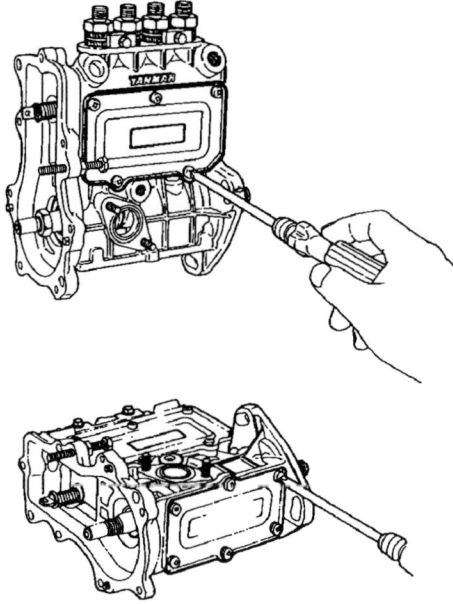

NOTE: Fit double nuts to turn the camshaft.

(18) Tighten the delivery valve retainer.

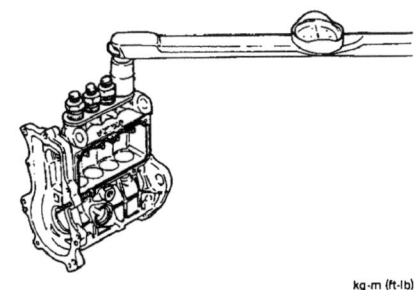

	kg-m (ft-lb)
Tightening torque	3.5 ~ 4.0 (25.31 ~ 28.93)

NOTE: 1. Tighten the retainer as far as possible by hand—
if the bolt gets hard to turn part way, the packing
or delivery valve are out of place. Remove, correct, and start tightening again.
2. Overtightening can result in malfunctioning of
the rack.

(19) Fit the delivery retainer stop and tighten the stop bolt.

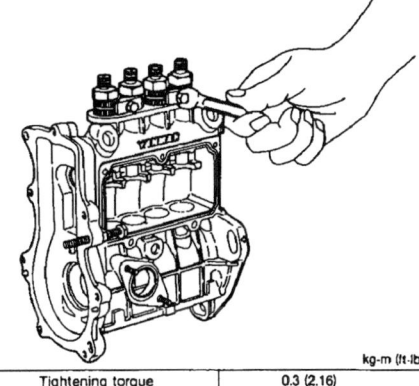

	kg-m (ft-lb)
Tightening torque	0.3 (2.16)

NOTE: Overtightening can upset the delivery retainer and
cause oil leakage.

(20) Mount the fuel feed pump

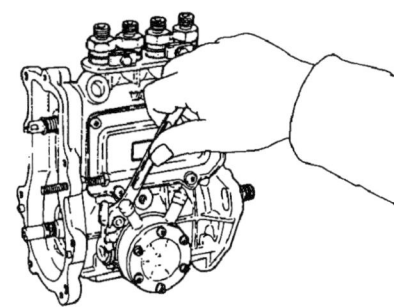

NOTE: Refer to the instructions for reassembly of the fuel
feed pump.

4. Adjustment of Fuel Injection Pump and Governor

Adjust the fuel injection pump after you have completed reassembly. The pump itself must be readjusted with a special pump tester when you have replaced major parts such as the plunger assembly, roller guide assembly, fuel camshaft, etc. Procure a pump tester like the one illustrated below.

4-1 Preparations

Prepare for adjustment of the fuel injection pump as follows:

(1) Adjusting nozzle assembly and inspection of injection starting pressure.

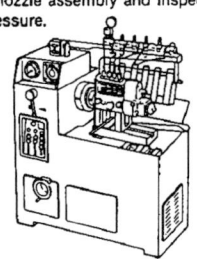

Adjusting nozzle type	YDN-12SD12
	kg/cm² (lb/in.²)
Injection starting pressure	165 ~ 175 (2346.85 ~ 2489.08)

(2) Adjusting injection pipe.

mm (in.)

Inner dia./outer dia. × length	2.0/6.0 × 600 (0.0787/0.2362 × 23.6220)
Minimum bending radius	25 (0.9842)

(3) Mount the fuel injection pump on the pump tester platform.

mm (in.)

Tester used	l_1	l_2	Part code number
Yanmar	110 (4.3307)	150 (5.9055)	158090-51010
Robert Bosch	125 (4.9212)	165 (6.4960)	158090-51020

(4) Remove the control rack blind cover and fit the rack indicator.

Next, turn the pinion from the side of the pump until the control rack is at the maximum drive side position, and set it to the rack indicator scale standard position. Then make sure that the control rack and rack indicator slide smoothly.

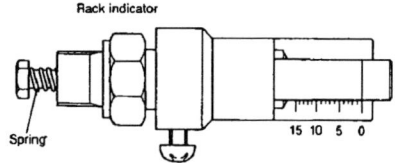

Rack indicator

Spring

15 10 5 0

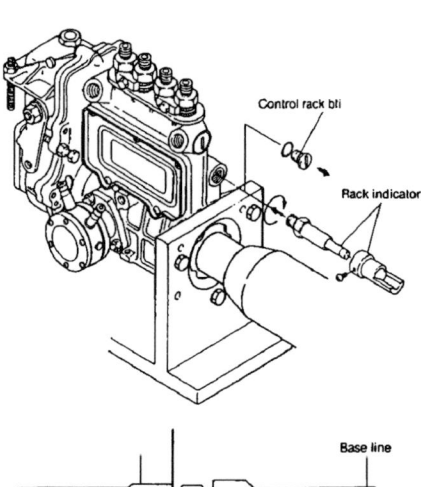

Control rack bli

Rack indicator

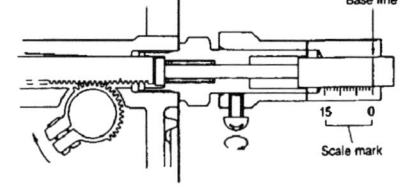

Base line

15 0

Scale mark

Part code number	158090-51500

3-23

(5) Check control rack stroke
Make sure the rack position is at 11.5 ~ 12.5mm (0.4527 ~ 0.4921in.) on the indicator scale when the governor control lever is set at the maximum operating position. If it is not at this value, change the link connecting the governor and control rack to adjust it.

NOTE: _Links are availabe in 1mm (0.0394in.) increments._

(6) Remove the plug in the oil fill hole on the top of the governor case, and fill the pump with about 200cc of pump oil or engine oil.

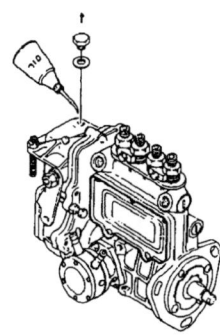

(7) Complete fuel oil piping and operate the pump tester to purge the line of air.
(8) Set the pressure of oil fed from the pump tester to the injection pump at 0.2 ~ 0.3kg/cm² (2.84 ~ 4.26 ln/in.²).

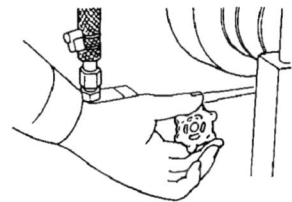

4-2 Adjustment of top clearance

Adjust the top clearance (the clearance between the top of plunger and the top of barrel with the cam at top dead center) of each cylinder plunger to bring it to the specified value by changing the thickness of the shims.

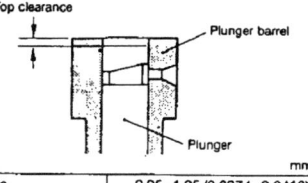

mm (in.)
Top clearance	0.95–1.05 (0.0374–0.0413)
Pre-stroke	2.5 (0.0984)
Standard shim thickness	1.2 (0.0472)

Relation between top clearance, standard shim thickness and pre-stroke.

mm (in.)
Adjusting shim thickness	1.0 (0.0394)
	1.2 (0.0472)
	1.3 (0.0512)
	1.4 (0.0551)
	1.5 (0.0591)
	1.6 (0.0630)
Part Code No.	129155–51600

(1) Place the top clearance gauge on a level surface and set the gauge to zero.

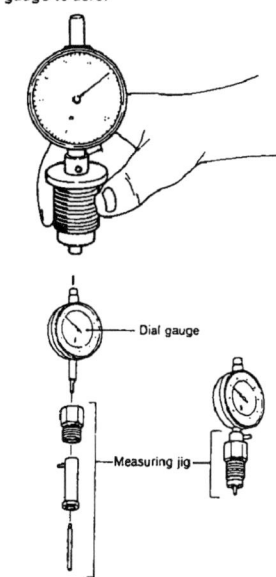

Dial gauge

Measuring jig

(2) Remove the injection pump delivery retainer, take out the delivery valve assembly, insert the top clearance gauge and tighten by hand.

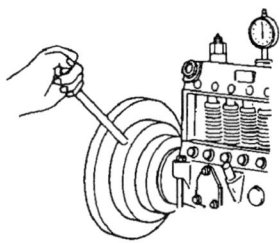

(3) Turn the camshaft, and bring the cam to the top dead center while watching the gauge needle.

3-24

(4) Read the gauge at this position, and adjust until the clearance is at the specified value by changing adjusting shims.
Tighten the adjusting screw after completing adjustment.

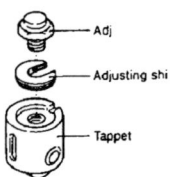

- Adj
- Adjusting shi
- Tappet

(Greater shim thickness decreases top clearance and smaller shim thickness increases top clearance).

NOTE: *Adjust while watching gauge, and then tighten.*

(5) After adjustment is completed, insert the delivery valve assembly and tighten the delivery retainer.

kg·m (ft·lb)

Delivery retainer tightening torque	3.5 ~ 4.0 (25.31 ~ 28.93)

Repeat the above procedure to adjust the top clearance of each cylinder.

4-3 Adjusting of injection timing

After adjusting the top clearance for all cylinders, check/adjust the injection timing.

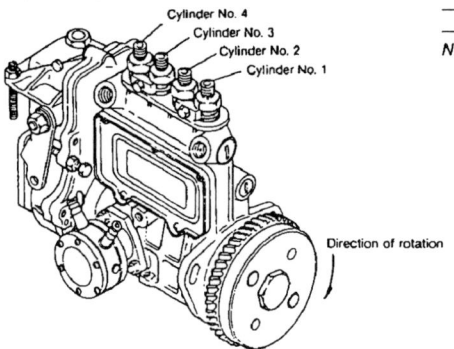

Cylinder No. 4
Cylinder No. 3
Cylinder No. 2
Cylinder No. 1

Direction of rotation

(1) Set the governor control lever to the operating position and fix (bring plunger to the effective injection range), turn the camshaft clockwise, and check the injection starting time (FID) of cylinder No.1 (start of discharge of fuel from the delivery retainer).

Cylinder no.	Count from the drive side
Direction of rotation	Right looking from drive side

(2) In the above state, set the tester needle to a position easy to read on the flywheel scale, and check the injection timing several times by reading the flywheel scale, according to the injection order.

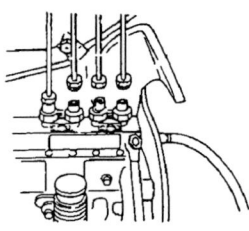

Injection order	1—3—4—2—1
Injection timing	90°
Allowable deviation	±30'

(3) Readjust the top clearance of cylinders that are not within the allowable deviation (increasing adjusting shim thickness makes injection timing faster, and decreasing makes it slower).
The change in injection timing effected by adjusting shims is as follows:

Change in shim thickness	Change in injection timing	
	Cam angle	Crank angle
0.1mm (0.0039in.)	0.5°	1.0°

(4) When you have readjusted top clearance, make sure it is within allowable values after completing adjustment.

mm (in.)

Allowable top clearance	0.3 (0.0118)

NOTE: *1. All cylinders must be readjusted it any one shows less than the allowable value.*
2. If the top clearance is less than the allowable value, the plunger will hit the delivery valve or the plunger flange will hit the plunger barrel.

4-4 Plunger pressure test

(1) Mount the pressure gauge to the delivery retai r of the cylinder to be tested.

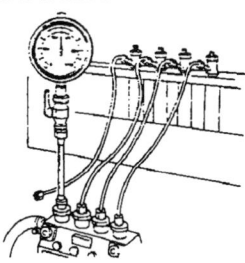

Max. pressure gauge reading	1000 kg/cm³ (14223 lb/in.³)
Connecting screw dimensions	M12 × 1.5

(2) Set the governor control lever to the stop position, operate the injection pump at about 200 rpm, and make sure that the pressure gauge reading is 500 kg/cm² (7110 lb/in.²) or more while lightly moving the control pinion gear towards full throttle (drive side) from the pump.
Replace the plunger if the pressure does not reach thi value.

(3) Immediately release the gear after the pressure rises to stop injection.
At the same time, check to see that oil is not leaking from the delivery retainer or fuel injection piping, and that there is no extreme drop in pressure.

4-5 Delivery valve pressure test

(1) Perform the plunger pressure test in the same way, bringing the pressure to about 120 kg/cm² (1706 lb/in.²), and then stopping injection.

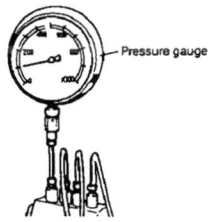

Pressure gauge

(2) After pressure rises to the above value, measure the time it takes to drop from 100 ~ 90 kg/cm² (1422 ~ 2702 lb/in.²).

100 → 90 kg/cm² (1422 ~ 1280 lb/in.²)	5 seconds (to drop 10 kg/cm² (142 lb/in.²))

If the pressure drops faster than this, wash the delivery valve, and retest. Replace the delivery valve if the pressure continues to drop rapidly.

4-6 Adjusting injection volume (uniformity of each cylinder)

The injection volume is determined by the fuel injection pump rpm and rack position. Check and adjust to bring to specified value.

4-6.1 Measuring injection volume

(1) Preparation
Set the pump rpm, rack position and measuring stroke to the specified value and measure:

Pump RPM	1800 rpm
Pump rotating direction	Right looking from drive side
Rack indicator scale reading	7mm (0.2756 in)

Remove the rack stop bolt behind the pump and screw in the rack fixing bolt to fix the rack.

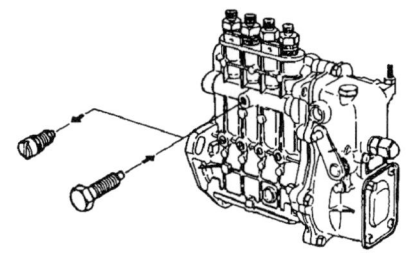

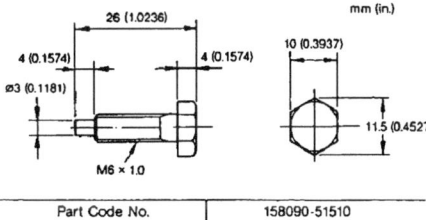

26 (1.0236) mm (in.)
4 (0.1574) 4 (0.1574) 10 (0.3937)
ø3 (0.1181)
11.5 (0.4527)
M6 × 1.0

Part Code No.	158090-51510

(2) Measuring injection volume
Measure the injection volume at the standard stroke, and adjust as follows if it is not within the specified value.

Measuring stroke	1,000 st
Specified injection volume at standard rack position	See injection pump service data
Nonuniformity of cylinders	±3%

4-6.2 Adjustment of injection volume

Measure the injection volume in measuring cylinders for each cylinder, and adjust if necessary to obtain the specified values.

(1) Push the control rack all the way to the drive side, stop with the rack fixing bolt, and loosen the pinion/sleeve fixing bolt 1/3 of a revolution.

Printed in Japan
_A0A1029-9002_

(2) When the control sleeve is turned to the right or left, the plunger is turned through the same angle to increase or decrease injection volume.
The injection volume is increased when the control sleeve is turned in the — direction and decreased when turned in the — direction in the following figure.

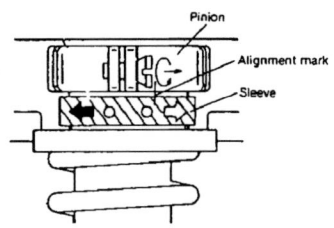

Pinion

Alignment mark

Sleeve

(3) Measure the injection volume of each cylinder again. Repeat this process until the injection volume for every cylinder is the same (within the specified limit).

(4) Next, measure the injection volumes under different conditions, and make sure the injection volume for every cylinder is within the specifications.
Replace the plunger if the injection volume is not within specifications.

NOTE: See adjustment data for the specified injecti volume value at other measuring points.

(5) After completing measurement, firmly tighten the piston/sleeve fixing screw.

(6) If not aligned with the match mark, make a new match mark.

4-7 Adjustment of governor

4-7.1 Adjusting fuel limit bolt

(1) Adjust the tightness of the fuel limit bolt to bring the rack position to the specified value (R₁) with the governor control lever all the way down towards the fuel increase position, while keeping the pump at rated rpm N₁.

(2) Measure fuel injection volume at rack position (R₁). Tightening of fuel limit bolt.

(3) If the injection volume is at the specified value, tighten the fuel limit bolt lock nut at that position.

4-7.2 Adjusting RPM limit bolt

(1) Gradually loosen the governor control lever while keeping the pump drive condition in the same condition as when the fuel limit bolt was adjusted, and adjust the tightness of the RPM limit bolt to the point where the rack position just exceeds the specified value (R₁).

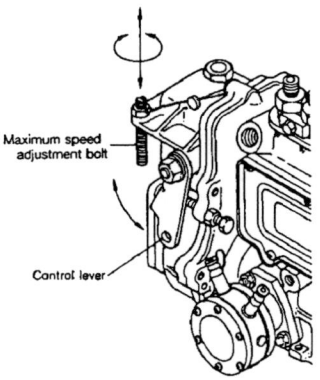

Maximum speed
adjustment bolt

Control lever

(2) Check maximum RPM at no load
Further increase rpm, and make sure that rack position $(R_2 = R_1 - L)$ corresponding to maximum rpm at no load is within specified value (N₂).

No load max. RPM (Pump RPM)	1950 rpm

4-7.3 Adjusting idling

(1) Maintain the pump rpm at specified rpm (N₃).

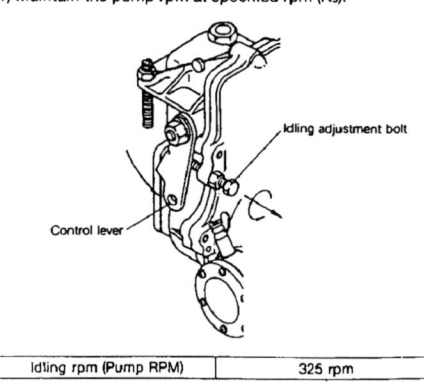

Idling adjustment bolt

Control lever

Idling rpm (Pump RPM)	325 rpm

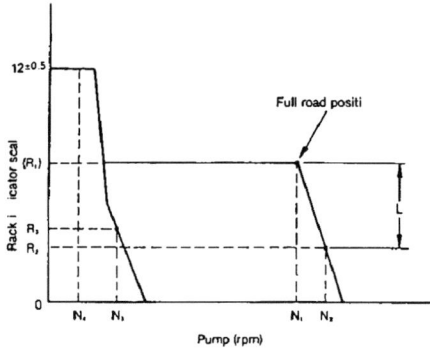

12±0.5

Full road positi

(R₁)

Rack i icator scal

R₁
R₂

0

N₄ N₃   N₅ N₂

Pump (rpm)

(2) Measure the injection volume while lowering the governor control lever to the idling position, and adjust the position of the control lever with the idling adjustment bolt to bring it to the specified value.

Measuring stroke	1000 st
Idling injection volume	See injection pump service data

4-7.4 Check injection volume when starting

(1) Make sure the control rack moves smoothly while gradually reducing idling rpm.
(2) Next, fix the governor control lever at the full load position with the pump at the specified rpm (N_4). Make sure that control rack is at the maximum rack position (11.05 ~ 12.05).
Measure the injection volume and check to make sure it is within the specified value.

Pump rpm (N^4)	200 rpm
Rack indicator scale	11.5~12.5mm(0.4527~0.4921 in.)
Measuring stroke	1000 st
Injection volume	See injection pump service data

Checking injection stop
Drive the pump at rated rpm (N_1) and standard rack position (R_1) with the governor control lever at the full load position, operate the stop lever on the back of the governor case, and make sure that injection to all cylinders is stopped.

NOTE: Be sure to remove the rack fixing bolt when doing this.

5. Fuel Feed Pump

The fuel feed pump pumps fuel from the fuel tank, passes it through the fuel filter element, and supplies it to the fuel injection pump.

The fuel feed pump is mounted on the side of this engine and is driven by the (eccentric) cam of the fuel pump camshaft. It is provided with a manual priming lever so that fuel can be supplied when the engine is stopped.

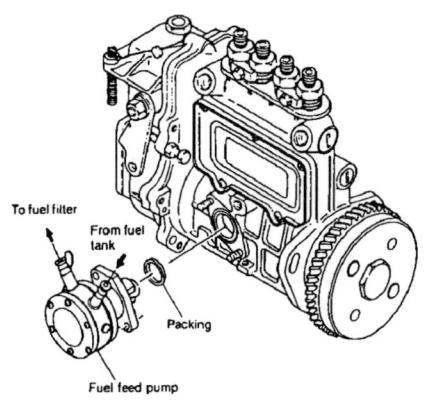

To fuel filter

From fuel tank

Packing

Fuel feed pump

5-1 Construction of fuel feed pump

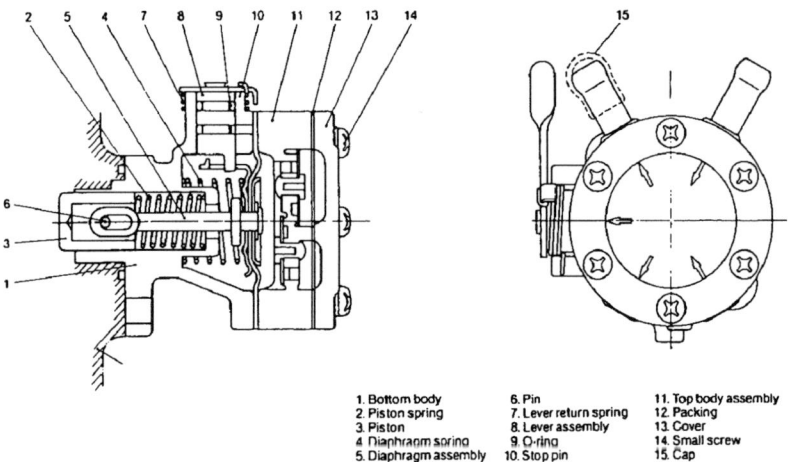

1. Bottom body	6. Pin	11. Top body assembly
2. Piston spring	7. Lever return spring	12. Packing
3. Piston	8. Lever assembly	13. Cover
4. Diaphragm spring	9. O-ring	14. Small screw
5. Diaphragm assembly	10. Stop pin	15. Cap

5-2 Fuel feed pump specifications

Head	1m (3.28 ft)
Discharge volume	230 cc/min (14.03 in.³/min) at 1500 cam rpm, discharge pressure of 0.2 kg/cm² (2.84 lb/in.³)
Closed off pressure	0.3 kg/cm² (4.26 lb/in.³) or more (at 400 cam rpm)

5-3 Disassembly and reassembly of fuel feed pump

5-3. 1 Disassembly

(1) Remove the fuel feed pump mounting nut, and take the fuel feed pump off the fuel injection pump.
(2) Clean the fuel feed pump assembly with fuel oil.
(3) After checking the orientation of the arrow on the cover, make match marks on the upper body and cover, remove the small screw, and disassemble the cover, upper body and lower body.

5-3. 2 Reassembly

(1) Clean all parts with fuel oil, inspect, and replace any defective parts.
(2) Replace any packings on parts that have been disassembled.
(3) Make sure that the intake valve and discharge valve on upper body are mounted in the proper direction, and that you don't forget the valve packing.
(4) Assemble the diaphragm into the body, making sure the diaphragm mounting holes are lined up (do not force).
(5) Align the match marks on the upper body of the pump and cover, and tighten the small screws evenly.

kg-cm (ft-lb)

Tightening torque	15 ~ 25 (1.08 ~ 1.80)

5-4 Fuel feed pump inspection

(1) Place the fuel feed pump in kerosene, cover the discharge port with your finger, move the priming lever and check for air bubbles (Repair or replace any part which emits air bubbles).

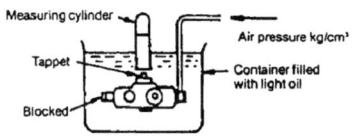

Measuring cylinder

Air pressure kg/cm³

Tappet

Container filled with light oil

Blocked

(2) Attach a vinyl hose to the fuel feed pump intake, keep the pump at the specified depth from the fuel oil surface, move the priming lever by hand and check for sudden spurts of fuel oil from the discharge port. If oil is not spurted out, inspect the diaphragm and diaphragm spring and repair/replace as necessary.
(3) Diaphragm inspection
Parts of the diaphragm that are repeatedly burned will become thinner or deteriorate over a long period of time. Check the diaphragm and replace if necessary.

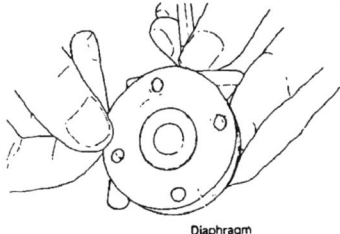

Diaphragm

(4) Valve contact/mounting
Clean the valve seat and valve with air to remove any foreign matter.

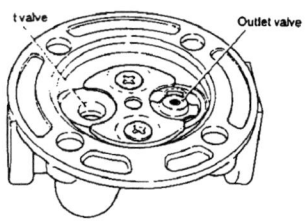

t valve   Outlet valve

(5) Inspect the diaphragm spring and piston spring for settling and the piston for wear, and replace as necessary.

NOTE: Replace parts as an assembly.

6. Fuel Injection Nozzle

When fuel oil pumped by the fuel injection pump reaches the injection nozzle, it pushes up the nozzle valve (held down by spring), and is injected into the combustion chamber at high pressure.
The fuel is atomized by the nozzle to mix uniformly with the air in the combustion chamber. How well the fuel is mixed with high temperature air directly affects combustion efficiency, engine performance and fuel economy.
Accordingly, the fuel injection nozzles must be kept in top-condition to maintain performance and operating efficiency.

6-1 Functioning of fuel injection nozzle

Fuel from the fuel injection pump passes through the oil port in the nozzle holder, and enters the nozzle body reservoir.
When oil reaches the specified pressure, it pushes up the nozzle valve (held by the nozzle spring), and is injected through the small hole on the tip of the nozzle body.
The nozzle valve is automatically pushed down by the nozzle spring and closed after fuel is injected.
Oil that leaks from between the nozzle valve and nozzle body goes from the hole on top of the nozzle spring through the oil leakage fitting and back into the fuel tank.
Adjustment of injection starting pressure is effected with the adjusting shims.

(1) Hole type fuel injection nozzle

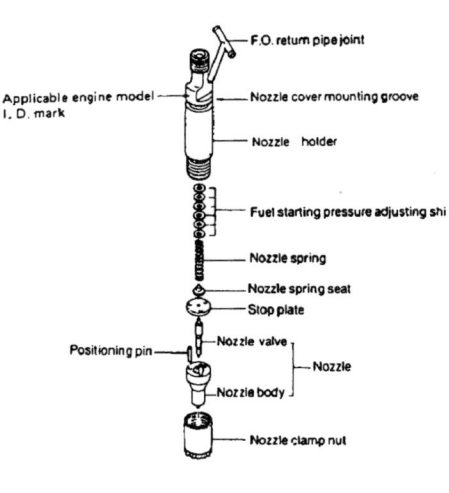

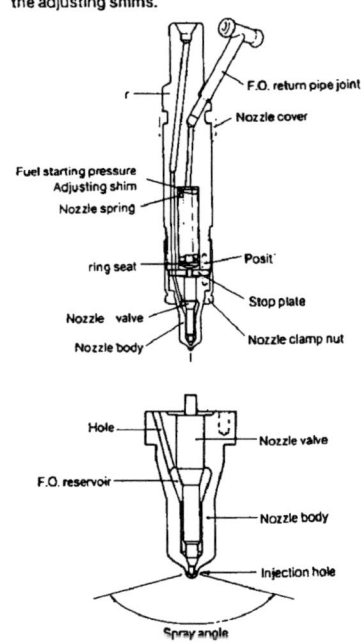

Engine model	4JH2E	4JH2-TE	4JH2-HTE	4JH2-DTE	4JH2-UTE
Nozzle I.D.Mark	155P235J20	140P255Z0	140P255Z0	140P265J20	140P255Z0
Spray angle	155°	140°	140°	140°	140°
No. of injection hole × dia	5 × 0.23mm	5 × 0.25mm	5 × 0.25mm	5 × 0.26mm	5 × 0.25mm
Nozzle opening pressure	195 ~ 205kg/cm² (2.773~2.915 lb/in.²)				

Nozzle body identification number
The type of nozzle can be determined from the number inscribed on the outside of the nozzle body.
1) Hole type fuel injection nozzles

Sample

Y DLL A — 150 P 244JO

- Design code
- Nozzle size P size / S size
- Spray angle
- Mounting angle of nozzle on cylinder head Code A: at angle No code: not at angle
- Type (DLL: semi-long type)

YANMAR

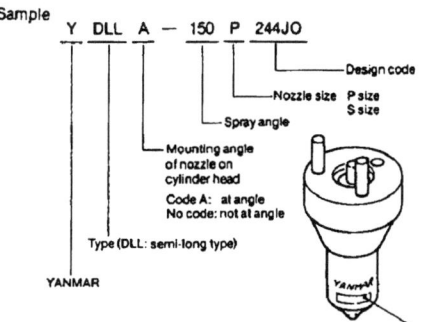

Identification number

6-2 Fuel injection nozzle disassembly

NOTE: 1. Disassemble fuel injection nozzle in a clean area as for the fuel injection pump.
2. When disassembling more than one fuel injection nozzle, keep the parts for each injection nozzle separate for each cylinder (i.e. the nozzle for cylinder 1 must be remounted in cylinder 1).

(1) When removing the injection nozzle from the cylinder head, remove the high pressure fuel pipe, fuel leakage pipe, etc., the injection nozzle retainer nut, and then the fuel injection nozzle.

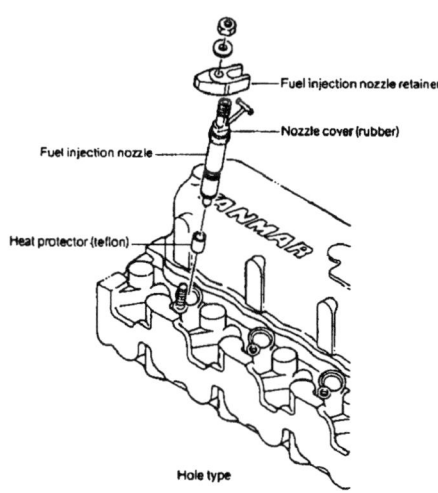

Fuel injection nozzle retainer
Nozzle cover (rubber)
Fuel injection nozzle
Heat protector (teflon)
Hole type

(2) Put the nozzle in a vise
NOTE: Use the special nozzle holder for the hole type injection nozzle so that the high pressure mounting threads are not damaged.
(3) Remove the nozzle nut

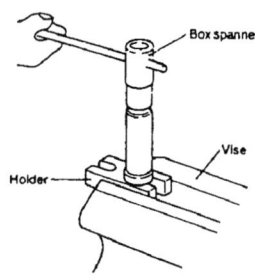

Box spanner
Vise
Holder

NOTE: Use a special box spanner for the hole type (the thickness of the two nozzle nuts is 15mm (0.5906in.)).

(4) Remove the inner parts

NOTE: Be careful not to loosen the spring seat, adjusting shims or other small parts.

6-3 Fuel injection nozzle inspection
6-3. 1 Washing

(1) Be sure to use new diesel oil to wash the fuel injecti nozzle parts.
(2) Wash the nozzle in clean diesel oil with the nozzle cleaning kit.

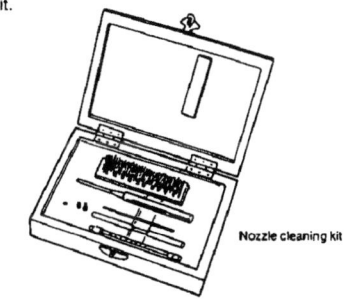

Nozzle cleaning kit

1) Diesel Kiki nozzle cleaning kit:
   Type NP-8486B No. 5789-001
2) Anzen Jidosha Co., Ltd. nozzle cleaning kit:
   Type NCK-001

(3) Clean off the carbon on the outside of the nozzle body with a brass brush.

(4) Clean the nozzle seat with cleaning spray.

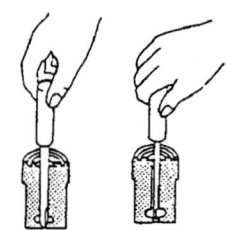

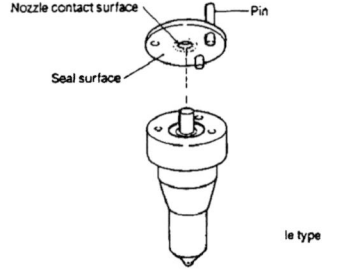

Nozzle contact surface — Pin

Seal surface

le type

	mm (in.)
Nozzle contact surface wear limit	0.1 (0.0039)

(5) Clean off the carbon on the tip of nozzle with a piece of wood.

(6) Clean hole type nozzles with a nozzle cleaning needle.

Nozzle cleaning needle (piano wire)
0.2mm dia. wire, 22mm long × 5 wires

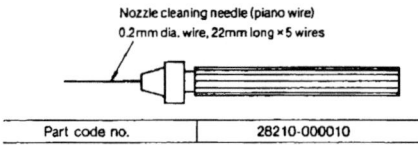

Part code no.	28210-000010

(4) Inspecting nozzle spring
Replace the nozzle spring if it is extremely bent, or the surface is scratched or rusted.

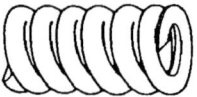

6-4. 2 Nozzle inspection

(1) Inspect for scratches/wear
Inspect oil seals for abnormal scratches or wear and replace the nozzle if the nozzle sliding surface or seat are scratched or abnormally worn.

(2) Check nozzle sliding
Wash the nozzle and nozzle body in clean diesel oil, and make sure that when the nozzle is pulled out about half way from the body, it slides down by itself when released.
Rotate the nozzle a little; replace the nozzle/nozzle body as a set if there are some places where it does not slide smoothly.

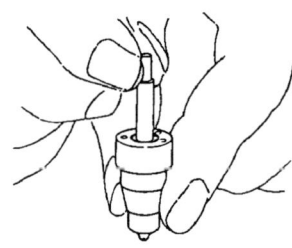

(5) Nozzle holder
Check the oil seal surface for scratches/wear; replace if the wear is excessive.

6-5 Fuel injection nozzle reassembly

The fuel injection nozzle is reassembled in the opposite order to disassembly.
(1) Insert the adjusting shims, nozzle spring and nozzle spring seat in the nozzle holder, mount the stop plate with the pin, insert the nozzle body/nozzle set and tighten the nut.
(2) Use the special holder when tightening the nut for the hole type nozzle as in disassembly.

Nozzle nut tightening torque	kg·m (ft-lb)
Hole type nozzle	4 ~ 4.5 (28.9 ~ 32.5)

(3) Inspecting stop plate (inter-piece)
Check for scratches/wear in seals on both ends, check for abnormal wear on the surface where it comes in contact with the nozzle; replace if the stop plate is excessively worn.

6-6 Adjusting fuel injection nozzle

6-6. 1 Adjusting opening pressure

Mount the fuel injection nozzle on the nozzle tester and use the handle to measure injection starting pressure. If it is not at the specified pressure, use the adjusting shims to increase/decrease pressure (both hole and pintle types).

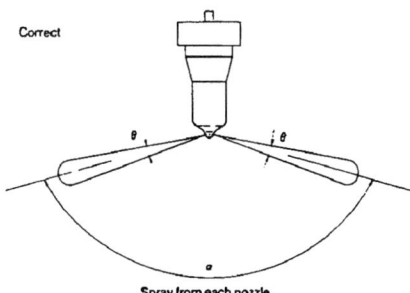

Correct

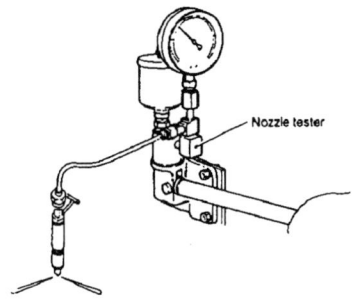

Nozzle tester

Spray from each nozzle hole is uniform

Poor

Injection starting pressure

	kg/cm² (lb/in.')
Injection starting pressure	195 ~ 205 (2773 ~ 2915)

7-6. 2 Injection test

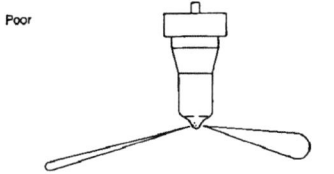

After adjusting the nozzle to the specified starting pressure, check the fuel spray condition and seat oil tightness.

(1) Check seat oil tightness

After two or three injections, gradually increase the pressure up to 20 kg/cm² (284 lb/in.') before reading the starting pressure, maintain the pressure for 5 seconds, and make sure that no oil is dripping from the tip of the nozzle.

Test the injection with a nozzle tester; retighten and test again if there is excessive oil leakage from the overflow coupling.

Replace the nozzle as a set if oil leakage is still excessive.

(2) Injection spray condition

Operate the nozzle tester lever once to twice a second and check for abnormal injection.

1) Hole type nozzles

Replace hole type nozzles that do not satisfy the following conditions:

* Proper spray angle (θ)
* Correct injection angle (α)
* Complete atomization of fuel
* Prompt starting/stopping of injection

• Excessive difference in spray angle (θ)
• Excessive difference in injection angle (α)
• Incomplete atomization
• Sluggish starting/stopping of injection

7. Troubleshooting

7-1 Troubleshooting of fuel injection pump

Complete repair means not only replacing defective parts, but finding and eliminating the cause of the trouble as well. The cause of the trouble may not necessarily be in the pump itself, but may be in the engine or the fuel system. If the pump is removed prematurely, the true cause of the trouble may never be known. Before removing the pump from the engine, at least go through the basic check points given here.

Basic check points
* Check for breaks or oil leaks throughout the fuel system, from the fuel tank to the nozzle.
* Check the injection timings for all cylinders. Are they correctly adjusted? Are they too fast or too slow?
* Check the nozzle spray.
* Check the fuel delivery. Is it in good condition? Loosen the fuel pipe connection at the injection pump inlet, and test operate the fuel feed pump.

7-2 Major faults and troubleshooting

Fault		Cause	Remedy
1. Engine won't start.	Fuel not delivered to injection pump.	(1) No fuel in the fuel tank.	Resupply
		(2) Fuel tank cock is closed.	Open
		(3) Fuel pipe system is clogged.	Clean
		(4) Fuel filter element is clogged.	Disassemble and clean, or replace element
		(5) Air is sucked into the fuel due to defective connections in the piping from the fuel tank to the fuel pump.	Repair
		(6) Defective valve contact of feed pump.	Repair or replace.
		(7) Piston spring of feed pump is broken.	Replace
		(8) Inter-spindle or tappets of feed pump are stuck.	Repair or replace
	Fuel delivered to injection pump.	(1) Defective connection of control lever and accel. rod of injection pump.	Repair or adjust
		(2) Plunger is worn out or stuck.	Repair or replace
		(3) Delivery valve is stuck.	Repair or replace
		(4) Control rack doesn't move.	Repair or replace
		(5) Injection pump coupling is damaged, or the key is broken.	Replace
	Nozzle doesn't work.	(1) Nozzle valve doesn't open or close normally.	Repair or replace
		(2) Nozzle seat is defective.	Repair or replace
		(3) Case nut is loose.	Inspect and tighten
		(4) Injection nozzle starting pressure is too low.	Adjust
		(5) Nozzle spring is broken.	Replace
		(6) Fuel oil filter is clogged.	Repair or replace
		(7) Excessive oil leaks from the nozzle sliding area.	Replace the nozzle assembly
	Injection timing is defective.	(1) Injection timing is retarded due to failure of the coupling.	Adjust
		(2) Camshaft is excessively worn.	Replace camshaft
		(3) Roller guide incorrectly adjusted or excessively worn.	Adjust or replace
		(4) Plunger is excessively worn.	Replace plunger assembly
2. Engine starts, but immediately stops.		(1) Fuel pipe is clogged.	Clean
		(2) Fuel filter is clogged.	Disassemble and clean, or replace the element.
		(3) Improper air-tightness of the fuel pipe connection, or pipe is broken and air is being sucked in.	Replace packing; repair pipe
		(4) Insufficient fuel delivery from the feed pump.	Repair or replace

Fault		Cause	Remedy
3. Engine's output is insufficient.	Defective injection timing. and other failures.	(1) Knocking sounds caused by improper (too fast) injection timing.	Inspect and adjust
		(2) Engine overheats or emits large amount of smoke due to improper (too slow) injection timing.	Inspect and adjust
		(3) Insufficient fuel delivery from feed pump.	Repair or replace
	Nozzle movements is defective	(1) Case nut loose.	Inspect and retighten
		(2) Defective injection nozzle performance.	Repair or replace nozzle
		(3) Nozzle spring is broken.	Replace
		(4) Excessive oil leaks from nozzle.	Replace nozzle assembly
	Injection pump is defective.	(1) Max. delivery limit bolt is screwed in too far.	Adjust
		(2) Plunger is worn.	Replace
		(3) Injection amount is not uniform.	Adjust
		(4) Injection timings are not even.	Adjust
		(5) The 1st and 2nd levers of the governor and the control rack of the injection pump are improperly lined up.	Repair
		(6) Delivery stopper is loose.	Inspect and retighten
		(7) Delivery packing is defective.	Replace packing
		(8) Delivery valve seat is defective.	Repair or replace
		(9) Delivery spring is broken.	Replace
4. Idling is rough.		(1) Movement of control rack is defective.	
		1) Stiff plunger movement or sticking.	Repair or replace
		2) Rack and pinion fitting is defective.	Repair
		3) Movement of governor is improper.	Repair
		4) Delivery stopper is too tight.	Inspect and adjust
		(2) Uneven injection volume.	Adjust
		(3) Injection timing is defective.	Adjust
		(4) Plunger is worn and fuel injection adjustment is difficult.	Replace
		(5) Governor spring is too weak.	Replace
		(6) Feed pump can't feed oil at low speeds.	Repair or replace
		(7) Fuel supply i insufficient at low speeds due to clogging of fuel filter.	Disassemble and clean, or replace element
5. Engine runs at high speeds, but cuts out at low speeds.		(1) The wire or rod of the accel. is caught.	Inspect and repair
		(2) Control rack is caught and can't be moved.	Inspect and repair
6. Engine doesn't reach max. rpm.		(1) Governor spring is broken or excessively worn.	Replace
		(2) Injection performance of nozzle is poor.	Repair or replace
7. Loud knocking.		(1) Injection timing is too fast or too slow.	Adjust
		(2) Injection from nozzle is Improper. Fuel drips after each injection.	Adjust
		(3) Injection nozzle starting pressure is too high.	Adjust
		(4) Uneven injection.	Adjust
		(5) Engine overheats, or insufficient compression.	Repair
3. Engine exhausts too much smoke.	When exhaust smoke is black:	(1) Injection timing is too fast.	Adjust
		(2) Air volume intake is insufficient.	Inspect and repair
		(3) The amount of injection is uneven.	Adjust
		(4) Injection from nozzle Is improper.	Repair or replace
	When exhaust smoke Is white:	(1) Injection timing is too slow.	Adjust
		(2) Water is mixed in fuel.	Inspect fuel system, and clean
		(3) Shortage of lube oil in the engine.	Repair
		(4) Engine is over-cooled.	Inspect

8. Tools

Name of tool	Shape and size	Application
Pump mounting scale for Yanmar tester 158090-51010 for Bosch (tester) 158090-51020		
Measuring device (cam backlash) 158090-51050		
Plunger insert 158090-51100		
Tappet holder 158090-51200		
Weight extractor 158090-51400		

3-37

Name of tool	Shape and size	Application
Rack indicator 158090-51500		
Rack lock screw 158090-51010		
Dummy nut 158090-51520		
Nozzle plate 158090-51700		
Plunger gauge 121820-92540		
Top clearance gauge 158090-51300		
Timer extraction tool		

Printed in Japan
A0A1029-9002

9. Fuel Filter

The fuel filter is installed between the fuel feed pump and fuel injection pump, and removes dirt/foreign matter from the fuel pumped from the fuel tank.
The fuel filter element must be changed periodically. The fuel pumped by the fuel feed pump goes around the element, is fed through the pores in the filter and discharged from the center of the cover. Dirt and foreign matter in the fuel are deposited in the element.

9-1 Fuel filter specifications

Filtering method	filter paper
Filtering area	840cm² (130.20in.²)
Maximum flow	0.25 ℓ/min (15.25 in.³/min)
Pressure loss	100mm (3.9370in.) Hg or less
Max. dia. of unfiltered particle	5μ

9-2 Fuel filter inspection

The fuel strainer must be cleaned occasionally. If there is water or foreign matter in the strainer bowl, disassemble the strainer and wash with clean fuel oil to completely remove foreign matter. Replace the element every 300 hours of operation.
Replace the filter prior to this if the filter is very dirty, deformed or damaged.

Element changes	every 300 hours
Element part code number	129470-55700

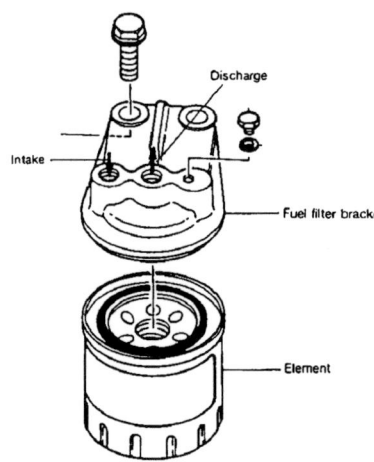

Discharge

Intake

Fuel filter bracket

Element

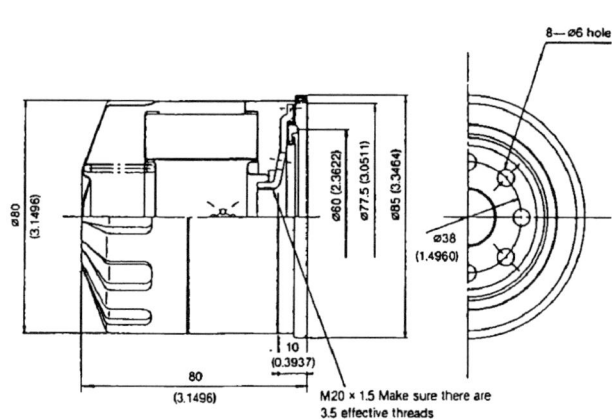

8—⌀6 hole

⌀60 (2.3622)
⌀77.5 (3.0511)
⌀85 (3.3464)

⌀38 (1.4960)

⌀80 (3.1496)

10 (0.3937)

80 (3.1496)

M20 × 1.5 Make sure there are 3.5 effective threads

10. Fuel Tank

A triangular 30 liter fuel tank with a 2000mm (78.7402in.) rubber fuel hose to fit all models is available as an option. A fuel return connection is provided on top of the tank to which a rubber hose can be connected to return fuel from the fuel nozzles.

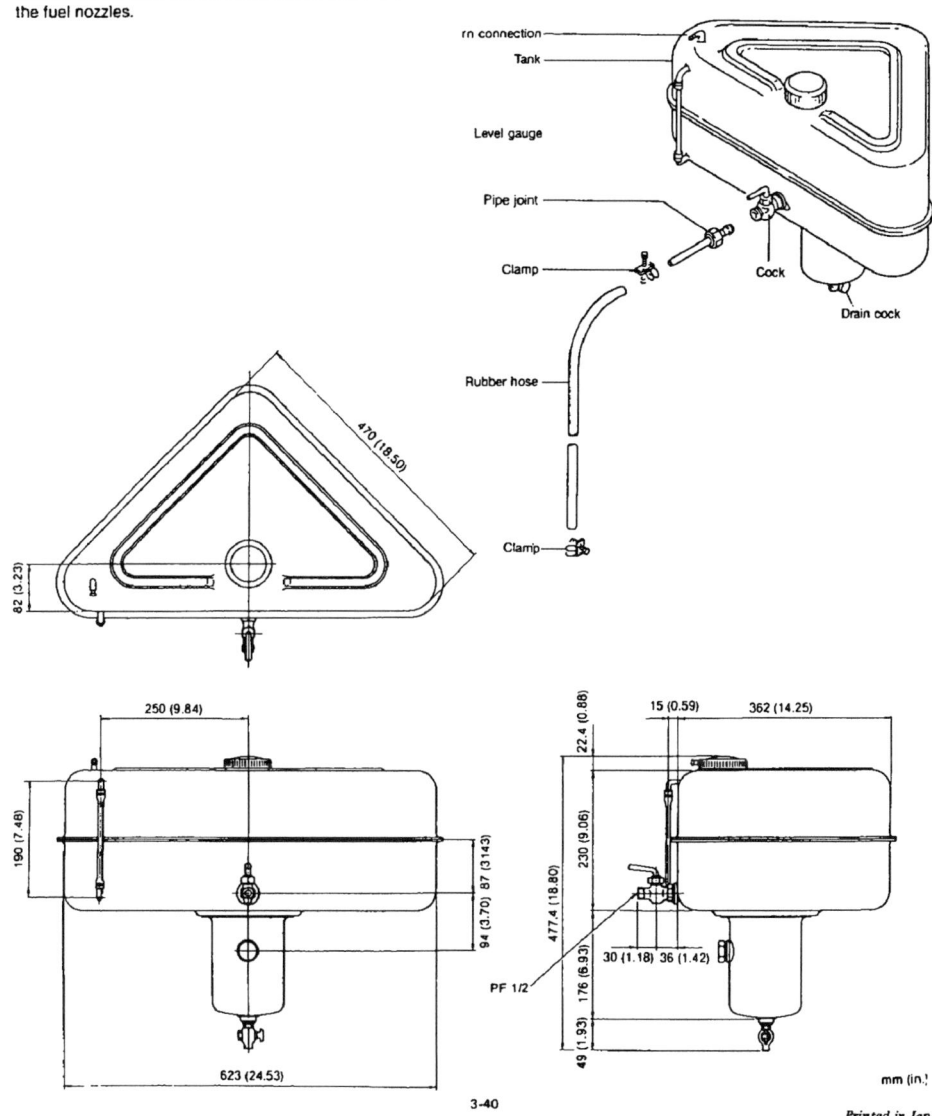

rn connection

Tank

Level gauge

Pipe joint

Clamp

Cock

Drain cock

Rubber hose

Clamp

470 (18.50)

82 (3.23)

250 (9.84)

190 (7.48)

94 (3.70) 87 (3143)

623 (24.53)

22.4 (0.88)

15 (0.59)   362 (14.25)

230 (9.06)

477.4 (18.80)

176 (6.93)   30 (1.18) 36 (1.42)

49 (1.93)

PF 1/2

mm (in.)

3-40

Printed in Japan
A0A1029-9002

11. Fuel Supply System (4JH2-UTE)

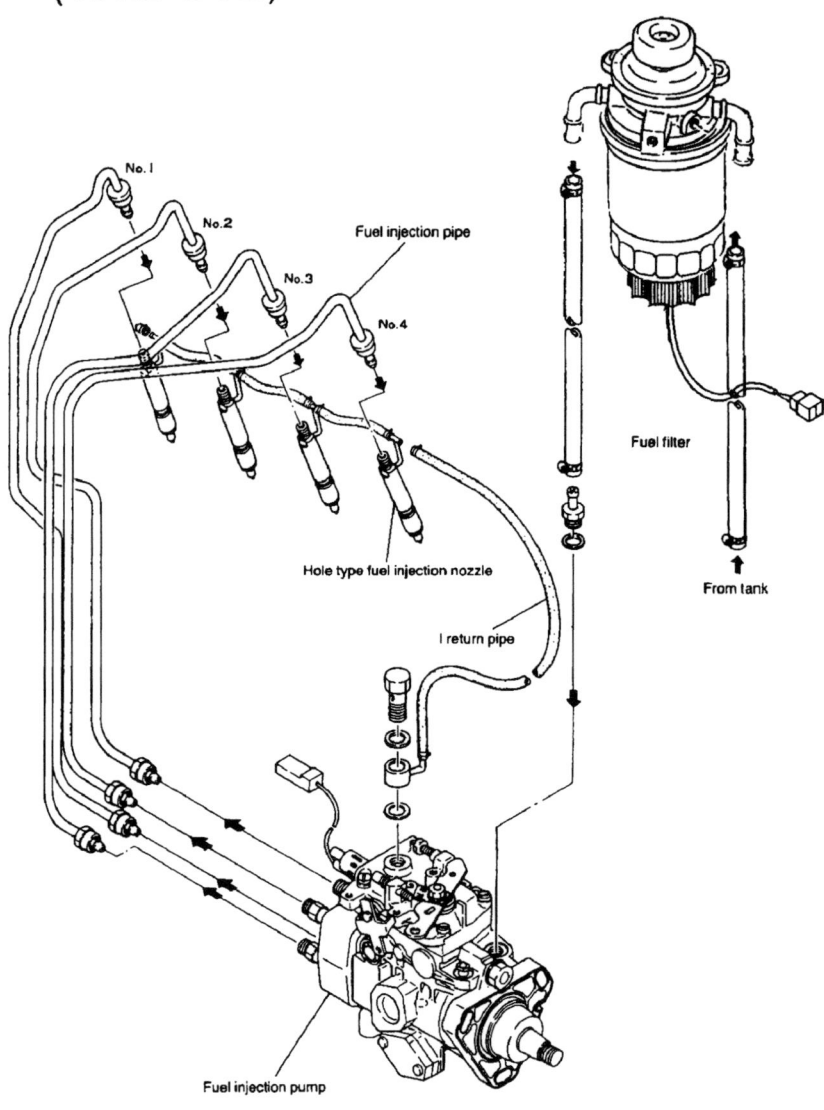

No. I

No.2

Fuel injection pipe

No.3

No.4

Fuel filter

Hole type fuel injection nozzle

From tank

I return pipe

Fuel injection pump

12. Bleeding and Checking Injection Timing(4JH2-UTE)

1. Air bleeding in the fuel system

If the engine is operated when the fuel tank is empty, or with the fuel tank outlet cock closed, air is sucked into the fuel oil system, and the engine stops. When this happens, vent the air as follows:

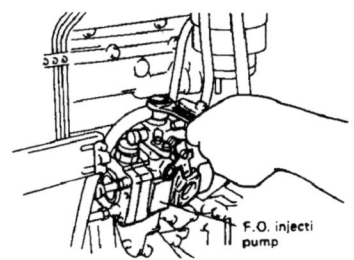

(1) Add fuel to the fuel tank.

(2) Loosen the air-vent screw on the fuel oil filter, and push the fuel feed pump priming lever several times.
When no air is observed in the fuel, tighten the air-vent screw firmly.

F.O. injecti
pump

(4) Next, vent air in the fuel injection piping. Loosen the fuel injection pipe nipple on the fuel injection valve side.
Put the remote control handle in the intermediate speed position, and the key switch in the "ST" position to run the engine. Repeat this procedure several times. After venting, tighten the fuel injection pipe nipple firmly.

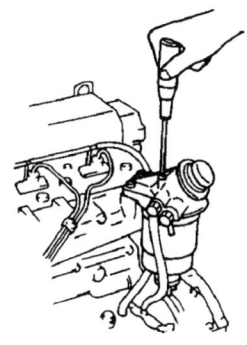

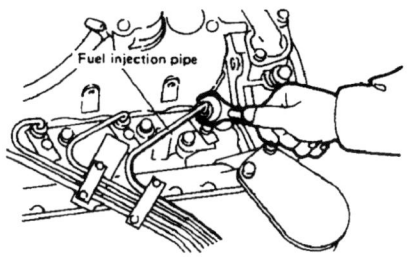

Fuel injection pipe

(3) Loosen the hexagonal bolt on the fuel pump. Push the fuel feed pump priming lever to vent the air. After venting the air, firmly tighten the hexagonal bolt.

(5) After bleeding air from all of the cylinders, turn the engine with the starter motor.
Make sure that the fuel injection for each cylinder gives off a high-pitched hissing sound.

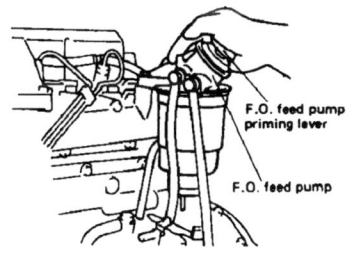

F.O. feed pump
priming lever

F.O. feed pump

Printed in Japan
AOA1029-9109SP

2. Check the fuel injection timing as follows:

(1) Remove the high pressure pipe from the fuel injection pump.

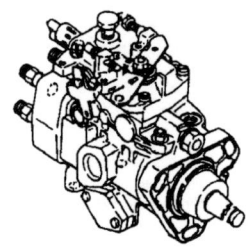

(2) Pull the engine warm up knob out and place the control lever in the "half speed" position.

(3) Insert a turning bar into the hole on the crank pulley on the front side. Crank the engine lightly to check the fuel injection timing.

(4) Timing marks on the flywheel can be seen through the hole on the flywheel housing

NOTE

3. Removal and Installation of Injection pump

(1) Remove the fuel injection pump gear cover from the timing gear housing cover.

(2) Make mating marks on the idle gear and the injecti pump gear using white paint for reinstallation.

(3) Remove the pump drive shaft end nut, the washer, the pump gear from the shaft, three pump retaining bolts, and two pump support bolts. Remove the injection pump.

NOTE: When removing the pump;
  1) Do not drop keys from the drive shaft into the gear housing.
  2) Avoid damage to O-rings on the pump.
  3) Do not hit the shaft end with a hammer.

(4) When installing the pump, match the mating marks on the bracket and the pump flange.

(5) While aligning the mating marks on the idle gear and the pump gear, install the pump to the pump gear.

(6) Tighten the drive shaft end nut to 7kg-m (51 lb-ft.).

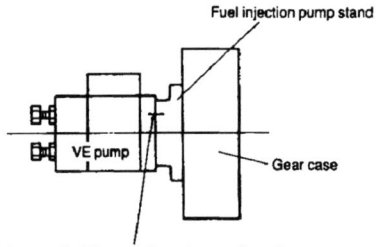

Fuel injection pump stand

VE pump

Gear case

Make sure that the match marks are aligned.
(With alignment of these marks, injection timing is automatically adjusted)

13. Fuel Injection Pump Outline(4JH2-UTE)

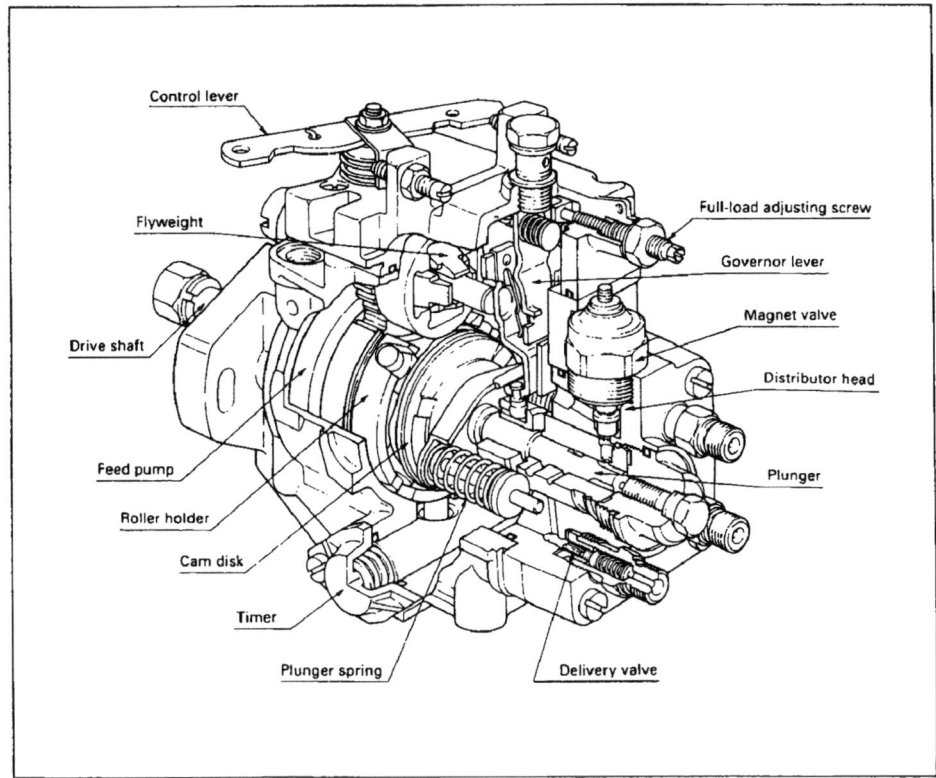

Fig. 1 VE type injection pump construction

With the PE type (in-line type) injection pump, the number of pump elements (plunger assemblies) must be the same as the number of engine cylinders. However, with the VE type (distributor type) injection pump, the number of plungers has no relationship to the number of engine cylinders, and there is only one plunger. This single plunger reciprocates while rotating, and fuel oil is injected into each cylinder through the injection pipes in accordance with the engine's firing order. As well as this, the governor, timer, feed pump etc. installed on the outside of the PE type injection pump are equipped within the VE type injection pump.

In comparison with the PE type, the VE type injection pump has less than half the number of component parts, and was developed in order to satisfy the need for a small, light-weight and high-speed injection pump.
In response to operator requirements, it was possible to design a pump with acceleration close to that of gasoline vehicles.
A VE type injection pump for direct injection system engines has recently been developed, and is expected to be adopted in a wide range of fields, including construction machinery, medium-sized trucks etc.

14. Fuel System (4JH2-UTE)

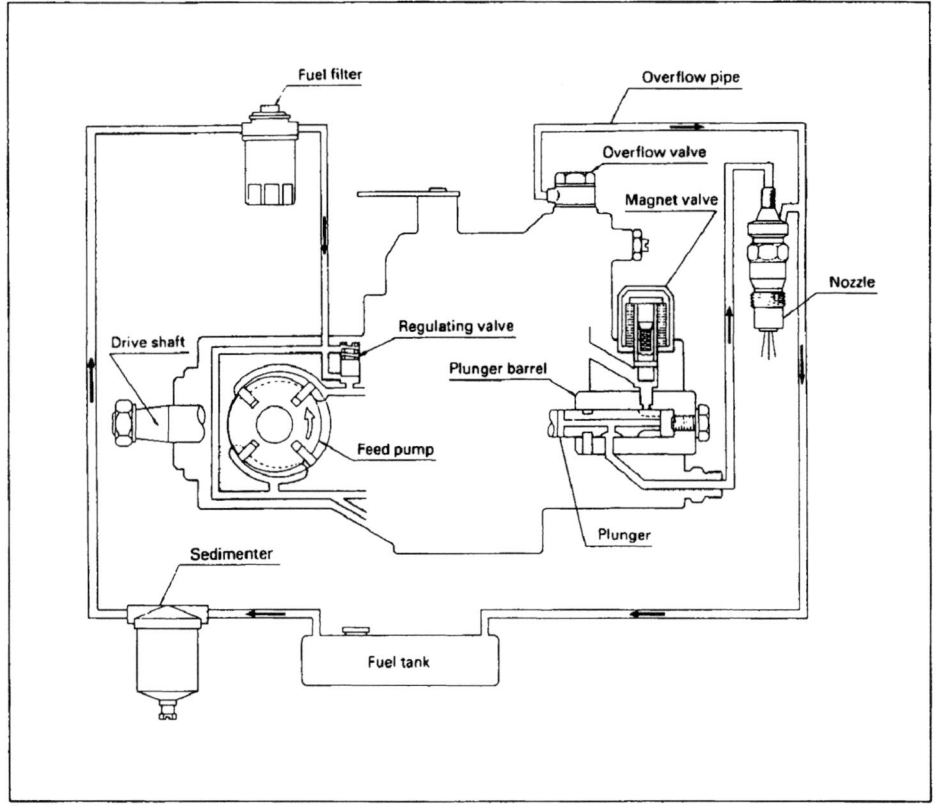

Fig. 2 Fuel system

Figure 2 shows an example of a fuel system. The injection pump drive shaft is turned by the engine's timing belt (or gear) and fuel oil is drawn by the injection pump's feed pump through the sedimenter and fuel filter to the injection pump's fuel oil inlet.

The fuel filter acts to filter the fuel oil, and the sedimenter is located in the lower portion of the fuel filter to remove moisture from the fuel system.

With drive shaft rotation the fuel oil sucked into the feed pump is pressurized by the feed pump and fills the injection pump chamber. The fuel oil pressure is proportional to drive shaft speed, and when it exceeds a specified pressure excess fuel again returns to the inlet side through a regulating valve located at the feed pump's fuel oil outlet.

The fuel oil in the injection pump chamber flows through the distributor head inlet into the pressure chamber, where plunger rotation and reciprocating motion increase its pressure. The fuel oil is then delivered through the injection pipe to the nozzle and nozzle holder.

An overflow valve located at the top of the injection pump functions to maintain a constant fuel oil temperature in the pump chamber by returning excess fuel oil to the fuel tank.

15. Injection Pump Construction and Operation (4JH2-UTE)

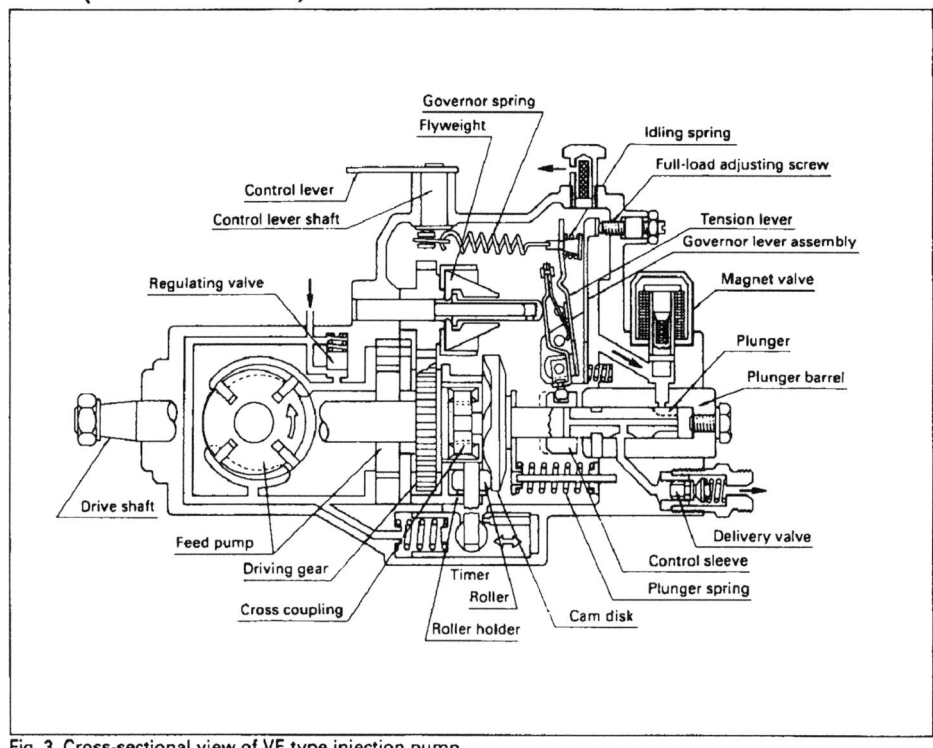

Fig. 3 Cross-sectional view of VE type injection pump

Fuel Delivery

The drive shaft, rotated by the engine's timing belt (or gear), rotates the cam disk through a cross coupling. The cam disk's press-fitted pin fits into a groove in the plunger to rotate the plunger. To reciprocate the plunger, the cam disk is also equipped with the same number of raised face cams, arranged uniformly around the circumference of the cam disk, as the number of cylinders. The cam disk's face cams are always in contact with the roller holder assembly's rollers because the cam disk and the plunger are pressed against the roller holder assembly by the set force of the two plunger springs. Because of this the plunger can follow cam disk movement. Therefore, as the cam disk is rotated on the roller holder assembly by the drive shaft, simultaneous plunger rotation and reciprocating movement is possible.

The roller holder assembly construction is such that it can only rotate in a certain angle range in accordance with timer operation.

Printed in Japan
A0A1029-9109SP

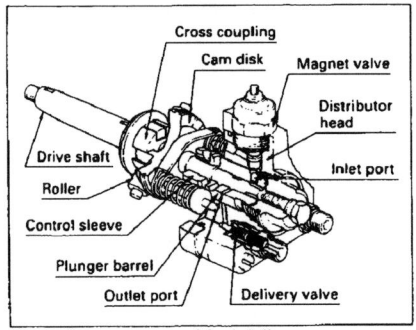

Cross coupling
Cam disk
Magnet valve
Distributor head
Drive shaft
Inlet port
Roller
Control sleeve
Plunger barrel
Outlet port
Delivery valve

Fig. 4 Cutaway view of fuel delivery

Because the plunger rotates and reciprocates simultaneously, suction of the fuel oil into the pressure chamber, pressurization in the pressure chamber and delivery into the engine cylinder are all possible.

Speed Governing

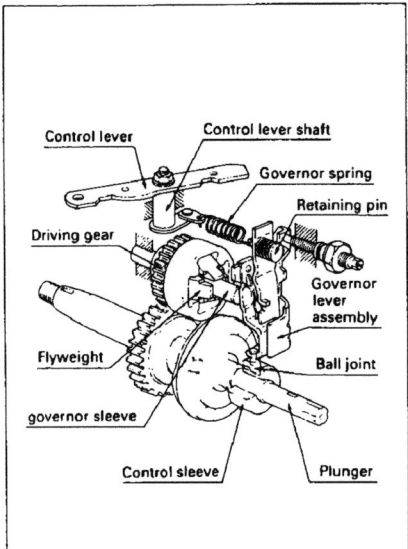

Control lever
Control lever shaft
Governor spring
Retaining pin
Driving gear
Governor lever assembly
Flyweight
Ball joint
governor sleeve
Control sleeve
Plunger

Fig. 5 Cutaway view of speed governing

The governor is located in the upper part of the injection pump chamber. Four flyweights and a governor sleeve are held in the flyweight holder, which is mounted on the governor shaft. The flyweight holder is rotated and accelerated by the drive shaft gear, through rubber dampers.

The governor lever assembly is supported by pivot bolts in the pump housing, and the ball joint at the bottom of the lever assembly is inserted into the control sleeve, which slides over the outside surface of the plunger. The top of the lever assembly (the tension lever) is connected to the governor spring by a retaining pin, while the opposite end of the governor spring is connected to the control lever shaft. The control lever shaft is inserted into the governor cover and a control lever is attached to the control lever shaft. The accelerator pedal is connected directly to the control lever by a linkage, and the governor spring set force changes in response to the control lever position (i.e. accelerator pedal position).

Injection quantity control is governed by the mutually opposing forces of the flyweights' centrifugal force and the governor spring's set force.

The flyweights' centrifugal force, which changes in response to engine speed, acts on the governor lever through the governor sleeve.

The governor spring's set force, which is dependant on control lever position, i.e. accelerator pedal position, acts on the governor lever through the retaining pin.

Injection Timing Control

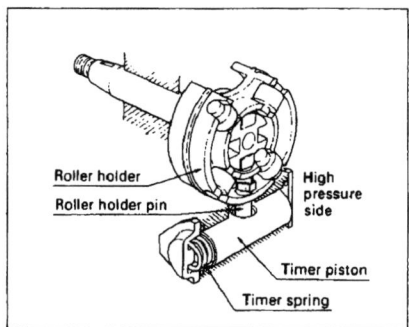

Roller holder
Roller holder pin
High pressure side
Timer piston
Timer spring

Fig. 6 Cutaway view of injection timing control

The piston is positioned in the center of the timer in the lower part of the injection pump. On the low pressure side of the timer piston there is a timer spring with a predetermined set force; the pump chamber fuel oil pressure acts on the opposite side (high pressure side). The timer piston position changes in accordance with the balance of these two forces. to rotate the roller holder via the roller holder pin. When the timer piston compresses the timer spring, the injection timing is advanced (the roller holder rotates in the reverse rotation direction), and due to timer piston movement in the opposite direction the injection timing is retarded. Injection timing is controlled by the above.

Feed Pump

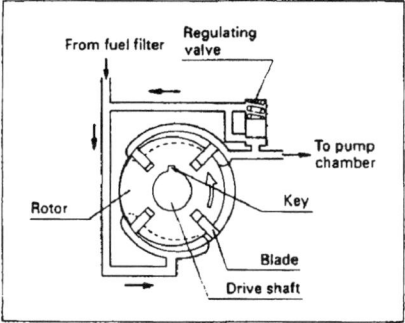

From fuel filter
Regulating valve
To pump chamber
Rotor
Key
Blade
Drive shaft

Fig. 7 Feed pump operation

The feed pump comprises a rotor, blades and liner.
Drive shaft rotation is transmitted through a key to rotate the rotor
The inside circumference of the liner is eccentric to the centre of rotor rotation. Four blades are installed in the rotor Centrifugal force forces the blades outwards during rotation to contact the inside surface of the liner and form four fuel oil chambers. The volume of these four chambers increases through rotor rotation to suck fuel oil from the fuel tank. Conversely, when the volume of these four chambers decreases fuel oil is pressurized.

Regulating Valve

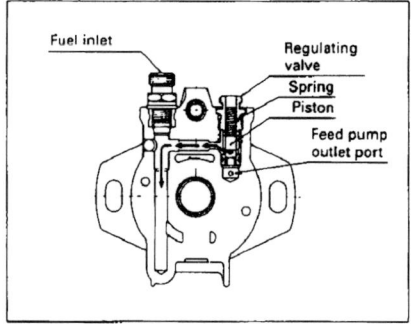

Fuel inlet

Regulating valve

Spring

Piston

Feed pump outlet port

Fig. 8 Regulating valve operation

Feed pump fuel oil delivery pressure increases proportionately with an increase in injection pump speed.
However, the total fuel oil injection quantity necessary for the engine is considerably less than that delivered by the feed pump. Therefore, in order to prevent an excessive increase in the pump chamber pressure caused by the excess fuel oil, and to adjust the pump chamber pressure so that it is usually within the specified limit, a regulating valve is installed near the feed pump outlet. The timer performs timing control using the pump chamber pressure, which is regulated by the regulating valve.

Plunger Operation

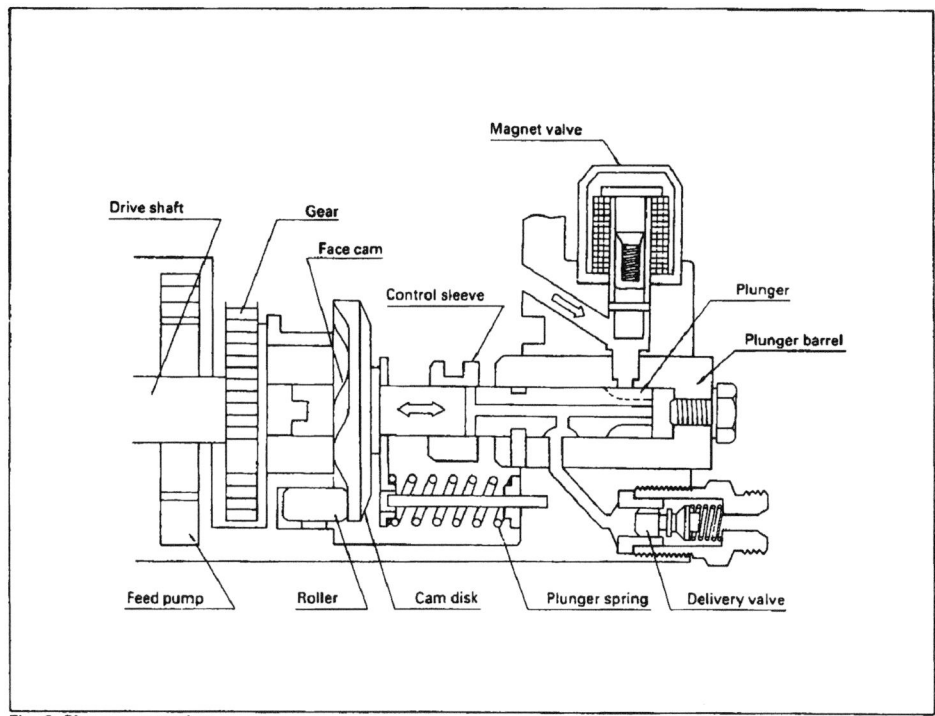

Fig. 9 Plunger operation

The drive shaft drives the feed pump, the cam disk and the plunger simultaneously. Plunger reciprocating movement is accomplished through the movement of the cam disk's face cams over the roller holder assembly's rollers. When the plunger's inlet slit and the inlet port of the plunger barrel, press-fitted to the distributor head are aligned, fuel oil is sucked into the pressure chamber. After the plunger barrel's inlet port has been closed by the plunger, the plunger rises.

Once the plunger's outlet slit and the plunger barrel's outlet port are aligned, and the pressure chamber pressure exceeds the injection pipe's in-line residual pressure and the delivery valve spring's set force, the delivery valve opens, fuel oil flows to the injection pipe, and is then injected from the nozzle into the engine cylinder.

Then, when the plunger's cut-off port aligns with the control sleeve's end face, plunger fuel delivery is completed.

The plunger barrel has only one inlet port, but it has an outlet port for each engine cylinder

However, although the plunger has the same number of inlet slits as engine cylinders, it has only one outlet slit and one equalizing slit.

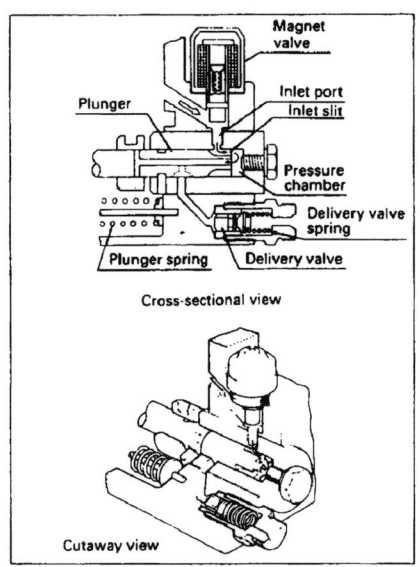

Cross-sectional view

Cutaway view

Fig. 10 Plunger operation: suction stroke

Suction stroke

During the plunger's return stroke, when the plunger barrel's inlet port and the plunger's inlet slit are aligned, pressurized fuel oil in the pump chamber is sucked into the pressure chamber. (Fig. 10)

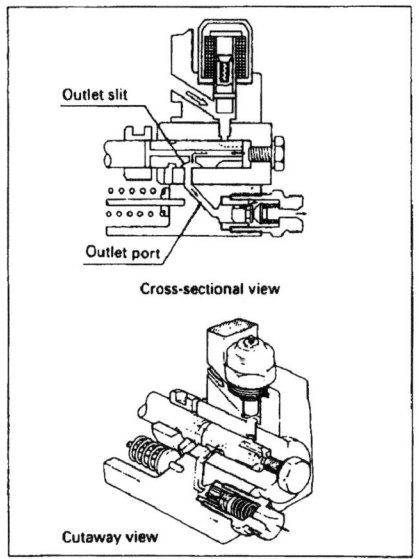

Cross-sectional view

Cutaway view

Fig. 11 Plunger operation: delivery stroke

Delivery stroke

As the plunger is rotated and lifted by the cam disk, the plunger's outside face blocks the plunger barrel's inlet port and compression of fuel oil begins. At almost the same time the plunger's outlet slit meets the plunger barrel's outlet port. As a result of this, the fuel oil pressurized by the plunger lift overcomes the set force of the delivery valve spring and the injection pipe's in-line residual pressure, and opens the delivery valve. The fuel oil is then injected through the nozzle and nozzle holder into the engine's combustion chamber. (Fig. 11)

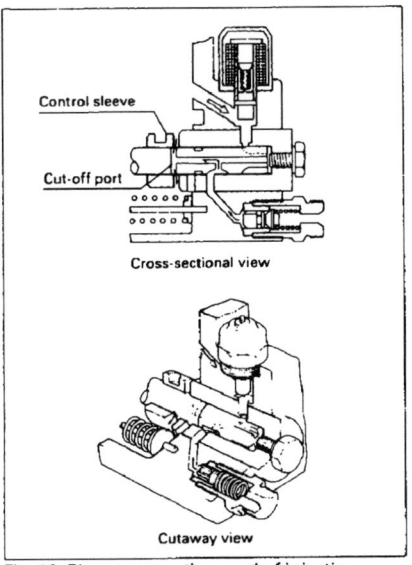

Control sleeve

Cut-off port

Cross-sectional view

Cutaway view

Fig. 12 Plunger operation; end of injection

End of injection

When the end face of the control sleeve meets the plunger's cut-off port, the fuel oil in the plunger (i.e. the pressure chamber), which is at a much higher pressure than that in the pump chamber, returns to the pump chamber through this cut-off port. The pressure then suddenly decreases, the delivery valve is closed by the spring, and fuel oil delivery finishes. These operations occur instantaneously. (Fig. 12)

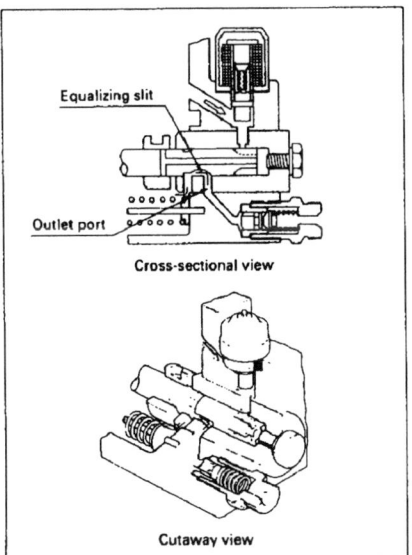

Equalizing slit

Outlet port

Cross-sectional view

Cutaway view

Fig. 13 Plunger operation; equalizing stroke

Equalizing stroke

Following the end-of-injection the plunger rotates 180° and the plunger barrel's outlet port meets the plunger's equalizing slit.
Then, the pressure of the fuel oil in the injection passage between the plunger barrel's outlet port and the delivery valve decreases to that of the fuel oil in the pump chamber.
This stroke equalizes each cylinder's outlet port pressure at injection for every revolution, therefore assuring stabilized injection. (Fig. 13)

The above operations are performed in the order of injection for each (pump) revolution.

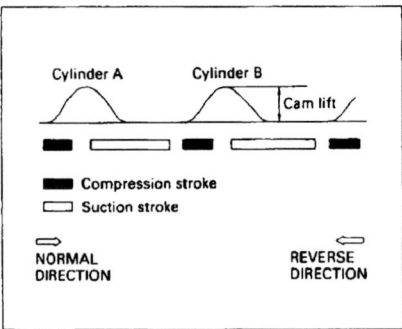

Fig. 14 Plunger strokes for cylinders A and B

Reverse rotation prevention

While the plunger is moving in the normal direction of rotation, the inlet port is open during the plunger's return stroke and sufficient fuel oil is sucked into the pressure chamber. During the compression stroke the inlet port is closed and injection is performed.

However, should the engine rotate in the reverse direction (e.g. when a stationary, parked vehicle begins to roll backwards and the engine is rotated, etc.) the plunger barrel's inlet port and the plunger's inlet slit will align during plunger lift, the fuel oil cannot be pressurized and non-injection will result.

Because of this the engine will immediately stop.

Injection quantity control

Fuel injection quantity is increased or decreased by the effective stroke, which is varied by the position of the control sleeve.

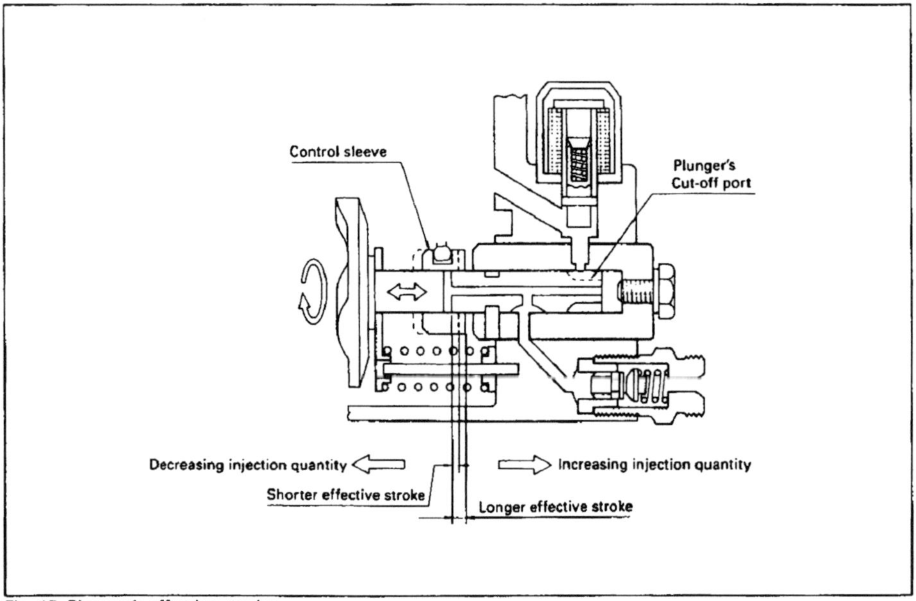

Fig. 15 Plunger's effective stroke

This effective stroke is the plunger stroke from the plunger's cut-off port to the control sleeve's end-face during the delivery stroke, after the plunger barrel's inlet port and the plunger's inlet slit are closed.
It is proportional to the fuel injection quantity. As can be seen in Fig. 15, control sleeve travel to the left decreases the effective stroke, and conversely control sleeve travel to the right increases the effective stroke and the fuel injection quantity.
Although the beginning-of-injection position is constant, end-of-injection varies according to the control sleeve position. The control sleeve position is determined by the governor.

Delivery Valve and Damping Valve

When the increased fuel oil pressure resulting from the plunger's compression stroke has overcome the delivery valve spring's set force and the injection pipe's in-line residual pressure, the delivery valve opens and fuel oil is delivered to the nozzle holder and the nozzle. (Fig. 16-A)
Then, when nozzle opening pressure is reached, initial injection into the engine cylinder occurs.

When the plunger has lifted and injection has ended, the pressure in the pressure chamber suddenly decreases and the delivery valve spring closes the delivery valve. In order to prevent delayed injection it is necessary to maintain the residual pressure of the fuel oil in the injection pipe for the next injection. The delivery valve functions to prevent reverse fuel oil flow during the plunger's suction stroke.

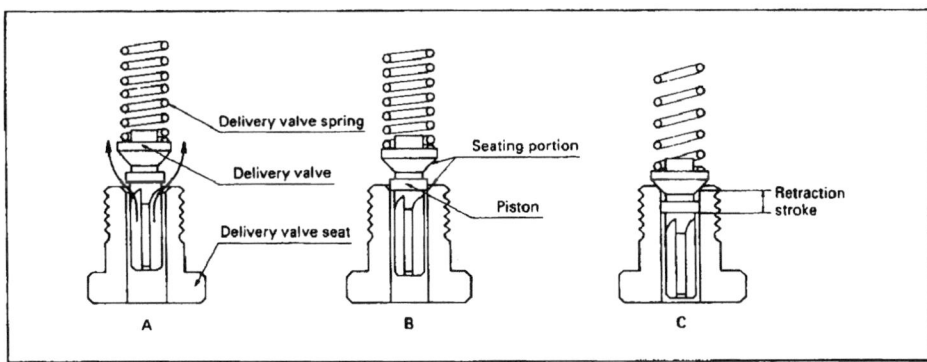

Fig. 16 Delivery valve operation

In the centre of the delivery valve is a piston. After injection has ended and the piston edge is contacting the top of the valve seat (Fig. 16-B), the amount by which the injection pipe's in-line pressure is reduced is proportional to the volume of fuel retracted up to the time that the delivery valve is completely closed.

$$\left[\frac{\pi(\text{piston diameter})^2}{4} \times \text{retraction stroke} \right]$$

Because of this, cut-off of injection occurs immediately after the end-of-injection and subsequent dripping is prevented. (Fig. 16-C)

Printed in Japan
A0A1029-9109SP

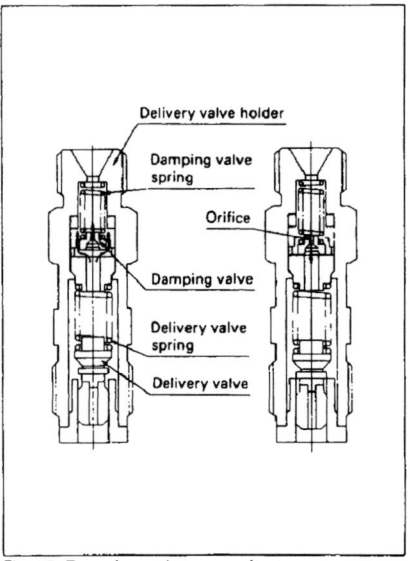

Fig. 17 Damping valve operation

The damping valve is a component of the delivery valve and its construction is shown in Fig. 17

The damping valve compresses the damping valve spring and opens almost simultaneously with the opening of the delivery valve. Fuel oil delivered by the plunger through the injection pipe is then delivered to the nozzle holder and the nozzle. After the end-of-injection the damping valve is closed more quickly (seated) than the delivery valve by the set force of the damping valve spring.

Following this, because only the retracted fuel oil is returned through the small orifice in the centre of the damping valve up until the time that the delivery valve is seated, a sudden reduction in the injection pipe's in-line pressure can be prevented.

A sudden reduction in pressure may sometimes result in negative pressure, thereby causing cavitation. This may result in corrosion of the injection pipes and finally the danger of pipe breakage.

The damping valve is installed to prevent the above problems.

16. Governing Mechanism(4JH2-UTE)

Depending on the purpose of use, mechanical governors (those utilizing a flyweight) are divided into three types:

1. The variable speed governor
2. The combination governor
3. The minimum-maximum speed governor

Variable Speed Governor Construction and-Operation

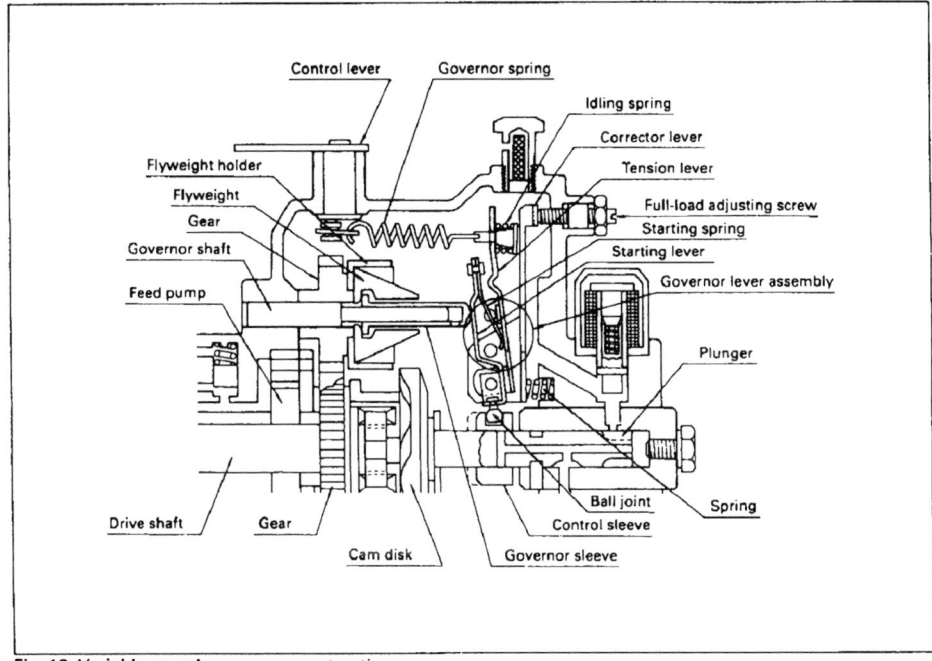

Fig. 18 Variable speed governor construction

The construction of the variable speed governor is shown in Fig. 18.
The rotation of the drive shaft (equipped with two rubber dampers) is conveyed through an acceleration gear to the flyweight holder mounted on the governor shaft.

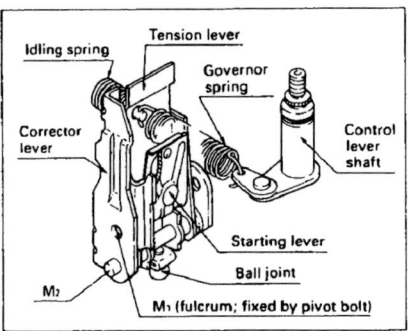

Fig. 19 Variable speed governor lever assembly

Four flyweights are mounted in the flyweight holder, and with rotation these open outward through centrifugal force. This movement moves the governor sleeve in an axial direction, resulting in the governor sleeve pushing the governor lever assembly.
The governor lever assembly consists of the corrector lever, tension lever, start lever, start spring and the ball joint. (Fig. 19)

The corrector lever's fulcrum M_1 is fixed at the pivot bolts in the pump housing and as its bottom portion is being pushed by the springs in the distributor head, and the top portion is being pushed by the full-load adjusting screw, the corrector lever cannot move at all.
The starting lever, separated from the tension lever by the starting spring only at engine starting, moves the governor sleeve to close the flyweights. As a result of this the ball joint at the bottom of the starting lever, pivoting around the tension and starting levers' common fulcrum M_2, can move the control sleeve in the fuel-increase direction (i.e. toward the distributor head side) for engine starting.

During engine operation the starting lever and the tension lever are in contact and move together as a single component. The top of the tension lever is connected to the control lever through the governor spring.
An idling spring is mounted on the retaining pin at the top of the tension lever.
Governor construction is such that governor control over the entire speed range is performed by the operation of all these springs.

Engine starting

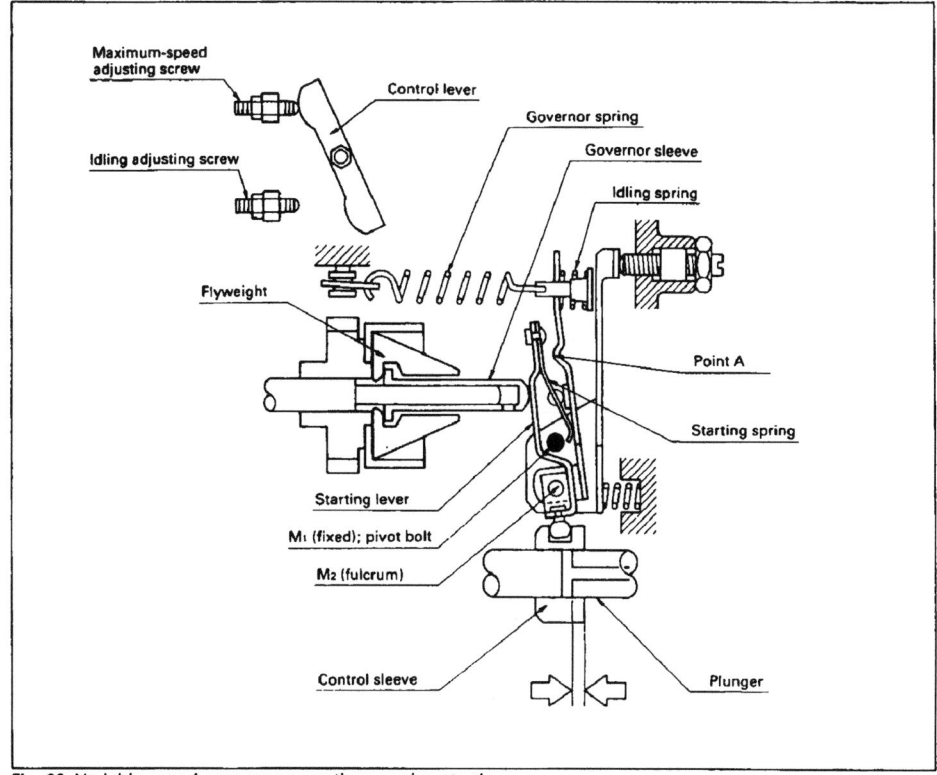

Fig. 20 Variable speed governor operation: engine starting

To improve starting characteristics at engine starting, the normal full-load injection quantity is exceeded and excess fuel for starting is supplied.

When the accelerator pedal is depressed while the engine is stationary, the starting lever is separated from the tension lever by the starting spring and moves to push the governor sleeve.

Because of this the control sleeve is moved to the right (the maximum injection quantity direction; Fig. 20) by the starting lever pivoting around M2.

Therefore, through lightly depressing the accelerator the engine can be easily started.

After engine starting centrifugal force is generated by the flyweights, the governor sleeve acts to compress the weak starting spring and the starting lever is pressed against the tension lever.

Through this movement the control sleeve is moved in the fuel-decrease direction, injection is returned to the full-load injection quantity range and the supply of excess fuel for starting is completed. Following this, the tension lever and the starting lever, in contact at point A (Fig. 20), move together as a single component.

Printed in Japan
A0A1029-9109SP

Idling operation

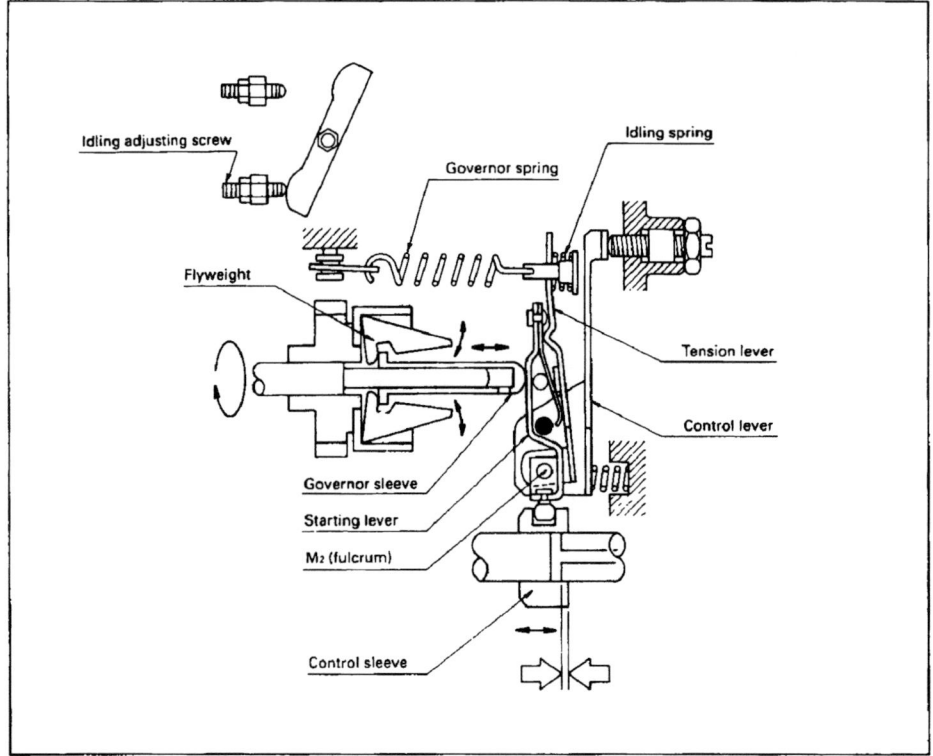

Fig. 21 Variable speed governor operation: idling operation

Once the engine has started the accelerator pedal is returned to its original position. The control lever is also returned to its original position and the governor spring tension becomes "0". The flyweights then open, the starting lever is pressed against the tension lever and compression of the idling spring begins.

The control sleeve then travels in the fuel-decrease direction and stops in the position where the flyweights centrifugal force and the idling spring force are balanced. In this position stable idling operation can be obtained.

Full-load and no-load maximum speed control

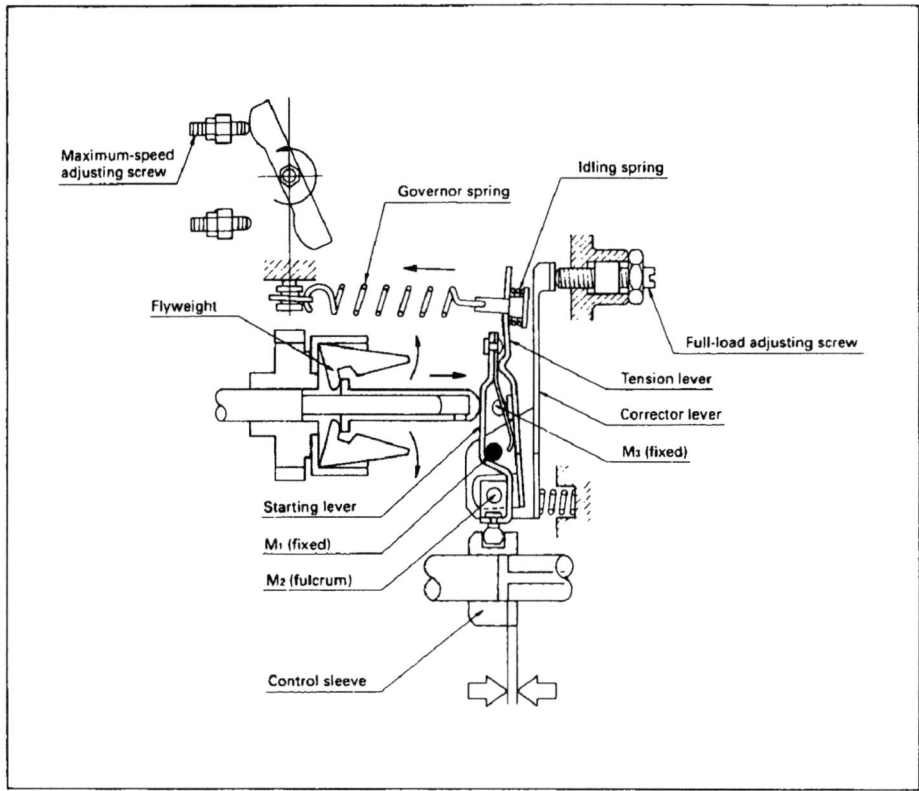

Fig. 22 Variable speed governor operation: full-load operation maximum speed control

When the accelerator pedal is fully depressed and the control lever has contacted the maximum speed adjusting screw, the tension lever contacts the pin (M3) press fitted to the pump housing (i.e. where the full-load injection quantity is obtained) and can move no further. At this time the governor spring set force is at a maximum. Because of this, the idling spring is fully compressed and the flyweights, being pushed by the governor sleeve, are closed. Then, although the centrifugal force of the flyweights increases with the increase in engine speed, the flyweights cannot move the governor sleeve until the governor spring's set force has been overcome.

Printed in Japan
A0A1029-9109SP

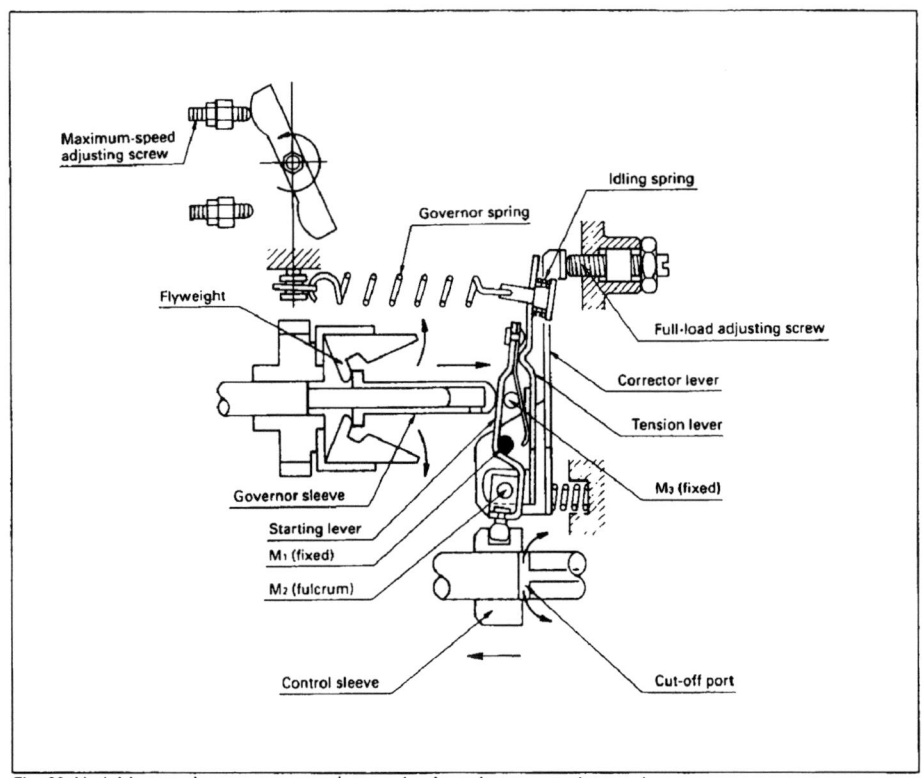

Fig. 23 Variable speed governor operation: no-load maximum speed control

Furthermore, with an increase in engine speed after both are balanced, the flyweights' centrifugal force will overcome the governor spring's set force, and will extend the spring while moving the governor lever assembly.

Therefore, the fuel injection quantity will be decreased and high speed control will be performed so that the specified maximum speed is not exceeded.

When the accelerator pedal is not fully depressed, the governor spring set force may be varied freely so that governor control may be performed in response to partial load conditions.

The full-load injection quantity is determined according to the amount that the full-load adjusting screw is screwed in. When the full-load adjusting screw is screwed in, the corrector lever pivots to the left (Fig. 22; counterclockwise direction) around point M_1 and the control sleeve moves in the fuel-increase direction. Unscrewing the full-load adjusting screw moves the control sleeve in the fuel-decrease direction.

Combination Governor Construction and Operation

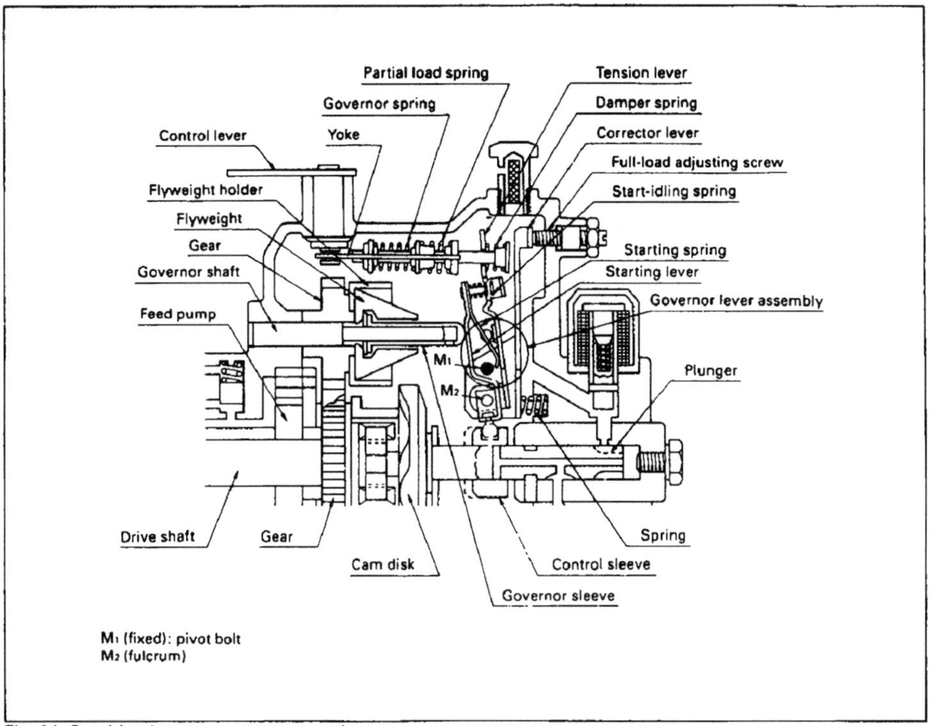

Partial load spring
Governor spring
Control lever
Yoke
Flyweight holder
Flyweight
Gear
Governor shaft
Feed pump

Tension lever
Damper spring
Corrector lever
Full-load adjusting screw
Start-idling spring
Starting spring
Starting lever
Governor lever assembly
Plunger

M_1
M_2

Drive shaft
Gear
Cam disk
Spring
Control sleeve
Governor sleeve

M_1 (fixed): pivot bolt
M_2 (fulcrum)

Fig. 24 Combination governor construction

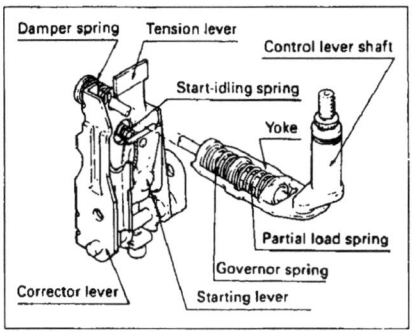

Damper spring   Tension lever
Control lever shaft
Start-idling spring
Yoke
Partial load spring
Governor spring
Corrector lever
Starting lever

Fig. 25 Combination governor lever assembly

When comparing the construction of the combination governor with that of the variable speed governor, the governor spring and the governor lever assembly of the combination governor differ from those of the variable speed governor.

As shown in Fig. 24 a yoke is attached to the control lever shaft assembly, and the governor spring and the partial load spring, with a preset force, are installed inside the yoke. A damper spring is installed at the end of the yoke.

Idling control is performed by the start-idling spring, which is installed between the top of the tension lever and the starting lever in the governor lever assembly.

3-62

Engine starting

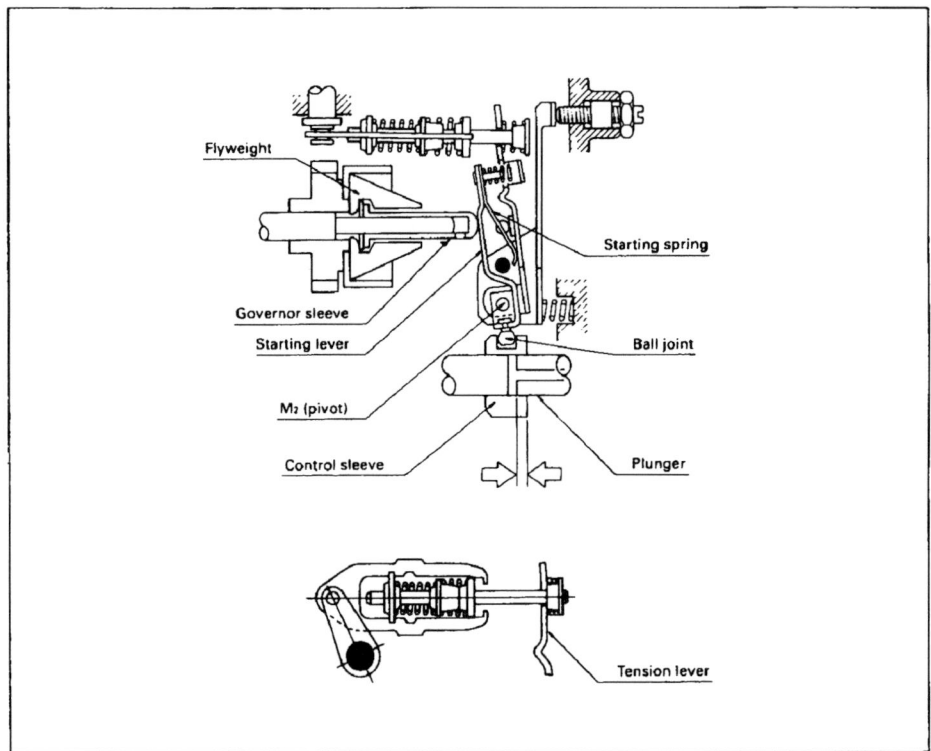

Fig. 26 Combination governor operation: engine starting

Depressing the accelerator pedal lightly at engine starting results in the control lever shaft assembly pulling the tension lever to the left (Fig. 26), and through the action of the starting spring (leaf spring) the starting lever pushes the governor sleeve. Through this movement the ball joint, with point M_2 as the fulcrum, moves the control sleeve to the position where excessive fuel for starting can be obtained, and the engine can be easily started.

Once the engine has been started, the centrifugal force generated by the flyweights pushes the governor sleeve against the weak force of the starting spring. The control sleeve is then moved in the fuel-decrease direction and the supply of excessive fuel for starting is completed.

Idling operation

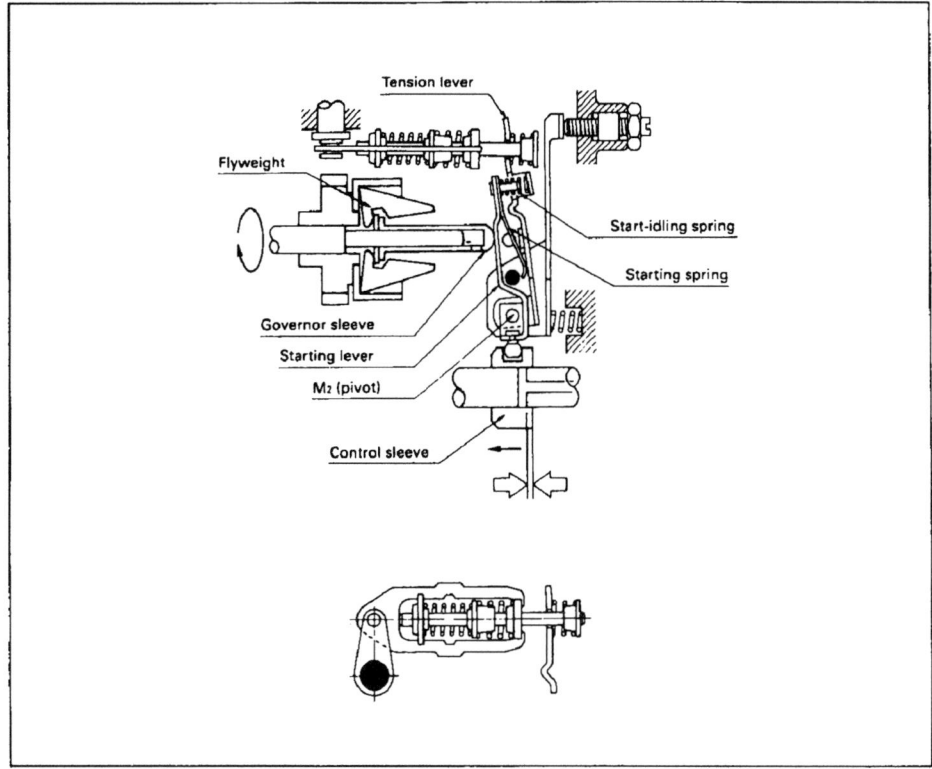

Fig. 27 Combination governor operation: idling operation

On releasing the accelerator pedal the control lever is returned to the idling position and the tension lever is freed.

Through the flyweights' centrifugal force the governor sleeve pushes the starting lever. After the start-idling spring has contacted the tension lever, the combined forces of the start-idling spring and the starting spring balance the flyweights' centrifugal force and the starting lever becomes stationary.

This starting lever movement moves the control sleeve directly in the fuel-decrease direction and stabilized idling operation can begin.

Printed in Japan
A0A1029-9109SP

Partial load operation

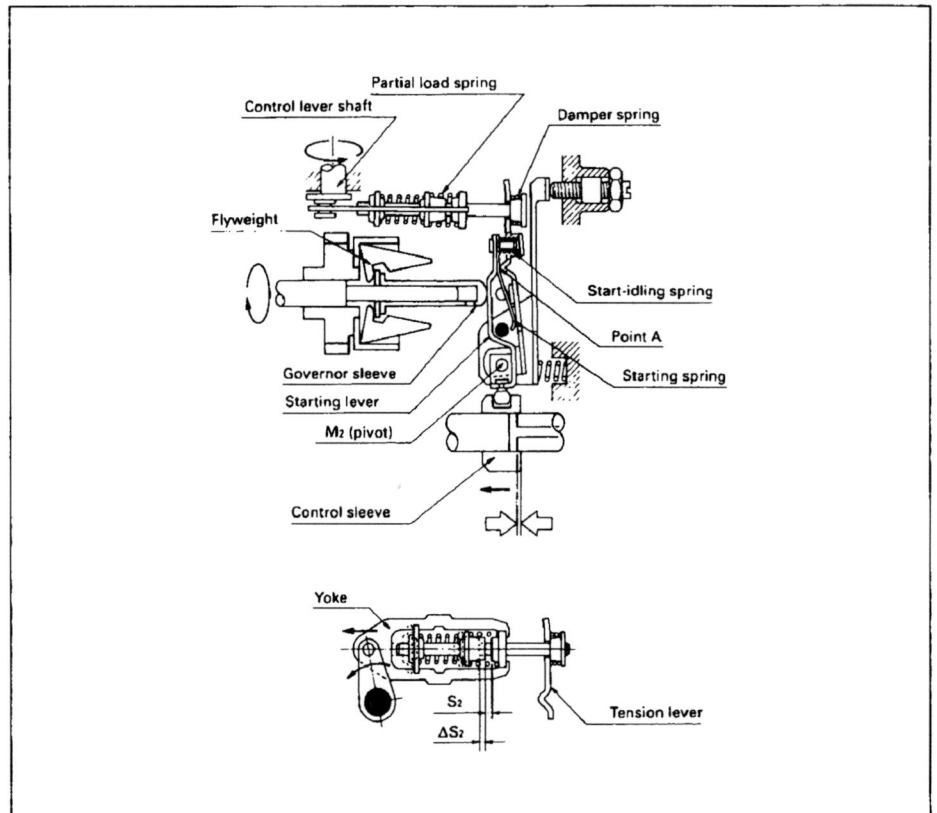

Fig. 28 Combination governor operation: partial load operation

In the speed range exceeding idling the starting spring and the start-idling spring are already compressed, and the starting lever and the tension lever, which are in contact at the convex point A, both move together as one. (Fig. 28)

Therefore, during partial load operation the damper spring and the partial load spring are acted upon by (and oppose) the flyweights' centrifugal force.

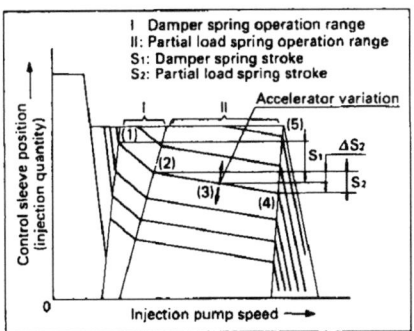

Fig. 29 Combination governor characteristics

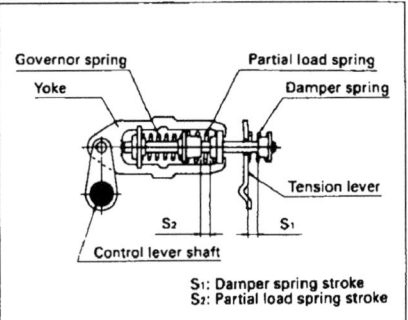

Fig. 30 Control lever shaft assembly

In low speed range I the control sleeve's position is controlled by the balance of the flyweights' centrifugal force and the damper spring force.
(e.g. control sleeve movement from (1) to (2) i Fig. 29)

In the intermediate-high speed range II (where the flyweights' centrifugal force exceeds the damper spring force, but is less than the governor spring's set force) the damper spring is fully compressed, and the partial load spring in the yoke is compressed an amount equal to ΔS_2 (Fig. 29). ΔS_2 varies according to the balance of the flyweights' centrifugal force with each spring's set force (i.e. engine speed and engine load).

If an uphill slope is negotiated after travelling on a level road with the control lever position fixed and the control sleeve positioned at point (3), because the engine speed decreases, the control sleeve position will shift in the direction of point (2) through the action of the partial load spring and the fuel injection quantity will be increased.

Conversely, if a downhill slope is negotiated, the fuel injection quantity will be decreased as engine speed increases.

Furthermore, if the amount that the accelerator pedal is depressed is altered, the control sleeve position will move in the direction of the arrow in Fig. 29.

Full-load and no-load maximum speed control

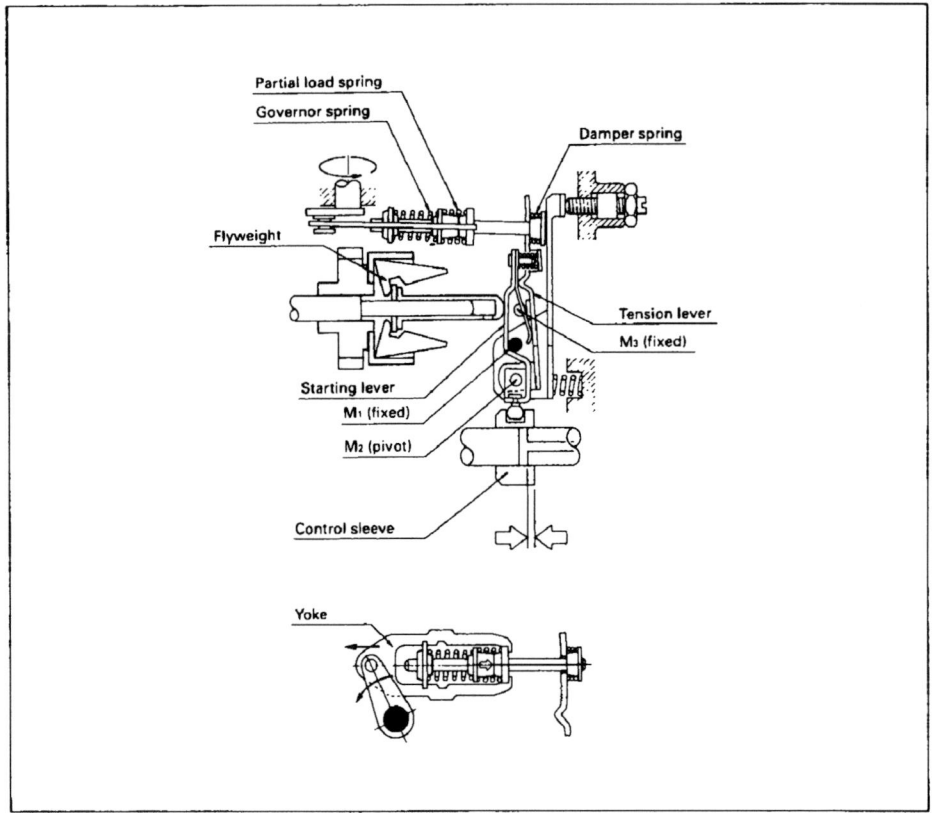

Fig. 31 Combination governor operation: full-load maximum speed operation

On moving the control lever until it contacts the maximum speed stopper bolt, the tension lever contacts the pin (or the stop lever of the BCS or ACS) M3 press-fitted to the pump housing and can move no further. Consequently, the damper spring and the partial load spring are fully compressed and the control sleeve travels to the position where the full-load injection quantity can be obtained.

Following this engine speed increases and, at the point where the flyweights' centrifugal force balances the combined forces of the yoke springs (point (5) in Fig. 29), the full-load maximum speed of maximum engine output is reached.

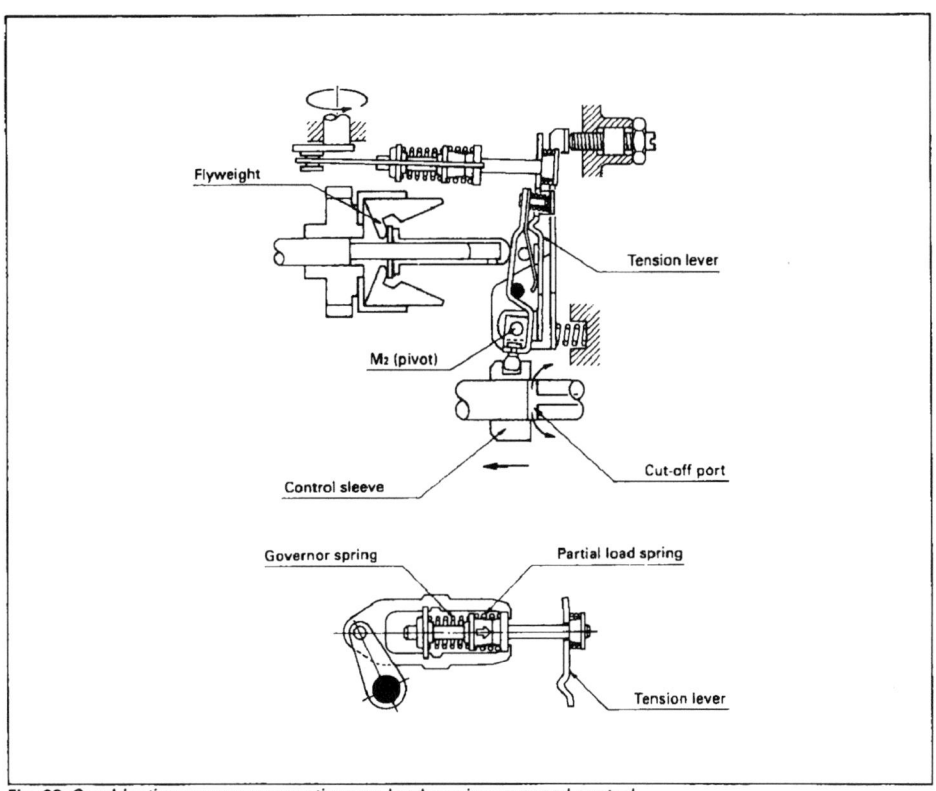

Fig. 32 Combination governor operation: no-load maximum speed control

To prevent the engine from exceeding the specified maximum speed when pump speed increases further, due to variations in load etc, the flyweights begin to compress the governor spring and the tension lever is pivotted clockwise around point M_2 to move the control sleeve in the non-injection direction.

The governor therefore controls the engine speed so that it does not exceed the engine's specified maximum speed.

Variable Speed Governor and Combination Governor

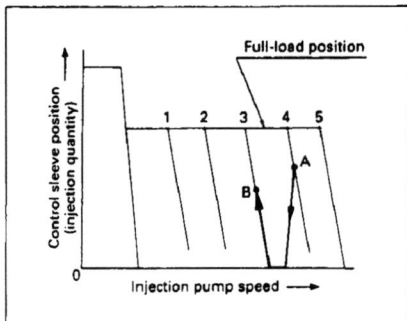

Fig. 33 Variable speed governor characteristics

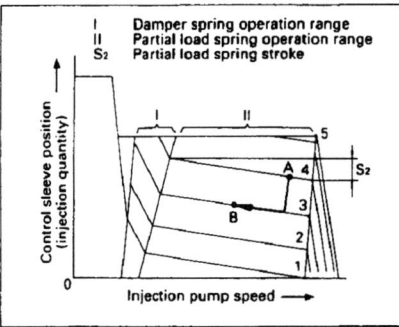

Fig. 34 Combination governor characteristics

The governor spring's set force in a variable speed governor changes in accordance with changes in the accelerator pedal position. (Fig. 33: points 1–5).

For example, when the flyweights' centrifugal force and the governor spring's set force are balanced (Fig. 33; point A) and the accelerator pedal is released a little to decrease speed, the control sleeve will move to the non-injection position as shown by the solid line in Fig. 33.

Then, in response to the change in the governor spring's set force (gradient 3), the control sleeve will move in the fuel-increase direction and will stop in the positon where the injection quantity necessary for the load at this time can be obtained (i.e. point B ; the flyweights' centifugal force and the governor spring's set force are balanced). The variable speed governor governs in the engine's all-speed range in response to accelerator pedal position or variations in engine load.

With the combination governor the set force of the partial load spring and the control sleeve position (Fig. 34 lines 1–5) are varied in response to accelerator pedal position to regulate the fuel injection quantity.

If the accelerator pedal is released slightly to decrease speed during partial load operation (Fig. 34 point A), when the flyweights' centrifugal force and the partial load spring's set force are balanced, the control sleeve will move from point A to point B, as shown by the solid line in Fig. 34.

As can be seen from the solid line in Fig. 34 showing control sleeve movement when speed decreases, the combination governor's control sleeve travel is less, and the variation in fuel injection quantity is also decreased.

This results in a reduction in the shock caused by sudden variations in fuel injection quantity and an improvement in accelerator "feeling" when speed is reduced.

Governor Equipped with Negative Torque Control Device

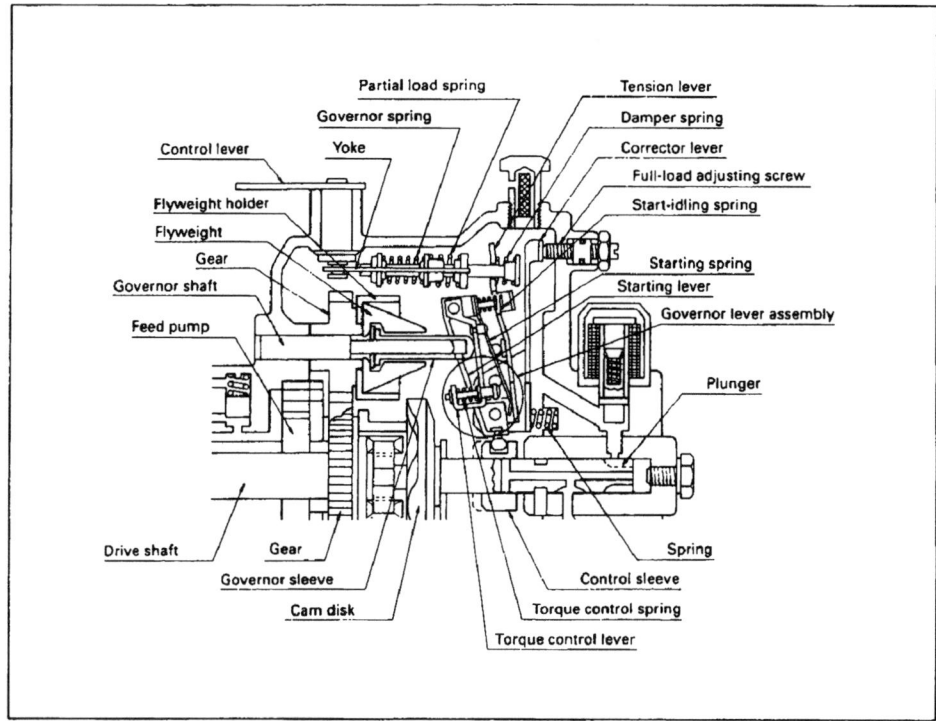

Fig. 35 Construction of governor equipped with negative torque control device

A negative torque control device is provided through the installation of a torque control lever to the governor lever assembly's starting lever.

The torque control lever is fitted with a torque control spring, the set force of which varies according to the torque control stroke.

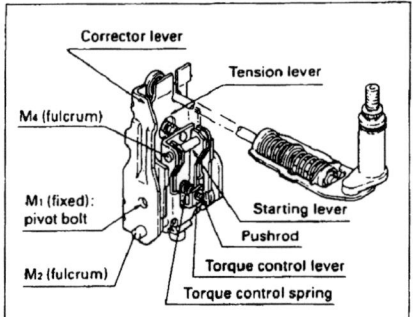

Fig. 36 Governor lever assembly equipped with
negative torque control device

The negative torque control device moves the
control sleeve through the torque control
stroke (S₃ in Fig. 37) in the governor's
intermediate-speed control range to increase
the injection quantity in proportion to engine
speed and therefore prevent insufficient engine output resulting from insufficient fuel injection at high speeds. (Refer to Fig. 37.)
Figure 37 shows the control characteristics of a
combination governor equipped with the negative torque control device.

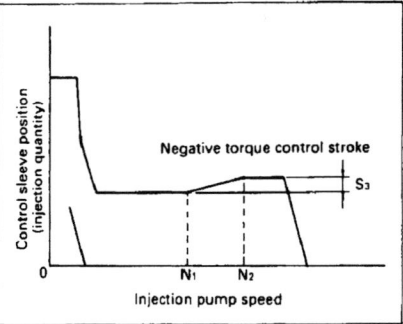

Fig. 37 Negative torque control characteristic

Engine starting

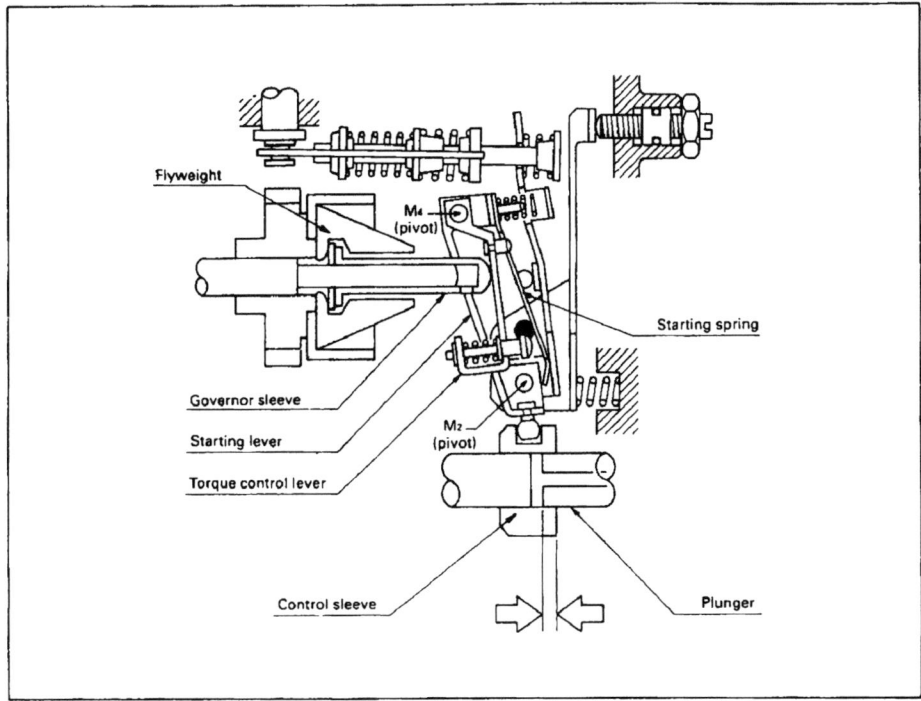

Fig. 38 Operation of governor equipped with negative torque control device: engine starting

As in the variable speed governor or the combination governor, the governor equipped with the torque control device controls starting through the action of the starting spring (a leaf spring) mounted on the starting lever.
At starting the action of the starting spring pivots both the starting lever and the torque control lever (connected at M4) in a counterclockwise direction around point M2, thus moving the control sleeve in the fuel-increase direction to supply a fuel injection quantity sufficient for starting.

Idling operation

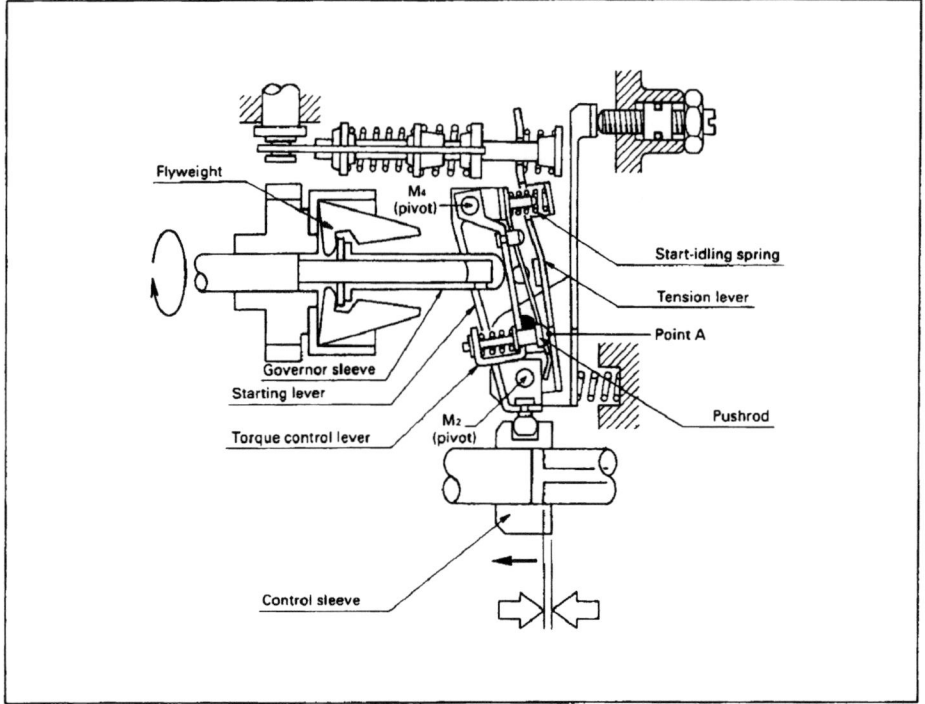

Fig. 39 Operation of governor equipped with negative torque control device: idling operation

On starting, the centrifugal force of the flyweights causes the governor sleeve to move to the right (Fig. 39). The governor sleeve then contacts and moves the torque control lever. The torque control lever pushrod then contacts the tension lever at point A, and the torque control lever then pivots around point A to compress the start-idling spring until its set force is overcome by the flyweights' centrifugal force. Consequently the starting lever will pivot clockwise around M_2, thus moving the control sleeve in the fuel decrease direction until an injection quantity suitable for idling is attained.

Partial load operation

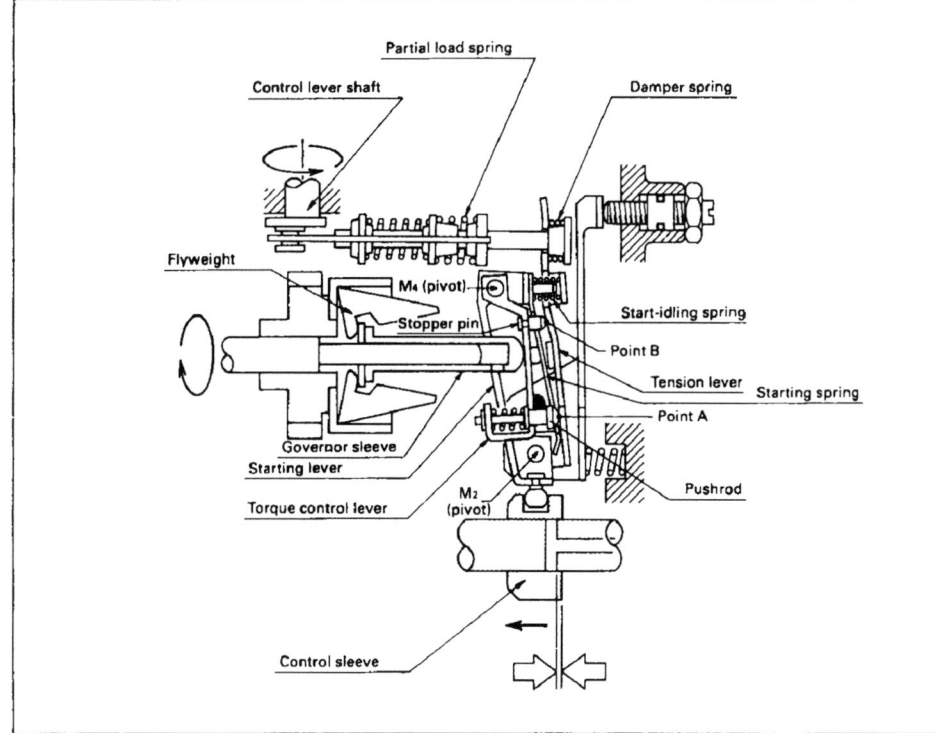

Fig. 40 Operation of governor equipped with negative torque control device: partial load operation

In the speed range exceeding idling operation, and the range where the control lever is positioned between the idling position and the maximum speed position, the starting spring and start-idling spring are already fully compressed, and the torque control lever and the tension lever (which are in contact at points A and B through the torque control lever pushrod and stopper pin), and the starting lever, move together as one (Fig. 40).

Therefore, during partial load operation the damper spring and the partial load spring are acted upon by (and oppose) the flyweights' centrifugal force.

If the speed increases during partial load operation in accordance with a change in the control lever position (i.e. the control sleeve position) after the accelerator pedal is depressed, the consequent increase in the flyweights' centrifugal force moves the governor sleeve to the right, thereby pushing the torque control lever to the right. Then, as the torque control lever, the starting lever and the tension lever behave as one component, movement of the governor sleeve by the flyweights' centrifugal force compresses the damper spring and the partial load spring, and pivots the starting lever around M2. Thus, the control sleeve is moved to the left to decrease the fuel injection quantity. As a result of this, the speed is decreased to maintain a suitable engine speed, and an injection quantity corresponding to the engine load etc. is obtained at the point where the flyweights' centrifugal force is balanced with the combined forces of the damper and partial load springs.

Printed in Japan
A0A1029-9109SP

Full-load maximum speed operation

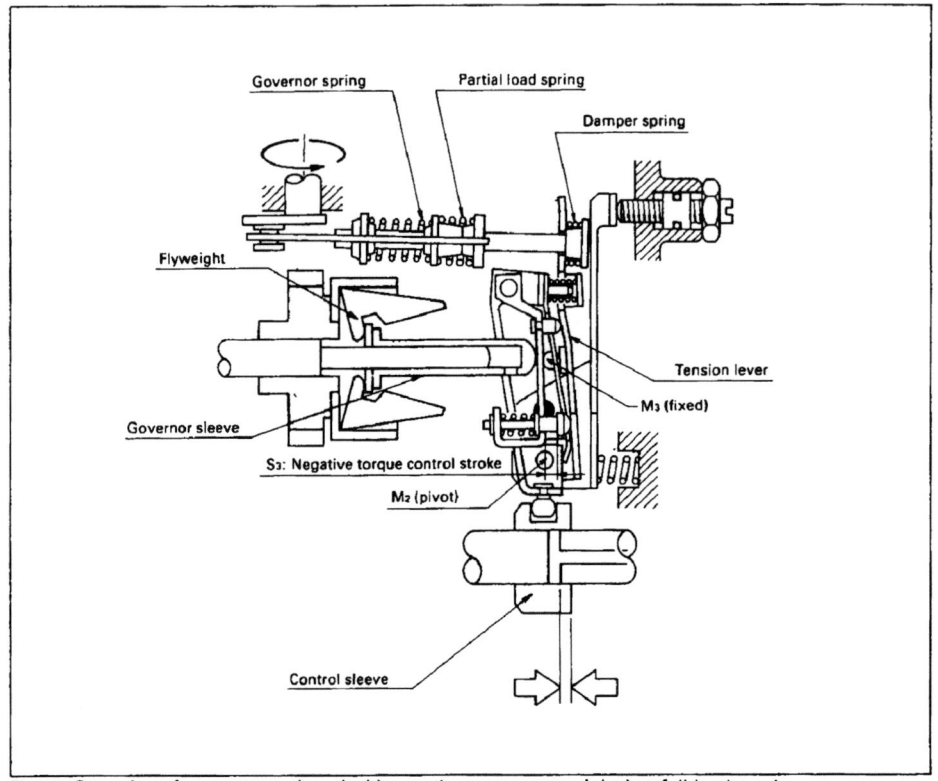

Fig. 41 Operation of governor equipped with negative torque control device: full-load maximum speed operation

When the control lever is moved until it contacts the maximum speed stopper, engine speed is increased until the full-load maximum speed is reached. At this time the yoke is pulled to the extreme left (refer to Fig. 41), the partial load spring is fully compressed, the governor spring is compressed and the tension lever is pulled to the left until it contacts the stopper pin M_3 (i.e. where the full-load injection quantity is obtained).

With an increase in speed the flyweights' centrifugal force increases and the governor sleeves acts to move the tension lever against the force of the governor spring to move the control sleeve and maintain full-load maximum speed operation.

Negative torque control stroke operation

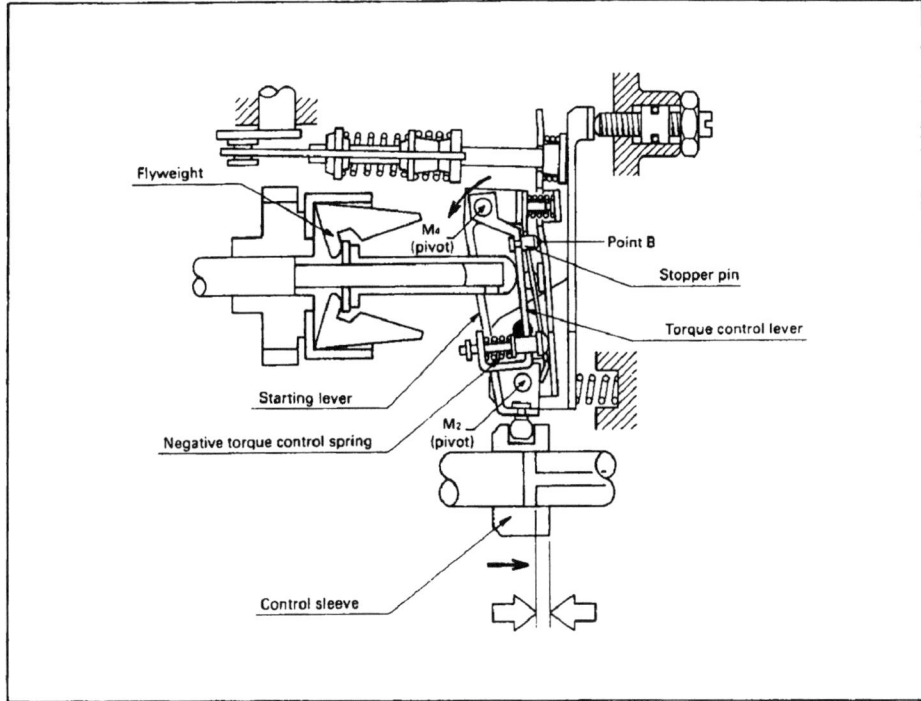

Fig. 42 Operation of governor equipped with negative torque control device: negative torque control stroke operation

When the engine speed exceeds N_1 r.p.m (refer to Fig. 37) the centrifugal force of the flyweights will continue to increase, resulting in compression of the negative torque control spring.

The torque control lever will therefore pivot counterclockwise around point B (the torque control lever stopper pin), pivoting the starting lever counterclockwise around M_2 to move the control sleeve in the fuel-increase direction. The increase in the fuel injection quantity is determined by the negative torque control stroke S_3 (refer to Fig. 41).

Printed in Japan
A0A1029-9109SP

No-load maximum speed operation

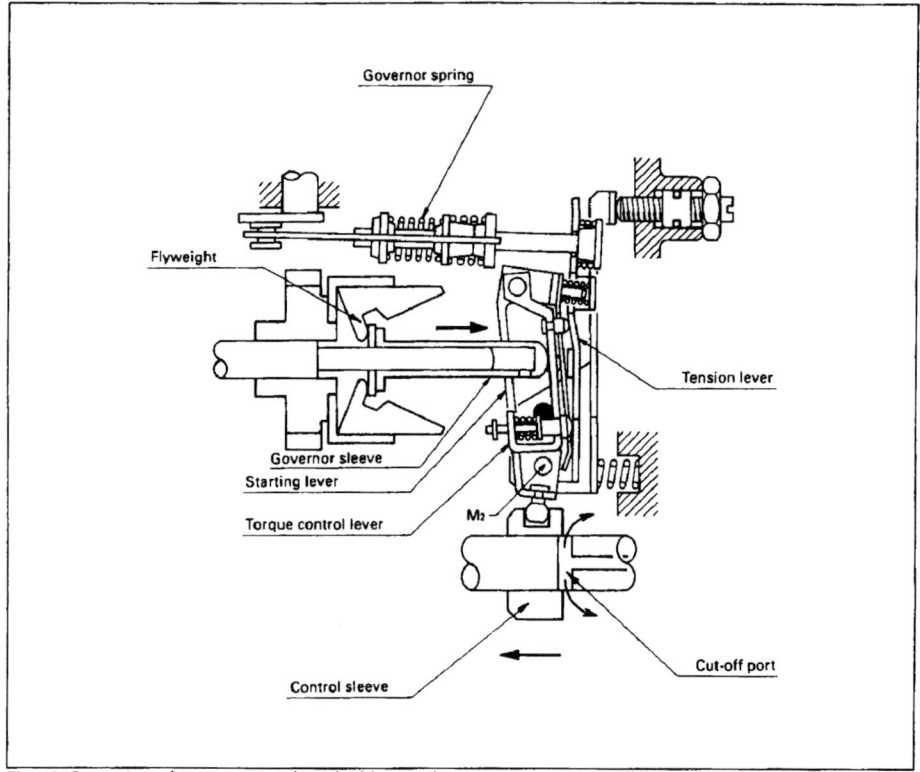

Fig. 43 Operation of governor equipped with negative torque control device: no-load maximum speed control

When the negative torque control stroke is completed and engine speed increases further, the flyweights' centrifugal force will move the governor sleeve to the right (Fig. 43). The starting lever and the tension lever (through the torque control lever) are then moved to compress the governor spring until the governor spring tension is balanced with the flyweights' centrifugal force in the no-load maximum speed position. If engine speed further increases, the control sleeve will move to the left until the plunger's cut-off port enters the pump chamber, resulting in non-injection so that the engine's specified maximum speed will not be exceeded.

17. Timer Construction and Operation (4JH2-UTE)

It is well-known that the relationship between fuel injection timing and engine performance (power, exhaust gas, engine vibration) is very important.
If actual fuel injection timing differs only slightly from the standard specified timing, then diesel engine performance will be adversely effected.

Because the ignition lag arising during diesel engine combustion increases as engine speed increases, it is necessary to compensate for this ignition lag by advancing injection timing.
To do this, a timer is installed at the bottom of the injection pump.

Standard Type Timer (Speed Timer)

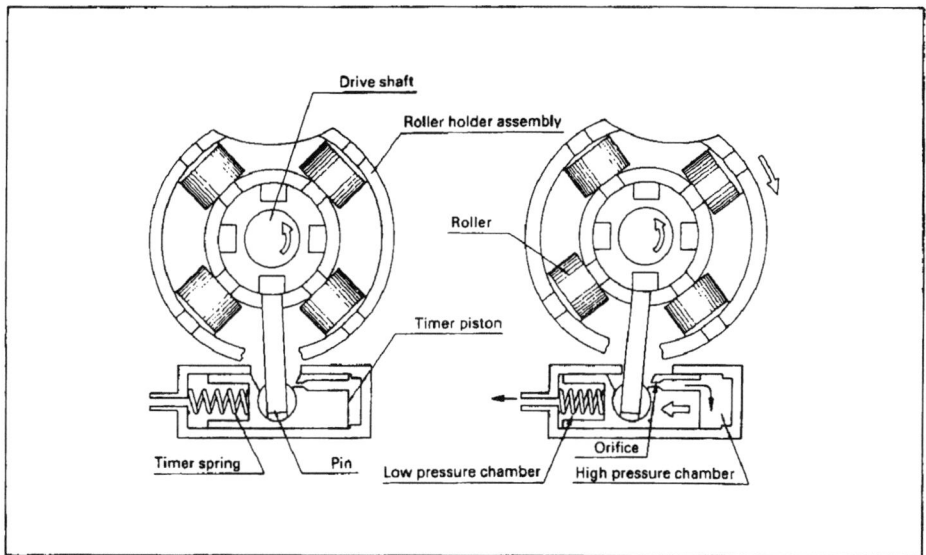

Fig. 44 Speed timer construction and operation

As shown in Fig. 44, a timer spring is installed in the low pressure chamber of the timer. Pump chamber pressure, passing through the timer piston orifice, acts on the high pressure side of the timer piston.
This timer piston orifice acts to prevent timer piston pulsation generated by fuel pressure fluctuations.
Timer piston movement results in the pin moving the roller holder assembly in the direction opposite to injection pump rotation.
When pump chamber pressure exceeds the set force of the timer spring due to an increase in pump speed, the timer piston compresses the timer spring and turns the roller holder assembly in the direction opposite to that of injection pump rotation. With this movement the cam disk's face cams contact the roller holder's rollers more quickly and injection timing is advanced.

When pump speed decreases and the timer spring set force exceeds the pump chamber pressure, the roller holder assembly is moved in the direction to retard injection timing.

Additional devices such as the solenoid timer, cold start device (C.S.D.) and the load timer etc. are also used with this standard-type timer to vary the injection timing in the specified range of engine speeds and loads.

Servo Valve Timer

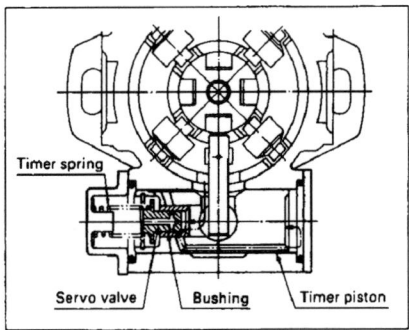

Timer spring

Servo valve / Bushing / Timer piston

Fig. 45 Servo valve timer construction

As shown in Fig. 45, through the addition of some parts (e.g. servo valve), the alteration of other parts (e.g. timer piston, cover and spring) and alterations to the fuel oil transfer passage, the servo valve timer differs from the standard type timer.

With the servo valve timer, pump chamber pressure does not act directly on the timer's high pressure chamber, but flows through the servo valve before acting on the timer's high pressure chamber.

The timer spring force does not push the timer piston, but pushes the servo valve against pump chamber pressure. The servo valve position depends on the balance of these two opposing forces, and timer characteristics in turn depend on the servo valve position.

For example, if the timer piston is moved in the retard direction by fluctuations in the driving reaction force, the servo valve position will not change, as the pump chamber pressure does not change. The servo valve then functions to compensate for the fluctuations in the driving reaction force by allowing the supply of pump chamber pressure to the high pressure side of the timer piston. The timer piston is therefore returned to its original position. In other words, the timer piston position is dependant on the servo valve position.

From the above, the servo valve timer's absorbing of the effect of the driving reaction force on injection timing can be seen.

As the effective pressure area directly acted upon by the pump chamber pressure decreases, and correspondingly the spring constant decreases, an improvement in response and a decrease in hysteresis can be obtained.

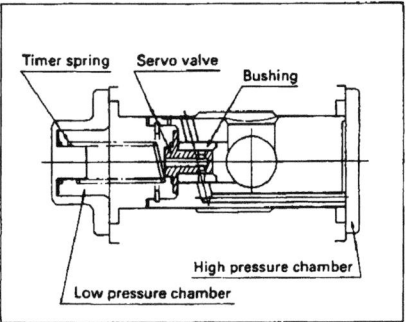

Fig. 46 Servo valve timer operation: when
advance angle is "0"

When advance angle is "0" (Low pump chamber pressure)

The pump chamber pressure, compared to the timer spring force, is still low, and the servo valve and the timer piston are pushed fully in the retard direction by the timer spring. The passage between the pump chamber (high pressure side) and the timer's high pressure chamber is closed, and the timer's high pressure chamber is connected to the timer's low pressure chamber (fuel inlet side) by the servo valve.

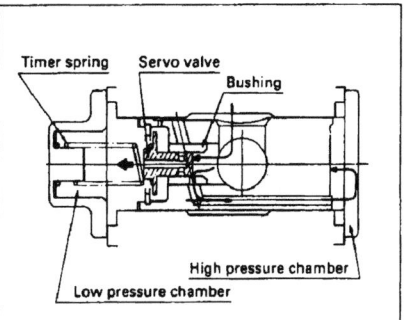

Fig. 47 Servo valve timer operation: when
pump chamber pressure has increased

When pump chamber pressure has increased

The pump chamber pressure has increased, the pump chamber pressure exceeds the timer spring set force, and the servo valve has been moved to the left (Fig. 47).
The passage between the pump chamber and the timer's high pressure chamber is open and the pump chamber pressure acts on the timer's high pressure chamber. Due to this the timer piston is moved in the advance direction (to the right in Fig. 47).

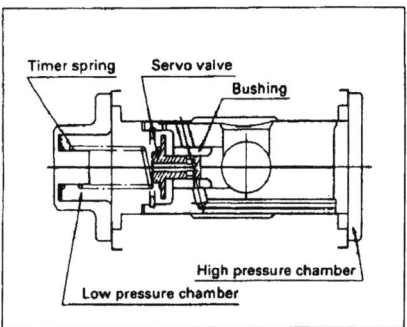

Fig. 48 Servo valve timer operation: stable
condition (balanced)

Stable condition (balanced)

The pump chamber pressure and the timer spring force are balanced, and the servo valve is stationary in a suitable position. The timer piston moves until the bushing hole is closed by the servo valve.
When the bushing hole is completely closed, there will be no change in the timer's high pressure chamber pressure and the timer piston will be stationary.

Printed in Japan
A0A1029-9109SP

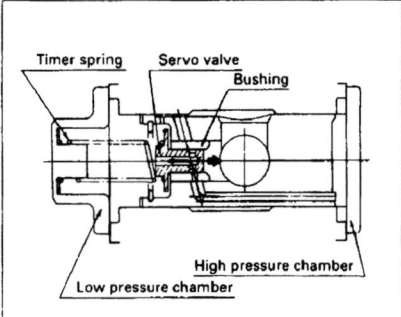

Fig. 49 Servo valve timer operation: when
pump chamber pressure has decreased

When pump chamber pressure has decreased

From the stable condition, pump chamber pressure has decreased and the servo valve is moved to the right (Fig. 49) by the timer spring force. The timer's high pressure chamber and the timer's low pressure chamber are connected through the passage in the servo valve. Therefore the timer high pressure chamber's high pressure escapes to the timer's low pressure chamber and the timer piston moves in the retard direction (to the right in Fig. 49), and, as in the above, a stable condition results.

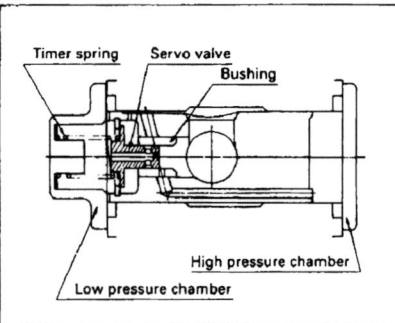

Fig. 50 Servo valve timer operation: maximum
advance position

Maximum advance position

As the pump chamber pressure has completely overcome the timer spring force, the timer piston moves until its end face contacts the timer cover's low pressure chamber side. That is, if pump chamber pressure further increases, the timer piston cannot move further in the advance direction. This position is the maximum advance position.

According to the above, if the timer piston is moved through the driving reaction force, operations identical to the above (when pump chamber pressure has increased or decreased) will be repeated until the stable condition is attained.

Load Timer

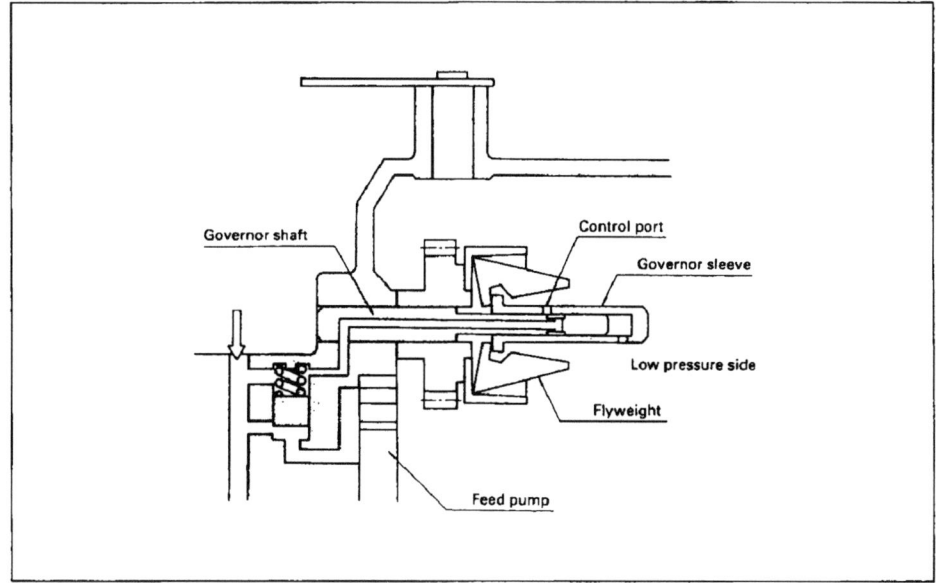

Fig. 51 Load timer construction and operation

The load timer functions to retard injection timing under partial loads in the low and intermediate speed range, and to reduce exhaust emission and engine noise.

With the load timer, the governor sleeve, the governor shaft, and the injection pump housing are specially constructed to facilitate the escape of fuel oil in the injection pump chamber from the governor sleeve control port, through a passage in the governor shaft and pump housing to the low pressure side.

When the flyweights are closed, the control port and the governor shaft passage are not aligned.

When the flyweights begin to open with an increase in the engine speed, the control port and the governor shaft passage barely align and injection pump chamber pressure begins to decrease as the pump chamber fuel oil flows to the fuel inlet (i.e. low pressure side) through this passage. When fully open pressure reduction is complete.

As a result, the timer's advance angle is only retarded an amount equal to the value of the pressure reduction.

Furthermore, the flyweights' (governor sleeve's) position changes in accordance with control lever position (engine load).

Printed in Japan
A0A1029-9109SP

18. Magnet Valve

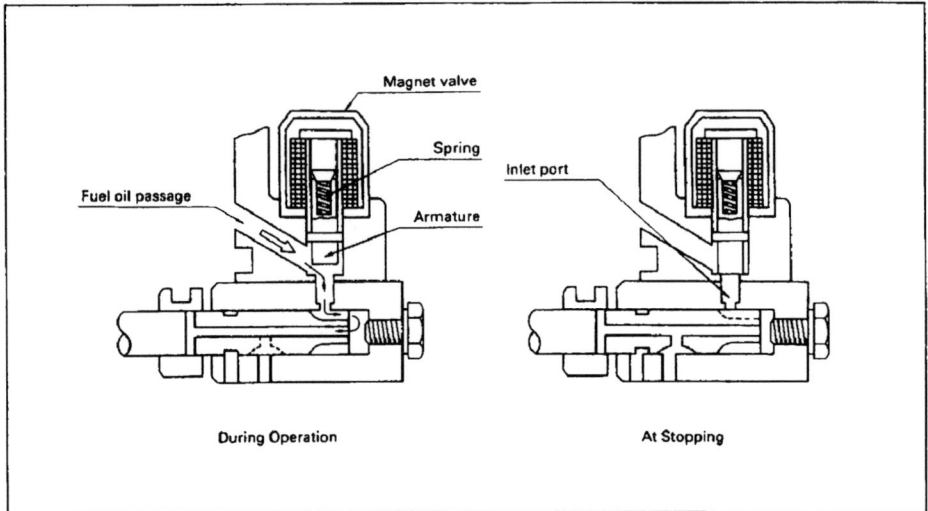

Fig. 52 Magnet valve construction and operation

The magnet valve is turned on and off by the vehicle's ignition switch to open and close the fuel oil passage leading to the plunger barrel's inlet port.
When the ignition switch is ON, current flows through the magnet valve, the armature in the centre of the magnet valve is attracted upwards and fuel oil from the pump chamber is supplied to the plunger barrel's inlet port.
When the ignition switch is turned OFF, the force of the spring inside the armature moves the armature downwards. Therefore, the fuel passage leading to the plunger barrel's inlet port is blocked and, as fuel oil injection to the engine combustion chamber is prevented, the engine can be stopped immediately.

19. Pump Reassembly, Adjustment and Inspection
(4JH2-UTE)

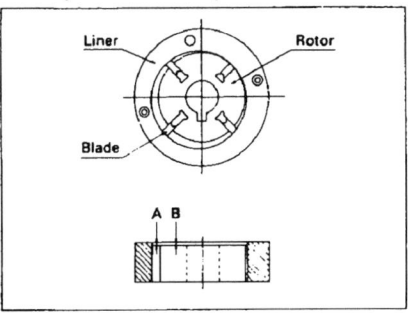

Fig. 1

1. Feed Pump Assembly

Set the rotor and blades inside the liner as a unit, so that their axial clearance will be within the specified tolerance. (The feed pump is delivered as a pre-adjusted assembly.)

Clearance between liner and rotor   A
0.010–0.020 mm.
Clearance between liner and blades: B
0.010–0.020 mm.

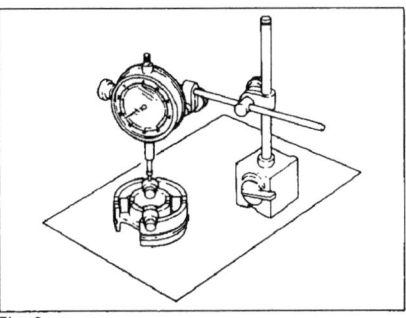

Fig. 2

2. Roller Height

When reassembling the roller holder, select the roller so that the difference in height (See Fig. 2) will be within the specified tolerance. (The roller holder is delivered as a pre-adjusted assembly.)

Difference in roller height:
±0.02 mm.

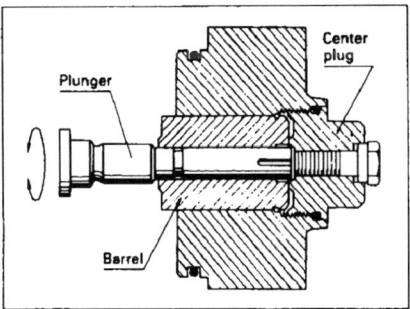

Fig. 3

3. Distributor Head Inspection

a) Plunger barrel movement.
With the center plug tightened to the head at the specified torque (6-8 kg.m) insert the plunger into the barrel. Confirm that in any position the plunger slides smoothly in the barrel.

Printed in Japan
A0A1029-9109SP

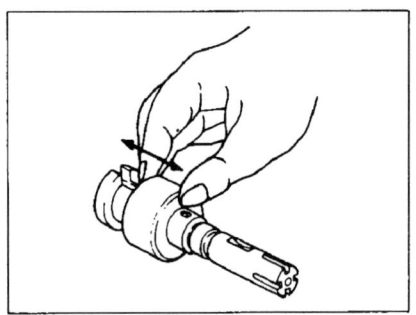

Fig. 4

b) Plunger control sleeve movement
Move the control sleeve 4 mm in an axial direction either side of the cut-off port. Rotate control sleeve and repeat. The control sleeve must slide smoothly in any position.

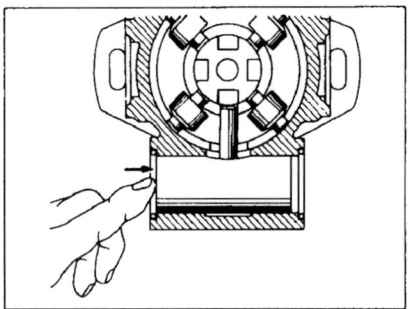

Fig. 5

4. Timer Movement Inspection

Position the plunger in the bottom dead center position. Push the timer piston from the retard side and observe timer movement. The timer must move smoothly. The force required for this movement should not exceed the specified value (Max 0.1 Kg.)

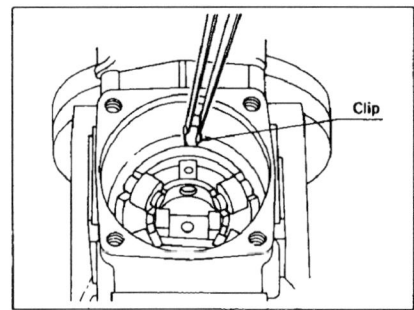

Clip

Fig. 6

5. Visual Inspection of Timer Lock Pin

Visually check that the timer connection lock pin [(25) in Fig. 25] is set correctly. Ensure a new clip (26) is installed at every service.

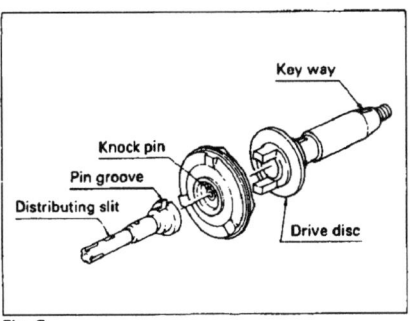

Fig. 7

6. Drive Shaft Key Way and Pin Groove

Visually check that the drive shaft key way and plunger pin groove are properly aligned.

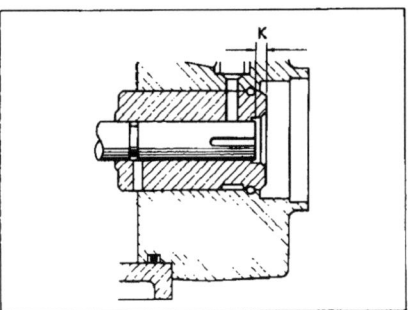

Fig. 8

7. Plunger Position Adjustment

a) VE type pump without plunger pre-stroke
Adjust the plunger position in the distributor head so that the dimension "K" is as specified. "K" is the distance from the end face of the distributor barrel to the plunger tip when the plunger is in the bottom dead center position. Adjust the shim [(52) in Fig. 25] on the plunger bottom, referring to the specified "K" dimension.

Clearance "K" 3.3 $^{\pm.1}$ mm

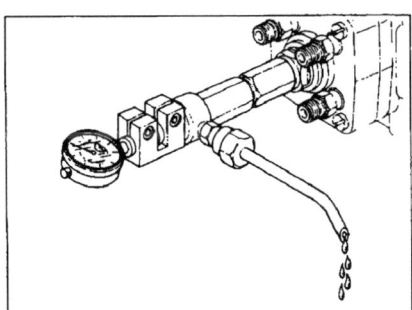

Fig. 9

b) VE type pump with plunger pre-stroke
The plunger position must be adjusted by checking the port closure point hydraulically on a pump test bench. With the plunger in the bottom dead center position, apply feed pressure of 0.2 Kg/cm^2. Test oil should flow out of the measuring device over-flow tube. Manually rotate the pump in the proper direction. Read the dial indicator when test oil stops flowing, and adjust the shim [(52) in Fig. 25] on the plunger bottom so that the dial reading is as specified.

Printed in Japan
A0A1029-9109SP

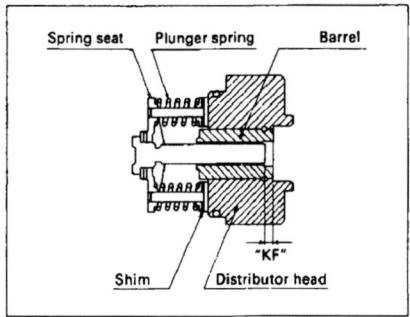

Fig. 10

8. Measurement of Plunger Spring Set Length

Install the plunger and plunger spring in the distributor head without the shim [(48) in Fig. 25]. Push the plunger bottom lightly in an axial direction and measure the dimension "KF" "KF" is the distance from the end face of the distributor barrel to the plunger tip. Adjust the shim (48) refering to the specified "KF" dimension.

Cam Lift (mm)	Dimensi "KF" (mm)
3	5.3 ±.1
2.8	5.3 ± 1
2.5	5.3 ± 1
2.2	5.8 ±.1
2.0	6.0 ± 1
1.56	6.64± 1

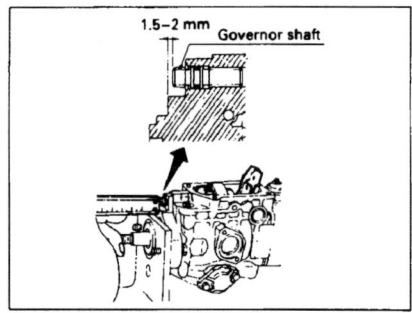

Fig. 11

9. Governor Shaft Installation

Install the governor shaft [(108) in Fig. 25] so that the distance from the end face of the pump housing flange to the governor shaft end face is 1.5–2.0 mm.

For an injection pump installed with a Load Timer, screw in the governor shaft so that the distance from the end of the governor shaft to the pump housing flange surface is 3 mm. After adjustment, tighten the locknut to the specified torque.

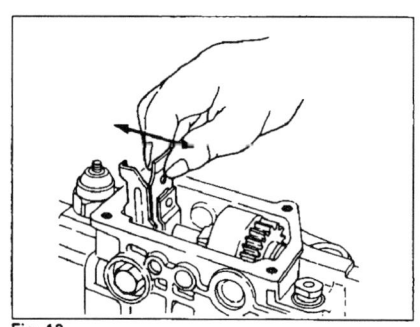

Fig. 12

10. Testing Governor Lever Action

After reassembly, manually check the movement of the start lever, governor lever assembly and control sleeve.

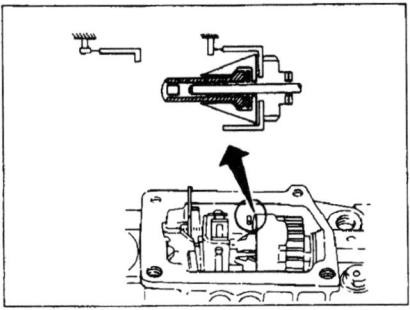

Fig. 13

11. Flyweight Assembly Clearance

Using a thickness gauge measure the clearance between the flyweight holder end face and the stopper pin (marked in Fig. 13.) Adjust the clearance using the shim [(110) in Fig. 25] at the back of the governor flyweight assembly.

Clearance:
   With straight pin: $0.15^{+0.2}$ mm
   With stepped pin $0.35^{+0.2}$ mm

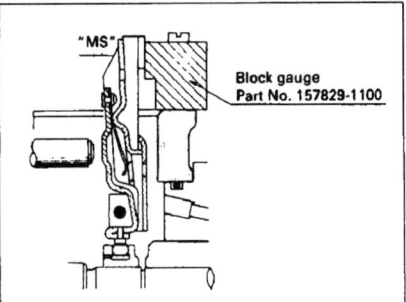

Block gauge
Part No. 157829-1100

Fig. 14

12. Starting Stroke "MS" Adjustment

"MS" is the distance from the closing plug installed on the governor sleeve to the starting lever, and determines the fuel injection quantity for engine starting. Method of measurement varies, depending on the type of governor lever assembly, as shown below.

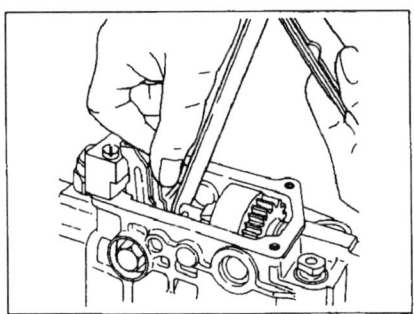

Fig. 15

a) Standard type
   Hold the corrector lever against the block gauge (Part No. 157829-1100) installed as shown in Fig. 15, and keep the tension lever against the stopper pin press-fitted into the pump housing.
   Then, hold the starting lever against the tension lever with the start spring compressed.
   Using a thickness gauge measure dimension "MS"

Printed in Japan
A0A1029-9109SP

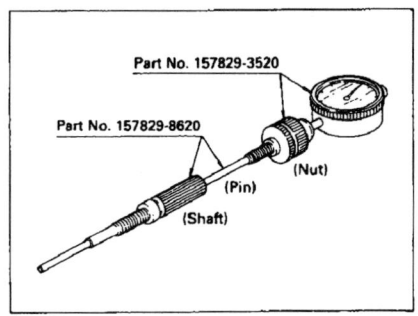

Part No. 157829-3520

Part No. 157829-8620

(Nut)

(Pin)

(Shaft)

Fig. 16

b) Negative torque control type
(1) Use "MS" measuring device (Part No. 157829-8620), block gauge (Part No. 157829-1100) and Plunger lift stroke measuring device (Part No. 157829-3520.) Before measurement, the pin of the plunger lift stroke measuring device (Part No. 157829-3520) must be replaced with the pin of the "MS" measuring device (Part No. 157829-8620.)

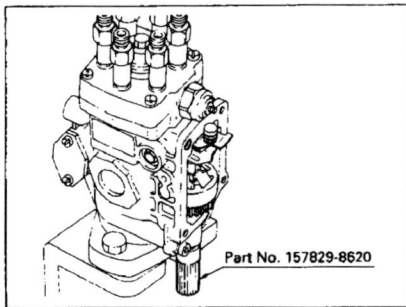

Part No. 157829-8620

Fig. 17

(2) Position the pump upright, loosen the nut (107) (See Fig. 25) and remove the governor shaft (108).
Install the shaft of "MS" measuring device (Part No. 157829-8620) in place of the governor shaft.
Take care not to drop the washer (111) and shim (110) (See Fig. 25), by holding the flyweight.
For an injection pump installed with a Load Timer, screw in the governor shaft so that the distance from the end of the governor shaft to the pump housing flange surface is 3 mm. After adjustment, tighten the locknut to the specified torque.

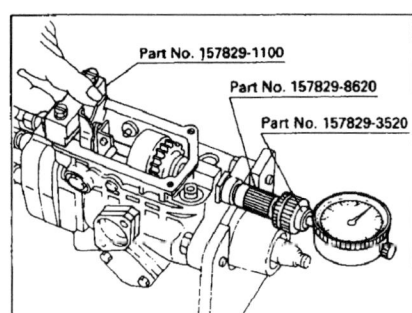

Part No.]57829-1100

Part No. 157829-8620

Part No. 157829-3520

Fig. 18

(3) Install the block gauge (Part No. 157829-1100) as shown in Fig. 18. Insert the pin of the plunger lift stroke measuring device (Part No. 157829-3520) into the measuring device shaft, already fixed in step b-(2). Secure the dial using the nut. To set the dial's zero point, slightly push the dial so that the dial reads between 2 to 3 mm (the tip of the pin touches the rear side of the closing plug.) Ensure the governor sleeve is pushed toward the flyweight side.
Hold the corrector lever against the block gauge, and push the tension lever against the stopper pin, press-fitted into the pump housing. Next, push the sleeve until the start lever contacts the tension lever, and will not move any further.
Next, read the dial and select the proper sized closing plug, to ensure dimension "MS" is as specified.

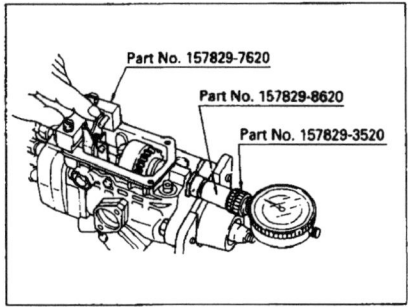

Part No. 157829-7620

Part No. 157829-8620

Part No. 157829-3520

Fig. 19

c) Boost compensator stopper and aneroid compensator type
Install the block gauge (Part No. 157829-7620) as shown in Fig. 19. Insert the pin of the plunger lift stroke measuring device (Part No. 157829-3520) into the device shaft, already fixed in step b-(2). Secure the dial with the nut. To set the dial's zero point, lightly push the dial so that the dial reads between 2 and 3 mm (the tip of the pin touches the rear side of the closing plug.) Ensure the sleeve is pushed toward the flyweight side.
Hold the corrector lever against the block gauge and push the tension lever against the stopper pin press-fitted into the block gauge. Next, push the governor sleeve until the start lever contacts the tension lever, and will not move any further. Then, read the dial and select the proper sized closing plug to ensure that dimension MS is as specified.

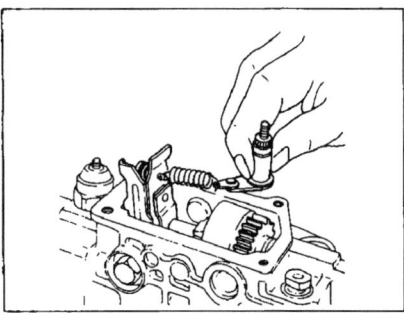

Fig. 20

13. Governor Spring Installation (Variable governor)

Attach the governor spring to the control lever shaft so that the hook faces downward.

Printed in Japan
A0A1029-9109SP

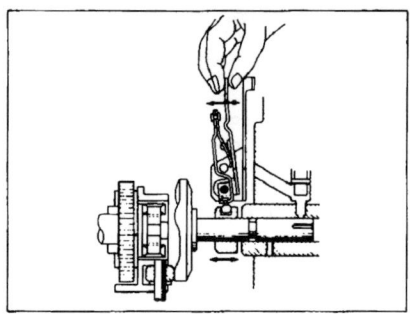

Fig. 21

14. Testing Governor Lever Assembly Movement

Position the cam in the top dead end position, and manually check governor lever assembly (control sleeve) movement. Perform this test over the entire cam profile.

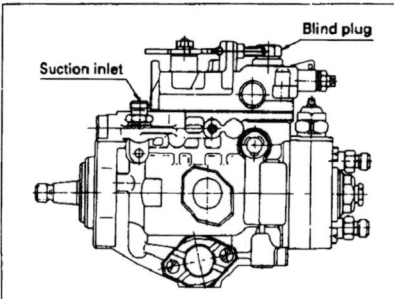

Blind plug

Suction inlet

Fig. 22

15. Air-tightness Test

After completion of assembly, perform an air-tightness test as described below.
a) Tightly screw in the pump cover overflow outlet plug (with a gasket).
b) Supply compressed air (approx. 4 Kg/cm^2) to the pump through the suction inlet.
c) Immerse the pump in light oil.
d) Check for bubbles indicating pump leakage (particularly at the drive shaft oil seal).

16. Handling of O-Rings

a) Rubber O-rings must be stored unexpanded.
b) When reassembling the pump after test immersion or actual use, replace all O-rings.

20. Test Bench Adjustment of VE Pump(4JH2-UTE)

* For adjustment specifications, refer to the individual test standards.

* Adjustment conditions:

Nozzle	DKKC Part No. 105780-0060 (NP-DN0SD1510)
Nozzle holder	DKKC Part No. 105780-2150

Nozzle opening pressure	133 kg/cri
Injection li	$6 \times 2-450$mm
Test oil	SAE Standard Test Oil (SEA J967d) or ISO 4113 test oil
Fuel oil temperature (fuel tank)	45^{+5} °C
Supply pressure	0.2 Kg/cm^2

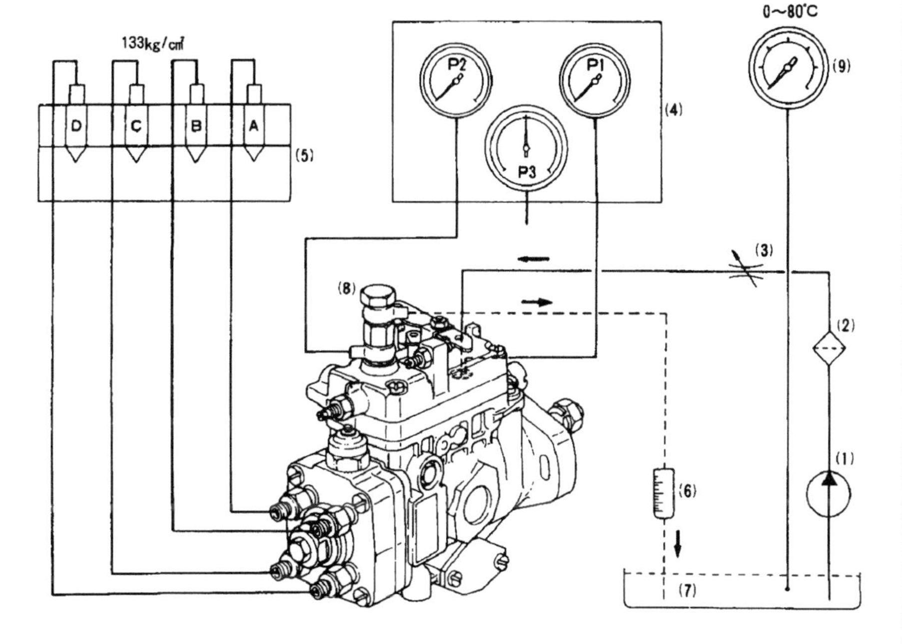

(1) Pre-supply pump
(2) Filter
(3) Regulator valve inlet
(4) Accumulator
P1: Test oil inlet pressure 0-1 Kg/cm^2
P2: Pump chamber pressure 0-15 Kg/cm^2
P3: Positive & Negative pressure;
    Positive: Boost compensator
    0-2 Kg/cm^2
    Negative: Aneroid compensator
    0-76 cmHg
(5) Nozzle opening pressure 133 Kg/cm^2
(6) Measuring cylinder for overflow fuel volume
(7) Fuel tank
(8) Overflow valve
(9) Thermometer (fuel tank)

Fig. 23 TEST BENCH PIPING DIAGRAM FOR PUMP PERFORMANCE TEST

Printed in Japan
A0A1029-9109SP

* Warm-up operation: refer to the following:

1. Standard Type VE Pump

Attach the pump to the pump test bench and connect the injection lines.
Using the thermometer (see Fig. 23) measure the fuel oil temperature in the fuel tank. Before starting operation, fill the pump with test oil.

a) Apply the specified voltage to test the pump's magnetic valve.
Fix the control lever in the maximum-speed position.
Operate the pump at the rated speed for approx. 10 minutes.

b) Timer adjustment
Install the timing measuring device and connect the pressure gauge.
Total timer stroke is determined by the timer piston length.
The start of the timer piston stroke depends on the spring tension force and the fuel oil feed pressure; the spring tension force is determined by the shims inside the timer cover. Usually, at least one shim (0.6 mm) is placed on each side of the timer spring.
Adjust the regulating valve so that the timer advances at the specified speed.

c) Supply pressure test
During timing adjustment, the pump chamber pressure must be within the specified range.

d) Full-load fuel injection quantity adjustment
Adjust the full-load fuel injection quantity through the full-load adjustment screw, and by adjusting the tension lever attached to the control sleeve.
Before adjustment, confirm that at the measuring point speed is as specified. Set the control lever to the maximum-speed position by rotating the adjusting screw. Adjust the full-load point by measuring the fuel injection quantity and referring to the specifications. The measuring point at all speeds must be within the specified range. The fuel injection quantity for each cylinder must not exceed the specified quantity.

e) Idling adjustment
Adjust the idling fuel injection quantity using the control lever.
The fuel injection quantity for each cylinder must not exceed the specified quantity

f) Governing adjustment
Adjust the governing performance using the control lever. The governing point is reached when the full-load fuel injection quantity begins to decrease, provided the adjusting screw is set at a position ensuring governor operation.

g) Measurement of overflow quantity
Measure the overflow quantity at the specified speeds using a measuring cylinder. Compare the measurement with the specified quantities.

h) Measurement of fuel injection quantity for engine starting
Control the starting fuel injection quantity at the specified speeds. Set the control lever to the maximum-speed position to adjust the starting stroke.

i) Control lever angle (see Fig. 24)
Adjust the control lever angles and dimensions given below, referring to the specifications.

α; Idling position/center position angle
β; Idling/maximum-speed position angle
γ; Idling/partial load position angle
a; Distance from the end of idling stopper to its boss portion
b; Distance from control lever idling position to maximum-speed stopper
c; Distance from control lever partial load position to idling stopper

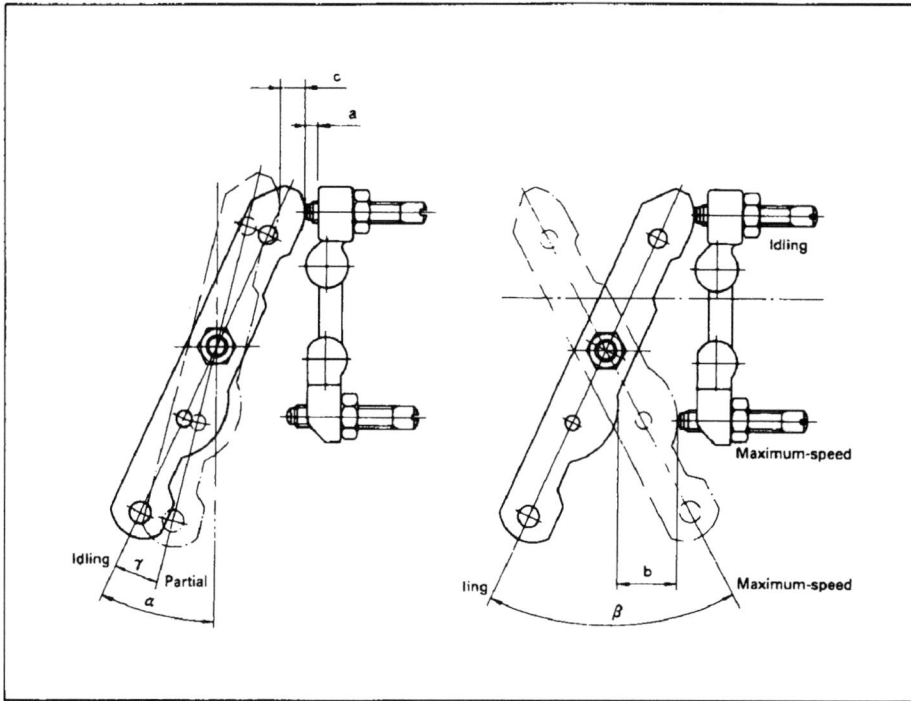

Fig. 24

2. VE Pump Special Specifications

a) Pump equipped with load timer
For a pump equipped with a load timer, move the control lever in the idling direction until the specified fuel injection quantity is reached at the specified test speed, and fix. Then, adjust the governor shaft so that the timer advances as specified.

b) Electrical shut-off
(1) Actuating voltages.
Check, as follows, at speeds as specified in the test standard.
Raise the voltage from 0 volts until the magnet actuates. Note the voltage and compare with the specifications.
(2) Fuel injection stop control
Cut off the voltage at the specified speed and ensure the fuel injection quantity is zero.

Printed in Japan
A0A1029-9109SP

21. Troubleshooting

Malfunctions	Causes	Remedies
The engine does not operate		
1 Fuel oil is not injected from the injection pump	1 There is no fuel oil in the fuel tank	Supply fuel and bleed the system
	2. The fuel line from the fuel tank is blocked	Clean or replace
	3. The fuel filter is clogged	Clean or replace
	4. There is air in the fuel filter or the pump chamber	Bleed the system
	5. The accelerator linkage is not properly connected	Repair
	6. The magnet valve wiring is broken or its armature is sticking	Repair or replace
	7 The feed pump blades are sticking, and therefore not operating	Repair or replace
	8. The drive gear or woodruff key is broken	Replace
2. Injection timing is incorrect	1 The drive gear or belt connections are incorrect	Repair
	2. The injection pump is incorrectly installed on the engine	Repair and adjust injection timing
	3. The roller holder assembly's roller or pin is worn excessively	Replace the assembly
	4. The plunger is worn excessively	Replace the distributor assembly
3. The nozzle does not operate	1 The nozzle or nozzle holder is functioning incorrectly	Inspect, then repair or replace
The engine operates, but only for a short time	1. The pipe(s) to the injection pump is blocked, or the fuel filter is clogged	Clean or replace the pipe(s) or fuel filter
	2. The fuel oil contains air or water	Bleed of air or replace the fuel oil
	3. The feed pump's delivery quantity (or pressure) is insufficient	Repair or replace
The engine "knocks"	1. The injection timing is too advanced	Readjust the timing
	2. The nozzle or nozzle holder is functioning incorrectly	Inspect, then repair or replace

Malfunctions	Causes	Remedies
The engine exhaust contains smoke and the engine "knocks"	1 The injection timing is incorrect 2. The nozzle or nozzle holder is functioning incorrectly 3. The injection quantity is excessive	Readjust the timing Inspect, then repair or replace Readjust
The engine output is unstable	1. The fuel filter element is clogged and fuel oil delivery is poor 2. The amount of fuel or pressure delivered by the feed pump is too little 3. The injection pump is sucking air 4. The regulating valve is stuck in the open position 5. The plunger is sticking and does not travel its full stroke 6. The plunger spring is broken 7 The control sleeve is not sliding smoothly 8. The governor lever is not operating properly or is worn excessively 9. The delivery valve spring is broken 10. The delivery valve is not sliding properly 11. The nozzle or the nozzle holder is not functioning properly 12. The injection timing is incorrect	Clean or replace Inspect and repair Inspect and repair Replace Replace the distributor assembly Replace Repair or replace Repair or replace Replace Repair or replace Inspect, and then repair or replace Readjust
Insufficient output 1 The injection quantity is insufficient	1. The specified full-load injection quantity is not delivered 2. The control lever is not reaching the maximum speed position 3. The governor spring is weak and therefore the governed speed is too low 4. The plunger is worn 5. The delivery valve seating portions are damaged	Readjust Readjust Replace Replace the distributor assembly Replace
2. The injection timing is too advanced and the engine is "knocking"		Readjust

Printed in Japan
A0A1029-9109SP

Malfunctions	Causes	Remedies
3. The injection timing is too retarded and the engine is overheating or the exhaust contains smoke		Readjust
4. The nozzle or the nozzle holder is not functioning properly		Inspect, and then repair or replace
The engine cannot reach its maximum speed	1. The governor spring is too weak or is improperly adjusted	Readjust or replace
	2. The control lever is not reaching the maximum-speed position	Readjust
	3. The nozzle's injection operation is poor	Repair or replace
The engine's maximum speed is too high	1 The governor spring is too strong or is improperly adjusted	Readjust or replace
	2. The governor flyweights or governor sleeve movement is not smooth	Repair or replace
Idling is unstable	1 The injection quantities are not uniform (the delivery valve is not operating properly)	Inspect or replace
	2. The governor's idling adjustment is improperly adjusted	Readjust
	3. The plunger is worn	Replace the distributor assembly
	4. The plunger spring is broken	Replace
	5. The rubber damper is worn.	Replace
	6. The governor lever shaft pin is worn excessively	Replace
	7 The feed pump blades are not operating properly	Repair or replace
	8. The regulating valve is stuck in the open position	Replace
	9. The fuel filter element is clogged and therefore fuel oil delivery is poor	Clean or replace
	10. The nozzle or the nozzle holder is not functioning properly	Inspect and then repair or replace

Fuel injection pump test data.

	Pump speed						rpm		
	500	750	1000	1350	1700	1800	1990	325	100
Fuel delivery cc/1000sts	37.2	37.4	46.1	58.9	68.0 ~ 70.0	66.5	8.0 ~ 17.0	10.6 ~ 17.0	57 ~ 97

Specification

	Model		NP-VE4/11F1800RNP1026
Pump	Cam Lift		2.8mm
	Pulunger diameter		ϕ 11 mm
	Cut-off poat		2 × ϕ4.0 a=0
	Pulunger pre-stroke		0.45
	Pulunger spring		k= 11.7kg / mm
	Delivery valve opening		22.6kg / cm²
	Delivery valve spring		k= 1.0kg / mm
Governor	Control speed		325 ~ 1800 rpm
Timer	Timer spring		k= 4.1 kg / mm
	Timer / piston stroke		1 deg/0.82mm
	Advance adjustment angle		3 deg/600 ~ 1500rpm
	Piston stroke	1000 rpm	0.8 ~ 1.6mm
		1500 rpm	2.0 ~ 2.9mm
	Pump pressure	1000 rpm	3.4 ~ 4.2 kg / cm²
Nozzle (Only for rig test)	Model		NP-DN0SD1510
	Nozzle opening pressure		133 kg / cm²
	Injection pipe		ϕ 8/ ϕ 2 × 450mm
	Feed pressure		0.2kg / cm²
	Nozzle holder Model		105780-2150

Printed in Japan
A0A1029-9109SP

INTAKE AND EXHAUST SYSTEM

Printed in Japan
A0A1029-9002

1. Intake and Exhaust System

1-1 4JHE engine

Air enters in the intake silencer mounted at the end of the intake manifold, is fed to the intake manifold and then on to each cylinder.

Exhaust gas goes into the exhaust manifold (in the fresh water tank) mounted on the cylinder head discharge. After cooling it enters the mixing elbow which is directly connected with the exhaust manifold, and is discharged from the ship along with waste cooling water.

Intake system

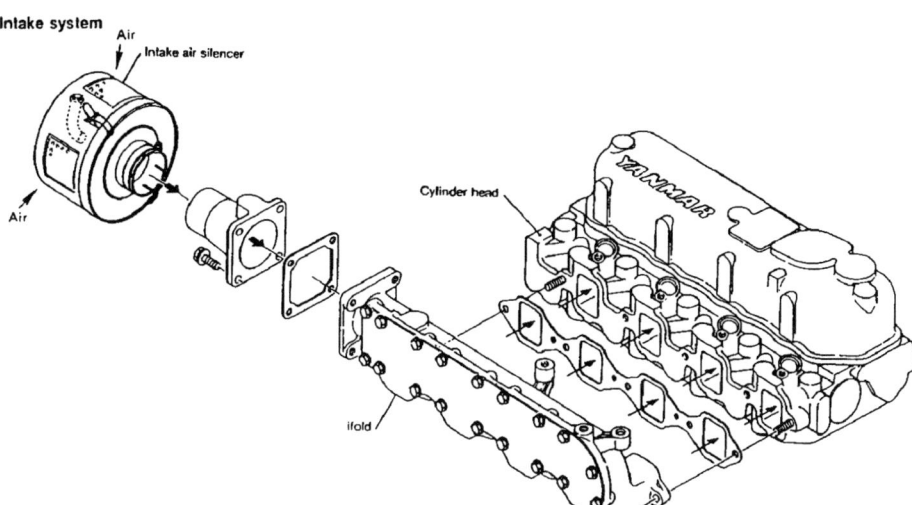

Exhaust system

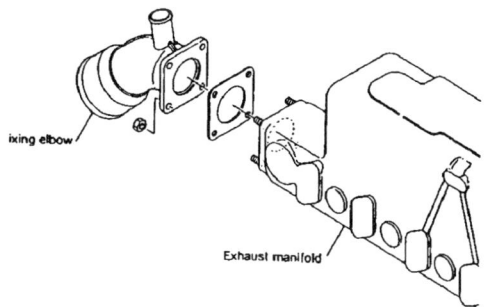

1-2 4JH-TE engine

Intake system

Air goes from the intake manifold mounted to the turbo-charger, through the turbocharger and a rubber hose to the intake manifold and is fed to each cylinder.

Exhaust gas goes from the exhaust manifold to the turbocharger connected to the exhaust manifold, to the mixing elbow mounted to the turbocharger, and is discharged from ship along with waste cooling water.

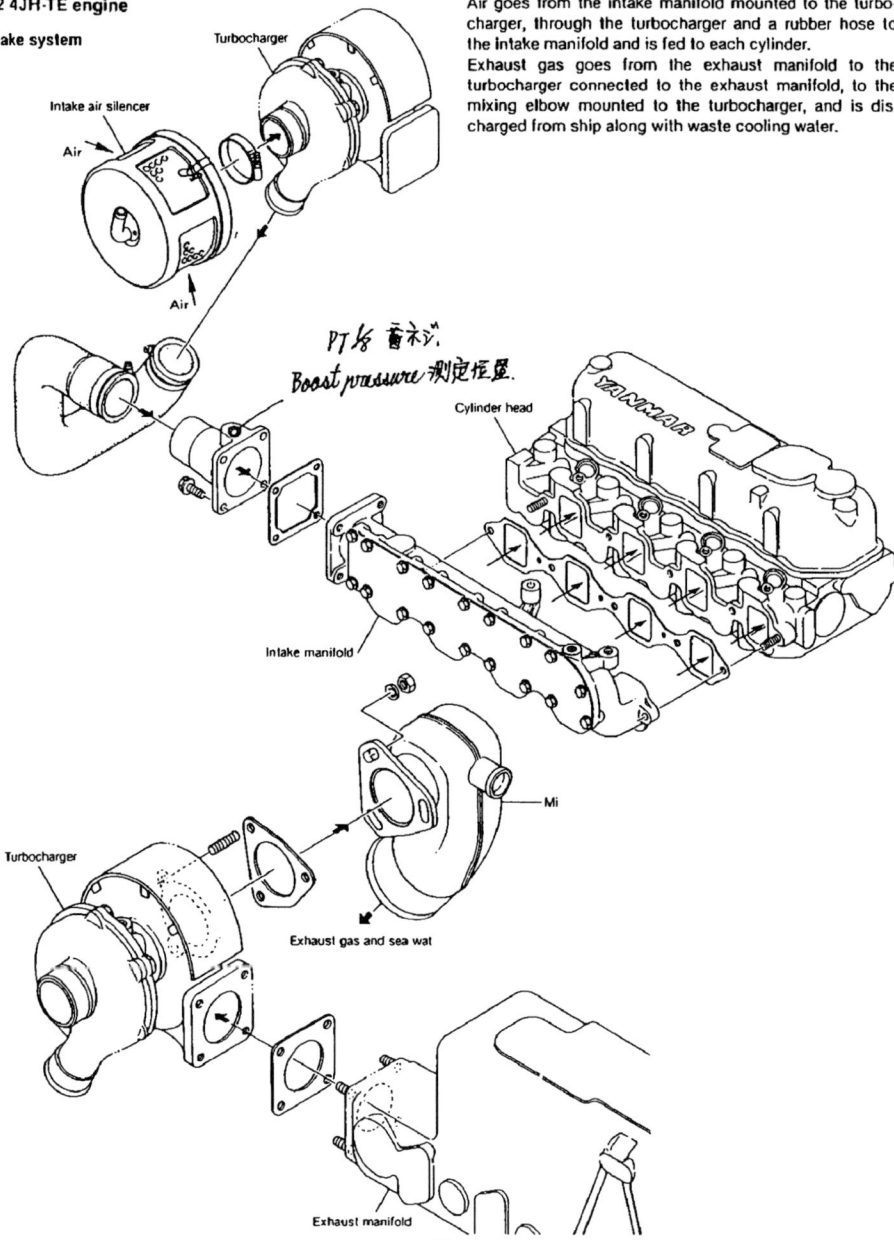

Air Cooler for Models 4JH2-HTE, 4JH2-DTE and 4JH2-UTE

Air introduced from the intake air silencer passes through the air duct to the air cooler where it is cooled, and is the distributed to each cylinder via the intake manifold.
Exhaust gases pass through the water-cooled turbocharger to the mixing elbow and are discharged with the sea water

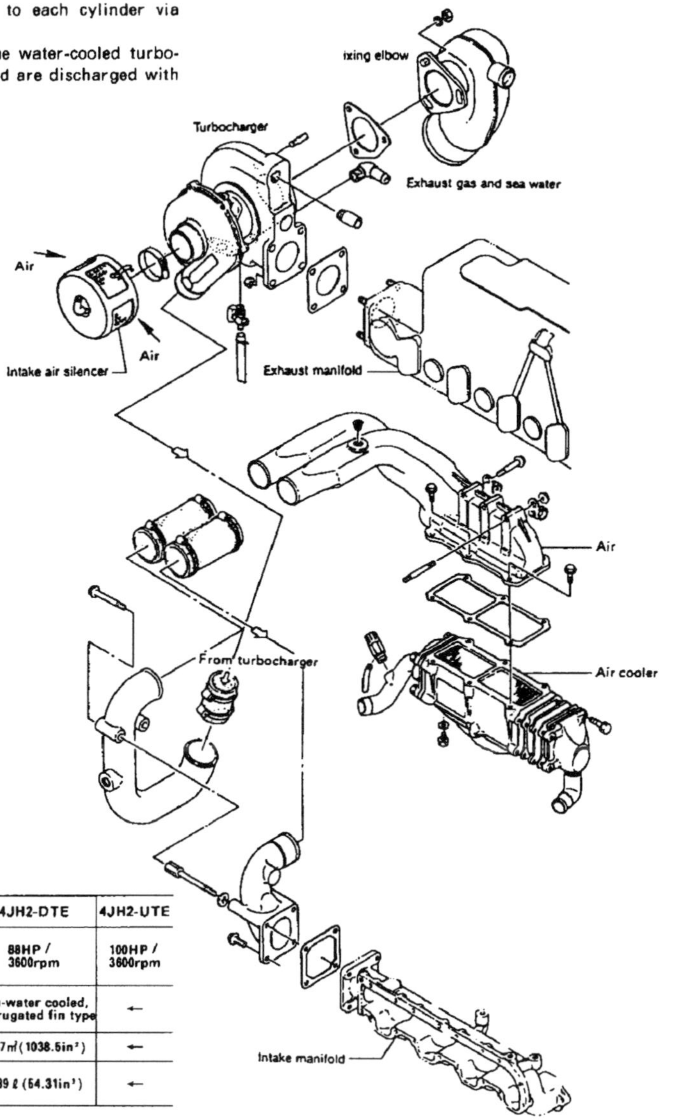

Mixing elbow

Turbocharger

Exhaust gas and sea water

Air

Intake air silencer

Air

Exhaust manifold

Air

From turbocharger

Air cooler

Air Cooler Specifications

Engine model	4JH2-HTE	4JH2-DTE	4JH2-UTE
Output Din6270B Rating	75HP / 3600rpm	88HP / 3600rpm	100HP / 3600rpm
Type	Sea-water cooled, Plate fin type	Sea-water cooled, Corrugated fin type	←
Radiation area	0.76 ㎡ (1178in²)	0.67 ㎡ (1038.5in²)	←
Sea-water capacity	0.85 ℓ (51.87in³)	0.89 ℓ (54.31in³)	←

Intake manifold

NOTE: → Charging Air
→ Exhaust gas and Sea-water

2. Turbocharger

2-1 Specifications

Turbocharger maker	ISHIKAWAJIMA-HARIMA HEAVY INDUSTRIAL CO.,LTD.(IHI)			
Turbine type	Radial flow			
Blower type	Centrifugal			
Bearing type	Full foating			
Lubrication method	Outer lubrication			
Cooling method	Air cooled	Water cooled		
Continuous rated rpm	155,000	165,000	160,000	
Max. gas inlet temp. (continuous allowable)	700℃			
Dry weight, approx.	4.2kg(9.26lb.)			
Turbocharger model	—	MY67	MY60	MY34
Applicable engine model	4JH2-TE	4JH2-HTE	4JH2-DTE	4JH2-UTE

2-2 Construction

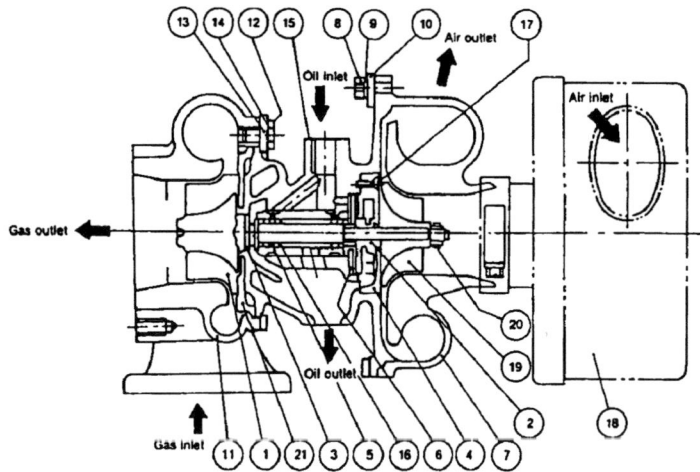

1. Turbine shaft
2. Oil thrower
3. Turbine side seal ri
4. Seal plate
5. Floating bearing
6. Thrust bearing
7. Blower wheel chamber
8. M5 hexagonal bolt
9. M5 lock washer
10. Blower side top plate
11. Turbine wheel chamber
12. M6 hexagonal bolt
13. Turbine side locking plate
14. Lock washer
15. Bearing chamber
16. Stop ring
17. Screw M3
18. Intake silencer
19. Blower wheel fixing nut
20. Blower wheel
21. Heat insulating board

Printed in Japan
A0A1029-9109SP

2-3 Interchangeability of turbochargers

The IHI-make turbocharger used for the 4JH series differ according to the engine model. Care should therefor be taken to assemble only components for the turbocharger used in your engine when replacing parts. The use of incorrect turbocharger components will detract from the performance of the engine. Turbocharger models can be distinguished by their name plates.

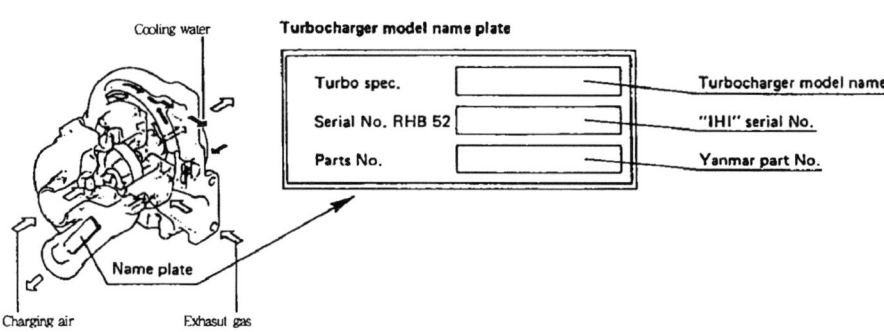

Engine model	Turbocharger model (spec.)	YANMAR parts No.	Turbine & Blower Spec.	
			Turbine	Blower
4JH2-TE	MY67	129571-18000	5200IIHP12NW	BRL3511E
4JH2-HTE	MY60	129474-18001	9000IVHP12NF	BRL3511E
4JH2-DTE	MY34	129473-18000	5200IIHP15NW	BRL3511E
4JH2-UTE	MY34	129473-18000	5200IIHP15NW	BRL3511E

2-4 Interchangeability of turbocharger components

The inspection procedures and adjustment standard are identical for all turbocharger models. Please note, however, that the asterisked (*) components differ according to the turbocharger model and are not interchangeable.

ide top plate

*Blower wheel

Thrust bushing

* Blower wheel chamber

Seal platet

*Bearing chamber

Oil thrower

Heat insulating board

Thrust bearing

* Turbine shaft

Floating bearing

ine housing

Lock washer

Plate

Lagging

Components Parts No.

Part name	MY67	MY60	MY34
Turbine housing		X-NE929010	X-NN139402
Bearing chamber		X-NE923300	X-NN133442
Turbine shaft		X-NN13570	X-NN131502
Blower wheel		X-NN136606	X-NN136606
Blower wheel chamber		X-NE924350	X-NN134092
Applicable engine model	4JH2-TE	4JH2-HTE	4JH2-DTE·4JH2-UTE

Printed In Japan
A0A1029-9109SP

2-5 Disassembly, assembly

2-5.1 Preparations for disassembly

The following special tools are required for disassembly of
the turbocharger, in addition to the standard tools.

Name of tool	Use	Illustration
Bar	To remove thrust metal and thrust bushings	mm (in.) 75 (2.9527) Ø7.5 (0.2952) Material: Copper or brass
Pliers	To remove floating bushing stop ring	
	To remove seal ring	
Torque driver (Phillips) 5 ~ 50kg/cm² (71.11 ~ 711.16 lb/in.²)	To mount thrust metal and seal plate (+)	Standard Model
Box wrench	To tighten turbine shaft 10mm (0.3937in.) × 12 square	Box only may be used

Torque wrench	For following bolts
	M6: 10mm (0.3937in.)
	    110kg/cm² (1564.56 lb/in.²)
	M5: 8mm (0.3149in.)
	    45 kg/cm² (64.005 lb/in.²)
	M5: 8mm (0.3149in.)
	    20 kg/cm² (284.46 lb/in.²)	

Gauge wire	To measure play in shaft and axial direction (horizontal and vertical)	R10 (0.3937) Ø5 (0.1968) mm (in.) R5 (0.1968) 7 (0.2755) M26 P0.45 1 (0.0393) 8 (0.3149) 40 (1.5748) 10 (0.3937) 15 (0.5905) Mount to dial gauge

2-5.2 Inspection prior to disassembly

(1) Make sure that the turbine and blower blades are not in contact and that the rotor rotates smoothly.

(2) Measuring rotor play.

mm (in.)

	Standard	Wear limit
Rotor play in direction of shaft	0.03 ~ 0.06 (0.0011 ~ 0.0023)	0.09 (0.0035)
Rotor play in axial direction	0.08 ~ 0.13 (0.0031 ~ 0.0051)	0.17 (0.0066)

2-5.3 Disassembly

Make match marks before disassembling the turbocharger to show how the super charger is mounted on the engine. This determines the angle at which the turbine chamber, bearing chamber and blower chamber are mounted.

(1) Removing blower chamber
  1) Remove the M5 mounting bolts, spring washers and blower side retaining plate.
  2) Remove the blower chamber.

NOTE: 1. The blower chamber and bearing chamber mounting surfaces are coated with a liquid gasket.
  2. Be careful not to scratch the blower blade when disassembling the blower chamber.

(2) Removing blower blade
  1) Fit a box wrench (10mm (0.3937in.)) to the end of the turbine side of the turbine shaft and remove the shaft end nut.

NOTE: The box end nut has left handed threads.

  2) Remove the blower blade.

(3) Removing turbine chamber, lagging.
  1) Remove the turbine chamber mounting bolts and the turbine side retai ing plate for lagging.
  2) Remove the lagging and turbine chamber.

(4) Pulling the turbine shaft
  1) Lightly hold the heat shield by hand and pull out the turbine shaft.

NOTE: If the turbine shaft is hard to pull out, lightly tap the blower side end of the shaft with a wooden mallet.

  2) Remove the heat shield.

NOTE: If the heat shield is hard to remove, tap it lightly with a caulking chisel.

(5) Removing the seal plate
  1) Loosen the M3 flat seal plate mounting screws with a plus screwdriver and remove them along with the double grip (tooth) washers.
  2) Remove the seal plate.

NOTE: The seal plate and bearing chamber mounting surfaces are coated with a liquid gasket.

  3) Remove the oil ring seal from the seal plate.

(6) Removing the thrust metal and thrust bushing.
  1) Loosen the M3 flat seal plate mounting screws with a plus screwdriver and remove them along with the double grip washers.
  2) Use a copper rod to remove the thrust metal and thrust bushing.

(7) Removing the floating metal (bushing)
  1) Remove the round R stop ring from the bearing chamber with stop ring pliers.
  2) Remove the floating metal from the bearing chamber.

(8) Removing seal ring
  1) Remove the turbine side seal ring from the turbine shaft.
  2) Remove the large and small blower side seal rings from the oil seal.

2-5.4 Preparations for reassembly

(1) When the turbocharger is reassembled, special tools, liquid gasket (Three Bond No.1207S or Three Bond No.1215) and burning preventative agent are needed in addition to the standard tools.

(2) Always replace the following with new parts when reassembling the turbocharger:

Turbine side seal rings
Blower side seal rings (large)
Blower side seal rings (small)
M3 flat screws
Bent washers
Double grip washers

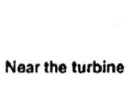

Near the turbine

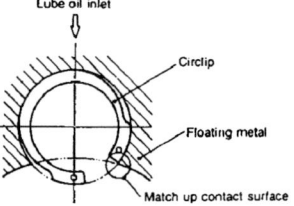

Lube oil inlet

Circlip

Floating metal

Match up contact surface

All other cases

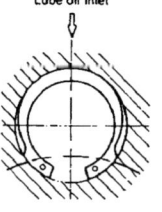

Lube oil inlet

Looking from turbine si

2-5.5 Reassembly

(1) Reassembly of floating metal
1) Mount the inside round R stop ring in the bearing chamber with stop ring pliers.
2) Fit the floating metal in the bearing chamber.
3) Mount the outside round R stop ring in the bearing chamber.

NOTE: 1. The round R stop ring opening should be mounted as shown in the illustration. The round part of the stop ring should be mounted on the metal.
2. When mounting, coat the floating metal with engine oil.

(2) Reassembly of the turbine shaft
1) Insert the seal ring in the turbine shaft.
2) Mount the heat shield on the turbine side bearing chamber.
3) Coat the journal of the turbine shaft with engine oil and insert from the turbine side of the bearing chamber.

NOTE: Take adequate care not to scratch the floating metal with the turbine shaft.
The seal ring opening should face the oil intake and be inserted aligned with the turbine shaft center.

(3) Reassembly of the thrust metal
1) Insert the thrust bushing in the turbine shaft.
2) Coat the thrust metal with engine oil and mount it i the bearing chamber.
3) Put the double grip washers on the thrust metal mounting M3 flat screws and tighten with the torque driver.

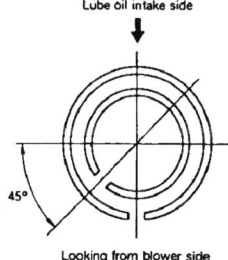

Lube oil intake side

45°

Looking from blower side

	kg-cm (ft-lb)
Tightening torque	12 ~ 14 (0.86 ~ 1.01)

(4) Mounting seal plate
1) Insert the seal ring in the oil drai
2) Insert the seal plate in the oil drain.

NOTE: The seal ring opening should face the direction i dicated in the upper right illustration.

3) Coat the blower side seal plate mounting surface of the bearing chamber (20) with the liquid gasket (Three Bond No.1207S or Three Bond No.1215).

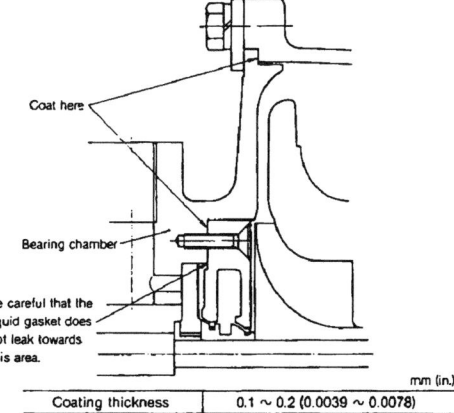

Coat here

Bearing chamber

Be careful that the liquid gasket does not leak towards this area.

	mm (in.)
Coating thickness	0.1 ~ 0.2 (0.0039 ~ 0.0078)

NOTE: See the illustration for where to coat it.

4) Mount the sealing plate on the bearing chamber.
5) Put the double grip washers on the sealing plate mounting M3 flat screws and tighten with the torque driver.

	kg-cm (ft-lb)
Tightening torque	12 ~ 14 (0.86 ~ 1.01)

(5) Mounting blower blade
1) Put the blower blade on the turbine shaft.
2) Tighten the turbine side shaft end nut of the turbine shaft with a box wrench (10mm (0.3937in.)).

NOTE: The shaft end nut has a left handed thread.

	kg-cm (ft-lb)
Tightening torque	18 ~ 22 (1.30 ~ 1.59)

(6) Mounting turbine chamber
1) Mount the turbine chamber, aligned with the match marks made before disassembly.

NOTE: When replacing parts, mount after checking the oil intake/discharge and exhaust gas intake positions.

2) Lugging
Put on the turbine side retainer plate for lugging and the bent washer, and tighten with the M6 hex bolt. Make sure to bend the washer after tightening the M6 hex bolt.

	kg-cm (ft-lb)
Tightening torque	105 ~ 115 (7.59 ~ 8.31)

(7) Mounting blower chamber
1) Coat the blower side flange surface of the seal plate with the liquid gasket (Three Bond No.1207S or Three Bond No.1215).

NOTE: Refer to page (21) for where to coat.

	mm (in.)
Coating thickness	0.1 ~ 0.2 (0.0039 ~ 0.0078)

2) Align the match marks made before disassembly and mount the seal plate in the blower chamber.

NOTE: When replacing parts, mount only after checking oil intake/discharge and air discharge positions.

3) Replace on the blower side retaining plate and spring washer and tighten with the M5 hex bolt.

	kg-cm (ft-lb)
Tightening torque	40 ~ 50 (2.89 ~ 3.61)

(8) Measuring rotor play
See item 3-2 on inspection procedure—the measuring procedure is the same.
Rotor play above the standard is usually due to improper assembly or use of the wrong part—reassemble.

mm (in.)

	Standard
Rotor play in direction of shaft	0.03 ~ 0.06 (0.0011 ~ 0.0023)
Rotor play in axial direction	0.08 ~ 0.13 (0.0031 ~ 0.0051)

2-5.6 Disassembly/reassembly precautions

Observe the following during and after mounting the turbocharger on the engine.
Be especially careful to prevent the entrance of foreign matter into the turbocharger.
(1) Precautions on mounting the turbocharger.

Lube oil system
1) Run new engine oil through the oil intake holes before mounting on the engine, turn the turbine shaft by hand and lubricate the journal metal (bushings) and thrust metal.
2) Wash the engine oil intake pipe and oil discharge pipe, check for damage and make sure it is not clogged up with dirt or other foreign matter.
3) Make sure that there is no oil leakage from the oil pipes and joints after assembly.

Intake system
1) Make sure that there is no dirt or other foreign matter in the air intake system.
2) Make sure that there is no air leakage from the air supply duct/air cleaner connections.

Exhaust system
1) Make sure that there is no dirt or other foreign matter in the exhaust gas system.
2) Make sure not to mix up the special heat resistant bolts and nuts with the regular bolts when mounting the parts. Coat the bolts, nuts, etc. with burning preventive agent.
(Heat resistant hex bolts are used for the turbi chamber.)
3) Make sure that there is no gas leakage from exhaust piping/connections.

2-6 Inpsection and maintenance

2-6.1 Washing

(1) Inspection prior to washing
Make a visual inspection of disassembled parts before washing to check for burning, wear, foreign, matter and carbon build-up. Make an especially thorough inspection in case of breakdowns as a step towards determining the cause of the breakdown.

Major items

Inspection	Location
Carbon build-up	1) Turbine turbine side seal ring and back of blade. 2) Around the heat shield mounting of the bearing chamber and the inside wall of the bearing chamber.
Lubrication (wear, burning, discoloration)	1) Turbine shaft journal, thrust bushing, oil drain. 2) Floating metal and thrust metal. 3) Around the inner bearing race of the bearing chamber.
Oil leakage	1) Inside wall of the turbine chamber. 2) Outer circumference of the bearing chamber and around the heat shield mounting. 3) Turbine side seal ring of the turbine shaft and the back of the blade. 4) Inside wall of the blower chamber. 5) Back of the blower blade. 6) Back of the seal plate and place where the seal ring is inserted.

(2) Washing procedure
Keep the following in mind when washing the parts.

Item	Tools/Cleaning Agent	Procedure
(1) Turbine shaft	1. Tools (1) Bucket (500 × 500) (2) Heat source steam or gas burner (3) Brush 2. Cleaning agent Standard carbon removing agent	(1) Boil the turbine shaft in the washing bucket. Do not hit the blade to remove the carbon. (2) Soak in the cleaning agent until the carbon and other materials adhering to the surface become soft. (3) Use a plastic scrubber or hard hair remove the softened foreign matter. (4) Be very careful not to scratch the turbine shaft bearing surface or the seal ring grooves. (5) Any foreign matter will unbalance the turbine shaft, so be sure to clean it well. Do not use a wire brush.
(2) Turbine chamber	1. Tools same as for turbine shaft 2. Cleaning agent same as for turbine shaft	(1) Boil the turbine chamber in the washing bucket. (2) Soak in the cleaning agent until all the material adhering to the surface becomes soft. (3) Use a plastic scrubber or hard hair brush to remove the foreign matter.
(3) Blower blade, blower chamber	1. Tools (1) Bucket (500 × 500) (2) Brush 2. Cleaning agent	(1) Soak in the cleaning agent until the foreign matter adhering to the surface becomes soft. (2) Use a plastic scrubber or hard hair brush to remove the softened foreign matter. Do not use a wire brush.
(4) Other parts	(1) Wash all other parts with diesel oil. (2) Clean all lube oil lines with compressed air. (3) Be careful not to scratch parts or allow them to rust.	

2-6.2 Inspection procedure

(1) Blower chamber
Inspect for scratches caused by contact with the blower blade, scratches in the mounting surface, any galling or cracks.
Replace if necessary.

(2) Turbine chamber
Inspect for scratches caused by contact with the turbine blade, flaking due to oxidation of the skin, and deformation due to heat or cracks.
Replace if necessary.

(3) Blower blade
Inspect for scratches caused by contact, and for breakage, corrosion or deformation.
Replace if necessary.

(4) Turbine shaft
1) Inspect the portion around the turbine blade for scratches, breakage, discoloration or deformation, and inspect the shaft for bending, discoloration of journal, abnormal wear, seal ring groove scratches or wear.
Replace if necessary.
2) Measure the outer diameter of turbine shaft journal (A) and seal ring groove width (E), and replace if beyond the wear limit.

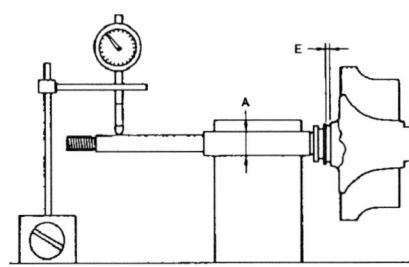

mm (in.)

		Wear limit
Journal outer dia.	A	7.98 (0.3141)
Seal ring groove width	B	1.29 (0.0507)

3) Measure turbine shaft undulation and replace if it exceeds 0.011mm (0.0004in.).

(5) Head shield
Inspect for scratches due to contact, deformation due to heat, and corrosion.
Replace if necessary.

(6) Thrust bushing, oil seal and thrust metal. Inspect for wear, scratches, discoloration, etc., and replace if necessary, even if they remain within the wear limit.

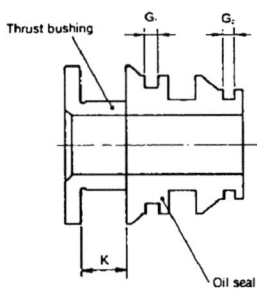

1) Thrust bush
Measure the thrust bush groove clearance (K), and replace if it exceeds the wear limit.

mm (in.)

		Wear limit
Thrust bush groove clearance	K	4.07 (0.1602)

2) Oil ring
Measure the seal ring groove width (G_1), (G_2) and replace if it exceeds the wear limit.

mm (in.)

		Wear limit
Seal ring groove width	G_1	1.31 (0.0515)
	G_2	1.11 (0.0437)

3) Thrust metal
Measure the thrust metal width (J), and replace if it exceeds the wear limit.

mm (in.)

		Wear limit
Thrust metal width	J	3.98 (0.1566)

(7) Floating metal
1) Inspect for abnormal wear, discoloration, scratches, etc., and replace if necessary.
2) Measure the inner diameter (C) and outer diameter (D) of the metal, and replace if either exceeds the wear limit.

mm (in.)

		Wear limit
Floating metal outer dia.	C	12.31 (0.4846)
Floating metal inner dia.	D	8.04 (0.3185)

(8) Bearing chamber
1) Inspect for flaking due to oxidation of the skin, galling and scratches, and replace if necessary.
2) Inspect the round R stop ring for breakage or cracks and replace if necessary.
3) Measure the (B) and (F) dimensions of the bearing chamber as shown in the illustration on the right, and replace if either exceeds the wear limit.

Printed in Japan
A0A1029-9002

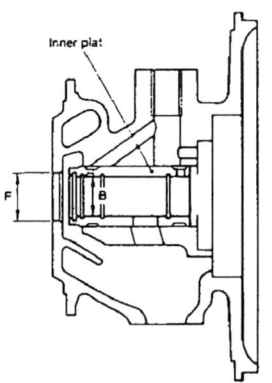

Inner plat

F

B

mm (in.)

		Wear limit
Bearing chamber Inner dia.	B	12.42 (0.4889)
Turbine side seal ring area Inner dia.	F	15.05 (0.5925)

(9) Seal plate
1) Inspect for scratches due to contact, scratches in mounting surface, galling and cracks and replace if necessary.
2) Measure the blower side seal ring area (H_1, H_2) and replace if either exceeds the wear limit.

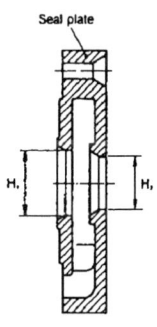

Seal plate

H_1

H_2

mm (in.)

		Wear limit
Blower side seal ring area inner dia.	H_1	12.45 (0.4901)
	H_2	10.05 (0.3956)

(10) Seal ring
Inspect for wear or deformation and replace if necessary.
(11) Inspect retaining plates, bolts and spring washers for deformation and replace if necessary. Always replace the M3 flat screw bend washer and grip washer.

2-6.3 Periodic inspection

(1) Periodically inspect the overall condition of supercharger and the amount of dirt build-up. Inspect at the intervals specified in the following chart.

Item	Interval		
	3 months or 1500 hours	6 months or 3000 hours	12 months or 6000 hours
Rotation of rotor	O		
Rotor play		O	
Disassembly, cleaning and inspection of entire unit			O
Cleaning and inspection of air filter	Every 300 hours		

(2) Inspection Procedure
1) Rotation of rotor
The rotation of the rotor is checked by listening for any abnormal noise when it is rotating. Use a listening bar, placing the tip of the bar firmly against the turbocharger and gradually increasing engine rpm. If a loud noise is emitted every 2 or 3 seconds, rotation is abnormal. The turbocharger should be replaced or repaired as something may be wrong with the metal or rotor.
2) Rotor play
Remove the turbocharger from the engine and check the play in the shaft axial and radial directions as shown below.
3) Rotor play in the shaft axial directi

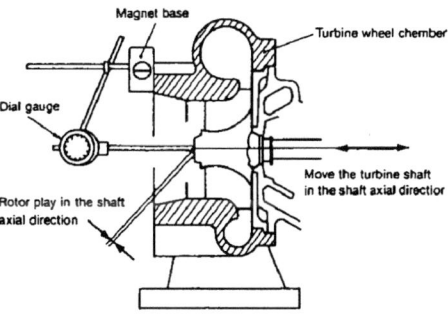

Magnet base

Turbine wheel chember

Dial gauge

Rotor play in the shaft axial direction

Move the turbine shaft in the shaft axial directior

mm (in.)

	Standard	Wear limit
Rotor play in shaft axial direction	0.03 ~ 0.06 (0.0018 ~ 0.0023)	0.09 (0.0035)

4) Rotor play in shaft radial direction.

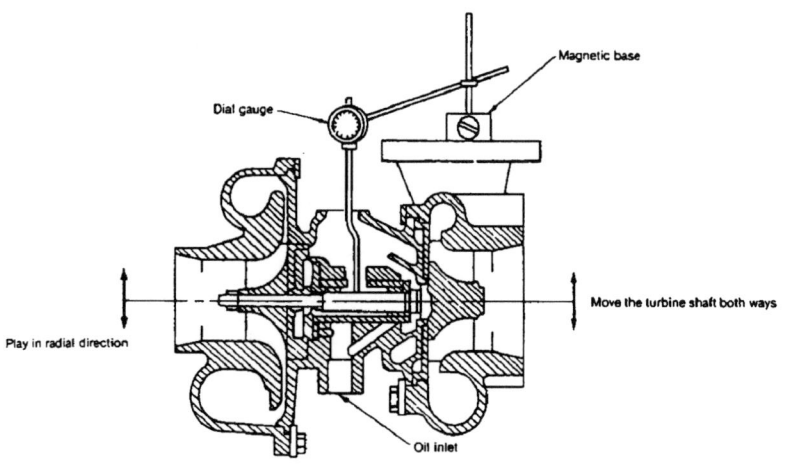

	Standard	Wear limit
		mm (in.)
Rotor play in the shaft radial direction	0.08 ~ 0.13 (0.0031 ~ 0.0051)	0.17 (0.0066)

5) Boost pressure

mmHg(inHg)

Eng. Model	4JH2-TE	4JH2-HTE	4JH2-DTE	4JH2-UTE
	Standard			
Boost pressure	750~900 (29.53~35.43)	925~1075 (36.42~42.32)	885~1035 (34.84~40.75)	870~1020 (34.25~40.16)
Exhaust gas pressure at turbocharger inlet	835 (32.87)	980 (38.58)	875 (34.45)	885 (34.84)
Testing condition	Max. rating output and back pressure 300mmAq (11.81 inAq)			

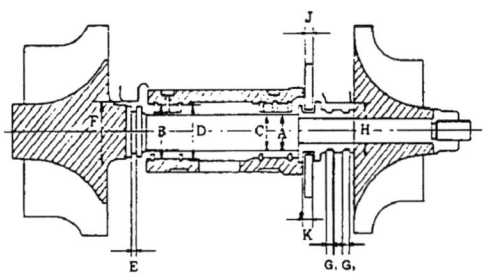

	Items to check	Standard	Wear limit
			mm (in.)
Turbine shaft	Turbine shaft journal outer dia. (A)	7.99 ~ 8.00 (0.3145 ~ 0.3149)	7.980 (0.3141)
	Turbine side seal ring groove width (E)	1.25 ~ 1.28 (0.0492 ~ 0.0503)	1.210 (0.0476)
	Blower side seal ring groove width (G_1)	1.22 ~ 1.23 (0.0480 ~ 0.0484)	1.310 (0.0515)
	Blower side seal ring groove width (G_2)	1.02 ~ 1.03 (0.0401 ~ 0.0405)	1.110 (0.0437)
	Turbine shaft play	0.01 (0.0003)	0.011 (0.0004)
Bearing	Floating bearing inner dia. (C)	8.01 ~ 8.03 (0.3153 ~ 0.3161)	8.040 (0.3165)
	Floating bearing inner dia. (D)	12.32 ~ 12.33 (0.4850 ~ 0.4854)	12.310 (0.4846)
	Bearing set ring inner dia. (B)	12.40 ~ 12.41 (0.4881 ~ 0.4885)	12.420 (0.4889)
Thrust bearing	Thrust bearing width (J)	3.99 ~ 4.01 (0.1570 ~ 0.1578)	3.980 (0.1566)
	Thrust bushing groove dimension (K)	4.04 ~ 4.05 (0.1590 ~ 0.1594)	4.070 (0.1602)
Seal ring fixing area	Turbine side (bearing wheel chamber) (F)	15.00 ~ 15.02 (0.5905 ~ 0.5913)	15.050 (0.5925)
	Blower side (seal plate) (H_1)	12.40 ~ 12.42 (0.4881 ~ 0.4889)	12.450 (0.4901)
	Blower side (seal plate) (H_2)	10.00 ~ 10.02 (0.3937 ~ 0.3944)	10.050 (0.3956)
Play of rotor in shaft axial direction		0.03 ~ 0.06 (0.0011 ~ 0.0023)	0.090 (0.0035)
Play of rotor in radial direction		0.08 ~ 0.13 (0.0031 ~ 0.0051)	0.170 (0.0066)

Tightening torque

	Screw dia. mm	Tightening torque kg-cm (ft-lb)
Turbine chamber set bolt	M6	105 ~ 115 (7.59 ~ 8.31)
Blower chamber set bolt	M5	40 ~ 45 (2.89 ~ 3.25)
Thrust metal set screw	M3	12 ~ 14 (0.86 ~ 1.01)
Seal plate set screw	M3	12 ~ 14 (0.86 ~ 1.01)
Blower blade nut	left hand screw M5	18 ~ 22 (1.30 ~ 1.59)

2-7 Troubleshooting

The engine will not produce the required output if the turbocharger breaks down. If the engine output drops, first check the engine to see if anything is wrong, and then check the turbocharger according to the following procedure if there is nothing wrong with the engine.

2-7.1 Excessive smoke

(1) Insufficient air intake

Cause	Remedy
1) Air cleaner is clogged up.	• Replace or wash the element.
2) Air intake is closed.	• Open to proper position.
3) Leakage from air intake system connections.	• Inspect and repair

(2) Turbocharger does not rotate

Cause	Remedy
1) Build-up of foreign matter in oil on seals inhibiting turbine shaft rotation.	• Disassemble and clean turbocharger and change engine oil.
2) Burned metal • Insufficient oil or clogging up of supply pipe.	• Disassemble turbocharger and repair. • Inspect engine oil supply system, repair any parts as necessary and change the engine oil.
• Oil temperature too high. Rotating parts are out of balance. • Insufficient warming up or sharp stopping.	• Wash or replace rotating parts. • Read operation manual and operate engine accordingly.
3) Turbine or blower blade knocking something or broken. • Excessive rpm • Excessive exhaust gas temperature rise. • Entrance of foreign matter. • Worn metal (bushings) • Improper reassembly	• Inspect engine parts and adjust. • Disassemble and thoroughly remove any foreign matter, inspect the air cleaner, and engine parts, and repair as necessary. • Disassemble turbocharger and repair. • Reassemble

(3) Excessive exhaust gas drag (resistance)

Cause	Remedy
1) Insufficient turbocharger rpm due to leakage of exhaust gas before entry into turbocharger.	• Inspect fittings and repair.
2) Insufficient turbocharger rpm due to deformation of exhaust system piping.	• Repair

2-7.2 White exhaust smoke

Cause	Remedy
1) Oil leaking on blower side or turbine side due to clogging or deformation of return piping.	• Repair or replace pipe.
2) Seal ring excessively worn or broken due to excessive metal wear.	• Disassemble turbocharger and repair.

2-7.3 Excessive oil consumption

Cause	Remedy
1) Seal ring excessively worn or broken due to excessive metal wear.	• Disassemble turbocharger and repair.

2-7.4 Decrease in (engine) output

Cause	Remedy
1) Gas leakage from exhaust gas system. 2) Air leakage from blower side discharge.	• Inspect parts and repair.
3) Air cleaner element clogged up.	• Clean or replace element.
4) Turbocharger dirty or damaged.	• Disassemble turbocharger and repair, or replace.

2-7.5 Poor (slow) turbocharger responsiveness (starting)

Cause	Remedy
1) Carbon build-up on turbine side (blade seal) inhibiting turbine shaft rotation.	• Disassemble and wash turbocharger and replace engine oil.
2) Incomplete combustion.	• Inspect engine fuel system and improve combustion efficiency.

2-7.6 Abnormal noise or vibrati

(1) Abnormal noise

Cause	Remedy
1) Blower discharge air flows back (surges) when the gas line area is considerably reduced due to closing of the turbine chamber nozzle or during acceleration.	• Disassemble and clean turbocharger.
2) Rotating parts knocking something.	• Disassemble turbocharger and repair or replace.

(2) Vibration

Cause	Remedy
1) Fittings connecting turbocharger and exhaust gas piping/oil pipe have become loose.	• Inspect fittings and retighten/repair as necessary.
2) Rotating parts making contact with surrounding parts because of metal failure, or turbine blade or blower blade damaged due to entrance of foreign matter.	• Disassemble turbocharger and repair or replace. Thoroughly remove any foreign matter.
3) Rotating parts out of balance.	• Repair or replace rotating parts.

2-8 Turbocharger blower washing procedure

2-8.1 General

(1) Use "Blower Wash" and clean water to wash the blower.

(2) Make it a general practice to wash the turbocharger blower when the air supply pressure has decreased by about 10 percent. The frequency of this will differ greatly depending on working conditions, but about once a week is generally sufficient.

(3) This prodecure cannot be used for cleaning the entire turbocharger. It must be periodically disassembled and cleaned.

(4) Only remove the inlet cap when washing the blower — it must not be removed under any other circumstances.

2-8.3 Blower washer parts cord

Cord number	Volume × Q'ty
919200—10000	4 liters × 4cans
919200—20000	150 cc × 6 bottles × 15 sets
919200—30000	18 liters × 1 box

2-8.2 Procedure

(1) Run the engine at normal load (3/4 ~ 4/4 load) and apply Blower Wash for 4 ~ 5 seconds with a 20cc standard oiler.

(2) 3 ~ 5 minutes after application of the Blower Wash the dirt will be loosened up. Slowly put in 20cc of water (over about 4 ~ 10 seconds).

(3) Use a vinyl container to feed in the cleaning agent or water. If too much cleaning agent or water enters suddenly there might be a breakdown or breakage of the blower blade. Be sure to feed in the cleaning agent or water at the correct speed.

(4) If there is no change in the air supply pressure or exhaust gas temperature after washing, repeat the washing after about 10 minutes.
No change after washing the blower 3 ~ 4 times indicates that either the blower is extremely dirty or something else is out of order. Disassemble and clean the washer, and take any other action as necessary.

(5) Run the engine under load to dry for at least 15 minutes after feeding in the agent or water.

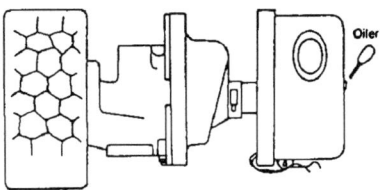

Clean the blower: Every 150 hours

3. Mixing Elbow

3-1 Construction

Threre are two types of mixing elbows for the 4JHE engine: the L and U types. Both types are bolted to the exhaust mainfold.

There are also L and U types for the 4JH-TE, 4JH-HTE and 4JH-DTE engines.

Both are mounted on the turbocharger discharge.

3-2 Mixing elbow inspection

(1) Clean dirt and scale out of the air and cooling water lines.

(2) Repair cracks or damage to welds, or replace.

(3) Inspect the gasket packing and replace as necessary.

For model 4JH2E

(Option)

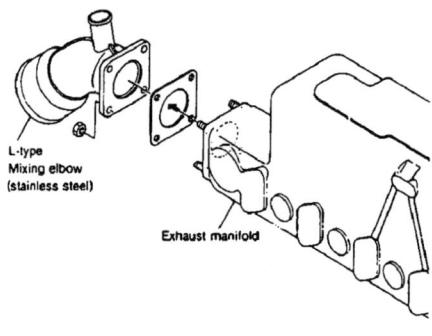

L-type
Mixing elbow
(stainless steel)

Exhaust manifold

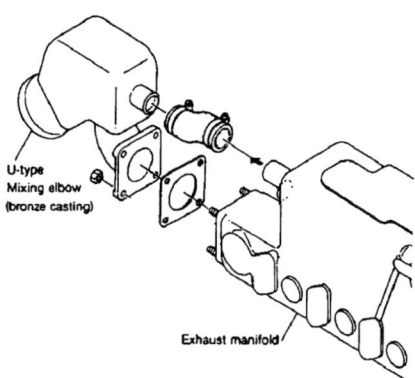

U-type
Mixing elbow
(bronze casting)

Exhaust manifold

For models 4JH2-TE, 4JH2-HTE and 4JH2-DTE

(Option)

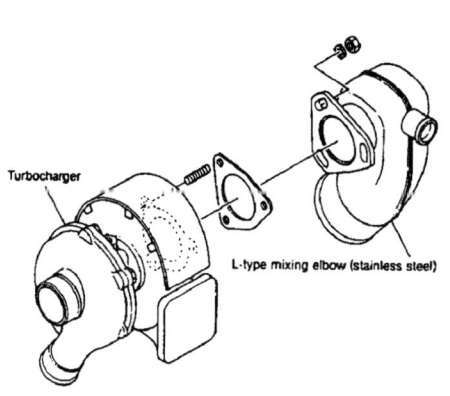

Turbocharger

L-type mixing elbow (stainless steel)

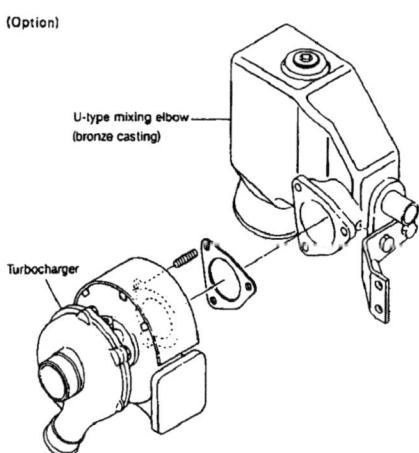

U-type mixing elbow
(bronze casting)

Turbocharger

4-18

LUBRICATION SYSTEM

Printed in Japan
A0A1029-9002

1. Lubrication System

The lube oil in the oil pan Is pumped up through the intake filter and intake piping by the lube oil pump, through the holes in the cylinder body and on to the discharge filter.

The lube oil which flows from the holes in the cylinder body through the bracket to the oil element is filtered and sent to the oil cooler. It returns from the oil cooler to the bracket, the pressure is regulated, and it is fed back to main gallery in the cylinder body.

The lube oil which flows in the main gallery goes to the crankshaft journal, lubricates the crank pin from the crankshaft journal, and a portion of the oil is fed to the camshaft bearings.

Oil is sent from the gear case camshaft bearings through the holes in the cylinder body and cylinder head to the valve arm shaft to lubricate the valve arm and valves.

Oil is also sent from the main gallery to the piston cooling nozzle to cool the piston surface, and is sent through the intermediate gear bearing (oil) holes to lubricate the intermediate gear bearings and respective gears.

Lube oil for the fuel injection pump Is sent by pipe from the main gallery to the fuel injection pump.

Part of the lube oil is sent from the oil cooler discharge to the supercharger in engines fitted with one, and is then piped back from the supercharger to the oil pan.

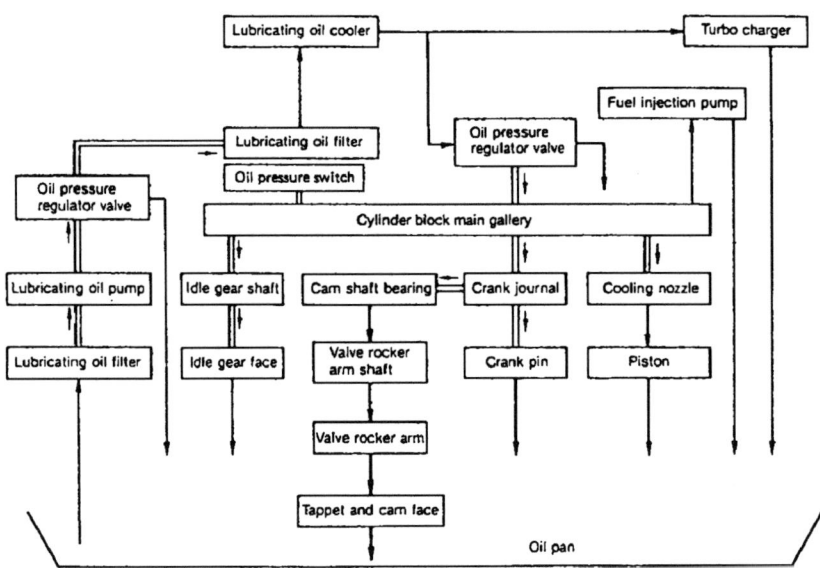

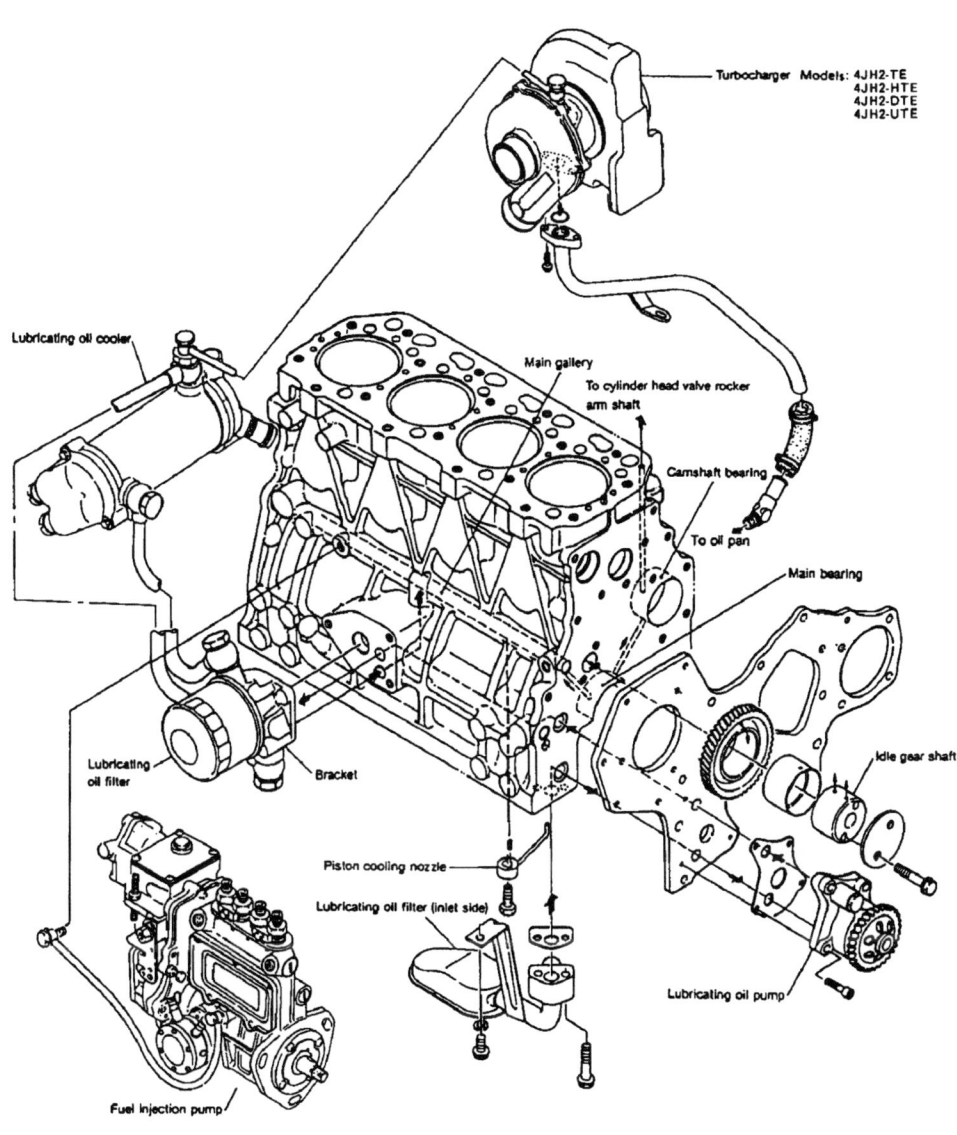

Turbocharger Models: 4JH2-TE
4JH2-HTE
4JH2-DTE
4JH2-UTE

Lubricating oil cooler

Main gallery

To cylinder head valve rocker arm shaft

Camshaft bearing

To oil pan

Main bearing

Idle gear shaft

Lubricating oil filter

Bracket

Piston cooling nozzle

Lubricating oil filter (inlet side)

Lubricating oil pump

Fuel injection pump

2. Lube Oil Pump

2·1 Lube oil pump construction

The trochoid type lube oil pump is mounted on the gear case side engine plate, and the rotor shaft gear is driven by the crankshaft gear.

The lube oil flows from the intake filter mounted on the bottom of the cylinder body through the holes in the cylinder body and engine plate, and out from the holes in the engine plate and cylinder body to the discharge filter.

The lube oil pump is fitted with a pressure regulating valve which maintains the discharge pressure at 3kg/cm².

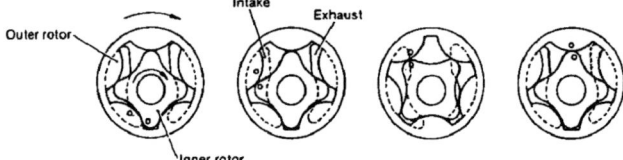

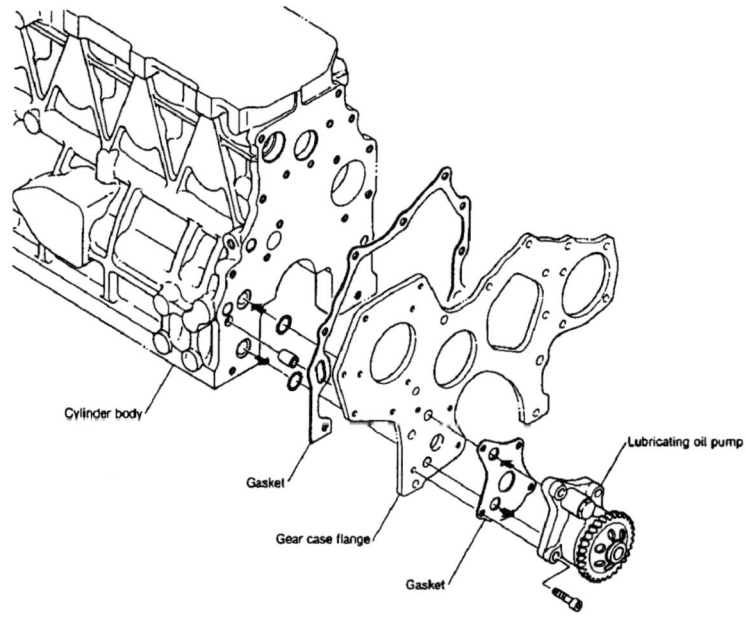

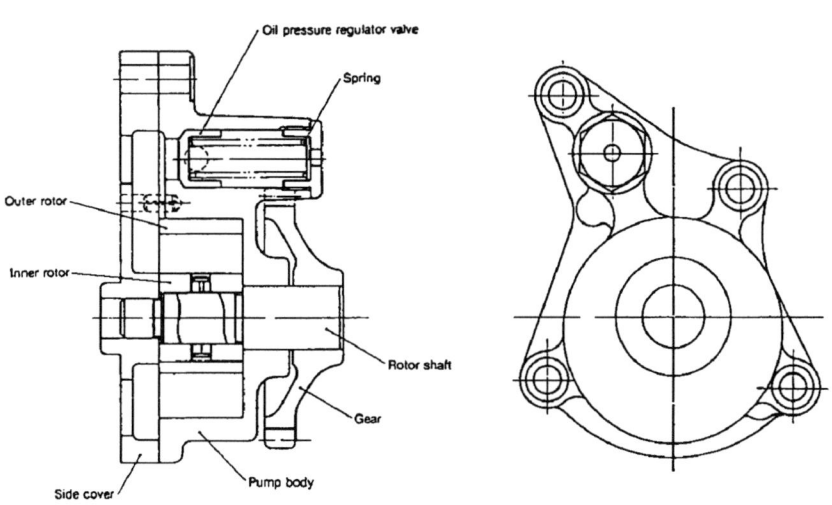

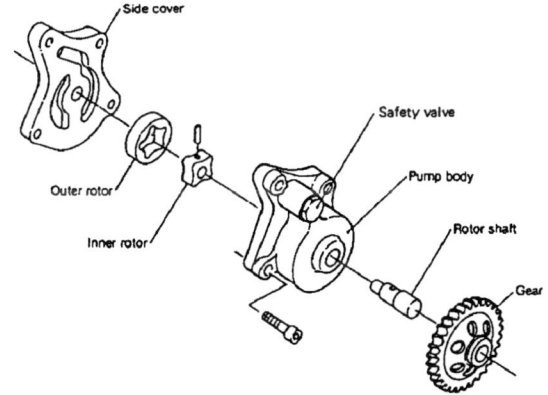

2-2 Specifications of lube oil pump

Engine speed	3600 rpm
Gear ratio (crank gear/pump gear)	28/29
Pump speed	3477 rpm

2-3 Lube oil pump disassembly

(1) Remove the lube oil pump assembly from the engine plate.

(2) The lube oil pump cover may be disassembled, but do not disassemble the rotor, rotor shaft or drive gear. The oil pressure regulating valve plug is coated with adhesive and screwed in, so it cannot be disassembled. These parts cannot be reused after disassembly. Replace if necessary as an assembly.

2-4 Lube oil pump inspection

(1) Clearance between outer rotor and pump body
Insert a feeler gauge between the outer rotor and pump body to measure the clearance, and replace if it exceeds the limit.

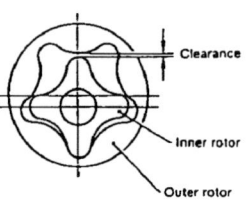

	Standard	mm (in.) Wear limit
Outer rotor and inner rotor clearance	0.050 ~ 0.105 (0.0019 ~ 0.0041)	0.15 (0.0059)

(3) Clearance between pump body and inner rotor side of outer rotor
Place a straight-edge against the end of the pump body and insert a feeler gauge between the straight-edge and the rotor to measure side clearance. Replace the assembly if the clearance exceeds the limit.

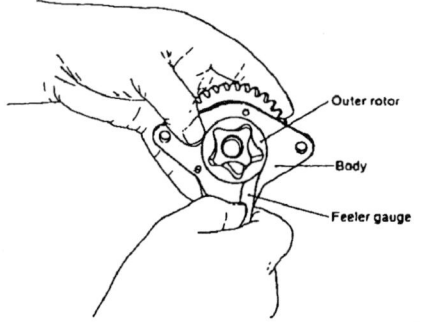

	Standard	mm (in.) Wear limit
Outer rotor and pump body clearance	0.100 ~ 0.170 (0.0039 ~ 0.0066)	0.25 (0.0098)

(2) Clearance between outer rotor and inner rotor
To measure clearance, insert a feeler gauge between the top of the inner rotor tooth and the top of the outer rotor tooth, and replace if it exceeds the limit.

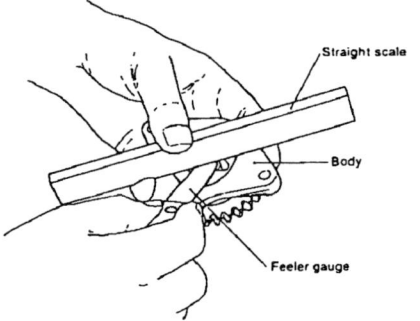

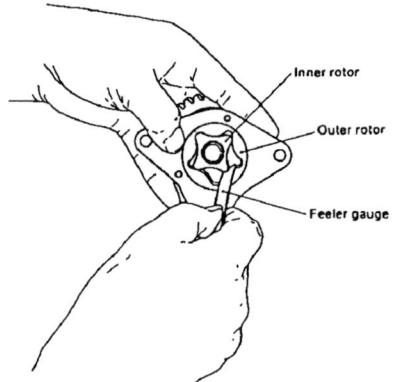

	Standard	mm (in.) Wear limit
Pump body and inner rotor, outer rotor clearance	0.03 ~ 0.09 (0.0011 ~ 0.0035)	0.13 (0.0051)

(4) Clearance between rotor shaft and side cover
Measure the rotor shaft outer diameter and the side cover hole diameter, and replace the entire assembly if the clearance exceeds the limit.

	Standard	mm (in.) Wear limit
Rotor shaft and body clearance	0.013 ~ 0.043 (0.0005 ~ 0.0016)	0.2 (0.0078)

(5) Check for looseness of driver gear/rotor shaft fitting, and replace the entire assembly if loose or wobbly.

(6) Push the oil pressure regulating valve piston from the oil hole side, and replace the assembly if the piston does not return due to spring breakage, etc.

(7) Make sure that the rotor shaft rotates smoothly and easily when the drive gear is rotated.

Turning torque	less than 1.5 kg-cm (0.108 ft-lb)

3. Lube Oil Filter

3-1 Lube oil filter construction

The lube oil filter is a full-flow paper element type, mounted to the side of the cylinder body with the filter bracket. The cartridge type filter is easy to remove.
To prevent seizure in the event of the filter clogging up, a bypass circuit is provided in the oil filter. The bypass valve in the filter element opens when the difference in the pressure in front and behind the paper element reaches 0.8 ~ 1.2kg/cm^2 (11.38 ~ 17.06 lb/in.^{2}).

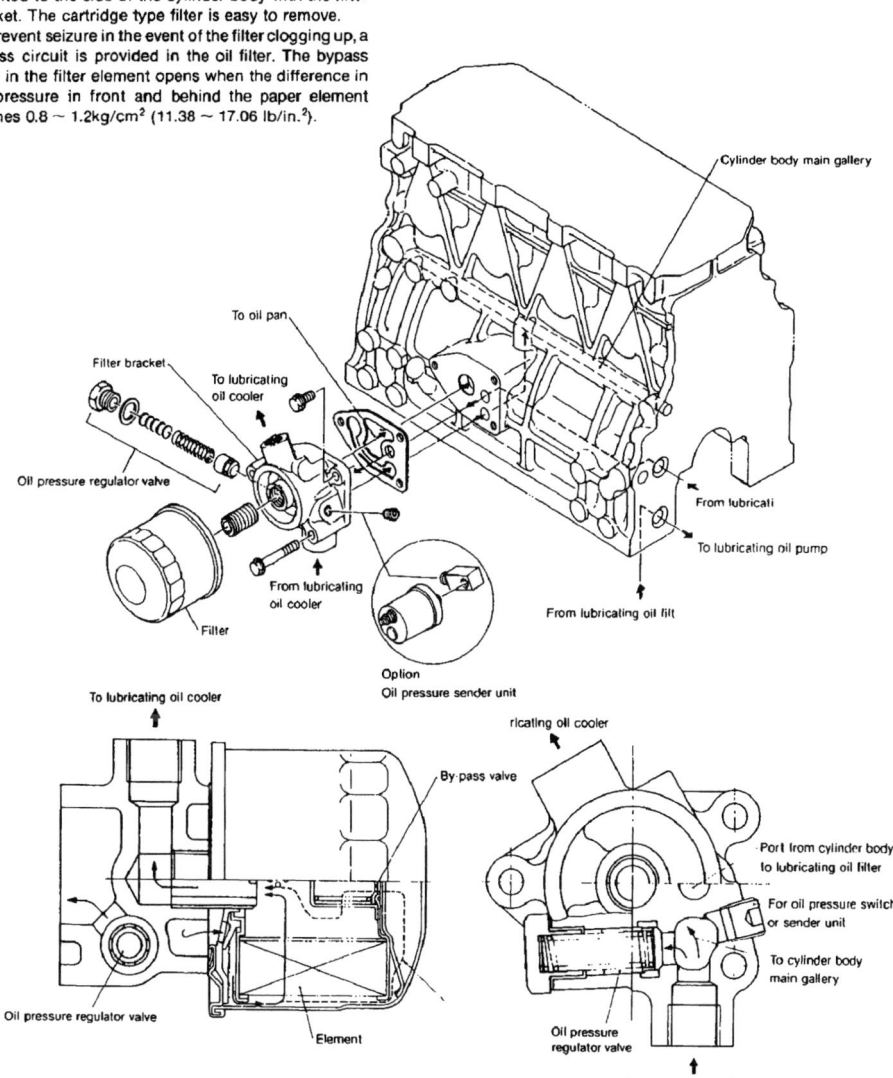

Cylinder body main gallery

To oil pan

Filter bracket

To lubricating oil cooler

Oil pressure regulator valve

From lubricati

To lubricating oil pump

From lubricating oil cooler

From lubricating oil filt

Filter

Option
Oil pressure sender unit

To lubricating oil cooler

ricating oil cooler

By-pass valve

Port from cylinder body to lubricating oil filter

For oil pressure switch or sender unit

To cylinder body main gallery

Oil pressure regulator valve

Element

Oil pressure regulator valve

From lubricating oil cooler

Printed in Japan
A0A1029-9002

Type	Full flow, paper element
Filtration area	0.10m² (155 in.²)
Discharge volume	30 l/min (1830 in.³/min)
Pressure loss	0.3 ~ 0.5 kg/cm² (4.26 ~ 7.11 lb/in.²)
By-pass valve regulating pressure	0.8 ~ 1.2 kg/cm² (11.37 ~ 17.06 lb/in.²)

3-2 Lube oil filter replacement

(1) Period

The paper element will get clogged up with dirt after long hours of usage, and eventually unfiltered oil will be fed to the engine through the bypass circuit. Replace the filter according to the following standard, as the dirt in unfiltered oil will of course have a detrimental affect on the engine.

Oil filter replacement period	Every 300 hours of engine operation

(2) Replacement

1) Remove the lube oil filter with the special tool.
2) Clean the filter mounting surface on the filter bracket and mounting screws.
3) Coat the filter rubber packing with lube oil.
4) Screw in the filter until the rubber packing comes in contact with the bracket mounting surface, and then 2 ~ 3 turns more.
5) Run the engine after mounting the filter, and make sure that there is no oil leakage.

4. Oil Pressure Control Valve

4-1 Oil pressure control valve construction

The oil pressure control valve built into the oil filter bracket controls the oil pressure from the time the lube oil leaves the filter and is cooled in the lube oil cooler until just before it enters the cylinder body main gallery.

When the pressure of lube oil entering the cylinder body main gallery exceeds the setting, the control valve piston opens the bypass hole and lube oil flows back into the oil pan.

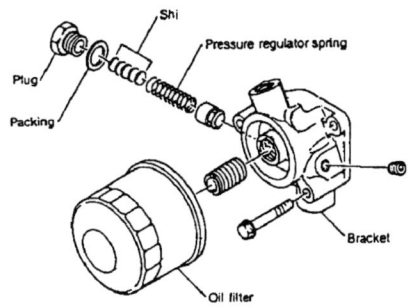

Regulating pressure	3.5 ~ 4.5 kg/cm² (49.78 ~ 64.00 lb/in.²)

4-2 Oil pressure control valve replacement

The control valve has been adjusted and assembled at the factory, so it should not be disassembled without good reason.

If the oil pressure control valve is disassembled due to spring trouble, etc., mount a pressure gauge on the oil pressure sender unit mounting washer, and adjust the pressure with adjustment shims until it is at the specified value.

Shim thickness	Shim part No.
0.2mm (0.0078 in.)	121850-35210
0.5mm (0.0196 in.)	121850-35220
1.0mm (0.0393 in.)	121850-35230

4-3 Vibration preventing damper

The filter bracket hydraulic (oil pressure) sender unit mount is constructed so that a vibration preventing damper can be mounted on it.

The hydraulic sender unit is mounted on the damper.

5. Lube Oil Cooler [Applicable Engine Model 4JH2E

5-1 Lube oil cooler construction

The spiral thread of the inner pipe is in contact with the inner surface of the outer pipe. This forms a spiral passageway.
The lube oil flows through this passageway and is cooled by the cooling water (sea water) flowing through the inner pipe.

There are two such pipes, connected side by side, designed so that the lube oil and sea water flow in the opposite directions.

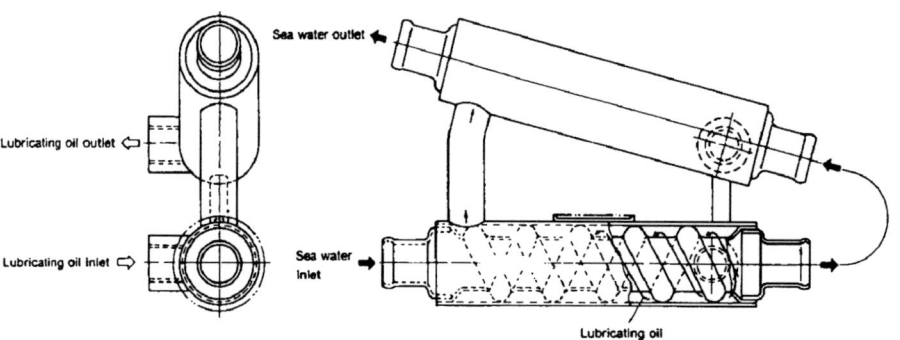

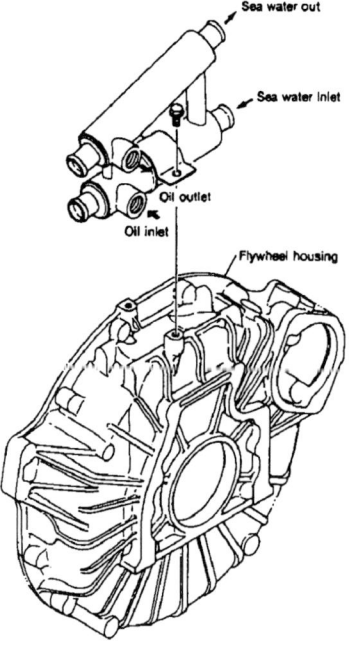

Cooling area	0.0192m² (29.76 in.²)
Cooling water discharge volume	3773 l/hr (230228 in.³/h)
Lubricating oil discharge volume	2160 l/hr (131803 in.³/h)
Lubricating oil temperature at 40°C room air	Model 4JHE: 110°C or below Model 4JH-TE: 115°C or below

5-2 Inspecting the lube oil cooler

(1) Clean the inside of the sea water pipes with a wire brush to prevent the build-up of scale.
(2) If the rubber hose connection or welds are corroded, repair or replace the cooler.
(3) Apply the following water pressures to the sea water and lube oil lines to check for any leakage. Repair or replace the cooler if there are any leaks.

	Test pressure
Lubricating oil circuit	8 kg/cm² (113.78 lb/in.²)
Sea water circuit	4 kg/cm² (56.89 lb/in.²)

4JH2-TE
4JH2-HTE
Lube Oil Cooler [Applicable Engine Model 4JH2-DTE]
4JH2-UTE

5-1 Lube oil cooler construction

The lube oil cooler is comprised of 36 cooling pipes and 9 internal baffle plates.
The lube oil flows through this passageway and is cooled by the cooling water (sea water) flowing through the inner pipe.

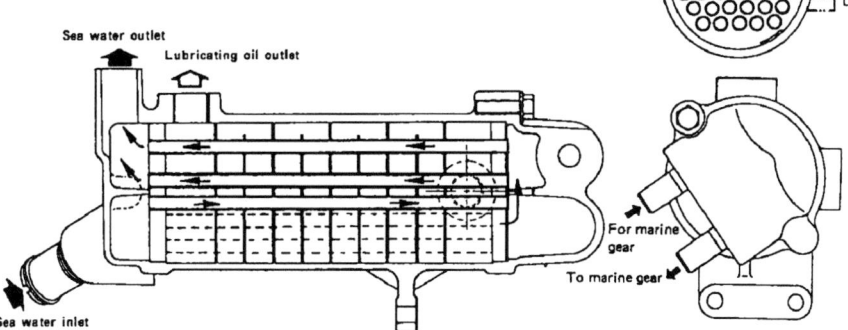

5-2 Inspecting the lube oil cooler

	Test pressure
Lubricating oil circuit	15kg/cm² (213.30 lb/in.²)
Sea water circuit	4 kg/cm² (56.89 lb/in.²)

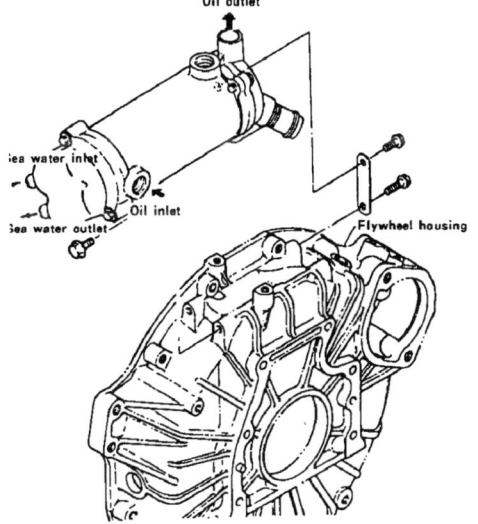

Cooling area	0.165m³ (255.75 in.³)
Cooling water discharge volume	3500ℓ/hr (213570 in³/h)
Lubricating oil discharge volume	2160 ℓ/hr (131803 in.³/h)
Lubricating oil temperature at 40°C room temperature	100°C or below

5-2 Inspecting the lube oil cooler

(1) Clean the inside of the sea water pipes with a wire brush to prevent the build-up of scale.
(2) If the rubber hose connection or welds are corroded, repair or replace the cooler.
(3) Apply the following water pressures to the sea water and lube oil lines to check for any leakage. Repair or replace the cooler if there are any leaks.

	Test pressure
Lubricating oil circuit	15kg/cm² (213.30 lb/in.²)
Sea water circuit	4 kg/cm² (56.89 lb/in.²)

6. Piston Cooling Nozzle

6-1 Piston cooling nozzle construction

A nozzle made from steel piping is mounted on the lower part of cylinder body main gallery. Lube oil from the main gallery is sprayed out in a jet from the steel tip (∅1.77mm (0.0697in.)) of this pipe.
This jet spray cools the piston surface when the piston goes down.

6-2 Inspection of piston cooling nozzle

(1) Check the nozzle tip hole to see if it is clogged up with dirt or other foreign matter, and clean.
(2) Inspect the pipe mounting to see if it is or may become loose or come off due to vibration, etc., and replace if necessary.

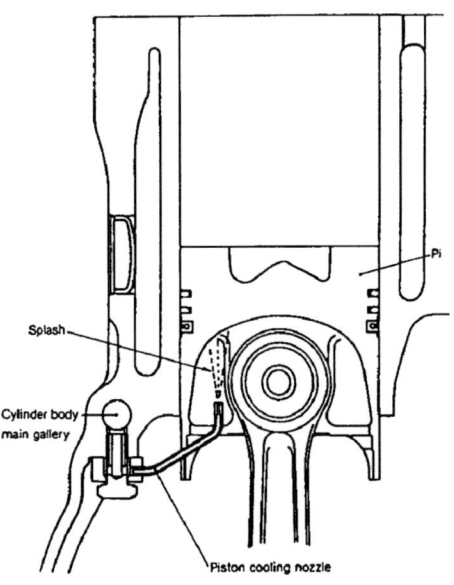

Splash
Cylinder body main gallery
Pi
Piston cooling nozzle

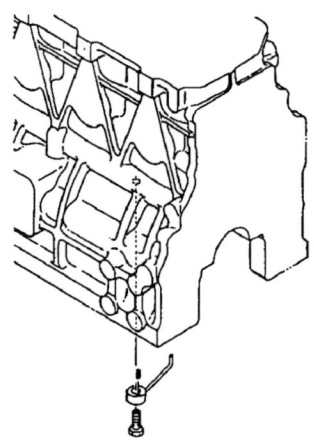

Oil injection volume	1.3 ℓ/min. (79.32 in.³/min)
Oil injection pressure	3.5 kg/cm² (49.78 lb/in.²)

Printed in Japan
A0A1029-9002

7. Rotary Waste Oil Pump (Optional)

A rotary waste oil pump to pump out waste oil during oil
changing is available as an option.
This is a vane type pump. Turning the handle
rotates the vanes and pumps out lube oil.

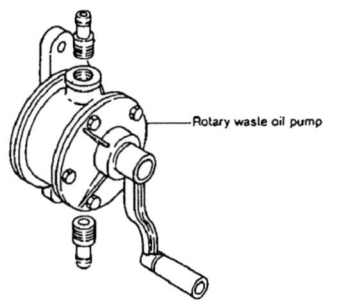

Rotary waste oil pump

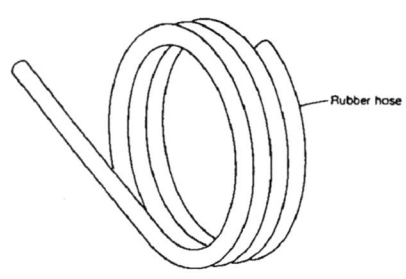

Rubber hose

7-1 Constructi

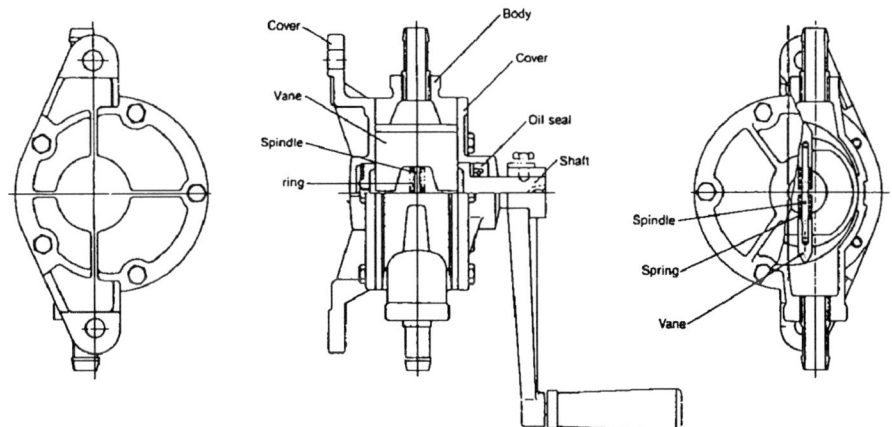

Cover Body
Cover
Vane
Oil seal
Spindle
Shaft
ring
Spindle
Spring
Vane

Rotary waste oil pump

Delivery capacity of one stroke	0.13ℓ (7.93 in.³)
Delivery pressure	1.5 kg/cm² (21.33 lb/in.²) or below
Suction head	less than 1m (39.37 in.)
Part No.	43600-002311

Rubber hose

Inner dia. × length	Ø12 × 1000mm (0.4724 × 39.37 in.)
Part No. of rubber hose	43720-001220

7-2 Inspecting the waste oil pump

(1) Disassemble the waste oil pump and check for spring
breakage or vane damage when there is an extreme
drop in discharge volume, and replace if necessary.
(2) Replace the oil seal if there is excessive oil leakage
from the handle shaft.
(3) Replace the impeller if there is an excessive gap
between the impeller and the covers on both sides of
casing. This will cause a drop in discharge volume.
(4) The hose coupling is coated with adhesive and screwed in. It therefore cannot be disassembled.

COOLING WATER SYSTEM

Printed in Japan
A0A1029-9002

1. Cooling Water System

The cooling water system is of the indirect sea water cooled, fresh water circulation type. The cylinders, cylinder heads, turbocharger and exhaust manifold are cooled with fresh water, and the lube oil cooler air cooler and fresh water cooler (heat exchanger) use sea water.

Sea water pumped in from the sea by the sea water pump cools the intercooler the lube oil in the lube oil cooler and then goes to the heat exchanger, where it cools the fresh water. Then it is sent to the mixing elbow and is discharged from the ship with the exhaust gas.

Fresh water is pumped by the fresh water pump from the fresh water tank to the cylinder jacket to cool the cylinders, the cylinder head and then turbocharger. The fresh water pump body also serves as a discharge passage-way (line) at the cylinder head outlet, and is fitted with a thermostat.

The thermostat is closed when the fresh water temperature is low, immediately after the engine is started and during low load operation, etc. Then the fresh water flows to the fresh water pump inlet, and is circulated inside the engine without passing through the heat exchanger.

When the temperature of the fresh water rises, the thermostat opens, fresh water flows to the heat exchanger, and it is then cooled by the sea water in the tubes as it flows through the cooling pine. The temperature of the fresh water is thus kept within a constant range by the thermostat.

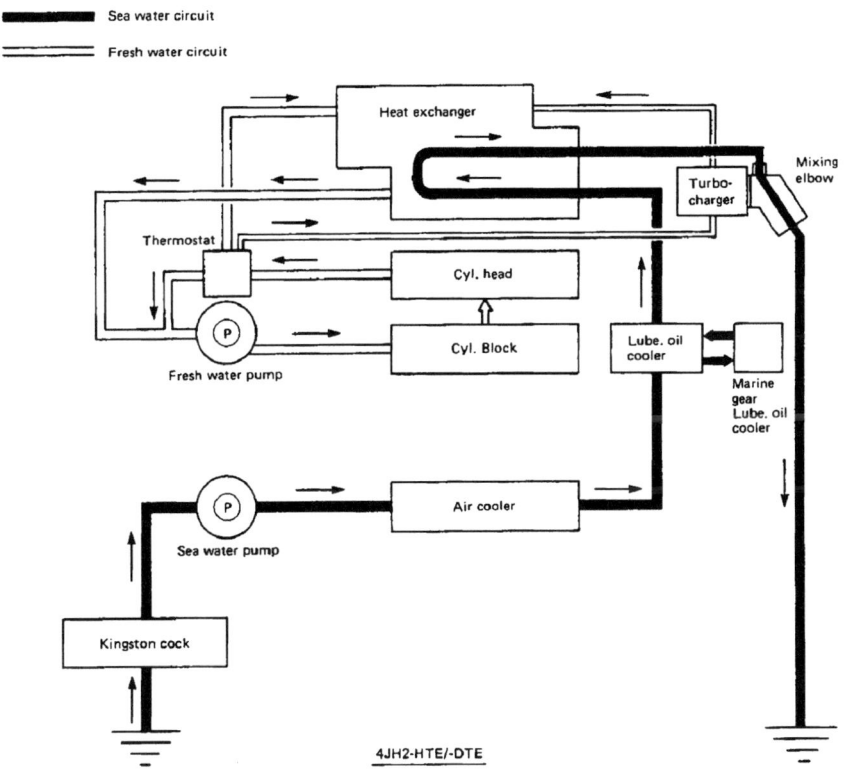

4JH2-HTE/-DTE

Fresh water line [ENGINE MODEL: 4JH2E & 4JH2-TE]

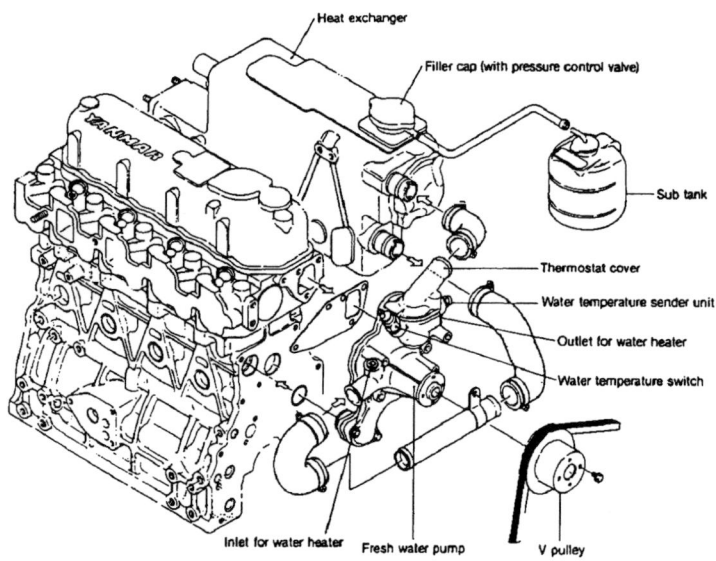

Sea water line [ENGINE MODEL: 4JH2E & 4JH2-TE]

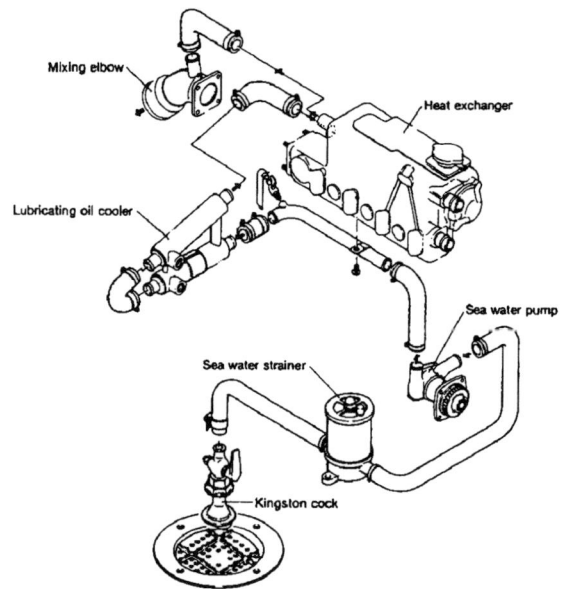

Fresh water line [ENGINE MODEL: 4JH2-HTE, 4JH2-DTE, 4JH2-UTE]

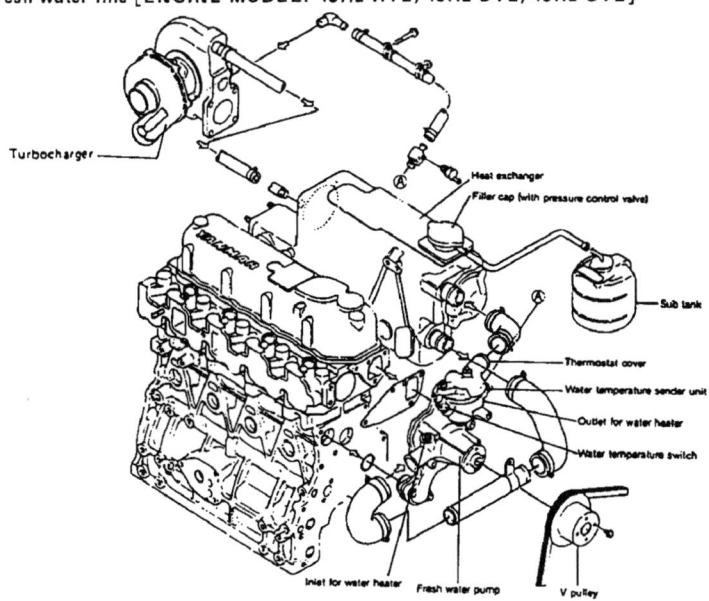

Turbocharger

Heat exchanger

Filler cap (with pressure control valve)

Sub tank

Thermostat cover

Water temperature sender unit

Outlet for water heater

Water temperature switch

Inlet for water heater

Fresh water pump

V pulley

Sea water line [ENGINE MODEL: 4JH2-DTE, 4JH2-UTE]

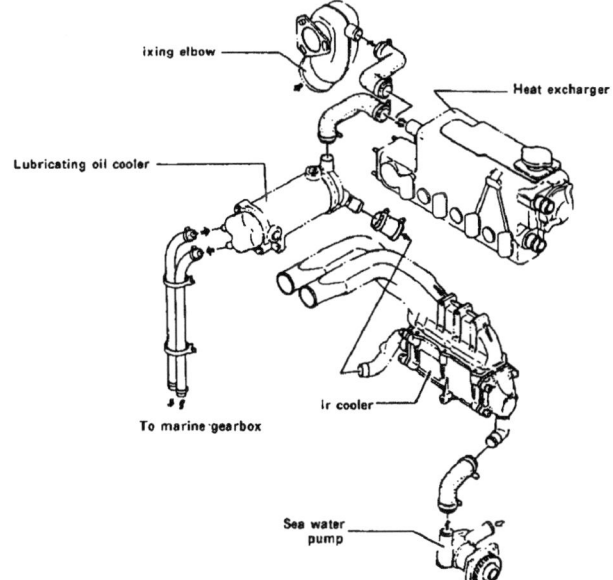

ixing elbow

Heat excharger

Lubricating oil cooler

ir cooler

To marine gearbox

Sea water pump

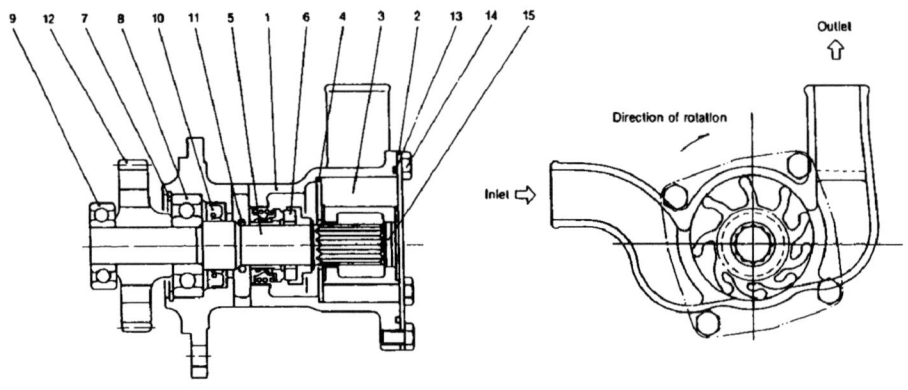

9 12 7 8 10 11 5 1 6 4 3 2 13 14 15

Outlet ⇧

Direction of rotation

Inlet ⇨

1. Sea water pump body	6. Mechanical seal	11. Water seal ring
2. Side cover	7. Circlip	12. Gear
3. Impeller (C-type)	8. Bearing	13. O ring
4. Wear plate	9. Bearing	14. Hexagonal bolt
5. Pump shaft	10. Oil seal	15. Impeller blind cover

2-2 Specifications of sea water pump

Engine speed (max.)	3600 rpm
Gear ratio (crank gear/pump gear)	28/31
Pump speed	3252 rpm
Suction head	0.5m (1.66 ft)
Total head	9.5m (31.16 ft)
Delivery capacity	3250 l/h (198315 in.³/h)

2-3 Sea water pump disassembly

(1) Remove the rubber hose from the sea water pump outlet and then the sea water pump assembly from the gear case.

(2) Remove the sea water pump cover and take out the O-ring, impeller and wear plate.

(3) Remove the mechanical seal side stop ring.

(4) Insert pliers from the drive gear long hole and remove the stop ring that holds the bearings.

(5) Lightly tap the pump shaft from the impeller side and remove the pump shaft, bearings, and drive gear as a set.

(6) Remove the oil seal and mechanical seal if necessary.

2-4 Sea water pump inspection

(1) Inspect the rubber impeller, checking for splitting around the outside, damage or cracks, and replace if necessary.

mm (in.)

	Standard	Clearance at assembly	Maximum allowable clearance	Wear limit
Impeller width	31.6 ~ 31.8 (1.2440 ~ 1.2519)			31.3 (1.2322)
Wear plate thickness	2 (0.0787)	0 ~ 0.3 (0 ~ 0.0118)	0.8 (0.0314)	1.8 (0.0708)
Housing width	33.8 ~ 33.9 (1.3307 ~ 1.3346)			—
Side plate thickness	2 (0.0787)			1.8 (0.0708)

Printed in Japan
A0A1029-9109SP

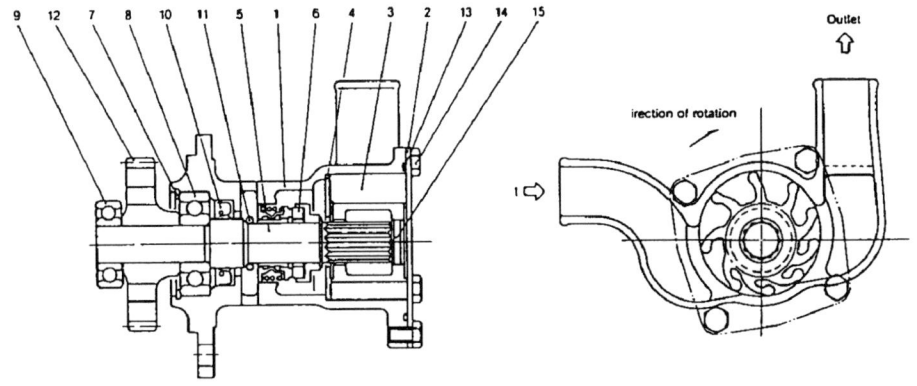

1. Sea water pump body
2. Side cover
3. Impeller (C-type)
4. Wear plate
5. Pump shaft
6. Mechanical seal
7. Circlip
8. Bearing
9. Bearing
10. Oil seal
11. Water seal ring
12. Gear
13. O ring
14. Hexagonal bolt
15. Impeller blind cover

2-2 Specifications of sea water pump

Engine speed (max.)	3600 rpm
Gear ratio (crank gear/pump gear)	28/31
Pump speed	3252 rpm
Suction head	0.5m (1.66 ft)
Total head	9.5m (31.16 ft)
Delivery capacity	3750 ℓ/h (228825in.³/h)

2-3 Sea water pump disassembly

(1) Remove the rubber hose from the sea water pump outlet and then the sea water pump assembly from the gear case.
(2) Remove the sea water pump cover and take out the O-ring, impeller and wear plate.
(3) Remove the mechanical seal side stop ring.
(4) Insert pliers from the drive gear long hole and remove the stop ring that holds the bearings.
(5) Lightly tap the pump shaft from the impeller side and

remove the pump shaft, bearings, and drive gear as a set.
(6) Remove the oil seal and mechanical seal if necessary.

2-4 Sea water pump inspection

(1) Inspect the rubber impeller, checking for splitting around the outside, damage or cracks, and replace if necessary.

mm (in.)

	Standard	Clearance at assembly	Maximum allowable clearance	Wear limit
Impeller width	31.6 ~ 31.8 (1.2440 ~ 1.2519)			31.3 (1.2322)
Wear plate thickness	2 (0.0787)	0 ~ 0.3 (0 ~ 0.0118)	0.8 (0.0314)	1.8 (0.0708)
Housing width	33.8 ~ 33.9 (1.3307 ~ 1.3346)			—
Side plate thickness	2 (0.0787)			1.8 (0.0708)

6-5

(3) Inspect the mechanical seal and replace if the spring is damaged, or the seal is corroded. Also replace the mechanical seal if there is considerable water leakage during operation.

Cooling water leakage	less than 3 cc/h (0.18 in.³/h)
Parts No. of oil seal	129795-42670

(4) Make sure the ball bearings rotate smoothly. Replace if there is excessive play.

2-5 Sea water pump reassembly

(1) When replacing the mechanical seal, coat the No.1101 oil seal and pressure fit. Coat the sliding surface with a good quality silicon oil, taking sufficient care not to cause any scratches.

(2) When replacing the oil seal, coat with grease and i sert.

(3) Mount the pump shaft, ball bearing and gear assembly to the pump unit and fit the bearing stop ring. Be sure not to forget the water O-ring when doing this.

NOTE: Coat the shaft with grease.

(4) After inserting the mechanical seal stop ring, mount the wear plate and impeller.

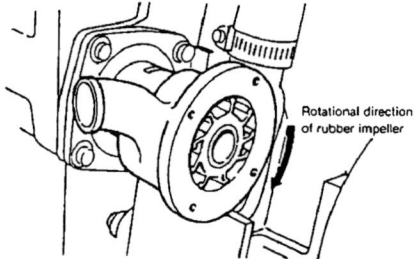

Rotational direction of rubber impeller

NOTE: 1. When inserting the impeller in the pump, make sure that the impeller lies in the proper direction.
2. Coat the inside of pump body impeller housing with grease.

(5) Mount the O-ring side cover.

NOTE: Replace the O-ring.

3. Fresh Water Pump

3-1 Fresh water pump construction

The fresh water pump is of the centrifugal (volute) type, and circulates water from the fresh water tank to the cylinders and cylinder head.

The fresh water pump consists of the pump body, impeller, pump shaft, bearing unit and mechanical seal. The V pulley on the end of the pump shaft is driven by a V belt from the crankshaft.

The bearing unit assembled in the pump shaft uses grease lubricated ball bearings and cannot be disassembled. The totally enclosed mechanical seal spring presses the impeller seal mounted on the impeller side away from the pump body side. This prevents water from leaking along the pump shaft.

As the impeller and pulley flanges are press fit assembled, they cannot be disassembled.

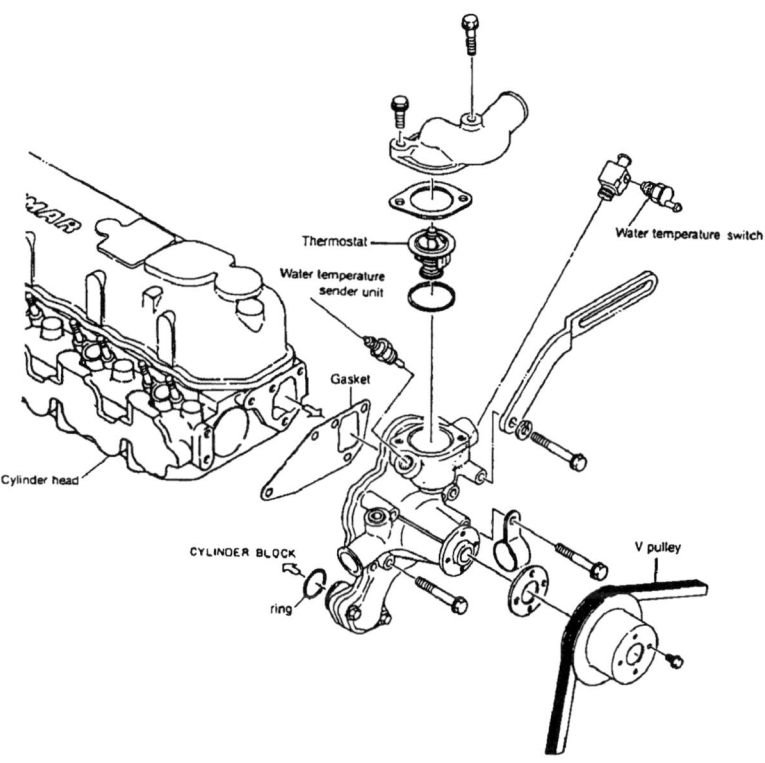

Thermostat

Water temperature sender unit

Gasket

Water temperature switch

Cylinder head

CYLINDER BLOCK

ring

V pulley

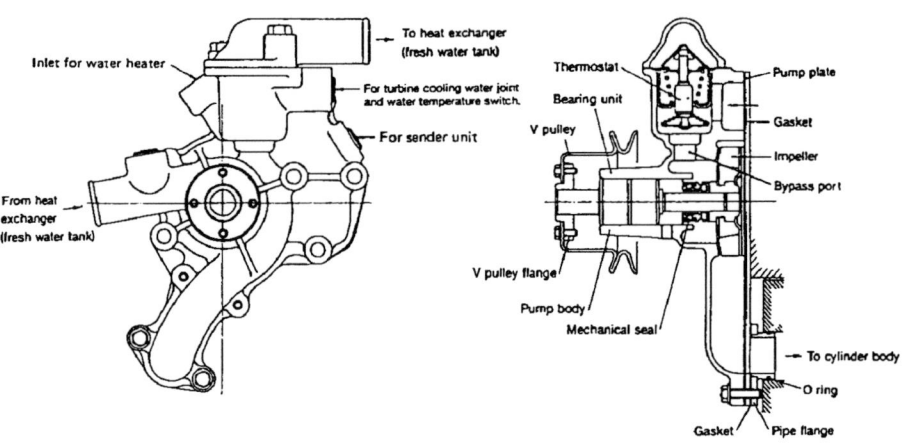

3-2 Specifications of fresh water pump

Crank shaft speed (max.)	3600 rpm
Pulley ratio (crank shaft/pump shaft)	Ø134/Ø120
Pump shaft speed	4020 rpm
Delivery capacity	86.8 *l*/min (5284 in.³/min)
Total head	4m (13.12 ft)

3-3 Fresh water pump disassembly

(1) Do not disassemble the fresh water pump. It is difficult to disassemble and, once disassembled, even more difficult to reassemble. Replace the pump as an assembly in the event of trouble.

(2) When removing the fresh water pipe as an assembly from the cylinder and cylinder head, replace the cylinder intake pipe O-ring.

(3) When the fresh water pump body and cylinder intake flange and/or fresh water pump and pump plate are disassembled, retighten to the specified torque.

Tightening torque for pump setting bolts	70 ~ 110 kg-cm (5.06 ~ 7.94 ft-lb)

3-4 Fresh water pump inspecti

(1) Bearing unit inspection
Rotate the impeller smoothly. If the rotation is not smooth or abnormal noise is heard due to excessive bearing play or contact with other parts, replace the pump as an assembly.

(2) Impeller inspection
Check the impeller blade, and replace if damaged or corroded, or if the impeller blade is worn due to contact with pump body.

(3) Check the holes in the cooling water and bypass lines, clean out any dirt or other foreign matter and repair as necessary.

(4) Replace the pump as an assembly if there is excessive water leakage due to mechanical seal or impeller seal wear or damage.

(5) Inspect the fresh water pump body and flange, clean off scale and rust, and replace if corroded.

(6) Measure the clearance between the impeller and the pump body, and the impeller and the plate.
Measure the clearance between the impeller and the pump body by pushing the impeller all the way towards the body, and inserting a thickness gauge diagonally between the impeller and the body.
Measure the clearance between the impeller and the plate (pump body bracket) by placing a straight-edge against the end of the pump body and inserting a thickness gauge between the impeller and the straight-edge.

Printed in Japan
A0A1029-9002

Measuring clearance between impeller and pump body.

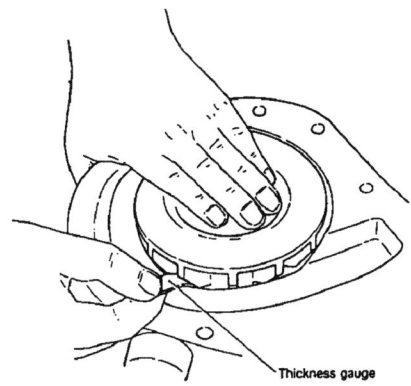

Thickness gauge

Measuring clearance between impeller and pump body bracket.

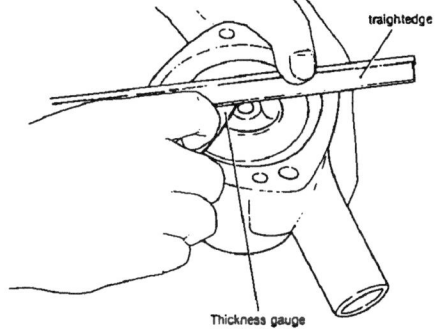

straightedge

Thickness gauge

	Standard	mm (in.) Wear limit
Clearance between impeller and body	0.3 ~ 1.1 (0.0118 ~ 0.0433)	1.5 (0.0590)
Clearance between impeller and plate	1.5 (0.0590)	—

4. Heat Exchanger

4-1 Heat exchanger construction

The heat exchanger cools the hot fresh water that has cooled the inside of the engine with sea water.

The inside of the heat exchanger cooling pipe consists of 36 small dia. tubes and baffle plates.

The sea water flows through the small dia. tubes and the fresh water flows through the maze formed by the baffle plates.

There is a reservoir at the bottom of the cooling pipe which serves as the fresh water tank. There is an exhaust water passageway (line) in the reservoir which forms a water cooled exhaust gas manifold.

The filler cap on top of the heat exchanger has a pressure valve, which lets off steam through the overflow pipe when pressure in the fresh water system exceeds the specified value. It also takes in air from the overflow pipe when pressure in the fresh water system drops below the normal value.

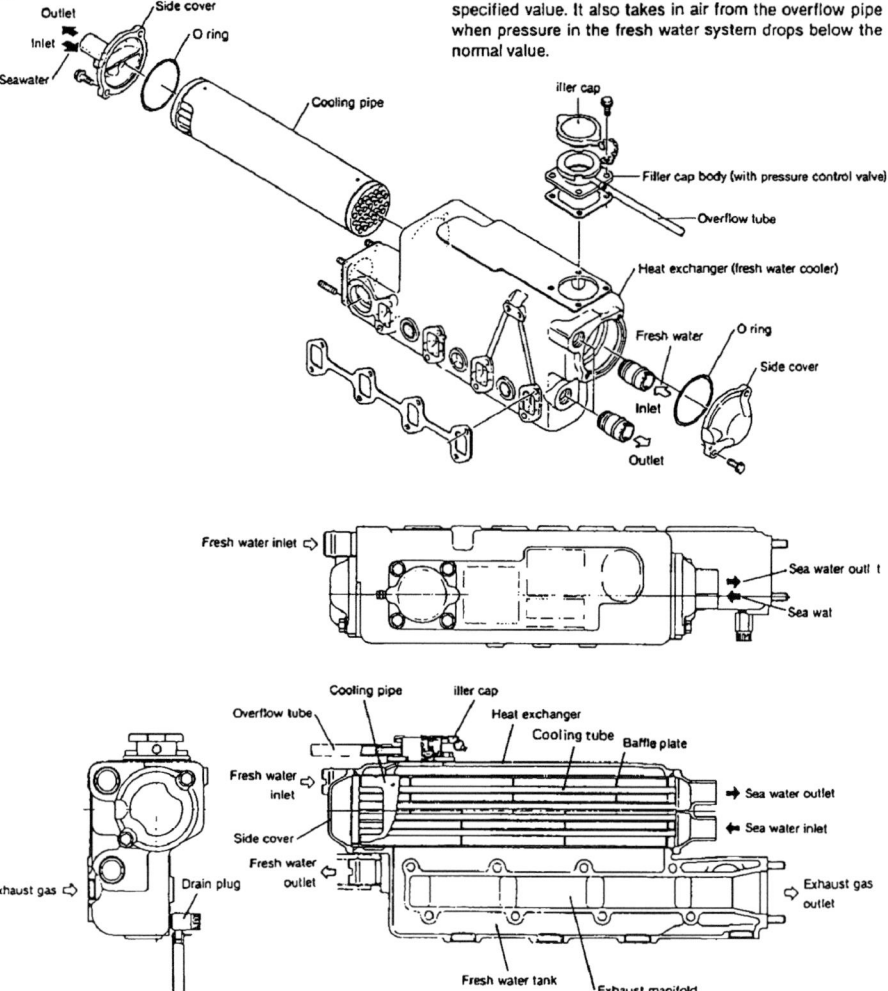

4-2 Specifications of heat exchanger

Model of engine		4JH2E	4JH2-TE	4JH2-HTE	4JH2-DTE	4JH2-UTE
Output(DIN6270 B rating)	HP/rpm	50/3600	62/3600	75/3600	88/3600	100/3600
Pipe dia. × Pieces	mm(in.)	φ6.4/φ 8 ×36 (0.2519/0.3149)		φ6.8/φ 8 ×44, φ4.75/φ6.35× 2 φ0.2677/φ0.3150) (φ0.1870/φ0.2500)		
Radiation area	㎡(in.²)	0.298	0.298	0.416(644.8)	0.416(644.8)	0.416(644.8)
Radiation area/HP	㎡/HP(in./HP)	0.00596(9.24)	0.00481(7.457)	0.00555(8.604)	0.00473(7.333)	0.00416(6.445)
Fresh water discharged volume	ℓ/hr(in.³/hr)	5562(339393)				
Sea water discharged volume	ℓ/hr(in.³/hr)	3500(213570)				
Fresh water flow speed in cooling pipe	m/s(ft/s)	1.53(5.02)				
Sea water flow speed in cooling tube	m/s(ft/s)	1.34(4.39)				
Fresh water capacity	ℓ (in.³)	6.7(408.8)				

4-3 Disassembly and reassembly of the heat exchanger

(1) Remove the covers on both sides and take out the cooling pipe and O-ring(s).

NOTE: *Replace the O-ring(s) when you have removed the cooling pipe.*

(2) Remove the filler assembly.

4-4 Heat exchanger inspecti

(1) Cooling pipe inspection

1) Inspect the inside of the tubes for rust or scale buildup from sea water, and clean with a wire brush if necessary.

NOTE: *Disassemble and wash when the cooling water temperature reaches 85°C.*

2) Check the joints at both ends of the tubes for looseness or damage, and repair if loose. Replace if damaged or corroded.

3) Check tubes and replace if leaking.

4) Clean any scale or rust off the outside of the tubes.

(2) Heat exchanger body inspection

1) Check heat exchanger body and side cover for dirt and corrosion. Replace if excessively corroded, or cracked.

2) Inspect sea water and fresh water inlets and outlets, retighten any joints as necessary and clean the insides of the pipes.

3) Check the exhaust gas intake flange and line, and replace if corroded or cracked.

(3) Heat exchanger body water leakage test

1) Compressed air/water tank test

Fit rubber covers on the fresh water and sea water inlets and outlets. Place the heat exchanger in a water tank, feed in compressed air from the overflow pipe and check for any (water) leakage, (air bubbles).

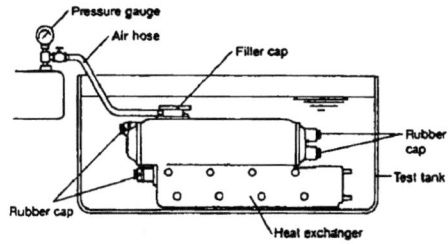

Test pressure	2 kg/cm² (28.44 lb/in.²)

2) Use of the tester

Fit the fresh and sea water inlets and outlets with rubber covers and fill the fresh water tank with fresh water. Fit a pressure cap tester in ·place of the pressure cap, operate the pump for one minute and set the pressure at 1.5kg/cm² (21.33lb/in.²). If there are any leaks the pressure will not rise. If no leaks the pressure will not fall.

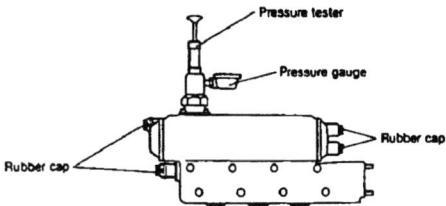

5. Pressure Cap and Sub Tank

5-1 Pressure cap construction

The pressure cap mounted on the fresh water filler neck incorporates a pressure control valve. The cap is mounted on the filler neck cam by placing it on the rocking tab and rotating. The top seal of the cap seals the top of the filler neck, and the pressure valve seals the lock seat.

5-2 Pressure cap pressure control

The pressure valve and vacuum seal both seal the valve seat when the pressure in the fresh water system is within the specified value of 0.9kg/cm^2 (12.80lb/in.^{2}). This seals the fresh water system.

When the pressure within the fresh water system exceeds the specified value, the pressure valve opens, and steam is discharged through the overflow pipe. When the fresh water is cooled and the pressure within the fresh water system drops below the normal value, atmospheric pressure opens the vacuum valve, and air is drawn in through the overflow pipe.

5-3 Pressure cap inspecti

Precautions

Do not open the pressure cap while the engine is running or right after stopping because high temperature steam will be blown out. Remove the cap only after the water has had a chance to cool down.

(1) Remove scale and rust, check the seat and seat valve, etc. for scratches or wear, and the spring for corrosi or settling. Replace if necessary.

NOTE: Clean the pressure cap with fresh water as it will not close completely if it is dirty.

(2) Fit the adapter on the tester to the pressure cap. Pump until the pressure gauge is within the specified pressure range (0.75 ~ 1.05kg/cm^2 (10.67 ~ 14.91lb/in.^{2})) and note the gauge reading. The cap is normal if the pressure holds for six seconds. If the pressure does not rise, or drops immediately, inspect the cap and repair or replace as necessary.

Pressure valve operation

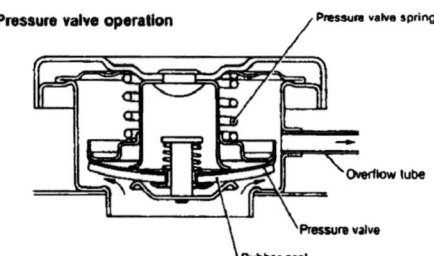

Pressure valve spring

Overflow tube

Pressure valve

Rubber seal

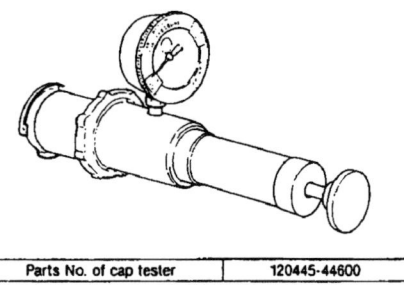

Parts No. of cap tester	120445-44600

5-4 Function of the sub tank

The pressure valve opens to discharge steam when the steam pressure in the fresh water tank exceeds 0.9kg/cm^2 (12.80lb/in.^{2}).

This consumes water. The sub tank maintains the water level by preventing this discharge of water.

The steam discharged into the sub tank condenses into water, and the water level in the sub tank rises.

When the pressure in the fresh water system drops below the normal value, the water in the sub tank is sucked back into the fresh water tank to raise the water back to its original level.

The sub tank facilitates long hours of operation without water replacement and eliminates the possibility of burns when the steam is ejected from the filler neck becase the pressure cap does not need to be removed.

Vacuum valve operation

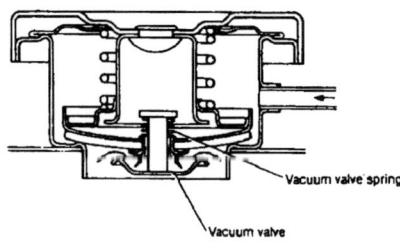

Vacuum valve spring

Vacuum valve

The sub tank, (which will be described later), keeps the water level from dropping due to discharge of steam when the pressure valve opens.

Action of pressure control valve

Pressure valve	Open at 0.9 kg/cm^{2}G (12.80 lb/in.^{2})
Vacuum valve	Open at 0.05 kg/cm^{2}G (0.71 lb/in.^{2}) or below

Printed in Japan
A0A1029-9109SP

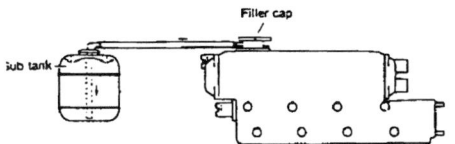

5-7 Precautions on usage of the sub tank

(1) Check the sub tank when the engine is cool and refill with fresh water as necessary to bring the water level between the low and full marks.
(2) Check the overflow pipe and replace if bent or cracked. Clean out the pipe if it is clogged up.

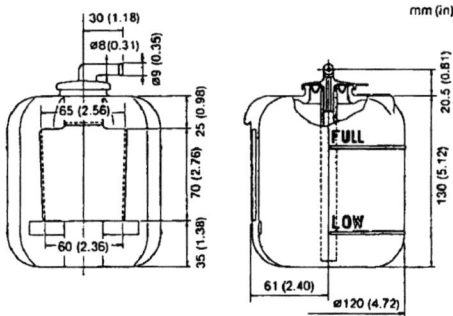

5-5 Specifications of sub tank

Subtank capacity	Overall capacity	1.25ℓ (76.27 in.³)
	Full-scale position	0.8ℓ (48.81 in.³)
	Low-scale position	0.2ℓ (12.20 in.³)
Part No. of subtank		120445-44530

5-6 Mounting the sub tank

(1) The sub tank is mounted at approximately the same height as the heat exchanger (fresh water tank).
(allowable difference in height: 300mm (11.8110in.) or less)
(2) The overflow pipe should be less than 1000mm (39.3701in.) long, and mounted so that it does not sag or bend.

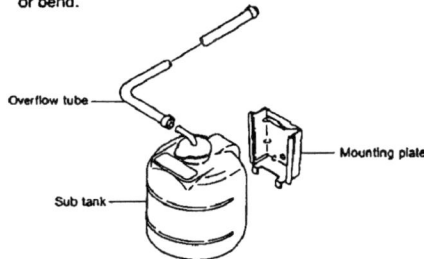

NOTE: *Make sure that the overflow pipe of the sub tank is not submerged in bilge. If the overflow pipe is submerged in bilge, water in the bilge will be siphoned into the fresh water tank when the water is being cooled.*

6. Thermostat

6-1 Functioning of thermostat

The thermostat opens and closes a valve according to changes in the temperature of the fresh water inside the engine, controlling the volume of water flowing to the heat exchanger from the cylinder head, and in turn maintaining the temperature of the fresh water in the engine at a constant level.

The thermostat is bottom bypass type. It is located in a position connected with the cylinder head outlet line at the top of the top of fresh water pump unit.

When the fresh water temperature is low (75.0 ~ 78.0°C or less), the thermostat is closed, and fresh water goes from the bypass line to the fresh water pump intake and circulates in the engine.

When the fresh water temperature exceeds the above temperature, the thermostat opens, and a portion of the water is sent to the heat exchanger and cooled by sea water, the other portion going from the bypass line to the fresh water pump intake.

The bypass line is closed off as the thermostat valve opens, and is completely closed when the fresh water temperature reaches 81.5°C (valve lifts 4mm (0.1575in.)), sending all of the water to the heat exchanger.

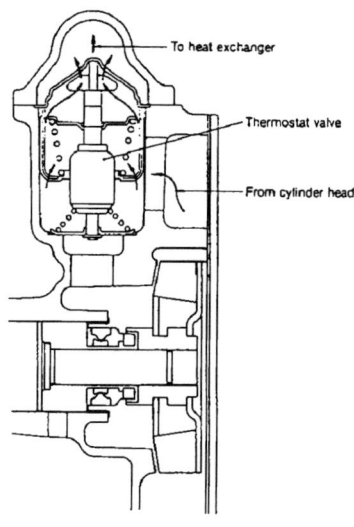

- To heat exchanger
- Thermostat valve
- From cylinder head

When valve is opened (by-pass passage is closed)

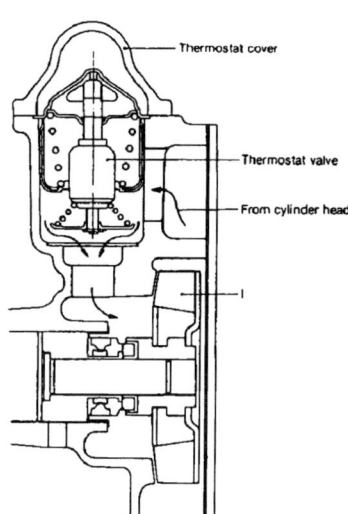

- Thermostat cover
- Thermostat valve
- From cylinder head

When valve is closed (by-pass passage is opened)

6-2 Thermostat construction

The thermostat used in this engine is of the wax pellet type, with a solid wax pellet located in a small chamber. When the temperature of the cooling water rises, the wax melts and increases in volume. This expansion and construction is used to open and close the valve.

6-3 Characteristics of thermostat

Opening temperature	75 ~ 78°C (167 ~ 174°F)
Full open temperature	90° (194°F)
Valve lift at full open	8mm (0.3149 in.)
By-pass valve lift	3.7mm (0.1456 In.)
By-pass valve close temperature	81.5°C (178°F)

6-4 Thermostat inspection

Remove the thermostat cover on top of the fresh water pump and take out the thermostat. Clean off scale and rust and inspect, and replace if the characteristics (performance) have changed, or if the spring is broken, deformed or corroded.

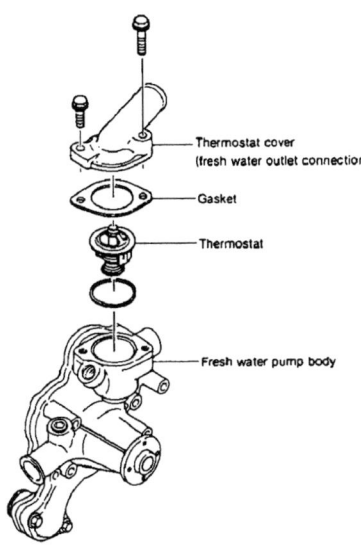

Thermostat cover
(fresh water outlet connection)

Gasket

Thermostat

Fresh water pump body

6-5 Testing the thermostat

(1) Put the thermostat in a beaker with fresh water, and heat it on an electric stove. The thermostat is functioning normally if it starts to open between 75 ~ 78°C, and opens 8mm (0.3150in.) or more at 90°C. Replace the thermostat if it is not functioning normally.

(2) Normally, the thermostat should be inspected every 500 hours of operation, but, it should be inspected before this if the cooling temperature rises abnormally or white smoke is emitted for a long time after engine starting.

(3) Replace the thermostat every year or 2000 hours of operation (whichever comes first).

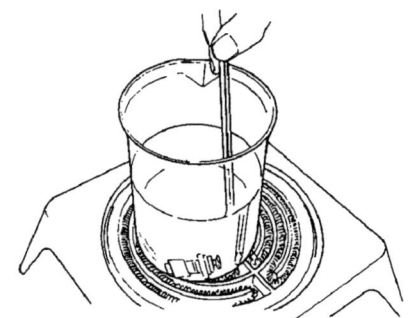

Part No. of thermostat	129470-49800

7. Kingston Cock (Optional)

7-1 Construction

The Kingston cock, installed on the bottom of the hull, controls the intake of cooling water into the boat. The Kingston cock serves to filter the water so that mud, sand, and other foreign matter in the water does not enter the water pump. '

Numerous holes are drilled in the water side of the Kingston cock, and a scoop strainer i installed to prevent the sucking in of vinyl, etc.

7-3 Inspection

When the cooling water volume has dropped and the pump is normal, remove the vessel from the water and check for clogging of the Kingston cock.

If water leaks from the cock, disassemble the cock and inspect it for wear, and repair or replace it.

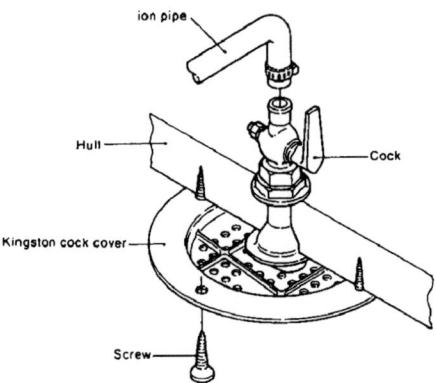

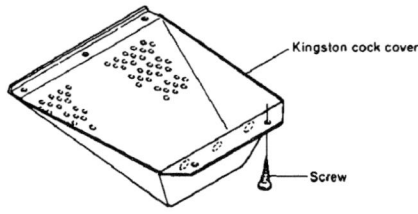

7-2 Handling precautions

Caution the user to always close the Kingston cock after each day of use and to confirm that it is open before beginning operation.

If the Kingston cock is left open, water will flow in reverse and the vessel will sink if trouble occurs with the water pump.

On the other hand, if the engine is operated with the Kingston cock closed, cooling water will not be able to get in, resulting in engine and pump trouble.

Printed in Japan
A0A1029-9002

8. Sea Water Filter (Optional)

When operating the engine in areas where the sea water contains a large amount of mud, sand or other foreign matter, a sea water filter should be provided between the kingston cock and the sea water pump.
Occasionally inspect the sea water filter and clean the dirt and scale off the element. Remove the dirt and sand from the bottom of the filter.

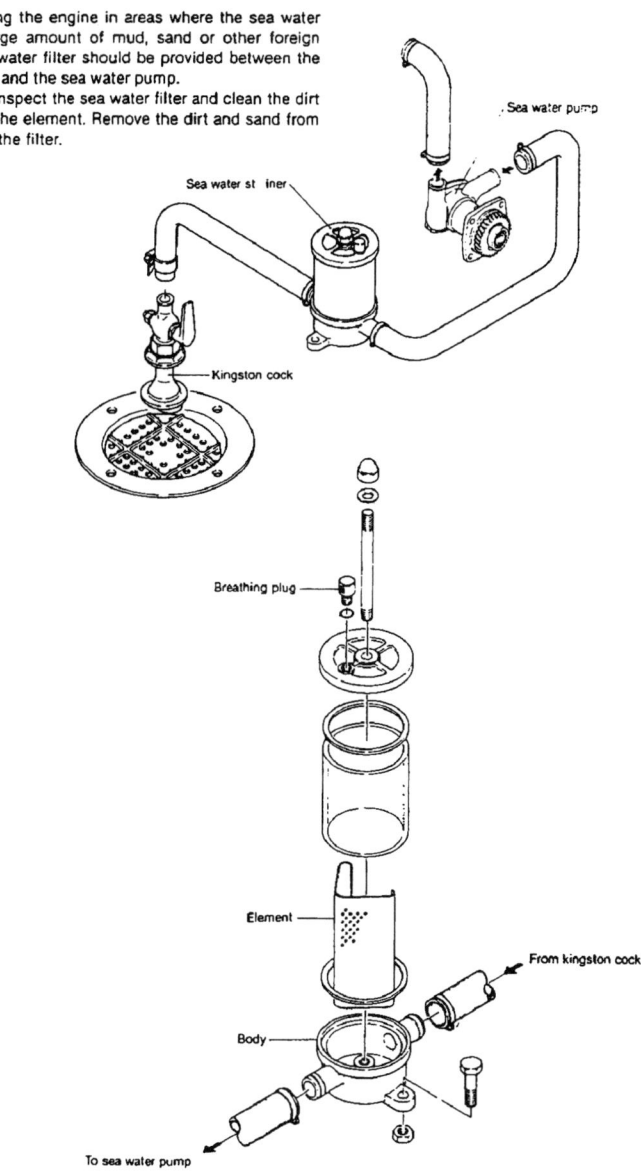

Sea water pump

Sea water st iner

Kingston cock

Breathing plug

Element

From kingston cock

Body

To sea water pump

9. Bilge Pump and Bilge Strainer (Optional)

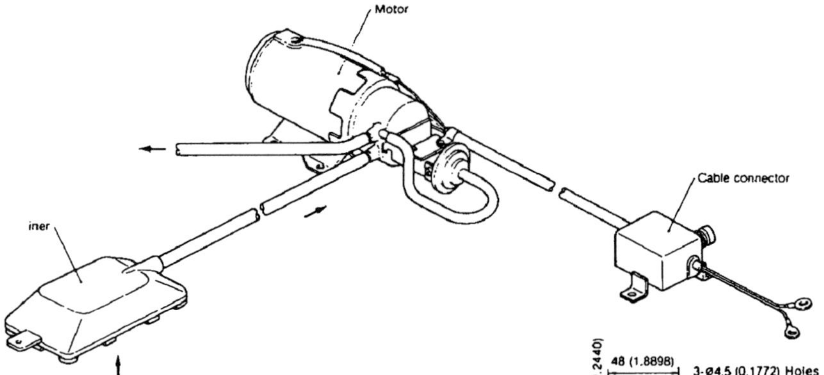

Motor

Cable connector

iner

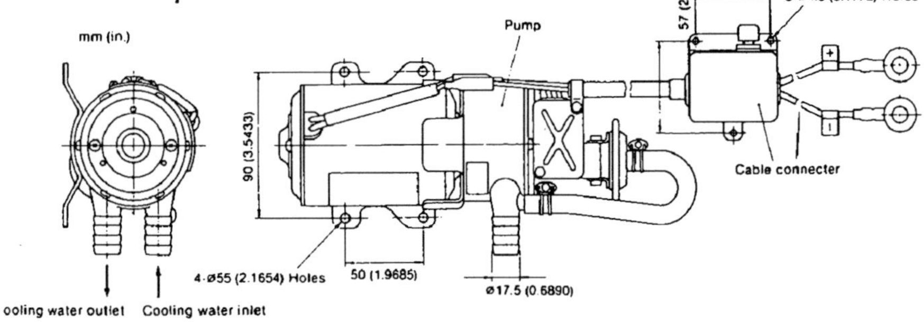

mm (in.)

48 (1.8898)

57 (2.2440)

3-ø4.5 (0.1772) Holes

Pump

90 (3.5433)

Cable connecter

4-ø55 (2.1654) Holes   50 (1.9685)

ø17.5 (0.6890)

ooling water outlet   Cooling water inlet

9-1 Bilge pump

9-1.1 Specifications

Code No.	120345-46010 (with strainer)
Model No.	BP190-10
Rating	60 min.
Voltage	12V
Output	90W
Weight	3.0kg (6.6 lb)

9-1.2 Performance of pump (in pure water)

Suction performance	Voltage	11.5V
	Max. suction lift	1.2m (3.94 ft)
	Suction time	4 sec.
Pumping lift performance	Voltage	11.5V
	Current	8A
	Total lift	1m (3.28 ft)
	Lifting volume of water	17 *l*/min

9-2 Bilge strainer

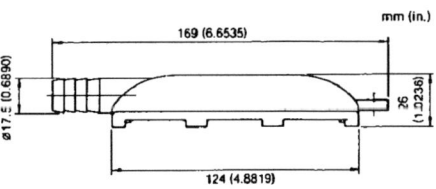

mm (in.)

169 (6.6535)

ø17.5 (0.6890)

26 (1.0236)

124 (4.8819)

Printed in Japan
A0A1029-9002

REDUCTION
AND REVERSING GEAR

Printed in Japan
A0A1029-9002

Marine Gear Model
KBW20/KBW21

1. Construction

1-1 Construction

The Kanzaki-Carl Hurth KBW20 and KBW21 reduction reversing gears were developed jointly by Kanzaki Precision Machine Co., Ltd. a subsidiary of Yanmar and one of Japan's leading gear manufacturers, and Carl Hurth Co.

The KBW20 and KBW21 consist of a multi-disc clutch and reduction gear housed in a single case. They are small, light, simply constructed and extremely reliable.

• The force required to shift between forward and reverse can be controlled by a cable type remote control system much smaller and simpler than other types of reduction reversing gears.

• The friction discs are durable sinter plates, and the surface fo the steel plates are corrugated in a sine curve shape to ensure positive engagement and disengagement and minimum loss of transmission force.

• Because of the special construction of this gear, the optimum pressure is automatically applied to the clutch plate in direct proportion to the input shaft torque.

1-2 Specifications

Engine model			4JH2E			4JH2-TE		
Marine gear model			KBW20					
Reduction system			One-stage reduction, helical gear					
Reversing system			Constant mesh gear					
Clutch			Wet type multi-disc, mechanically operated					
Reduction ratio	Forward		2.17	2.62	3.28	2.17	2.62	3.28
	Reverse		3.06			3.06		
Diection of rotation	Input shaft		Counterclockwise as viewed from stern					
	Output shaft	Forward	Clockwise as viewed from stern					
		Reverse	Counterclockwise as viewed from stern					
Lubricating oil			DEXRON, ATF					
Lubricating oil capacity			1.2ℓ					

Engine model			4JH2-HTE		4JH2-DTE	4JH2-UTE
Marine gear model			KBW21			
Reduction system			One-stage reduction, helical gear			
Reversing system			Constant mesh gear			
Clutch system			Wet type multi-disc, mechanically operated			
Reduction ratio	Forward		2.17	2.62	2.17	2.62
	Reverse		3.06		3.06	
Direction of rotation	Input shaft		Counterclockwise as viewed from stern			
	Output shaft	Forward	Clockwise as viewed from stern			
		Reverse	Counterclockwise as viewed from stern			
Lubricating oil			DEXRON,ATF			
Lubricating oil capacity			1.2 ℓ			
lube oil cooler			Sea-water cooling			

IMPORTANT:
Differences between Marine Gear Models KBW20 and KBW21
KBW 21 is provided with a lube oil cooler (of side cover monoblock construction).
The dimensions of all KBW21 internal marine gear box components are identical to those of KBW20. However, all

KBW21 gears are provided with higher strength through a gear teeth hardening process.
Accordingly, KBW21 can be used both for models 4JHE and 4JH-TE, however, KBW20 cannot be used for models 4JH-HTE and 4JH-DTE since KBW20 is not durable enough for these engine models.

1-3 Power transmission system

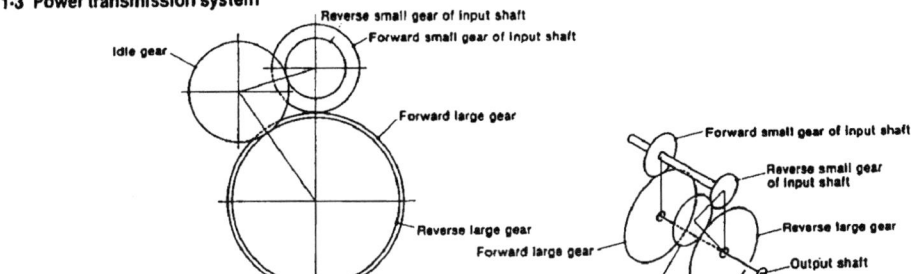

Forward			Reverse			
Number of teeth		Reduction ratio	Number of teeth			Reduction ratio
Forward small gear of input shaft	Forward large gear		Reverse small gear of input shaft	Idle gear	Reverse large gear	
24	52	52/24 = 2.17	18	25	55	55/18 = 3.06
21	55	55/21 = 2.62				
18	59	59/18 = 3.28				

Forward

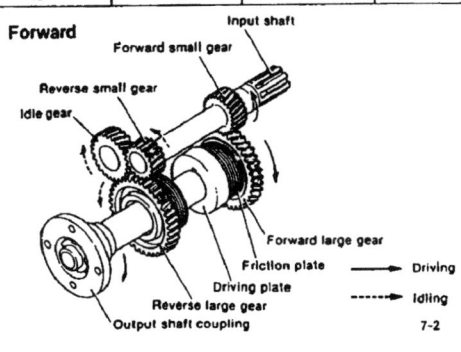

Reverse

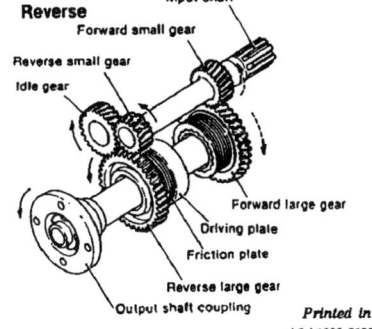

1-4 Drawing

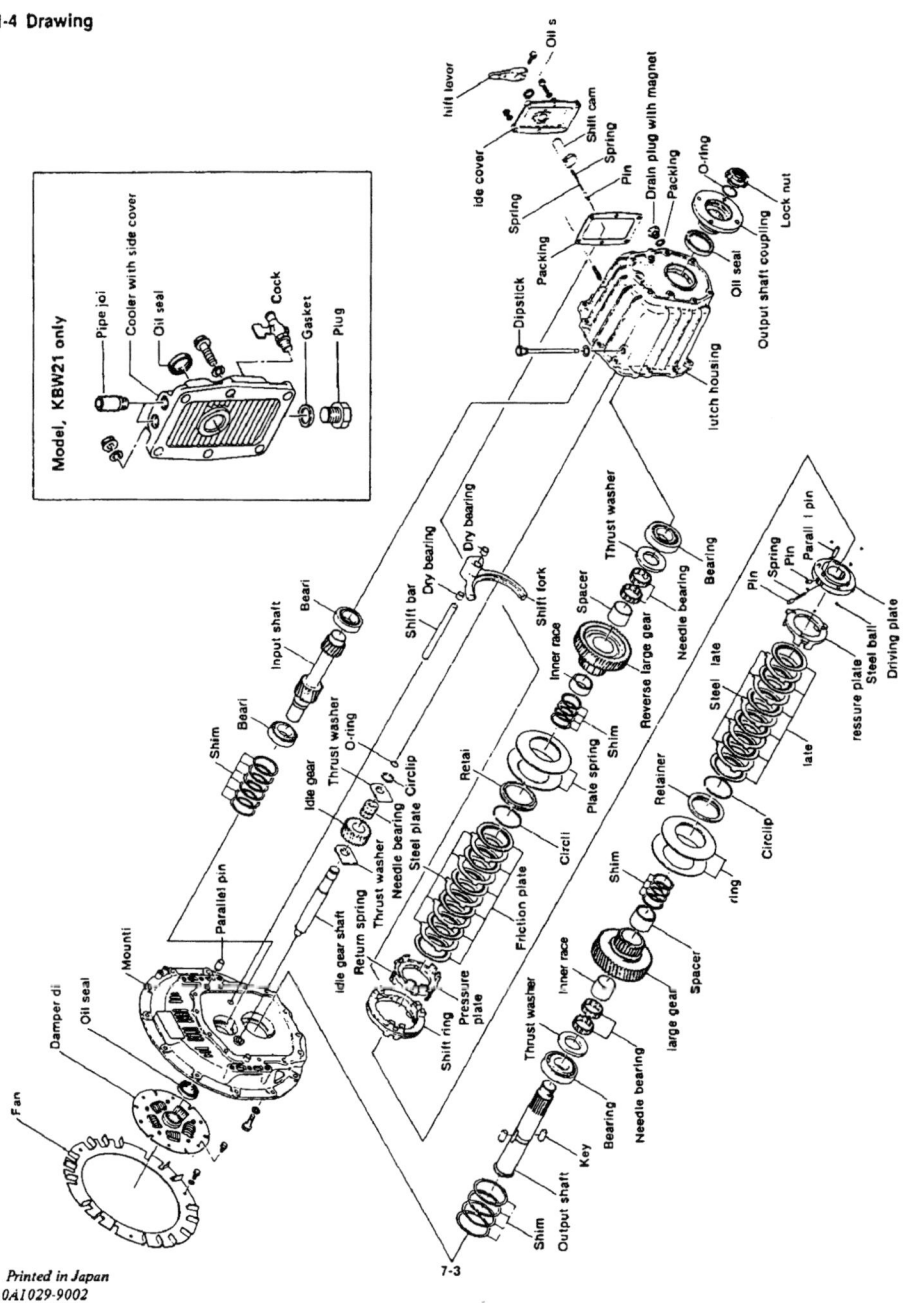

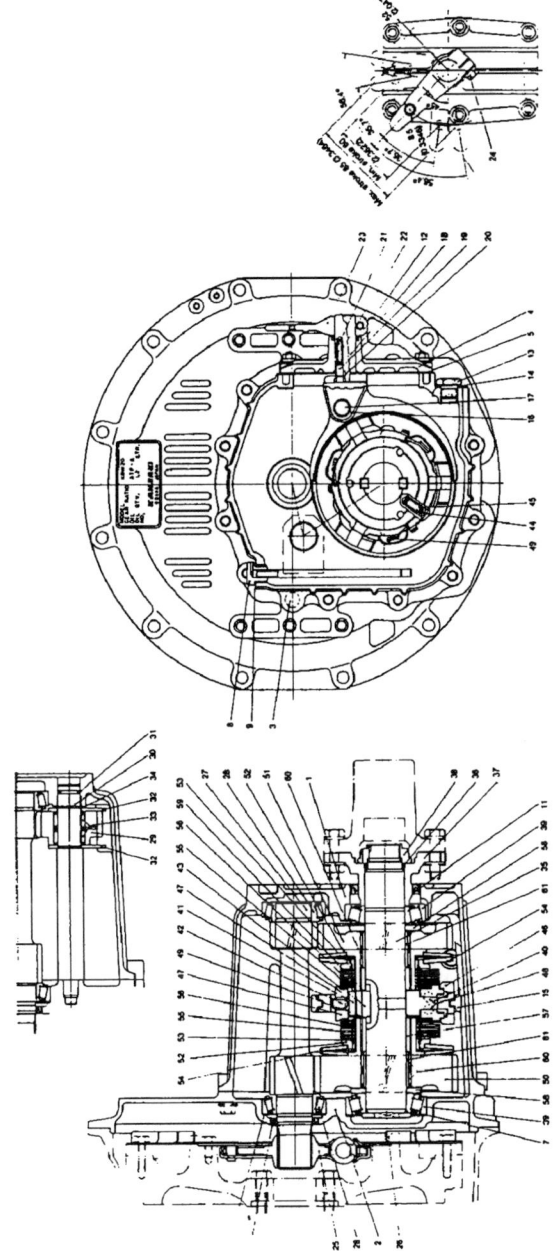

1-5 Cross section

Model: KBW20

1. Clutch housing
2. Mounting flange
3. Parallel pin
4. Side cover
5. Packing
6. Shim (input shaft)
7. Shim (output shaft)
8. Dipstick
9. Packing
10. Oil seal (input shaft)
11. Oil seal (output shaft)
12. Oil seal (shift lever)
13. Plug
14. Packing
15. Shift fork

16. Dry bearing
17. Shift bar
18. Shift cam
19. Pin
20. Circlip
21. Packing
22. Spring
23. Shift lever
24. Dipstick
25. Damper disc
26. Fan
27. Inner shaft
28. Roller bearing
29. Idle gear shaft
30. Idle gear shaft

31. O-ring
32. Thrust washer
33. Needle bearing
34. Circlip
35. Output shaft
36. O-ring
37. Output shaft coupling
38. Lock nut
39. Roller bearing
40. Driving plate
41. Parallel pin
42. Parallel pin
43. Key
44. Key
45. Spring

46. Shift ring
47. Pressure plate
48. Steel ball
49. Return spring
50. Forward gear
51. Forward gear
52. Retainer
53. Circlip
54. Plate spring
55. Friction disc
56. Steel plate
57. Steel plate
58. Thrust washer
59. Shim (output shaft)
60. Needle bearing

1. Inner race

Cross section

Model: KBW21

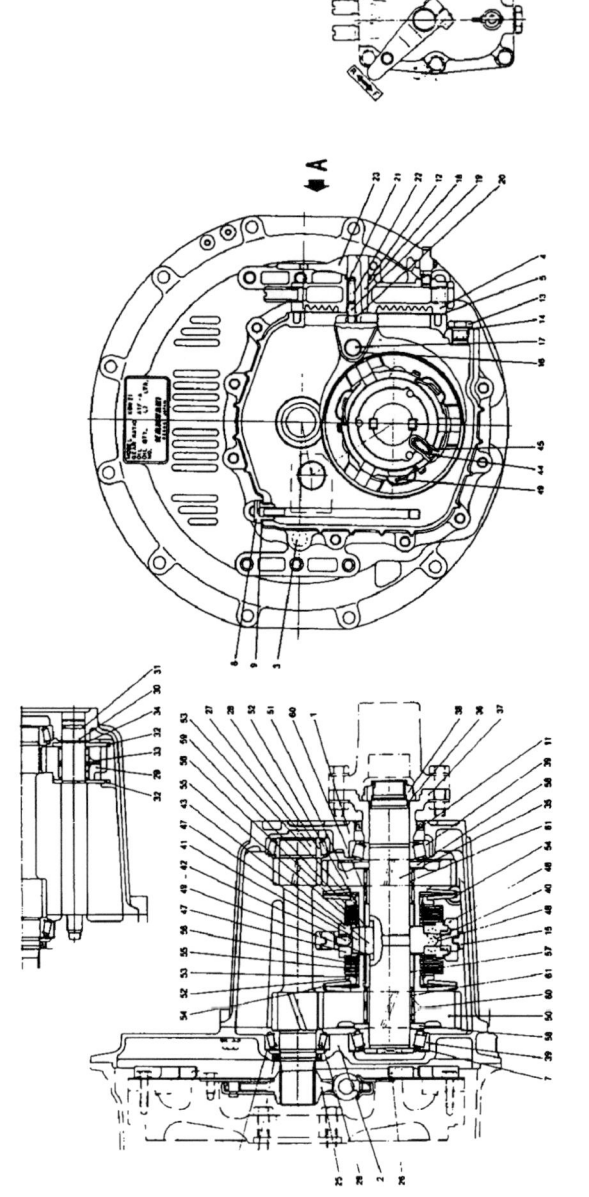

1. Clutch housing
2. Mounting flange
3. Spacer pin
4. Side cover
5. Packing
6. Pulley (input shaft)
7. Shim (output shaft)
8. Dowels
9. Packing
10. Oil seal (input shaft)
11. Oil seal (output shaft)
12. Plug
13. Plug
14. Packing
15. Shift fork

16. Dry bearing
17. Shift bar
18. Shift cam
19. Pin
20. Circlip
21. Spring
22. Spring
23. Shift lever
24. Ball
25. Damper disc
26. Fan
27. Wheel shaft
28. Roller bearing
29. Idle gear
30. Idle gear shaft

31. O-ring
32. Thrust washer
33. Needle bearing
34. Circlip
35. Output shaft
36. O-ring
37. Output shaft coupling

38. Needle bearing
39. Roller bearing
40. Damping plate
41. Parallel pin
42. Parallel pin
43. Key
44. Pin
45. Spring

46. Shaft ring
47. Pressure plate
48. Steel ball
49. Return spring
50. Forward gear
51. Reverse gear
52. Retainer
53. Circlip
54. Spring
55. Friction disc
56. Steel plate
57. Spacer
    Thrust washer
    Shim (output shaft)
    Needle bearing

1. Inner race

2. Installation

2-1 Installation angle

During operation the angular inclination of the gearbox in the longitudinal direction must be less than 20° relative to the water line.

2-2 Remote control unit

This marine gearbox is designed for single lever control to permit reversing at full engine speed (to avoid danger, etc.). Normally, Morse or Teleflex single lever control is employed. During installation, make sure that the remote control lever and shift lever on the marine gearbox are coordinated. Shifting the lever toward the propeller side produces forward movement, while moving the lever toward the engine side causes the vessel to move in the reverse direction.

To connect the linkage, the operating cable must be positioned at right angles to the shift lever when the shift lever is in the neutral position.

The shift play, measured at the pivot point of the shift lever, must be at least 30mm (1.1811in.) on each side (reverse and forward) of the neutral position. Greater shift play has no adverse effect on the marine gearbox. After connecting the linkage, confirm that the remote control and the shift lever on the marine gearbox work properly.

A typical linkage arrangement is illustrated in the figure below.

When the cable is attached to the hole 52mm (2.0472in.) from the center of the rotation of the shift lever, these strokes must be 30mm (1.1811in.)

mm(in.)

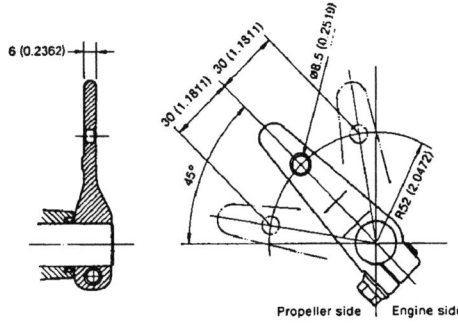

Propeller side | Engine side

Side view of clutch

2-3 Clutch operation force (reference value)

Operation direction \ Operation position	Operation lever position at 52mm (2.0472in.)	Remarks
Engaging stroke	Approx. 9.5kg (20.94 lb)	Engine speed at 1000 rpm
Disengaging stroke	Approx. 11.5kg (25.35 lb)	

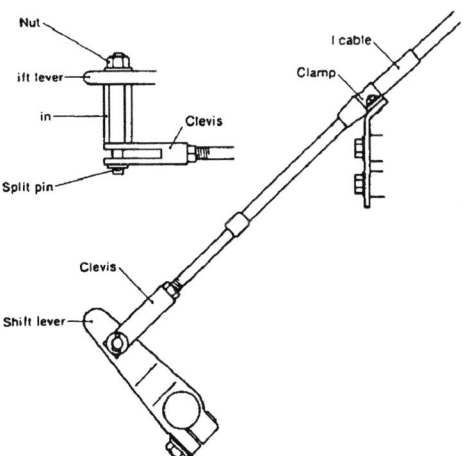

3. Operation and Maintenance

3-1 Lube oil

(1) Oil level

The oil level should be checked each month and must be maintained between the groove and the end of the dipstick. The groove indicates the maximum oil level and the end of the dipstick is the minimum oil level. When checking the oil level with the dipstick, do not screw in the oil filler screw; it should rest on top of the oil filler hole.

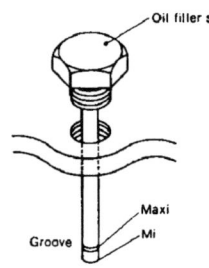

Oil filler screw

Maxi

Groove

Mi

lobe and groove are engaged properly there will be no clearance between the body and the side cover. Use packing when installing the side cover.

—After making sure that the cam lobe and notches are aligned properly, securely tighten all the bolts. After tightening the bolts, move the lever back and forth. Positive contact should be felt and a click should be clearly audible as the gears shift; otherwise, the cam and notch are not properly engaged, and the cover must be loosened and readjusted until proper engagement is achieved.

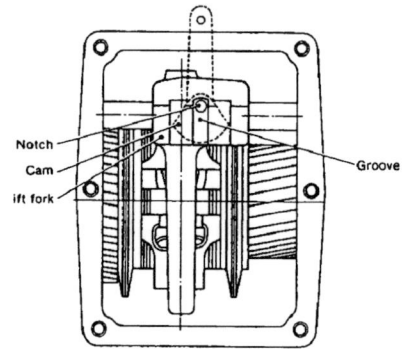

Notch

Cam

ift fork

Groove

(2) Oil change

Change the oil after the first 50 hours of operation, and every 150 hours of operation thereafter. When adding oil between oil changes, always use the same type of oil as i in the marine gearbox.

(3) Recommended brands of lube oil

Supplier	Brand name
SHELL	SHELL DEXRON
CALTEX	TEXAMATIC FLUID (DEXRON)
ESSO	ESSO ATF
MOBIL	MOBIL ATF220
B.P. (British Petroleum)	B.P. AUTRAN DX

3-2 Precautions

Do not stop the shift lever halfway between the neutral and forward or reverse positions. The lever must be set to the neutral position or shifted into forward or reverse in a single motion.

3-3 Side cover

The internal shifting mechanism has been carefully aligned at the factory. Improper removal of the side cover can cause misalignment. If the side cover must be removed, proceed as follows:

—Before removing the cover, put alignment marks on the side cover and the case to facilitate accurate installation.

—When installing the side cover, put the shift lever in neutral so that the cam lobe on the shift lever engages the groove on the internal shift mechanism. When the cam

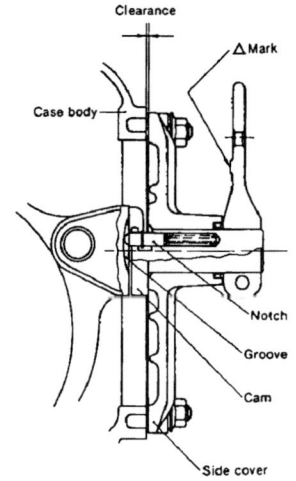

Clearance

△ Mark

Case body

Notch

Groove

Cam

Side cover

4. Inspection and Servicing

4-1 Clutch case

(1) Check the clutch case for cracking with a test hammer.
Perform a color check when required.
If the case is cracked, replace it.

(2) Check for staining on the inside surface of the bearing section.
Also, measure the inside diameter of the case.
Replace the case if it is worn beyond the wear limit.

4-2 Bearing

(1) Rusting and damage
If the bearing is rusted or the taper roller retai damaged, replace the bearing.

(2) Make sure that the bearings rotate smoothly.
If rotation is not smooth, if there is any binding, or if an abnormal sound is heard, replace the bearing.

4-3 Gear

(1) Tooth surface wear
Check the tooth surface for pitching, abnormal wear, dents, and cracks. Repair lightly damaged gears and replace heavily damaged gears.

(2) Tooth surface contact
Check the tooth surface contact. The amount of tooth surface contact between the tooth crest and tooth flank must be at least 70% of the tooth width.

(3) Backlash
Measure the backlash of each gear, and replace the gear when it is worn beyond the wear limit.

mm (in.)

	Standard	Wear limit
Input shaft forward gear and output shaft forward gear	0.1 ~ 0.2 (0.0039 ~ 0.0078)	0.3 (0.0118)
Input shaft reverse gear and intermediate gear	0.1 ~ 0.2 (0.0039 ~ 0.0078)	0.3 (0.0118)
Intermediate gear and output shaft reverse gear	0.1 ~ 0.2 (0.0039 ~ 0.0078)	0.3 (0.0118)

(4) Forward/reverse gear spline
1) Check the spline for damage and cracking.
2) Step wear of spline
Step wear depth limit:
0.1mm (0.0040in.)

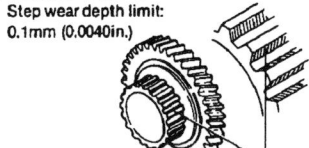
Step wear of spli

(5) Forward/reverse gear needle bearing
When an abnormal sound is produced at the needle bearing, visually inspect the rollers; replace the bearing if the rollers are faulty.

Rollers

4-4 Steel plate

(1) Burning, scratching, cracking
Replace any steel plates that are discolored or cracked.

(2) Warping measurement

mm (in.)

	Standard	Wear limit
Warping	1.49 ~ 1.70 (0.0586 ~ 0.0669)	1.4 (0.0551)

(3) Steel plate pawl width measurement

Pawl

Measure the width of the steel plate pawl and the width of the pressure plate; replace the plate when the clearance exceeds the wear limit.

Steel plate width
Wear must be under 0.2mm (0.0079 in.)

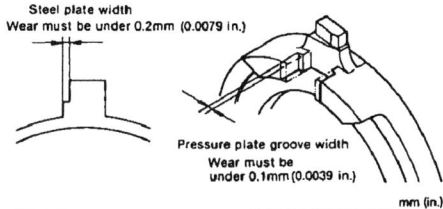

Pressure plate groove width
Wear must be under 0.1mm (0.0039 in.)

mm (in.)

	Standard	Wear limit
Steel plate width	11.8 ~ 12.0 (0.4645 ~ 0.4724)	Worn 0.2 (0.0078)
Pressure plate groove	12.0 ~ 12.1 (0.4724 ~ 0.4763)	Worn 0.1 (0.0039)
Clearance	0 ~ 0.3 (0 ~ 0.0118)	0.3 ~ 0.6 (0.0118 ~ 0.0236)

4-5 Friction plate

(1) Check the friction plate for burning, scoring, or cracking. Repair the plate when the damage is light and replace the plate if the damage is heavy.

(2) Friction surface wear
Measure the thickness of the friction plate, and replace the plate when it is worn beyond the wear limit.

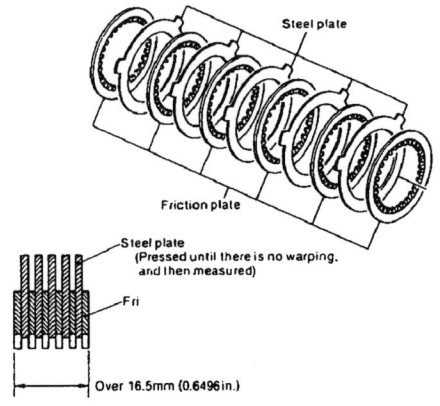

Steel plate

Friction plate

Steel plate
(Pressed until there is no warping, and then measured)

Fri

Over 16.5mm (0.6496 in.)

mm (in.)

	Standard	Wear limit
Friction plate thickness	1.65 ~ 1.70 (0.0649 ~ 0.0669)	1.5 (0.0590)

The assembled friction plate and steel plate dimensi must be over 16.5mm (0.6496in.).

Both sides of the friction plate have a 0.35mm (0.0138in.) copper sintered layer. Replace the friction plate when this layer is worn more than 0.2mm (0.0079in.) on one side (standard thickness 1.65 ~ 1.70 (0.0650 ~ 0.0670in.)). However, the sum of the wear of the six friction plates must not exceed 1.2mm (0.0472in.). When this value is exceeded, replace all friction plates. In unavoidable circumstances, it is permissible to replace only the friction plate with the greatest amount of wear.

(3) Friction plate and gear spline back clearance
Measure the clearance between the friction plate spline collar and the output shaft gear spline, and replace the plate or spline when they are worn beyond the wear limit.

mm (in.)

	Standard	Wear limit
Standard backlash	0.20 ~ 0.61 (0.0078 ~ 0.0240)	0.9 (0.0354)

4-6 Pressure plate

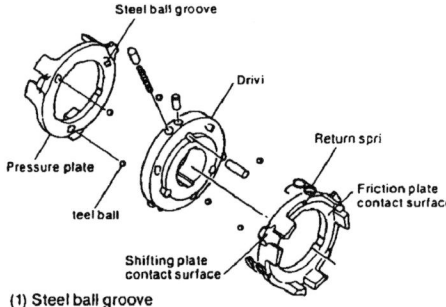

Steel ball groove

Drivi

Return spri

Pressure plate

teel ball

Friction plate contact surface

Shifting plate contact surface

(1) Steel ball groove
Check the steel ball groove for stains and wear. Replace the pressure plate if the groove is noticeably worn.

(2) Friction plate contact surface
Check the contact face for stains and damage.

(3) Shifting plate contact surface

(4) Worn parts measurement

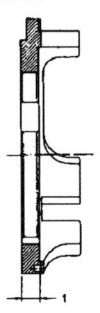

mm (in.)

	Standard	Wear limit
Thickness: t	8.0 ~ 8.1 (0.3149 ~ 0.3188)	7.9 (0.3110)

(5) Return spring permanent strain.
Make sure the length (free length) is within the values specified in the figure.

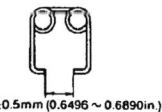

17 ±0.5mm (0.6496 ~ 0.6890in.)

4·7 Driving plate

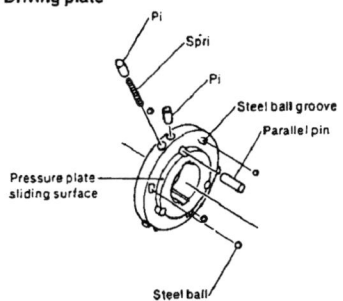

(1) Check the key groove for scoring and cracking, and the output shaft fitting section for burning. Repair if the damage is light and replace the driving plate if the damage is heavy.

(2) Outside diameter of pressure plate sliding part; others

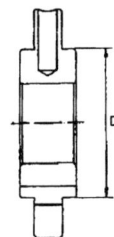

mm (in.)

	Standard	Wear limit
Outside diameter: D	Ø68.366 ~ 68.440 (2.6915 ~ 2.6944)	Ø68.3 (2.6889)

(3) Steel ball groove wear and stains.
(4) Determine the amount of wear and play of both the axial and circumferential direction pins.
(5) Permanent spring strain.

mm (in.)

	Standard	Wear limit
Spring free length	32.85 (1.2933)	32 (1.2598)

(6) Pin end wear.

4-8 Retainer

(1) Check for stains and damage on the friction plate contact surface.
(2) Check for wear and cracking on the plate spring contact surface.
(3) Measurement of dimensions

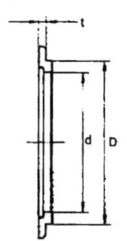

mm (in.)

	Standard	Wear limit
d	Ø67.060 ~ 67.106 (2.6401 ~ 2.6419)	Ø67.3 (2.6496)
D	Ø75.9 ~ 76.0 (2.9881 ~ 2.9921)	Ø75.7 (2.9803)
t	4.95 ~ 5.05 (0.1948 ~ 0.1988)	4.8 (0.1889)

4-9 Plate spring

(1) Permanent strai

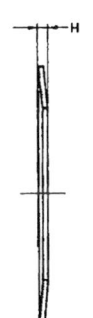

mm (in.)

	Standard	Wear limit
H: when plate spring is free	7.2 ~ 7.6 (0.2834 ~ 0.2992)	7.05 (0.2775)

4-10 Thrust collar

The gear side of the thrust washer has a 0.3mm (0.0118in.) copper sintered layer. Replace the thrust collar when the thickness is less than 5.75mm (0.2263in.) (Standard thickness: 5.9 ~ 6.0mm (0.2322 ~ 0.2362).

4-11 Shift ring

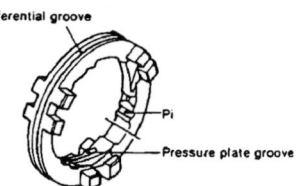

Circumferential groove

Pi

Pressure plate groove

(1) Circumferential groove wear.

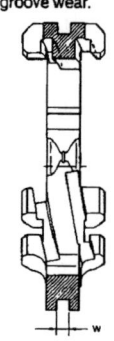

w

mm (in.)

	Standard	Wear limit
Shifting groove: w	6.0 ~ 6.1 (0.2362 ~ 0.2401)	6.3 (0.2480)

(2) Pressure plate groove wear.
Whenever uneven wear and/or scratches are found, replace with a new part.
(3) Parallel pin contact part wear.
Whenever uneven wear and/or scratches are found, replace with a new part.

4-12 Shift fork and shift lever

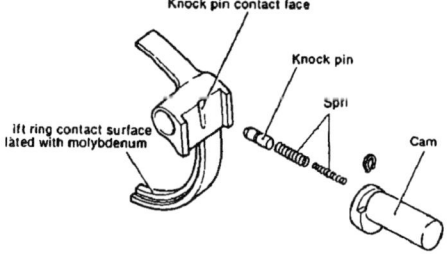

Knock pin contact face

Knock pin

Spri

ift ring contact surface
lated with molybdenum

Cam

(1) End wear.
The shift ring contact surface of the shift fork is plated with molybdenum (thickness: 0.04 ~ 0.05mm (0.0016 ~ 0.0020in.)). If this plating is peeled or worn to such an extent that the base metal of the shift fork is exposed, replace the shift fork.
(2) Cam surface wear and stains.
Whenever uneven wear and/or scratches are found, replace with a new part.
(3) Pin part play.
Whenever uneven wear and/or scratches are found, replace with a new part.
(4) Notch end wear.
Whenever uneven wear and/or scratches are found, replace with a new part.

4-13 Output shaft

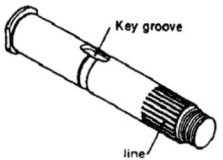

Key groove

line

(1) Key groove.
Whenever uneven cracks and/or stai   re found, replace with a new part.

4-14 Damper disc

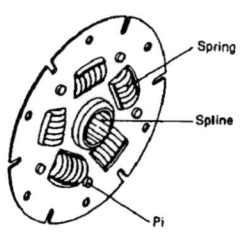

Spring

Spline

Pi

(1) Spline part
Whenever uneven wear and/or scratches are found, replace with a new part.
(2) Spring.
Whenever uneven wear and/or scratches are found, replace with a new part.
(3) Pin wear.
Whenever uneven wear and/or scratches are found, replace with a new part.

4-15 Input shaft

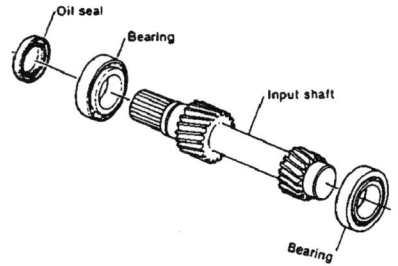

(1) Spline part
Whenever uneven wear and/or scratches are found, replace with a new part.
(2) Surface of oil seal.
If the sealing surface of the oil seal is worn or scratched, replace.

4-16 Intermediate shaft

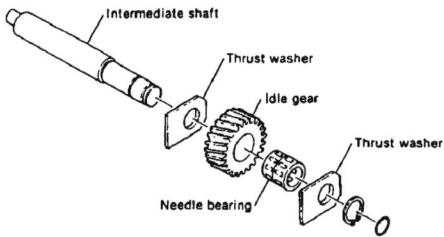

(1) Needle bearing dimensions, staining.
Check the surface of the roller to see whether the needle bearing sticks or is damaged. Replace if necessary.

5. Disassembly

5-1 Disassembling the clutch and accessories
(1) Remove the drain plug and packing, and drain the oil from the clutch.
(2) Uncaulk the output shaft lock nut, and remove the nut using a disassembly tool.

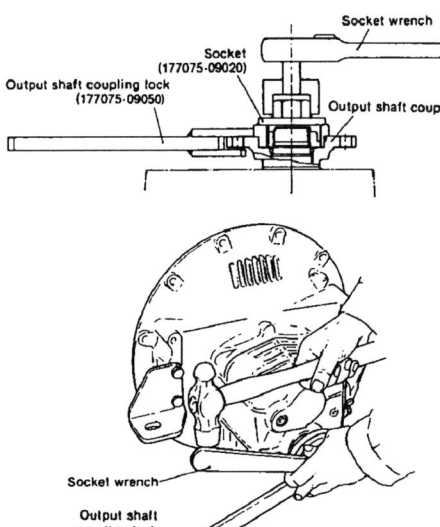

Socket wrench

Socket (177075-09020)

Output shaft coupling lock (177075-09050)

Output shaft coupli

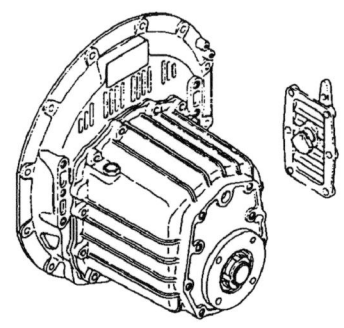

(6) Remove the M10 bolt and super lock washer on the mounting flange.

(7) Screw the M10 bolt into the M10 pulling bolt hole of the mounting flange, and remove the mounting flange. Do not remove the parallel pin.

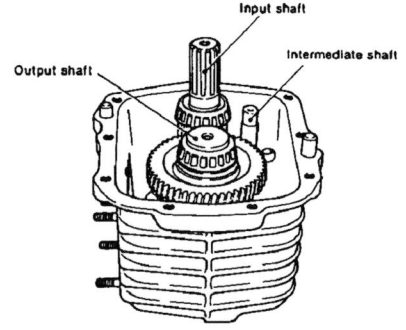

Input shaft

Intermediate shaft

Output shaft

Socket wrench

Output shaft coupling lock

(3) Remove the output coupling with O-ring.

(8) Remove the output shaft, intermediate shaft, and input shaft from the case, in that order.

(9) Remove the shift bar from the moving flange side.

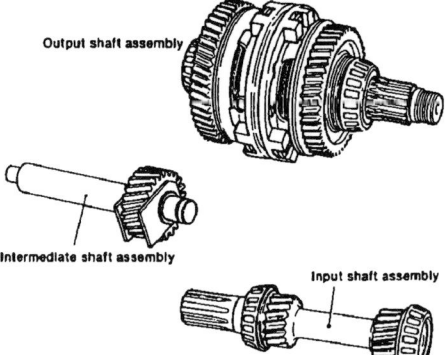

Output shaft assembly

Intermediate shaft assembly

Input shaft assembly

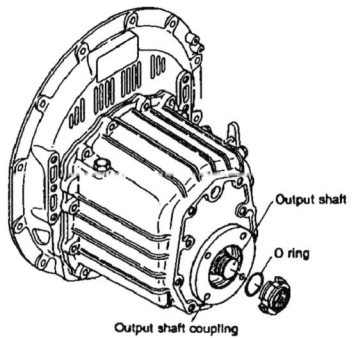

Output shaft

O ring

Output shaft coupling

(4) Remove the dipstick and packing.
(5) Remove the case cover M8 nut and M8 bolt; remove the case cover, with the operating lever, shift cam, etc. in position.

(10) Heat the case body to about 100°C and remove the outer race of the input shaft and output shaft bearings. If the outer races are difficult to remove, tap them out with a plastic hammer from the rear of the case, or pull them by using the pulling groove in the case at the rear of the races.

(11) Remove the outer race of the bearing from the mounting flange as described in step (11) above.

(12) Remove the input shaft and output shaft adjusting plates.

NOTE: If the following parts are not replaced, the adjusting plates may be reused without readjustment. However, if even one part is replaced, readjustment is necessary.

Input shaft part: 24-2, 24-31
Output shaft part: 26-6, 26-9, 26-26, 26-27, 26-28, 26-30

(13) Pull the oil seal from the case.

(14) Pull the oil seal from the mounting flange.

5-2 Disassembling the input shaft
Pull the bearing from the input shaft.
NOTE: Do not disassemble unless the input shaft parts are damaged.

5-3 Disassembling the output shaft
(1) Remove the O-ring.
(2) Remove the output shaft by pressing the threaded end of the output shaft with a press, or tapping it with a hammer.

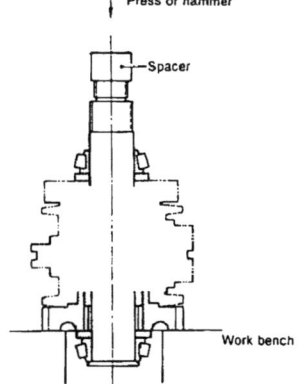

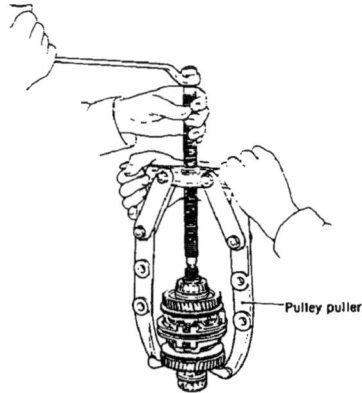

NOTE 1: When removing the shaft, place spacers between the shaft and the press to prevent damage.

NOTE 2: Make sure that the forward large gear parts and reverse large gear parts are not mixed together once they are removed.

(3) Remove the adjusting plate.
NOTE: Record the thickness of the adjusting plate to facilitate reassembly.
If the parts are not replaced, the adjusting plate may be reused without readjustment. However, if even one part is replaced, readjustment is required.

(4) Remove the key.
To facilitate removal, clamp the key with a vi

(5) Remove the adjusting plate.
NOTE: Record the thickness of the adjusting plate to facilitate reassembly.
If the parts are not replaced, the adjusting plate may be reused without adjustment. However, if even one part is replaced, readjustment is required.

(6) Remove the spacer and needle bearing.

(7) Cover the outer race of the forward bearing, and pull out the output shaft about 10mm (0.3937in.) by pressing the threaded end of the output shaft with a press, or tapping it with a hammer.
NOTE: Do not pull it out more than 10mm (0.3937in.); otherwise damage may result.

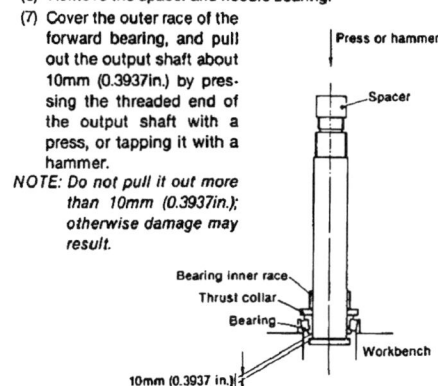

(8) Insert the disassembly tool between the collar of the output shaft and the bearing; next remove the bearing inner race, thrust collar, and bearing from the output shaft with a press or hammer.

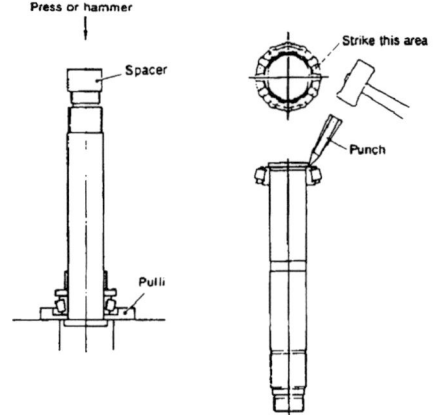

(9) Remove the friction plates and steel plates from the forward large gear.

(10) Using a disassembly tool, compress the plate spring and remove the circlip from the forward large gear.

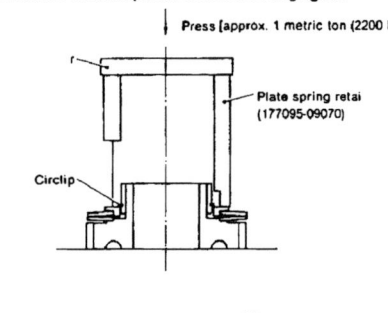

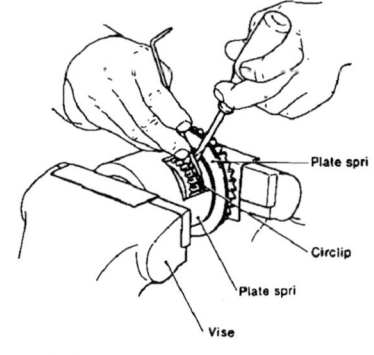

(11) Remove the retainer and plate spring.

(12) Remove the parts from the reverse large gear as described in steps (9)—(11) above.

(13) Remove the pressure plate return spring; remove the pressure plate and steel ball.

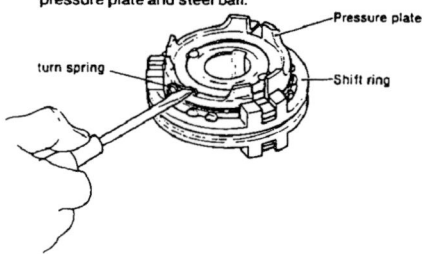

(14) Remove the shift ring.
To disassemble, remove the three knock pins. When disassembling the shift ring, cover it with a cloth to prevent it being lost.

(15) Remove the knock pin and spring from the driving plate.

5-4 Disassembling the intermediate shaft

(1) Place a spacer against the case side end of the intermediate shaft and remove the shaft from the case by tapping the spacer with a hammer.

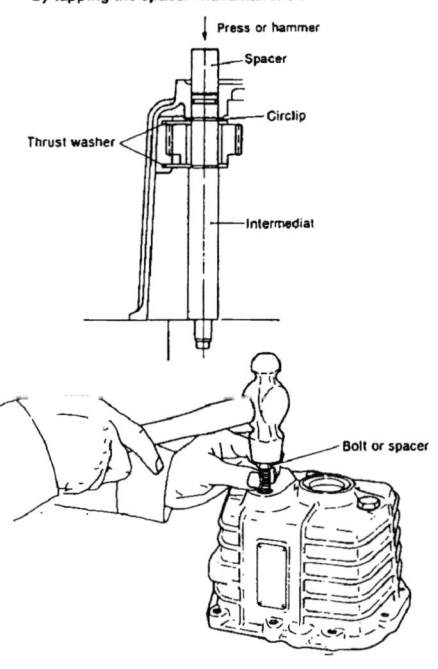

(2) Remove the O-ring, and then remove the circlip.
(3) Remove the idle gear, needle bearing, and thrust washer.

5-5 Disassembling the operating system
(1) Loosen the M8 bolt of the shift lever; remove the shift lever.
(2) Pull the shift cam.
(3) Push in the knock pin and remove the circlip.
(4) Remove the knock pin and spring.
(5) Pull the oil seal from the case side cover.

Printed in Japan
A0A1029-9002

6. Reassembly

6-1 Reassembly precautions
(1) Before reassembling, clean all parts in washing oil, and replace any damaged or worn parts.
Remove non-dry packing agent from the mating surface with a blunt knife.
(2) Pack the oil seal and O-ring parts with grease.
(3) Coat the mating surfaces of the case with wet packing.

6-2 Reassembling the output shaft
(1) Reassembling forward large gear and plate spring
  1) Insert the two plate springs of the forward large gear so that their large diameter sides are opposite each other.
  2) Insert the retainer and install the circlip.
  3) Compress the plate spring, using the disassembly tool, and snap the circlip into the groove on the outside of the spline of the forward large gear.

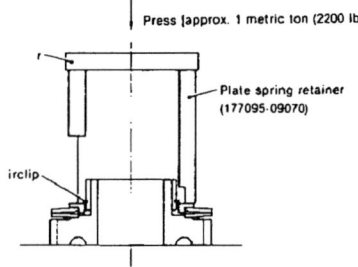

Press [approx. 1 metric ton (2200 lb)]

Plate spring retainer
(177095-09070)

irclip

(2) Reassemble the reverse large gear and plate spring retainer, and the circlip as described in step (1) above.
(3) Determi ing the forward adjusting plate thickness

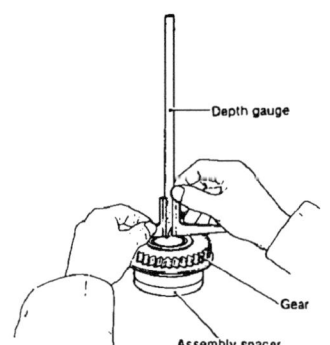

Depth gauge

Gear

Assembly spacer

NOTE: As mentioned in section 5-3. (5), if no parts need to be replaced, the adjusting plate can be reused without adjustment.

1) Position the assembled large gear on the assembly tool so that the spline part is on the bottom; insert the spacer and bearing inner race into the gear.

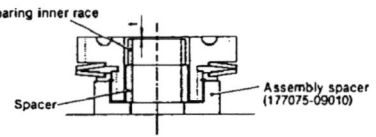

Bearing inner race

Spacer

Assembly spacer
(177075-09010)

2) Three adjustment plates of 0.5mm (0.0196in.), 0.4mm (0.0157in.) and 0.3mm (0.0118in.) are available.
3) Measure the "t" dimension. Combine these plates to obtain a dimension from (t-0.5)mm to (t-0.5)mm.

(4) Determine the thickness of the reverse adjusting plate by following the procedure described in step(3)above.
(5) First, insert a friction plate into the spline part of the forward large gear; next insert steel plates and friction plates alternately. Finally, insert a friction plate (six friction plates and five steel plates).
(6) Insert the friction plates and steel plates into the spline part of the reverse large gear in the same manner as described in step (5) above (six friction plates and five steel plates).
(7) Press the inner race of the bearing onto the output shaft up to the collar, using an assembly tool.
NOTE: The inner race can be installed easily by preheating it to approximately 100°C.

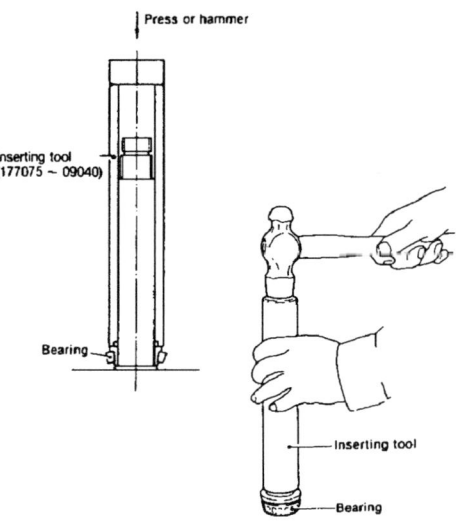

Press or hammer

Inserting tool
(177075 ~ 09040)

Bearing

Inserting tool

Bearing

(8) Insert the thrust collar, with the sintered surface (brown surface) facing the gear side.
(9) Press the bearing inner race onto the output shaft, using an assembly tool.

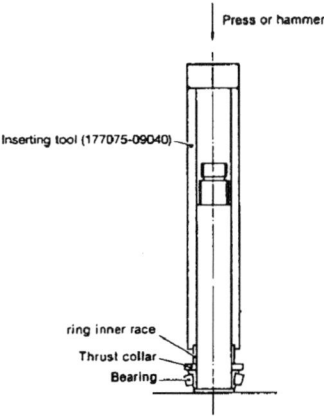

Press or hammer

Inserting tool (177075-09040)

ring inner race
Thrust collar
Bearing

(10) Insert the needle bearing.
(11) Insert the spacer and adjusting plate.
(12) Fit the key so that the fillet side is facing the threaded part of the output shaft.

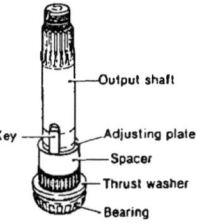

Output shaft
Key
Adjusting plate
Spacer
Thrust washer
Bearing

(13) Insert the forward large gear, together with the friction plates and steel plates. At this time, align the three pawls on the outside of the steel plates.

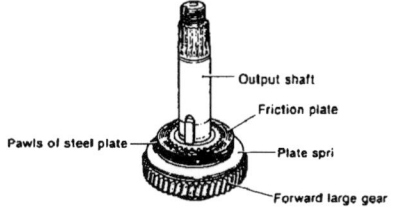

Output shaft
Friction plate
Pawls of steel plate
Plate spri
Forward large gear

(14) Cover the friction plates and steel plates with the pressure plate so that the pawls of the steel plate fit into the three notches on the pressure plate.
(15) Insert the three steel balls into the three grooves in the pressure plate.

(16) Insert the drive plate into the output shaft so that the side with the identification groove faces the forward large gear side.
NOTE: *Make sure that the three steel balls are in the three grooves of the driving plate.*
At the same time, make sure that the pin for the driving plate fits into the groove of the torque limiter for the pressure plate.

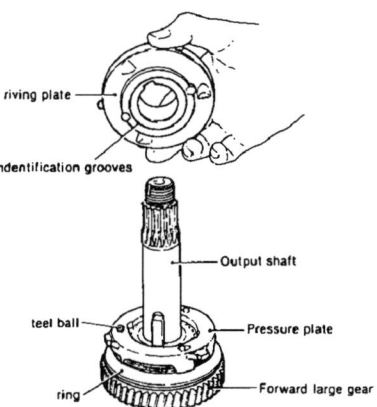

riving plate
Indentification grooves

Output shaft
teel ball
Pressure plate
ring
Forward large gear

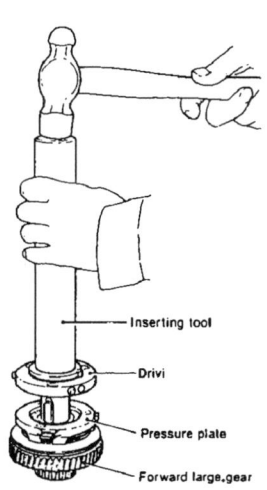

Inserting tool
Drivi
Pressure plate
Forward large.gear

(17) Insert the adjusting plate and spacer.
(18) Press the bearing inner race, using an assembly tool.

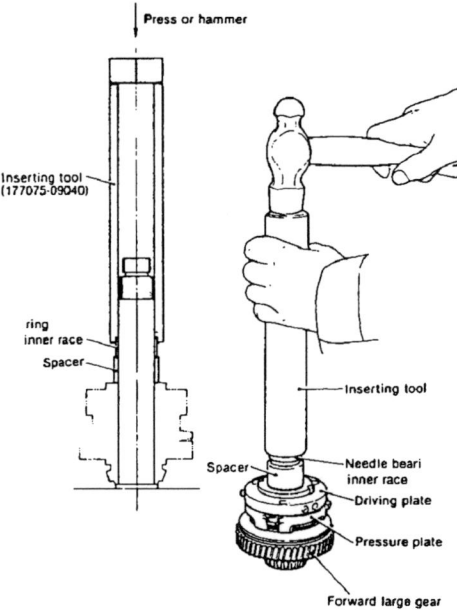

(19) Insert the knock pins and springs into the three holes around the circumference of the driving plate.
(20) Cover the driving plate with the shift ring so that the side with the identification groove faces the forward large gear side; install the ring so that the knock pins are pushed in.

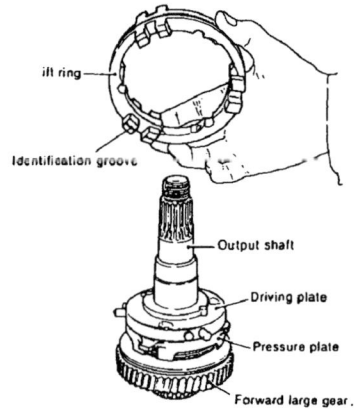

(21) Insert the three steel balls into the three grooves in the driving plate.
(22) Place the pressure plate onto the driving plate so that the steel balls enter the three grooves of the pressure plate.
(23) Insert the three pressure plate return springs between the shift ring and the driving plate, and attach them to the small holes in the side of the pressure plate.
(24) Insert the reverse large gear [see step (6)] so that the three pawls of the steel plates enter the notches around the circumference of the pressure plate.
(25) Insert the needle bearing.
(26) Insert the thrust washer so that the sintered side (brown side) faces the gear side.
(27) Press the inner race of the bearing, using an assembly tool. At this time, make sure that the direction of the bearing is correct.
NOTE: The bearing inner race can be installed easily by preheating it to approximately 100°C.

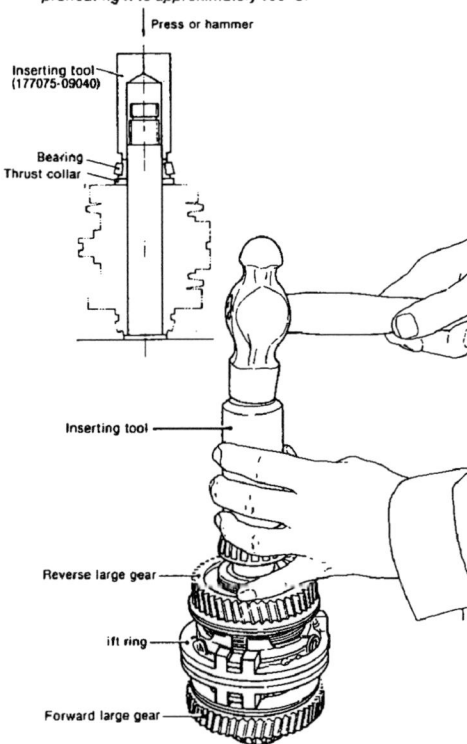

Insert the O-ring.
(28) With the shift ring in the reverse position, check the forward large gear to make sure it rotates smoothly. Next, with the shift ring in the forward position, check the reverse large gear to make sure it rotates smoothly.

6-3 Reassembling the input shaft
Press the inner race of the bearing onto the input shaft. At this time, make sure that the direction of the bearing is correct.
NOTE: The bearing inner race can be easily installed by preheating it to approximately 100°C.

6-4 Reassembling the intermediate shaft
NOTE: Assemble the intermediate shaft as described i section 6-5. (5).
(1) Insert the thrust washer the needle bearing and idle gear on the intermediate shaft. Then insert the thrust washer.
NOTE: Pay careful attention to the assembling direction of the thrust washer.

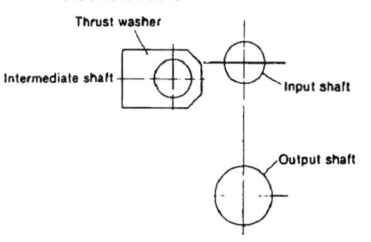

(2) Insert the circlip on the intermediate shaft, and then insert the O-ring.
(3) Press the assembled intermediate shaft into the case with a press or hammer.

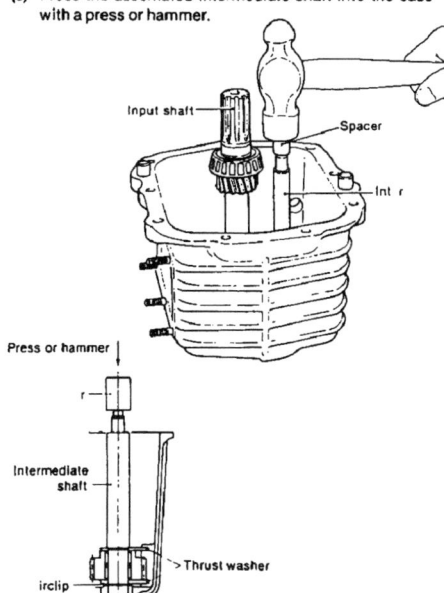

(4) Make sure that the idle gear rotates smoothly.

6-5 Installing the input shaft and output shaft
(1) Determining the thickness of the input shaft adjusting plate and output shaft adjusting plate
NOTE: As mentioned in section 5-1. (13), when none of the parts are replaced the adjusting plate can be reused without readjustment.
  1) Measure length "A" "D" between the cases of each shaft of the case body and mounting flange.
  2) Cover each bearing with the bearing outer race, and measure length "B" "C" between the bearings.

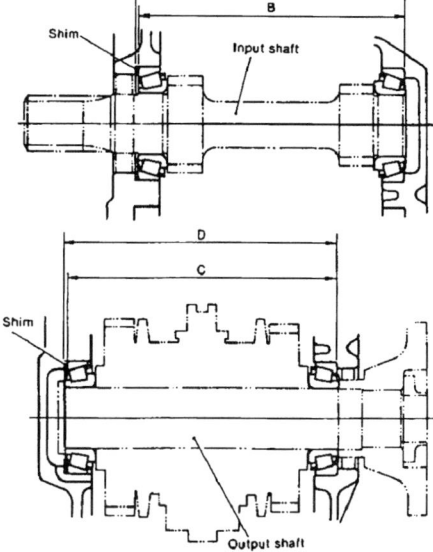

3) Adjust the input shaft adjusting plate thickness so that the clearance or tightening allowance is less than 0.05mm (0.0020in.).
4) Adjust the output shaft adjusting plate thickness so that the tightening allowance is within 0 ~ 0.1mm (0~0.0040in.).
5) Three adjustment plates of 0.5mm (0.0196in.), 0.4mm (0.0157in.) and 0.3mm (0.0118in.) are available.
Combine these plates to obtain the desired adjusting plate measurement.
(2) Insert the adjusting plate into the mounting flange, and press the outer race of the bearing.
Also, press the outer race of the bearing into the case.
NOTE: The outer race can be installed easily by heating the mounting flange and case to approximately 100°C, or by cooling the bearing outer race with liquid nitrogen, etc.
(3) Coat the circumference of the oil seal with a liquid packing agent, and press it onto the mounting flange and case so that the spring part of the oil seal is inside the case.

(4) Coat the mating surfaces of the mounting flange and case with a liquid packing agent.
Wipe off oil and dirt on the mating surface of the case and coat with a thin film of liquid packing agent.

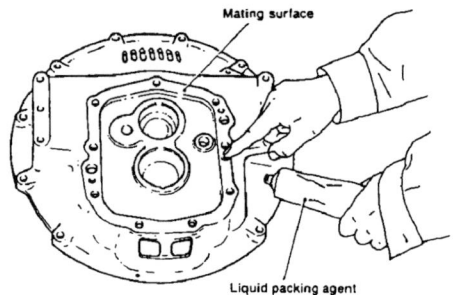

(5) Insert the input shaft into the case, assemble the intermediate shaft as described in section 6-4 and then insert the output shaft into the case, mounted with shift fork and shift ring.

(6) Align the mounting flange with the case, and insert the parallel pin by tapping the mounting flange with a plastic hammer.

(7) Insert the super lock washer and tighten the M10 bolt.

(8) Install the dipstick and packing.

(9) Install the drain plug and packing.

6-6 Reassembling and installing the operating system

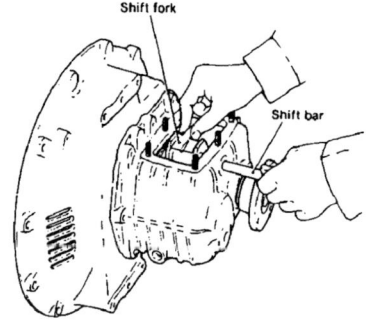

(1) Put the shift fork into neutral before installing.

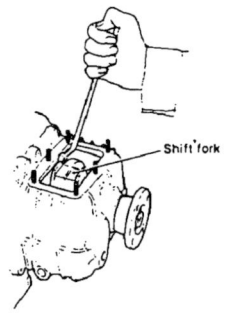

(3) Coat the circumference of the oil seal with a liquid packing agent and press the seal against the case cover.

(4) Insert the spring into the shift cam.

(5) Insert the knock pin into the shift cam from the front end, and lock with the circlip.

(6) Insert the assembled shift cam into the case cover.

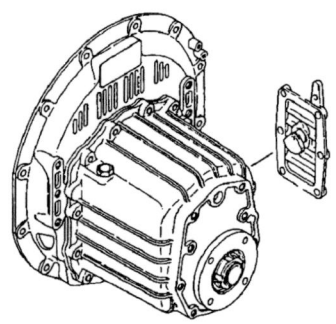

(7) Fit the shift lever to the shift cam, and tighten the M8 bolt.

NOTE: The shift cam must rotate smoothly.

(8) Replace the packing if it is damaged.

(9) Attach the case side cover with operating system in the case body.
At this time, make sure that the shift cam is fitted to the shift fork, and that the shift lever is in neutral.

NOTE: Put the shift fork into neutral before installing.

(10) Insert the super lock washer, and tighten the M8 nut.

(11) Shift the shift lever to forward and reverse to make sure that the lever operates normally.
If the lever does not operate normally, loosen the M8 nut, slide the case side cover forward, backward, and to the left and right, then re-tighten with the M8 nut in the position at which the lever operates normally.

NOTE: If the lever operates normally a click will be heard when it is put into forward and reverse.

6-7 Installing the output shaft coupling

(1) Install the output shaft coupling on the output shaft and then insert the O-ring in the groove between the output shaft and the output shaft coupling.

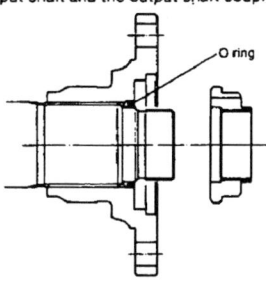

O ring

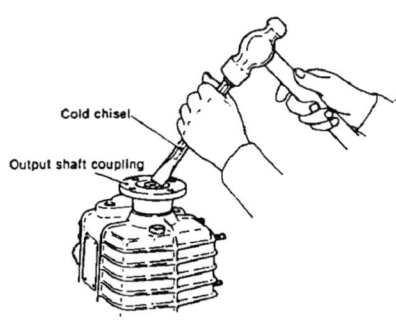

Cold chisel

Output shaft coupling

(2) Tighten and caulk the output shaft lock nut, using the assembly tool.
Tightening torque.........15kg-m (108.5ft-lb)

(3) Shift the shift lever to the neutral position and make sure the clutch engages when the shift lever is put into forward and reverse.
The input/output shafts will not rotate smoothly if the side gap of the bearing is too small in relation to the thickness of the adjusting plate.

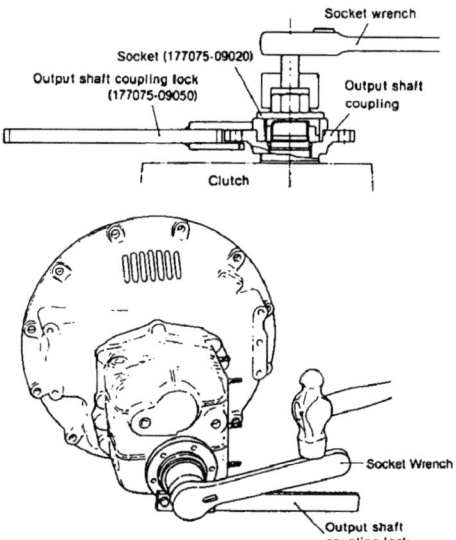

Socket wrench

Socket (177075-09020)

Output shaft coupling lock (177075-09050)

Output shaft coupling

Clutch

Socket Wrench

Output shaft coupling lock

7. Special Tools

Name of tool	Part number	Illustration	Application
Socket	177075-09020		For removing and tightening the output shaft nuts.
Output shaft coupling lock	177075-09050		For removing and tightening the output shaft nut.
Plate for spring retai	177095-09070		For removing and installing the plate spring, retainer and circlip of the large gear (forward and reverse).
Assembly spacer	177075-09010		For determining the thickness of adjusting plate.
Inserting tool	177075-09040		For installing the spacer and needle bearing inner race of the output shaft (reverse small gear side).
Inserting tool	177075-09030		For installing the thrust bearing of the input shaft.

7-23

Marine Gear Model
KM4A

for Engine Models 4JH2-BE, 4JH2-TBE, 4JH2-HTBE and 4JH2-DTBE

1. Construction

1-1 Construction

The clutch is a cone-type, mechanically operated clutch. When the drive cone (which is connected to the clutch shaft by the lead spline) is moved forward or backward, its taper contacts with the clutch gear and transfers power to the output shaft.

The construction is simple compared with other types of clutch and serves to reduce the number of components, making for a lighter, more compact unit which can be operated smoothly. Although it is small, the power transmission efficiency is high even under a heavy load. It is also durable and reliable because high grade materials are used for the shaft and gear, and a taper roller bearing is incorporated. Power transmission is smooth because connection with the engine is made through the damper disc.

- The drive cone is made from special aluminum bronze which has high wear-resistance and durability. The drive cone is connected with the clutch shaft. The taper angle, diameter of the drive cone, twist angle, and diameter of the involute spline, are designed to give the greatest efficiency, thus ensuring that the drive cone can be readily engaged or disengaged.
- Helical gears are used for greater strength. The intermediate shaft is supported at 2 points to reduce deflection and gear noise.
- The clutch case and mounting flange are made from an aluminum alloy of special composition to reduce weight. This is non-corrosive in seawater.
- The damper disc is fitted to the input shaft, so power can be transmitted smoothly. Springs of different strengths are used for the damper disc so that two stages of torque and twist angle are applied. That is, in the first stage, only the weak spring is used, and the strong spring comes into action for a torque higher than a predetermined value.

This prevents gear noise due to torsional vibration, well as absorbing shock when engaging.

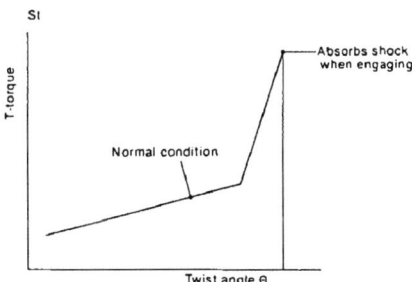

There is a small clearance between the dipstick and the inside of the dipstick tube. A small hole in the dipstick works as a breather.

- When the load on the propeller is removed, the engagement of the drive cone and the clutch gear is maintained by the shifter and V-groove of the drive cone. Even when the drive cone's tapered area and V-groove are worn, this engagement is maintained by the shift lever device. Accordingly no adjustment of the remote control cable is required.
- The cup spring on the rear of the clutch gear absorbs rotational fluctuations and stabilizes the engagement of the drive cone and the clutch gear. Thus, the durability of the cone against wear is enhanced.

Printed in Japan
A0A1029-9002

- A torque limiter is built into the input shaft gear to prevent damage caused by excessive torque.
- The lube oil temperature can be controlled because in addition to the input shaft gear which functions as a centrifugal pump, an oil cooler is also equipped.
- The oil cooler is equipped with a cooling water drain cock to prevent cracks caused by freezing in cold weather. It is therefore easy to drain the water.
- The propeller shaft can rotate in both counter clockwise (C.C.W.) and clockwise (C.W.) directions.

NOTE: *Since the difference in reduction gear ratio between C.C.W. and C.W. rotations is within 0.07%, no problem occurs in operation.*

1-2 Specifications of Angle Drive Marine Gear

Model		KM4A		
For engine models		4JH2 E , 4JH2-TE, 4JH2-HTE,4JH2-DTE, 4JH2-UTE		
Down angle		7 degree		
Clutch		Constant mesh gear with servo cone clutch (wet type)		
Direction of rotation	Input shaft	Counter-clockwise, viewed from stern.		
	Output shaft	Bi-rotation		
Reduction ratio		3.30	2.63	2.14
Propeller shaft rpm at cont, rating		1062	1332	1637
Remote control	Control head	Single lever control		
	Cable	Morse, 33-C (Cable travel 76.2mm or 3 in.)		
	Clamp	YANMAR Made, standard accessory		
	Cable connector	YANMAR Made, standard accessory		
Output shaft coupling	Outer diameter	ϕ120mm (4.72")		
	Pitch circle diameter	ϕ100mm (3.93")		
	Connecting bolt holes	4—ϕ10.5mm (4—ϕ0.41")		
Position of shift lever		Right side, viewed from stern.		
Lubricating oil		Same as Engine lube oil		
Lubricating oil capacity		1.3ℓ		
Lube oil cooler		Sea-water cooling		

1-3 KM4A Sectional View

1 Clutch case	16 Bearing
2 Shim	17 End nut
3 Bearing	18 Name plate
4 Thrust collar(A)	19 Shim
5 Spring retainer	20 Shim
6 Cup spring	21 Output shaft cover
7 Clutch gear(A)	22 Bearing
8 Needle bearing	23 End nut
9 Thrust collar(B)	24 O ring
10 Snap ring	25 Oil seal
11 Drive cone	26 Output shaft coupli
12 Clutch gear B	27 Bolt
13 Drive gear	28 Output shaft
14 Key	29 Bearing
15 Clutch shaft	30 Shim
	31 Bolt
	32 Washer
	33 Bearing
	34 Ball bearing
	35 Snap ring
	36 Cup spring
	37 Spacer
	38 Input shaft gear
	39 Plate(A)
	40 Plate(B)
	41 Lock nut
	42 O-ring
	43 Ball bearing
	44 Mounting flange
	45 Lube oil filter case
	46 End nut
	47 Lube oil filter
	48 Pin
	49 Centering bush
	50 Dumper disk
	51 Input shaft
	52 Oil seal
	53 Shim
	54 Bearing
	55 Nut
	56 Washer
	57 O-ring
	58 Dip stick
	59 Spring
	60 Cover
	61 O-ring
	62 Location pin
	63 Spring pin
	64 Shift lever shaft
	65 O-ring
	66 Washer
	67 Split space pin
	68 Pivot
	69 Oil seal
	70 Spring
	71 Shim
	72 Stopper bolt
	73 Shifter
	74 Bolt (M8 × 30)
	75 Side cover
	76 Oil - cooler body
	77 Pipe
	78 Shim
	79 O-ring
	80 Bolt
	81 Washer
	82 Cooler
	83 Cock
	84 Drain plug
	85 Washer
	86 End nut
	87 Washer
	88 Shim
	89 Bearing
	90
	91 Idle gear
	92
	93 Bearing
	94 Intermediate shaft gear
	95 Washer
	96 Lock nut
	97 Bolt
	98 Cable clamp
	99 Cable blacket
	100 Shift lever
	101 Bolt(M8 × 25)

7-26

1-4 Power Transmission System

1-4-1 Arrangement of shafts and gear

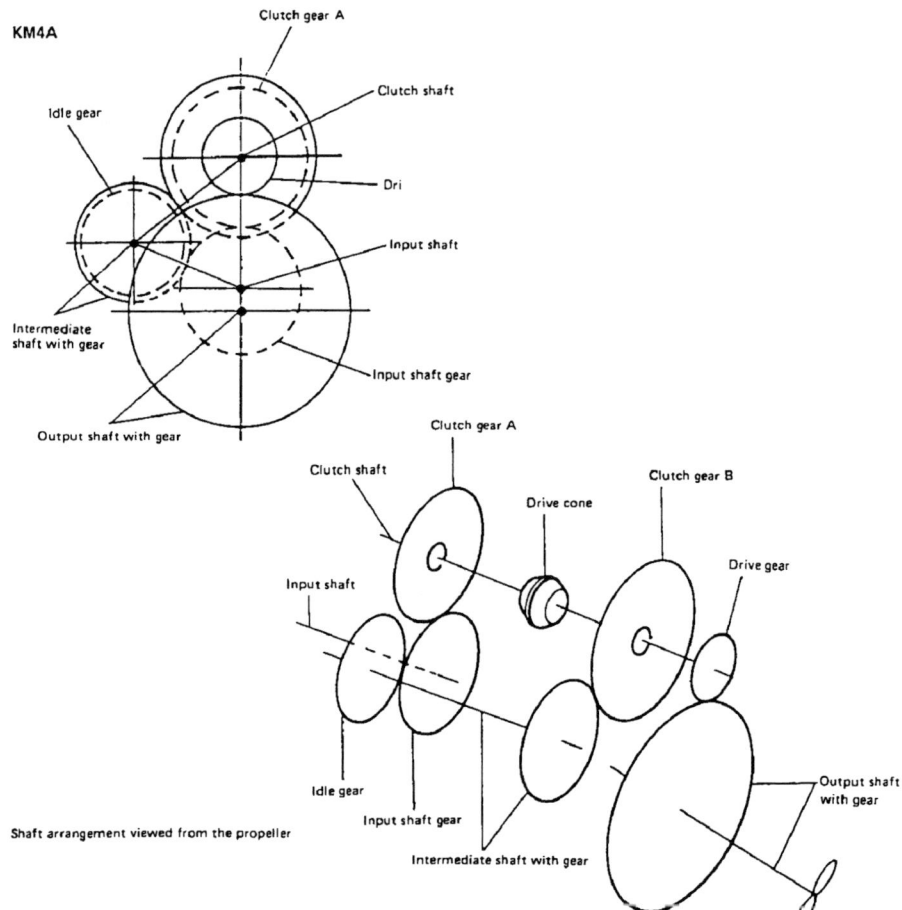

KM4A

Clutch gear A

Idle gear

Clutch shaft

Dri

Input shaft

Intermediate shaft with gear

Input shaft gear

Output shaft with gear

Clutch gear A

Clutch shaft

Drive cone

Clutch gear B

Drive gear

Input shaft

Idle gear

Input shaft gear

Intermediate shaft with gear

Output shaft with gear

Shaft arrangement viewed from the propeller

1-4-2 Reduction ratio

Input shaft gear	Clutch gear		Intermediate shaft		Drive gear	Output shaft with gear	Reduction ratio
	A	B	Idle gear	Shaft gear			
39	41	45	31	34	30	61	2.14
					26	65	2.63
					22	69	3.30

Printed in Japan
A0A1029-9002

2. Shifting Device

2-1 Construction of shifting mechanism

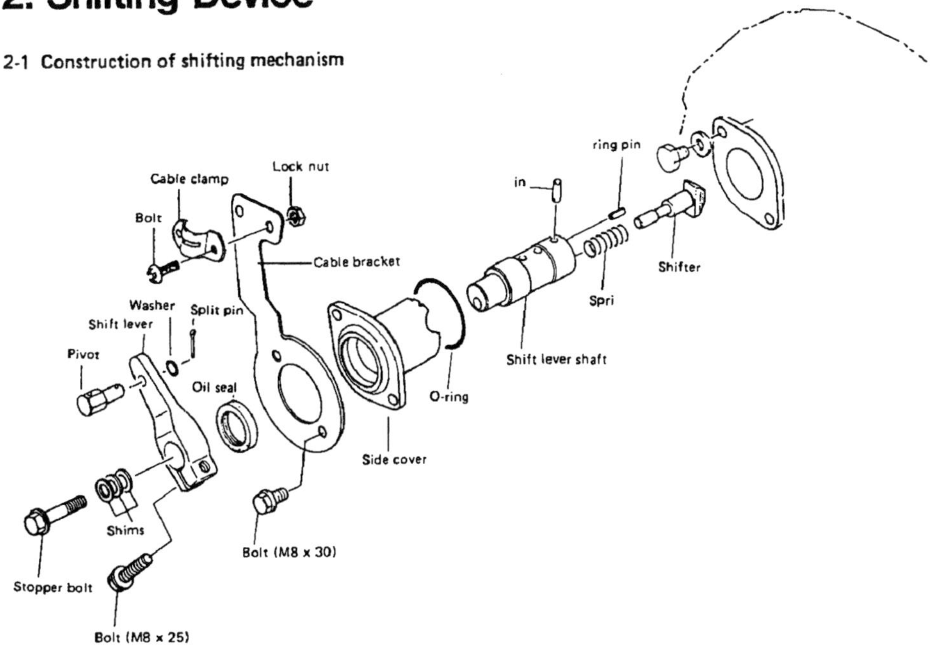

Cable clamp
Lock nut
ring pin
in
Bolt
Cable bracket
Shifter
Washer
Split pin
Spri
Shift lever
Pivot
Shift lever shaft
Oil seal
O-ring
Side cover
Shims
Bolt (M8 x 30)
Stopper bolt
Bolt (M8 x 25)

The shift lever shaft is installed on the side cover with neutral, clutch gear (A) and clutch gear (B) positions provided on the cover. The neutral, clutchgear (A) and clutch gear (B) location pins of the shift lever shaft are constantly inserted into their respective grooves on the shift lever by the tension of the shifter spring. The shifter is set on the eccentric hole of the shift lever shaft and moves the drive cone in the neutral position either to the clutch gear (A) or clutch gear (B) positions, and then back to the neutral position. (The shift lever shaft moves slightly to the shift lever (or drive cone) side when the shift lever is placed in the clutch gear (A) or clutch gear (B) positions.)

NOTE:1 Clutch gear (A) position: clockwise propeller rotation viewed from propeller side (C.C.W.)
NOTE:2 Clutch gear (B) position: Counterclockwise propeller rotation viewed from propeller side (C.W.)

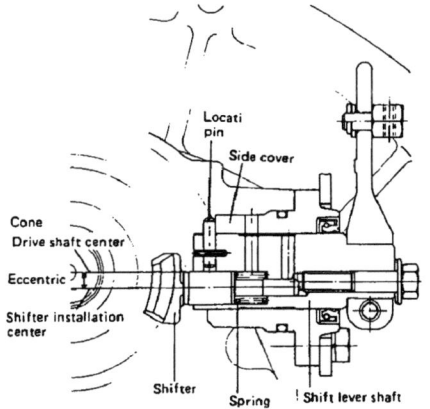

Locati
pin
Side cover
Cone
Drive shaft center
Eccentric
Shifter installation
center
Shifter
Spring
Shift lever shaft

2-2 Clutch gear (A) and clutch gear (B) operation (Neutral ⇒ clutch gear (A), Neutral ⇒ clutch gear (B))

When the shift lever is moved to the clutch gear (A) position from the neutral position, the shift lever shaft starts to revolve, and the location pin disengages from the neutral V-groove position of the side cover. (The shift lever moves approx. 0.5mm to the drive cone side.) At this time the shifter, which is set on the eccentric hole of the shift lever shaft, moves the drive cone's V-groove to the clutch gear (A).

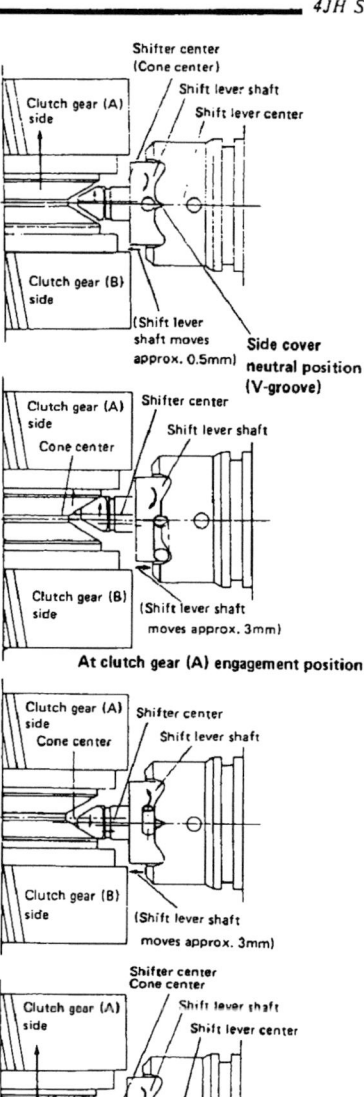

When the location pin of the shift lever shaft falls into the clutch gear (A) position groove on the side cover, the shift lever shaft moves approx. 3mm to the shift lever side, and the shifter starts to press the drive cone V-groove to the clutch gear (A) side by spring force.

2-3 Engagement and disengagement of clutch (Clutch gear (A) ⇒ Neutral, Clutch gear (B) ⇒ Neutral)

When the shift lever is moved to the clutch gear (A) position from the neutral position, the shift lever shaft starts to revolve, and the location pin disengages from the clutch gear (A) position groove on the side cover. (The shift lever shaft moves approx. 3mm to the drive cone side.) At this time, the shifter which is set on the eccentric hole of the shift lever shaft, is moved to the neutral side (clutch gear (B) side). The drive cone, however, is engaged with the clutch gear (A) as the torque force produced by the revolving centrifugal force.

Further, when the shift lever shaft starts to revolve, and the positioning pin falls into the neutral V-groove position of the side cover (the shift lever shaft travels approx. 5mm to the shift lever side), the shifter moves to the shift lever side (to the spring side) while moving the V-groove of the drive cone to the clutch gear (B) side. The movement of the shifter to the shift lever side, however, is stopped when the shifter end contacts the stopper bolt. The shifter only works to press the V-groove of the drive cone to the clutch gear (B) side. Thus, the drive cone is disengaged from the clutch gear (A). After this disengagement, the transmission torque of the drive cone is decreased to zero and the shift lever is returned to the neutral position by spring force.

2-4 Clutch shifting force

Shifting position / Shifting direction	Shift lever position at 56mm	Remote control handle position at 170mm (Cable length, 4m)
Engaging force at 1000 rpm	3 ~ 4 kg (6.6 ~ 8.8 lbs)	4 ~ 5 kg (8.8 ~ 11.0 lbs)
Disengaging force at 1000 rpm	3.5 ~ 5 kg (7.7 ~ 11.0 lbs)	4 ~ 6 kg (8.8 ~ 13.2 lbs)

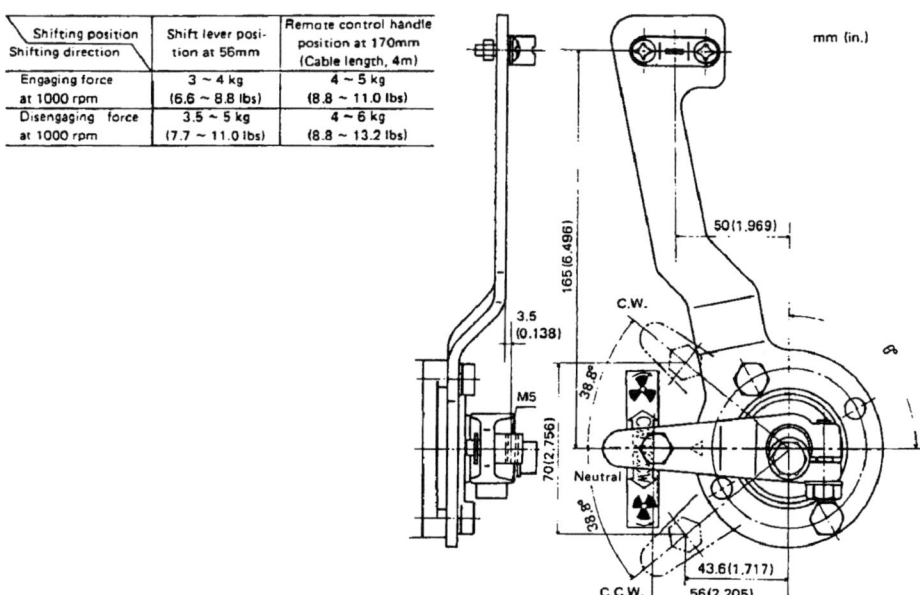

mm (in.)

2-5 Adjustment of shifting device

Whenever the side cover, shift lever shaft, shifter, stopper bolt or drive cone is replaced, be sure to adjust the clearance between the shifter end and the stopper bolt with shims. When the adjustment of this clearance is inadequate, the drive cone may not connect properly when the shift lever is moved to the neutral position, either from the clutch gear (A) or clutch gear (B) position.

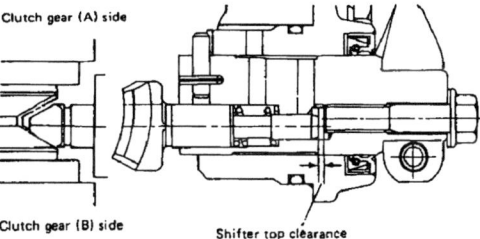

Clutch gear (A) side

Clutch gear (B) side

Shifter top clearance

Printed in Japan
A0A1029-9002

2-5-1 Measurement and adjustment of clearance

(mm)

(1)Assemble the shifting mechanism (without installing the stopper bolt of the shifter) to the marine gear case.

NOTE: Ensure the correct alignment of the shifter before assembly.

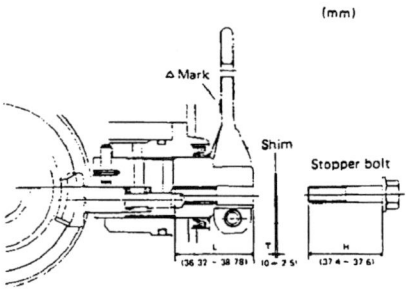

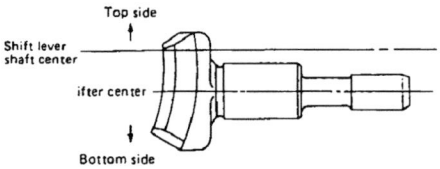

(2)Turn the shift lever 10 ~ 15 degrees either to the clutch gear (A) or clutch gear (B) position from the neutral position.

(3)Measure the L-distance between the shift lever shaft end surface and the shifter end.

(4)Measure the H-distance (the distance from the neck of the stopper bolt to its end).

(5)Obtain the shim thickness "T" by the following formula.

$$T = (H - L + 1.25) \pm 0.1mm (0.0039in.)$$

NOTE: Shim set includes one each of 1mm, 0.4mm, 0.3mm, 0.25mm shims.
(YANMAR Part No. 177088-06380)

(6)Insert shim (s) of proper thickness to the stopper bolt side and tighten to the shift lever shaft.

NOTE: When tightening the stopper bolt, apply either a non-drying type liquid packing (THREE BOND No.1215), or a seal tape around the bolt threads.

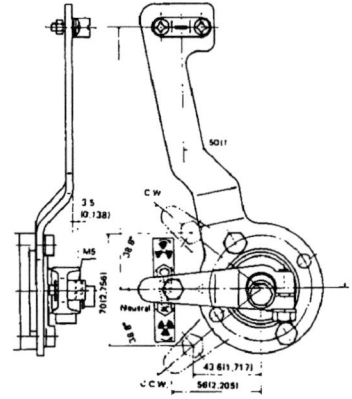

NOTE. Shift lever must be installed in the direction of the Δ-mark ensuring the specified installation angle (θ).

$$\theta = 90°$$

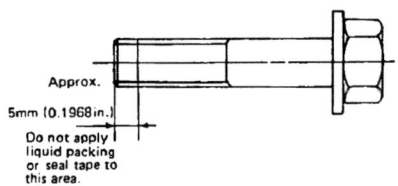

Approx.
5mm (0.1968in.)
Do not apply liquid packing or seal tape to this area.

2-5-2 Inspect for the following points (to be inspected every 2-3 months)

(1)Looseness at the connection of the cable connector and the remote control cable.

(2)Looseness of the attaching nut of the cable connector and the shift lever.

2-6 Adjustment of the remote control head Marine gearbox control side

(1)Equal distribution of the control lever stroke.

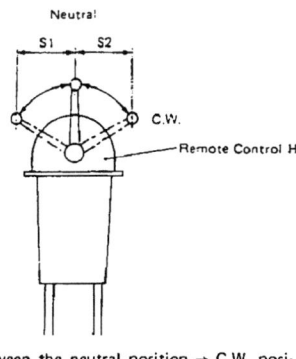

Neutral

The stroke between the neutral position → C.W. position (S2), and the neutral position → C.C.W. position (S1) must be equalized.

When either stroke is too short, clutch engagement becomes faulty.

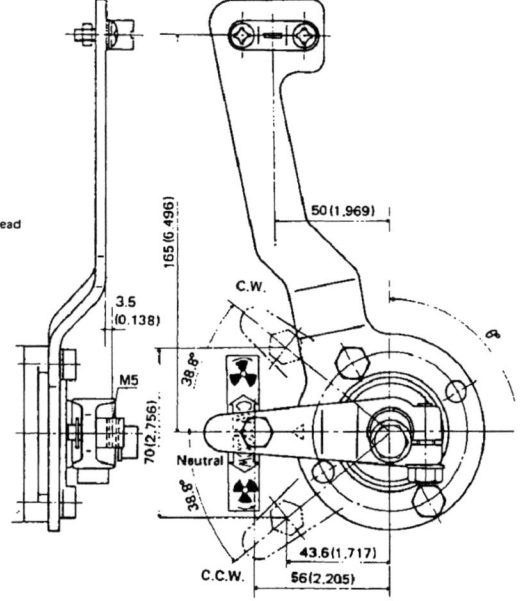

(2)Equalizing the travel distance of the control cable.

After ensuring the equal distribution of the stroke described in (1), connect the cable to the control head. Adjust so that the cable shift travel of the S1 and S2 control lever strokes becomes identical.

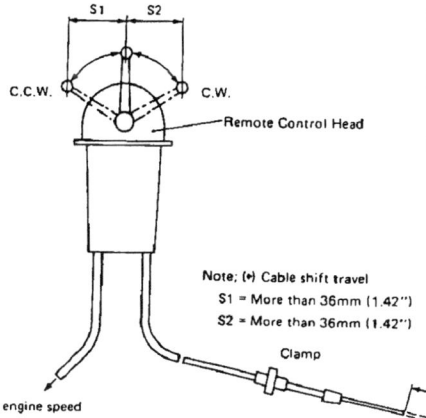

Note; (•) Cable shift travel
S1 = More than 36mm (1.42″)
S2 = More than 36mm (1.42″)

Clamp

To engine speed

2-7 Cautions

(1)Always stop the engine when attaching, adjusting, and inspecting.

(2)When conducting inspection immediately after stopping the engine, do not touch the clutch. The oil temperature is often raised to around 90°C (194°F).

(3)Half-clutch operation is not possible with this design and construction. Do not use with the shift lever halfway to the engaged position.

(4)Set the idling engine speed at between 800 and 850 rpm.

NOTE: The dual(Two) lever remote control device cannot be used.

3. Inspection and Servicing

3-1 Clutch case and cover

(1)Check the clutch case and cover for cracking with a test hammer.

Perform a color check when required.

If the case and cover are cracked, replace those together.

(2)Check for   ining on the inside surface of the bearing section.

Also, measure the inside diameter of the case and cover Replace the case and cover if these are worn beyond the wear limit.

3-2 Bearing

(1) Rusting and damage.

If the bearing is rusted or the taper roller retainer i damaged, replace the bearing.

(2) Make sure that the bearings rotate smoothly.

If rotation is not smooth, if there is any binding, or if any abnormal sound is evident, replace the bearing.

3-3 Gear

Check the surface, tooth face conditions and backlash of each gear. Replace any defective part.

(1)Tooth surface wear.

Check the tooth surface for pitting, abnormal wear, dents, and cracks.   Repair the lightly damaged gears and replace heavily damaged gears.

(2)Tooth surface contact.

Check the tooth surface contact. The amount of tooth surface contact between the tooth crest and tooth flank must be at least 70% of the tooth width.

(3)Backlash.

Measure the backlash of each gear, and replace the gear when it is worn beyond the wear limit.

3-4 Clutch gear (A) and (B)

(1)Contact surface with drive cone.

Visually inspect the tapered surface of the clutch gears (A) and (B) where they make contact with the drive cone to check if there is any abnormal condition or sign of overheating.

If any defect is found,

replace the gear.

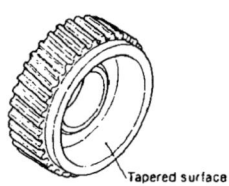

Tapered surface

3-5 Drive cone

(1)Visually inspect that part of the surface that comes into contact with the circumferential triangular slot to check for signs of scoring, overheating or wear. If deep scoring or signs of overheating are found, replace the cone.

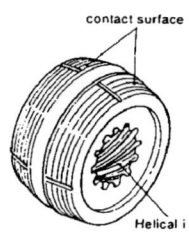

contact surface

Helical i

(2)Check the helical involute spline for any abnormal condition on the tooth surface, and repair or replace the part should any defect be found.

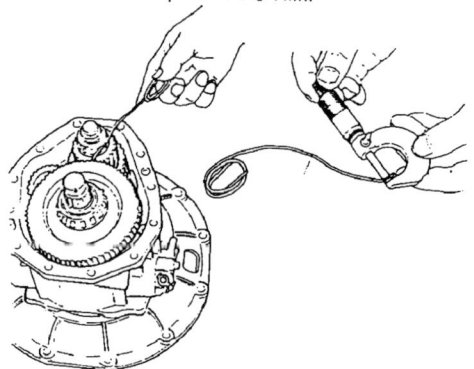

	Maintenance Standard	Wear limit
		mm (in.)
All gears	0.08 ~ 0.16 (0.0031 ~ 0.0063)	0.3 (0.0118)

(3)Measure the amount of wear on the tapered contact
surface of the drive cone, and replace the cone when the
wear exceeds the specified limit.

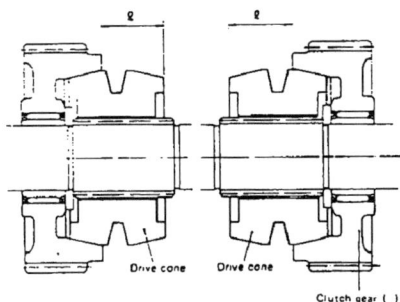

Drive cone   Drive cone

Clutch gear ( )

mm(in.)

	Standard dimensions	Limited dimensions
Dimensions ℓ	29.2 ~ 29.8	28.1
	(1.1496 ~ 1.1732)	(1.1063)

NOTE: When dismantled, the forward or reverse direction
of the drive cone must be clearly identified.

(4)If the wear of the V-groove of the dri
sive, replace the part.

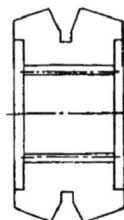

NOTE:When replacing the drive cone, the drive cone
and clutch gears (A) and (B) must be lapped prior
to assembly.
The lapping procedure is described below.

Printed in Japan
A0A1029-9002

3-5-1 Lapping Procedure for Drive Cone

(1) Coat the lapping powder onto the cave of the clutch gear (Lapping powder: 67 micron silicon carbide =280)

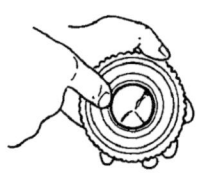

(2) Set the clutch gear on the clutch shaft with a needle bearing and then set the drive cone on the clutch shaft

(3) Lap the clutch gear's cave and drive cone, pushing them together by hand

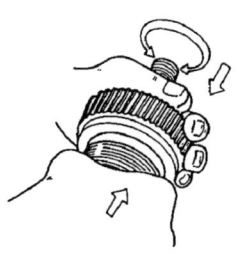

(4) Push and turn the clutch gear about 5 times both clockwise and counter-clockwise.

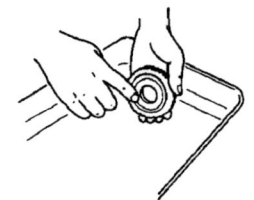

(5) After lapping them, wash them with washing oil. The lapped parts should be cleaned completely.

Small

I.D. mark "O".

Large

NOTE: Do not mix the combination of the lapped parts. The washing oil should be changed frequently in order to prevent residual powder being left on the parts.
When assembling the drive cone, be sure to check its alignment.
The larger chamferring face should be on the clutch gear (A) side.

3-6 Thrust coller A and B for clutch shaft

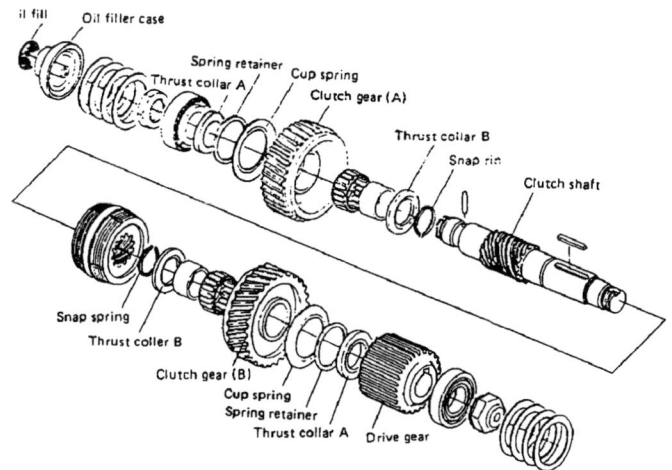

(1) Visually inspect the sliding surface of thrust collar A or B to check for signs of overheating, scoring, or cracks. Replace the collar if any abnormal condition is found.
(2) Measure the thickness of thrust collar A or B, and replace it when the dimension exceeds the specified limit.

3-7 Cup spring and spring retainer

(1) Check for cracks and damage to the cup spring and spring retainer. Replace the part if defective.
(2) Measure the free length of the cup spring and the thickness of the spring retainer. If the length or the thickness deviates from the standard size, replace the part.

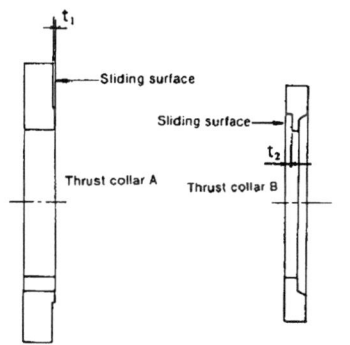

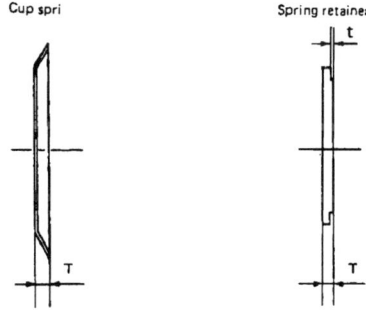

mm (in.)

Stepped wear	Standard		Limit
Thrust collar A, t_1	t_1	0.1 (0.0039)	0.05 (0.0020)
Thrust collar B, t_2	t_2	1.0 (0.0394)	0.20 (0.0079)

mm (in.)

	Standard	Limit
Cup spring, T	2.8 ~ 3.1 (0.1102 ~ 0.1220)	2.6 (0.1024)
Spring retainer, T	2.92 ~ 3.08 (0.1150 ~ 0.1213)	2.8 (0.1102)
Spring retainer, t	—	0.1 (0.0039)

Printed in Japan
A0A1029-9002

3-8 Input shaft

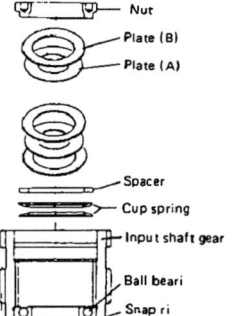

Input shaft gear

Roller bearing

mm(in.)

	Standard	Limit
Cup spring, T	2.75 ~ 3.05 (0.1083 ~ 0.120)	2.6 (0.1024)

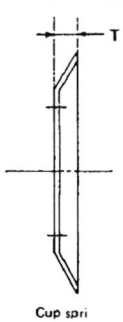

Cup spri

(1) Spline part.
Whenever uneven wear and/or scratches are found, replace with a new part.
(2) Surface of oil seal.
If the sealing surface of the oil seal is worn or scratched, replace.

(3)Torque limiter parts.
If the torque limiter has slipped due to excessive torque, measure the size of the inner parts listed top right. If the parts are excessively damaged replace.

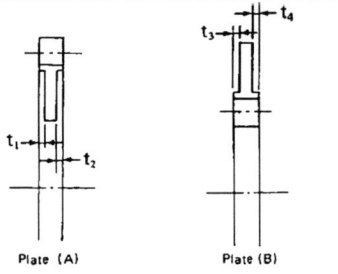

Nut
Plate (B)
Plate (A)

Spacer
Cup spring
Input shaft gear
Ball beari
Snap ri

3-9 Output shaft

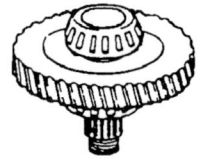

(1)Visually inspect the spline, oil seal and O-ring, and repair or replace a part when any abnormal condition is found on its surface.

Plate (A) and (B)

mm(in.)

Stepped wear	Standard	Limit	Q'ty/unit
Plate (A) ($t_1 + t_2$)	0.95 ~ 1.05 (0.0374 ~ 0.0413)	0.92 (0.0362)	15
Plate (B) ($t_3 + t_4$)	0.35 ~ 0.45 (0.0138 ~ 0.0177)	0.32 (0.0126)	

Plate (A)

Plate (B)

3-10 Intermediate shaft

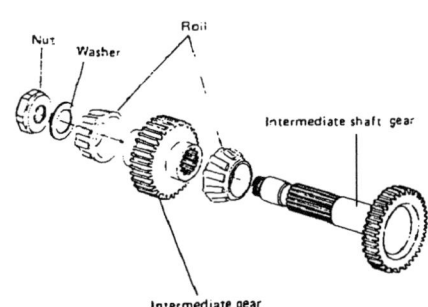

Intermediate gear

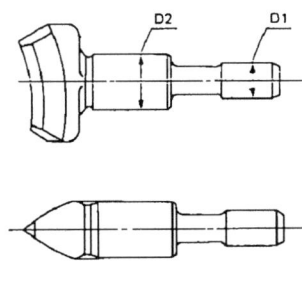

(1)Visually inspect the spline and repair or replace a part when any abnormal condition is found on its surface.

mm (in.)

	Standard	Limit
D1	6.69 ~ 6.70 (0.2634 ~ 0.2638)	6.50 (0.2559)
D2	11.966 ~ 11.984 (0.4711 ~ 0.4718)	11.95 (0.4705)
Shift lever shaft, Shifter insertion hole	12.0 ~ 12.018 (0.4724 ~ 0.4731)	12.05 (0.4744)

3-11 Shifting device

3-11-1 Shifter

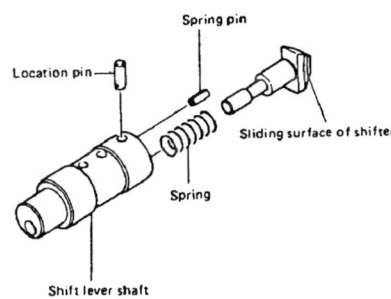

(1)Visually inspect the surface which contacts with the drive cone, and replace the shifter when signs of over-heating, damage or wear are found.

(2)Measure the shaft diameter of the shifter. Replace the shaft if the size deviates from the standard.

3-11-2 Shift lever shaft and location pin

(1)Check the shift lever shaft and location pin for damage or distortion, and replace defective parts. If the location pin must be replaced, replace it together with the shift lever shaft.

(2)Measure the diameter of the shift lever shaft and the shifter insertion hole. Replace the part if the size deviates from the standard value.

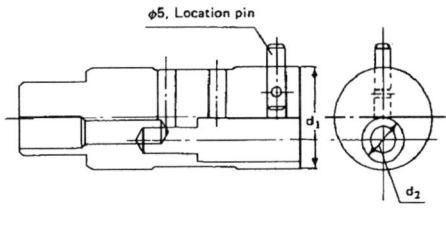

mm (in.)

	Standard	Limit
d_1	27.959 ~ 27.98 (1.1001 ~ 1.1016)	27.90 (1.0984)
d_2	12.0 ~ 12.018 (0.4724 ~ 0.4731)	12.05 (0.4744)
Side cover, Shift insertion hole	28.0 ~ 28.021 (1.1024 ~ 1.1032)	28.08 (1.1055)

7-38

3-11-3 Shifter spring

(1)Check the spring for scratches or corrosion.
(2)Measure the free length of the spring.

Shifter spring	Standard		Limit
Free length	22.6 mm	(0.890in.)	19.8 mm (0.780in.)
Spring constant	0.854 kg/mm	(1.88 lbs/0.04in.)	
Length when attached	14.35 mm	(0.5650 in.)	
Load when attached	7.046 kg	(15.54 lbs)	6.08 kg (13.41 lbs)

3-11-4 Stopper bolt

Check the stopper bolt. If it is worn or stepped, replace.

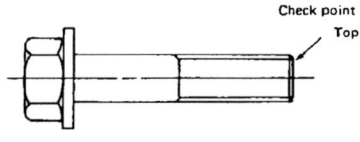

Check point
Top

3-11-5 Side cover and oil seal

(1)Check the neutral, clutch gear (A) and clutch gear (B) position grooves. Replace if the grooves are worn.
(2)Measure the insertion hole of the shift lever shaft. Replace if the size deviates from the standard value.
(3)Check the oil seal and the O-ring for damage. Replace if the part is defective.

3-12 Damper disc

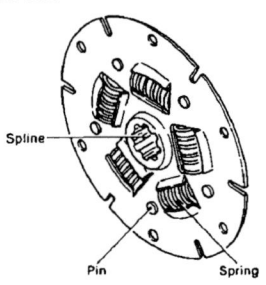

Spline
Pin   Spring

(1) Spline part.
Whenever uneven wear and/or scratches are found, replace with a new part.
(2) Spring.
Whenever uneven wear and/or scratches are found, replace with a new part.
(3) Pin wear.
Whenever uneven wear and/or scratches are found, replace with a new part.
(4) Whenever a crack or damage to the spring slot is found replace the defective part with a new one.

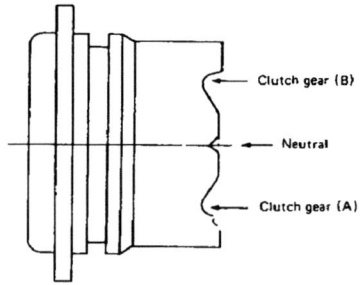

Clutch gear (B)

Neutral

Clutch gear (A)

3-13 Shim adjustment for output and input shafts

Check the thickness of the shims for the intermediate, clutch, input and output shafts. When the component parts are not replaced after dismantling, the same shims can be reused. When the clutch case, mounting flange and clutch case cover or any one of the following parts is replaced, the shim thickness must be determined in the following manner.

For input shaft parts	input shaft, bearing.
For output shaft parts:	output shaft, bearing.
For intermediate shaft parts	intermediate shaft, spacer, gear bearing.
For clutch shaft parts	clutch shaft, thrust collar (A), (B), gear, bearing.

(1) Input Shaft

Measure the distance A and B.
Thickness of Shim t_1

$$t_1 \quad (A - B)^{\pm 0.05}$$

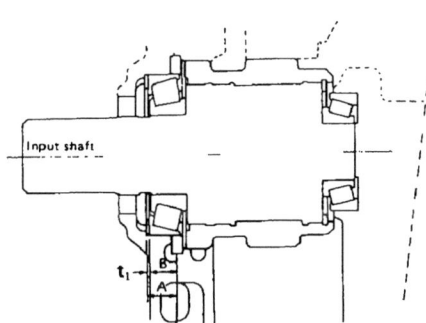

(2) Intermediate Shaft

Measure the distance C and thickness D

$$t_2 \quad (C - D)^{\pm 0.05}$$

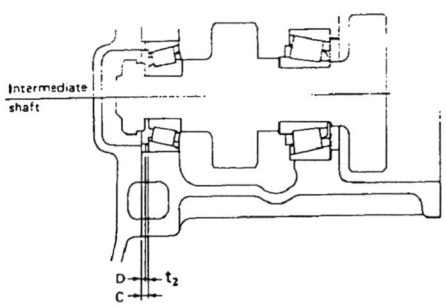

(3) Clutch Shaft

Measure the distance E, F and G.

$$t_3 \quad \left(78 - E - F - \frac{G}{2}\right)^{\pm 0.05}$$

NOTE: When measuring the distances F and G, the clutch gears must be pushed in the direction of the drive cone.

Then measure distances H and I.

$$t_4 = (H - I)^{\pm 0.05}$$

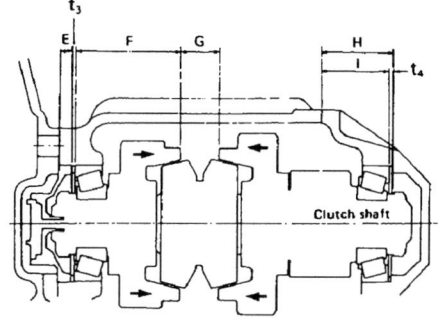

(4)Output Shaft

Adjust the thickness of Shim t_5 to make the backlash
of gear at 0.08~0.16mm (0.0032~0.0063in).
Then measure the distances J and K.

$$t_6 = (J - K)^{-0}_{-0.1}$$

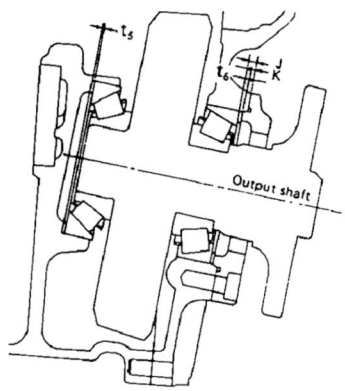

(5)Standard size of parts

mm (in.)

A	B	C	D	E	F	G	H	I	J	K	Drive cone neutral center position
14.0 ~ 14.2 (0.551 ~ 0.559)	11.4 ~ 12.9 (0.449 ~ 0.508)	2.3 ~ 3.7 (0.091 ~ 0.146)	1.9 ~ 2.1 (0.075 ~ 0.083)	7.4 ~ 7.5 (0.291 ~ 0.295)	57.8 ~ 58.7 (2.276 ~ 2.311)	20.3 ~ 21.2 (0.799 ~ 0.835)	39.9 ~ 40.3 (1.571 ~ 1.587)	37.7 ~ 39.5 (1.484 ~ 1.555)	3.6 ~ 4.7 (0.142 ~ 0.185)	2.4 ~ 2.6 (0.094 ~ 0.102)	78 (3.071)

NOTE: Compare your measurements with the above standard
size. If your measurements differ greatly from the
standard sizes, the measurements may not be correct.
Check and measure again.

Adjusting point	Part No.	Thickness. mm (in.)	No. of shims
t1	177095-02150	0.1 (0.0039) 0.3 (0.0118) 0.5 (0.0197) 1.0 (0.0394)	2 1 2 1
t2	177090-02250	0.1 (0.0039) 0.3 (0.0118) 0.5 (0.0197) 1.0 (0.0394)	2 1 1 1
t3 & t4	177075-02150	0.3 (0.0118) 0.4 (0.0157) 0.5 (0.0197)	4 4 4
t5 & t6	177090-02310	0.1 (0.0039) 0.3 (0.0118) 0.5 (0.0197) 1.0 (0.0394)	4 2 2 2

Printed in Japan
A0A1029-9002

4.Special Tools

Name of tool	Shape and size mm(in.)	Application
Part No. 177075-09030	10 (0.394) 190 (7.480) ø35.2 (1.386) ø40 (1.575) ø42.7 (1.681)	
Inserting tool Part No. 177088-09150	88 (3.465) 2 (0.079) ø30 (1.181)	For installing intermediate shaft and clutch shaft bearings.
Part No. 177073-09020	5 (0.197) 30 (1.181) ø44 (1.732) ø44 (1.732) 30 (1.181)	For checking limiter torque of the torque limiter
Ring nut Part No. 177073-09010	210 (8.268) ø12 (0.472) 50 (1.969) (1.575) 40	For removing and tightening the torque limiter

Printed in Japan
A0A1029-9002

Special tools

Name of tool	Shape and size mm (in.)	Application
Part No. 177075-09050	100 (3.937) 20 (0.787) 150 (5.906) 8 (0.315) 5 (0.197) 20 (0.787) 35 (1.378) 30 (1.181) 12 (0.472)	For removing and ti output shaft nut.
Socket Part No. 177073-00050	20 (0.786) 16 (0.629) φ55 (2.165) φ40.5 (1.595) 9.5 (0.374) 30 (1.181)	For removing and ti output shelf nut.
Part No. 177073-09030	100 (3.937) φ28.3 (1.114) φ32.2 (1.268) φ38 (1.496) 5 (0.197)	For installing the clutch shaft bearing

Printed in Japan
A0A1029-9002

5.Disassembly

5-1 Disassembling the clutch and accessories.

(1)Remove the remote-control cable and the C.W. hose of L.O. cooler.

(2)Dismount the clutch main body from the mounting flange.

(3)Drain the lubricating oil

Drain the lubricating oil by loosening the plug at the bottom of the clutch case. Also remove the dipstick from the clutch case at the same time.

(4)Remove the drain plug and pull out the L.O.

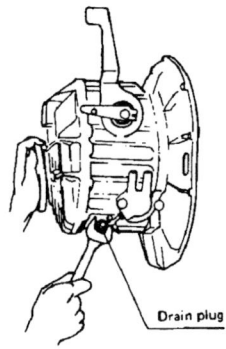

Drain plug

(5) Remove the dipstick.

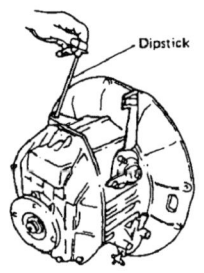

Dipstick

(6) Remove the end nut and output shaft coupling
   1) Loosen the calking of the endnut.

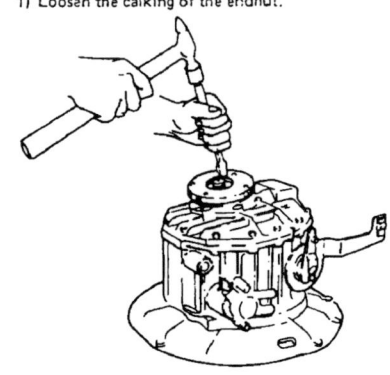

NOTE: Loosen the endnut with the special tool and a torque wrench.

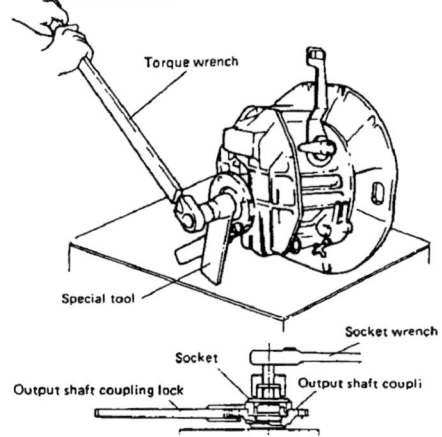

Torque wrench

Special tool

Socket wrench

Socket

Output shaft coupling lock

Output shaft coupli

2)Remove the output shaft coupling

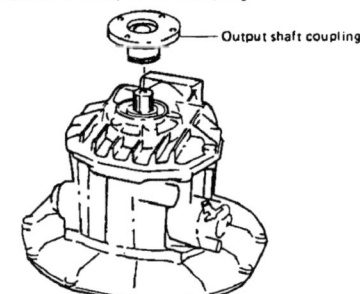

Output shaft coupling

(7)Remove the fixing bolts on the side cover of clutch case, and also remove the shift lever shaft assembly.

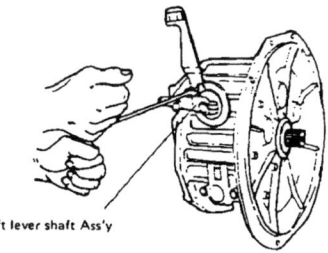

ift lever shaft Ass'y

(8) Remove the clutch case cover.

1) Remove the bolt of the clutch case cover

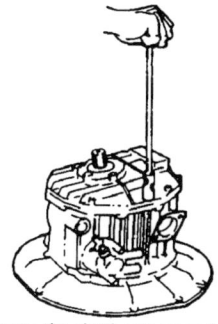

2) Remove the clutch case cover from the clutch case.

Clutch case cover

Clutch case

Clutch shaft ass'y

Output shaft ass'y

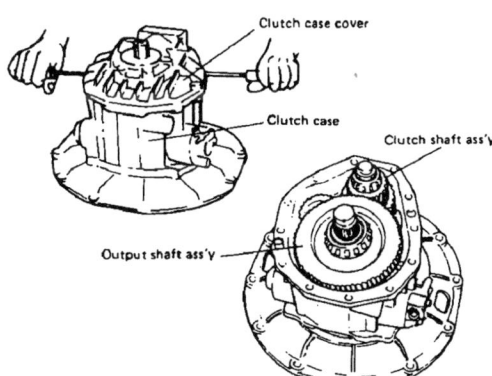

NOTE:To remove the case cover and the case, insert two drivers into the two depressed points at the joint between the case cover and the case. This makes removal easy.

(9)Removing the output shaft assembly and clutch shaft assembly.

Clutch shaft ass'y

Output shaft

Intermediate shaft ass'y

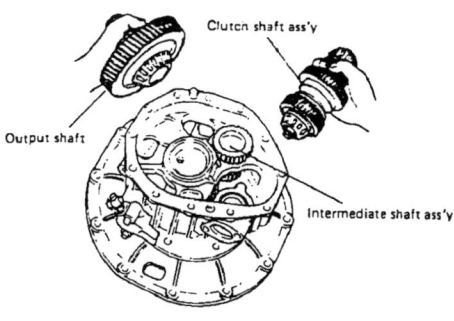

(10)Removing the mounting flange

Remove the fastening bolt of the mounting flange and then remove the mounting flange.

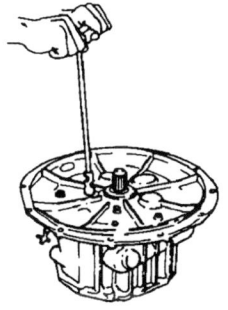

(11)Removing the input shaft assembly.
Draw out from the mounting flange side of the case.

Input shaft ass'y

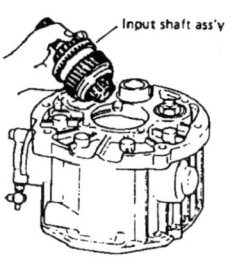

Printed in Japan
A0A1029-9002

(12)Removing the intermediate shaft.

1) Loosen the calking of locknut of the intermediate shaft.

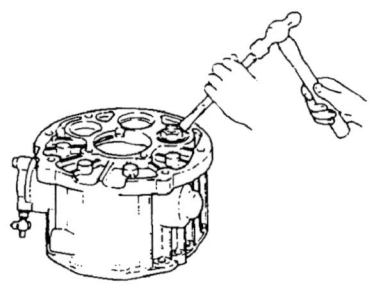

2) Remove the locknut.

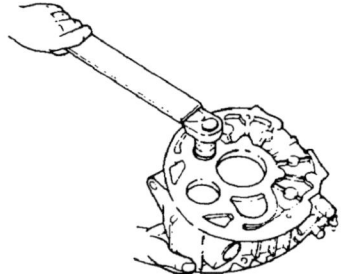

NOTE: *Thread of the locknut is left-handed.*

3) Draw out the intermediate shaft tapping to the case cover side with a plastic-headed hammer.

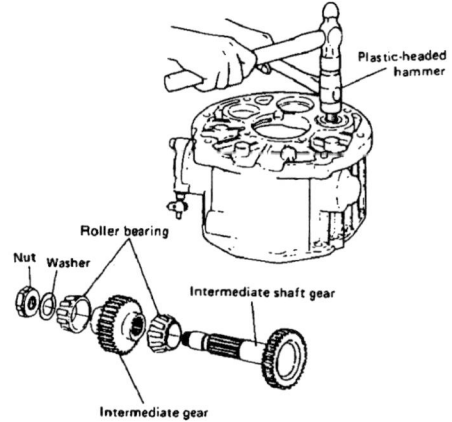

Plastic-headed hammer

Roller bearing

Nut   Washer

Intermediate shaft gear

Intermediate gear

(11)Removing the oil-cooler.

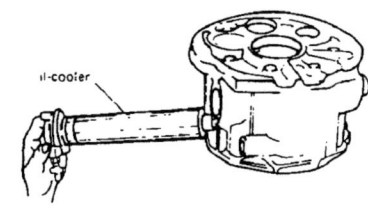

il-cooler

Spri

(14)Draw out the outer bearing races.

1) Remove the outer bearing races of the mounting flange, the case cover and the case.

NOTE: Remove the outer bearing races with a special tool.

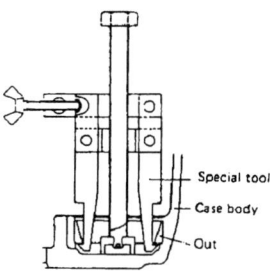

Special tool
Case body
Out

(15) Remove the oil seals of the mounting flange and the case cover.

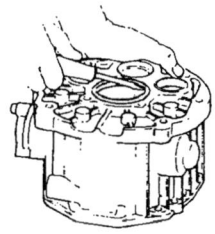

Printed in Japan
A0A1029-9002

5-2 Disassembling the clutch shaft.

5-2-1 Clutch gear (A) side

(1) Loosen the calking of the end nut and remove the nut. Remove the nut by a torque wrench, fixing the clutch shaft in a vice.

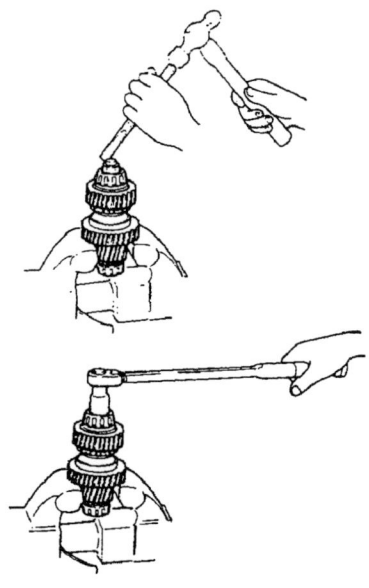

NOTE: *Remember that the nut has a left-handed thread.*

(2) Take out the clutch gear (A), Thrust collar (A), cup spring, spring retainer and inner bearing trace. The clutch gear (A) must be withdrawn using a pulley extracter, with the clutch shaft fixed in a vice.

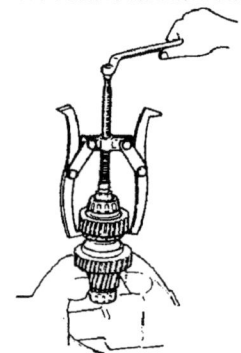

(3) Remove the pi

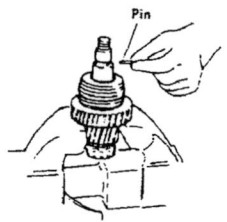

Pin

(4) Withdraw the thrust collar (B), inner needle bearing by pulley extractor.

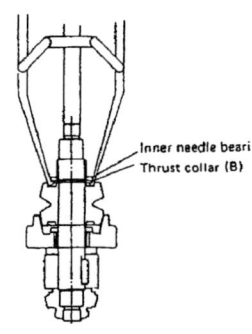

Inner needle beari
Thrust collar (B)

5-2-2 Clutch gear (B) side

(1) Loosen the calking of the end nut and remove the nut. Remove the nut by a torque wrench, with the clutch shaft fixed in a vice.

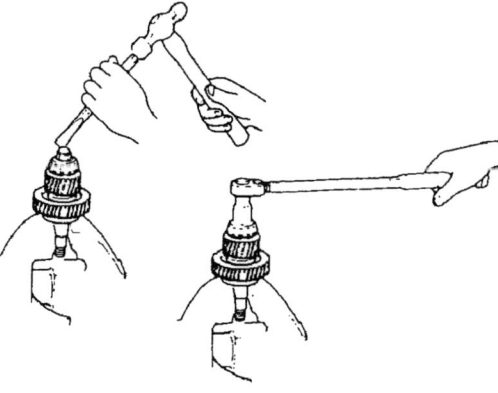

NOTE: *Remember that as the nut has a left-handed thread.*

(2)Withdraw the large gear (B), thrust collar (A), cup-spring, spring retainer, drive gear and inner bearing race.
Use a pulley extracter, with the clutch shaft fixed in a vice.

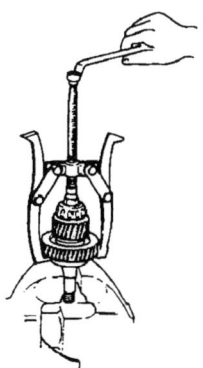

(3)Remove the key

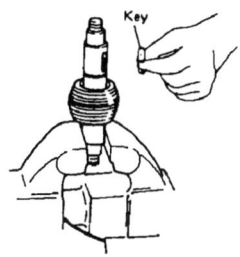

Key

(4)Withdraw the thrust collar (B) and inner needle bearing race with the pulley extractor.

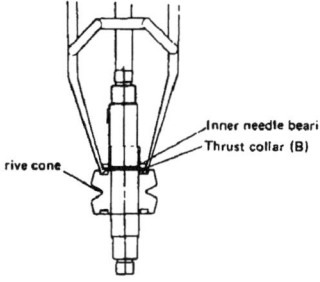

Inner needle beari
Thrust collar (B)
rive cone

(5)Remove the snap rings

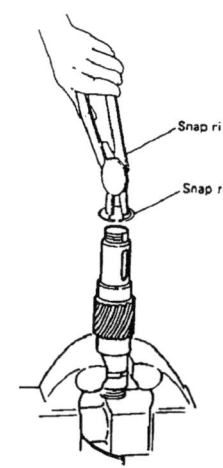

Snap ri
Snap ri

(6)Draw out the drive cone.

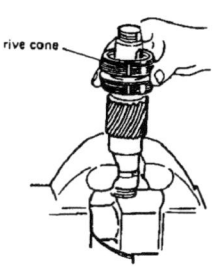

rive cone

5-3 Disassembling the input shaft.

1) Draw out the input shaft tapping to the small roller bearing side with a steel bar.

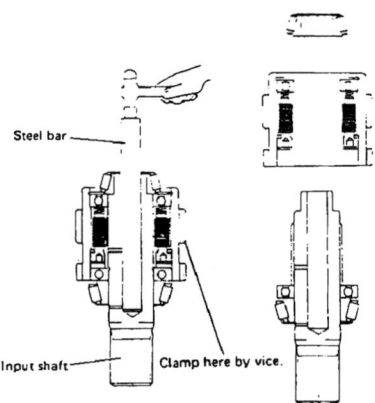

Steel bar

Input shaft | Clamp here by vice.

(2) Fix the input shaft gear in a vice, and remove the lock nut with a special tool.

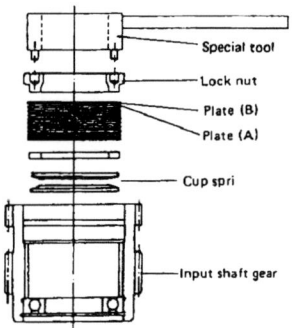

Special tool
Lock nut
Plate (B)
Plate (A)
Cup spri
Input shaft gear

5-4 Disassembling the output shaft

(1) Remove the bearing inner race from the output shaft. Use a pulley extracter, fixing the output shaft in a vice.

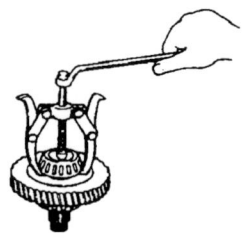

5-5 Disassembling the shifting device

(1)Take out the shifter and shifter spring

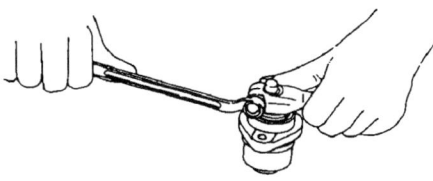

(2)Remove the stopper bolt of the shifter and shim.

(3)Loosen the belt of the shift lever and remove the shift lever and cable bracket

(4)Remove the shift lever to the anti-shift lever side.

(5)Remove the oil-seal and O-ring.

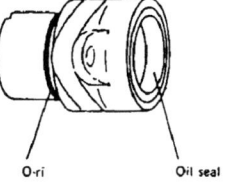

O-ri   Oil seal

6.Reassembly

6-1 Reassembly of clutch shaft

6-1-1 Clutch gear (B) side

(1) Fit the clutch gear (B) side snap ring and thrust collar (B) onto the shaft.

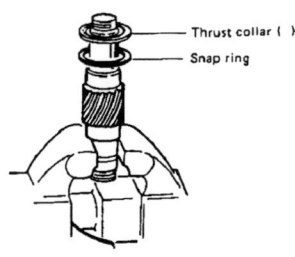

Thrust collar ( )
Snap ring

(2) Drive in the inner needle bearing race using the inserting tool.

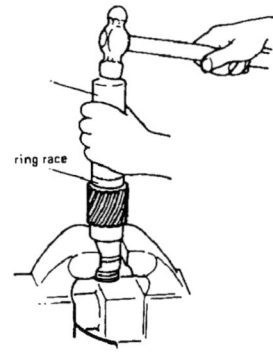

ring race

(3) Assemble the needle bearing and clutch gear (B)

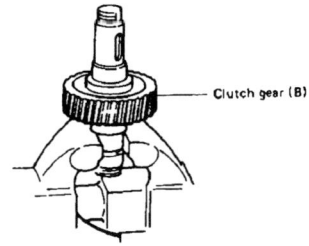

Clutch gear (B)

NOTE: Check that the clutch gear (B) rotates smoothly.

(4) Fit the cup spring, spring retainer, thrust collar (A).

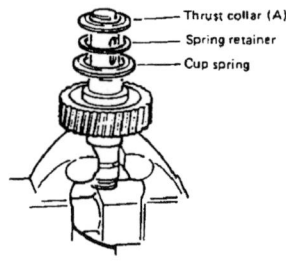

Thrust collar (A)
Spring retainer
Cup spring

NOTE: 1) Drive in with a plastic headed hammer. Do not hit hard.

2) When fitting the thrust collar (A), note the fitting direction. Fit it keeping the stepped surface toward the drive gear side.

3) Check that the clutch gear (B) rotates smoothly.

(5) Fit the key

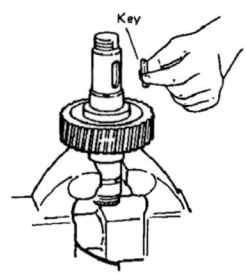

Key

(6)Drive in the driving gear and inner bearing race using the inserting tool.

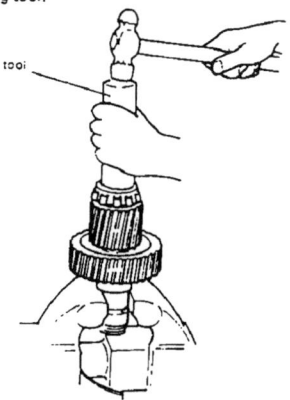

tool

(7)Set and tighten the clutch gear (B) end nut
Fit the clutch shaft in a vice, and tighten the nut with a torque wrench.

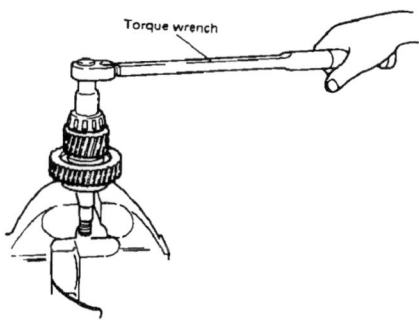

Torque wrench

Tightening torque	8.5 – 11.5 kg-m (61.5 – 83.2 ft-lb)

NOTE: 1) Remember it is a left-handed thread.

2) Use the clutch gear (A) side nut which was used before dismantling for the clutch gear (B) end nut. This is to provide effective calking to the nut.

(8)Calking the end nut and clutch shaft.

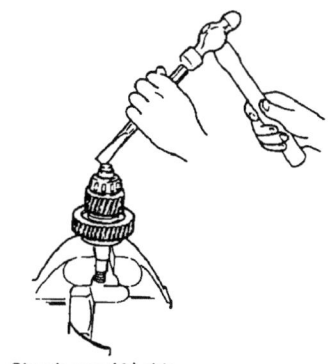

6-1-2 Clutch gear (A) side

(1)Insert the drive cone, snap ring and thrust collar (B).

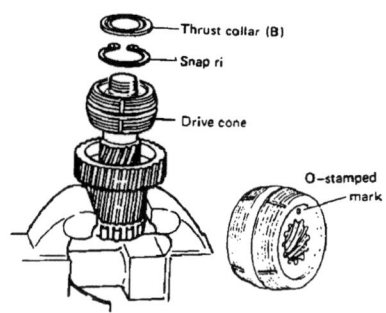

Thrust collar (B)

Snap ri

Drive cone

O-stamped mark

NOTE: Insert it keeping the O-stamped mark surface toward the clutch gear (B) side.

(2)Drive in the inner needle bearing race, using an inserting tool.

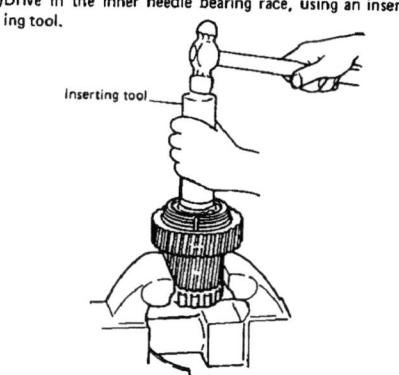

Inserting tool

Printed in Japan
A0A1029-9002

(3)Assemble the needle bearing and clutch gear (A)

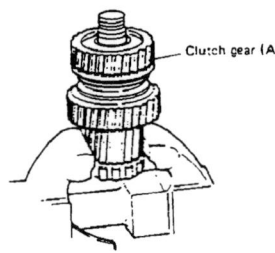

Clutch gear (A)

NOTE: Check that the clutch gear (A) rotates smoothly.

(4)Insert the pin.

Pin

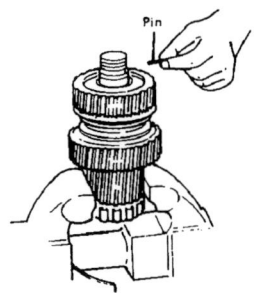

(5)Fit the cup spring, spring retainer and thrust collar (A) and drive in the inner bearing race using the inserting tool.

NOTE:1) When fitting the thrust collar (A), note the fitting direction. Fit it keeping the stepped surface toward the roller bearing side.

2) The pin cannot be fitted after the inner bearing race has been driven in.

3) Check that the large gear (B) rotates smoothly.

(6)Set and tighten the clutch gear (A) end nut. Fix the clutch shaft in a vice and tighten the nut with a torque wrench.

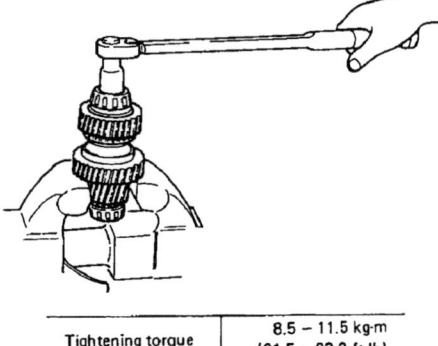

Tightening torque	8.5 – 11.5 kg·m (61.5 – 83.2 ft-lb)

NOTE: 1) Remember it is a left-handed thread.

(7)Calk the end nut and clutch shaft.

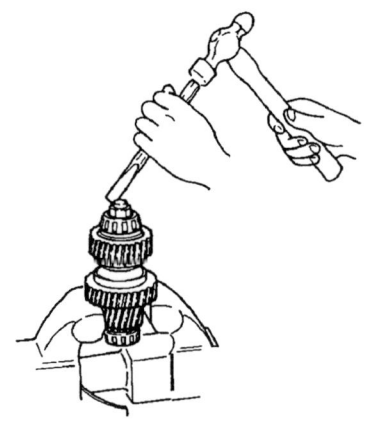

NOTE: Use the clutch gear (A) side nut which was used before dismounting for the clutch gear (B) end nut. This to provide effective calking to the nut.

6-2 Reassembly of input shaft

(1)Drive in the ball bearing and fit the snap ring into the input shaft gear.

(2)Insert the cup springs, spacer, plates (A) and plates (B) and temporarily lock the lock nut.

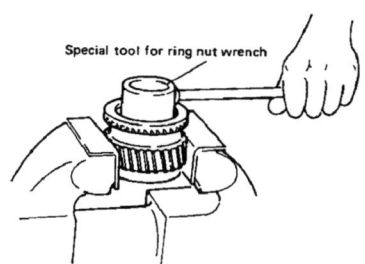

Special tool for ring nut wrench

NOTE: Apply lube oil to each insert part.

(3)Fit the O-ring onto the input shaft.

(4)Drive the ball bearing and the inner bearing race using an inserting tool.

(5)Insert the input shaft into the plate (A).

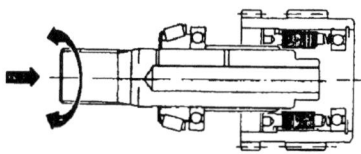

(6)Take the input shaft out again.

(7)Tighten the nut firmly using the special tool, then return the nut by 45 — 90 degrees.

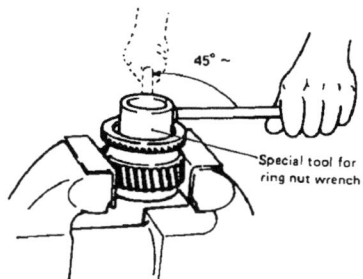

45° ~

Special tool for ring nut wrench

(8)Insert the input shaft, then measure its torque using a torque wrench.

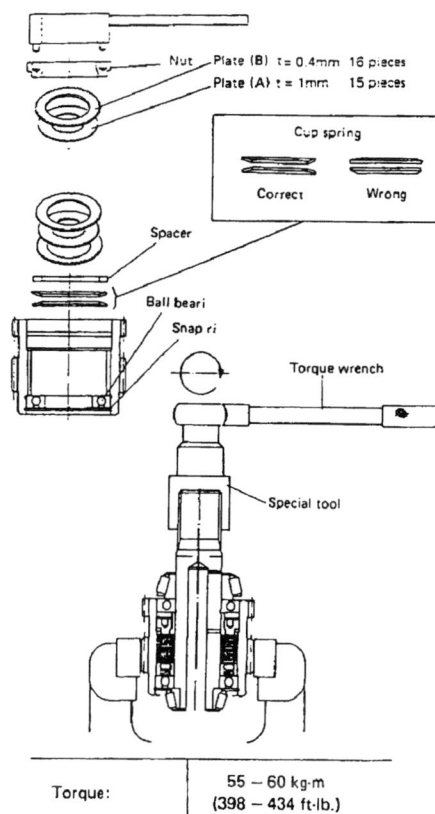

Nut — Plate (B) t = 0.4mm 16 pieces
Plate (A) t = 1mm 15 pieces

Cup spring

Correct   Wrong

Spacer

Ball beari
Snap ri

Torque wrench

Special tool

Torque:	55 — 60 kg·m (398 — 434 ft·lb.)

NOTE: Match up the teeth of plate (A).

(9)Take out the input shaft and caalking at the lock nut end ot the thread.

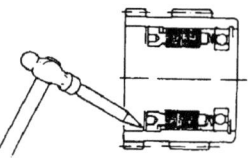

(10)Insert the input shaft into the input gear assembly.
(11)Drive the inner bearing race onto the input shaft end.

6-3 Reassembly of the clutch case

6-3-1 Reassembly of the intermediate shaft

(1) Drive in the outer bearing race (large) into the clutch case.

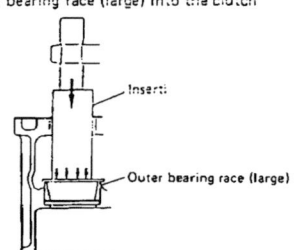

Insert

Outer bearing race (large)

(2) Insert the inner bearing races and idle gear and drive in the intermediate shaft

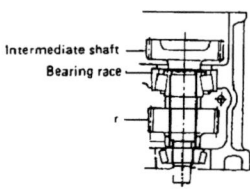

Intermediate shaft
Bearing race
r

(3) Drive the outer bearing race into the clutch case.

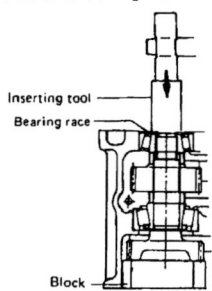

Inserting tool
Bearing race

Block

(4) Insert the washer and tighten the end nut using a torque wrench.

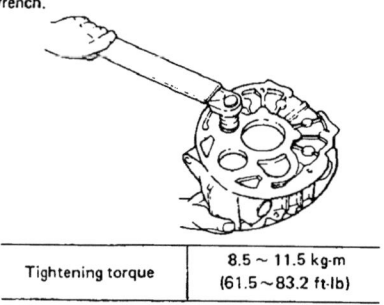

Tightening torque	8.5 ~ 11.5 kg-m (61.5 ~ 83.2 ft-lb)

NOTE: Remember it is a left-handed thread

(5) Calk the end nut

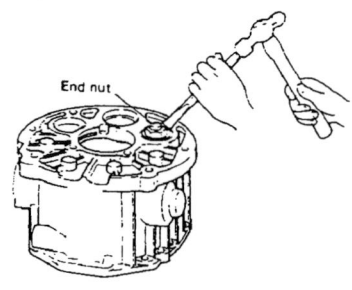

End nut

(6) Insert the shims into the clutch case.

6-3-2 Reassembly of the bearing outer races and shims in the clutch case

(1) Drive the input shaft outer bearing race and clutch shaft outer bearing race into the clutch case.

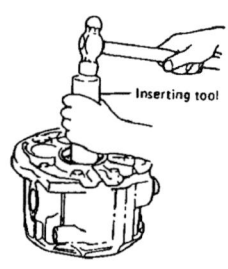

Inserting tool

(2) Insert the clutch shaft shim, lube oil filter case and filter into the clutch case.

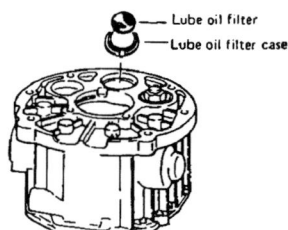

Lube oil filter
Lube oil filter case

6-3-3 Reassembly of the input shaft

(1)Insert the input shaft assembly into the clutch case.

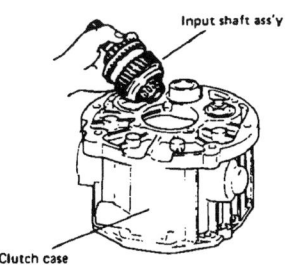

Input shaft ass'y

Clutch case

(2)Drive the centering bush into the clutch case.

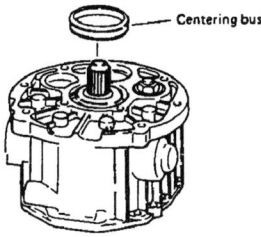

Centering bush

6-3-4 Reassembly of the mounting flange

(1)Insert the oil seal and the shim into the mounting flange.

(2)Drive the outer bearing race into the mounting flange.

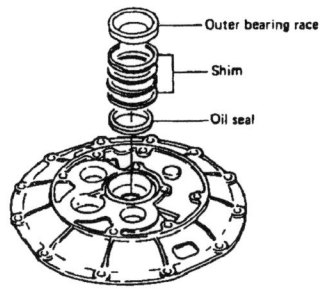

Outer bearing race

Shim

Oil seal

(3)Fit the mounting flange onto the clutch case, and tighten the bolt.

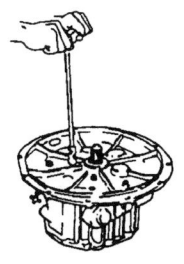

Tightening torque	5 – 6 kg-m (36.2 – 43.4 ft-lb)

NOTE: Apply non-drying liquid packing to the matching surface of the mounting flange and the clutch case.

6-3-5 Reassembly of the oil cooler

NOTE: Fasten taking care not to allow the spring at the tip of the oil cooler to drop out.

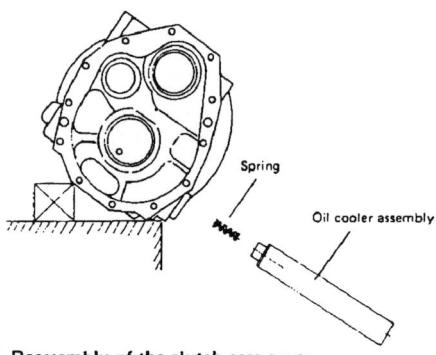

Spring

Oil cooler assembly

6-3-6 Reassembly of the clutch case cover.

(1)Drive the output shaft shim and the outer bearing race into the clutch case.

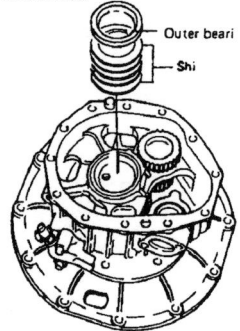

Outer beari

Shi

(2)Drive the shims and the outer bearing races into the clutch case cover

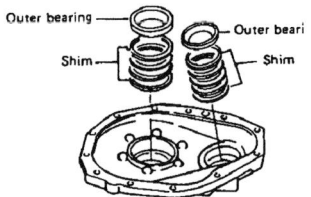

Outer bearing

Outer beari

Shim

Shim

(3)Insert the clutch shaft assembly and the output shaft into the clutch case.

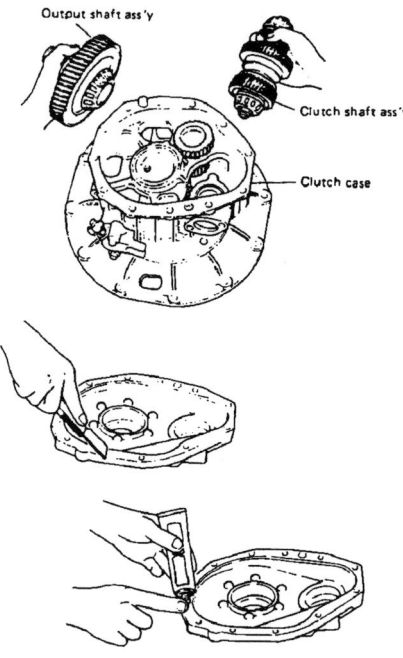

Output shaft ass'y

Clutch shaft ass'y

Clutch case

NOTE: Apply non-drying liquid packing to the maching surface of the clutch case cover and the clutch case.

(4)Fit the clutch case cover on the clutch case, and tighten the bolt.

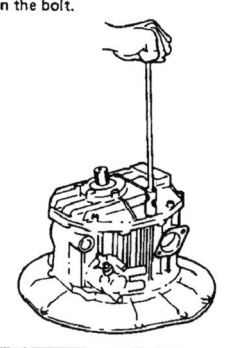

Tightening torque	2.3 – 2.8 kg-m (16.6 – 20.3 ft-lb)

(5)Insert the outer bearing race, shim and the output shaft cover, and tighten the bolt.

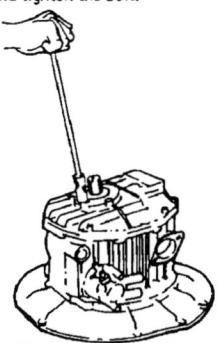

(6)Insert the oil seal, output shaft coupling, O-ring and the end nut into the output shaft.

(7)Tighten the end nut with the special tool and a torque wrench, then calk it.

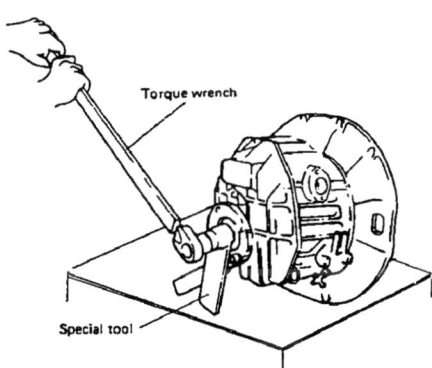

Torque wrench

Special tool

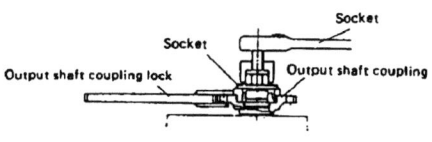

Socket

Socket

Output shaft coupling lock

Output shaft coupling

Tightening torque	54 – 56 kg-m (391 – 405 ft-lb)

6-3-7 Reassembly of the shifting device

(1)Fit the oil seal and O-ring to the side cover

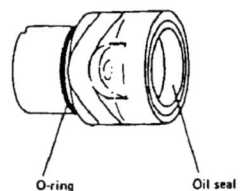

O-ring   Oil seal

(2)Insert the shift lever shaft to the side cover

(3)Fit the shift lever to the shift lever shaft

NOTE: Check the direction of the shift lever △ mark.

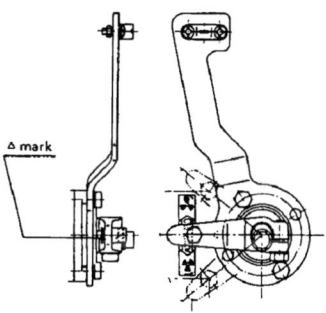

△ mark

(4)Insert the shifter spring and shifter to the shift lever shaft

Shifter   Spring

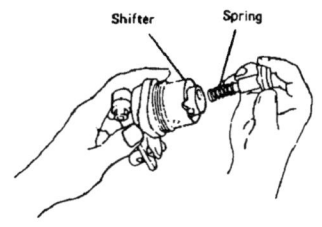

(5)Fit the side cover assembly and the remote control bracket to the clutch case.

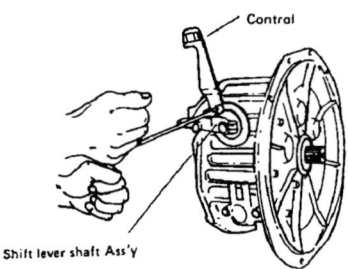

Control

Shift lever shaft Ass'y

NOTE: 1) Check the direction of the shifter (Top and bottom side)
2) The shift lever may not turn smoothly if the clutch case is not filled with lubricating oil.

(6)Fit the shim and stopper bolt to the shift lever shaft.

NOTE:Apply non-drying liquid packing or seal tape to the thread of the stopper bolt.

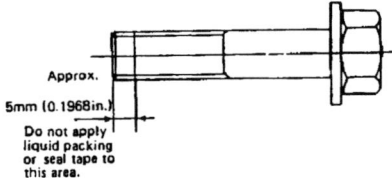

Approx.
5mm (0.1968in.)
Do not apply
liquid packing
or seal tape to
this area.

(7)Fit the pivot to the shift lever.

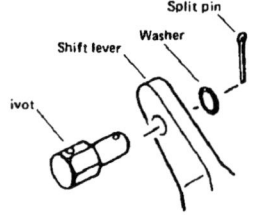

Split pin
Washer
Shift lever
ivot

6-3-8 Reassembly of the lube oil drain plug and the dipstick

Drain plug

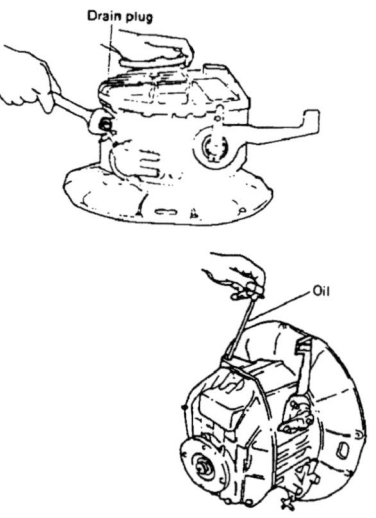

Oil

Marine Gear Models
KM3P2

for Engine Models 4JH2E

1. Construction

1-1 Construction

This clutch is a cone-type, mechanically operated clutch. When the drive cone (which is connected to the output shaft by the lead spline) is moved forward or backward, its taper contacts with the large gear and transfers power to the output shaft.

The construction is simple when compared with other types of clutch and if serves to reduce the number of components, making for a lighter, more compact unit which can be operated smoothly. Although it is small, the power transmission efficiency is high even under a heavy load. Its durability is high and it is also reliable because high grade materials are used for the shaft and gear, and a taper roller bearing is incorporated. Power transmission is smooth because connection with the engine is made through the damper disc.

- The drive cone is made from special aluminum bronze which has both higher wear-resistance and durability. The drive cone is connected with the output shaft through the thread spline. The taper angle, diameter of the drive cone, twist angle, and diameter of the thread spline, are designed to give the greatest efficiency, thus ensuring that the drive cone can be readily engaged or disengaged.

- Helical gears are used for greater strength. The intermediate shaft is supported at 2 points to reduce deflection and gear noise.

- The clutch case and mounting flange are made from an aluminum alloy of special composition to reduce weight. It is also anticorrosive against seawater.

- As the damper disc is fitted to the output shaft, power can be transmitted smoothly. For the damper disc, springs of different strengths are used so that two stages of torque and twist angle are applied. That is, in the first stage, only the weak spring is used, and the strong spring comes into action for a torque higher than a predetermined value.

This prevents gear noise due to torsional vibration as well as absorbing shock when engaging.

Stage arrangement

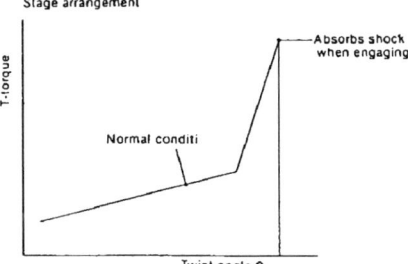

- There is a small clearance between the dipstick and the inside of the dipstick tube. A small hole in the dipstick works as a breather.

- When the load on the propeller is removed, the engagement of the drive cone and the large gear is maintained by the shifter and V-groove of the drive cone. Even when the drive cone's tapered area and V-groove are worn, this engagement is maintained by the shift lever device and accordingly no adjustment of the remote control cable is required.

- The cup spring on the rear of the larger gear absorbs rotational fluctuations and stabilizes the engagement of the drive cone and the larger gear. Thus, the durability of the cone against wear is enhanced.

1-2 Specifications

Model			KM3P2	
For engine models			4JH2E	
Clutch			Constant mesh gear with servo cone clutch (wet type)	
Reduction ratio	Forward		2.36	2.61
	Reverse		3.16	3.16
Propeller shaft rpm (Forward)			1441	1303
irection of rotation	Input shaft		Counter-clockwise, viewed from stern	
	Output shaft	Forward	Clockwise, viewed from stern	
		Reverse	Counter-clockwise, viewed from stern	
Remote control	Control head		Single lever control	
	Cable		Morse, 33-C (cable travel 76.2mm or	
	Clamp		YANMAR made, standard accessory	
	Cable connector		YANMAR made, standard accessory	
Output shaft coupling	Outer diameter		∅100mm (3.93")	
	Pitch circle diameter		∅78mm (3.07")	
	Connecting bolt holes		4—∅10.5mm (4—∅0.41")	
Position of shift lever			Left side, viewed from stern	
Lubricating oil			SAE 20/30	
Lubricating oil capacity			0.35 ℓ	
Dry weight			11.5 kg (25.4 lbs)	

1-3 Power transmission system

1-3.1 Arrangement of shafts and gears

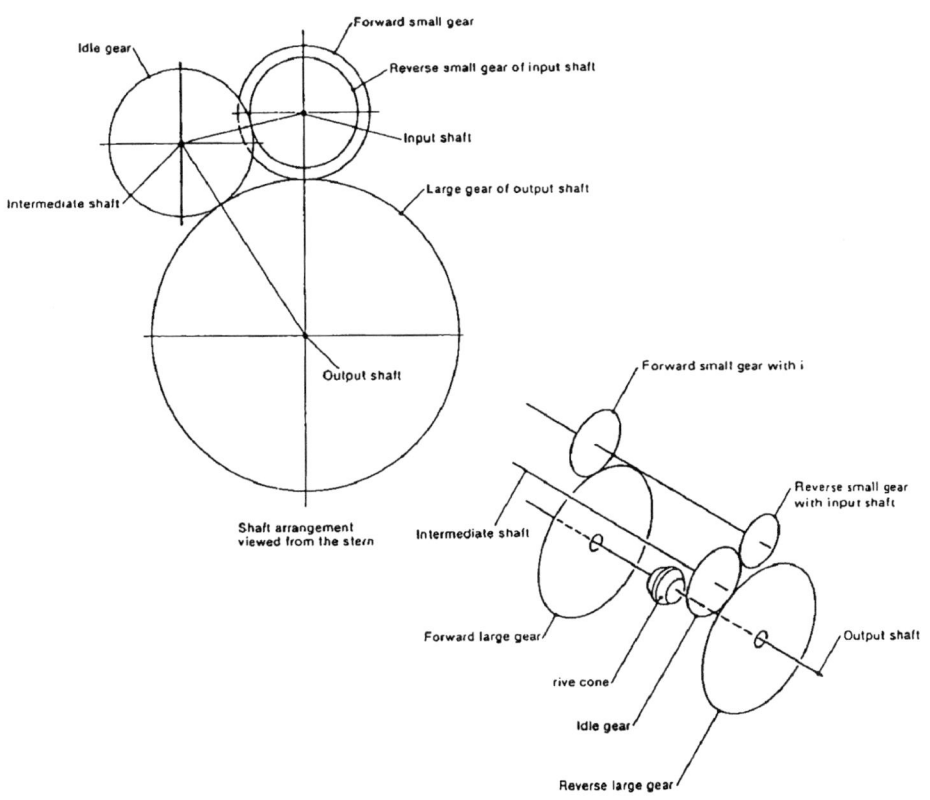

1-3.2 Reduction ratio

Forward

Model	No. of teeth of forward small gear Zif	No. of teeth of forward large gear Zof	Reduction ratio Zof/Zif
KM3P2	25	59	59/25 = 2.36
	23	60	60/23 = 2.61

Reverse

Model	No. of teeth of reverse small gear Zir	No. of teeth of intermediate shaft gear Zl	No. of teeth of reverse large gear Zdr	Reduction ratio Zil/Zir·Zdr/Zl
KM3P2	19	26	60	60/19 = 3.16

Printed in Japan
A0A1029-9002

1-3.3 Power transmission routine — Forward

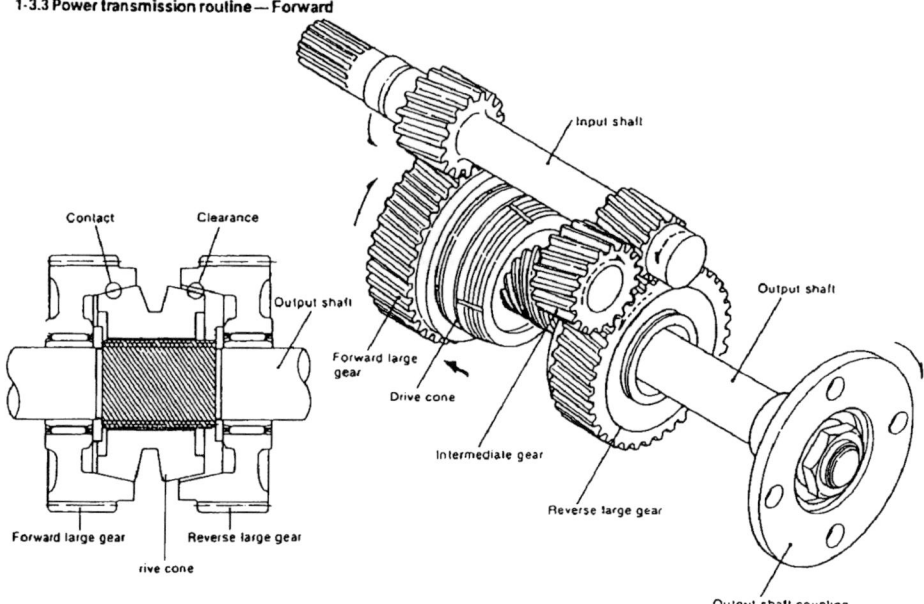

Contact   Clearance

Output shaft

Input shaft

Output shaft

Forward large gear

Drive cone

Output shaft

Intermediate gear

Reverse large gear

Forward large gear   Reverse large gear

rive cone

Output shaft coupling

1-3.4 Power transmission routine — Reverse

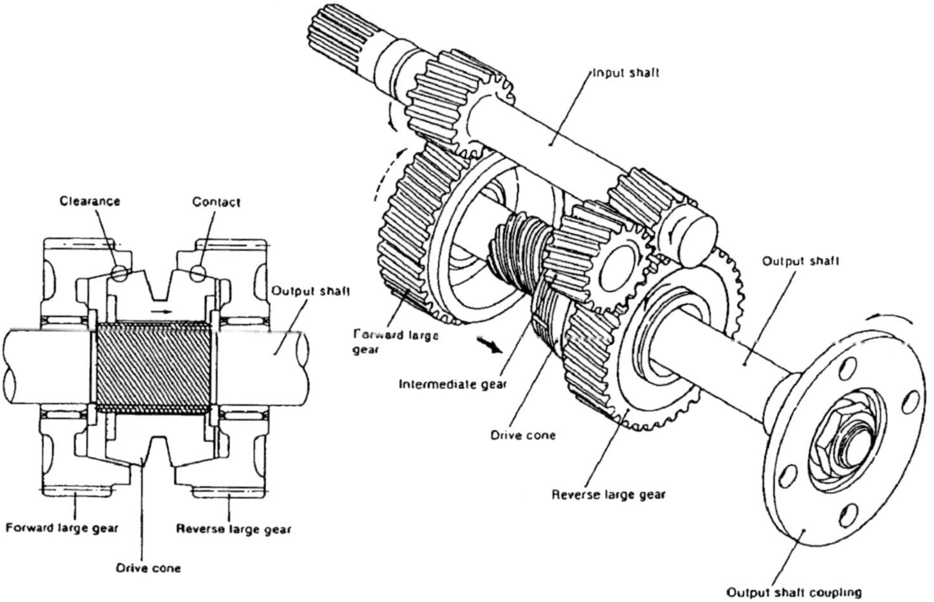

Clearance   Contact

Output shaft

Input shaft

Output shaft

Forward large gear

Intermediate gear

Output shaft

Drive cone

Reverse large gear

Forward large gear   Reverse large gear

Drive cone

Output shaft coupling

1-4 Drawing

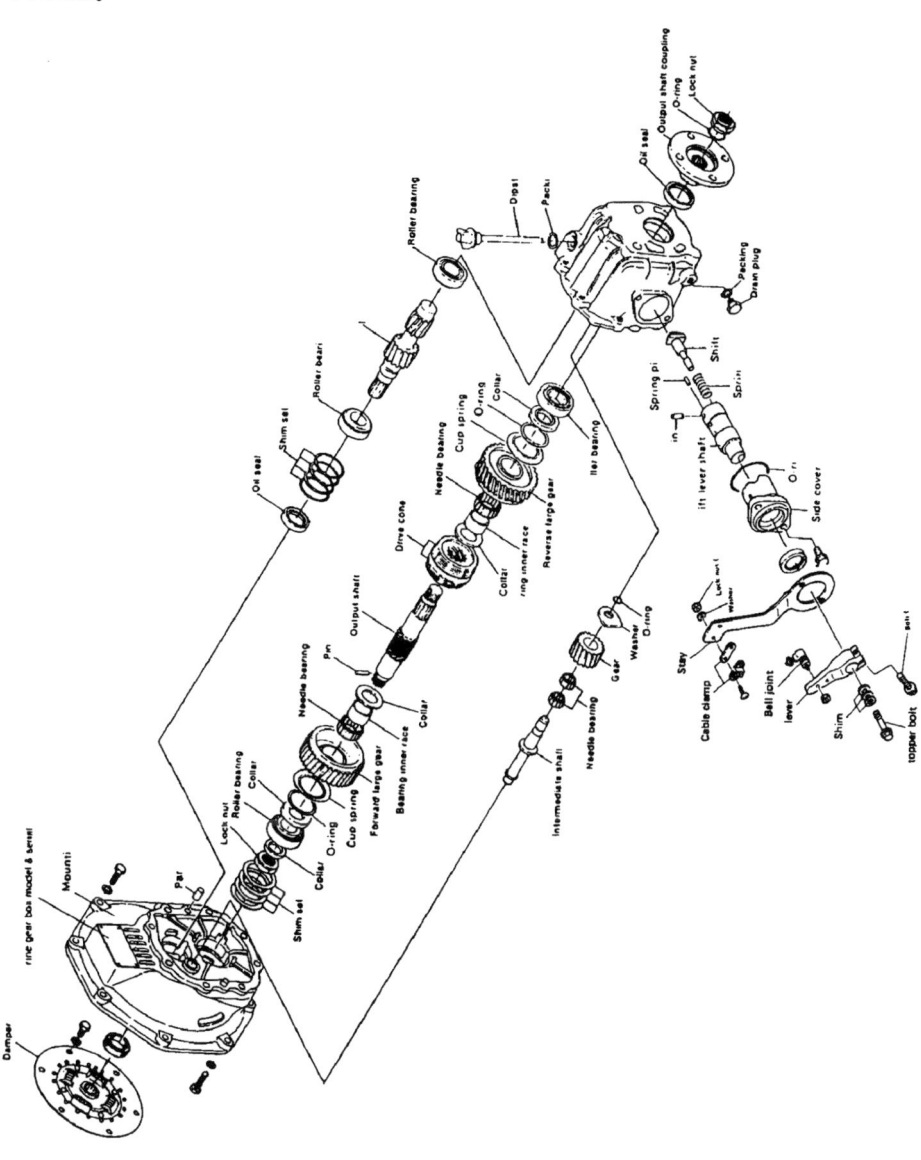

1·5 Sectional view

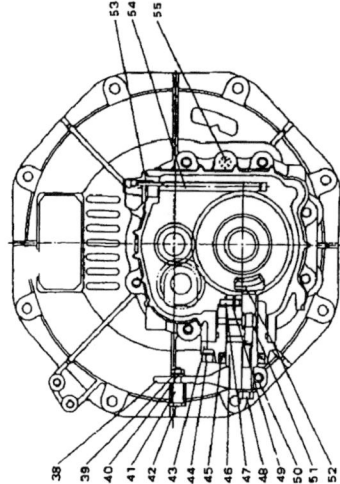

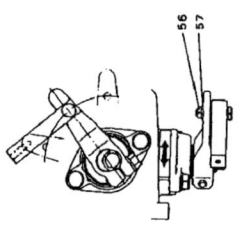

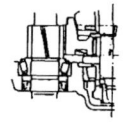

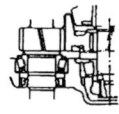

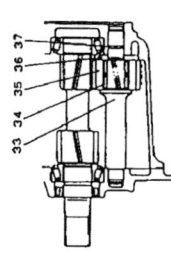

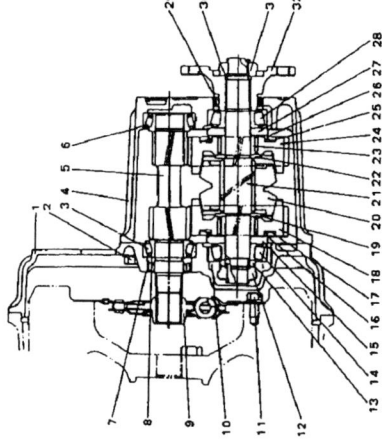

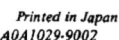

1	Mounting flange
2	Bolt M8 x 25
3	Bearing
4	Clutch case
5	Input shaft
6	Bearing
7	Oil seal
8	Shim
9	Dumper disk
10	Shim
11	Bolt M8 x 14
12	Lock nut
13	Collar
14	Bearing
15	Thrust coll r A
16	Spring retainer
17	Cup spring
18	Forward gear
19	Thrust collar B
20	Drive cone
21	Output shaft
22	Thrust collar B
23	Inner rase
24	Reverse gear
25	Cup spring
26	Spring retainer
27	Thrust collar A
28	Bearing
29	Oil seal
30	O-ring
31	Lock nut
32	Coupling
33	Idle gear shaft
34	Bearing
35	Idle gear
36	Thrust washer
37	O-ring
38	Shift lever
39	Lock nut
40	Washer
41	Holder
42	Connector
43	Side cover
44	Bolt M8 x 25
45	Oil seal
46	Shift lever shaft
47	Location pin
48	Stopper bolt
49	Spring pin
50	Bolt M8 x 25
51	Spring
52	Shifter
53	Washer
54	Dipstick
55	Parallel pin
56	Lock nut
57	Washer

2. Shifting Device

2-1 Construction of shifting mechanism

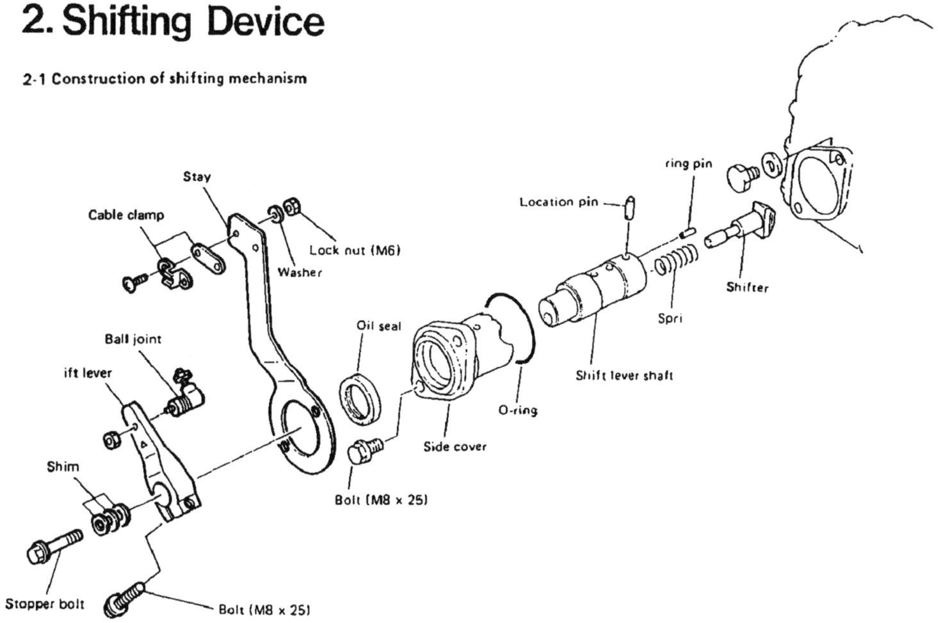

Stay

Cable clamp

Lock nut (M6)

Washer

ring pin

Location pin

Shifter

Spri

Ball joint

Oil seal

ift lever

Shift lever shaft

Shim

O-ring

Side cover

Bolt (M8 x 25)

Stopper bolt

Bolt (M8 x 25)

The shift lever shaft is installed on the side cover with neutral, forward and reverse positions provided on this cover The neutral, forward and reverse location pins of the shift lever shaft are constantly inserted into their respective grooves on the shift lever by the tension of the shifter spring. The shifter is set on the eccentric hole of the shift lever shaft and moves the drive cone in the neutral position either to the forward or reverse positions, and then back to the neutral position. (The shift lever shaft moves slightly to the shift lever or drive cone side when the shift lever is placed in the forward or reverse positions.)

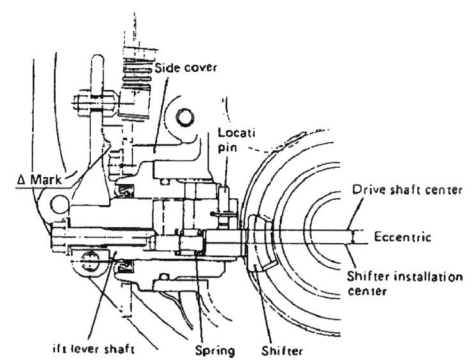

Side cover

Locati pin

△ Mark

Drive shaft center

Eccentric

Shifter installation center

ift lever shaft

Spring

Shifter

Printed in Japan
A0A1029-9002

2-2 Forward and reverse clutch operation
(Neutral ⇒ Forward; Neutral ⇒ Reverse)

When the shift lever is moved to the forward position from the neutral position, the shift lever shaft starts to revolve, and the location pin disengages from the neutral V-groove position of the side cover. (Shift lever moves approx. 0.5mm to the drive cone side.) At this time the shifter, which is set on the eccentric hole of the shift lever shaft, moves the drive cone's V-groove to the forward large gear.

When the location pin of the shift lever shaft falls in the forward position groove of the side cover, the shift lever shaft moves approx. 3mm to the shift lever side, and the shifter starts to press the drive cone V-groove to the forward large gear side through the spring force.

2-3 Engagement and disengagement of clutch
(Forward ⇒ Neutral; Reverse ⇒ Neutral)

When the shift lever is moved to the forward position from the neutral position, the shift lever shaft starts to revolve, and the location pin disengages from the forward position groove of the side cover. (The shift lever shaft moves approx. 3mm to the drive cone side.) At this time, the shifter which is set on the eccentric hole of the shift lever shaft is moved to the neutral side (reverse large gear side). The drive cone, however, is engaged with the forward large gear through the torque force produced by the revolving centrifugal force.

Further, when the shift lever shaft starts to revolve, and the positioning pin falls in to the neutral V-groove position of the side cover (the shift lever shaft travels approx. 5mm to the shift lever side), the shifter moves to the shift lever side (to the spring side) while moving the V-groove of the drive cone to the reverse large gear side. The movement of the shifter to the shift lever side, however, is stopped when the shifter end contacts the stopper bolt. The shifter only works to press the V-groove of the drive cone to the reverse large gear side. Thus, the drive cone is disengaged from the forward large gear. After this disengagement, the transmission torque of the drive cone is decreased to zero and the shift lever is returned to the neutral position by the spring force.

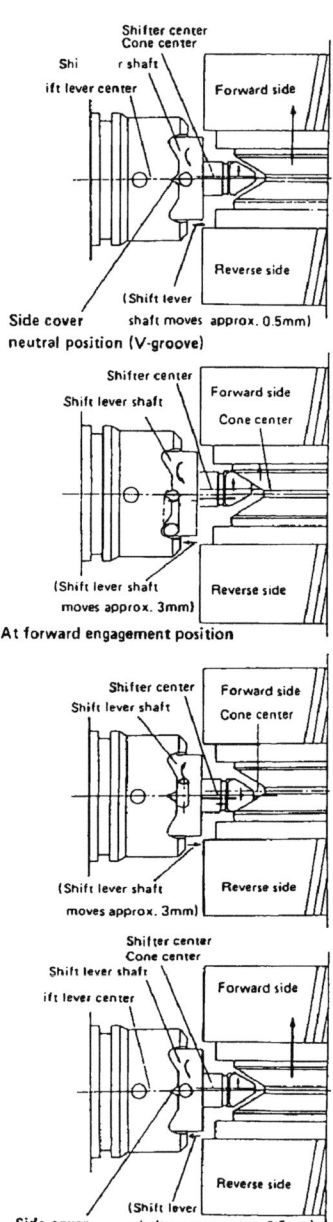

Side cover neutral position (V-groove)

At forward engagement position

Side cover neutral position (V-groove)

2-4 Clutch shifting force

Shifting direction \ Shifting position	Shift lever position at 56mm	Remote control handle position at 170mm (Cable length, 4m)
Engaging force at 1000 rpm	3 ~ 4 kg (6.6 ~ 8.8 lbs)	4 ~ 5 kg (8.8 ~ 11.0 lbs)
Disengaging force at 1000 rpm	3.5 ~ 5 kg (7.7 ~ 11.0 lbs)	4 ~ 6 kg (8.8 ~ 13.2 lbs)

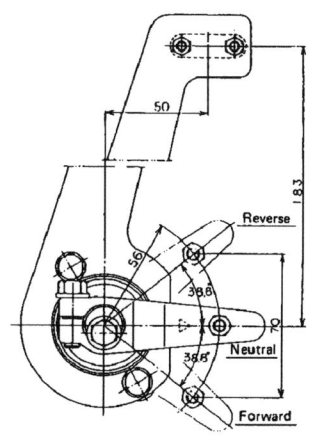

2-5 Adjustment of shifting device

Whenever the side cover, shift lever shaft, shifter, stopper bolt or drive cone is replaced, be sure to adjust the clearance between the shifter end and the stopper bolt by using shims. When the adjustment of this clearance is not proper the drive cone may be improperly fitted when the shift lever is moved to the neutral position from either the forward or the reverse position.

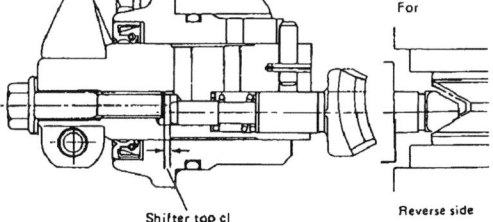

Shifter top cl

2-5.1 Measurement and adjustment of clearance

(a)Assemble the shifting mechanism (without installing the stopper bolt of the shifter) to the marine gear case.

NOTE:Ensure the correct direction of the shifter before assembly.

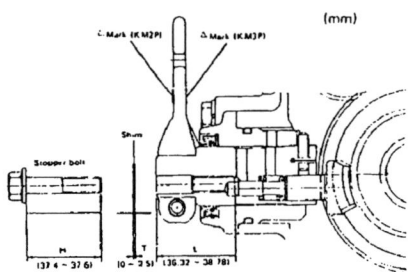

(mm)

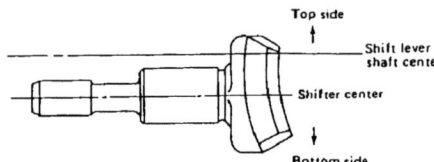

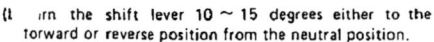

(b)Turn the shift lever 10 ~ 15 degrees either to the forward or reverse position from the neutral position.

(c)Measure the L-distance between the shift lever shaft end surface and the shifter's end.

(d)Measure the H-distance (the distance from the neck of the stopper bolt to its end).

(e)Obtain the shim thickness "T" by the following formula.

$$ T = (H - L + 1.25) \pm 0.1mm\ (0.004in.) $$

NOTE:Shim set includes one piece each of 1mm, 0.4mm, 0.3mm, 0.25mm shims.
(YANMAR Part No.177088-06380)

(f)Insert shim (s) of proper thickness to the stopper bolt side and tighten it to the shift lever shaft.

NOTE:When tightening the stopper bolt, apply either a non-drying type liquid packing (TREE BOND No.1215), or a seal tape around the bolt threads.

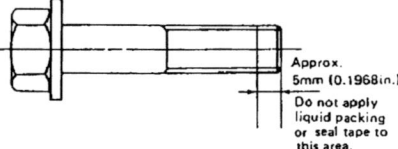

Approx.
5mm (0.1968in.)

Do not apply liquid packing or seal tape to this area.

2-5.2 Inspect for the following points
(to be inspected every 2-3 months)

(1)Looseness at the connection of the cable connector and the remote control cable.

(2)Looseness of the attaching nut of the cable connector and the shift lever.

2-6 Adjustment of the remote control head
Marine gearbox control side
(1)Equal distribution of the control lever stroke.

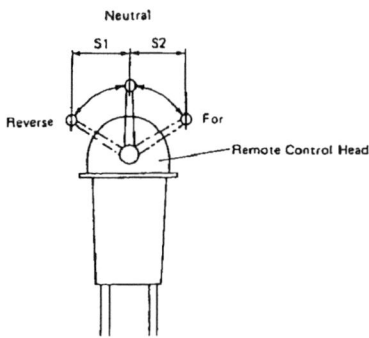

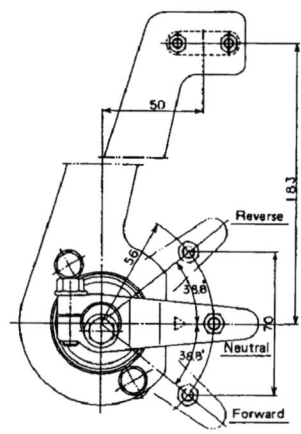

The stroke between the neutral position → forward position (S2), and the neutral position → reverse positon (S1) must be equalized.
When either stroke is too short, clutch engagement becomes faulty.

(2)Equalizing the travel distance of the control cable.

After ensuring the equal distribution of the stroke described in (1), connect the cable to the control head. Adjust so that the cable shift travel of the S₁ and S₂ control lever strokes becomes identical.

2-7 Cautions
(1)Always stop the engine when attaching, adjusting, and inspecting.
(2)When conducting inspection immediately after stopping the engine, do not touch the clutch. The oil temperature is often raised to around 90°C (194°F).
(3)Half-clutch operation is not possible with this design and construction. Do not use with the shift lever halfway to the engaged position.
(4)Set the idling engine speed at between 750 and 800 rpm.

NOTE: The dual(Two) lever remote control device cannot be used.

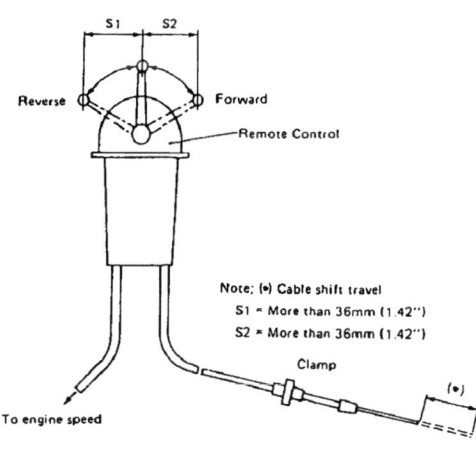

3. Inspection and Servicing

3-1 Clutch case

(1) Check the clutch case with a test hammer for cracking.
Perform a color check when required.
If the case is cracked, replace it.

(2) Check for staining on the inside surface of the bearing section.
Also, measure the inside diameter of the case.
Replace the case if it is worn beyond the wear limit.

3-2 Bearing

(1) Rusting and damage.
If the bearing is rusted or the taper roller retainmaged, replace the bearing.

(2) .nake sure that the bearings rotate smoothly.
If rotation is not smooth, if there is any binding, or if any abnormal sound is evident, replace the bearing.

3-3 Gear

Check the surface, tooth face conditions and backlash of each gear. Replace any defective part.

(1) Tooth surface wear.
Check the tooth surface for pitting, abnormal wear, dents, and cracks. Repair the lightly damaged gears and replace heavily damaged gears.

(2) Tooth surface contact.
Check the tooth surface contact. The amount of tooth surface contact between the tooth crest and tooth flank must be at least 70% of the tooth width.

(3) Backlash.
Measure the backlash of each gear, and replace the gear when it is worn beyond the wear limit.

mm (in.)

	Maintenance standard	Wear limit
..put shaft forward gear and output shaft forward gear	0.06 ~ 0.12 (0.0024 ~ 0.0047)	0.2 (0.0079)
Input shaft reverse gear and intermediate gear	0.06 ~ 0.12 (0.0024 ~ 0.0047)	0.2 (0.0079)
Intermediate gear and output shaft reverse gear	0.06 ~ 0.12 (0.0024 ~ 0.0047)	0.2 (0.0079)

3-4 Forward and reverse large gears

(1) Contact surface with drive cone.
Visually inspect the tapered surface of the forward and reverse large gears where they make contact with the drive cone to check if any abnormal condition or sign of overheating exists.
If any defect is found, replace the gear.

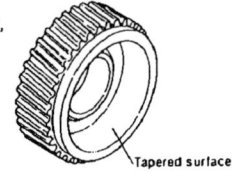
Tapered surface

(2) Forward/reverse gear needle bearing.
When an abnormal sound is produced at the needle bearing, visually inspect the rollers; replace the bearing if the rollers are faulty.

Rollers

3-5 Drive cone

(1) Visually inspect that part of the surface that comes into contact with the circumferential triangular slot to check for signs of scoring, overheating or wear. If deep scoring or signs of overheating are found, replace the cone.

contact surface

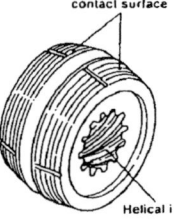
Helical i

(2) Check the helical involute spline for any abnormal condition on the tooth surface, and repair or replace the part should any defect be found.

(3) Measure the amount of wear on the tapered contact surface of the drive cone, and replace the cone when the wear exceeds the specified limit.

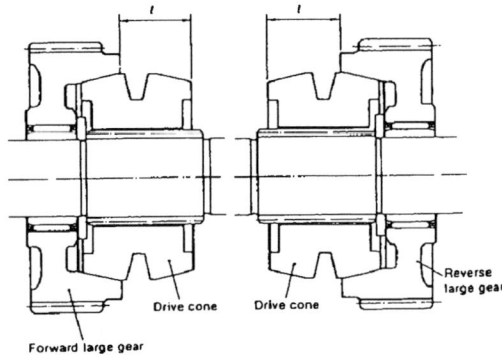
Drive cone Drive cone
Reverse large gear
Forward large gear

Printed in Japan
A0A1029-9002

mm (in.)

		Standard dimensions	Limited dimensions
Dimensions *l*	KM3P2	32.7 ~ 33.3 (1.2874 ~ 1.3110)	32.4 (1.2756)

NOTE: *When dismantled, the forward or reverse direction of the drive cone must be clearly identified.*

(4) If the wear of the V-groove of the drive cone is excessive, replace the part.

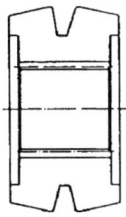

3-6 Thrust collar

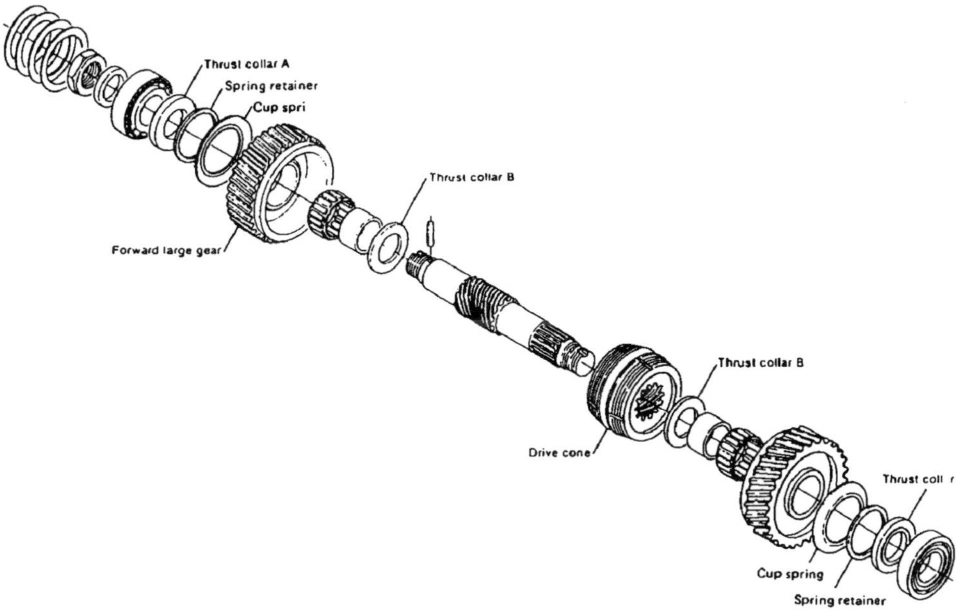

Thrust collar A
Spring retainer
Cup spri
Thrust collar B
Forward large gear
Thrust collar B
Drive cone
Thrust coll r
Cup spring
Spring retainer

(1) Visually inspect the sliding surface of thrust collar A or B to check for signs of overheating, scoring, or cracks. Replace the collar if any abnormal condition is found.

(2) Measure the thickness of thrust collar A or B, and replace it when the dimension exceeds the specified limit.

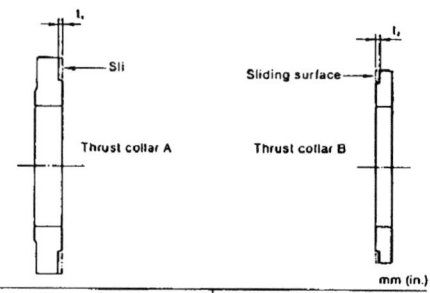

Stepped wear	Limit for use
Thrust collar A, t_1	0.05 (0.0020)
Thrust collar B, t_2	0.20 (0.0079)

mm (in.)

3-7 Cup spring and spring retainer

(1) Check for cracks and damage to the cup spring and spring retainer. Replace the part if defective.

(2) Measure the free length of the cup spring and the thickness of the spring retainer. If the length or the thickness deviates from the standard size, replace the part.

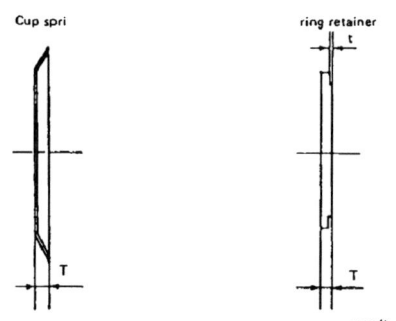

mm (in.)

	Standard	Limit
Cup spring, T	2.8 ~ 3.1	2.6
	(0.1102 ~ 0.1220)	(0.1024)
Spring retainer, T	2.92 ~ 3.08	2.8
	(0.1150 ~ 0.1213)	(0.1102)
Spring retainer, t	—	0.1
		(0.0040)

3-8 Oil seal of output shaft

Visually inspect the oil seal of the output shaft to check if there is any damage or oil leakage; replace the seal when any abnormal condition is found.

3-9 Input shaft

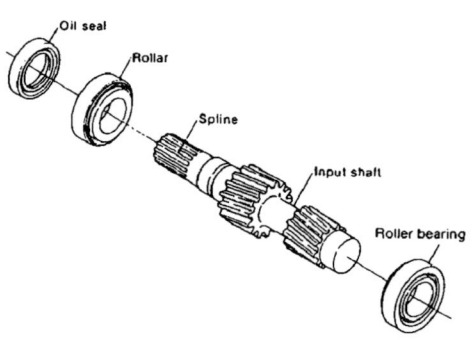

(1) Spline part.
   Whenever uneven wear and/or scratches are found, replace with a new part.

(2) Surface of oil seal.
   If the sealing surface of the oil seal is worn or scratched, replace.

3-10 Output shaft

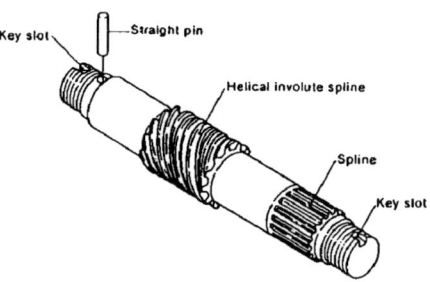

(1) Visually inspect the spline and the helical involute spline, and repair or replace a part when any abnormal condition is found on its surface.

3-11 Intermediate shaft

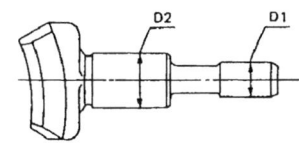

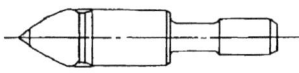

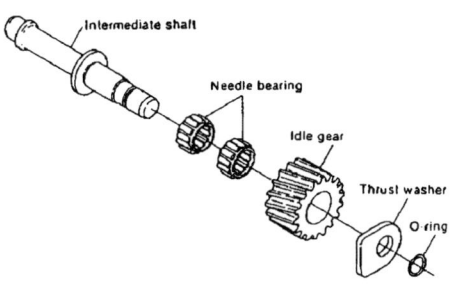

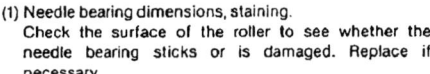

		Standard	Limit
D1		66.9 ~ 67.0	65
		(2.6338 ~ 2.6378)	(2.5591)
D2		11.966 ~ 11.984	11.95
		(0.4711 ~ 0.4718)	(0.4705)
Shift lever shaft,		12.0 ~ 12.018	12.05
Shifter insert hole		(0.4724 ~ 0.4731)	(0.4744)

mm (in.)

(1) Needle bearing dimensions, staining.
Check the surface of the roller to see whether the needle bearing sticks or is damaged. Replace if necessary.

3-12.2 Shift lever shaft and location pin
(1)Check the shift lever shaft and location pin for damage or distortion, and replace defective parts. If the location pin must be replaced, replace it together with the shift lever shaft.
(2)Measure the diameter of the shift lever shaft and the shifter insertion hole. Replace the part if the size deviates from the standard value.

3-12 Shifting device

3-12.1 Shifter

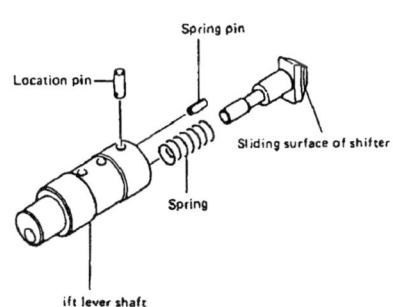

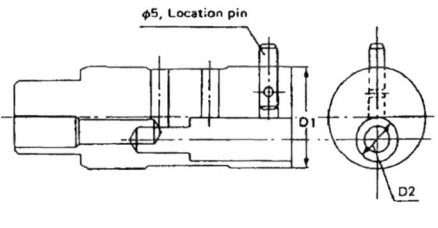

		Standard	Limit
D1		27.959 ~ 27.98	27.90
		(1.1001 ~ 1.1016)	(1.0984)
D2		12.0 ~ 12.018	12.05
		(0.4724 ~ 0.4731)	(0.4744)
Side cover,		28.0 ~ 28.021	28.08
Shift insert hole		(1.1024 ~ 1.1032)	(1.1055)

mm (in.)

(1)Visually inspect the surface in contact with the drive cone, and replace the shifter when signs of overheating, damage or wear are found.
(2)Measure the shaft diameter of the shifter. Replace the shaft if the size deviates from the standard.

7-76

Printed in Japan
A0A1029-9002

3-12.3 Shifter spring
(1)Check the spring for scratches or corrosion.
(2)Measure the free length of the spring.

Shifter spring	Standard		Limit
Free length	22.6 mm	(0.890in.)	19.8 mm (0.780in.)
Spring constant	0.854 kg/mm	(1.88 lbs/0.04in.)	
Length when attached	14.35 mm	(0.5650 in.)	
Load when attached	7.046 kg	(15.54 lbs)	6.08 kg (13.41 lbs)

3-12.4 Stopper bolt
Check the stopper bolt. If it is worn or stepped, replace.

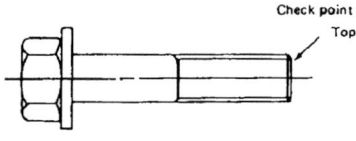

Check point
Top

3-12.5 Side cover and oil seal
(1)Check the neutral, forward and reverse position grooves.
Replace if the grooves are worn.
(2)Measure the insertion hole of the shift lever shaft.
place if the size deviates from the standard value.
(3) Check the oil seal and the O-ring for damage.
Replace if the part is defective.

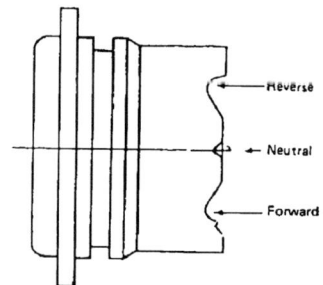

Reverse
Neutral
Forward

3-13 Damper disc

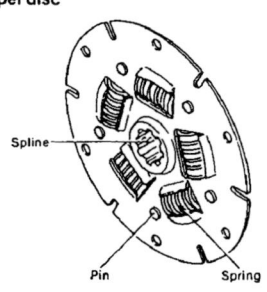

Spline
Pin
Spring

(1) Spline part.
Whenever uneven wear and/or scratches are found,
replace with a new part.
(2) Spring.
Whenever uneven wear and/or scratches are found,
replace with a new part.
(3) Pin wear.
Whenever uneven wear and/or scratches are found,
replace with a new part.
(4) Whenever a crack or damage to the spring slot is found
replace the defective part with a new one.

3-14 Shim adjustment for output and input shafts
Check the thickness of shims for both input and output
shafts. When the component parts are not replaced after
dismantling, the same shims can be reused. When the clutch
case and flange or any one of the following parts is
replaced the thickness of the shim must be determined in
the following manner.

For input shaft parts: input shaft, bearing.
For output shaft parts: output shaft, thrust collar A,
thrust collar B, gear, bearing.

(1)Shim thickness (T1) measurement of input shaft

(a)Measure the bearing insertion hole depth (A) of the mounting flange, and the bearing insertion hole depth (A') of the clutch case.

(b)Measure the length (B) between the bearing outer races of the input shaft assembly.

(c)Obtain the (T1) thickness by the following formula:

$$T_1 = A + A' - B \quad (T_1 : \text{Clearance } \pm 0.05 \text{mm})$$

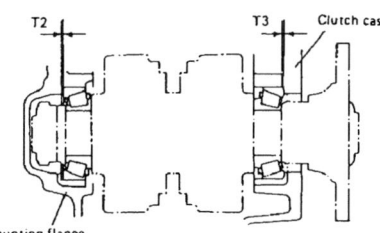

Mounting flange

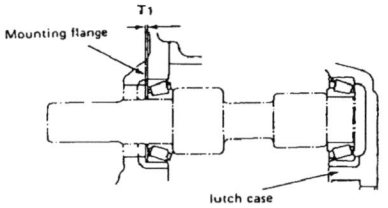

Mounting flange

lutch case

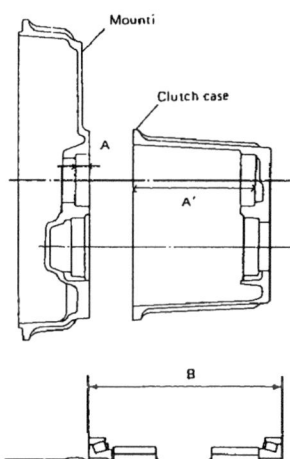

Mounti

Clutch case

A

A'

B

Input shaft ass'y

(c)Measure lengths (F) and (E) from the outer race end of the clutch case bearing included in the output shaft assembly.

NOTE: Before measuring length (F) and (E), press the forward large gear and the reverse large gear to the drive cone until there is no clearance.

(d)Obtain thicknesses (T2) and (T3) by the following formulas:

$$T_2 = C + C' - D - T_3 \quad (T_2 : \text{Clearance } \pm^{0.1mm}_{0})$$

$$T_3 \text{ (KM3P)} = C' - 47.3 - \frac{E}{2} - F \quad (\text{Tolerance } \pm 0.05 \text{mm})$$

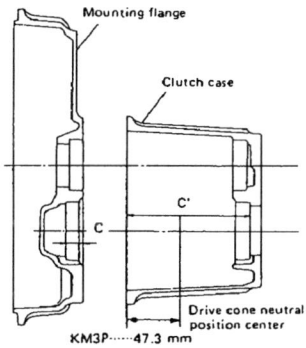

Mounting flange

Clutch case

C'

C

Drive cone neutral position center

KM3P······47.3 mm

Output shaft ass'y

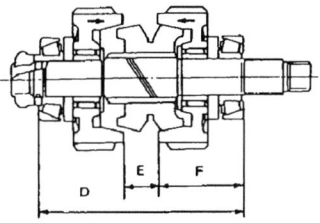

E   F

D

(2)Shim thickness (T2, T3) measurement of output shaft

(a)Measure the bearing insertion hole depth (C) of the mounting flange, and the bearing insertion hole depth (C') of the clutch case.

(b)Measure the length (D) between the bearing outer races.

NOTE: Tighten the mounting flange nut of the output shaft assembly with the specified torque. Press-fit the inner race of the clutch case roller bearing to the large gear side.

(3)Standard size of parts

mm (in.)

	A + A'	B	C + C'	D	E	F	Drive cone neutral center position
KM3P2	132.40 ~ 132.75 (5.2126 ~ 5.2264)	131.20 ~ 132.10 (5.1654 ~ 5.2008)	141.20 ~ 141.55 (5.5591 ~ 5.5728)	139.56 ~ 141.00 (5.4945 ~ 5.5512)	23.50 ~ 24.10 (0.9252 ~ 0.9488)	57.83 ~ 58.65 (2.2768 ~ 2.3091)	47.3 (1.8622)

*NOTE:Compare your measurements with the above
standard size. If your measurements differ largely
from the standard sizes, measurements may not be
correct. Check and measure again.*

(4) Adjusting shim set

	Part No.	Thickness.mm(in.)	No. of shims
	177088-02350	0.5 (0.0197)	1
		0.4 (0.0157)	1
		0.3 (0.0118)	2
	177088-02300	1.0 (0.0394)	1
		0.5 (0.0197)	1
		0.3 (0.0118)	2
		0.1 (0.0039)	3

13-13. Torque limiter

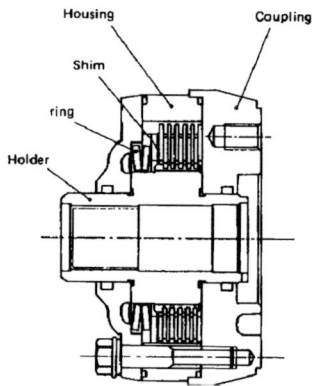

Housing   Coupling

Shim

ring

Holder

4. Disassembly

4-1 Dismantling the clutch

(1) Remove the remote control cable.
(2) Remove the clutch assembly from the engine mounting flange.

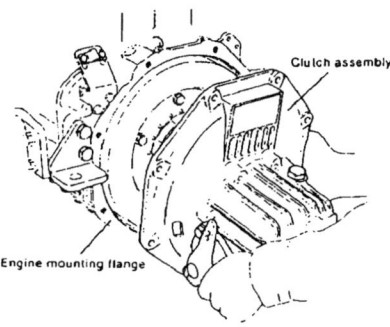

Clutch assembly

Engine mounting flange

(3) Drain the lubricating oil.
Drain the lubricating oil by loosening the plug at the bottom of the clutch case.

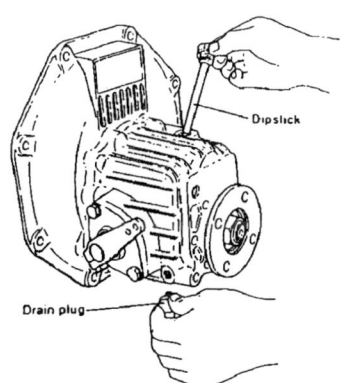

Dipstick

Drain plug

(4) Remove the end nut and output shaft coupling.

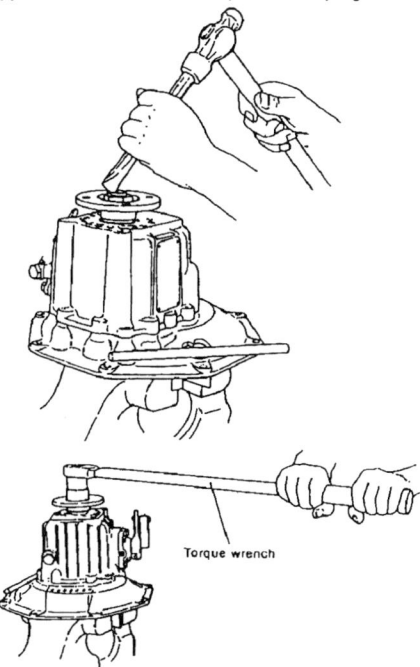

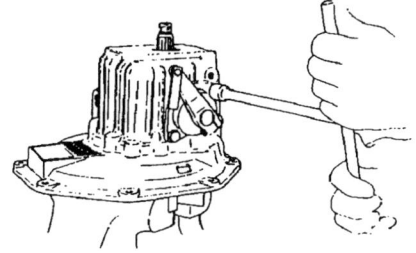

Torque wrench

NOTE: *Take care as it has a left-handed thread.*

(5) Remove the oil dip stick and O-ring.
(6) Remove the fixing bolts on the side cover, and also remove the shift lever shaft, shift lever and shifter.

(7) Remove the bolts which secure the mounting flange to the case body, give light taps to the left and right with a plastic headed hammer while supporting the clutch case with your hand, then remove the mounting flange.

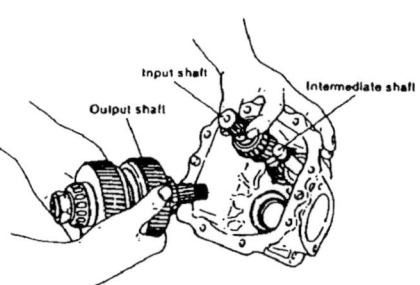

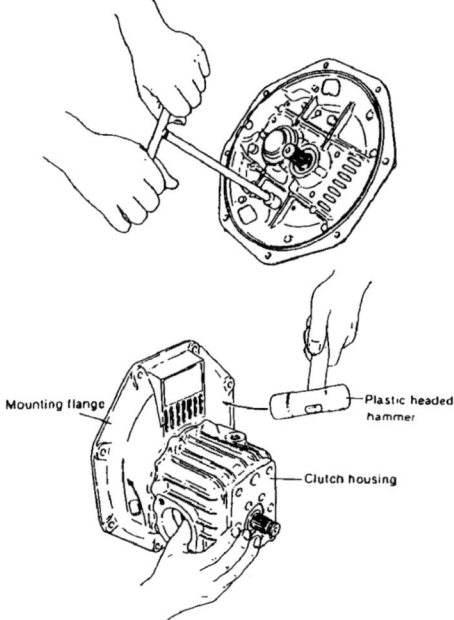

(9) Take out the intermediate shaft and input shaft. When taking out the intermediate shaft, place a bolt or spacer on the shaft hole of the case, and drive the shaft out by tapping it lightly.

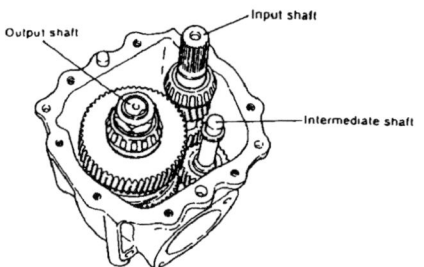

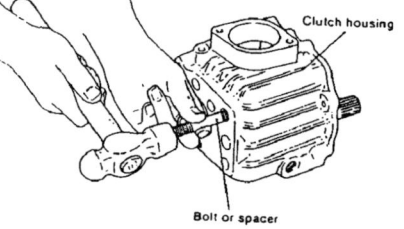

(8) Withdraw the output shaft assembly.

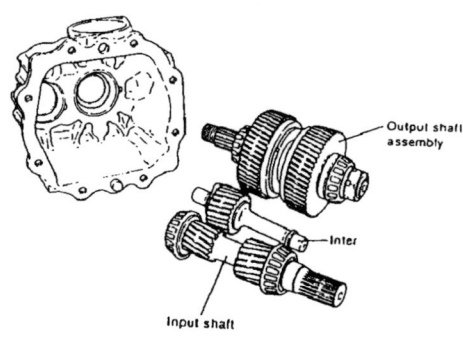

(10) Remove the oil seal of the output shaft from the case body.

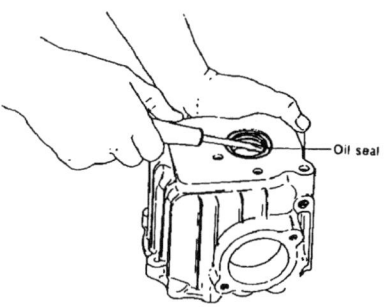

Oil seal

(11) Remove the outer bearing race from the case body by using the special tool.

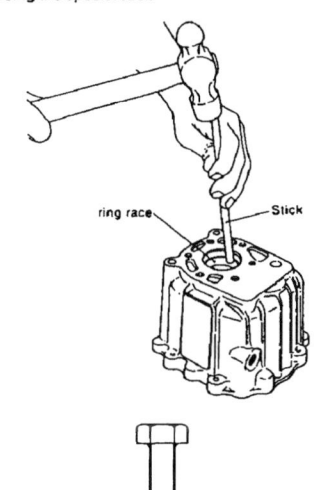

ring race — Stick

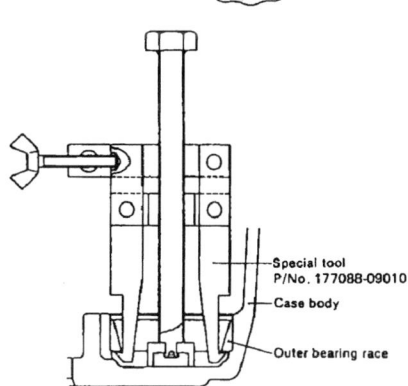

Special tool P/No. 17708B-09010
Case body
Outer bearing race

(12) Remove the oil seal of the input shaft from the mounting flange.

(13) Remove the outer bearing race from the mounting flange in the same way as with the case body.

(14) Remove each adjusting plate from the input or output shaft.

NOTE: *The same adjusting plates can be reused when the following parts are not replaced. When any part is replaced however, re-adjustment is necessary.*

4-2 Removal of the output shaft

(1) Take out the reverse large gear, thrust collar A, cup spring, spring retainer and inner bearing race.

The reverse large gear must be withdrawn using a pulley extracter, by fixing the nut at the forward end in a vice.

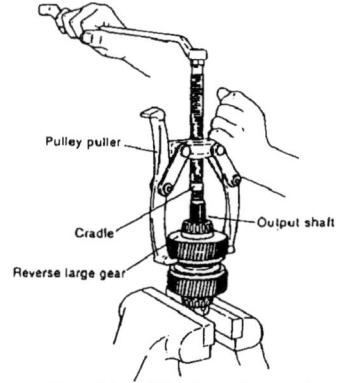

Pulley puller
Cradle — Output shaft
Reverse large gear

(2) Loosen the calking of the forward nut and remove the nut and spacer.

Remove the nut by using a torque wrench after setting the output shaft coupling and fixing the coupling bolt in a vice.

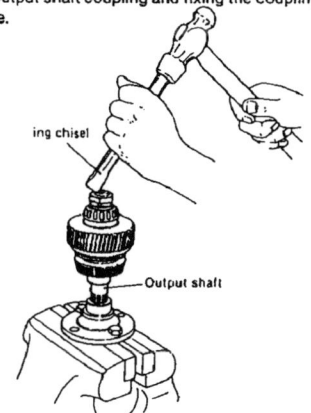

ing chisel
Output shaft

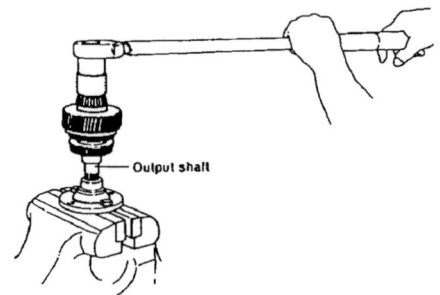

Output shaft

(3)Place the pulley extractor against the end surface of the forward large gear, and withdraw the forward large gear, thrust collar A, cup spring, spring retainer and inner bearing race.

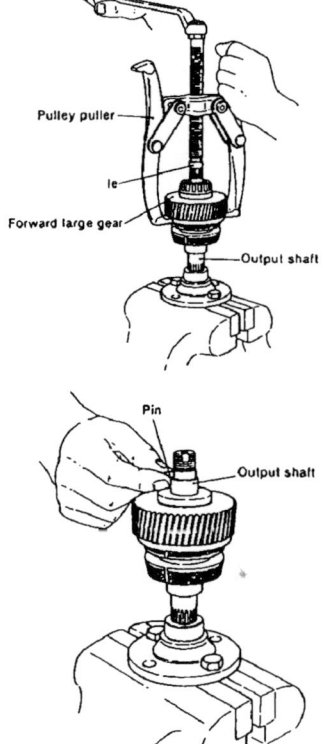

Pulley puller

le

Forward large gear

Output shaft

Pin

Output shaft

(4)While gripping the drive cone, tap the end of the shaft with a plastic headed hammer, and withdraw the thrust collar B and inner needle bearing race. A pulley extractor may be used.

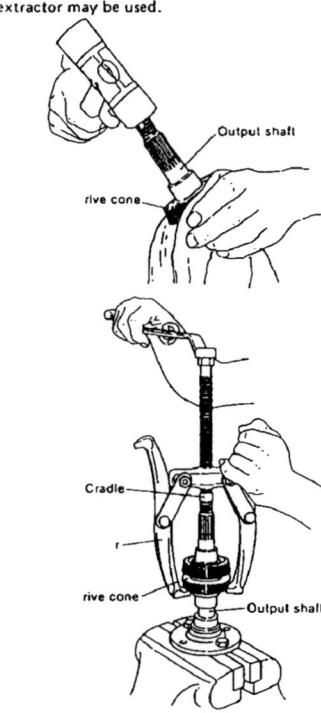

Output shaft

rive cone

Cradle

r

rive cone

Output shaft

4-3 Removal of the intermediate shaft

(1) Remove the "O" ring.
(2) Remove the thrust washer.
(3) Remove the intermediate gear and needle bearing.

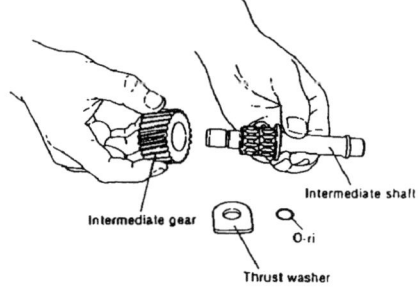

Intermediate shaft

Intermediate gear

O-ri

Thrust washer

NOTE: Take care as the nut has left-handed thread.

4-4 Dismantling the shifting device
(1)Take out the shifter and shifter spring.

(4)Remove the shift lever to the anti-shift lever side.

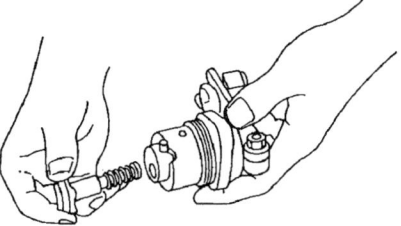

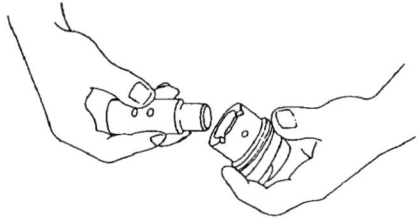

(2)Remove the stopper bolt of the shifter and shim.

(5)Remove the oil-seal and O-ring.

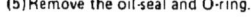

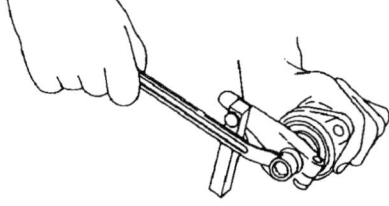

(3)Loosen the bolt of the shift lever and remove the shift
lever from the shift lever shaft.

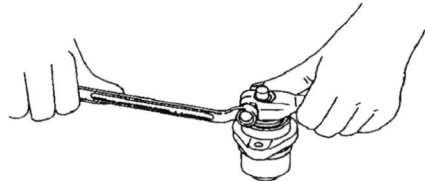

5. Reassembly

5-1 Reassembly of output shaft

(1) Fit the forward side thrust collar B onto the shaft.
(2) Drive in the forward end inner needle bearing race using a jig.

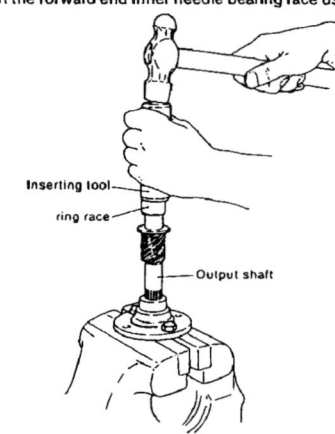

(3) Assemble the needle bearing and forward large gear.
NOTE: Check that the forward large gear rotates smoothly.
(4) Fit the cup spring, spring retainer, thrust collar A and pin, and drive in the inner bearing race using a jig.

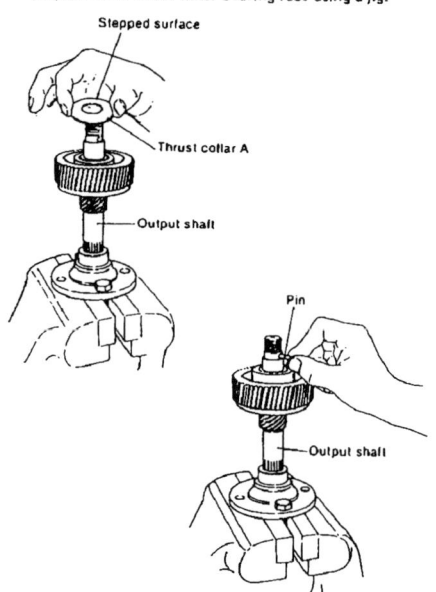

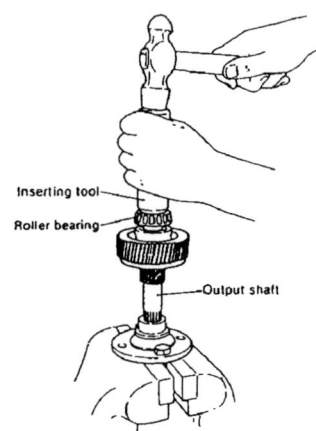

NOTE: 1)Drive in with a plastic headed hammer. Do not hit it hard.
2)When fitting the thrust collar A, note the fitting direction. Fit it keeping the stepped surface toward the roller bearing side.
3)Note that the pin cannot be fitted after the i bearing race has been driven in.
4)Check that the forward large gear smoothly.

(5) Assemble the collar and pin so that the pin is in the groove of the collar.
(6) Set and tighten the forward end nut. Insert the bolt into the coupling, and fix it in a vice, keeping the spline part upward.
Insert the shaft into the spline of the coupling, fit the spacer, and tighten the nut with a torque wrench.

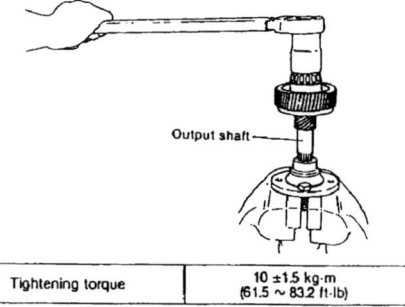

Tightening torque	10 ±1.5 kg·m (61.5 ~ 83.2 ft·lb)

(The same torque applies to both models KM2P and KM3P)

NOTES: 1) Take care as it is a left-handed thread.
2) Use the reverse side nut used before dismantling at the forward eng. This is to provide effective calking to the nut by changing the calking position.

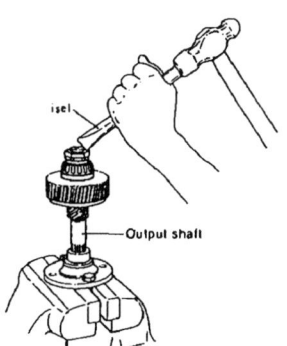

(7) Insert the drive cone while keeping the output shaft set for reverse.

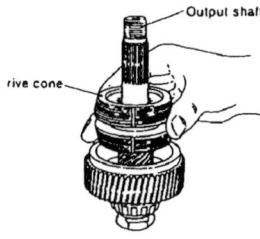

(8) Apply procedures 1 through 4 to the forward end.

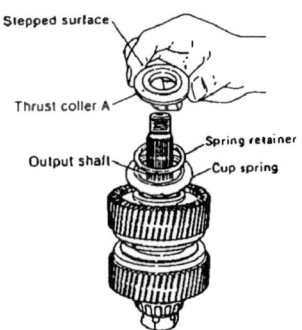

NOTE: 1) Fit thrust collar A so that the stepped surface faces the roller bearing side.
2) Check that the reverse large gear rotates smoothly.

5-2 Reassembly of the clutch
(1) Fit the oil seal, bearing outer races and shim (output shaft side) in the clutch case.
(2) Insert the input shaft into the clutch case.
(3) Drive the intermediate shaft into the clutch case.

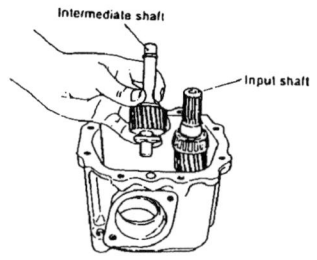

NOTES: 1) If the output shaft is not fitted into the clutch case before driving-in the intermediate shaft, it cannot be assembled.
2) Note the assembly direction of the thrust washer.

(4) Insert the output shaft into the clutch case.

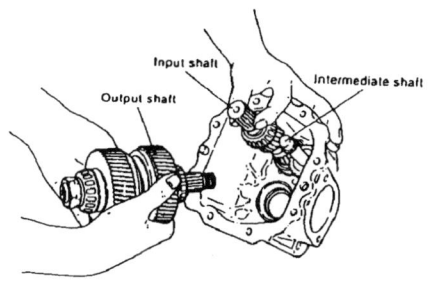

(5) Fit the adjusting plate to the mounting flange, and drive in the outer bearing race.

NOTE: The outer bearing race can be easily driven in by heating the mounting flange to about 100°C, or by cooling the outer race with liquid hydrogen.

(6) Apply non-drying liquid packing around the outer surface of the oil seal, and insert the oil seal into the mounting flange while keeping the spring part of the oil seal facing the inside of the case.

(7) Apply non-drying liquid packing to the matching surfaces of the mounting flange and the case body.

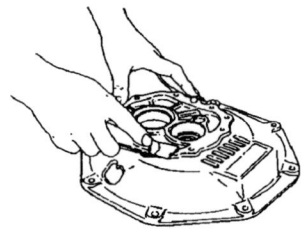

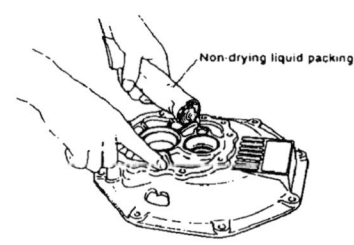

Non-drying liquid packing

(8) Insert the input shaft and output shaft into the shaft holes of the mounting flange, assemble the mounting flange on the case body, and tighten the bolt.

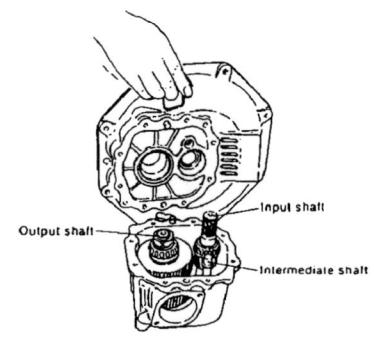

Output shaft — Input shaft
Intermediate shaft

NOTE: Apply non-drying liquid packing to either the mounting flange or the case body.

(9) Assemble the output shaft coupling on the output shaft, and fit the O-ring.

(10) Tighten the end nut by using a torque wrench, then calk it.

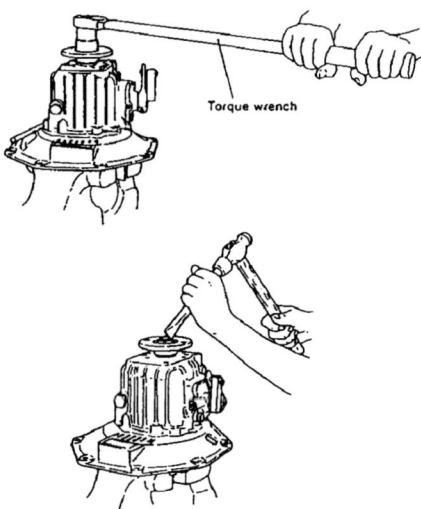

Torque wrench

NOTE: Take care as it is a left-handed thread.

Tightening torque	10 ±1.5 kg·m (61.5 ~ 83.2 ft·lb)

(The same torque applies to both models KM2P and KM3P).

5·3 Reassembly of the shifting device
(1)Fit the oil seal and O-ring to the side cover.

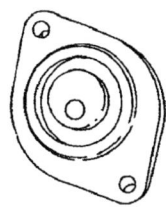

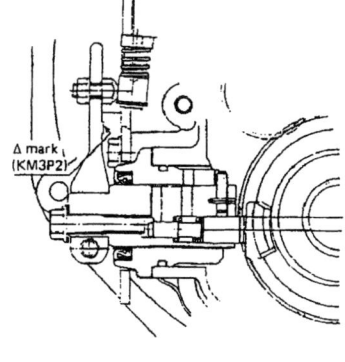

△ mark
(KM3P2)

(2)Insert the shift lever shaft to the side cover.

(4)Insert the shifter spring and shifter to the shift lever shaft.
(5)Fit the side cover assembly to the clutch case.

NOTE: 1) Check the direction of the shifter (Top and bottom side).
2) The shift lever may not turn smoothly if the clutch case is not filled with lubricating oil.

(6)Fit the shim and stopper bolt to the shift lever shaft.

NOTE: Apply non-drying liquid packing or seal-tape to the thread of the stopper bolt.

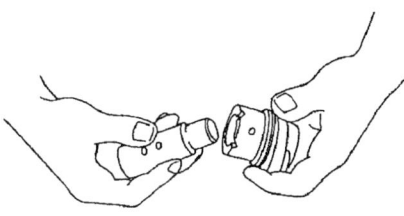

(3)Fit the shift lever to the shift lever shaft.

NOTE: Check the direction of the shift lever △ mark.

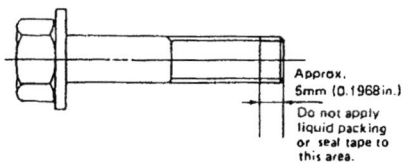

Approx.
5mm (0.1968in.)
Do not apply
liquid packing
or seal tape to
this area.

(7)Fit the cable connector to the shift lever.

Side cover

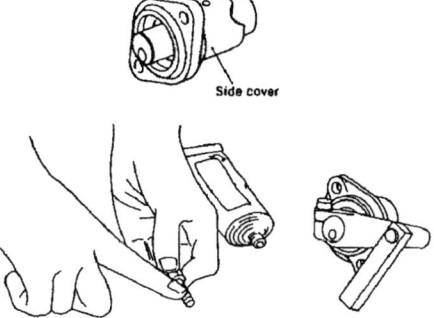

REMOTE CONTROL (OPTIONAL)

Printed in Japan
A0A1029-9002

1. Remote Control System

1-1 Construction of remote control system

The remote control permits one handed control of the engine speed, changing from forward to reverse, and stopping.

Fittings which allow for easy connection of the remote control cables with the fuel injection pump and transmission are provided with the remote control set.

The use of Morse remote control cables, clamps and a remote control head, are also provided for. The device to stop the engine is electric and will be explained under the section on electrical equipment.

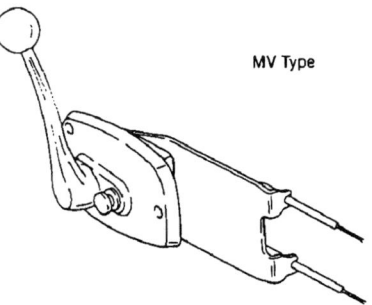

MV Type

1-2 Remote control device components

	Morse description	Yanmar Part No.
Remote control head	Morse MT2 top mounting single lever	41730-000680
	Morse MV side mounting single lever	128170-86500
Remote control cable	Morse 33C x 4m (13.12ft.)	41710-000360
	Morse 33C x 7m (23.00ft.)	129470-86500
Engine stop cable	Yanmar 4m (13.12ft)	129470-67550
	Yanmar 7m (22.96ft)	129470-67560

(1) Remote control handle

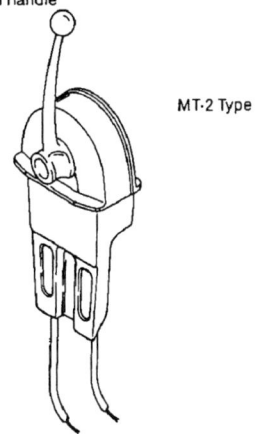

MT-2 Type

The model MT-2 remote control has been designed so that operation of the clutch (shift) and governor (throttle) can be effected with one lever.

Two cables are required for the MT-2 single, one for the clutch and the other for the governor.

When warming up the engine, to freely control the governor separately from the clutch put the lever in neutral, the central position, and pull the knob in the center of the control lever. When the lever is returned to the neutral position, the knob automatically returns to its original position, and the clutch is free. The governor can then be freely operated.

The MV type controller has been designed so that operation of the clutch and throttle can be effected with one lever. When the button next to the control lever is pulled out with the lever in the central position, it holds the clutch in the neutral position so that the throttle can be opened all the way and warm up the engine.

When the engine is warmed up, return the handle to the central position and push the button back in. Control of the clutch and throttle is thus effected with one handle.

(2) Remote control cable

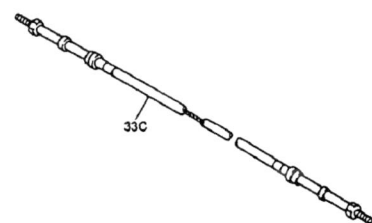

33C

Use only Super-Responsive Morse Control Cables. These are designed specifically for use with Morse control heads. This engineered system of Morse cables, control head and engine connection kits ensures dependable, smooth operation with an absolute minimum of backlash.

(3) Engine stop cable

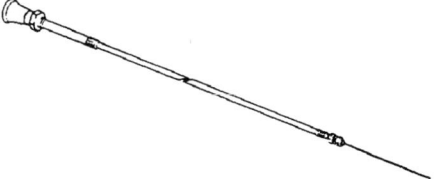

2. Remote Control Installation

2-1 Speed control

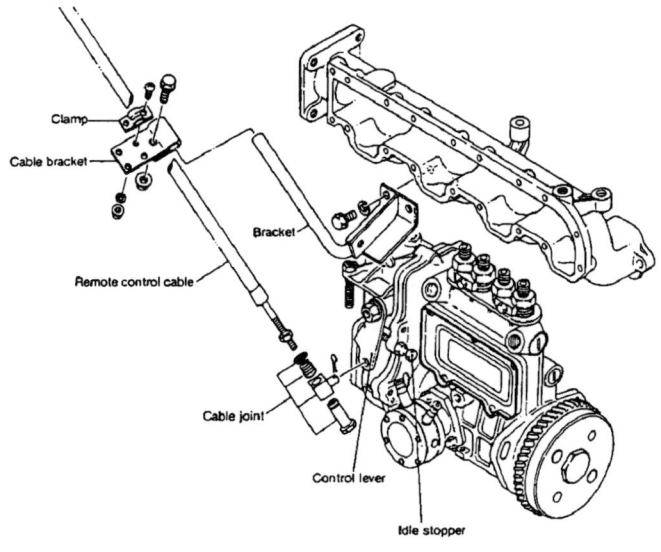

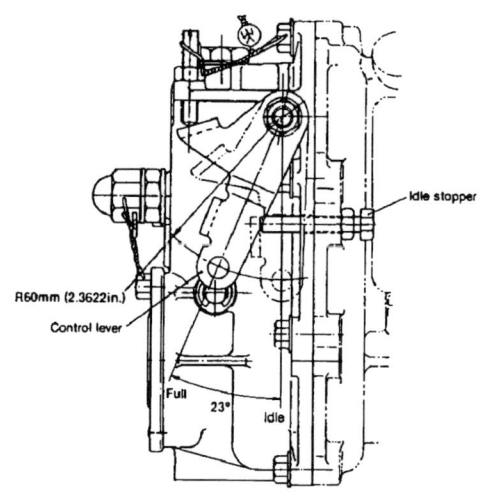

2-2 Clutch control

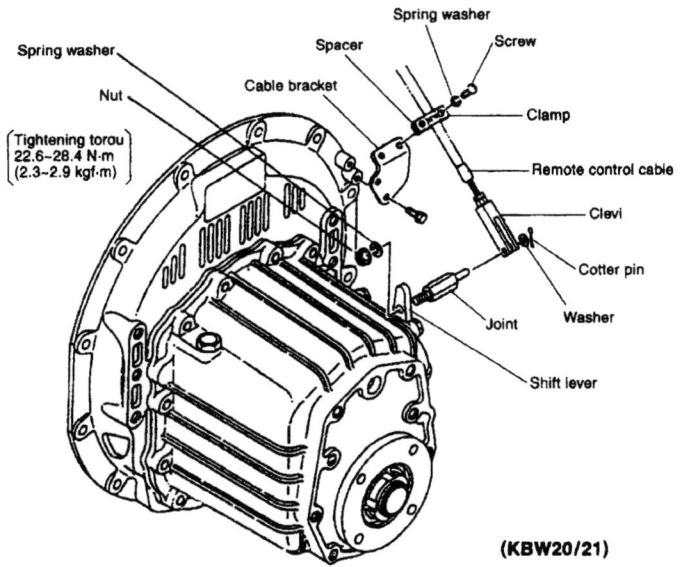

Spring washer
Spacer
Screw
Spring washer
Cable bracket
Nut
Clamp
Tightening torou
22.6~28.4 N·m
(2.3~2.9 kgf·m)
Remote control cable
Clevi
Cotter pin
Joint
Washer
Shift lever

(KBW20/21)

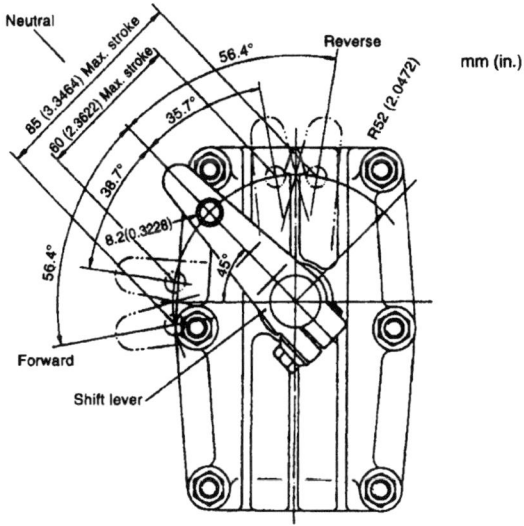

Neutral
Max. stroke
Reverse
56.4°
mm (in.)
85 (3.3464) Max. stroke
80 (2.3622) Max. stroke
R52 (2.0472)
35.7°
38.7°
8.2(0.3228)
45°
56.4°
Forward
Shift lever

2-3 Engine stop

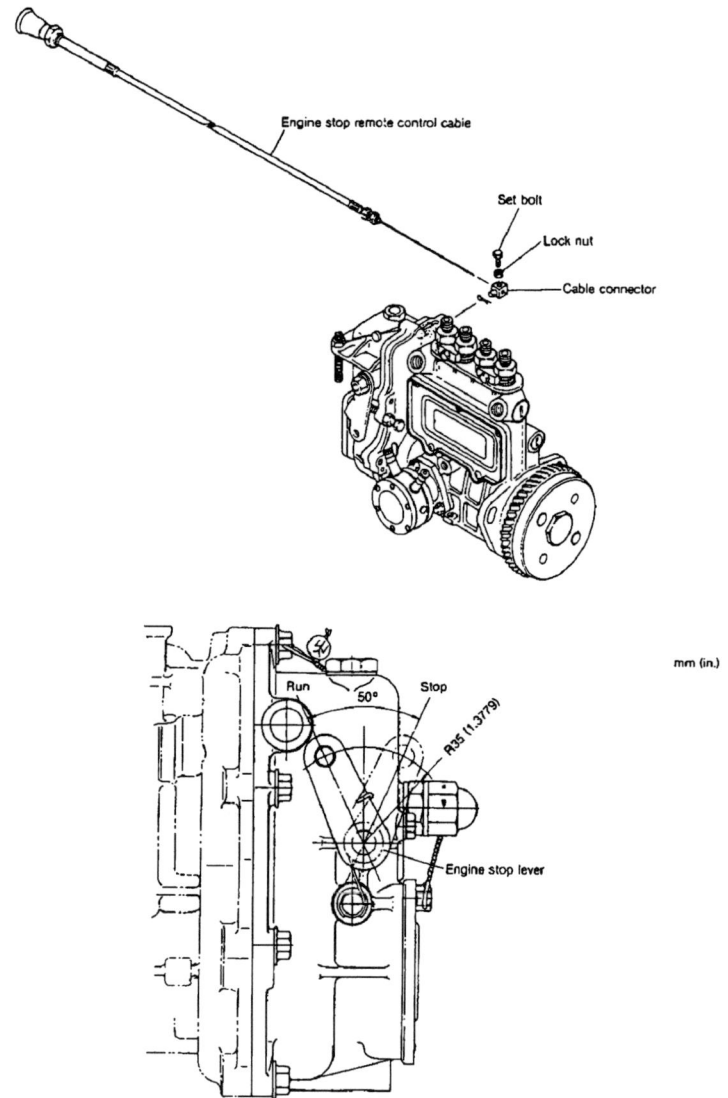

Engine stop remote control cable

Set bolt

Lock nut

Cable connector

mm (in.)

Run

50°

Stop

R35 (1.3779)

Engine stop lever

3. Remote Control Inspection

(1) When the control lever movement does not coincide with operation of the engine, check the cable end stop nut to see whether or not it is loose, and readjust/ retighten when necessary.

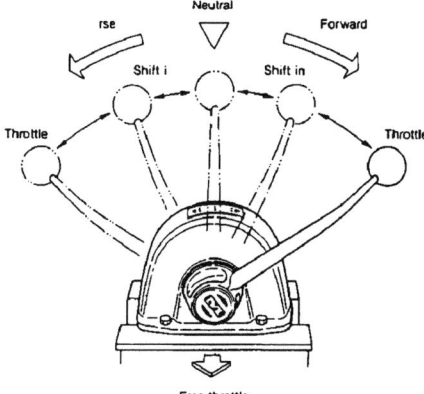

(2) Too many bends (turns) in the cable or bends at too extreme an angle will make it difficult to turn the handle. Reroute the cable to reduce the number of bends or enlarge the bending radius as much as possible (to 200mm or more).
(3) Check for loose cable bracket/clamp bolts or nuts and retighten as necessary.
(4) Check cable connection screwheads, cable sleeves and other metal parts for rust or corrosion. Clean off minor rust and wax or grease the parts. Replace if the parts are heavily rusted or corroded.

4. Remote Control Adjustment

(1) Shift lever adjustment

Move the lever several times—the movement of the clutch lever on the engine from forward, neutral and reverse must coincide with the forward, neutral and reverse on the control lever. If they do not coincide, adjust the fittings as necessary (first engine side, then controller side).

(2) Throttle lever adjustment

Move the control lever all the way to full throttle several times, and then return. The throttle lever on the engine must lightly push against the idle switch when it is returned. If it is properly adjusted, the knob can be easily pulled out when the lever is in the neutral position, and will automatically return when the control lever is brought back to the neutral position. If the control lever presses too hard against the knob, it may not return automatically, in which case the cable end must be adjusted as explained for the clutch. The knob cannot be pulled out when the lever is not in the neutral (central) position.

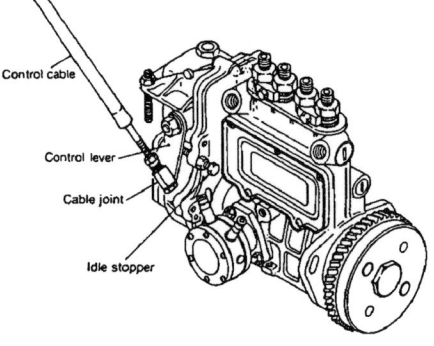

Control cable

Control lever

Cable joint

Idle stopper

ELECTRICAL SYSTEM

Printed in Japan
A0A1029-9002

1. Electrical System

System diagram of electric parts (B2-type)

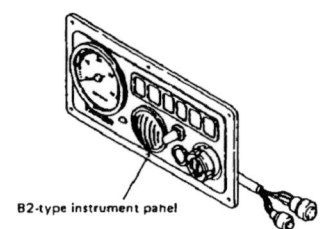

B2-type instrument panel

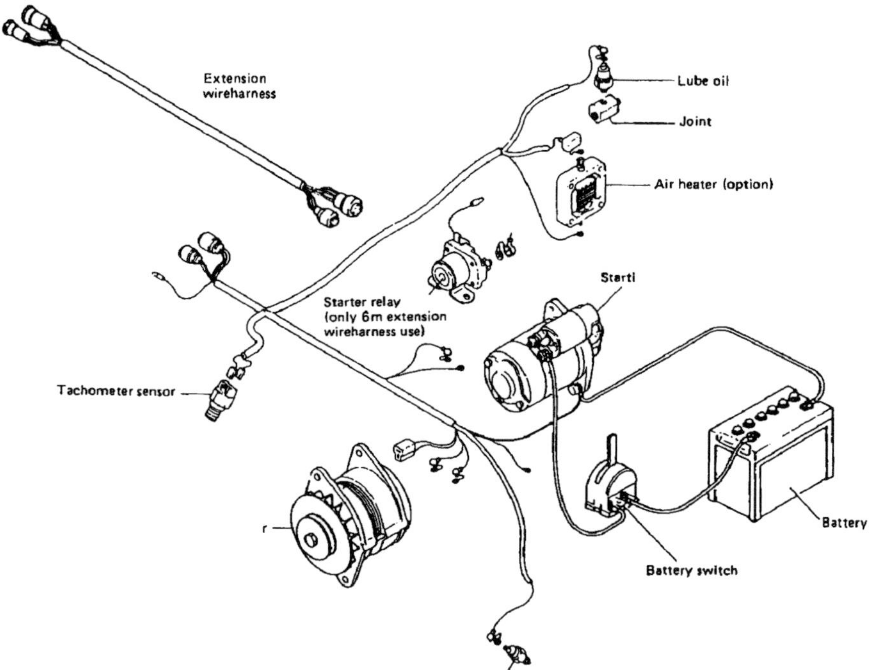

Extension
wireharness

Lube oil

Joint

Air heater (option)

Starter relay
(only 6m extension
wireharness use)

Starti

Tachometer sensor

Battery

r

Battery switch

Water temperature switch

C-type, D-type and E-type

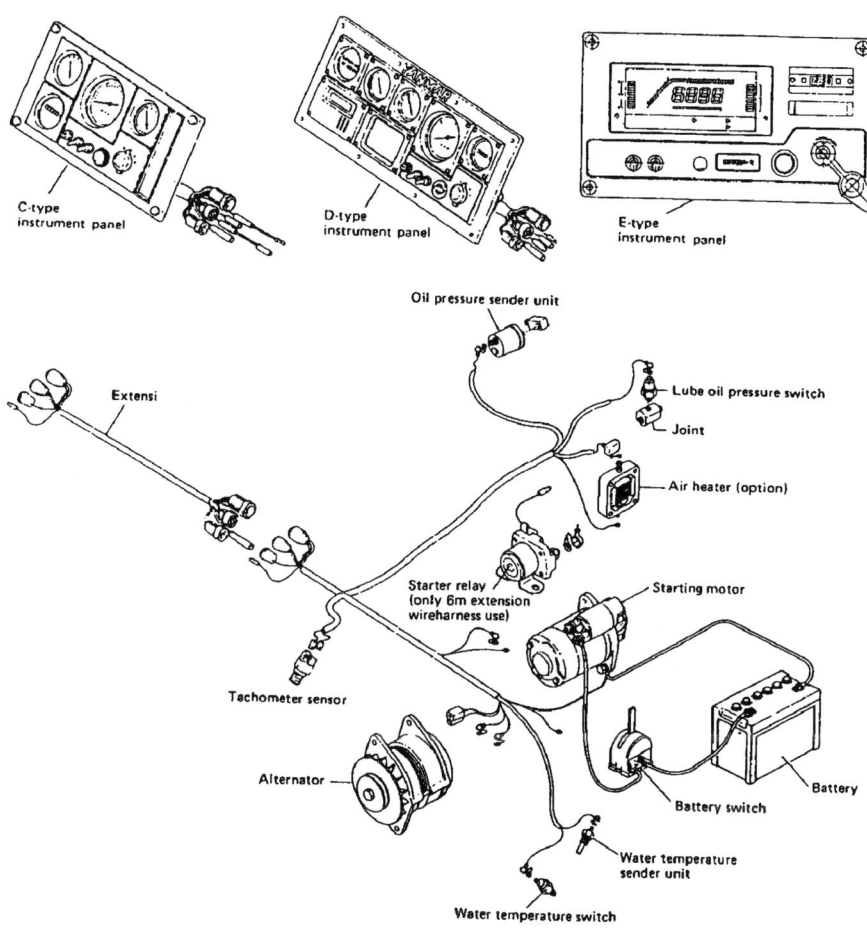

C-type
instrument panel

D-type
instrument panel

E-type
instrument panel

Oil pressure sender unit

Extensi

Lube oil pressure switch

Joint

Air heater (option)

Starter relay
(only 6m extension
wireharness use)

Starting motor

Tachometer sensor

Alternator

Battery

Battery switch

Water temperature
sender unit

Water temperature switch

1-2 Wiring diagram

1-2.1 For B-type instrument panel

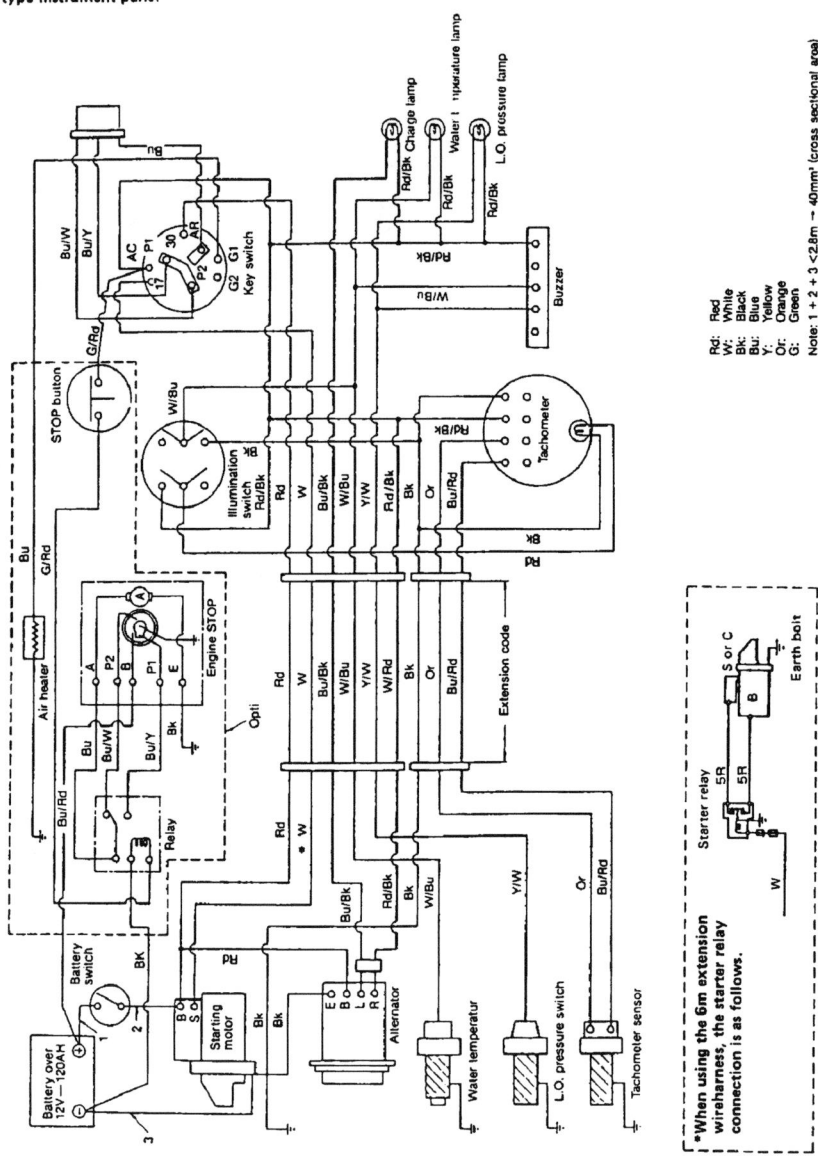

1·2.2 For C-type instrument panel

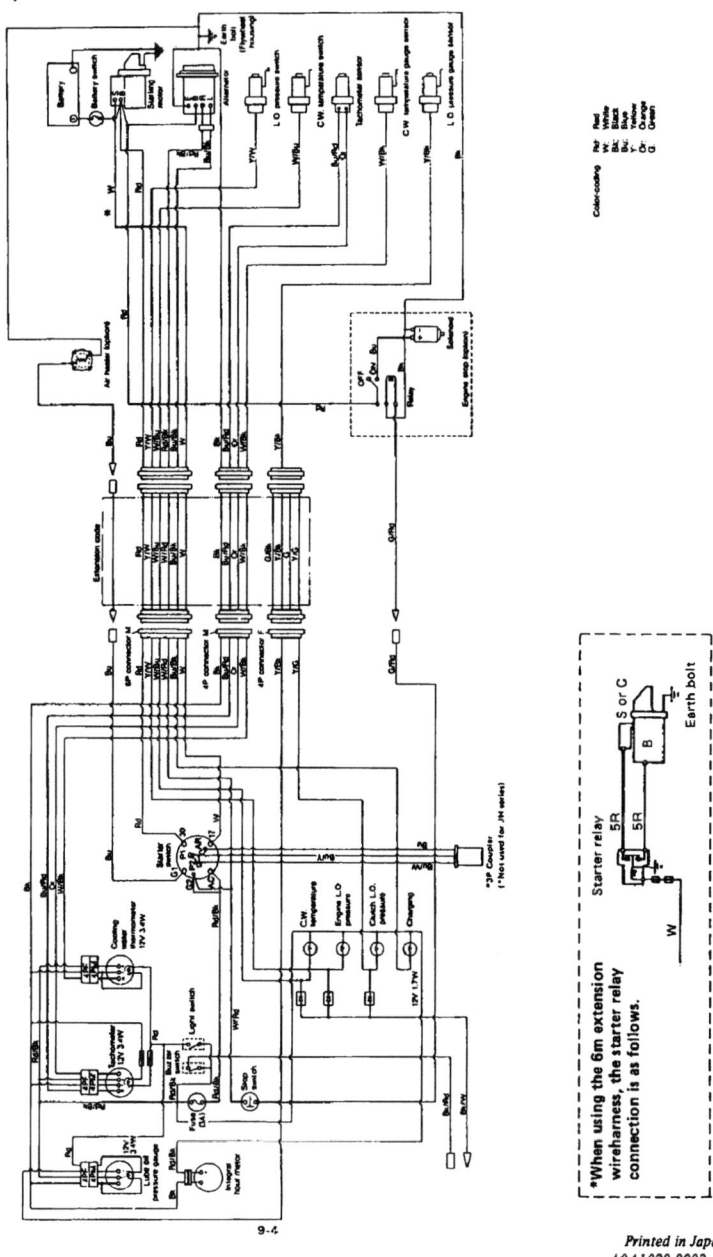

9-4

1-2.3 D-type instrument panel

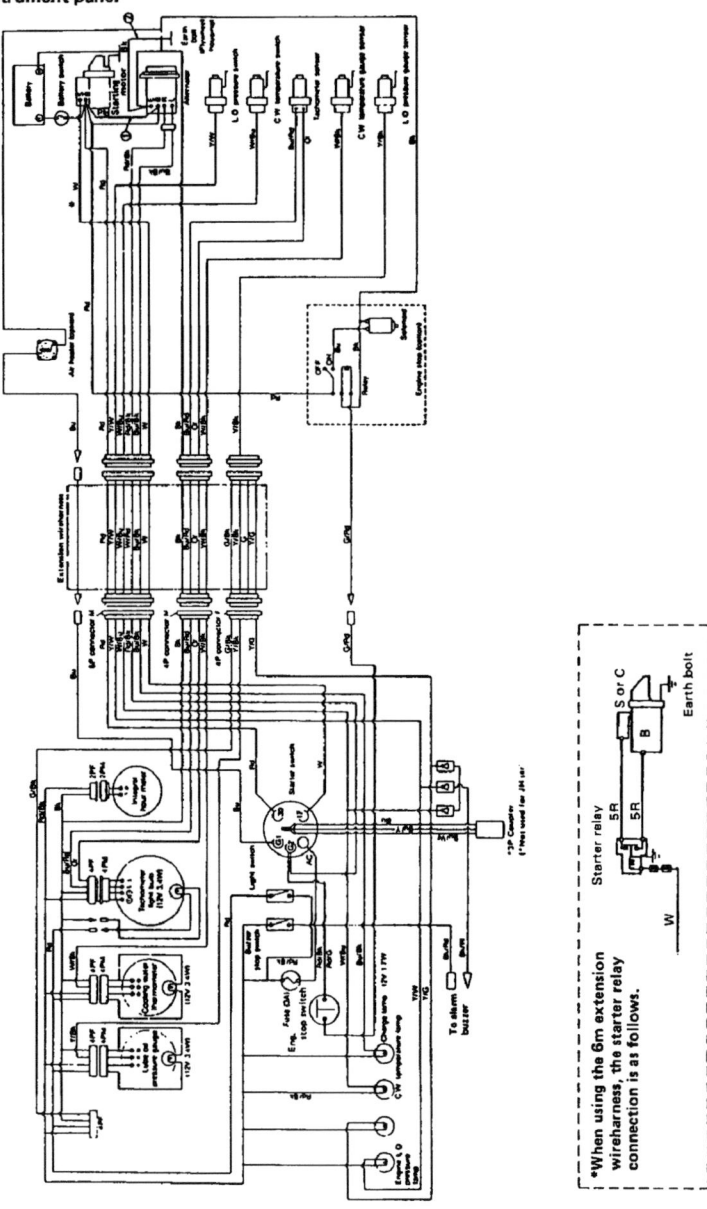

1-2.4 For E-type instrument panel

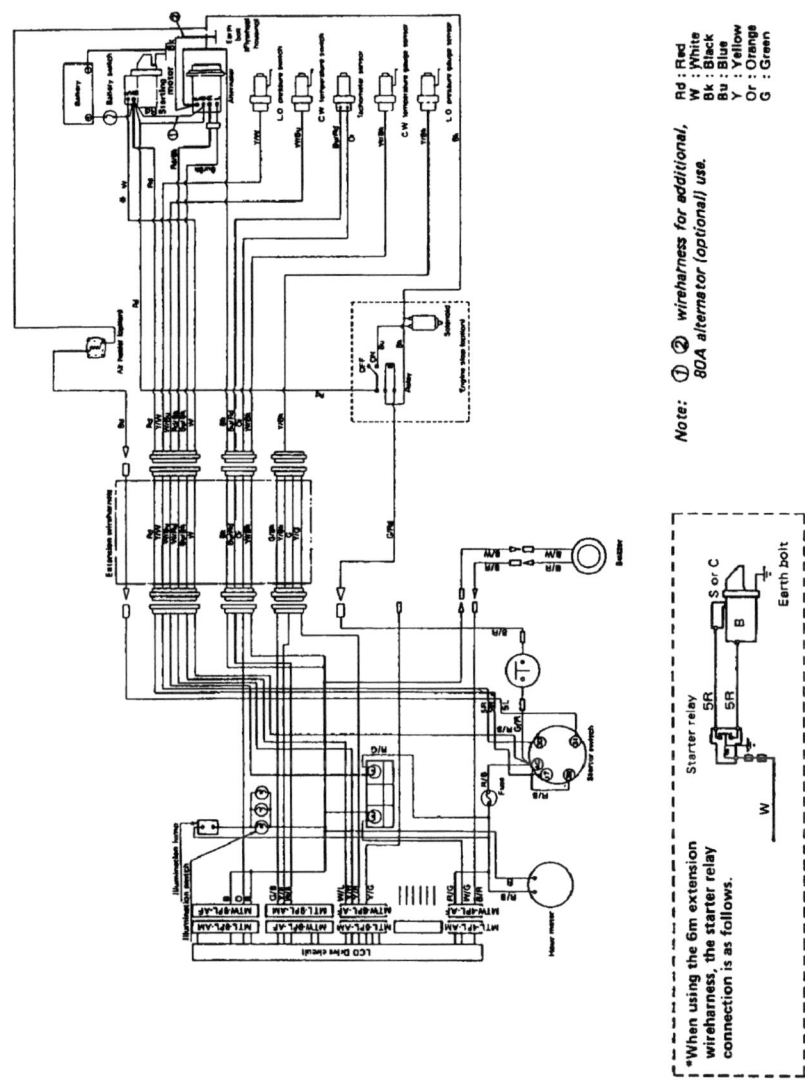

2. Battery

2-1 Construction

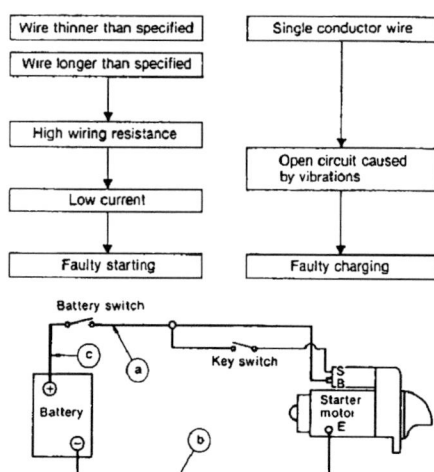

```
┌─────────────────────────────┐   ┌─────────────────────────┐
│ Wire thinner than specified │   │ Single conductor wire   │
└─────────────────────────────┘   └─────────────────────────┘
┌─────────────────────────────┐
│ Wire longer than specified  │
└─────────────────────────────┘
           │                                  │
┌─────────────────────────────┐               │
│ High wiring resistance      │               │
└─────────────────────────────┘   ┌─────────────────────────┐
           │                      │ Open circuit caused     │
┌─────────────────────────────┐   │ by vibrations           │
│ Low current                 │   └─────────────────────────┘
└─────────────────────────────┘
           │                                  │
┌─────────────────────────────┐   ┌─────────────────────────┐
│ Faulty starting             │   │ Faulty charging         │
└─────────────────────────────┘   └─────────────────────────┘
```

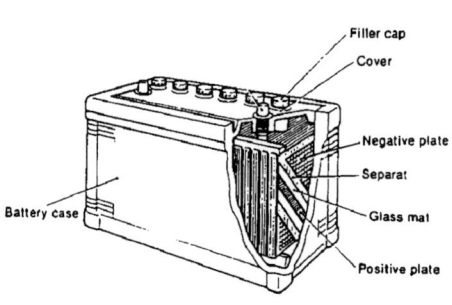

The battery utilizes chemical action to convert chemical energy to electrical energy. This engine uses a lead acid battery which stores a fixed amount of power that can be used when required. After use, the battery can be recharged and used again.

As shown in the figure, a nonconductive container is filled with dilute sulfuric acid electrolyte. Lead dioxide positive plates and lead dioxide negative plates separated by glass mats are stacked alternately in the electrolyte. The positive and negative plates are connected to their respective terminals.

Power is removed from the battery by connecting the load across these two terminals.

When the battery is discharging, an electric current flows from the positive plates to the negative plates. When the battery is being charged, electric current is passed through the battery in the opposite direction by an external power source.

2-2 Battery capacity and battery cables

2-2.1 Battery capacity

Since the battery has a minimum capacity of 12V, 70AH, it can be used for 100 ~ 150AH.

	minimum	12V — 100AH
Battery capacity	standard	12V — 120AH
	cold weather	12V — 150AH
Full charged specific gravity		1.26

2-2.2 Battery cable

Wiring must be performed with the specified electric wire. Thick, short wiring should be used to connect the battery to the starter, (soft automotive low-voltage wire [AV wire]). Using wire other than that specified may cause the following troubles:

The overall lengths of the wire between the battery (+) terminal and the starter (B) terminal, and between the battery (–) terminal and the starter (E) terminal, should be determined according to the following table.

Voltage system	Allowable wiring voltage drop	Conductor cross-section area	a + b + c allowable length
0.2V or less/100A		20mm² (0.0311 in.²)	Up to 2.5m (98.43 in.)
		40mm² (0.062 in.²)	Up to 5m (196.87 in.)

Note: Excessive resistance in the key switch circuit (between the battery and start [S] terminals) can cause improper pinion engagement. To prevent this, follow the wiring diagram carefully.

2-3 Inspection

The quality of the battery governs the starting performance of the engine. Therefore the battery must be routinely inspected to ensure that it functions perfectly at all times.

2-3.1 Visual inspection

(1) Inspect the case for cracks, damage and electrolyte leakage.

(2) Inspect the battery holder for tightness, corrosion, and damage.

(3) Inspect the terminals for rusting and corrosion, and check the cables for damage.

(4) Inspect the caps for cracking, electrolyte leakage and clogged vent holes.

Correct any abnormal conditions found. Clean off rusted terminals with a wire brush before reconnecting the battery cable.

2-3.2 Checking the electrolyte
(1) Electrolyte level

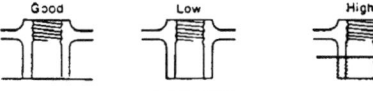

Good   Low   High

Check the electrolyte level every 7 to 10 days. The electrolyte must always be 10 ~ 20mm (0.3937 ~ 0.7874in.) over the top of the plates.

NOTES: 1. The "LEVEL" line on a transparent plastic bat-
tery case indicates the height of the elec-
trolyte.
2. Always use distilled water to bring up the elec-
trolyte level.
3. When the electrolyte has leaked out, add dilute
sulfuric acid with the same specific gravity as
the electrolyte.

(2) Measuring the specific gravity of the electrolyte
1) Draw some of the electrolyte up into a hydrometer.

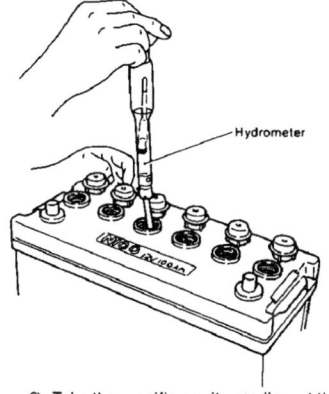

Hydrometer

2) Take the specific gravity reading at the top of the scale of the hydrometer.

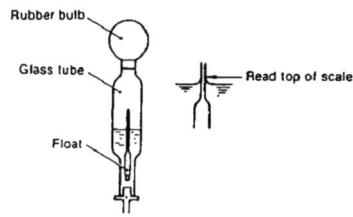

Rubber bulb

Glass tube

Read top of scale

Float

3) The battery is fully charged if the specific gravity is 1.260 at an electrolyte temperature of 20°C. The battery is discharged if the specific gravity is 1.200

(50%). If the specific gravity is below 1.200, recharge the battery.
4) If the difference in the specific gravity among the cells of the battery is ±0.01, the battery is OK.
5) Measure the temperature of the electrolyte. Since the specific gravity changes with the temperature, 20°C is used as the reference temperature.
Reading the specific gravity at 20°C
$S_{20} = St + 0.0007 (t - 20)$
S_{20}: Specific gravity at the standard temperature of 20°C
St: Specific gravity of the electrolyte at t°C
0.0007: Specific gravity change per 1°C
t: Temperature of electrolyte

2-3.3 Voltage test
Using a battery tester, the amount of discharge can be determined by measuring the voltage drop which occurs while the battery is being discharged with a large current.

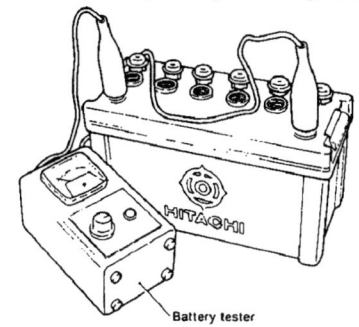

Battery tester

(1) Connect the tester to the battery.
12V battery tester
Adjust the current (A).
(2) Connect the (+) lead of the tester to the (+) battery terminal, and the (-) tester lead to the (-) battery terminal.
(3) Push the TEST button, wait 5 seconds, and then read the meter.
• Repeat the test twice to make sure that the meter indication remains the same.

2-3.4 Washing the battery
(1) Wash the outside of the battery with a brush while running cold or warm water over the battery. (Make sure that no water gets into the battery.)
(2) When the terminals or other metal parts are corroded due to exposure to electrolyte leakage, wash off all the acid.
(3) Check the vent holes of the caps and clean if clogged.
(4) After washing the battery, dry it with compressed air, connect the battery cable, and coat the terminals with grease. Since the grease acts as an insulator, do not coat the terminals before connecting the cables.

2-4 Charging

2-4.1 Charging methods

There are two methods of charging a battery: normal and rapid.

Rapid charging should only be used in emergencies.

• Normal charging...Should be conducted at a current of 1/10 or less of the indicated battery capacity (10A or less for a 100AH battery).

Rapid charging...Rapid charging is done over a short period of time at a current of 1/5 ~ 1/2 the indicated battery capacity (20A ~ 50A for a 100AH battery). However, since rapid charging causes the electrolyte temperature to rise too high, special care must be exercised.

2-4.2 Charging procedure

(1) Check the specific gravity and adjust the electrolyte level.
(2) Disconnect the battery cables.
(3) Connect the red clip of the charger to the (+) battery terminal and connect the black clip to the (−) terminal.

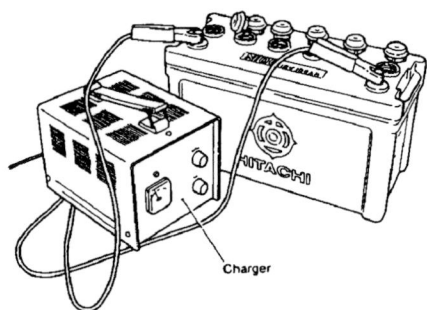

Charger

(4) Set the current to 1/10 ~ 1/5 of the capacity indicated on the outside of the battery.
(5) Periodically measure the specific gravity during charging to make sure that the specific gravity remains at a high fixed value. Also check whether gas is being generated.

2-4.3 Charging precautions

(1) Remove the battery caps to vent the gas during charging.
(2) While charging, ventilate the room and prohibit smoking, welding, etc.
(3) The electrolyte temperature should not exceed 45°C during charging.
(4) Since an alternator is used on this engine, when charging with a charger, always disconnect the battery (+) cable to prevent destruction of the diodes.
(Before disconnecting the (+) battery cable, disconnect the (−) battery cable [ground side].)

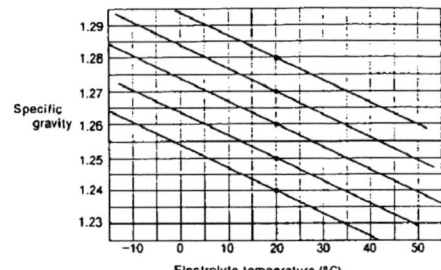

Electrolyte temperature and specific gravity

2-5 Battery storage precautions

The life of a battery depends considerably on how it is handled. Generally speaking, however, after about two years its performance will deteriorate, starting will become difficult, and the battery will not fully recover its original charge even after recharging. Then it must be replaced.

(1) Since the battery will self-discharge about 0.5%/day even when not in use, it must be charged 1 or 2 times a month when it is being stored.

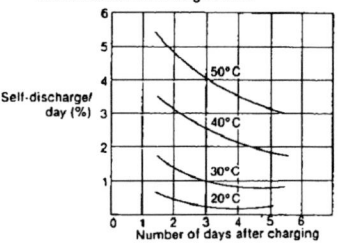

(2) If charging by the engine alternator is insufficient because of frequent starts and stops, the battery will rapidly lose power.
Charge the battery as soon as possible after it is used under these conditions.
(3) An easy-to-use battery charger that permits home charging is available from Yanmar. Take proper care of the battery by using the charger as a set with a hydrometer.
When the specific gravity has dropped to about 1.16 and the engine will not start, charge the battery up to a specific gravity of 1.26 (24 hours).
(4) Before putting the battery in storage for long periods, charge it for about 8 hours to prevent rapid aging.

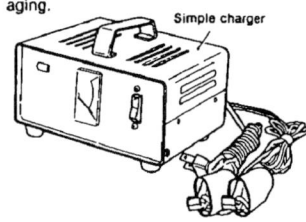

Simple charger

3. Starter Motor

1. The Reduction Starter System
    1-1 The Reduction Starters
    While these only had specialized applications in the past, they currently are being widely adopted because of their compact, lightweight design.
    Although smaller than the direct-drive type starter with its armature and pinion driven at the same speed, the gear reduction starter actually reduces the motor speed to approximately 27% prior to driving the pinion.
    It does this without reducing output, hence its name.
    Furthermore, use of heat-resistant insulating materials and advanced production technology makes the compact, light weight design possible and improves its starting capabilities in cold regions.

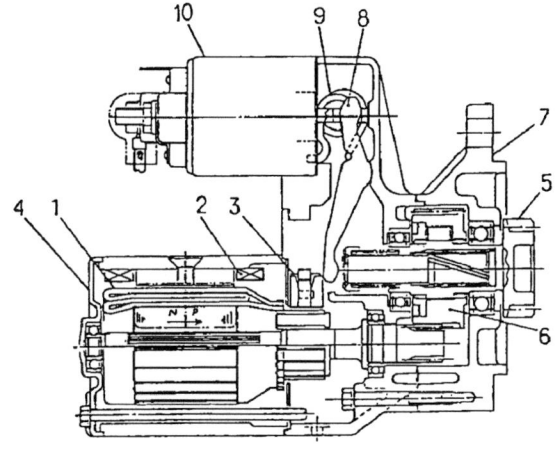

1. Armature	6. Pinion Clutch
2. Field Coil	7. Gear Case
3. Brush	8. Shift Lever
4. Rear Cover	9. Torsion Spring
5. Pinion Shaft	10. Magnetic Switch

Fig.1 Reduction Starter Construction

1-2 The Engagement Mechanism
This type utilizes the electromagnetic force. The pinion is engaged with the ring gear
by means of the torsion spring and shift lever. The plunger is shifted by the attracting
force and depresses the pinion. When the pinion does not strike the ring gear, smooth
engagement occurs, then the contacts close to start the motor.
Also, when the pinion strikes the ring gear teeth, it compresses the torsion spring and
loses the contacts. When the current flows through the motor and the armature starts
rotating, the pinion is depressed strongly on the ring gear and rotated by means of
torsion spring pressure and the helical spline's force. Then, the pinion teeth are
arranged in engagement with the ring gear teeth. When the key start switch is turned
OFF, the magnetic switch is demagnetized, and the pinion is returned by the torsion
spring force. Simultaneously, the contacts open to stop motor operation. In Fig. 2.
engagement between the pinion and ring gear is illustrated.

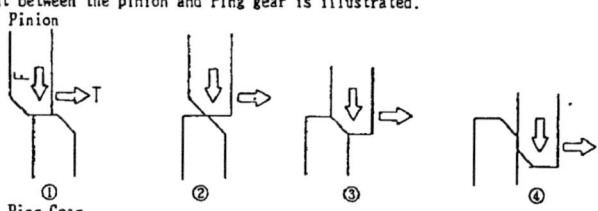

Fig. 2. Engagement of Pinion and Ring Gear

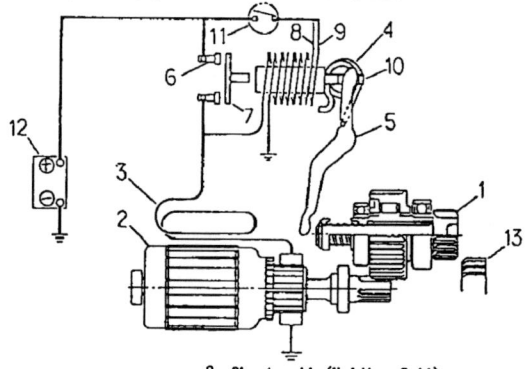

1. Pinion	8. Shunt coil (Holding Coil)
2. Armature	9. Series Coil (Attracting Coil)
3. Field Coil	10. Plunger
4. Torsion Spring	11. Key Start Switch
5. Shift lever	12. Battery
6. Stationary contact	13. Ring Gear
7. Movable Contactor	

Fig. 3. Schematic Layout of Reduction Starter's Electrical Circuit

2. Removal
1) Disconnect the battery's negative or ⊖ side cable at the battery.
2) Disconnect the battery's posistive or ⊕ cable and the main harness' feed wire from
the magnetic switch of the reduction starter.
3) Disconnect the battery's negative or ⊖ cable at the reduction starter.
4) Remove the reduction starter retaining bolts and lockwashers. Then withdraw the motor
assembly.

3. TROUBLESHOOTING THE STARTER SYSTEM

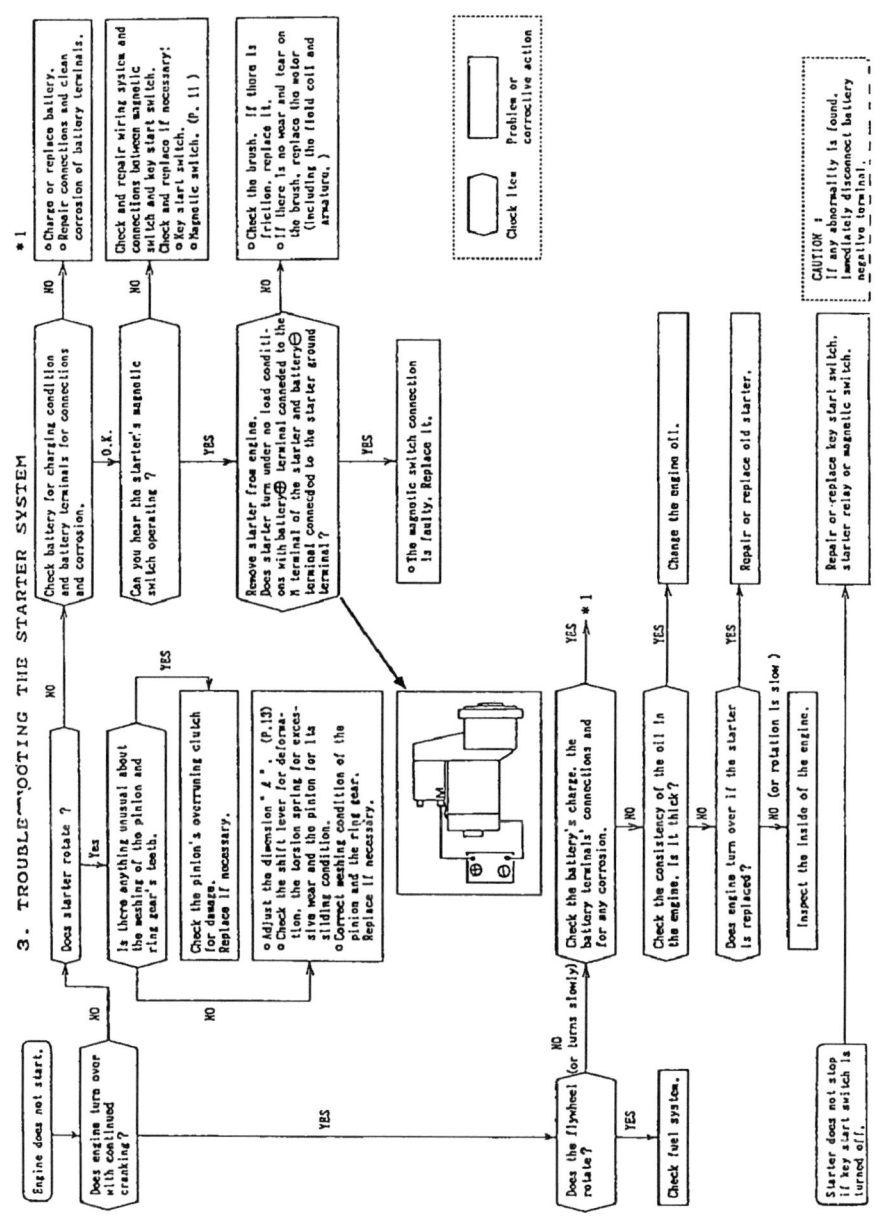

*1 Charge or replace battery.
o Repair connections and clean corrosion of battery terminals.

Check and repair wiring system and connections between magnetic switch and key start switch.
Check and replace if necessary:
o Key start switch.
o Magnetic switch. (P. 11)

o Check the brush. If there is friction, replace it.
o If there is no wear and tear on the brush, replace the motor (including the field coil and armature.)

[legend box]
Problem or corrective action
Check item

CAUTION :
If any abnormality is found, immediately disconnect battery negative terminal.

Check battery for charging condition and battery terminals for connections and corrosion. — NO

O.K.

Can you hear the starter's magnetic switch operating ? — NO / YES

Remove starter from engine. Does starter turn under no load conditions with battery⊕ terminal connected to the M terminal of the starter and battery⊖ terminal connected to the starter ground terminal? — NO / YES

o The magnetic switch connection is faulty. Replace it.

Engine does not start.

Does engine turn over with continued cranking? — NO

Does starter rotate ? — Yes / No

Is there anything unusual about the meshing of the pinion and ring gear's teeth. — YES

Check the pinion's overruning clutch for damage. Replace if necessary. — NO

o Adjust the dimension " ℓ ". (P.13)
o Check the shift lever for deformation, the torsion spring for excessive wear and the pinion for its sliding condition.
o Correct meshing condition of the pinion and the ring gear. Replace if necessary.

YES

Does the flywheel rotate ? — NO (or turns slowly) / YES

Check fuel system.

Check the battery's charge, the battery terminals' connections and for any corrosion. — NO

Check the consistency of the oil. Is it thick? — YES *1 / NO

Change the engine oil. — YES

Does engine turn over if the starter is replaced? — YES / NO (or rotation is slow)

Repair or replace old starter.

Inspect the inside of the engine.

Starter does not stop if key start switch is turned off.

Repair or replace key start switch, starter relay of magnetic switch.

4. Disassembly

▲ 1) The Magnetic Switch's 8 ㎝ Nut
  2) The 5 ㎜ Through Bolts (2)
▲ 3) The Rear Cover
▲ 4) The Brush Holder
  5) Yoke Assembly
▲ 6) Armature
  7) The 6 ㎜ Bolts (2)
  8) Magnetic Switch
▲ 9) Torsion Spring
 10) Dust Cover

▲11) Shift Lever
 12) The 6 ㎜ Bolts (3)
 13) Gear Case
▲14) Center Housing
▲15) The Pinion Stopper Clip
 16) Pinion Stopper
 17) Retaining Spring
 18) Pinion Shaft
▲19) Clutch Assembly

▲: Disassembly Reference Exhibit Is Provided

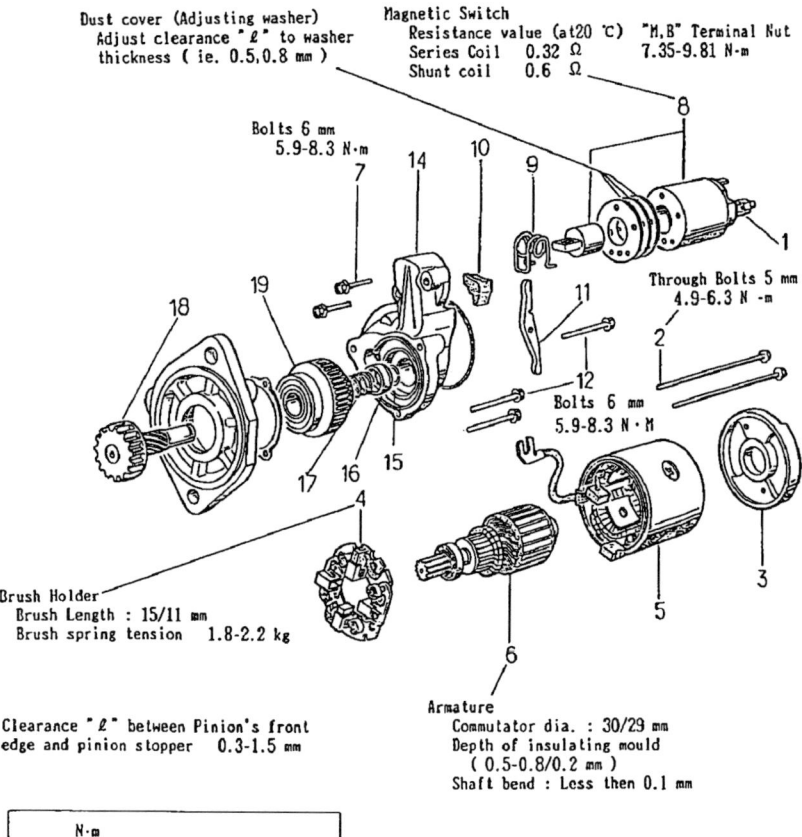

Dust cover (Adjusting washer)
Adjust clearance "ℓ" to washer
thickness (ie. 0.5,0.8 ㎜)

Magnetic Switch
Resistance value (at20 ℃)
Series Coil 0.32 Ω
Shunt coil 0.6 Ω

"M,B" Terminal Nut
7.35-9.81 N·m

Bolts 6 ㎜
5.9-8.3 N·m

Through Bolts 5 ㎜
4.9-6.3 N·m

Bolts 6 ㎜
5.9-8.3 N·M

Brush Holder
Brush Length : 15/11 ㎜
Brush spring tension 1.8-2.2 kg

Clearance "ℓ" between Pinion's front
edge and pinion stopper 0.3-1.5 ㎜

Armature
Commutator dia. : 30/29 ㎜
Depth of insulating mould
(0.5-0.8/0.2 ㎜)
Shaft bend : Less then 0.1 ㎜

	N·m
Unit	㎜ (Standard "New"/Limit "Used")

Fig. 4. Exhibit of Disassembled Parts

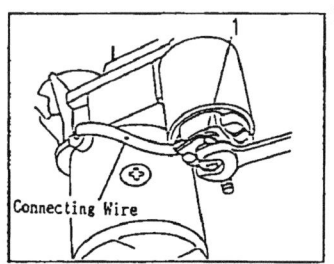

Fig. 5

1) The Magnetic Switch's 8 mm Nut

Remove the magnetic switch's 8 mm nut and disconnect the connecting wire.

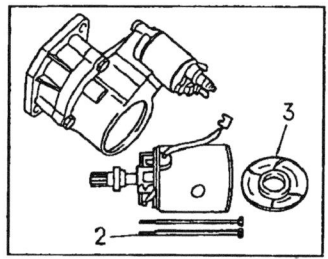

Fig. 6

2) The 5 mm Through Bolts (2)
3) The Rear Cover

The rear cover is disassembled by removing the 5 mm through bolts.

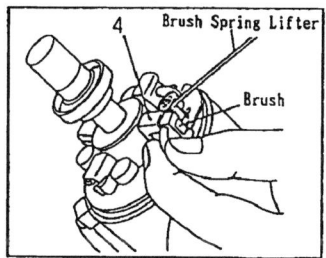

Fig. 7

4) The Brush Holder

Pull the brush spring up with a brush spring lifter tool so that the $\ominus$ side brush is separated from the surface of the commutator (otherwise, the brush holder keeps the brush in contact with the commutator). Remove the $\oplus$ side brush from the brush holder.

Fig. 8

5) Yoke Assembly
6) Armature

The armature and the yoke assembly can be disassembled once the brush holder is removed.

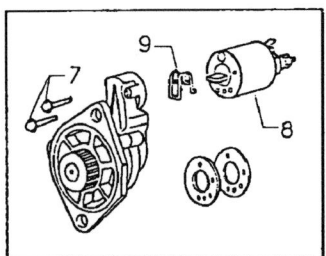

7) The 6 mm Bolts (2)
8) Magnetic Switch
9) Torsion Spring

The magnetic switch can be disassembled once the
6 mm Bolts are removed. Next, the torsion spring is
disassembled from the magnetic switch.

Fig. 9

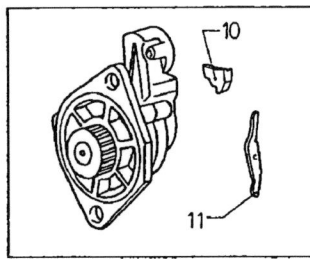

10) Dust Cover
11) Shift lever

The shift lever can be removed once the dust cover
is disassembled from the gear case.

Fig. 10

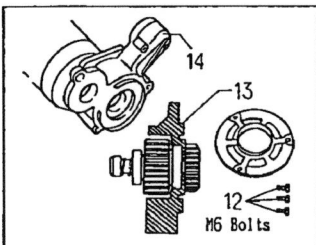

12) The 6 mm Bolts (3)
13) Gear Case and Pinion Clutch ASSY.
14) Center Housing
20) Gasket

The gear case and the Center Housing can disasembled
after the 6 mm Bolts have been removed.

Fig. 11

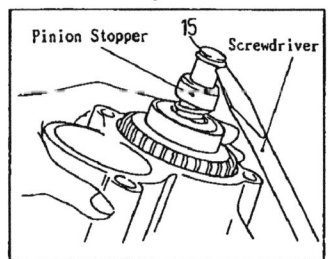

15) The Pinion Stopper Clip

The pinion stopper clip is removed with a standard
screwdriver while the pinion stopper is pushed toward
the pinion.

Fig. 12

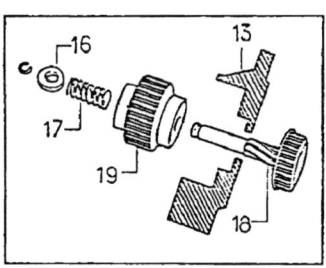

13) Gear Case
16) Pinion Stopper
17) Retaining Spring
18) Pinion Shaft
19) Clutch Assembly

The pinion stopper, retaining spring, pinion shaft and the clutch assembly can be disassembled once the pinion stopper clip has been removed.

-End of Disassembly-

Fig. 13

Printed in Japan
A0A1029-9002

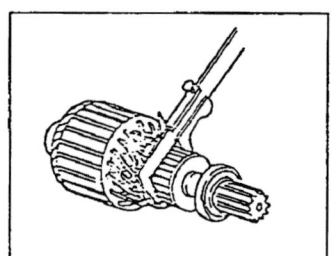

Fig. 14

5. Inspection and Repair

5-1 Armature
(1) Check the diameter of the Commutator

If the outside diameter of the commutator is below the minimum limit then replace it.

(mm)

Standard (New)	Limit (Used)
30	29

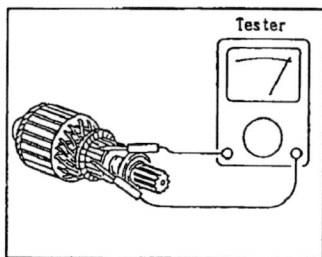

Fig. 15

(2) Continuity Test for the Armature Coil

Use a tester to check for continuity between parallel points on the commutator. If there is continuity, the armature is still good.

No continuity   (Disconnected coil)
                Replace the armature.

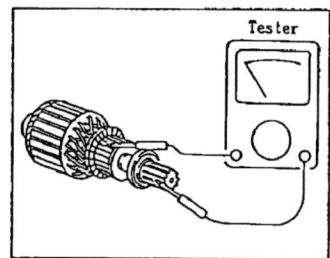

Fig. 16

(3) Insulation Test for the Armature Coil

Use a tester to check for continuity between a point on the commutator and the shaft or the core. If there is no continuity the armature is still good.

Continuity Exists   (Short circuited coil)
                    Replace the armature.

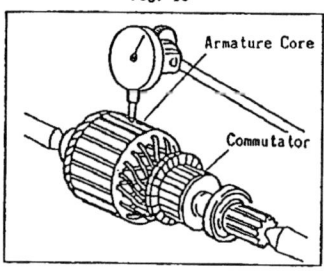

Fig. 17

(4) Check for Surface Distortion on the Armature and the Commutator

Use a dial gauge to measure the distortion of the outside surfaces of the armature core and the commutator. If it is above the limit, then repair or replace it.

(mm)

	Standard (New)	Limit (Used)
Armature	0.05 (MAX)	0.1
Commutator	0.05 (MAX)	0.1

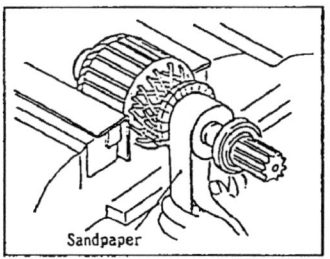

Fig. 18

(5) Check the Surface of the Commutat

If the commutator surface is rough, then please use No. 500-600 sandpaper to make it smooth.

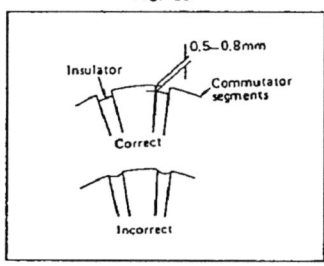

Fig. 19

(6) Check the Depth of Insulating Material from the Commutator Surface

If the depth of the insulating material from the commutator segments is less than the limit, than please repair it by filing it down.

(mm)

Standard (New)	Limit (Used)
0.5 ~ 0.8	0.2

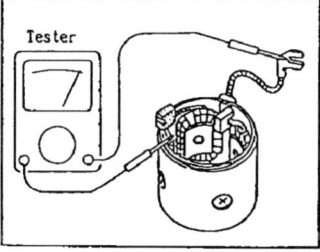

Fig. 20

5-2 The Field Coil
(1) Continuity Test for the Field Coil

Check for continuity between the field coils' terminals with a tester. If there is continuity, then it is still good.

No continuity   (Disconnected coil)
                 Replace the field coil.

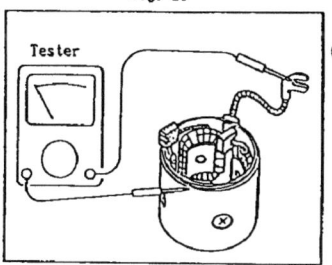

Fig. 21

(2) Insulation Test for the Field Coil

Check for continuity between the yoke and one terminals of each coil with a tester.
If there is no continuity the field coils are still good.

Continuity Exists   (Short circuited coil)
                     Replace the field coils.

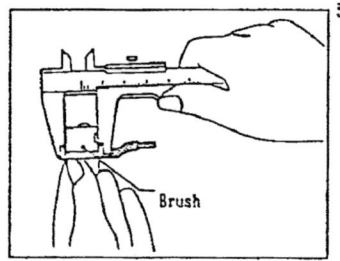

Fig. 22

5-3 Brushes

Measure the length of the brushes and if they are under the limit, replace them.

(mm)

Standard (New)	Limit (Used)
1 5	1 1

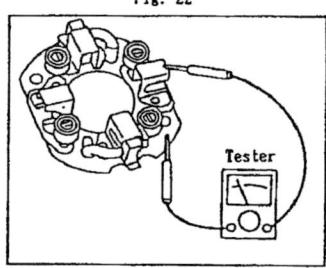

Fig. 23

5-4 Brush Holder

Insulation Test for the Brush Holder

Check for continuity between the brush holder's positive side and its base (negative side) with a tester. If there is no continuity the brush holder is still good.

Continuity Exists (Unsatisfactory insulation)
　　　　　　　　　　　Replace the brush holder.

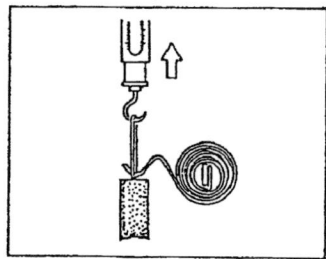

Fig. 24

(3) Inspection of the Brush Springs

Check the weight of the brush springs.

Standard Weight (Kg)
1.8 ~ 2.2

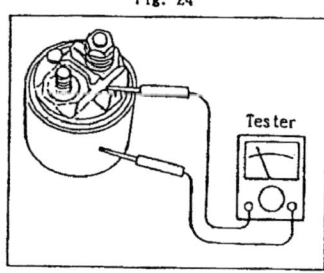

Fig. 25

5-5 Magnetic Switch

(1) Continuity Test for the Shunt Coil

Check for continuity between the "S" terminals and "M"(the switch body)with a tester. If there is continuity, then it is still good.

No continuity (Disconnected coil)
　　　　　　　　　Replace the magnetic switch.

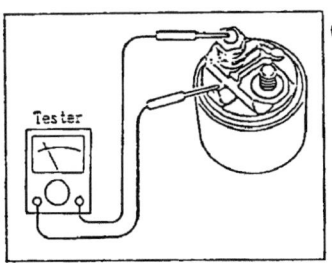

Fig. 26

(2) Continuity Test for the Series Coil

Check for continuity between the "S" and "M" terminals with a tester. If there is continuity, then it is still good.

No continuity   (Disconnected coil)
                 Replace the magnetic switch.

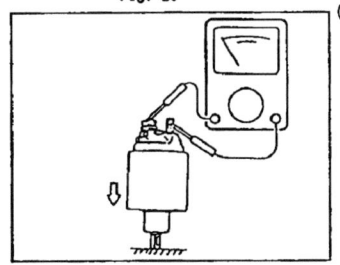

Fig. 27

(3) Continuity Test for Contact-Points

Put the plunger on the under side and then push the magnetic switch down. At this time, check for continuity between the "B" and "M" terminals with a tester. If there is continuity, then it is still good.

No continuity   (Insufficient Continuity)
                 Replace the magnetic switch.

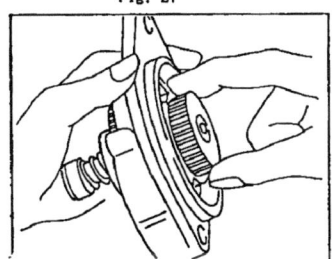

Fig. 28

5-6 Pinion Clutch

(1) Inspection of the Pinion

Rotate the pinion manually. While rotating it in the direction of normal operation, smoothly reverse the direction of rotation to confirm that it locks. In the event of any irregularity, replace it.

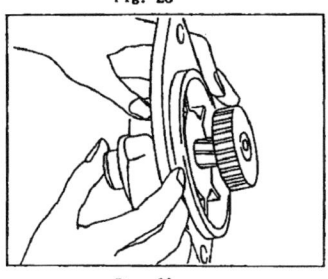

Fig. 29

(2) Pinion Sliding Test

Check to see if the pinion slides up smoothly when the end is pushed. If there are scratches, rust or if the required force seems too strong, please repair it. If too much grease is applied to the pinion shaft, Then it will seem hard to slide.

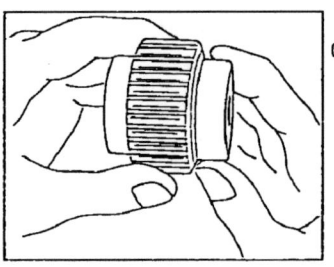

Fig. 30

(2) Inspection of the Ball Bearings

Rotate the ball bearings outer ring surface with
your finger tips and check to see if it rocks
perpendicularly to the direction of rotation.

6. R e a s s e m b l y

Reassembly is in the reverse order of disassembly. Howev r,note the following points.

1. Tightening Torques   Refer to page 5 of the reference materials for the tightening torques of particular screws.

2. The Places to Apply Grease :
   ① ⋯⋯ The moving parts of shift lever.
   ② ⋯⋯ The sliding surface of magnetic switch plunger.
   ⋮⋯ The surface of pinion.
   ③ ⋯⋯ The toothed wheel inside the gear case.

Part		①	②	③
Item	Grease	Shell Alvania Grease No. 2	Aero Shell Grease No. 7	Epnoc Grease No. 2
Worked Penetration 60 Times at 25℃		2 8 0	2 7 2	2 8 2
Dropping Point		1 8 2	2 6 0	2 0 0
Viscosity	at 37.8 ℃	1 4 5	———	———
	at 98.7 ℃	———	3 2	1 3. 9
Starting Torque /Running Torque (Ball Bearing Dia. 47 mm) g-cm	at-30 ℃	2 8 9 0／8 0 0	———	———
	at-40 ℃	———	5 2 0／1 4 0	———

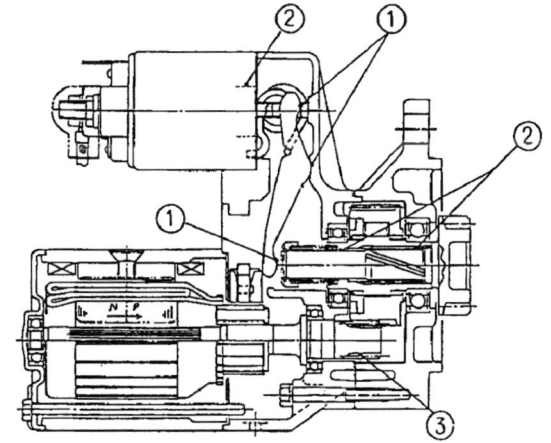

Fig. 31 Kind of Grease

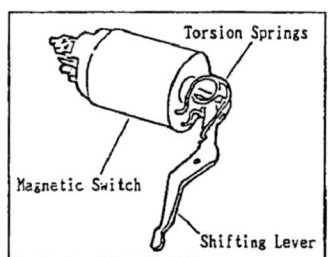

Fig. 32

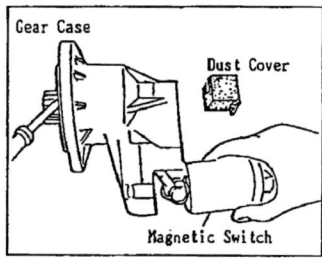

Fig. 33

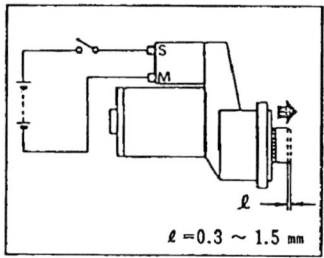

ℓ = 0.3 ~ 1.5 mm

Fig. 34

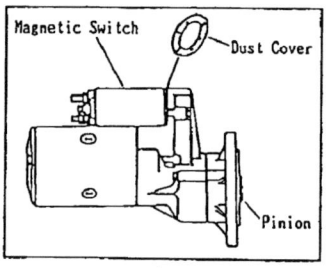

Fig. 35

3. Reassembly of the Magnetic Switch

(1) Introduce the torsion springs into the magnetic switch and connect the shifting lever.

(2) To connect and stabilize the magnetic switch to the gear case, pull out the pinion and connect the shift lever (connected to the magnetic switch) to the gear case with a 6 mm bolt.
Do not forget to reconnect the dust cover.

(4) Measurement of the Pinion's Motion

After connecting the positive ⊕ side of the battery to the "S"terminal and the negative ⊖ side to the "M" terminal and turning the switch on, measure the amount of movement " ℓ " in the direction of the pinion's thrust.

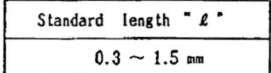

Standard length " ℓ "
0.3 ~ 1.5 mm

Note : When taking the measurement, do so by pushing the pinion softly in the direction of the large arrow.

(5) When the measurement " ℓ " is outside the standard range, adjust the dust cover by inserting it further or loosening it.

7. Operation Specifications Check

Perform the no-load test as instructed because this provides an easy way to confirm the specifications.
Note: The rating is 30 seconds, so perform the test quickly.

(1) The No-load Test

Set the starter securely on a test bench and lay the lines as shown in fig. 36. When the switch is turned off, the electric current flows into the starter in no-load operating conditions. With the electric current flowing, measure the voltage and the r.p.m. and see whether they satisfy the specifications.

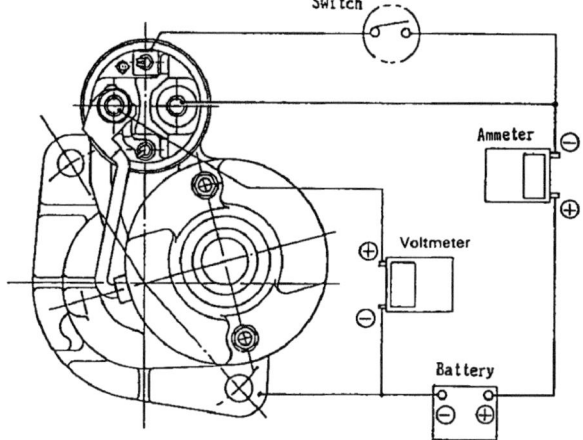

Fig. 36   The No-load Test

Printed in Japan
A0A1029-9002

8. Appendix

   (1) Specifications

Hitachi Model No.	S114-483
YANMAR Part No.	171008-77010
Yoke Diameter (mm)	80
Nominal power (kw)	1.4
Nominal voltage (V)	12
Rating (sec)	30
Direction of Rotation (Looking from the pinion side)	Clockwise
Number of Pinion Teeth	15
Weight (kg)	5.0

No load	Terminal voltage (V)	12
	Electric Current (A)	100 (MAX)
	Revolutions (rpm)	4300 (MIN)
Load	Terminal voltage (V)	9.8
	Electric Current (A)	200
	Torque (N · m)	4.5 (MIN)
	Revolutions (rpm)	1900 (MIN)

4. Alternator Standard, 12V/55A

The alternator serves to keep the battery constantly charged. It is installed on the cylinder block by a bracket, and is driven from the V-pulley at the end of the crankshaft by a V-belt.
The type of alternator used in this engine is ideal for high speed engines with a wide range of engine speeds. It contains diodes that convert AC to DC, and an IC regulator that keeps the generated voltage constant even when the engine speed changes.

4-1 Features

The alternator contains a regulator using an IC, and has the following features.
(1) The IC regulator is self-contained, and has no moving parts (mechanical contact points). It therefore has superior features such as freedom from vibration, no fluctuation of voltage during use, and no need for readjustment.
Also, it is of the over-heating compensation type and can automatically adjust the voltage to the most suitable level depending on the operating temperature.
(2) The regulator is integrated within the alternator to simplify external wiring.
(3) It is an alternator designed for compactness, lightness of weight, and high output.
(4) A newly developed U-shaped diode is used to provide increased reliability and easier checking and maintenance.
(5) As the alternator is to be installed on board, the following measures are taken to provide salt-proofing.
  1) The front and rear covers are salt-proofed.
  2) Salt-proof paint is applied to the diode.
  3) The terminal, where the inboard harness is connected to the alternator, is nickel plated.

4-2 Specifications

Model of alternator	LR155-20 (HITACHI)
Model of IC regulator	TRIZ-63 (HITACHI)
Battery voltage	12V
Nominal output	12V/55A
Earth polarity	Negative earth (⊖)
Direction of rotation (viewed from pulley end)	Clockwise
Weight	4.3kg (9.5lb.)
Rated speed	5000 rpm
Operating speed	1000 ~ 9000
Speed for 13.5V	1000 or less
Output current at 20°C	over 53A/5000 rpm
Regulated voltage	14.5 ±0.3V (Standard temperature voltage gradient, −0.01/°C)

4-3 Characteristics

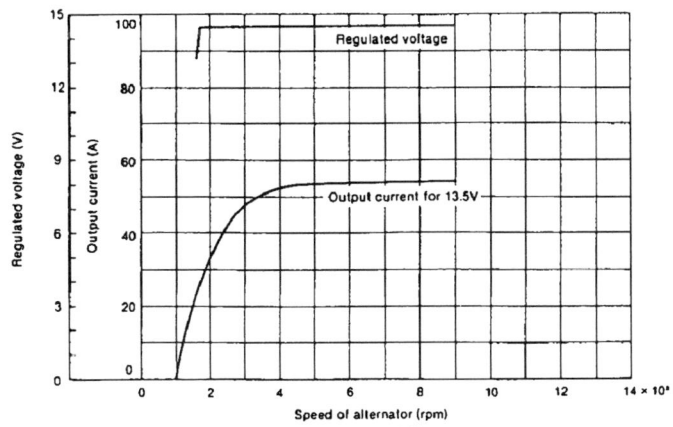

Speed of alternator (rpm)

9-26

4-4 Construction

This is a standard rotating field type three-phase alternator.
It consists of six major parts: the pulley, fan, front cover,
rotor, stator and rear cover. The IC regulator is an integral
part of the alternator.

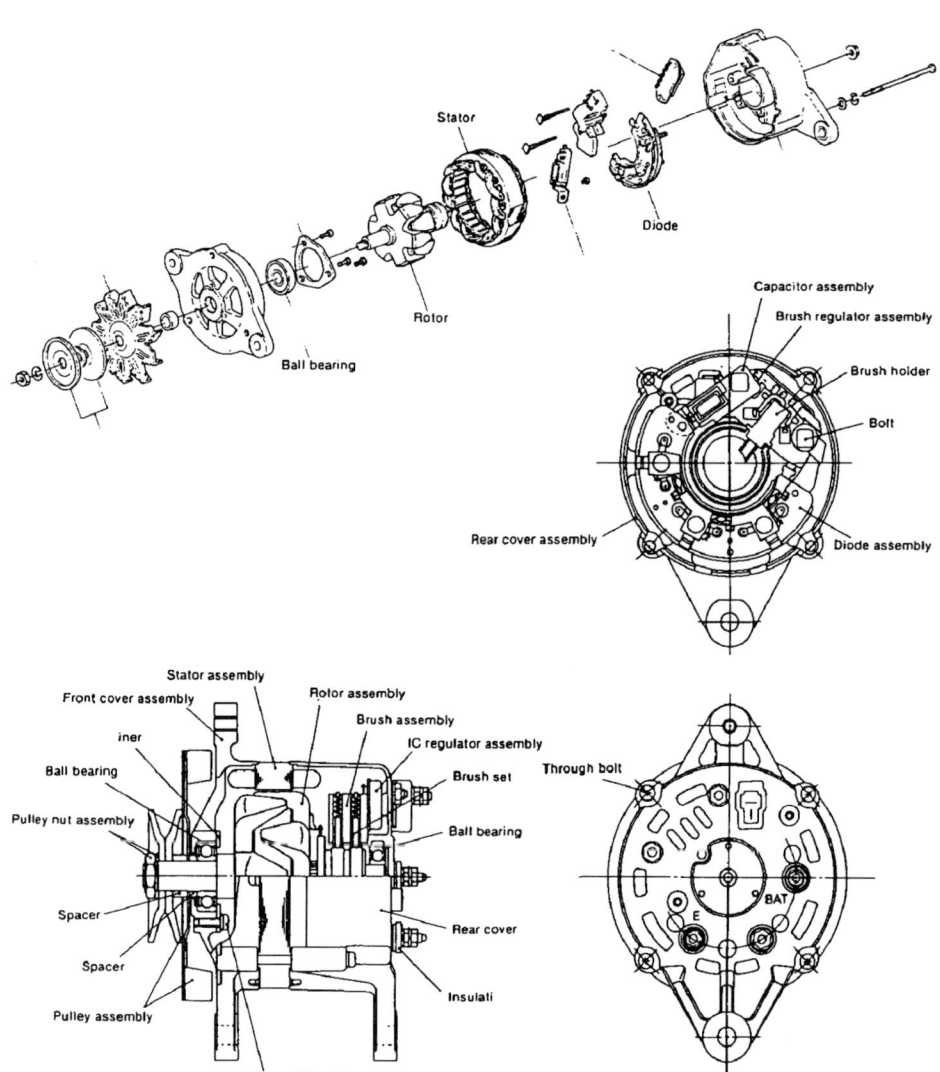

Stator

Diode

Capacitor assembly

Brush regulator assembly

Brush holder

Bolt

Rotor

Ball bearing

Rear cover assembly

Diode assembly

Stator assembly

Front cover assembly

Rotor assembly

Brush assembly

iner

IC regulator assembly

Ball bearing

Brush set

Through bolt

Pulley nut assembly

Ball bearing

Spacer

Rear cover

Spacer

Pulley assembly

Insulati

Screw (M5 × 0.8 × 14)

E

BAT

4-5 Alternator functioning

(1) IC regulator

The IC regulator is the transistor (Tr₁) which is series-connected with the rotor. The IC regulator controls the output voltage of the generator by breaking or conducting the rotor coil (exciting) current.

When the output voltage of the generator is within the standard value, the transistor (Tr₁) turns on. When the voltage exceeds the standard value, the Zener diode goes on and the transistor (Tr₁) turns off.

With the repeated turning on and off of the transistor, the output voltage is kept at the standard value. (Refer to the circuit diagram below.)

(2) Charge lamp

When the transistor (Tr₁) is on, the charge lamp key switch is turned to ON, and current flows to R₁, R₄ and to Tr₁ to light the lamp. When the engine starts to run and output voltage is generated in the stator coil, the current stops flowing to this circuit, turning off the charge lamp.

(3) Circuit diagram

4-6 Handling precautions

(1) Be careful of the battery's polarity (+, − terminals), and do not connect the wrong terminals to the wrong cables, or the battery will be short-circuited by the generator diode.

In this case too much current will flow, the IC regulator and diodes burn out, and the wire harness will burn.

(2) Make sure of the correct connection of each terminal.

(3) When quick-charging, etc., disconnect either the battery terminal on the AC generator or the terminal on the battery.

(4) Do not short-circuit the terminals.

(5) Do not conduct any tests using high tension insulation resistance. (The diodes and IC regulator will burn out.)

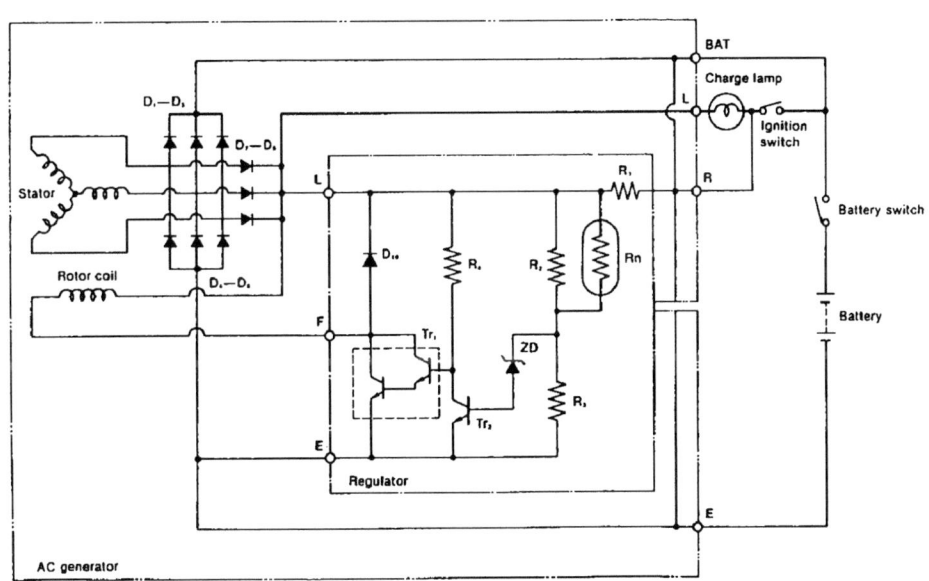

Generator output termi	D₁—D₆: Output commutation diode
IC protecting diode	R₁—R₄: Resistor
Charge lamp terminal	D₁—D₂: Charging lamp switching diode
Zener diode	F: To supply current to rotor coil
Earth	Rn: Thermistor
Transistor	(Temperature gradient resistance)

Printed in Japan
A0A1029-9002

4-7 Disassembling the alternator

(1) Remove the through-bolt, and separate the front assembly from the rear assembly.

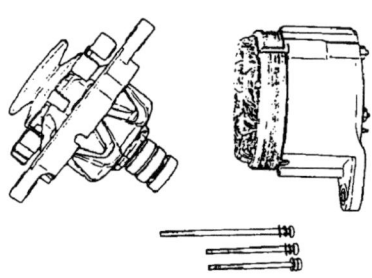

(2) Remove the pulley nut, and pull out the rotor from the front cover.

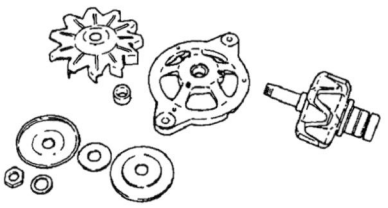

(3) Remove the ∅5mm (∅0.1969in.) screw from the front cover, and then remove the ball bearing.

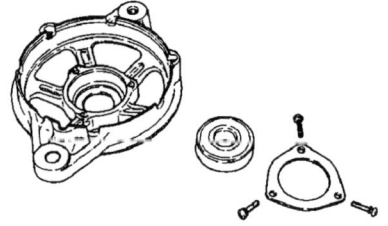

(4) Remove the nut, the brush-holder, and diode fixing nut at the BAT, and the terminal screws of the rear cover. Separate the rear cover from the stator (with the diode and brush holder).

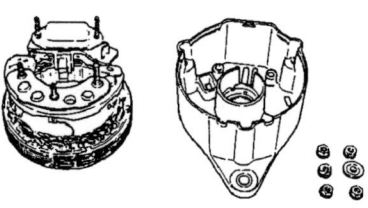

(5) Disconnect the soldered joint of the stator lead wir and remove the diode and brush regulator assembli from the stator at the same time.

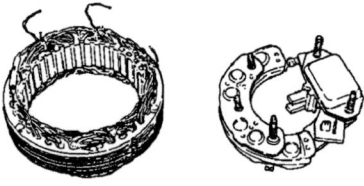

(6) Separating the regulator
1) To separate the regulator, remove the ∅3mm (∅0.1181in.) rivet which keeps the diode assembly and the brushless regulator in place, and the soldered joint of the L-terminal.

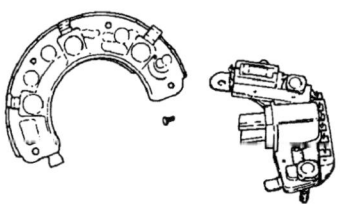

2) To replace the IC regulator, disconnect the soldered joint of the IC regulator and pull out the two bolts. Do not remove these two bolts except when replacing the IC regulator.

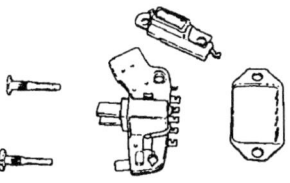

4-8 Inspection and adjustment

(1) Diode

Between terminals		BAT (+ side diode)	
	Tester wire	+ side	– side
U.V.W.	+ side		No continuity
	– side	Continuity	

Between terminals		E (– side diode)	
	Tester wire	+ side	– side
U.V.W.	+ side		Continuity
	side	No continuity	

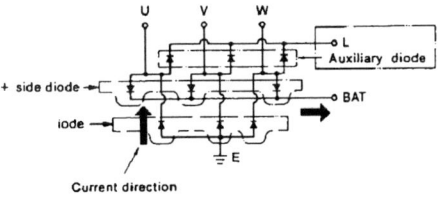

Current direction

U.V.W.: termi

Current flows only in one direction in the diode as shown in Fig. 181. Accordingly, when there is continuity between each terminal (e.g. BAT and U), the diode i in normal condition (photo). When there is no continuity, the diode is defective.
When the tester is connected in the reverse of above, there should be no continuity. If there is, the diode i defective.

After repeating the above test, if any diode is found to be defective, replace the diode assembly. Since there is no terminal on the auxiliary diode, check the continuity between both ends of the diode.

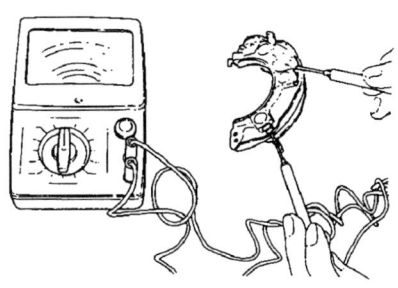

CAUTION: Do not use high tensile insulation resistance such as meggers, etc. for testing. The diode may burn out.

(2) Rotor
Inspect the slip ring surface, rotor coil continuity and insulation.

1) Inspecting the slip ring surface
Check if the surface of the slip ring is sufficiently smooth. If the surface is rough, grind the surface with No. 500—600 sand paper. If it is contaminated with oil, etc., wipe the surface clean with alcohol.

	Standard	Wear limit
Slip ring outer dia.	∅31.6mm (1.2441in.)	∅30.6mm (1.2049in.)

2) Rotor coil continuity test
Check the continuity in the slip ring with the tester. If there is no continuity, there is a wire break. Replace the rotor coil.

Resistance value	Approx. 3.34Ω at 20°C

Printed in Japan
A0A1029-9002

3) Rotor coil insulation test

Check the continuity between the slip ring and the rotor core, or the shaft. If there is continuity, insulation inside the rotor is defective, causing a short with the earth circuit. Replace the rotor coil.

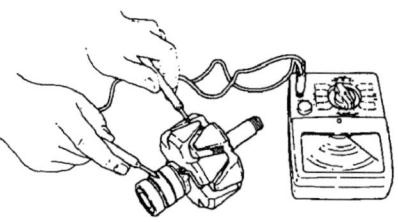

4) Check the rear side ball bearing. If the rotation of the bearing is heavy, or produces abnormal sounds, replace the ball bearing.

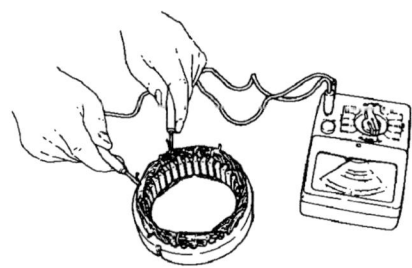

(3) Stator

1) Stator coil continuity test

Check the continuity between each terminal of the stator coil. If there is no continuity, there is a wire break in the stator coil. Replace the stator coil.

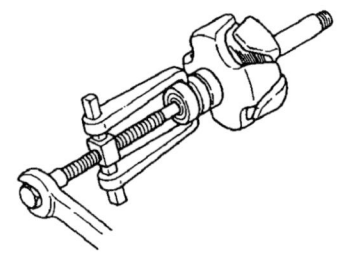

Resistance value	Approx. 0.077Ω at 20°C 1-phase resistance

2) Stator coil insulation test

Check the continuity between the terminals and the stator core. If there is continuity, insulation of the stator coil is defective. This will cause a short-circuit with the earth core. Replace the stator coil.

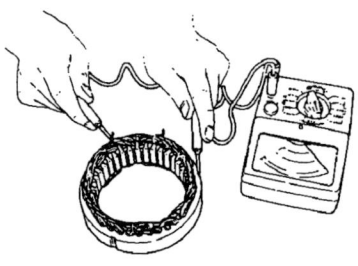

(4) Brush

The brush is hard and wears slowly, but when it is worn beyond the allowable limit, replace it. When replacing the brush, also check the strength of the brush spring. To check, push the spring down to 2mm (0.0787in.) from the end surface of the brush holder, and read the gauge.

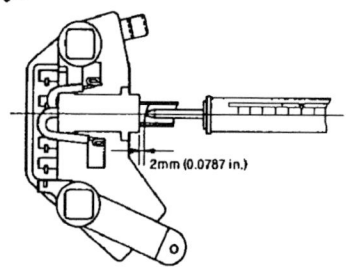

2mm (0.0787 in.)

Brush spring strength	255—345g (0.56 ~ 0.76lb.)

(5) Brush wear

Check the brush length.

The brush wears very little, but replace the brush if worn over the wear limit line printed on the brush.

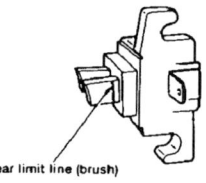

Wear limit line (brush)

mm (in.)

	Maintenance standard	Wear limit
Brush length	16 (0.6299)	9 (0.3543)

Printed in Japan
A0A1029-9002

(6) IC regulator

Connect the variable resistance, two 12V batteri resistcr, and voltmeter as shown in the diagram.

1) Use the following measuring devices.

Resistor (R.)	100Ω, 2W, 1pc.
Variable resistor (Rv)	0—300Ω, 12W, 1pc.
Battery (BAT., BAT₂)	12V, 2pcs.
DC voltmeter	0—30V, 0.5 class 1pc. (measure at 3 points)

2) Check the regulator in the following sequence, according to the diagram.
   a) Check V₂ (BAT₁ + BAT₂ voltage). If the voltage 20—26V, both BAT₁ and BAT₂ are normal.
   b) While measuring V₂ (F-E terminal voltage), move Rv gradually from the 0-position. Check if there is a point where the V₂ voltage rises sharply from below 2.0V to over 2.0V. If there is no such point, the regulator is defective. Replace the regulator. If there is a sharp voltage rise when testing, return the Rv to the 0-position, and connect the voltmeter to the V₁ position.
   c) While measuring V₁ (voltage between L-E terminals), move Rv gradually from the 0-position. There should be a point where the voltage of V₁ rises sharply by 2—6V. Measure the voltage of V₁ just before this sharp voltage rise. This is the regulating voltage of the regulator. If this voltage of V₁ is within the standard limit, the regulator is normal. If the voltage deviates from the limit, the regulator is defective. Replace the regulator.

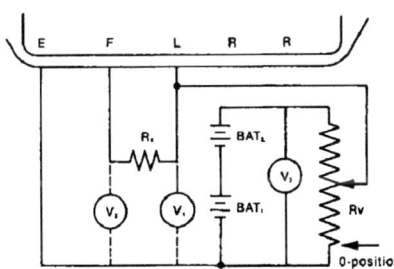

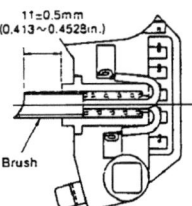

11±0.5mm
(0.413~0.4528in.)

Brush

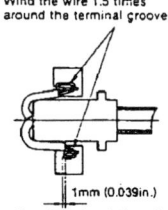

Wind the wire 1.5 times around the terminal groove.

1mm (0.039in.)

Mount the insulation tube on the terminal surface.

NOTES: 1. Use non-acid type paste.
2. The soldering iron temperature is 300 ~ 350°C.

2) Mount the IC regulator on the brush holder as illustrated, and press in the M5 bolt. Do not forget to assemble the bushing and the connecting plate at the same time.
(If the bushing is left out, the output terminal will be earthed and the battery short-circuited).

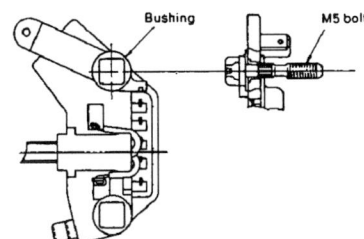

Bushing   M5 bolt

NOTES: 1. Insertion pressure is 100kg (220.5 lbs.)
2. Insert vertically.

(2) Connecting the brush regulator assembly and diode
1) Check the rivets
   Place the rivets as shown in the figure, and then calk them using the calking tool.

Calking torque	500kg (1102 lbs.)

2) Connect the brush to the diode.
   Insert the brush side terminal into the diode terminal, calk it, and then solder into place.

3.0 mm (0.11 1 in.) dia. rivet.

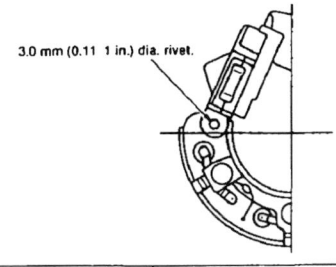

Rivetting pressure	500kg (1102 lbs.)

4-9 Reassembling the alternator

Reassembly is done in the reverse order of disassembly. For reassembly, be careful of the following points. (Refer to 4—7 disassembling alternator).
(1) Assembling the brush regulator
1) Solder the brush.
   Position the brush as shown in the drawing and solder it. Be careful not to let the solder drip into the pig tail (lead wire).

(3) Assembling the rear cover

Insert pins from the outside of the rear cover. Install the brush on the brush holder, then attach the rear cover. After assembly, pull out the pins.

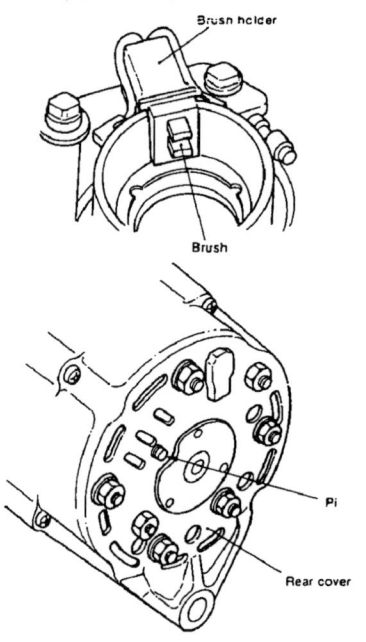

Brush holder

Brush

Pi

Rear cover

(4) Tightening torques

Positions	Tightening torque kg-cm (ft-lb)
Brush holder fixing	32 — 40 (2.31 ∼ 2.89)
Diode fixing	32 — 40 (2.31 ∼ 2.89)
Bearing retainer fixing	32 — 40 (2.31 ∼ 2.89)
Pulley nut tightening	400 — 600 (28.93 ∼ 43.40)
Through-bolt tightening	32 — 40 (2.31 ∼ 2.89)

4-10 Performance test

Conduct a performance test on the reassembled AC generator as follows. The following is the circuit for the performance test.

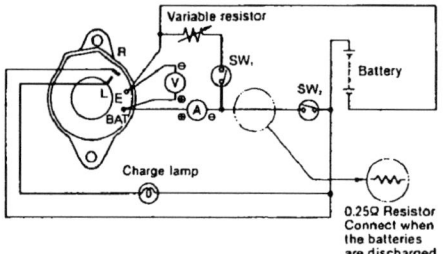

Variable resistor

R

SW,

V

Battery

SW,

BAT

Charge lamp

0.25Ω Resistor
Connect when
the batteries
are discharged

(1) Measuring devices

DC voltmeter	0 — 15V or 0 — 30V, 0.5 Class, 1pc.
DC ammeter	0 — 100A, 1.0 Class, 1pc.
Variable resistor	0 — 0.25Ω, 1kW, 1pc.
Lamp	12V, 3W
100Ω resistor	3W
0.25Ω resistor	25W

(2) Measuring the regulating voltage

1) When measuring devices are connected in the performance test circuit as shown above, the charge lamp lights.
2) Close SW, while keeping SW, open and run the AC generator. When the revolutions of the generator are gradually raised, the charge lamp goes off.
3) Raise the revolutions of the AC generator, and read the voltmeter gauge when the revolutions reach about 5,000 rpms.

NOTES: 1. *Make sure that the ammeter indication at this time is less than 5A. If the indication is over 5A, connect the 0.25Ω resistor. The voltmeter indication at this time must be within the prescribed regulating voltage value.*

2. *Raise the AC generator revolutions high to make sure the regulating voltage does not fluctuate along with changes in the revolution speed.*

(3) Precautions for measuring the regulating voltage

1) When measuring the voltage, measure the voltage between the AC generator BAT terminal, or Battery + terminal, and AC generator E-terminal.
2) Use a fully charged battery.
3) Measure the voltage quickly.
4) Keep SW, open for measurement.

4-11 Troubleshooting

(1) Charging failure

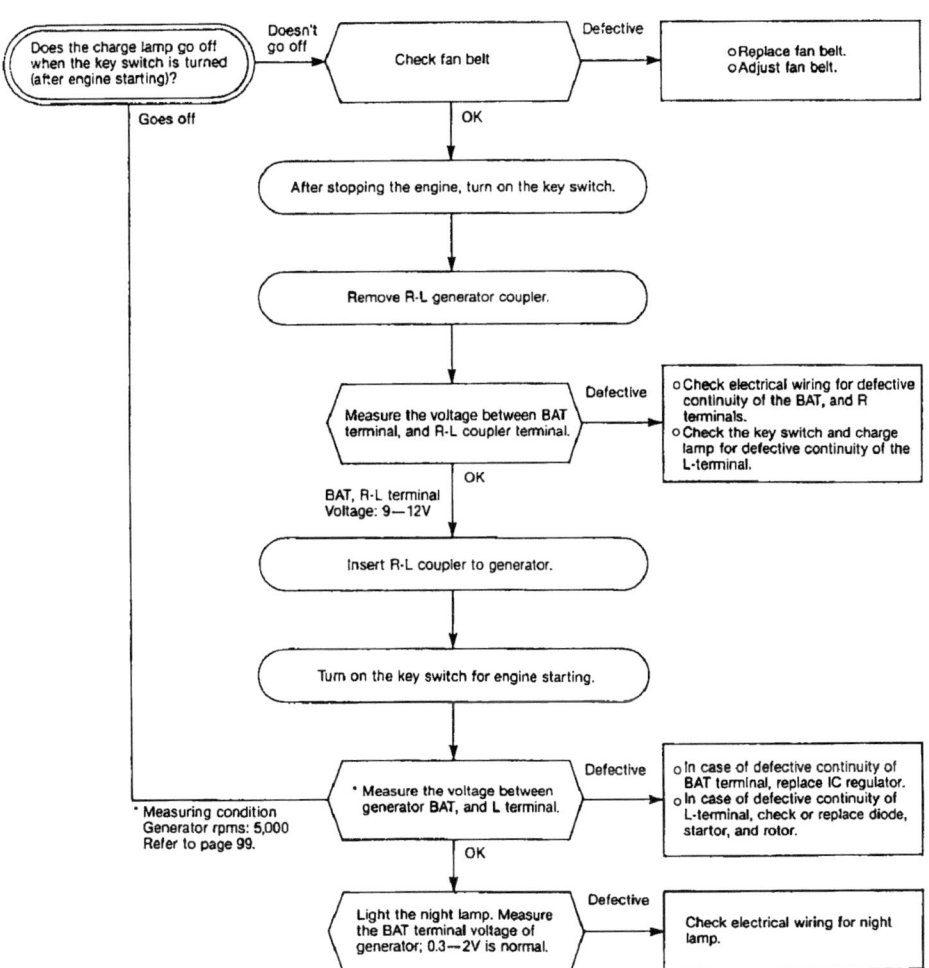

(2) Overcharging

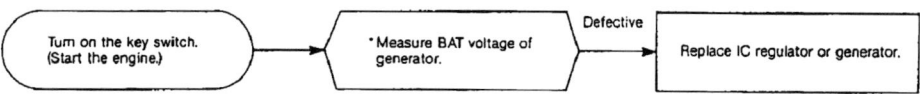

(3) Charge lamp failure

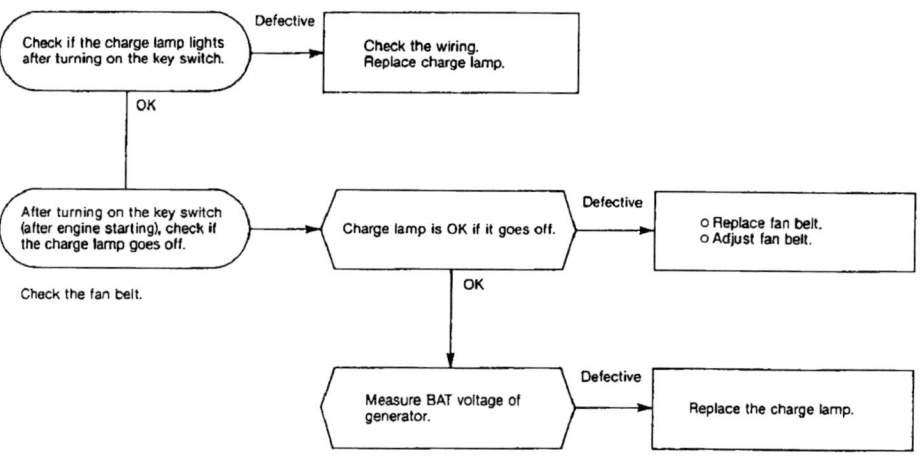

5. Instrument Panel

5-1　B2-type instrument panel with wiring

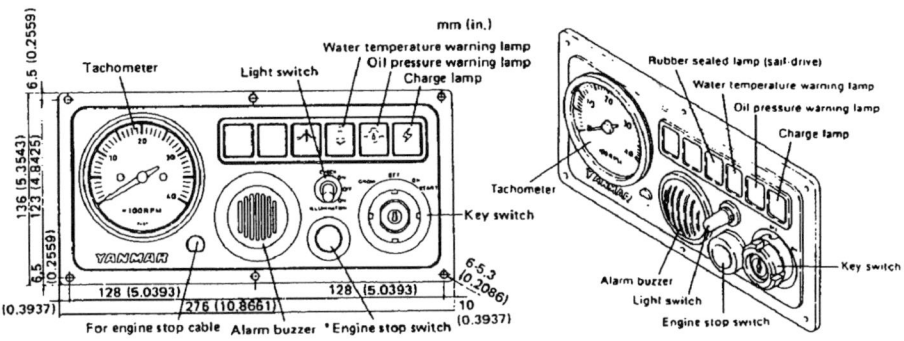

5-2　C-type instrument panel

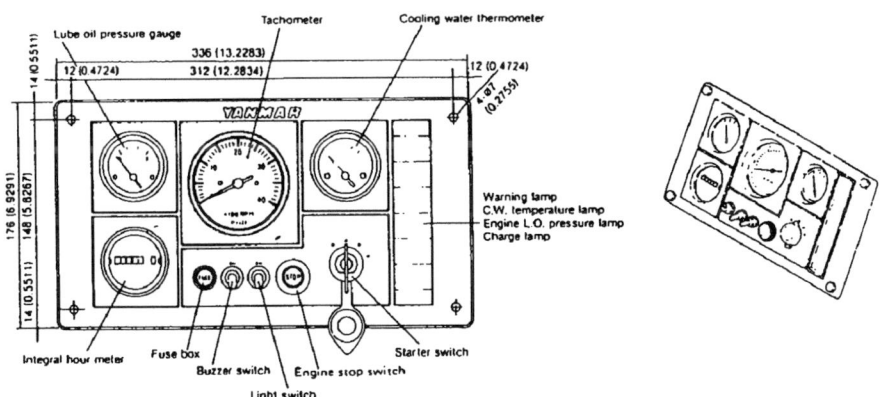

5-3 D-type instrument panel

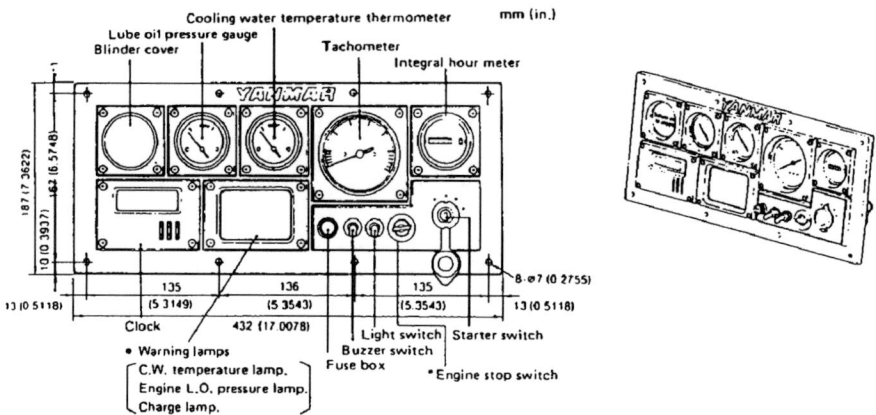

mm (in.)

Cooling water temperature thermometer
Lube oil pressure gauge
Blinder cover
Tachometer
Integral hour meter

187 (7 2622)
163 (6.5748)
10 (0 3937)

135 (5.3149)
136 (5.3543)
135 (5.3543)
8-ø7 (0 2755)

13 (0 5118)
432 (17.0078)
13 (0 5118)

Clock

• Warning lamps
  C.W. temperature lamp.
  Engine L.O. pressure lamp.
  Charge lamp.

Light switch Starter switch
Buzzer switch
Fuse box
* Engine stop switch

5-4 E-type instrument panel

mm (in.)

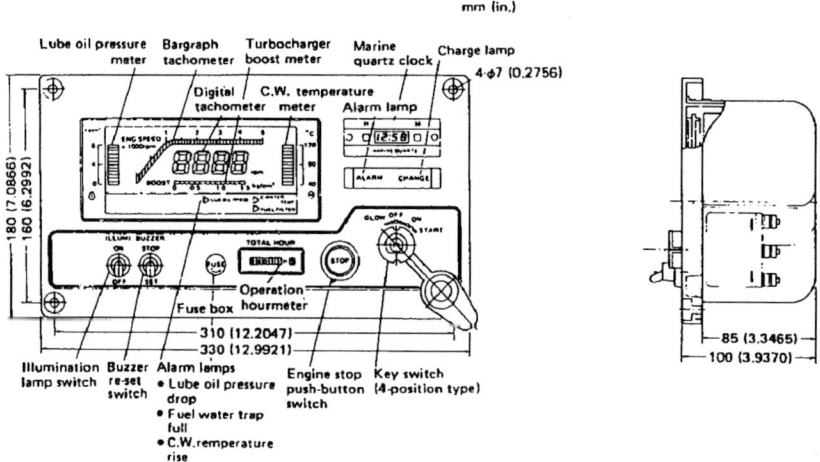

Lube oil pressure Bargraph Turbocharger Marine Charge lamp
meter tachometer boost meter quartz clock 4-ø7 (0.2756)

Digital C.W. temperature
tachometer meter
Alarm lamp

180 (7.0866)
160 (6.2992)

Operation
Fuse box hourmeter

310 (12.2047)
330 (12.9921)

Illumination Buzzer Alarm lamps
lamp switch re-set • Lube oil pressure
              switch   drop
                      • Fuel water trap
                        full
                      • C.W.remperature
                        rise

Engine stop Key switch
push-button (4-position type)
switch

85 (3.3465)
100 (3.9370)

5-5 Extension codes

Extension cord for B2-type instrument panel

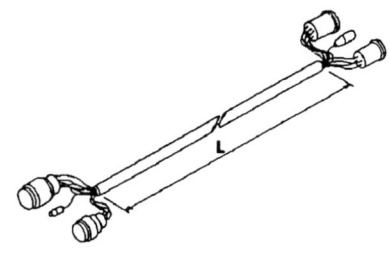

mm (in.)

	Part code No.	L
Extension cord 4M	129772-77500	3750 ~ 3850 (147.63 ~ 151.57)
Extension cord 2M	129470-77510	1750 ~ 1850 (68.89 ~ 72.83)
Extension cord 6M	129470-77530	5750 ~ 5850 (226.38 ~ 230.31)

Extension cord for C-type and D-type, E-type instrument panel

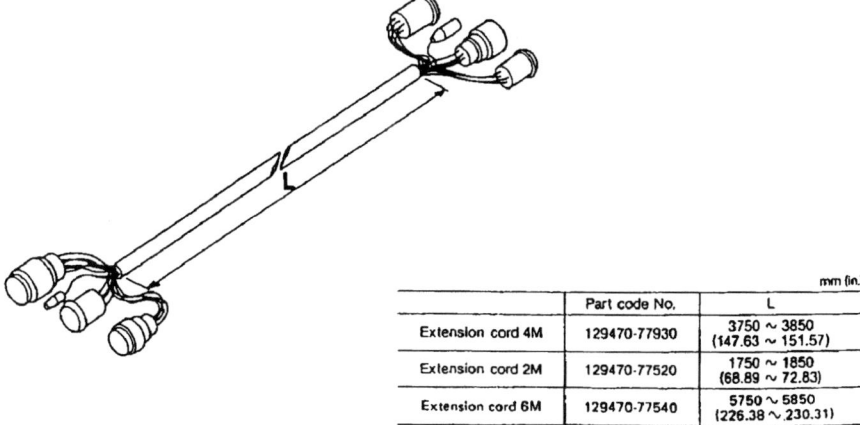

mm (in.)

	Part code No.	L
Extension cord 4M	129470-77930	3750 ~ 3850 (147.63 ~ 151.57)
Extension cord 2M	129470-77520	1750 ~ 1850 (68.89 ~ 72.83)
Extension cord 6M	129470-77540	5750 ~ 5850 (226.38 ~ 230.31)

6. Warning Devices

6-1 Oil pressure alarm

If the engine oil pressure is below $0.1 \sim 0.3$ kg/cm² ($1.42 \sim 4.26$ lb/in.²), with the main switch in the ON position, the contacts of the oil pressure switch are closed by a spring, and the lamp is illuminated through the lamp → oil pressure switch → ground circuit system. If the oil pressure is normal, the switch contacts are opened by the lubricating oil pressure and the lamp remains off.

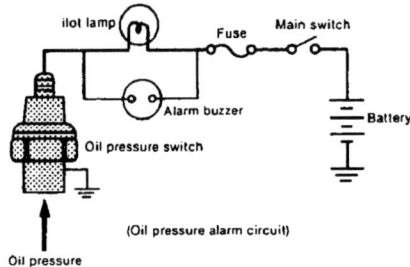

(Oil pressure alarm circuit)

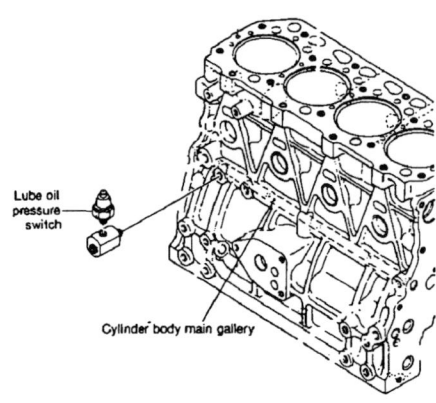

Oil pressure switch

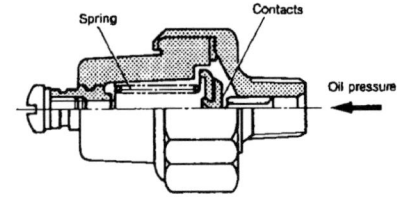

Part No.	124060-39451
Rated voltage	12V
Operation pressure	$0.1 \sim 0.3$kg/cm² ($1.422 \sim 4.266$lb/in.²)
Lamp capacity	5W

Inspection

Problem	Inspection Item	Inspection method	Corrective action
Lamp not illuminated when main switch set to ON	1. Oil pressure lamp blown out	(1) Visual inspection	Replace lamp
		(2) Lamp not illuminated even when main switch set to ON position and terminals of oil pressure switch grounded	
	2. Operation of oil pressure switch	Lamp illuminated when checked as described in (2) above	Replace oil pressure switch
Lamp not extinguished while engine running	1. Oil level low	Stop engine and check oil level with dipstick	Add oil
	2. Oil pressure low	Measure oil pressure	Repair bearing wear and adjust regulator valve
	3. Oil pressure faulty	Switch faulty if abnormal at (1) and (2) above	Replace oil pressure switch
	4. Wiring between lamp and oil pressure switch faulty	Cut the wiring between the lamp and switch and wire with separate wire	Repair wiring harness

9-39

6·2 Cooling water temperature alarm

A water temperature lamp and water temperature gauge, backed up by an alarm in the instrument panel, are used to monitor the temperature of the engine cooling water. A high thermal expansion material is set on the end of the water temperature unit. When the cooling water temperature reaches a specified high temperature, the contacts are closed, and an alarm lamp and buzzer are activated at the instrument panel.

Operating temperature	ON	93 ~ 97°C (199 ~ 206°F)
	OFF	88°C (190°F) or high
Electric capacity		DC 12V, 1A
Response time		with in 60 sec.
Indication color		Green
Part code No.		127610-91350
Tightening torque		2.40 ~ 3.20kg-m (17.35 ~ 23.14ft-lb)

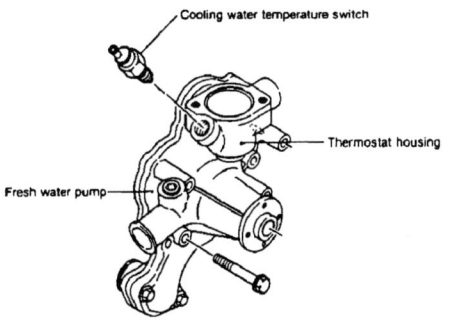

Cooling water temperature switch

Thermostat housing

Fresh water pump

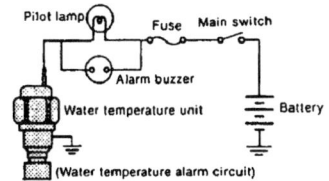

Pilot lamp   Fuse   Main switch

Alarm buzzer

Water temperature unit   Battery

(Water temperature alarm circuit)

6·3 Sender unit for lube oil pressure gauge

The sender unit for the lube oil pressure gauge has a mounting seat for mounting on the lube oil filter bracket. Oil pressure is measured when the oil enters into the main gallery after being fed from the lube oil cooler and passing through the oil pressure control valve. Be sure to mount a vibration damper when mounting the oil pressure sender unit.

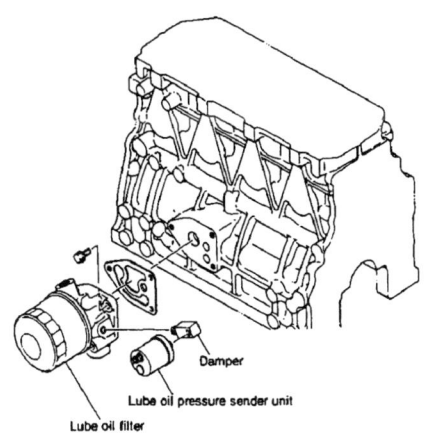

Damper

Lube oil pressure sender unit

Lube oil filter

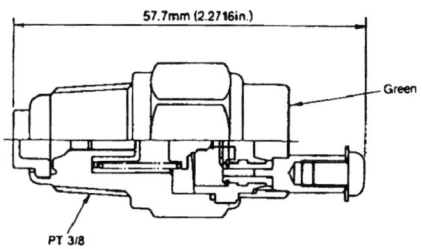

57.7mm (2.2716in.)

Green

PT 3/8

Printed in Japan
A0A1029-9002

Lube oil pressure sender unit

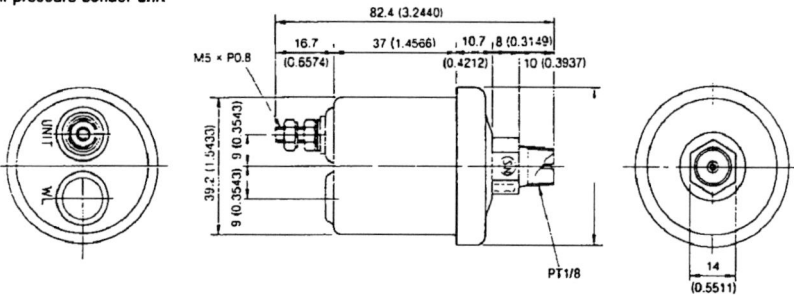

Damper

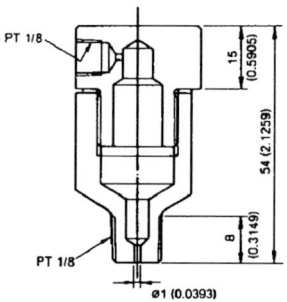

Type	Resistance switch
Rated voltage	DC 12/DC 24
Max. operating pressure	8kg/cm² (113.76 lb/in.²)
Part code No.	144626-31560

6-4 Sender unit for the cooling water temperature gauge

The water temperature sender unit has a mounting seat for mounting on the fresh water pump unit. Water temperature is measured when the cooling water flows into the thermostat housing after leaving the cylinder head.

mm (in.)

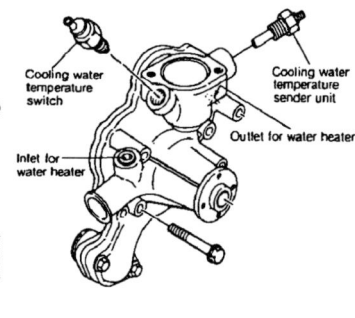

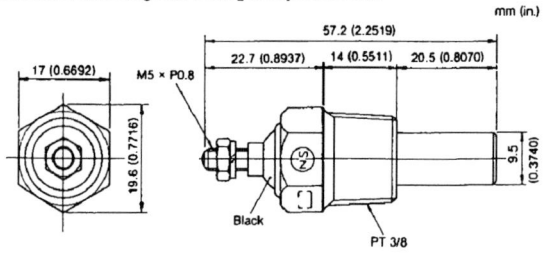

Type	Thermistor switch
Rated voltage	12V/24V
Part code No.	144626-91570

7. Air Heater (Optional)

An air heater is available for warming intake air when starting in cold areas in winter. The air heater is mounted between the intake manifold and intake manifold coupling. The device is operated by the glow switch on the instrument panel.

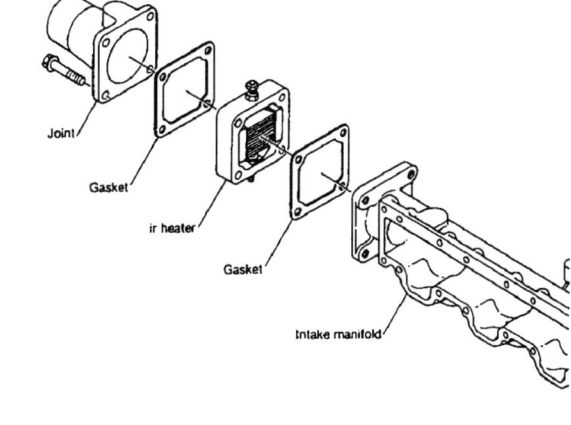

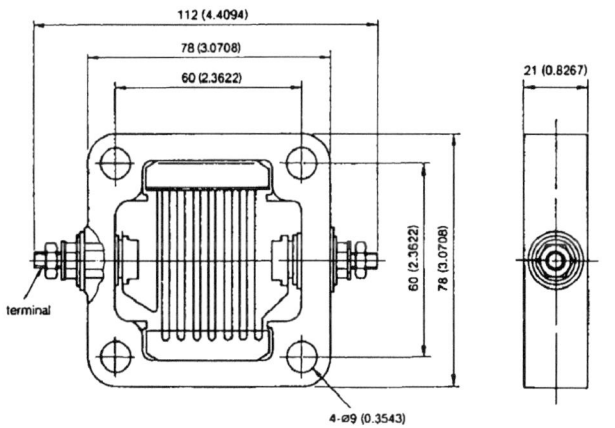

Rated output	400W
Rated current	33.3A
Rated voltage	DC 12V
Rated operating time	Engine operation: 60 sec. Engine stop: 30 sec.
Range of operating temperature	+50°C ~ 30°C (122°F ~ −22°F)
Part code No.	129400-77500

8. Electric type Engine Stopping Device (Optional)

To employ the electric engine stop device, the stop lever of the fuel injection pump is connected to the solenoid with a connection metal.
The device is operated by the stop switch on the instrument panel.

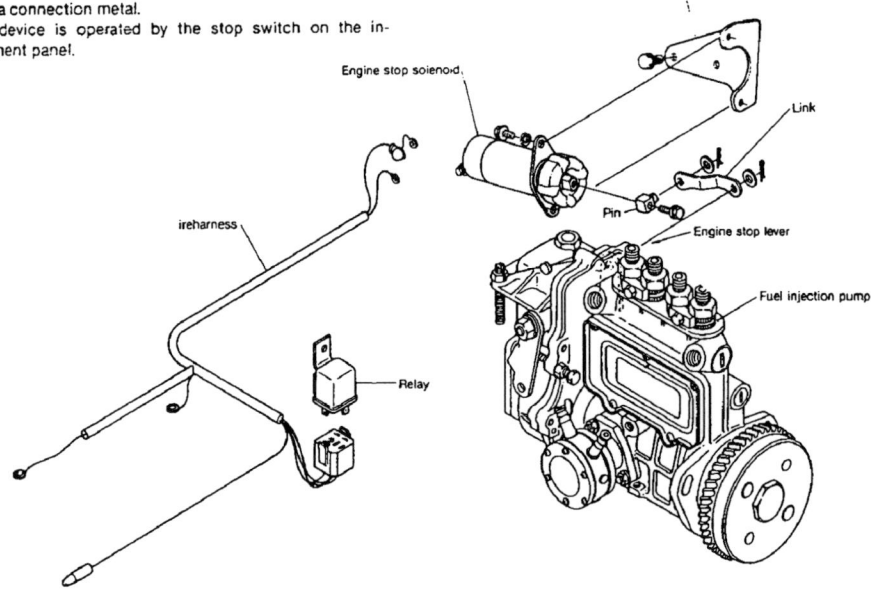

Solenoid bracket

Engine stop solenoid

Link

ireharness

Pin

Engine stop lever

Fuel injection pump

Relay

8-1 Solenoid

Solenoid model	1502-12A7U1B
Rated voltage	12V
Loaded current	30A
Loaded force	9kg (19.84lb)
No-load current	0.7A
No-load force	4kg (8.82lb)

mm (in.)

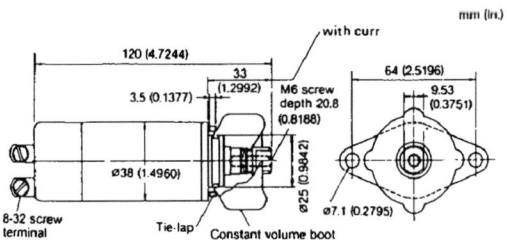

with curr

120 (4.7244)

33 (1.2992)

3.5 (0.1377)

M6 screw depth 20.8 (0.8188)

64 (2.5196)

9.53 (0.3751)

Ø38 (1.4960)

Ø25 (0.9842)

Ø7.1 (0.2795)

8-32 screw terminal

Tie-lap

Constant volume boot

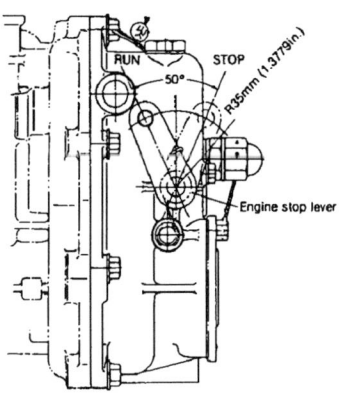

RUN   STOP
50°
R35mm (1.3779in.)

Engine stop lever

8-2 Relay

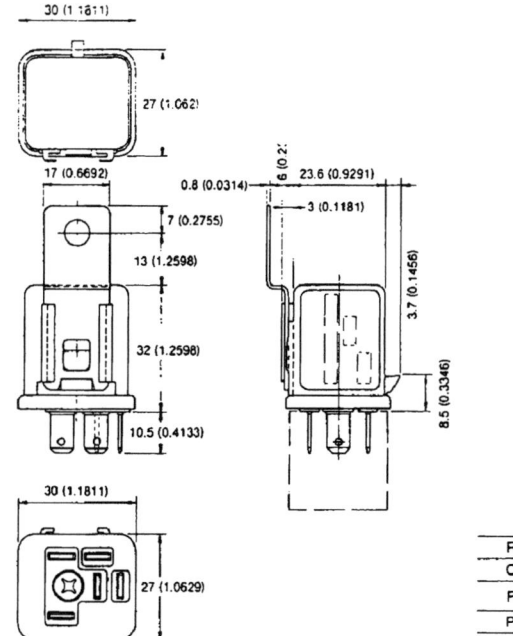

Rated voltage	12V
Contact current	Lamp: 20A, extra-lamp: 25A
Range of operation	−30°C ~ +90°C (−22°F ~ 194°F)
Part code No.	124617-91850

8-3 Wire harness of engine stop

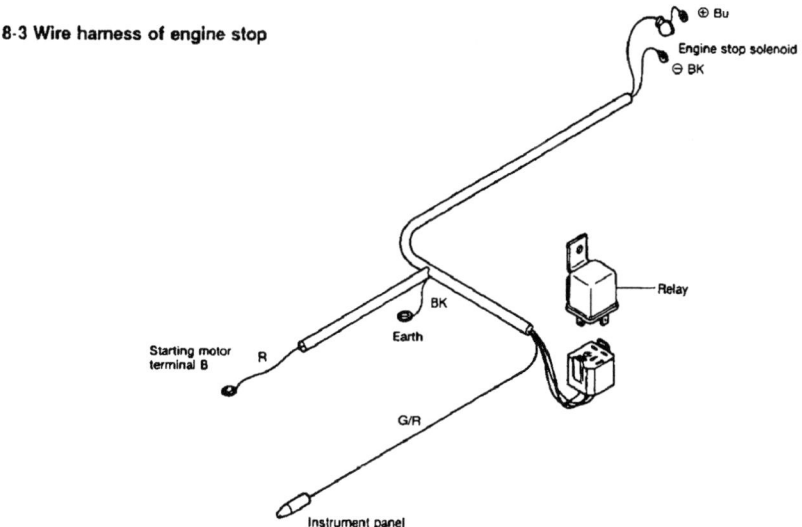

9. Tachometer

9-1 Construction of tachometer

The tachometer indicates the number of revolutions per minute by means of an electrical input signal which is generated as a pulse signal from the magnetic pickup sender (MPU sender).

The function of the sender is to convert the rotary motion into an electrical signal by counting the number of teeth of the ring gear connecting with the flywheel housing.

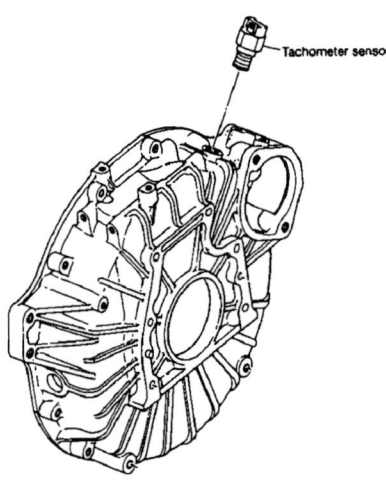

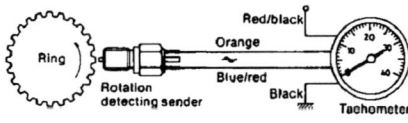

9-2 Specifications and dimensions of tachometer

(1) Specifications

Rated voltage		DC 12V
Range of operating voltage		10 ~ 15V
Illumination		3.4W/12V
Ring gear	No. of teeth	127
	Module	2.54
Part No. of tachometer		120130-91200 (128696-91100)
Part No. of sender unit		128170-91160

(2) Sensitivity limit of sender unit

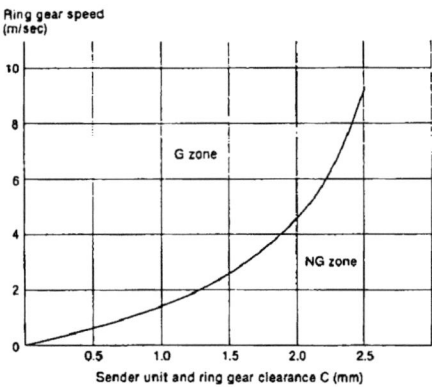

Sender unit and ring gear clearance C (mm)

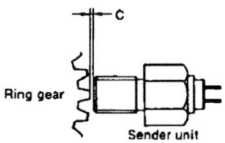

(3) Dimensions of sender unit

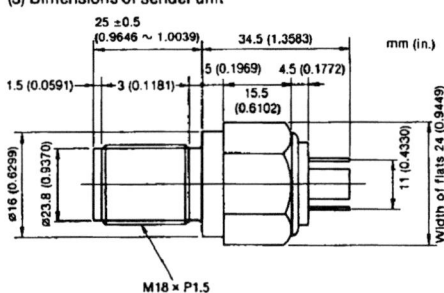

(4) Dimensions and shape of tachometer

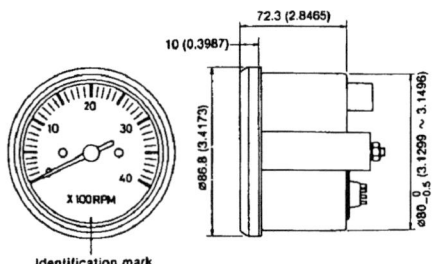

9-3 Measurement of sensor unit characteristics

(1) Measurement of output voltage

Output voltage	1.0V or higher

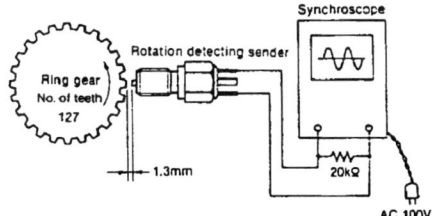

Synchroscope

* Check the output wave pattern and number of pulses when carrying out the output voltage measurement.

Measuring conditions

Number of teeth of ring gear	127
Gap between the ring gear and sender	1.3mm (0.0511 in.)
Resistance	20kΩ
Speed of ring gear	500 rpm (approx. 800Hz)
Measuring temperature	20°C (68°F)
Measuring instrument	Synchroscope

(2) Measurement of internal resistance

Measuring conditions

Measuring temperature	20°C (68°F)
Measuring instrument	Digital tester

Digital tester

1.600

kΩ

Rotation detecting sender

AC 100V

9-4

Fault	Diagnosis		Remedy
Does not function well. 1) Pointer does not move. 2) Functions intermittently.	Check if there is an open-circuit cable connection at the rear of the meter, a loose or disconnected terminal, or bad continuity due to corrosion.	Yes	Make good the connection.
	Disconnect at the instrument terminals, and measure the voltage between the cable terminals. (To be 10 ~ 16V) ↓ Satisfactory	No	If the input voltage is abnormal, check the cause. (e.g. short-circuit, disconnection, or blown fuse, etc.)

Printed in Japan
A0A1029-9002

Check if the sender is loosely fitted.	Yes	Fix the sender securely.
↓ No		
Measure the internal resistance of the sender. (To be 1.6 ±0.1kΩ at 20°C)	No	Replace the sender.
Measure the output voltage of the sender. (To be 1V or higher at 20°C)	No	Replace the sender.

10. Alternator 12V/80A (OPTIONAL)

The alternator serves to keep the battery constantly charged. It is installed on the cylinder block by a bracket, and is driven from the V-pulley at the end of the crankshaft by a V-belt.
The type of alternator used in this engine is ideal for high speed engines with a wide range of engine speeds. It contains diodes that convert AC to DC, and an IC regulator that keeps the generated voltage constant even when the engine speed changes.

10-1 Features

The alternator contains a regulator using an IC, and has the following features.

(1) The IC regulator is self-contained, and has no moving parts (mechanical contact points). It therefore has superior features such as freedom from vibration, no fluctuation of voltage during use, and no need for readjustment.
Also, it is of the over-heating compensation type and can automatically adjust the voltage to the most suitable level depending on the operating temperature.

(2) The regulator is integrated within the alternator to simplify external wiring.

(3) It is an alternator designed for compactness, lightness of weight, and high output.

(4) A newly developed U-shaped diode is used to provide increased reliability and easier checking and maintenance.

(5) As the alternator is to be installed on board, the following measures are taken to provide salt-proofing.
  1) The front and rear covers are salt-proofed.
  2) Salt-proof paint is applied to the diode.
  3) The terminal, where the inboard harness is connected to the alternator, is nickel plated.

10-2 Specifications

Model of alternator	LR180-03 (HITACHI)
Model of IC regulator	TRIZ-63 (HITACHI)
Battery voltage	12V
Nominal output	12V/80A
Earth polarity	Negative earth (⊖)
Direction of rotation (viewed from pulley end)	Clockwise
Weight	5.8kg (12.8lb.)
Rated speed	5000 rpm
Operating speed	1000 ~ 9000
Speed for 13.5V	1000 or less
Output current at 20°C	over 78A/5000 rpm
Regulated voltage	14.5 ±0.3V (Standard temperature voltage gradient, −0.01/°C)

10-3 Characteristics

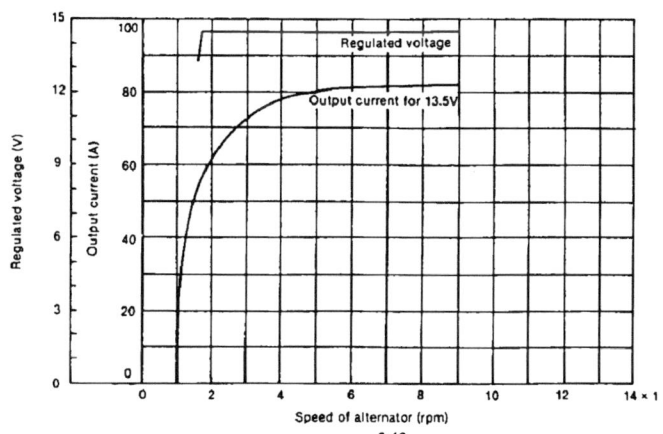

Speed of alternator (rpm)

9-48

10-4 Construction

This is a standard rotating field type three-phase alternator. It consists of six major parts: the pulley, fan, front cover, rotor, stator and rear cover. The IC regulator is an integral part of the alternator.

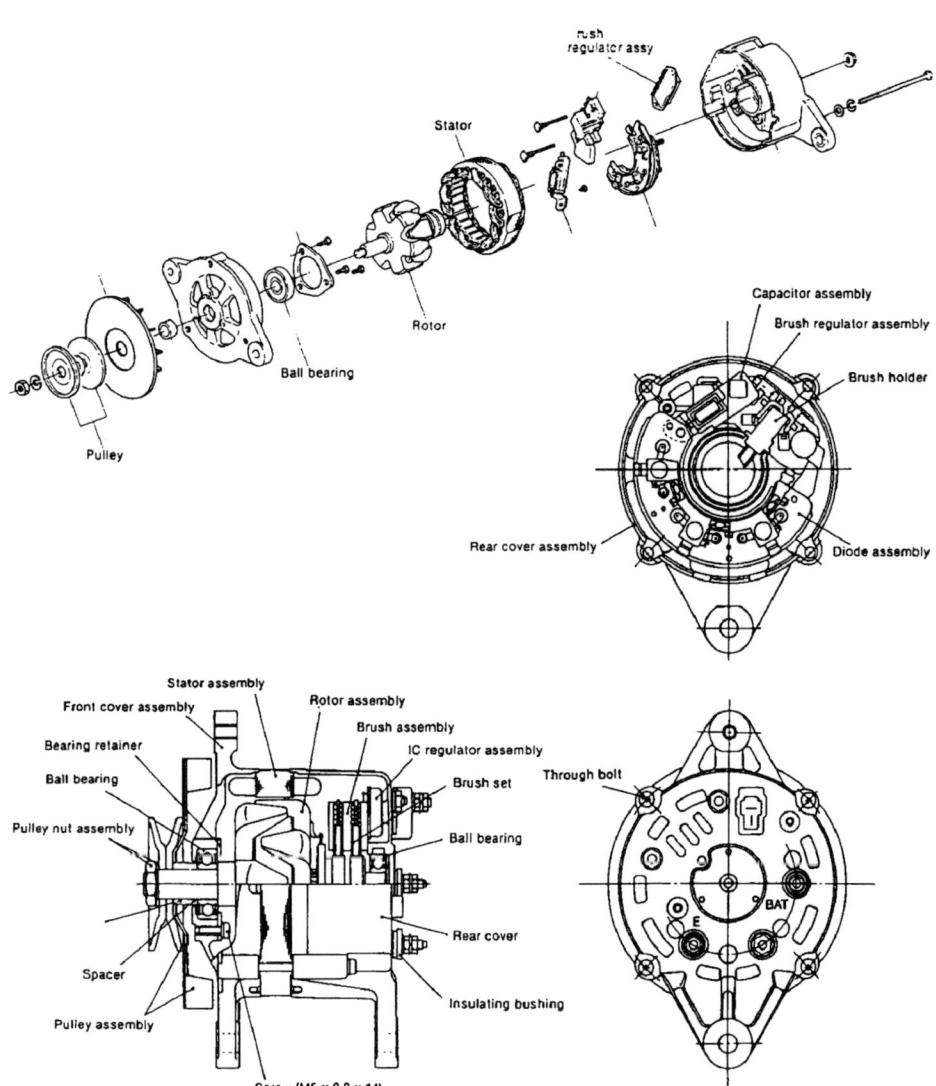

10-5 Alternator functioning

(1) IC regulator

The IC regulator is the transistor (Tr₁) which is series-connected with the rotor. The IC regulator controls the output voltage of the generator by breaking or conducting the rotor coil (exciting) current.

When the output voltage of the generator is within the standard value, the transistor (Tr₁) turns on. When the voltage exceeds the standard value, the Zener diode goes on and the transistor (Tr₁) turns off.

With the repeated turning on and off of the transistor, the output voltage is kept at the standard value. (Refer to the circuit diagram below.)

(2) Charge lamp

When the transistor (Tr₁) is on, the charge lamp key switch is turned to ON, and current flows to R₁, R₄ and to Tr₁ to light the lamp. When the engine starts to run and output voltage is generated in the stator coil, the current stops flowing to this circuit, turning off the charge lamp.

(3) Circuit diagram

10-6 Handling precautions

(1) Be careful of the battery's polarity (+, − terminals), and do not connect the wrong terminals to the wrong cables, or the battery will be short-circuited by the generator diode.

In this case too much current will flow, the IC regulator and diodes burn out, and the wire harness will burn.

(2) Make sure of the correct connection of each terminal.

(3) When quick-charging, etc., disconnect either the battery terminal on the AC generator or the terminal on the battery.

(4) Do not short-circuit the terminals.

(5) Do not conduct any tests using high tension insulation resistance. (The diodes and IC regulator will burn out.)

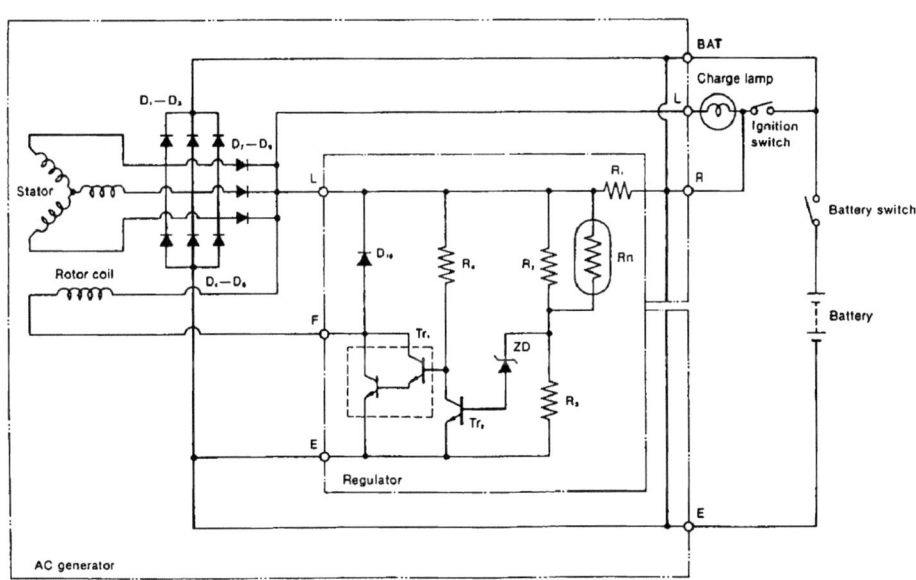

D₁−D₆:	Output commutation diode
R₁−R₄:	Resistor
D₇−D₈:	Charging lamp switching di
F:	To supply current to rotor coil
Rn:	Thermistor (Temperature gradient resistance)

Printed in Japan
A0A1029-9002

10-7 Disassembling the alternator

(1) Remove the through-bolt, and separate the front assembly from the rear assembly.

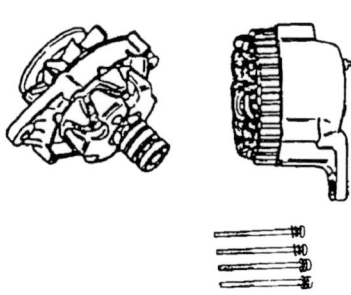

(2) Remove the pulley nut, and pull out the rotor from the front cover.

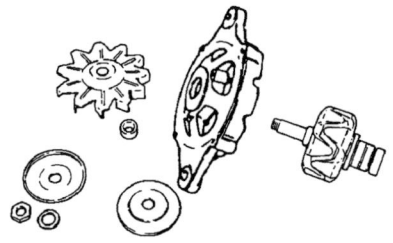

(3) Remove the ø5mm (ø0.1969in.) screw from the front cover, and then remove the ball bearing.

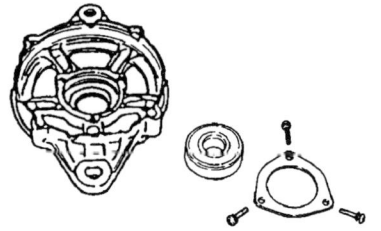

(4) Remove the nut, the brush-holder, and diode fixing nut at the BAT, and the terminal screws of the rear cover. Separate the rear cover from the stator (with the diode and brush holder).

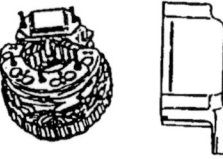

(5) Disconnect the soldered joint of the stator lead wir and remove the diode and brush regulator assemblies from the stator at the same time.

(6) Separating the regulator
1) To separate the regulator, remove the ø3mm (ø0.1181 in.) rivet which keeps the diode assembly and the brushless regulator in place, and the soldered joint of the L-terminal.

2) To replace the IC regulator, disconnect the soldered joint of the IC regulator and pull out the two bolts. Do not remove these two bolts except when replacing the IC regulator.

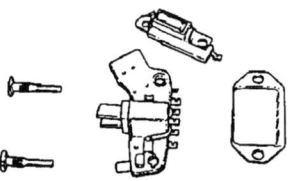

10-8 Inspection and adjustment

(1) Diode

Between terminals		BAT (+ side diode)	
	Tester wire	+ side	− side
U.V.W.	+ side		No continuity
	− side	Continuity	

Between terminals		E (− side diode)	
	Tester wire	+ side	− side
U.V.W.	+ side		Continuity
	− side	No continuity	

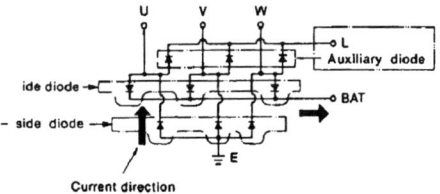

Current direction

U.V.W.: termi

Current flows only in one direction in the diode as shown in Fig. 181. Accordingly, when there is continuity between each terminal (e.g. BAT and U), the diode is in normal condition. When there is no continuity, the diode is defective.
When the tester is connected in the reverse of above, there should be no continuity. If there is, the diode i defective.

After repeating the above test, if any diode is found to be defective, replace the diode assembly. Since there is no terminal on the auxiliary diode, check the continuity between both ends of the diode.

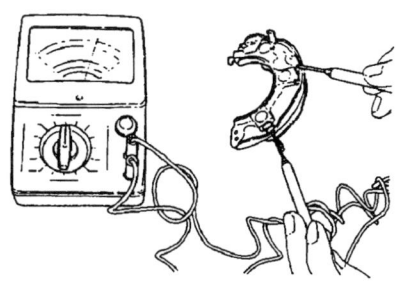

CAUTION: Do not use high tensile insulation resistance such as meggers, etc. for testing. The diode may burn out.

(2) Rotor
Inspect the slip ring surface, rotor coil continuity and insulation.
1) Inspecting the slip ring surface
Check if the surface of the slip ring is sufficiently smooth. If the surface is rough, grind the surface with No. 500—600 sand paper. If it is contaminated with oil, etc., wipe the surface clean with alcohol.

	Standard	Wear limit
Slip ring outer dia.	⌀31.6mm (1.2441in.)	⌀30.6mm (1.2049in.)

2) Rotor coil continuity test
Check the continuity in the slip ring with the tester. If there is no continuity, there is a wire break. Replace the rotor coil.

Resistance value	Approx. 2.58Ω at 20°C

3) Rotor coil insulation test
Check the continuity between the slip ring and the rotor core. or the shaft. If there is continuity, insulation inside the rotor is defective, causing a short with the earth circuit. Replacé the rotor coil.

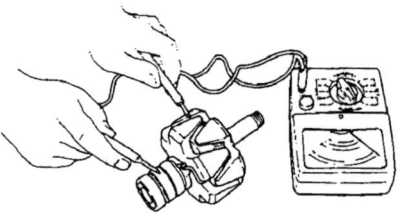

4) Check the rear side ball bearing. If the rotation of the bearing is heavy, or produces abnormal sounds, replace the ball bearing.

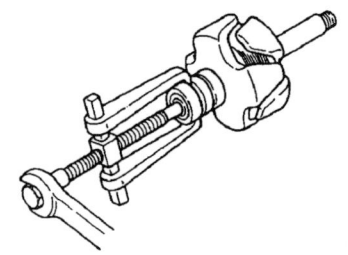

(3) Stator
1) Stator coil continuity test
Check the continuity between each terminal of the stator coil. If there is no continuity, there is a wire break in the stator coil. Replace the stator coil.

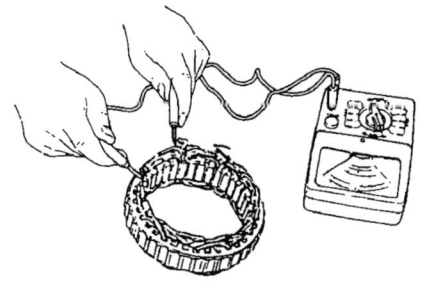

Approx. 0.041Ω at 20° C u, v-phase resistance
Approx. 0.036Ω at 20° C w-phase resistance

2) Stator coil insulation test
Check the continuity between the terminals and the stator core. If there is continuity, insulation of the stator coil is defective. This will cause a short-circuit with the earth core. Replace the stator coil.

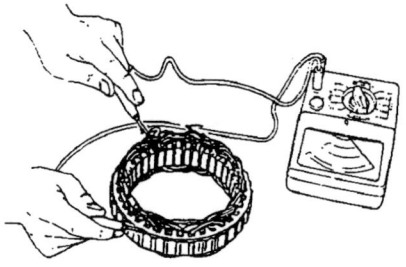

(4) Brush
The brush is hard and wears slowly, but when it is worn beyond the allowable limit, replace it. When replacing the brush, also check the strength of the brush spring. To check, push the spring down to 2mm (0.0787in.) from the end surface of the brush holder, and read the gauge.

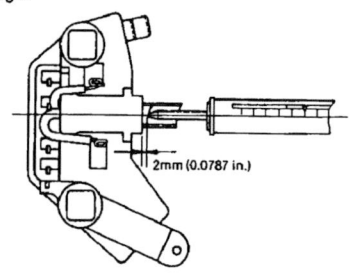

2mm (0.0787 in.)

Brush spring strength	255–345g (0.56 ~ 0.76lb.)

(5) Brush wear
Check the brush length.
The brush wears very little, but replace the brush if worn over the wear limit line printed on the brush.

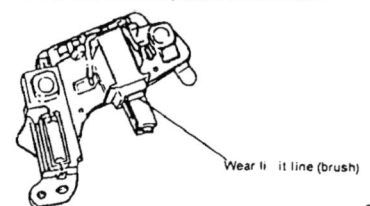

Wear limit line (brush)

mm (in.)

	Maintenance standard	Wear limit
Brush length	16 (0.6299)	9 (0.3543)

(6) IC regulator

Connect the variable resistance, two 12V batteries, resistor, and voltmeter as shown in the diagram.

1) Use the following measuring devices.

Resistor (R,)   100Ω, 2W, 1pc.
Variable resistor (Rv)   0—300Ω, 12W, 1pc.
Battery (BAT,, BAT,)   12V, 2pcs.
DC voltmeter   0—30V, 0.5 class 1pc.
                         (measure at 3 points)

2) Check the regulator in the following sequence, according to the diagram.
   a) Check V_2 (BAT, + BAT, voltage). If the voltage i 20—26V, both BAT, and BAT, are normal.
   b) While measuring V_3 (F-E terminal voltage), move Rv gradually from the 0-position. Check if there is a point where the V_3 voltage rises sharply from below 2.0V to over 2.0V. If there is no such point, the regulator is defective. Replace the regulator. If there is a sharp voltage rise when testing, return the Rv to the 0-position, and connect the voltmeter to the V_1 position.
   c) While measuring V_1 (voltage between L-E terminals), move Rv gradually from the 0-position. There should be a point where the voltage of V_1 rises sharply by 2—6V. Measure the voltage of V_1 just before this sharp voltage rise. This is the regulating voltage of the regulator. If this voltage of V_1 is within the standard limit, the regulator is normal. If the voltage deviates from the limit, the regulator is defective. Replace the regulator.

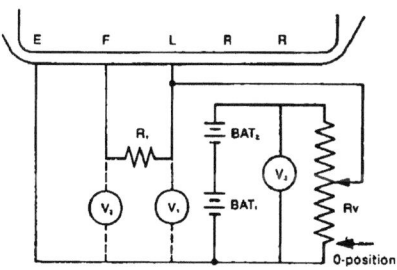

10-9   Reassembling the alternator

Reassembly is done in the reverse order of disassembly. For reassembly, be careful of the following points. (Refer to 4—7 disassembling alternator).

(1) Assembling the brush regulator
1) Solder the brush.
   Position the brush as shown in the drawing and solder it. Be careful not to let the solder drip into the pig tail (lead wire).

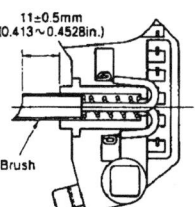

11±0.5mm
(0.413~0.4528in.)

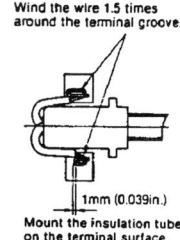

Wind the wire 1.5 times around the terminal groove.

Brush

1mm (0.039in.)

Mount the insulation tube on the terminal surface.

NOTES: 1. Use non-acid type paste.
         2. The soldering iron temperature is 300 ~ 350°C.

2) Mount the IC regulator on the brush holder as illustrated, and press in the M5 bolt. Do not forget to assemble the bushing and the connecting plate at the same time.
(If the bushing is left out, the output terminal will be earthed and the battery short-circuited).

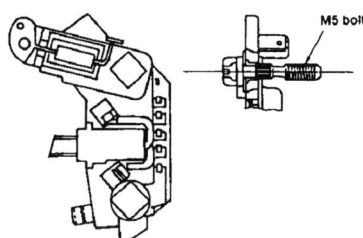

M5 bolt

NOTES: 1. Insertion pressure is 100kg (220.5 lbs.)
         2. Insert vertically.

(2) Connecting the brush regulator assembly and diode
1) Check the rivets
   Place the rivets as shown in the figure, and then calk them using the calking tool.

Calking torque	500kg (1102 lbs.)

2) Connect the brush to the diode.
   Insert the brush side terminal into the diode terminal, calk it, and then solder into place.

3.0 mm (0.11 1 in.) dia. rivet.

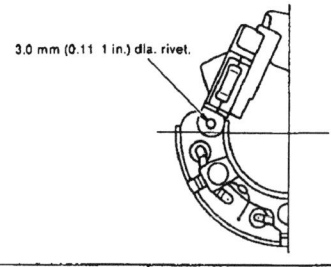

Rivetting pressure	500kg (1102 lbs.)

Printed in Japan
A0A1029-9002

(3) Assembling the rear cover

Insert pins from the outside of the rear cover. Install the brush on the brush holder, then attach the rear cover. After assembly, pull out the pins.

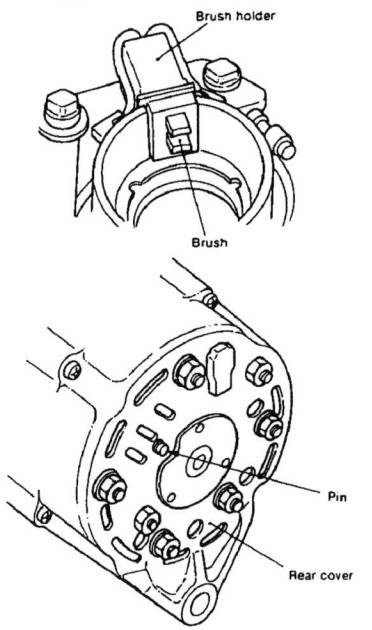

Brush holder

Brush

Pin

Rear cover

(4) Tightening torques

Positions	Tightening torque kg·cm (ft-lb)
Brush holder fixing	32—40 (2.31~2.89)
Diode fixing	60—70 (4.33~5.05)
Bearing retainer fixing	32—40 (2.31~2.89)
Pulley nut tightening	400—600 (28.93~43.40)
Through-bolt tightening	32—40 (2.31~2.89)

10-10 Performance test

Conduct a performance test on the reassembled AC generator as follows. The following is the circuit for the performance test.

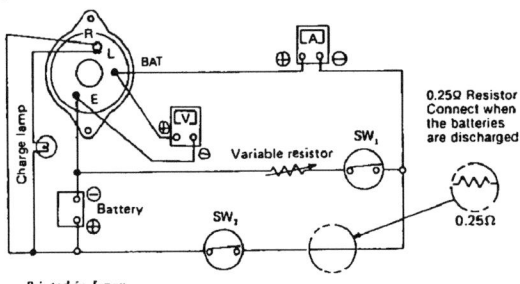

0.25Ω Resistor
Connect when
the batteries
are discharged

0.25Ω

Charge lamp

Battery

Variable resistor

SW₁

SW₂

(1) Measuring devices

DC voltmeter	0—15V or 0—30V, 0.5 Class, 1pc.
DC ammeter	0—100A, 1.0 Class, 1pc.
Variable resistor	0—0.25Ω, 1kW, 1pc.
Lamp	12V, 3W
100Ω resistor	3W
0.25Ω resistor	25W

(2) Measuring the regulating voltage

1) When measuring devices are connected in the performance test circuit as shown above, the charge lamp lights.

2) Close SW_2 while keeping SW_1 open and run the AC generator. When the revolutions of the generator are gradually raised, the charge lamp goes off.

3) Raise the revolutions of the AC generator, and read the voltmeter gauge when the revolutions reach about 5,000 rpms.

NOTES: 1. Make sure that the ammeter indication at this time is less than 5A. If the indication is over 5A, connect the 0.25Ω resistor. The voltmeter indication at this time must be within the prescribed regulating voltage value.

2. Raise the AC generator revolutions high to make sure the regulating voltage does not fluctuate along with changes in the revolution speed.

(3) Precautions for measuring the regulating voltage

1) When measuring the voltage, measure the voltage between the AC generator BAT terminal, or Battery + terminal, and AC generator E-terminal.

2) Use a fully charged battery.

3) Measure the voltage quickly.

4) Keep SW_1 open for measurement.

10-11 Troubleshooting

(1) Charging failure

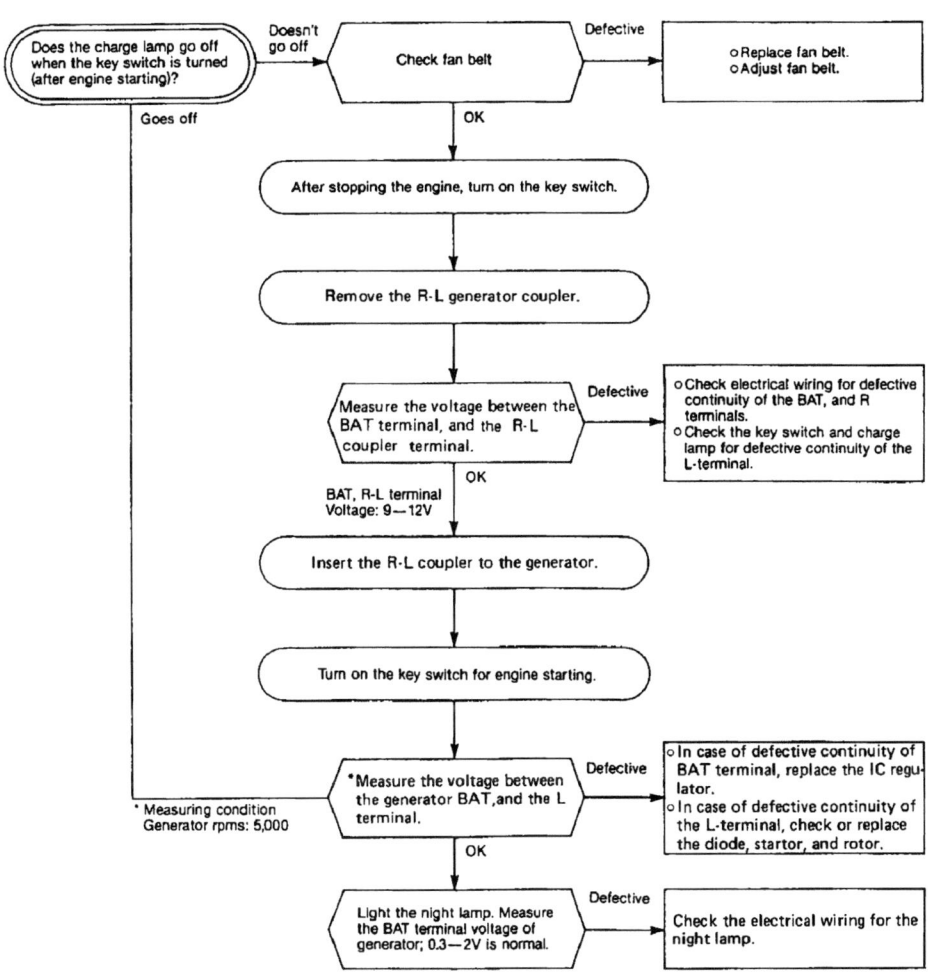

(2) Overcharging

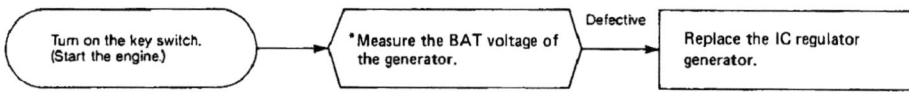

(3) Charge lamp failure

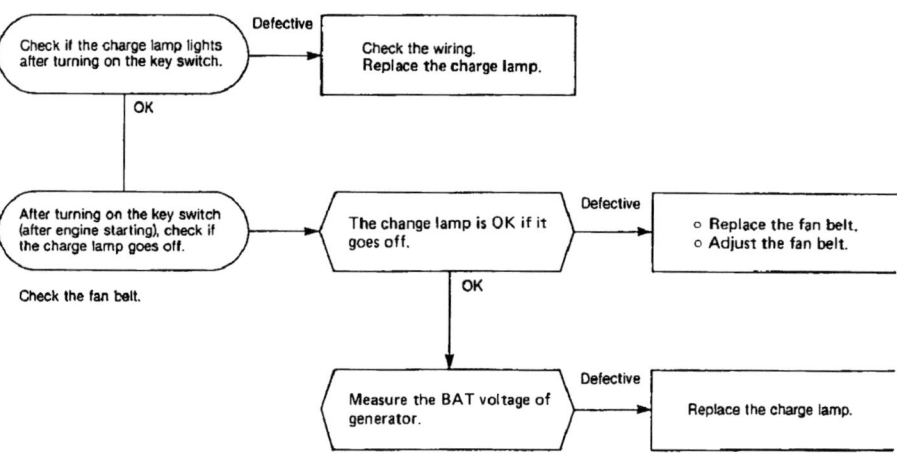

DISASSEMBLY
AND REASSEMBLY

Printed in Japan
A0A1029-9002

1. Disassembly and Reassembly Precautions

(1) Disassembly
- Take sufficient time to accurately pin-point the cause of the trouble, and disassemble only those parts which are necessary.
- Be careful to keep all disassembled parts in order.
- Prepare disassembly tools.
- Prepare a cleaner and cleaning can.
- Clear an adequate area for parts and prepare a container(s).
- Drain cooling water (sea water, fresh water) and lube oil.
- Close the Kingston cock.

(2) Reassembly
- Sufficiently clean and inspect all parts to be assembled.
- Coat sliding and rotating parts with new engine oil when assembling.
- Replace all gaskets and O-rings.
- Use a liquid packing agent as necessary to prevent oil/water leaks.
- Check the oil and thrust clearances, etc. of parts when assembling.
- Make sure you use the correct bolt/nut/washer. Tighten main bolts/nuts to the specified torque. Be especially careful not to overtighten the aluminum alloy part mounting bolts.
- Align match marks (if any) when assembling. Make sure that the correct sets of parts are used for bearings, pistons, and other parts where required.

2. Disassembly and Reassembly Tools

The following tools are required when disassembling and
reassembling the engine.
Please use them as instructed.

2-1. General Handtools

Name of tool	Illustration	Remarks
Wrench		Size:
Wrench		Size: 12 × 14
Wrench		Size: 17 × 19
Wrench		Size: 22 × 24
Screwdriver		
Steel hammer		Local supply

10-2

Name of tool	Illustration	Remarks
Copper hammer		Local supply
Mallet		Local supply
Nipper		Local supply
Pliers		Local supply
Offset wrench		Local supply 1 set
Box spanner		Local supply 1 set
Scraper		Local supply

Printed in Japan
A0A1029-9002

Name of tool	Illustration	Remarks
Lead rod		Local supply
File		Local supply 1 set
Rod spanner for hexagon socket head screws		Local supply Size: 6mm (0.2362in.) 8mm (0.3150in.) 10mm (0.3937in.)
Starling Pliers Hole type Shaft type	S→0 H4 ~ H8 S = Hole type H = Shaft type	Local supply

2-2 Special Handtools

Name of tool	Shape and size	Application
Piston pin insertion/ extraction tool	mm (in.) 20 (0.7874) 80 (3.1496) 12 (0.4724) 20 (0.7874) Part No. 128670-92260	Piston pin extractor Extraction of piston pin Insertion of piston pin
Connecting rod small end bushing insertion/ extraction tool	mm (in.) 20 (0.7874) 80 (3.1496) 25.4 ~ 25.7 (1.0000 ~ 1.0118) 28.4 ~ 28.7 (1.1181 ~ 1.1299)	Extraction
Intake and exhaust valve insertion/ extraction tool	mm (in.) ø25 (0.9843) ø100 (3.9370) 15 (0.5906) ø13.5 (0.5315)	
Lubricating oil No.2 filter case remover		

Printed in Japan
A0A1029-9002

Name of tool	Shape and size	Application
Piston ring compressor		Piston insertion guide
Valve lapping handle		Lapping tool
Valve lapping powder		
Feeler gauge		
Pulley puller	Local supply	Removing the coupling

Printed in Japan
A0A1029-9002

2-3 Measuring Instruments

Name of tool	Shape and size	Application
Vernier calipers		0.05mm (0.0020in.), 0 ~ 150mm (0 ~ 5.9055in.)
Micrometer		0.01mm (0.0004in.) 0 ~ 25mm (0 ~ 0.9843in.), 25 ~ 50mm (0.9843 ~ 1.9685in.), 50 ~ 75mm (1.9685 ~ 2.9528in.), 75 ~ 100mm (2.9528 ~ 3.9370in.), 100 ~ 125mm (3.9730 ~ 4.9213in.) 125 ~ 150mm (4.9213 ~ 5.9055in.).
Cylinder gauge		0.01mm (0.0004in.), 18 ~ 35mm (0.7087 ~ 1.3780in.), 35 ~ 60mm (1.3780 ~ 2.3622in.), 50 ~ 100mm (1.9685 ~ 3.9370in.).
Thickiness gauge		0.05 ~ 2mm (0.0020 ~ 0.0787in.)
Torque wrench		0 ~ 13kg-m. (0 ~ 94ft-lb)
Nozzle tester		0 ~ 500kg/cm² (0 ~ 7111.7lb/in.²)

Printed in Japan
A0A1029-9002

2-4 Other

Supplementary packing agent

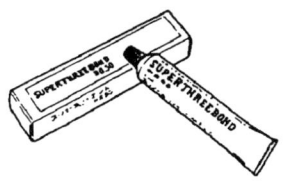

Type	Use
"Three Bond 3B8-005"	White. Since "Three Bond 3B8-005" is a nonorganic solvent, it does not penetrate asbestos sheets made principally or completely of asbestos. Always use it with grey asbestos sheet packing for complete oil tightness. When "Three Bond 3B8-005" is difficult to obtain, use silicon nonsolvent type "Three Bond No. 50."
"Three Bond No. 50"	Grey. Silicon nonsolvent type liquid packing. Semidry type packing agent coated on mating faces to prevent oil and gas leakage. Does not penetrate asbestos sheet and assures complete oil tightness.
"Three Bond No. 1"	Reddish brown. Paste type wet viscous liquid packing. Ideal for mating faces which are removed but reinstalled. Particularly used to prevent water leakage and to prevent seizing of bolts and nuts.

The surface to be coated must be thoroughly cleaned with thinner or benzene and completely dry. Moreover, coating must be thin and uniform.

Products of Three Bond Co., Ltd.

Paint

Color spray

Only Metallic Ecole Silver is used on this engine.

Wipe the surface to be painted with thinner or benzene, shake the spray can well, push the button at the top of the can and spray the paint onto the surface from a distance of 30 ~ 40 cm.

Paint

Type
White paint
(Mixed oil paint)

Usage point
Cylinder liner
insertion hole

Use
Paint parts that contact with the cylinder body when inserting the cylinder liner to prevent rusting and water leakage.

Yanmar cleaner (Ref.)

Cooling passage cleaner is mixed by adding one part "Unicon 146" to about 16 parts water (specific gravity ratio). To use, drain the water from the cooling system, fill the system with cleaner, allowing it to stand overnight (10 ~ 15 hours). Then drain out the cleaner, refill the system with water, and operate the engine for at least one hour.

NEJI LOCK SUPER   203M: a locking agent for screws (Ref.)

For coating on screws and bolts to prevent loosening, rusting, and leaking. To use, wipe off all oil and water on the threads of studs, coat the threads with screw lock, tighten the stud bolt, and allow them to stand until the screw lock hardens. Use screw lock on the oil intake pipe threads, oil pressure switch threads, fuel injection timing shim faces, and front axle bracket mounting bolts.

Printed in Japan
A0A1029-9002

3. Disassembly and Reassembly

3-1 Disassembly

For engines mounted in an engine room, remove the piping and wiring connecting them to the ship.

(1) Remove the remote control cable (from engine and marine gearbox).
(2) Unplug the extension cord for the instrument panel from the engine.
(3) Remove the wiring between the starting motor and the battery.
(4) Remove the exhaust rubber hose from the mixing elbow.
(5) Remove the fresh water sub-tank rubber hose from the filler cap.
(6) Remove the cooling water (sea water) pump sea water intake hose (after making sure the Kingston cock is closed).
(7) Remove the fuel oil intake rubber hose from the fuel feed pump.
(8) Remove the body fit (reamer) bolts and disassemble the propeller shaft coupling and thrust shaft coupling.
(9) If a driven coupling is mounted to the front drive coupling, disassemble.
(10) Remove the flexible mount nut, lift the engine, and remove it from the engine base.
(Leave the flexible mount attached to the engine base.)

3-1.1 Drain cooling water

(1) Open the sea water drain cock between the sea water pump and lube oil cooler to drain the sea water.
(2) Open the cylinder body drain cock to drain the fresh water from the cylinder head and cylinder body.
(3) Open the fresh water drain cock on the lower part of the fresh water tank to drain the fresh water.

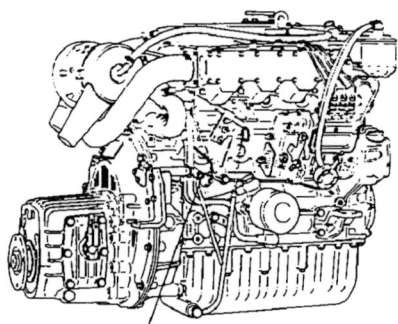

Fresh water drain cock (cylinder block)

3-1.2 Drain lube oil

(1) Remove the pipe coupling bolt which holds the lube oil dip stick guide, and drain the lube oil from the engine.
(2) Remove the drain plug on the lower part of the crank case control side, and drain the lube oil from the marine gearbox.

NOTE: If a lube oil supply/discharge pump is used for the engine, the intake hose is placed in the dip stick guide, and for the clutch side (gearbox) it is placed in the oil hole on top of the case.

3-1.3 Removing (electrical) wiring

Remove the wiring from the engine.

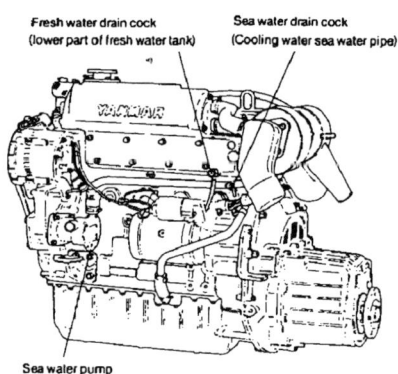

Fresh water drain cock
(lower part of fresh water tank)

Sea water drain cock
(Cooling water sea water pipe)

Sea water pump

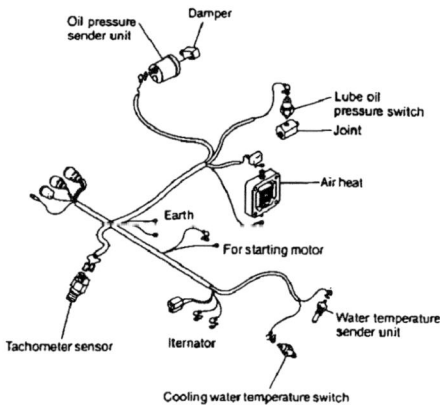

Oil pressure sender unit

Damper

Lube oil pressure switch
Joint

Air heat

Earth

For starting motor

Tachometer sensor

Iternator

Water temperature sender unit

Cooling water temperature switch

3-1.4 Removing the fuel oil filter & fuel oil pipe

(1) Remove the fuel oil pipe (fuel oil filter—fuel feed pump, fuel oil filter—fuel injection pump).

(2) Remove the fuel oil filter (with bracket) from the intake manifold.

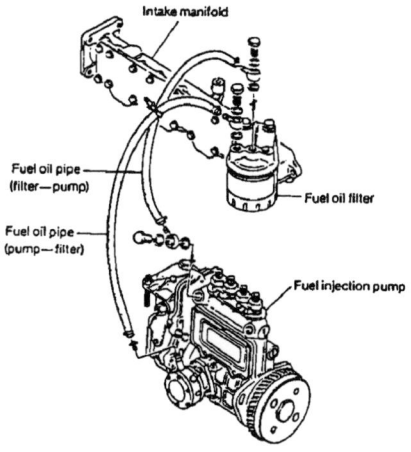

Intake manifold
Fuel oil pipe (filter—pump)
Fuel oil pipe (pump—filter)
Fuel oil filter
Fuel injection pump

3-1.5 Removing the intake silencer

(1) Remove the breather hose attached to the intake silencer—valve rocker arm chamber cover.

(2) Remove the intake silencer
N/A: from exhaust manifold outlet
T, T & A: from turbocharger outlet

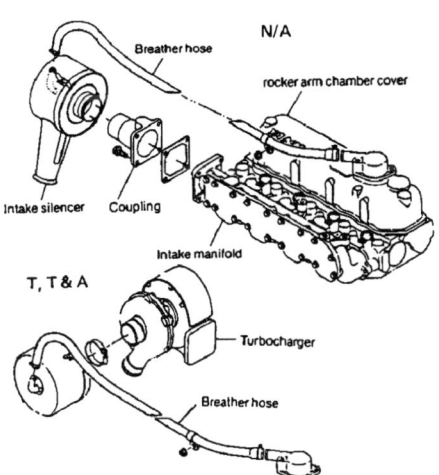

N/A
Breather hose
rocker arm chamber cover
Intake silencer   Coupling
Intake manifold
T, T & A
Turbocharger
Breather hose

3-1.6 Removing the mixing elbow

(1) Remove cooling water (sea water) pipe rubber (heat exchanger—mixing elbow).

(2) Remove the mixing elbow
N/A: from the intake manifold intake coupling
T, T & A: from the blower side of the turbocharger

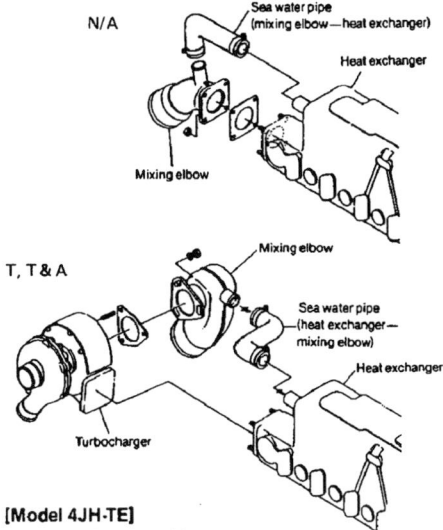

N/A
Sea water pipe (mixing elbow—heat exchanger)
Heat exchanger
Mixing elbow
T, T & A
Mixing elbow
Sea water pipe (heat exchanger—mixing elbow)
Heat exchanger
Turbocharger

[Model 4JH-TE]

3-1.7 Removing the turbine

(1) Remove the intake rubber hose (turbine—intake manifold).

(2) Remove the oil pan side rubber hose for the turbi lube oil return pipe from the oil pan, and the vibrati stop from the flywheel housing.

(3) Remove the turbine lube oil pipe (lube oil cooler—turbine).

(4) Remove the turbine from the exhaust manifold.

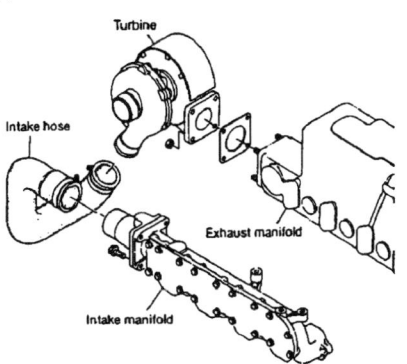

Turbine
Intake hose
Exhaust manifold
Intake manifold

Printed in Japan
A0A1029-9002

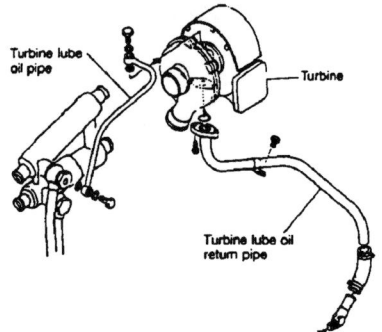

[Model: 4JH2-HTE, 4JH2-DTE & 4JH2-UTE]

Removing the air cooler
(1) Remove the intake rubber hoses.
    (Air duct-intake manifold, and turbocharger)
(2) Remove the sea-water rubber hoses.
    (Sea water pump — Air cooler — Lube oil cooler)
(3) Remove the air cooler from the heat exchanger,
    and cylinder block.

MODEL: 4JH2-HTE & 4JH2-DTE

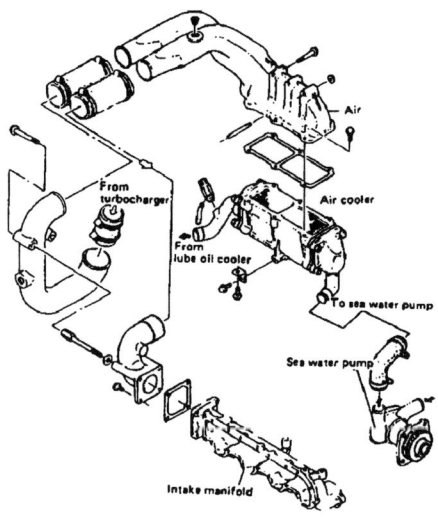

Removing the mixing elbow and the turbocharger.
(1) Remove the fresh water hoses.
    (Turbocharger — heat exchanger)
(2) Remove the lube oil pipes.
    (Lube oil cooler—Turbocharger—Lube oil pump)
(3) Remove the sea water hose.
    (Mixing elbow — heat exchanger)
(4) Remove the mixing elbow from turbocharger.
(5) Remove the air duct rubber hose.
    (Air duct — Turbocharger)
(6) Remove the turbocharger from exhaust mani-
    fold.

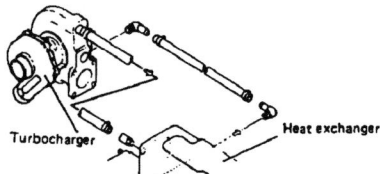

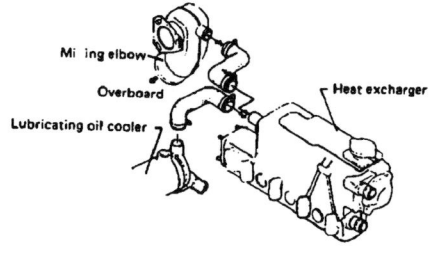

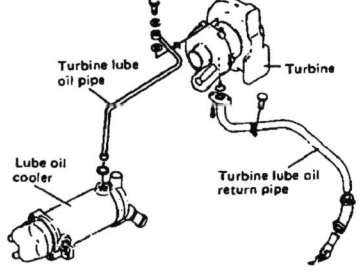

3-1.8 Removing the starting motor

Remove the starting motor from the flywheel housing.

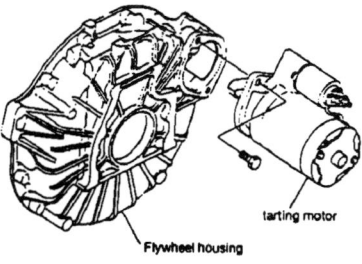

Flywheel housing

tarting motor

3-1.9 Removing the alternator

(1) Loosen the alternator adjuster bolt and remove the V-belt.
(2) Remove the adjuster from the fresh water pump, and remove the alternator from the gear case (with distance piece).

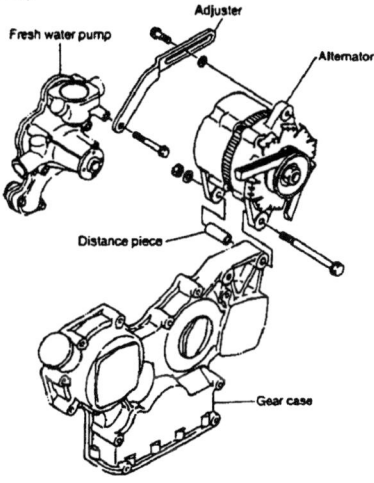

Fresh water pump

Adjuster

Alternator

Distance piece

Gear case

3-1.10 Removing the cooling water pipe

(1) Remove the cooling water (sea water) pipe (lube oil cooler — heat exchanger).
(2) Remove the cooling water (fresh water) pipe (heat exchanger — fresh water pump, fresh water pump — fresh water tank).
(3) Remove the cooling water pipe (lube oil cooler — marine gearbox)

[Model: 4JH2E 4JH2-TE]

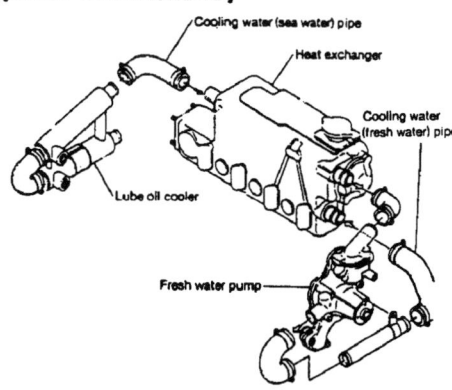

Cooling water (sea water) pipe

Heat exchanger

Cooling water (fresh water) pipe

Lube oil cooler

Fresh water pump

[Model: 4JH2-HTE, 4JH2-DTE, 4JH2-UTE]

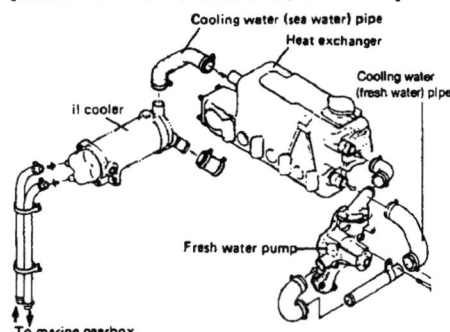

Cooling water (sea water) pipe

Heat exchanger

Cooling water (fresh water) pipe

il cooler

Fresh water pump

To marine gearbox

3-1.11 Removing the heat exchanger
(exhaust manifold, fresh water tank unit)

Remove the heat exchanger and gasket packing.

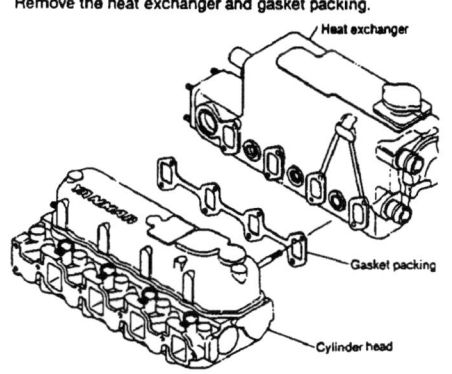

Heat exchanger

Gasket packing

Cylinder head

3-1.12 Removing the cooling water (sea water) pipe (sea water pump—lube oil cooler).

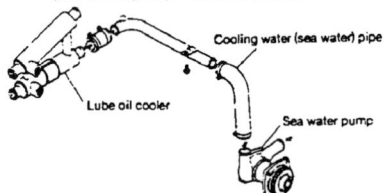

Cooling water (sea water) pipe
Lube oil cooler
Sea water pump

3-1.13 Removing the sea water pump

(1) Pull out the bearing mounts, receptacles from the sea water pump mounting side and from the opposite side of the gear case.
(2) Remove the sea water pump.

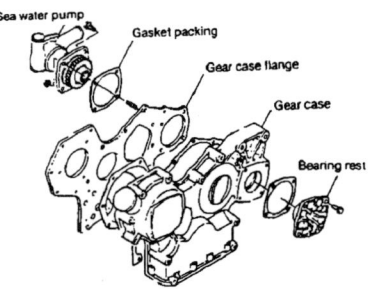

Sea water pump
Gasket packing
Gear case flange
Gear case
Bearing rest

3-1.14 Removing the lube oil filter

(1) Remove the lube oil pipe (lube oil cooler—filter bracket, filter bracket—lube oil cooler).
(2) Remove the filter bracket (with lube oil filter element) from the cylinder block.
(3) Remove the lube oil pipe (cylinder block—fuel injection pump).
(4) Remove the lube oil dipstick and guide.

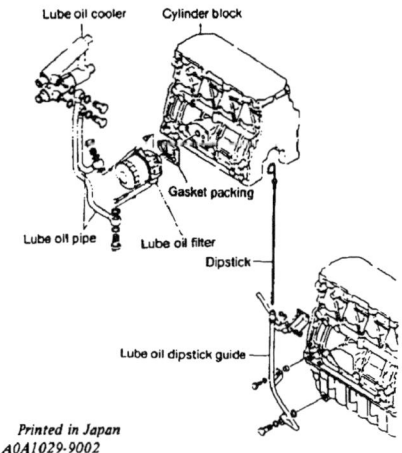

Lube oil cooler   Cylinder block
Gasket packing
Lube oil pipe   Lube oil filter
Dipstick
Lube oil dipstick guide

3-1.15 Removing the high pressure fuel pipe

(1) Remove the high pressure fuel pipe vibration stop from the intake manifold.
(2) Loosen the box nuts on both ends of the high pressure fuel pipe and remove the high pressure fuel pipe.
(3) Remove the fuel oil return pipe (fuel injection nozzle — fuel injection pump).

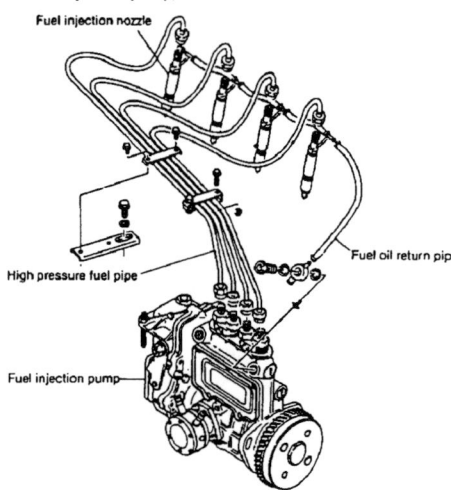

Fuel injection nozzle
Fuel oil return pipe
High pressure fuel pipe
Fuel injection pump

3-1.16 Removing the intake manifold

(1) Remove the governor speed remote control bracket.
(2) Remove the intake manifold and gasket packing.

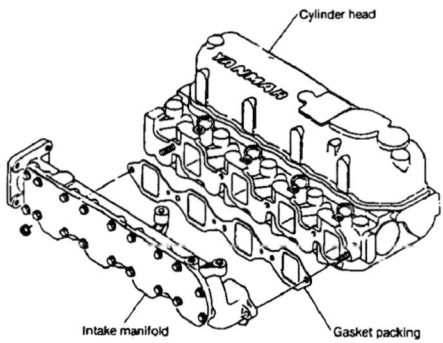

Cylinder head
Intake manifold   Gasket packing

3-1.17 Removing the fresh water pump

Remove the fresh water pump, gasket packing and O-ring.

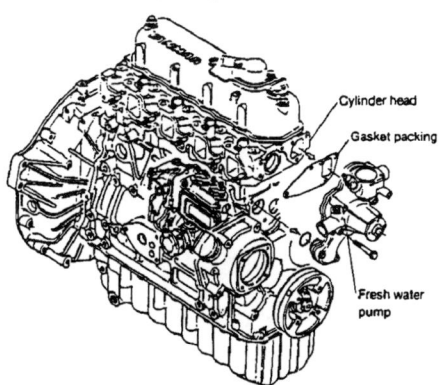

Cylinder head

Gasket packing

Fresh water pump

3-1.18 Removing the fuel injection nozzles

Remove the fuel injection nozzle retainer nut, and pull out the fuel injection nozzle retainer and fuel injection nozzle.

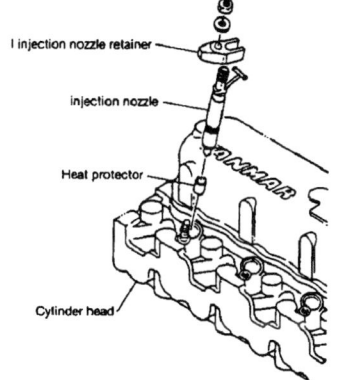

I injection nozzle retainer

injection nozzle

Heat protector

Cylinder head

NOTE: If the heat protector stays in the cylinder head, make a note of the cylinder no. and be sure to remove it when you disassemble the cylinder head.

3-1.19 Removing the valve elbow shaft assembly

(1) Remove the valve elbow chamber cover.
(2) Remove the valve elbow shaft support mounting bolts(s), and remove the entire valve elbow shaft assembly.
(3) Pull out the push rods.

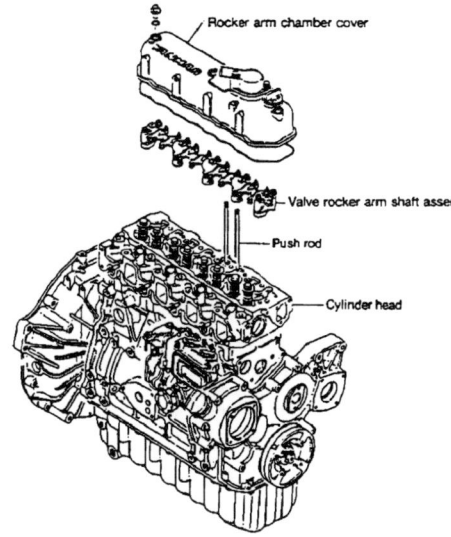

Rocker arm chamber cover

Valve rocker arm shaft assembly

Push rod

Cylinder head

3-1.20 Remvoing the cylinder head

(1) Remove the cylinder head bolts with a torque wrench, and remove the cylinder head.
(2) Remove the cylinder gasket packing.

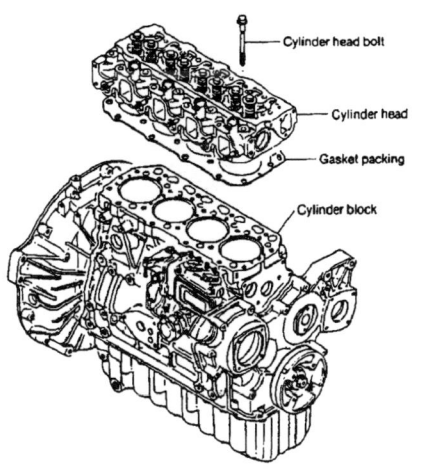

Cylinder head bolt

Cylinder head

Gasket packing

Cylinder block

3-1.21 Removing the crankshaft V-pulley

Remove the hex bolts holding the crankshaft V-pulley, and remove the crankshaft V-pulley with an extraction tool.

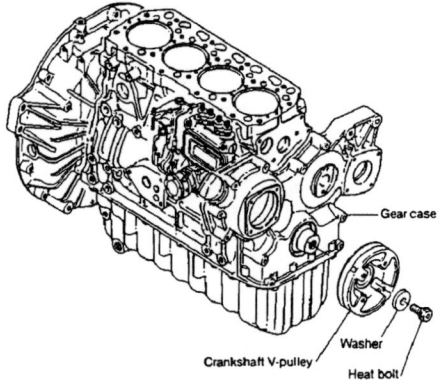

Gear case

Crankshaft V-pulley

Washer

Heat bolt

3-1.22 Removing the marine gearbox

(1) Remove the hex bolts from the clutch case flange, and remove the gearbox assembly.
(2) Remove the damper disk from the flywheel.
(3) Remove the fan from the flywheel.

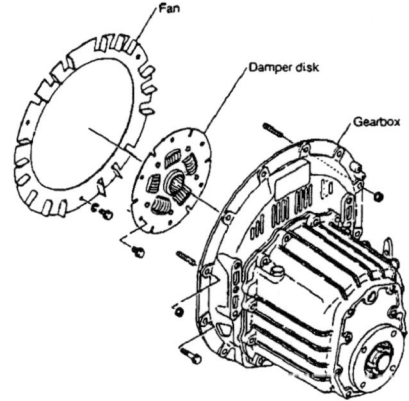

Fan

Damper disk

Gearbox

3-1.23 Removing the lube oil cooler

Remove the lube oil cooler from the upper part of the flywheel housing.

MODEL: 4JH2E

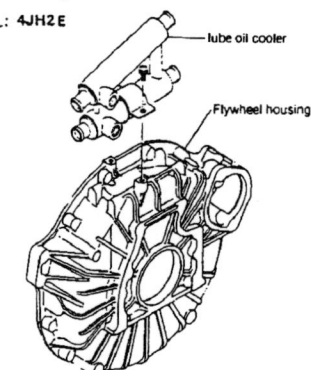

lube oil cooler

Flywheel housing

MODEL: 4JH2-TE
4JH2-HTE
4JH2-DTE

Lube oil cooler

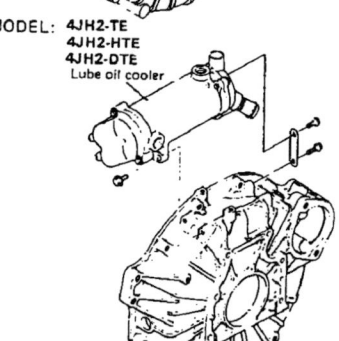

3-1.24 Removing the flywheel

Remove the flywheel mounting bolts and then the flywheel.

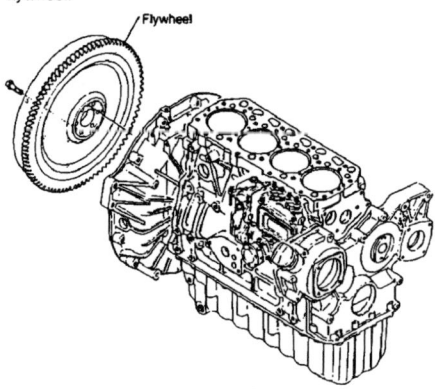

Flywheel

3-1.25 Turning the engine over

(1) Place a wood block of appropriate size on the floor, and stand up the engine on the flywheel housing.

(2) Remove the engine mounting feet.

3-1.26 Removing the oil pan

(1) Remove the bracket holding the oil pan and clutch housing.

(2) Remove the oil pan and gasket packing.

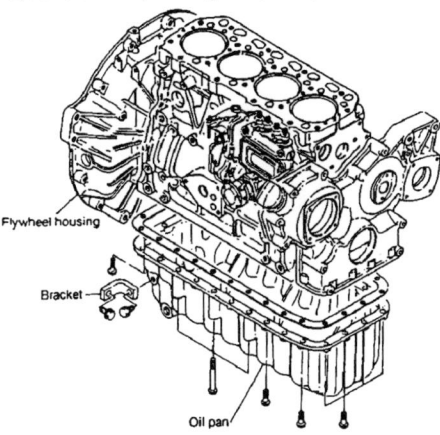

Flywheel housing

Bracket

Oil pan

3-1.27 Removing the lube oil intake pipe

Remove the lube oil intake pipe and gasket packing.

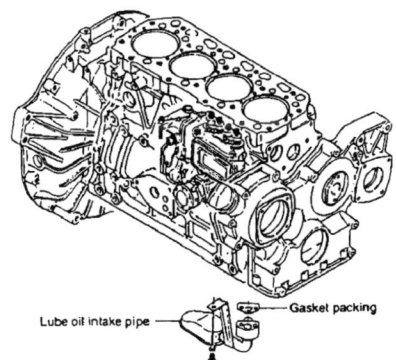

Lube oil intake pipe — Gasket packing

3-1.28 Removing the gear case

Remove the gear case mounting bolts, and remove the gear case from the cylinder block.

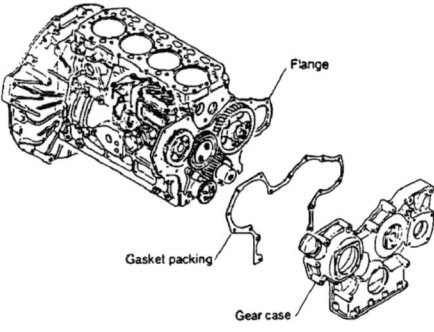

Flange

Gasket packing

Gear case

3-1.29 Removing the lube oil pump

Remove the lube oil pump and gasket packing from the gear case flange.

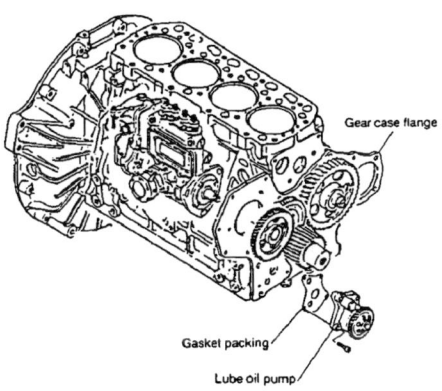

Gear case flange

Gasket packing

Lube oil pump

Printed in Japan
_A0A1029-9002_

3-1.30 Remove the fuel injection pump

(1) Remove the blind plug mounted to the hub of the automatic advancing timer.
(2) Remove the box nut, and pull out the fuel oil pump drive gear/automatic advancing timer assembly with an extraction tool.
(3) Remove the fuel injection pump and O-ring from the gear case flange.

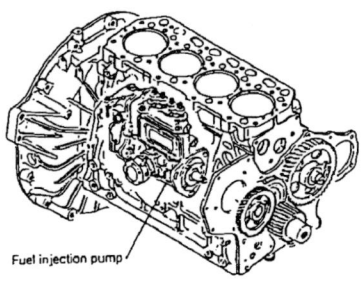

Fuel injection pump

3-1.31 Removing the idling gear

Remove the two hex bolts holding the idling shaft, and pull out the idling gear and idling shaft.

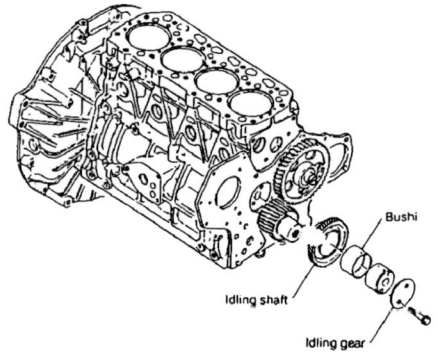

Bushi

Idling shaft

Idling gear

3-1.32 Removing the pistons and connecting rods

(1) Remove the connecting rod bolt and the large end cap.
(2) Push the connecting rod from the bottom and pull out the piston connecting rod assembly.

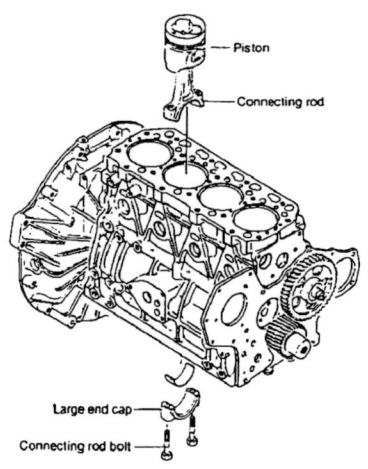

Piston

Connecting rod

Large end cap

Connecting rod bolt

NOTE: *Place a tool against the piston cooling nozzle to make sure the nozzle position does not change and it does not get scratches.*

3-1.34 Turning the engine over

Place a wood block of suitable size on the floor and turn the engine over, with the cylinder head mounting surface facing down.

NOTE: Make sure that the cylinder head positioning pins on the cylinder block do not come in contact with the wood block.

3-1.35 Removing the flywheel housing

Remove the flywheel housing from the cylinder block.

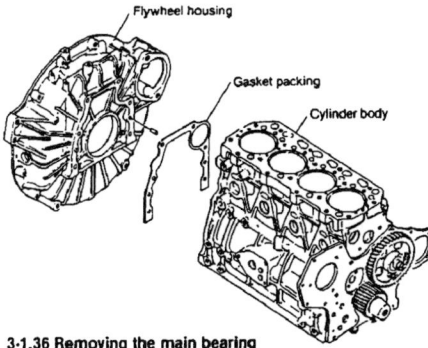

Flywheel housing

Gasket packing

Cylinder body

3-1.36 Removing the main bearing

(1) Remove the main bearing bolts.
(2) Remove the main bearing cap and lower main bearing metal.

NOTE: The thrust metal (lower) is mounted to the standard main bearing cap. Be sure to differentiate between mounting surfaces.

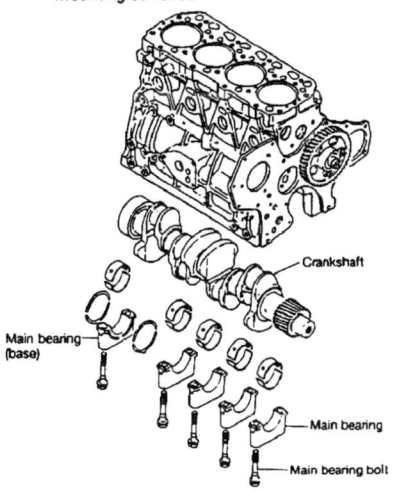

Crankshaft

Main bearing
(base)

Main bearing

Main bearing bolt

3-1.37 Removing the crankshaft

(1) Remove the crankshaft

NOTE: 1. The thrust metal (upper) is mounted to the standard main bearing. However, in some cases the thrust metal (upper) may be mounted to the crankshaft.
2. Remove the main bearing metal (upper) from the cylinder block.

3-1.38 Removing the camshaft

(1) Loosen the thrust rest mounting bolts out of the holes in the camshaft gear, and remove.
(2) Pull out the camshaft gear and camshaft assembly from the cylinder block.

NOTE: The camshaft gear and camshaft are shrunk fit. They must be heated to 180—200°C to disassemble.

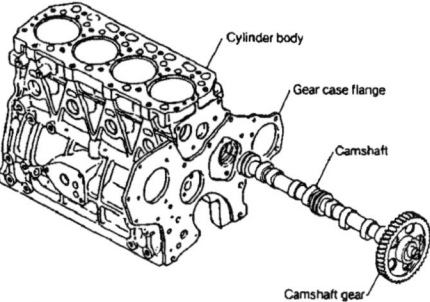

Cylinder body

Gear case flange

Camshaft

Camshaft gear

3-1.39 Removing the tappets

Remove the tappets from the tappet holes in the cylinder block.

3-1.40 Removing the gear case flange

(1) Remove the gear case flange from the cylinder block.
(2) Remove the two O-rings from the lube oil passage.

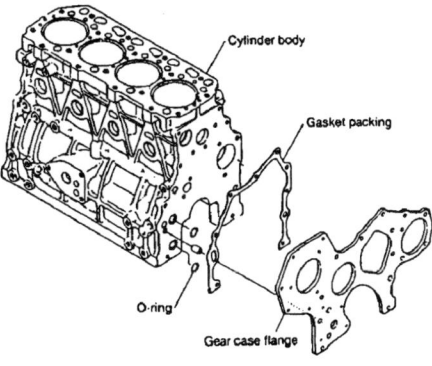

Cylinder body

Gasket packing

O-ring

Gear case flange

Printed in Japan
A0A1029-9002

3-1.41 Removing the piston cooling nozzle

Remove the piston cooling nozzle mounting nut and then the piston cooling nozzle from the cylinder block.

3-2 Reassembly

3-2.1 Mounting the piston cooling nozzle

Turn the cylinder block upside down and place it on appropriate wood blocks. Mount the piston cooling nozzles.

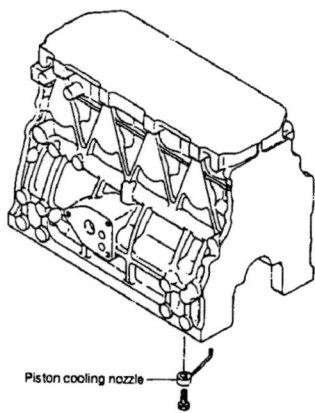

Piston cooling nozzle

3-2.2 Mounting the gear case flange

Mount the gear case flange, gasket packing and lube oil line O-ring onto the cylinder block.

NOTE: 1. When mounting the gear case flange, match up the two cylinder block pipe knock pins.
2. Be sure to coat the cylinder block lube oil line O-ring with grease when assembling, so that it does not get out of place.

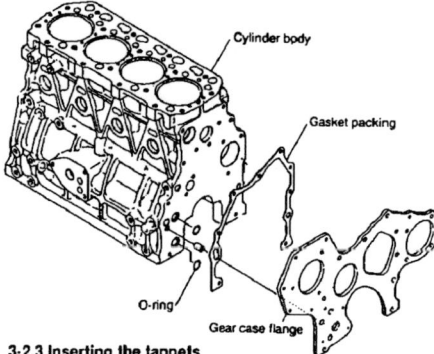

Cylinder body

Gasket packing

O-ring

Gear case flange

3-2.3 Inserting the tappets

Coat the inside of the cylinder block tappet holes and the outside circumference of the tappets with engine oil, and insert the tappets in the cylinder block.

NOTE: Separate the tappets to make sure that they are reassembled in the same cylinder, intake/exhaust manifold as they came from.

3-2.4 Mounting the camshaft

(1) If the camshaft and camshaft gear have been disassembled, shrink fit the camshaft and camshaft gear [heat the camshaft gear to 180—200°C (356—392°F) in the hot oil and press fit].

NOTE: When mounting the camshaft and camshaft gear, be sure not to forget assembly of the thrust rest. Also make sure they are assembled with the correct orientation.

(2) Coat the cylinder block camshaft bearings and camshaft with engine oil, insert the camshaft in the cylinder block, and mount the thrust rest with the bolt.

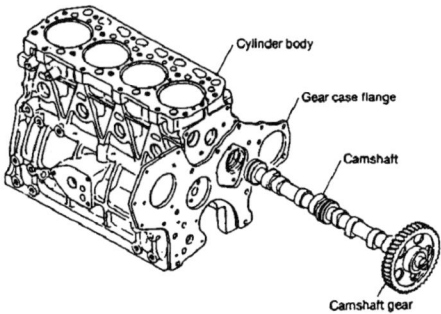

Cylinder body

Gear case flange

Camshaft

Camshaft gear

(3) Measure the camshaft side gap.

mm (in.)

Camshaft side gap	0.05 ~ 0.25 (0.0020 ~ 0.0098 in.)

(4) Make sure that the camshaft rotates smoothly.

3-2.5 Mounting the crankshaft

(1) The crankshaft and crankshaft gear are shrink fitted. If the crankshaft and crankshaft gear have been disassembled, they have to be shrink fitted [heat the crank shaft gear to 180°—200°C (356—392°F) in the hot oil and press fit].

(2) Coat the cylinder block crank journal holes and upper part of the main bearing metal with oil and fit the upper main bearing metal onto the cylinder block.

NOTE: 1. Be sure not to confuse the upper and lower main bearing metals. The upper metal has an oil groove.

2. When mounting the thrust metal, fit it so that the surface with the oil groove slit faces outwards, (crankshaft side).

(3) Coat the crank pin and crank journal with engine oil and place them on top of the main bearing metal.

NOTE: 1. Align the crankshaft gear and camshaft gear with the "A" match mark.

2 Position so that the crankshaft gear is on the gear case side.

3. Be careful not to let the thrust metal drop.

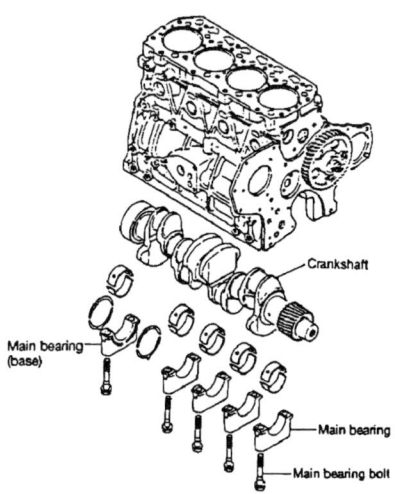

Crankshaft

Main bearing (base)

Main bearing

Main bearing bolt

3-2.6 Mounting the main bearing metal with engine oil, and mounting the main bearing cap.

NOTE: 1. The lower main bearing metal does not have an oil groove.

2. The standard bearing thrust metal is fitted with the oil groove slit facing outwards.

(2) Coat the main bearing cap bolt washer contact surface and threads with engine oil, place them on the crankshaft journal, and tighten the main bearing bolts to the specified torque.

kg-m (ft-lb)

Main bearing bolt tightening torque	9.5 ~ 10.5 (68.7 ~ 75.9)

NOTE: 1. The main bearing cap should be fitted with the arrow near the embossed letters "FW" on the cap pointing towards the flywheel.

2. Make sure you have the correct cylinder alignment no.

(3) Measure the crankshaft side clearance.

mm (in

Crankshaft side clearance	0.090 ~ 0.271 (0.0035 ~ 0.0107)

(4) Make sure that the crankshaft rotates smoothly and easily.

3-2.7 Mounting the flywheel housing

(1) Press fit the oil seal in the flywheel housing, and coat the lip of the oil seal with engine oil.

(2) Mount the flywheel housing and gasket packing, matching them up with the cylinder block positioning pins.

NOTE: Trim the gasket packing if it protrudes onto the oil pan mounting surface.

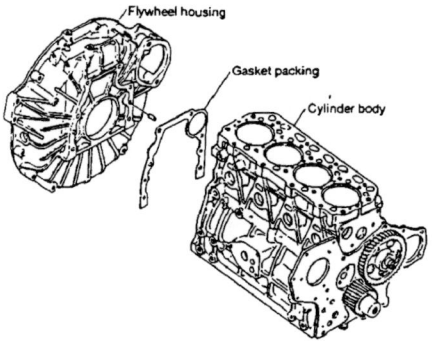

3-2.8 Stand up the cylinder block

On wood blocks, with the flywheel housing facing down. Take care that the gearbox mounting surface does not get scratched.

3-2.10 Mounting the piston and connecting rod

(1) Reassemble the piston and connecting rod.

NOTE: When reassembling the piston and connecting rod, make sure that the parts are assembled with the correct orientation.

(2) Each ring opening (piston/oil rings) should be staggered at gaps of 120°.

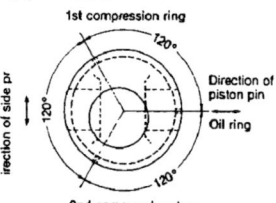

(3) Coat the outside of the piston and the inside of the connecting rod crank pin metal with engine oil and insert the piston with the piston insertion tool.

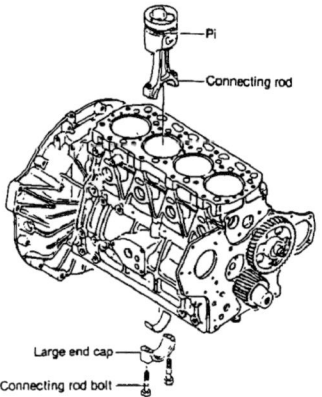

10-21

NOTE: 1. Insert the piston so that the match mark on the large end of the connecting rod faces the fuel feed pump, and the manufactuer's mark on the stem points toward the flywheel.
2. After inserting the piston, make sure the combustion chamber hollow is facing the fuel feed pump, looking from the top of the piston.

(4) Align the large end match mark, mount the cap, and tighten the connecting rod bolts.

	kg·m (ft-lb)
Connecting rod bolt tightening torque	4.5 ~ 5.0 (32.5 ~ 36.2)

NOTE: If a torque wrench is not available, match up with the mark made before disassembly.

3-2.11 Mounting the idling gear

(1) Fit the idling gear so that the side of the idling shaft with two oil holes faces up.
(2) Align the "A" and "C" camshaft gear and crankshaft gear match marks, match up with idling shaft retaining plate, and tighten the bolts.
(3) Measure the idling gear, camshaft gear and crankshaft gear backlash.

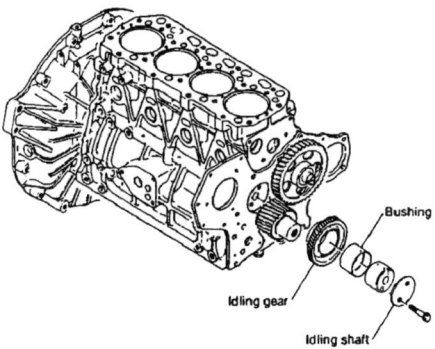

Bushing
Idling gear
Idling shaft

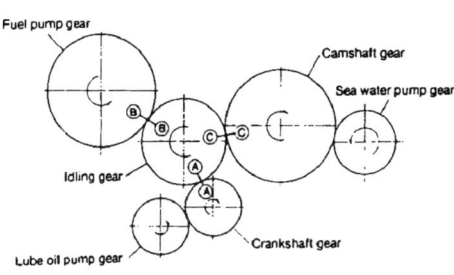

Fuel pump gear
Camshaft gear
Sea water pump gear
Idling gear
Crankshaft gear
Lube oil pump gear

Looking from gear case side

3-2.12 Mounting the fuel injection pump

Lightly fit the fuel injection pump on the gear case.

NOTE: 1. Be careful not to scratch the O-ring between the fuel injection pump and gear case flange.
2. Tighten the fuel injection pump all the way after adjusting injection timing.

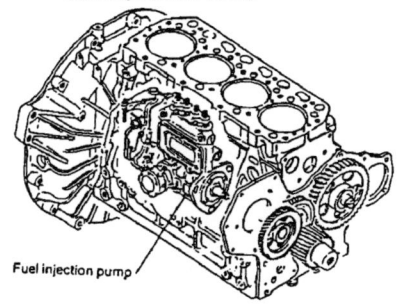

Fuel injection pump

3-2.13 Mounting the fuel feed pump drive gear and automatic advancing timer.

(1) When the drive gear and automatic advancing time have been disassembled, coat all sliding parts in bot assemblies with grease.
(2) Align the "B" match marks on the fuel pump drive gea and idling gear.
(3) Tighten all box nuts holding the fuel feed pump to th specified torque.

	kg·m (ft-l
Box nut tightening torque	6 ~ 7 (43.4 ~ 50.6)

(4) Grease parts around the box nuts (lithium grease) ar tighten the blind plug.
(5) Measure the backlash of the fuel feed pump drive geai

3-2.14 Mounting the lube oil pump

(1) Mount the lube oil pump on the gear case flange.
(2) Measure the backlash of the lube oil pump drive gear.

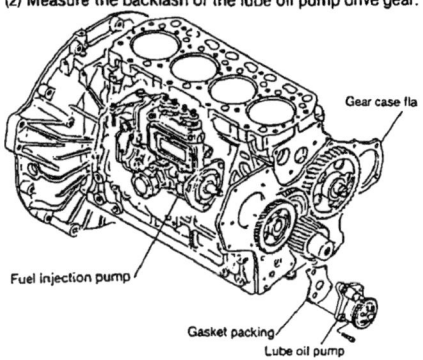

Gear case fla
Fuel injection pump
Gasket packing
Lube oil pump

3-2.15 Mounting the gear case

(1) Coat the inside and outside of the oil seals with engine oil, and press fit them into the gear case.

(2) Position the two pipe knock pins, and tighten the bolts holding the gear case and gasket packing.

NOTE: Trim the gasket packing if it protrudes onto the oil pan mounting surface.

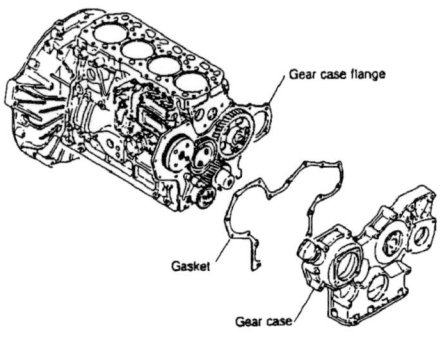

Gear case flange

Gasket

Gear case

3-2.16 Mounting the lube oil intake pipe

Mount the lube oil intake pipe on the bottom of the cylinder block, using new packing.

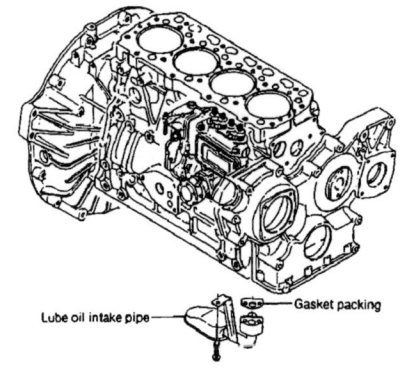

Lube oil intake pipe

Gasket packing

	kg-m (ft-lb)
lube oil intake pipe tightening torque	2.6 (18.8)

3-2.17 Mounting the oil pan

(1) Coat with three bond (3B-1114) the surfaces of the gear case, gear case flange and flywheel that contact with the cylinder block.

(2) Tighten the gasket packing/oil pan bolts.

(3) Mount the bracket that connects the flywheel with the oil pan.

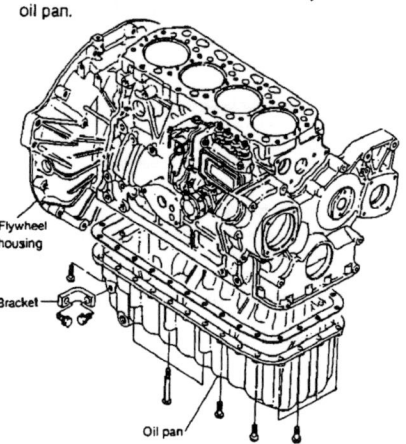

Flywheel housing

Bracket

Oil pan

3-2.18 Mounting the engine mounting feet and turning the engine upright.

Place suitable wood blocks below the oil pan and turn the engine upright.

3-2.19 Mounting the flywheel

(1) Coat the flywheel mounting bolt threads with engine oil.

(2) Align the positioning pins, and tighten the flywheel bolts to the specified torque.

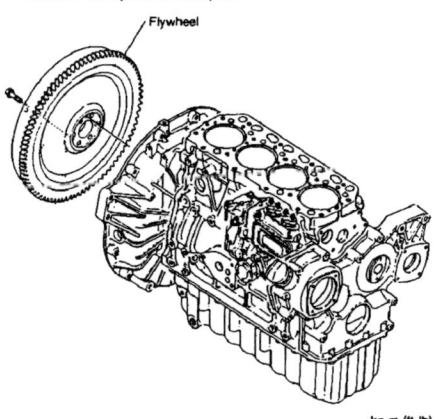

Flywheel

	kg-m (ft-lb)
Flywheel mounting bolt tightening torque	7.0 ~ 8.0 (50.6 ~ 57.9)

3-2.20 Mounting the marine gearbox

(1) Mount the fan and damper disk to the flywheel.
(2) Align the damper disk with the input shaft spline and insert. Tighten the flywheel housing and flange.

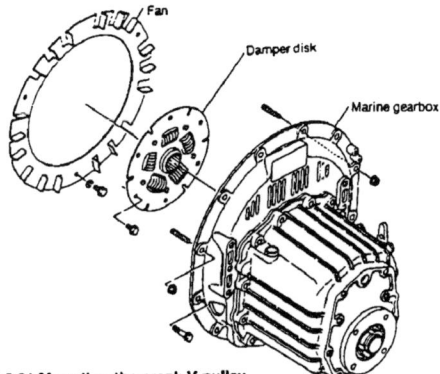

3-2.22 Mounting the cylinder head

(1) Fit the gasket packing against the cylinder block, aligning it with the cylinder block positioning pins.

NOTE: The side on which the engine model i inscribed should face up (cylinder head side).

(2) Lift the cylinder head horizontally and mount, aligning with the cylinder head gasket.
(3) Coat the mounting bolt washers and threads with engine oil, and lightly tighten the bolts in the specified order. Then tighten completely, in the same order.

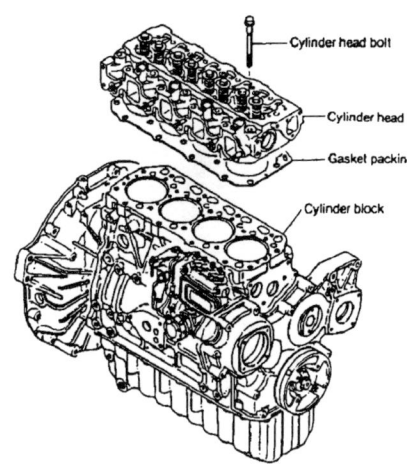

3-2.21 Mounting the crank V-pulley

(1) Coat the oil seal and the section of the shaft with which it comes in contact with oil.
(2) Tighten to the specfied torque.

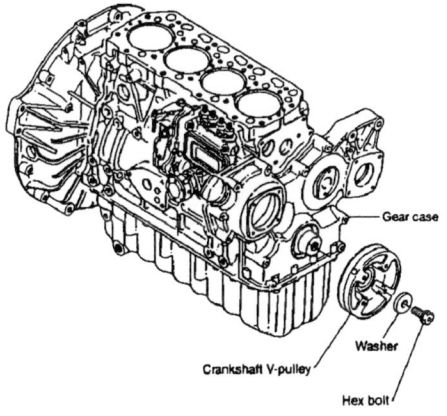

Tightening order

Exhaust manifold side

Intake manifold side

	kg-m (ft-lb)
V-pulley tightening torque	11.5 ~ 12.5 (83.2 ~ 90.4)

	kg-m (ft-l	
	Partial	Complete
Cylinder bolt tightening torque	3.5 ~ 4.5 (25.3 ~ 32.5)	7.5 ~ 8.5 (54.2 ~ 61.5)

(4) Measure the top clearance.
mm (I

Top clearance	0.71 ~ 0.89 (0.0279 ~ 0.0350)

3-2.23 Mounting the valve rocker arm shaft assembly pushrod

(1) Fit the pushrod to the tappet.

(2) Mount the valve rocker arm shaft assembly.

kg-m (ft-lb)

Valve rocker arm shaft support tightening torque	2.4 ~ 2.8 (17.4 ~ 20.4)

(3) Adjust valve clearance.

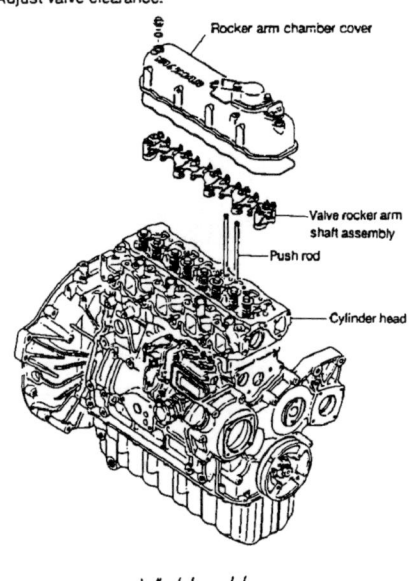

Rocker arm chamber cover

Valve rocker arm shaft assembly

Push rod

Cylinder head

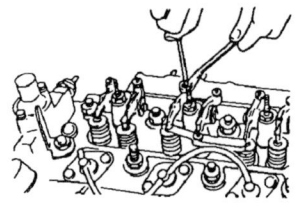

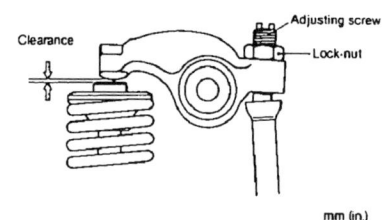

Adjusting screw

Lock-nut

Clearance

mm (in.)

Intake/discharge valve clearance	0.2 (0.0079)

(4) Coat the valve rocker arm and valve spring with engine oil, and mount the valve rocker arm chamber cover.

3-2.24 Mounting the fuel injection nozzle

(1) Mount the injection nozzle tip heat protector, and then the fuel injection nozzle.

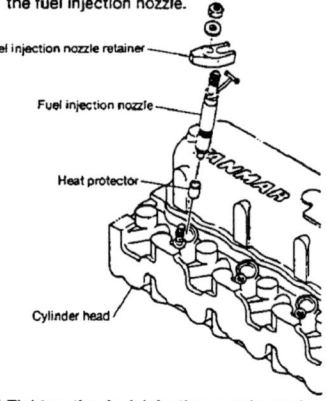

Fuel injection nozzle retainer

Fuel injection nozzle

Heat protector

Cylinder head

(2) Tighten the fuel injection nozzle retainer nut to the specified torque.

kg-m (ft-lb)

Fuel injection nozzle retainer tightening torque	2.0 ~ 3.0 (14.5 ~ 21.7)

3-2.25 Mounting the fresh water pump

(1) Thoroughly coat both sides of the packing with adhesive.

(2) Replace the O-ring for the connecting pipe which is inserted in the cylinder block, and tighten the fresh water pump to the specified torque.

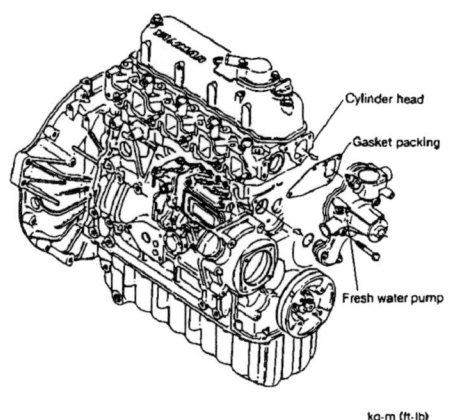

Cylinder head

Gasket packing

Fresh water pump

kg-m (ft-lb)

Fresh water pump tightening torque	0.7 ~ 1.1 (5.0 ~ 8.0)

3-2.26 Mounting the intake manifold

(1) Thoroughly clean the inside of the intake manifold, and mount the gasket packing and intake manifold.

(2) Mount the governor remote control bracket.

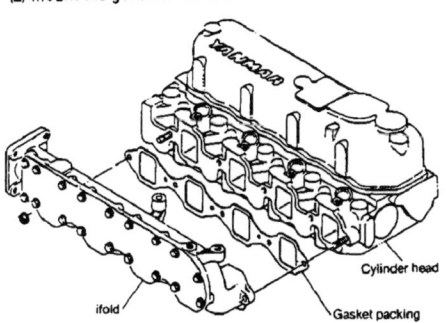

Cylinder head

ifold

Gasket packing

3-2.27 Mounting the high pressure fuel pipe and fuel oil return pipe

(1) Mount the high pressure fuel pipe and then the high pressure fuel pipe vibration stop.

NOTE: Lightly tighten the box nuts on both ends of the high pressure fuel pipe. Completely tighten after adjusting the injection timing.

(2) Mount the fuel oil return pipe with the hose clamp (fuel injection nozzle—fuel injection pump)

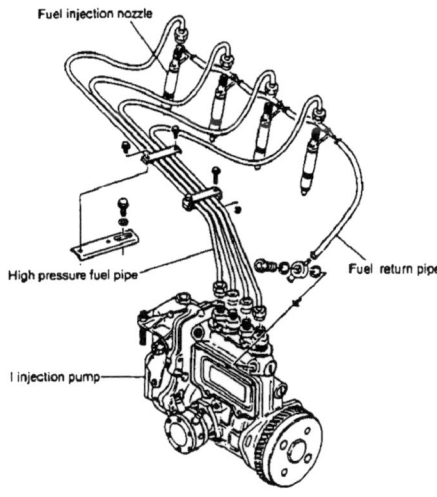

Fuel injection nozzle

High pressure fuel pipe

Fuel return pipe

I injection pump

3-2.28 Mounting the lube oil cooler

Mount the lube oil cooler to the top of the flywheel housing with the bracket.

MODEL: 4JHE
        4JH-TE

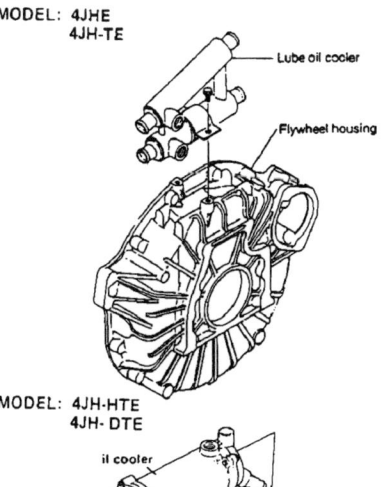

Lube oil cooler

Flywheel housing

MODEL: 4JH-HTE
        4JH- DTE

il cooler

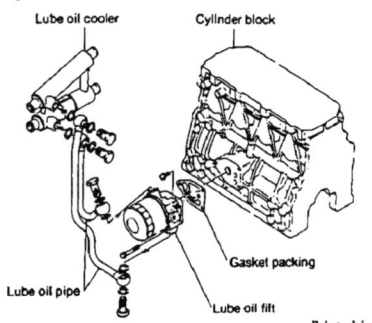

3-2.29 Mounting the lube oil filter

(1) Mount the filter bracket and packing on the cylinder block.

(2) Mount the filter element with the filter remover mounting tool.

Lube oil cooler   Cylinder block

Gasket packing

Lube oil pipe

Lube oil filt

10-26

3-2.30 Mounting the lube oil pipe

(1) Mount the lube oil pipe (filter—lube oil cooler, lube oil cooler—filter).
(2) Mount the lube oil pipe (cylinder block—fuel injecti pump).

3-2.31 Mounting the dipstick guide

Mount the dipstick and dipstick guide.

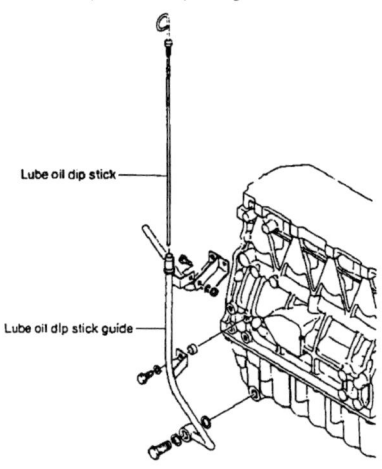

Lube oil dip stick

Lube oil dip stick guide

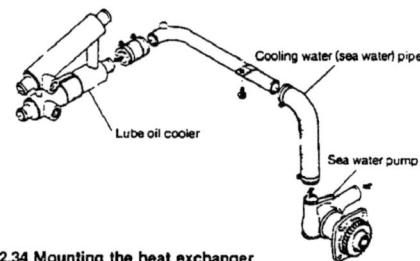

Cooling water (sea water) pipe

Lube oil cooler

Sea water pump

3-2.34 Mounting the heat exchanger (exhaust manifold, fresh water tank unit).

Mount the gasket packing and exhaust manifold.

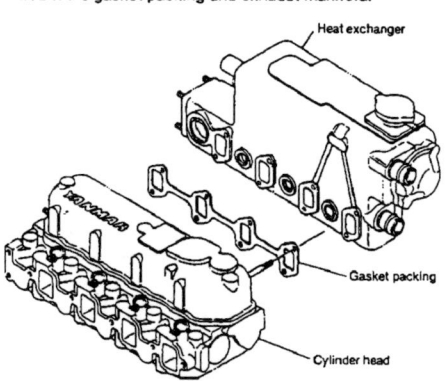

Heat exchanger

Gasket packing

Cylinder head

3-2.32 Mounting the sea water pump

(1) Mount the sea water pump assembly to the gear case flange.
(2) Lightly tap the gear case side bearing rest with a wood hammer, and tighten the mounting bolts.

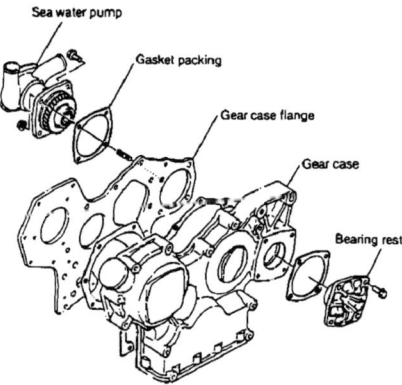

Sea water pump

Gasket packing

Gear case flange

Gear case

Bearing rest

3-2.35 Mounting the cooling water pipe

(1) Mount the cooling fresh water pipe with the hose clamp (fresh water tank — fresh water pump, fresh water pump—heat exchanger).
(2) Mount the cooling sea water pipe with the hose clamp (lube oil cooler — heat exchanger).
(3) Mount the cooling sea water pipe with the hose clamp (lube oil cooler — marine gearbox).

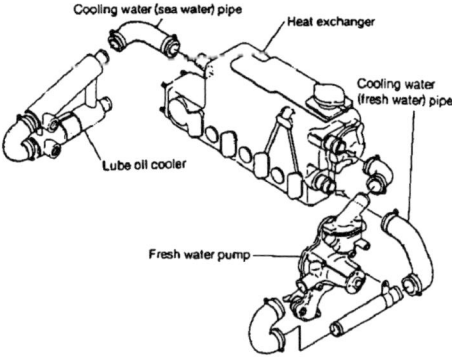

Cooling water (sea water) pipe

Heat exchanger

Cooling water (fresh water) pipe

Lube oil cooler

Fresh water pump

3-2.33 Mounting the cooling sea water pipe

Mount the cooling water pipe with the hose clamp (sea water pump—lube oil cooler).

MODEL: 4JH-HTE
4JH-DTE

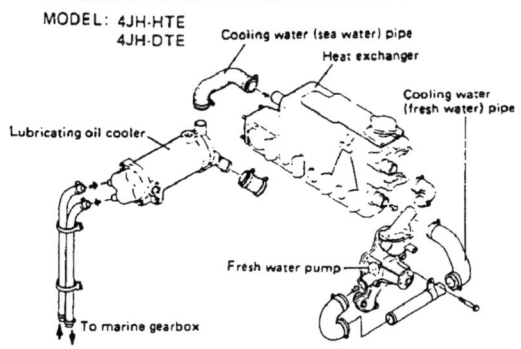

3-2.36 Mounting the alternator

(1) Mount the adjuster on the fresh water pump, the distance piece on the gear case, and then the alternator.

(2) Adjust V-belt tension with the adjuster, and tighten the mounting bolts.

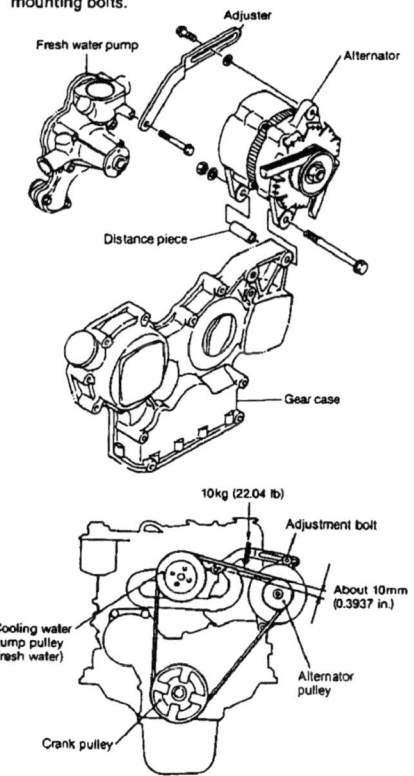

3-2.37 Mounting the starting motor

Fit the starting motor in the flywheel housing.

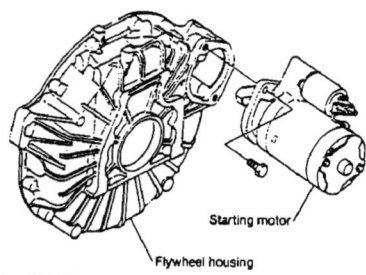

[Model 4JH-TE]

3-2.38 Mounting the turbine

(1) Mount the turbine on the exhaust manifold.

NOTE: First make sure to tighten the turbine lube oil return pipe.

(2) Mount the lube oil pipe (lube oil cooler—turbine).

(3) Insert the rubber hose at the end of the lube oil return pipe (turbine—oil pan) into the elbow on the oil pan, and mount with the hose grip.

(4) Mount the intake rubber hose (turbine—intake manifold).

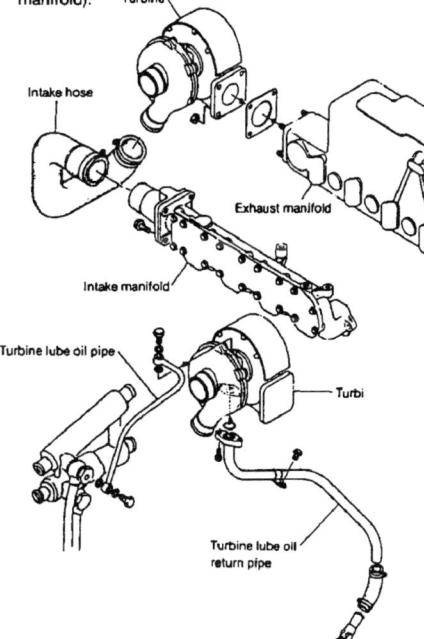

Printed in Japan
A0A1029-9002

3-2.39 Mounting the mixing elbow

(1) Mount the mixing elbow on the exhaust manifold outlet for model 4JHE, and on the turbocharger outlet for model 4JE-TE.
(2) Mount the cooling sea water pipe rubber hose with the hose grip (heat exchanger—mixing elbow).

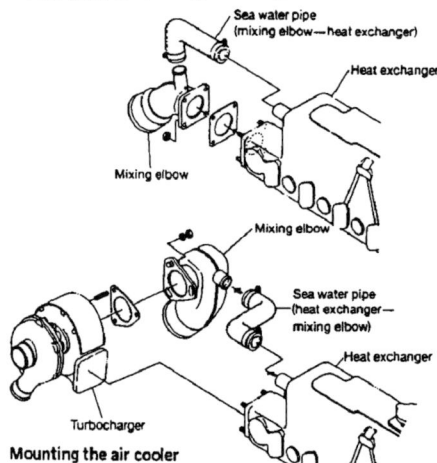

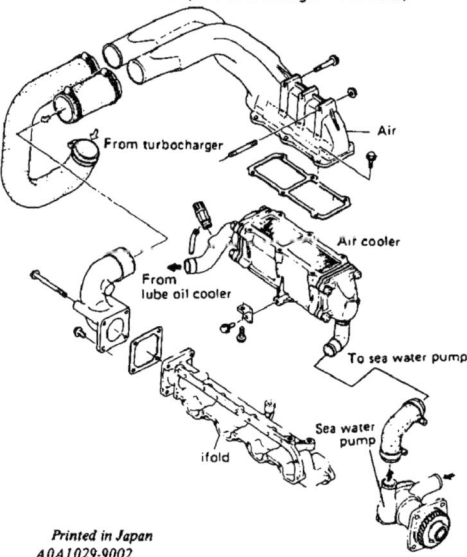

Mounting the air cooler

(1) Mount the air cooler on the heat exchanger, and cylinder block.
(2) Mount the sea-water rubber hoses.
   (Lube oil cooler — Air cooler — Sea water pump)
(3) Mount the intake rubber hoses
   (Intake manifold, and turbocharger — Air duct)

Mounting the mixing elbow and the turbocharger

(1) Mount the turbocharger on the exhaust mainfold.
(2) Mount the air duct rubber hose.
   (Turbocharger — Air duct)
(3) Mount the mixing elbow on the turbocharger.
(4) Mount the sea water hose.
   (Heat exchanger — Mixing elbow)
(5) Mount the lube oil pipes.
   (Lube oil pump — Turbocharger — Lube oil cooler)
(6) Mount the fresh water hoses.
   (Heat exchanger — Turbocharger)

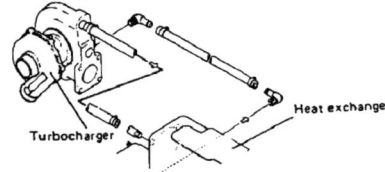

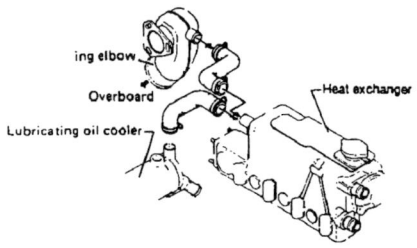

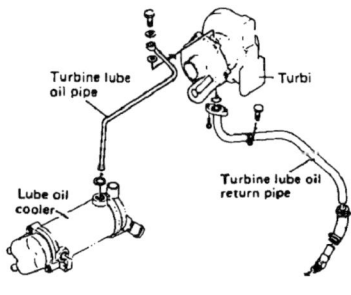

3-2.40 Mounting the intake silencer

(1) Mount the intake silencer on the intake manifold inlet coupling for model 4JHE, and on the turbocharger blower side for model 4JH-TE.
(2) Mount the breather hose with the hoe clamp (intake silencer—valve rocker arm chamber cover).

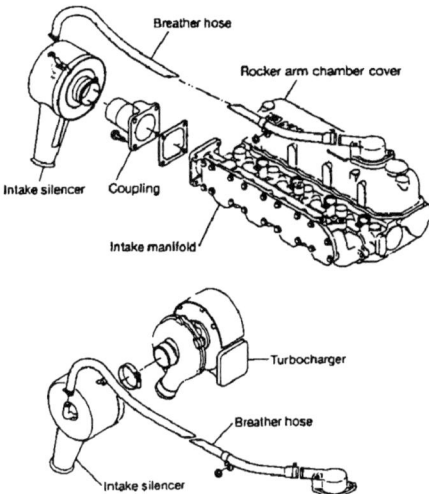

Breather hose

Rocker arm chamber cover

Intake silencer   Coupling

Intake manifold

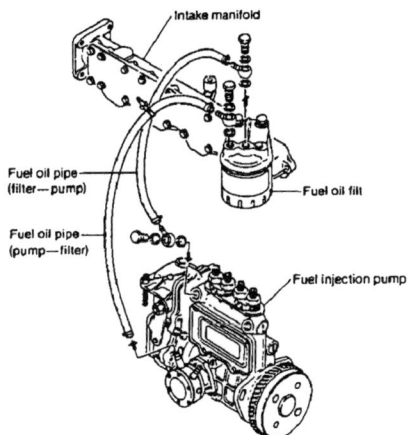

Turbocharger

Breather hose

Intake silencer

3-2.41 Mounting the fuel filter and fuel oil pipe

(1) Mount the fuel filter.
(2) Mount the fuel oil pipe (fuel feed pump—fuel filter, fuel filter—fuel injection pump).

Intake manifold

Fuel oil pipe
(filter—pump)

Fuel oil fill

Fuel oil pipe
(pump—filter)

Fuel injection pump

3-2.42 Electrical Wiring

Connect the wiring to the proper terminals, observing the color coding to make sure the connections are correct.

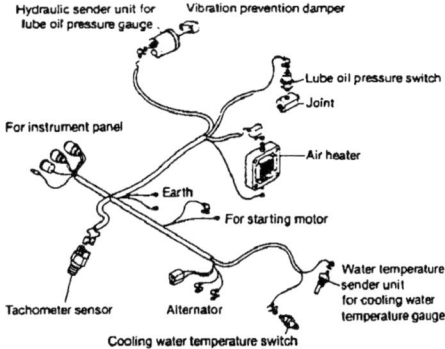

Hydraulic sender unit for lube oil pressure gauge   Vibration prevention damper

Lube oil pressure switch

Joint

For instrument panel

Air heater

Earth

For starting motor

Water temperature sender unit for cooling water temperature gauge

Tachometer sensor   Alternator

Cooling water temperature switch

3-2.43 Installation in the ship and completion of the piping and wiring

Mount the engine in the ship after all engine assembly has been completed. Connect the cooling water, fuel oil and other piping on the ship and the exhaust hoses. Connect the battery, instrument panel, remote control and other wiring.

3-2.44 Filling with lube oil

Fill the engine with lube oil from the supply port on top of the gear case and the marine gearbox supply port on top of the clutch case.

l (in.³)

Lube oil capacity	Engine	6.5 (396.63)
	Gearbox	1.2 (73.22)

3-2.45 Filling with cooling water

(1) Open the frssh water tank cap and fill with water.

	ℓ (in.³)
Fresh water tank capacity	6.7 (408.83)

(2) Fill with water until the level in the sub-tank is between the full and low marks.

	ℓ (in.³)	
	Full	Low
Sub-tank capacity	0.8 (48.82)	0.2 (12.20)

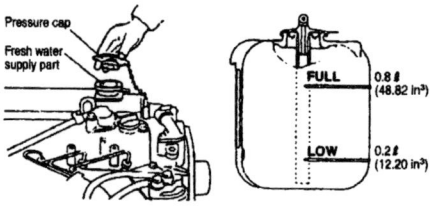

(3) If injection timing is off, change the mounting position using the long hole in the injection pump mounting flange. Turning the fuel feed pump towards the cylinder block slows timing down, while movement in the other direction makes it faster.

			ℓ (in.³)
Fuel injection timing (FID)		4JH2E	b.TDC 10°
		4JH2-TE	b.TDC 12°
		4JH2-HTE	b.TDC 14°
		4JH2-DTE	b.TDC 10°
		4JH2-UTE	b.TDC 12°

3-2.46 Check fuel injection timing

(1) Open the fuel tank cock and shift the fuel feed pump priming lever for air bleeding.

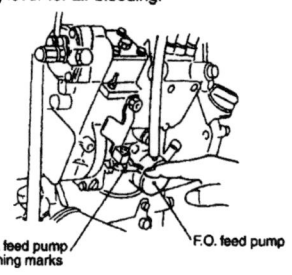

F.O. feed pump priming marks

F.O. feed pump

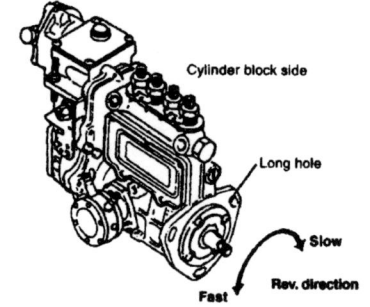

Cylinder block side

Long hole

Slow

Fast

Rev. direction

(2) Check injection timing by turning the flywheel and looking through the inspection hole in the flywheel housing.

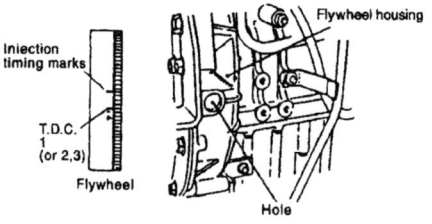

Flywheel housing

Injection timing marks

T.D.C.
1
(or 2,3)

Flywheel

Hole

4. Bolt/nut tightening torque

Engine

Description	Thread dia. x pitch mm	Tightening torque kg-m (ft-lb)	Wrench mm (in)
Cylinder head bolts	M10 x 1.25	7.5 ~ 8.5 (52.24 ~ 61.47)	14 (0.5512)
Connecting rod bolts	M9 x 1.0	5.0 ~ 5.5 (36.16 ~ 39.78)	13 (0.5118)
Flywheel bolts	M10 x 1.25	7.0 ~ 8.0 (50.63 ~ 57.86)	17 (0.6693)
Crankshaft V-pulley bolts	M14 x 1.5	11.5 ~ 12.5* (83.17 ~ 90.41) 8.5 ~ 9.5** (61.47 ~ 68.70)	19 (0.7480)
Main bearing bolts	M12 x 1.5	10.5 ~ 11.5 (75.94 ~ 83.17)	17 (0.6693)
Fuel pump gear nut	M12 x 1.75	6.0 ~ 7.0 (43.39 ~ 50.63)	17 (0.6693)

* For P.T.O. V-pulley (optional) (material: steel)
** For standard V-pulley (material: casting iron)

Turbocharger (RHB52)

Description	Thread dia. x pitch mm	Tightening torque kg-m (ft-lb)	Wrench mm (in)
Turbine chamber bolts	M6	10.0 ~ 11.0 (72.33 ~ 79.56)	10 (0.3937)
Blower chamber bolts	M5	3.5 ~ 4.5 (25.31 ~ 32.54)	8 (0.3150)
Thrust metal bolts	M3	0.7 ~ 0.9 (5.06 ~ 6.50)	—
Seal plate screws	M3	0.7 ~ 0.8 (5.06 ~ 5.78)	—
Blower blade nuts	M5	1.8 ~ 2.2 (13.01 ~ 15.91)	8 (0.3150)

Tightening torque of the standard bolts & nuts for general use.

[NOTICE]

● Apply the following tightening torque to bolts having " 7 " on the head.
(JIS strength classification : 7T)
○ Tighten bolts with no " 7 " mark to 60% tightening torque.
○ If the parts to be tightened are made from aluminum alloy, tighten the bolts to 80% tightening torque.

Bolt dia. x pitch mm	M6x1.0	M8x1.25	M10x1.5	M12x1.75	M14x1.5	M16x1.5
Tightening torque N·m (Kgf-m)	10.8±1.0 (1.1±0.1)	25.5±2.9 (2.6±0.3)	49.0±4.9 (5.0±0.5)	88.3±9.8 (9.0±1.0)	137±9.8 (14.0±1.0)	226±9.8 (23.0±1.0)

Name	Thread diameter	Tightening torque N·m (kgf-m)
PT plug	1/8	9.80 (1.0)
	1/4	19.61 (2.0)
	3/8	29.42 (3.0)
	1/2	58.83 (6.0)
Ball joint bolt	M8	14.70 (1.5)
	M12	29.42 (3.0)
	M14	44.12 (4.5)
	M16	53.93 (5.5)

Printed in Japan
A0A1015-0104

5. Test running

5-1. Preliminary Precautions

Before making a test run, make sure of the following points.

(1) Warm the engine up.
(2) Remove any precipitation from the F.O. filter, separator, and F.O. tank.
(3) Use only lube oil recommended by Yanmar.
(4) Be sure to add Yanmar anti-rust agent to fresh cooling water.
(5) During cold weather, add Yanmar anti-freeze to the cooling water.
(6) Provide good ventilation in the engine room

5-2 Check Points and Precautions During Running

Step	Item	Instructions	Precautions
1	Checks before operation	1) Make sure that the Kingston Cock is open. 2) Make sure there is enough lube oil and (fresh) cooling water. 3) Operate the remote control handle and check if the devices connected to the engine side work properly.	3) Lamp should go off when engine is running.
2	No load operation; warm up operation	1) Glow plug is provided to aid engine starts. When the lube oil temperature is raised to allow the engine to start, the pilot lamp goes off. 2) When the engine is started, check the following: • there is no water and no oil leakage. • gas does not leak when the engine is started. • there are no abnormal indications on the instrument panel. • there is no abnormality in cooling water discharge, engine vibrations, or engine sounds. 3) To warm up the engine, operate at low revolutions for about 5 minutes, then raise the revolutions to the rated rpms and then to max. rpms.	1) Even if one glow plug should break, the remaining plug works. 2) • Fix leaks if any. • Check the intake/exhaust valves, F.O. injection valve, and cylinder head. 3) Do not raise the engine revoluti abruptly.
3	Cruising (load) operation	1) Do not operate the engine at full load yet, but raise the rpms gradually for about 10 minutes until they reach rated rpms. 2) Make sure that exhaust color and temperature are normal. 3) Check the instrument panel and see if the water temperature and oil pressure are normal.	
4	Stopping the engine	1) Before stopping the engine, operate it at 650—700 rpms for about 5 minutes. 2) Raise engine rpms to 1,800 just before stopping the engine and idle the engine for about 3—4 seconds.	1) Stopping the engine suddenly during high speed operation increases the temperature of engine parts. 2) This procedure prevents carbon from being deposited on the valve seats, etc.
5	Checks after stopping the engine	1) Check again for water and oil leaks. 2) Make sure that no nuts and bolts are loose. 3) Close the Kingston and fuel cocks. 4) When the temperature is expected to fall below freezing, drain the cooling water (sea water). 5) Turn off the battery switch.	1) Check the oil seal area. 2) Especially the engine installation bolts. 4) Drain from the sea water pump.

4JHE/4JH2E PARTS DIFFERING IN SHAPE

No.	Part		Current 4JH-DTE	Specification — 4JH2E Series					Reason for Difference	Remarks
				4JH2E	4JH2-TE	4JH2-HTE	4JH2-DTE	4JH2-UTE		
1	Output	Cont rating	70HP/3500rpm	46/3400	57/3400	69/3400	80/3400			Indication in nameplate is for flywheel output.
		Max.	77HP/3600rpm	Clutch output 48/3600 Flywheel output 50/3600	Clutch output 60/3600 Flywheel output 62/3600	Clutch output 72/3600 Flywheel output 75/3600	Clutch output 85/3600 Flywheel output 88/3600	Clutch output 96/3600 Flywheel output 100/3600		
2	Cylinder block CMP		129472-01000 for cyl. w/sleeve	↑	↑	↑	129573-01000 for sleeveless cyl. Cyl. block: 129402-01010	↑	Bore enlargement by sleeveless structure	Design change in corner of main bearing(2→2.5)
3	Cylinder sleeve		[129472-011100]	↑	↑	↑	None	↑	Bore enlargement by sleeveless structure	
4	Cyl. head gasket		ø78mm bore, for cyl. w/sleeve. No grommets (at both ends)	↑	↑	Grommets (at both ends) 4JH2 sump	[129573-01340 (1.3t) -01350 (1.4t) -01360 (1.5t)] standard ø82mm for sleeveless cyl.	↑	Bore enlargement by sleeveless structure	
5	Engine name plate		[129473-07010] -07020 Model: 4JH-DTBE 4JH-DTE	[129570-07010] Model: 4JH2E	[129571-07010] Model: 4JH2-TE	[129572-07010] Model: 4JH2-HTE	[129573-07010] Model: 4JH2-DTE	[129574-07010] Model: 4JH2-UTE		
6	Metal cap tightening torque		10±0.5 kg-m	↑	↑	↑	11±0.5 kg-m	↑	P max. increase	JH2 mass-produced. As for JH, the torque will be changed to 11 kg-m.
7	Rocker arm support		[129150-11260] -11270 Made of FCD	↑	↑	↑	[129155-11260] -11270 Made of ACD	↑		Rocker arm support of current 4JH is to be changed also to of ADC.
8	Supercharger		[129474-18001] 9000 I VHP12NF BRL3511E "MY60"	None	[129571-18000] 5200 II HP12NW BRL3511E "MY67"	[129474-18001] Same as current 4JH-DTE "MY60"	[129473-18000] 5200 II HP15NW BRL3511E (Old type of 4JH-DTE) Abbreviation: "MY34"	↑	Combustion performance	RHB52 (Water cooling) MY60 MY34

No	Part name	Specification (left)		Specification (right)	Remarks	Notes
9	Crankshaft	[129474-21010] SCM440 Discrimination Stamp: C (on No.4 arm)	↓ (Same as left) ↓	[129573-21010] SCM440 Resintered Discrimination (on No.4 arm)	P max. increase	
10	Flywheel CMP	[129472-21590]	↑ ↑	[129573-21690]	To make it applicable to Bob tail	
11	Piston	[129474-22010] dia.78mm Troical	↑ [129570-22010] dia.82mm YPBC (Petal) Stamp A ↑ [129572-22010] dia.82mm YPBC (Petal) Stamp C	[129573-22010] dia.82mm YPBC (Petal) Stamp D; Set added for YX-15 (8-MBA: 6 points)	Bore enlarging. Combustion performance	4JH2-HTE & 4JH2-DTE differ in combustion chamber only.
12	Piston ring (Top)	[129550-22100] Chrome-plating on 3 faces	↑	[129573-22100] Chrome-plating on 3 faces	Bore enlargement	Differ in material
	Piston ring (2nd)	[129795-22120]	↑	[129351-22100]	Bore enlargement	
	Oil ring	[129795-22200]	↑	[129573-23010]	Bore enlargement	Differ in material
13	Conn. rod	[129150-23010] • Small end: Straight • Small end: Hole dia.=29mm • Tightening torque: 4.5~5.0 kg-m	↑	[129573-23010] • Small end: Taper • Small end: Hole dia.=31mm • Tightening torque: 5.0~5.5 kg-m	P max. increase	
14	Piston pin	[129150-22300] dia.26 × ℓ 66mm	↑	[129573-22300] dia.28 × ℓ 69mm	P max. increase	
15	Piston pin metal	[129100-23100] dia. 66mm Straight	↑	[129573-23100] dia. 28mm Taper	P max. increase	
16	Piston pin snap ring	[121100-22400] Coil(Round) For dia. 26mm hole	↑	[22252-000280] Circlip(Flat) For dia. 26mm hole		
17	Seawater pump	[129470-42500] Discharge capacity: 3250 ℓ/hr Cam lift: 4.5mm	↓	[129573-42500] Discharge capacity: 3750 ℓ/hr (Cam lift increased)5mm	Increase in heat exchanged calorie	
18	Fresh water cooler (Body)	[129470-44010] Cooler inset dia. 76.5mm Length: 451mm	↓	[129573-44010] Cooler inset dia. 83mm Length: 481mm	Increase in heat exchanged calorie	That for 4JH2 is changed in design and applied to current 4JH.

4JHE/4JH2E PARTS DIFFERING IN SHAPE

№	Part	Current 4JH-DTE	Specification 4JH2E Series					Reason for Difference	Remarks
			4JH2E	4JH2-TE	4JH2-HTE	4JH2-DTE	4JH2-UTE		
19	Freshwater cooler (Cooler core)	[129473-44111] Core dia. 76.5 mm A=0.328 m²	↓	↓	Stamp C	[129573-44111] Core dia. 83 mm A=0.416 m²	↓	Increase in heat exchanged calories	
20	Freshwater cooler (Side cover)	[129470-44450 -44440] Cooler inset die. 76.5 mm	↓	↓	Side cover / Emboss mark	[129573-44440 -44450] Cooler inset die. 83 mm	↓		
21	Fuel injection pump governor	Retraction volume 30 mm³/st Cut amt.: 0.05 mm W/O Boost compensator [729473-51300] (B364)	↑ [729570-51300] (B471)	Retraction volume 23.6 mm³/st Cut amt.: W/Boost compensator [729572-51300] (B445)	Same as right, differs in injection amount at B point only] (729572-51300) (B438)	Retraction volume 36 mm³/st Cut amt.:0.13 mm W/Boost compensator [729573-51300] (B434)	↓	Combustion performance Standization at acceleration	
22	Fuel injection nozzle	[729595-51300] 5-0.25 φ × 140° 140P255Z0	5-0.23 φ × 155° 155P235J20	↑	[729595-51300] 5-0.25 φ × 145° 140P255Z0	5-0.26 φ × 140° 140P265J20	5-0.25 φ × 150°	Combustion performance	
23	Push rod	[129150-14200] dia. 8 mm Material=5TK.H12C	↑	↑	↑	[119171-14400] dia. 8.5 mm Material=5TK.M16C yellow paint	↓	Stress relieving	
24	Cyl. head packing	Asbestos used	↑	↑	↑	Non-asbestos [Material: SF7000]	↓		Non-asbestos is also to be applied to current 4JH
25	Oil pan	E: Deep type BE: Shellow type	↑	↑	Shellow Type	(1) Hole added for front P.T.O bracket (2) Screw hole (M16 × 1.5) for dipstick Added also to non-control side	↓	To make it applicable to twin installe!	Oil pan for current 4JH is changed in design (Applied also to current 4JHE Series)
26	Cover (Thermostat)	[129470-49540]	↓	↑	↑	[129573-49540]	↓	Following elongation of fresh water cooler (No. 19, 20)	
27	Marine gear Model: KM4A	Input shaft				Input shaft		Measure for oil	

No.	Item						Remarks	
	Cooling fan	None	→			Shaft case: oil supply amt increased / Length: 7 mm increased	→	leak. Measure for wear out of friction plate. To make it applicable to the clutchless engines
28	Intercooler	[129473-18101] Corrugated type	None	None	(129474-18100) plate-fin type used also for 4JH-HT(E)	[129473-18101] Used also for 4JH-DT(B)(E)	→	Oil temp. reduced
29	Air intake duct	Bent: rubber hose	None	Aluminum pipe and rubber joint.	↑	Aluminum pipe and rubber joint.	→	Prevention of hose slipping off	A1 pipe is also to be applied to current 4JH-HTE/DTE
30	Starter	Conventional type [12450-77012]	→	→	↑	Reduction type [129573-77010]	→	Unification of parts
31	Wireharness Extension cord	Without relay (for all 2, 4, 6 m)	→	↑	↑	2 & 4 m: Without relay / 6 m: with/relay	→	Following change of starter	Optional
32	Marine gear Model: KBW	KBW21 [S] [G] [GG] Input shaft length	KBW20 [S] [G] [GG] Input shaft length: 7 mm up	KBW21 [S] [G]	KBW21 [S] [G] Input shaft length: 7 mm up	————(S)	→	Flywheel changed for application to Bobtail
	Cooling fan	None	Added Same as KM4A 177073-63190	↓	None	None	→	Same as above
33	Head bolt tightening torque	T=8±0.5 kg-m	↑	↑	↑	T=9±0.5 kg-m at shop assembly (T=8±0.5 kg-m at site reassembly)	→	P max. increase	Applied also to current 4JHE Series

YANMAR DIESEL ENGINE CO.,LTD.

OVERSEAS OPERATIONS DIVISION
1-32, CHAYAMACHI, KITA-KU, OSAKA 530-8311, JAPAN
TEL   81-6-6376-6411
FAX   81-6-6377-1242

YANMAR DIESEL AMERICA CORP.
951 CORPORATE GROVE DRIVE, BUFFALO GROVE, IL 60089-4508, U.S.A.
TEL   1-847-541-1900
FAX   1-847-541-2161

YANMAR EUROPE B.V.
BRUGPLEIN 11, 1332 BS ALMERE-DE VAART, THE NETHERLANDS P.O. BOX 30112, 1303
TEL   31-36-5493200
FAX   31-36-5493209

YANMAR ASIA (SINGAPORE) CORPORATION PTE LTD.
4 TUAS LANE. SHINGAPORE 638613
TEL   65-861-3855
FAX   65-862-5195

Printed in Japan
A0A1029-0104

YANMAR DIESEL ENGINE CO.,LTD.

1-32, CHAYAMACHI, KITA-KU, OSAKA 530 JAPAN   TEL.(06)376-6211 TELEX 63436 YANMARJ FAX.(06)372-2455

Printed in Japan
0000A0A102S-9004